AFTER CLARICE
READING LISPECTOR'S LEGACY IN THE TWENTY-FIRST CENTURY

LEGENDA

LEGENDA is the Modern Humanities Research Association's book imprint for new research in the Humanities. Founded in 1995 by Malcolm Bowie and others within the University of Oxford, Legenda has always been a collaborative publishing enterprise, directly governed by scholars. The Modern Humanities Research Association (MHRA) joined this collaboration in 1998, became half-owner in 2004, in partnership with Maney Publishing and then Routledge, and has since 2016 been sole owner. Titles range from medieval texts to contemporary cinema and form a widely comparative view of the modern humanities, including works on Arabic, Catalan, English, French, German, Greek, Italian, Portuguese, Russian, Spanish, and Yiddish literature. Editorial boards and committees of more than 60 leading academic specialists work in collaboration with bodies such as the Society for French Studies, the British Comparative Literature Association and the Association of Hispanists of Great Britain & Ireland.

The MHRA encourages and promotes advanced study and research in the field of the modern humanities, especially modern European languages and literature, including English, and also cinema. It aims to break down the barriers between scholars working in different disciplines and to maintain the unity of humanistic scholarship. The Association fulfils this purpose through the publication of journals, bibliographies, monographs, critical editions, and the MHRA Style Guide, and by making grants in support of research. Membership is open to all who work in the Humanities, whether independent or in a University post, and the participation of younger colleagues entering the field is especially welcomed.

ALSO PUBLISHED BY THE ASSOCIATION

Critical Texts
Tudor and Stuart Translations • *New Translations* • *European Translations*
MHRA Library of Medieval Welsh Literature

MHRA Bibliographies
Publications of the Modern Humanities Research Association

The Annual Bibliography of English Language & Literature
Austrian Studies
Modern Language Review
Portuguese Studies
The Slavonic and East European Review
Working Papers in the Humanities
The Yearbook of English Studies

www.mhra.org.uk
www.legendabooks.com

TRANSCRIPT

Transcript publishes books about all kinds of imagining across languages, media and cultures: translations and versions, inter-cultural and multi-lingual writing, illustrations and musical settings, adaptation for theatre, film, TV and new media, creative and critical responses. We are open to studies of any combination of languages and media, in any historical moments, and are keen to reach beyond Legenda's traditional focus on modern European languages to embrace anglophone and world cultures and the classics. We are interested in innovative critical approaches: we welcome not only the most rigorous scholarship and sharpest theory, but also modes of writing that stretch or cross the boundaries of those discourses.

Editorial Committee
Chair: Matthew Reynolds (Oxford)
Robin Kirkpatrick (Cambridge)
Laura Marcus (Oxford)
Patrick McGuinness (Oxford)
Ben Morgan (Oxford)
Mohamed-Salah Omri (Oxford)
Tanya Pollard (CUNY)
Yopie Prins (Michigan)

Advisory Board
Jason Gaiger (Oxford)
Alessandro Grilli (Pisa)
Marina Grishakova (Tartu)
Martyn Harry (Oxford)
Linda Hutcheon (Toronto)
Calin-Andrei Mihailescu (London, Ontario)
Wen-Chin Ouyang (SOAS)
Clive Scott (UEA)
Ali Smith
Marina Warner (Birkbeck)
Shane Weller (Kent)
Stefan Willer (Berlin)

Managing Editor
Dr Graham Nelson
41 Wellington Square, Oxford OX1 2JF, UK

www.legendabooks.com/series/transcript

TRANSCRIPT

1. *Adapting the Canon: Mediation, Visualization, Interpretation*, edited by Ann Lewis and Silke Arnold-de Simine
2. *Adapted Voices: Transpositions of Céline's Voyage au bout de la nuit and Queneau's Zazie dans le métro*, by Armelle Blin-Rolland
3. *Zola and the Art of Television: Adaptation, Recreation, Translation*, by Kate Griffiths
4. *Comparative Encounters between Artaud, Michaux and the Zhuangzi: Rationality, Cosmology and Ethics*, by Xiaofan Amy Li
5. *Minding Borders: Resilient Divisions in Literature, the Body and the Academy*, edited by Nicola Gardini, Adriana Jacobs, Ben Morgan, Mohamed-Salah Omri and Matthew Reynolds
6. *Memory Across Borders: Nabokov, Perec, Chamoiseau*, by Sara-Louise Cooper
7. *Erotic Literature in Adaptation and Translation*, edited by Johannes D. Kaminski
8. *Translating Petrarch's Poetry: L'Aura del Petrarca from the Quattrocento to the 21st Century*, edited by Carole Birkan-Berz, Guillaume Coatalen and Thomas Vuong
9. *Making Masud Khan: Psychoanalysis, Empire and Modernist Culture*, by Benjamin Poore
10. *Prismatic Translation*, edited by Matthew Reynolds
11. *The Patient, the Impostor and the Seducer: Medieval European Literature in Hebrew*, by Tovi Bibring
12. *Reading Dante and Proust by Analogy*, by Julia Caterina Hartley
13. *The First English Translations of Molière: Drama in Flux 1663-1732*, by Suzanne Jones
14. *After Clarice: Reading Lispector's Legacy in the Twenty-First Century*, edited by Adriana X. Jacobs and Claire Williams
15. *Uruguayan Theatre in Translation: Theory and Practice*, by Sophie Stevens
16. *Hamlet Translations: Prisms of Cultural Encounters across the Globe*, edited by Márta Minier and Lily Kahn
17. *The Foreign Connection: Writings on Poetry, Art and Translation*, by Jamie McKendrick
18. *Poetics, Performance and Politics in French and Italian Renaissance Comedy*, by Lucy Rayfield

After Clarice

*Reading Lispector's Legacy
in the Twenty-First Century*

Edited by
Adriana X. Jacobs and Claire Williams

Transcript 14
Modern Humanities Research Association
2022

Published by Legenda
an imprint of the Modern Humanities Research Association
Salisbury House, Station Road, Cambridge CB1 2LA

ISBN 978-1-78188-859-9 *(HB)*
ISBN 978-1-78188-860-5 *(PB)*

First published 2022

All rights reserved. No part of this publication may be reproduced or disseminated or transmitted in any form or by any means, electronic, mechanical, photocopying, recording or otherwise, or stored in any retrieval system, or otherwise used in any manner whatsoever without written permission of the copyright owner, except in accordance with the provisions of the Copyright, Designs and Patents Act 1988, or under the terms of a licence permitting restricted copying issued in the UK by the Copyright Licensing Agency Ltd, Saffron House, 6–10 Kirby Street, London EC1N 8TS, *England, or in the USA by the Copyright Clearance Center, 222 Rosewood Drive, Danvers MA 01923. Application for the written permission of the copyright owner to reproduce any part of this publication must be made by email to legenda@mhra.org.uk.*

Disclaimer: Statements of fact and opinion contained in this book are those of the author and not of the editors or the Modern Humanities Research Association. The publisher makes no representation, express or implied, in respect of the accuracy of the material in this book and cannot accept any legal responsibility or liability for any errors or omissions that may be made.

Trademark notice: Product or corporate names may be trademarks or registered trademarks, and are used only for identification and explanation without intent to infringe.

© *Modern Humanities Research Association 2022*

Texts by Clarice Lispector quoted in this book are used by permission of the Lispector Estate and are © *Paulo Gurgel Valente*

Copy-Editor: Richard Correll

CONTENTS

	Acknowledgements	ix
	Notes on the Contributors	xi
	Introduction: Afterthoughts and Afterwords	1

PART I: MAPS AND PLACES

1. A Walk through Clarice's Leme: One of the 'O Rio de Clarice' Guided Tours — 15
   TERESA MONTERO
2. In Search of Belonging: Places and Non-places in *Correspondências* and *Minhas queridas* — 39
   LAÍS MARIA ROSAL BOTLER
3. Bridging the Imaginary Gap between Distant Cartographies: The Visit that Never Was — 57
   DAFNA HORNIKE

PART II: ARCHIVES AND MANUSCRIPTS

4. Clarice Lispector's Unsettling Archive — 73
   ELVIA BEZERRA
5. And Now: A *Crônica* about My Encounter with the Manuscripts of *The Hour of the Star* — 87
   PALOMA VIDAL
6. Clarice Lispector the Conference Speaker: The Vanguard and the Right to Narrate — 105
   NÁDIA BATTELLA GOTLIB
7. Afterword to *The Besieged City* — 119
   GIOVANNI PONTIERO

PART III: THEORIZING CLARICE

8. 'Prender um inefável': Affect in Clarice's Fictions — 127
   MARTA PEIXOTO
9. 'My Error Is My Mirror': Clarice Lispector's Jewish Rhetoric of Mistakes — 139
   YAEL SEGALOVITZ
10. 'The error had often become my path': Lispector, Cixous and Ways of Reading — 157
    JULIE CÔTÉ
11. Clarice Lispector and World Literature: Is *The Hour of the Star* a Global Novel? — 169
    NELSON H. VIEIRA

PART IV: WRITING AND REWRITING

12 Clarice: The Visitor — 183
IDRA NOVEY

13 Capture — 189
HÉLIA CORREIA

14 Spectres of Clarice: Lispector's Literary Afterlives — 199
CLAIRE WILLIAMS

15 Rewriting Clarice Lispector in the Digital Age — 217
KARYN MOTA

PART V: THE POSTHUMAN

16 Writing Life beyond the Humanist Subject in *The Hour of the Star* and *A Breath of Life* — 239
KELLI D. ZAYTOUN

17 Reflections in the *Porta-espelho*: Clarice Lispector's Literary Theory of the Object — 255
AMI SCHIESS

18 Lispector and the Illogic of Matter — 273
MARTIN MACINNES

PART VI: TRANSMEDIALITY AND PERFORMANCE

19 The Mute Wide-Open Eye of All Things — 279
KIRAN LEONARD

20 Clarice Lispector: 'Unreal like Music' — 281
CARLOS MENDES DE SOUSA

21 The Body Speaks: Clarice Lispector on Screen — 301
MAGDALENA EDWARDS

22 Que(e)rying Femininities: Clarice Lispector's 'Correio Feminino' on TV Globo — 321
MARIELA MÉNDEZ

23 Mutatis Mutandis: Communicating Absence — 335
SARA ANDRÉ DA COSTA

PART VII: TRANSLATING CLARICE

24 Clarice Hebraica — 353
ADRIANA X. JACOBS

25 Marketing Lispector: Life Writing as Literary Criticism — 371
JÚLIA BRAGA NEVES

26 Clarice Lispector in English: Translation and Reception — 391
CYNTHIA BEATRICE COSTA AND LUANA FERREIRA DE FREITAS

27 Counterfeit Clarices: Performing Lispector — 411
KATRINA DODSON

28 We Are All Children of Babel: On Clarice Lispector's Chinese Translation — 425
MIN XUEFEI

Index — 435

ACKNOWLEDGEMENTS

This volume began as a conference that we co-organized in November 2017 in Oxford, 'After Clarice: Lispector's Legacy'. Commemorating forty years since the death of Clarice Lispector, it celebrated her place and status in twentieth- and twenty-first-century configurations of world literature by bringing together a variety of readers and scholars of her work. We are grateful to our colleague Jason Stanyek for hosting us at St John's College. The support of TORCH (The Oxford Research Centre in the Humanities), Oxford Comparative Criticism and Translation, the Oxford Centre for Hebrew and Jewish Studies, the Faculties of Medieval and Modern Languages and Oriental Studies, St John's College, the Modern Humanities Research Association, the British Comparative Literature Association, the Latin American Centre, the Camões Institute, and the Embassy of Brazil in London made the conference possible, and in so doing, this book became possible. In addition to the conference participants, our volume welcomes new voices into the conversations and collaborations that our conference encouraged; we are indebted and grateful to our contributors for their creativity, professionalism and patience as the book took shape. This Claricean network has proven vital to us, particularly in this time of pandemic, and we include here the translators of some of the chapters, our attentive and incisive peer reviewers, and our external reader above all, as well as copyeditor Richard Correll. They have been instrumental in developing this volume, as has Graham Nelson, Legenda's managing editor, who supported our vision for a hybrid academic volume from the start. We also thank Anna J. Davies for creating the index, and thank the University of Oxford's Humanities Division for awarding us a research support grant, which made it possible for us to include this vital navigational tool. We are thankful to the Oxford University Brazilian Society, in particular José Inácio da Costa Filho, for hosting the online pre-launch event which took place in December 2020.

We wholeheartedly thank Paulo Gurgel Valente for his enthusiasm for this project, and for generously granting us permission to use citations and images from across the range of Lispector's works and archival material, and colleagues at the Instituto Moreira Salles and the AMLB, Casa Fundação Rui Barbosa for providing some of the images. We are indebted to Mariana Valente for permission to use her spectacular collage on our conference poster and as the cover for this volume. The Agencia Carmen Balcells and Carcanet were generous in their permissions, allowing us to reproduce entire *crônicas* and excerpts from other texts by Lispector. Katrina Dodson's essay 'Counterfeit Clarices: Performing Lispector' first appeared in the magazine *The Believer*, and is reproduced here by kind permission of the publishers. We are particularly grateful to Teresa Montero for her encyclopedic knowledge about Lispector and to Professor Juan Sager, who passed away in February 2021, for kindly sharing Giovanni Pontiero's afterword to his unpublished translation of Lispector's *The Besieged City* with us.

We also wish to thank our dear friend and colleague Phillip Rothwell for having the foresight to introduce us years ago, and to our families, especially David Jacobs and Giles Ratcliffe. In the short foreword to *A paixão segundo G.H.*, Clarice Lispector explained to 'possible readers' that writing the character had brought her 'uma alegria difícil' [a difficult joy] (*The Passion According to G.H.*, trans. by Idra Novey (New York: New Directions, 2012), p. xi). We must confess that working together on this volume has been 'uma alegria fácil', the easy joy of a friendship that has developed during the process, in parallel with an ever deeper appreciation of Lispector's work, and will continue hereafter.

NOTES ON THE CONTRIBUTORS

Elvia Bezerra is the author of several biographical and literary studies, including *A trinca do Curvelo: Manuel Bandeira, Ribeiro Couto, Nise da Silveira* (Topbooks, 1995), which was awarded the Pen Clube do Brasil National Essay Prize, and *Meu diário de Lya* (Topbooks, 2002). She has published articles in numerous different periodicals. Between 2009 and 2019 she led the Literature Department at the Instituto Moreira Salles, where she was responsible for setting up two websites: the Correio IMS [IMS Mail], about letters and correspondence, and the Portal da Crônica Brasileira [Brazilian Crônica Portal]. Although retired, she continues to collaborate with the Instituto Moreira Salles.

Nádia Battella Gotlib has taught and researched Portuguese and Brazilian literature at the University of São Paulo, and other universities in and outside of Brazil, such as the University of Oxford and the University of Buenos Aires. She is the author of eleven books, two of them on Clarice Lispector: the literary biography *Clarice, uma vida que se conta* (1995), 7th edn revised and expanded (2013); and the photobiography *Clarice fotobiografia* (2008), 3rd edn revised and expanded (2014). These volumes have been translated into Spanish and published in Argentina (Adriana Hidalgo, 2007) and Mexico (Consejo Nacional para la Cultura y las Artes/Consultores de Diseño, 2015).

Laís Maria Rosal Botler received her PhD from the Department of Spanish and Latin American Studies at the Hebrew University of Jerusalem, where she developed research on places and non-places in the narrative of Clarice Lispector. She has a master's degree in Education from the Federal University of Pernambuco, Brazil and graduated in 'Letras' at the same institution. She is the leader of the study group 'Identity and Belonging' at the Hebrew University of Jerusalem.

Júlia Braga Neves teaches English Literature in the Anglo-German Languages Department at the Federal University of Rio de Janeiro. She has a PhD from Humboldt University Berlin and King's College London, where she wrote a thesis on queer historiography in contemporary British gay and lesbian literature. Her research interests include nineteenth-century travel writing, Brazilian contemporary literature and, of course, Clarice Lispector.

Hélia Correia is a Portuguese novelist, playwright, poet and translator who began her literary career in the 1980s and was awarded the prestigious Prémio Camões in 2015. Her short story 'Captura' was commissioned for the volume of Extratextos, *Clarice Lispector: personagens reescritos*, edited by Mayara R. Guimarães and Luis Maffei (Oficina Raquel, 2012), for which writers from across the Portuguese-speaking world contributed stories based on characters from Clarice Lispector's works.

Sara André da Costa is a Teaching Associate in Portuguese at the University of Nottingham. Her studies began at the University of Lisbon, where she completed a degree in General Linguistics and Romance Languages. At the University of Nottingham, in 2018, she was awarded a MA by Research in Portuguese and Lusophone Studies for her thesis on the Portuguese poet Herberto Helder, entitled 'herberto helder: os gestos do poema'. Since 2019, she has been a PhD candidate, also at the University of Nottingham, undertaking a comparative study of the literature of Clarice Lispector and Herberto Helder, entitled 'Clarice Lispector e Herberto Helder: do mito ao texto'.

Julie Côté is a PhD candidate in Comparative Literature at the Université de Montréal. Her doctoral dissertation is titled 'Les Amies qui m'accompagnent: la filiation textuelle de Clarice Lispector et Hélène Cixous'. She also teaches literature at Cégep Édouard-Montpetit.

Cynthia Beatrice Costa completed her PhD in Translation Studies at Universidade Federal de Santa Catarina, in 2016, with a dissertation on the English-language reception of Machado de Assis's famous novel *Dom Casmurro* (1899). She teaches Literary Studies and Translation at the Universidade Federal de Uberlândia and has published studies on translations of Machado de Assis and Clarice Lispector.

Katrina Dodson is a writer and translator in Brooklyn, New York. She is the translator of *The Complete Stories*, by Clarice Lispector, winner of the 2016 PEN Translation Prize and other awards. Her translation of Mário de Andrade's 1928 Brazilian modernist classic, *Macunaíma: The Hero With No Character* will be published by New Directions in 2023. She is currently adapting her Lispector translation journal into a book, and her writing has appeared in *The Paris Review*, *The Believer*, *McSweeney's*, and elsewhere. Dodson holds a PhD in Comparative Literature from the University of California, Berkeley and is an affiliated scholar of the Brazil LAB at Princeton University. She teaches translation at Columbia University.

Magdalena Edwards is a writer, actor, and translator based in Los Angeles, California. She holds a BA in Social Studies from Harvard and a PhD in Comparative Literature from UCLA. Her translations include the work of Clarice Lispector, Silviano Santiago, Márcia Tiburi, Noemi Jaffe, Oscar Contardo, Nicanor Parra, Raúl Zurita and Julio Cortázar. She plays Annie in Lucia Senesi's short film *A Short Story* (2019), which earned her Best Lead Actress at the Montreal International Indie Short Film Awards (2020). Magdalena performed the lead role of Virginia — a character inspired by Clarice Lispector's *The Chandelier* — for Heidi Duckler Dance's *Illuminating the Chandelier* (April 2020), the company's first original digital site-specific performance shared globally — and live — through Zoom's streaming platform. Magdalena's writing has appeared in *The Paris Review*, *Boston Review*, *Los Angeles Review of Books*, *London Review of Books*, *The Millions*, *The Point Magazine*, *Full Stop*, *Words Without Borders*, *The Critical Flame*, *El Mercurio*, and elsewhere.

Luana Ferreira de Freitas completed her PhD in Literary Studies at Universidade Federal de Santa Catarina and a post-doctorate at Vrije Universiteit in Brussels. She teaches Literary Studies at the Universidade Federal do Ceará (UFC). She is one of the founders and current coordinator of POET — Postgraduate Programme in Translation Studies — at UFC. Her research focuses on the internationalization of Brazilian literature.

Dafna Hornike completed her undergraduate degree in Latin American Studies and Gender Studies *magna cum laude* at the Hebrew University in Jerusalem. She subsequently continued her studies at the University of Calgary, where she wrote a thesis in the Department of French, Italian, and Spanish titled 'Si yo fuese yo: los sujetos nómadas en Clarice Lispector y Mayra Santos-Febres'. She conducted her PhD studies at the department of Romance Studies at Cornell University, from where she travelled to perform research in Rio de Janeiro and Mexico City. Her dissertation 'Orienting towards Home, or the Boundaries of the Nomad' is a comparative analysis of contemporary Latin American authors such as Clarice Lispector, Diamela Eltit, Carmen Boullosa and Ana Clavel. Her research focuses on the nuanced intersections between space, subjectivity, and gender, as they are articulated through the words of contemporary Latin American women writers. Preliminary parts of her research have been published in several reviews. Currently she teaches at the Hebrew University, while continuing to study Clarice Lispector's works.

Adriana X. Jacobs is Associate Professor of Modern Hebrew Literature at the University of Oxford and a Fellow of the Oxford Centre for Hebrew and Jewish Studies. She is the author of *Strange Cocktail: Translation and the Making of Modern Hebrew Literature* (University of Michigan Press, 2018). Her translation (from the Hebrew) of Vaan Nguyen's *The Truffle Eye* was published by Zephyr Press in March 2021.

Kiran Leonard is a musician and songwriter currently based in south London. His work has been profiled in publications such as *The Guardian*, *Pitchfork Media*, *The Quietus* and *Paste Magazine*, and he has been commissioned to write for both the Manchester International Festival and Manchester Central Library. He first read Clarice Lispector as an undergraduate; his favourite passage of hers is the scene in the bath from *Perto do coração selvagem*.

Martin MacInnes is the author of two novels. After the 2020 publication of *Gathering Evidence* (Atlantic), he was selected by the National Centre for Writing/British Council as one of ten writers shaping the UK's future. His first novel, *Infinite Ground* (Atlantic, 2016), was shortlisted for the Saltire Awards and won the 2017 Somerset Maugham award. He has previously won the Manchester Fiction Prize and the Scottish Book Trust New Writers Award.

Annie McDermott translates fiction and poetry from Spanish and Portuguese. She has previously lived and worked in Mexico City, Mexico, and São Paulo, Brazil, and is now based in Hastings, UK. Her translations include *Loop* (Charco, 2019), by the Mexican writer Brenda Lozano, *Empty Words* (Coffee House, 2019) and *The Luminous Novel* (And Other Stories, 2021) by the Uruguayan writer Mario Levrero, and *City of Ulysses* (Dalkey Archive Press, 2017) by the Portuguese writer Teolinda Gersão, co-translated with Jethro Soutar.

Mariela Méndez is Associate Professor and Chair in the Department of Latin American, Latino & Iberian Studies and Associate Professor of Women, Gender & Sexuality Studies at the University of Richmond. She is the author of the book *Crónicas travestis: el periodismo transgresor de Alfonsina Storni, Clarice Lispector y María Moreno* (Beatriz Viterbo, 2017), which won the 2019 Best Monograph Award from the Association for the Study of Genders and Sexualities. She has co-edited several editions of Argentinean writer Alfonsina Storni's chronicles as well as a book on the Latin American *crónica* of the 1930s to the 1970s. Méndez is also editor of *Journal of Lusophone Studies* 4.2, Special Dossier on Clarice Lispector's Journalism (Fall 2019) and, with Claudia Darrigrandi and Macarena Mallea, co-editor of *El arte de pensar sin riesgos: Cien años de Clarice Lispector* (Buenos Aires: Editorial Corregidor, 2021). She teaches at the intersection of Latin American Studies, Periodical Studies, Performance Studies, and Queer and Feminist Theory.

Min Xuefei is Associate Professor at Peking University, where she teaches Portuguese language and literature. She completed her doctoral thesis, 'Diluindo fronteiras: mal, amor, morte, corpo e mente em Clarice Lispector', at the University of Coimbra, in Portugal. She is a literary translator who has translated into Chinese works by Fernando Pessoa and Clarice Lispector, among others.

Teresa Montero is a teacher, actress, writer and biographer. Her doctoral thesis, defended in 2001 at the Pontifícia Universidade Católica in Rio de Janeiro was entitled 'Yes, nós temos Clarice: a divulgação da obra de Clarice Lispector nos Estados Unidos'. She has been promoting Clarice Lispector's work for over thirty years. She designed and leads the guided tour 'O Rio de Clarice', which she turned into a book in 2018. She has edited and organized several books about Clarice Lispector, including *Todas as cartas* (Rocco, 2020). Her 1999 biography, *Eu sou uma pergunta* was republished in a revised and expanded form in 2021, as *À procura da própria coisa. Uma biografia de Clarice Lispector* (Rocco).

Karyn Mota is a Brazilian journalist and PhD candidate in Portuguese and Brazilian Studies at Brown University. She has a master's degree in Communications from the Catholic University of Rio de Janeiro for the dissertation 'Clarice Lispector in the Digital Era: The Appropriation of the Writer on the Web' (2018). Mota has been a Visiting Research Fellow at Brown University, The Hebrew University of Jerusalem, and at Université Paris 8 Vincennes–Saint Denis. Her research interests include the life and works of Clarice Lispector, contemporary Brazilian literature, Afro-Latin American Studies, and Digital Humanities.

Idra Novey's forthcoming novel *Take What You Need* will be out from Viking Books in 2023. She is also the author of *Those Who Knew*, a finalist for the 2019 Clark Fiction Prize and a *New York Times* Editors' Choice. Her first novel *Ways to*

Disappear, received the 2017 Sami Rohr Prize, the 2016 Brooklyn Library Prize, and was a finalist for the L.A. Times Book Prize for First Fiction. Her poetry collections include *Exit, Civilian*, selected for the 2011 National Poetry Series, *The Next Country*, and *Clarice: The Visitor*, a collaboration with the artist Erica Baum. Her fiction and poetry have been translated into a dozen languages and she's written for *The New York Times*, *The Los Angeles Times*, *New York Magazine*, and *The Paris Review*. Her works as a translator include Clarice Lispector's novel *The Passion According to G.H.* and a co-translation with Ahmad Nadalizadeh of Iranian poet Garous Abdolmalekian, *Lean Against This Late Hour*, a finalist for the PEN America Poetry in Translation Prize in 2021. She teaches fiction at Princeton University.

Marta Peixoto recently retired as Associate Professor of Brazilian Literature at New York University. She has worked primarily on twentieth-century Brazilian literature, having published a book on a João Cabral de Melo Neto, *Poesia com coisas* (Perspectiva, 1983) and another on Clarice Lispector, *Passionate Fictions: Narrative, Gender, and Violence in Clarice Lispector* (University of Minnesota Press, 1994). She has published essays on Machado de Assis, on women's autobiographical writing, and on questions of urban crisis and artistic representation in literature and film, among other topics and writers. She is currently working on documentary film.

Giovanni Pontiero (1932–1996) was an academic and translator who specialized in Latin American Modernist literature. He studied at the University of Glasgow and went on to teach at the universities of Paraíba (Brazil), Liverpool and Manchester. He was a great advocate for and promoter of Portuguese and Brazilian literature and his prize-winning translations were instrumental in introducing the works of Clarice Lispector, José Saramago and others to an anglophone readership.

Ami Schiess holds a master's degree in Hispanic Literatures and Linguistics from the University of Massachusetts–Amherst and a PhD in Iberian and Latin American Cultures from Stanford University. Her research field is twentieth- and twenty-first-century Brazilian literature and criticism, with a critical focus on new materialisms, Translation Theory, and Comparative Anthropologies. Her dissertation, 'The Ethics of the Object in Modern Brazilian Literature' examines works that produce mixed imagetic fields of objectified people and personified objects, with examples culled from Brazilian *modernismo*, the late writings of Clarice Lispector, and essays in Translation Theory by Haroldo de Campos and others. Her current project is a critical translation of the avant-garde narrative poem *Cobra Norato* (1931) by Raul Bopp.

Yael Segalovitz is a Lecturer at the Department of Foreign Literatures and Linguistics at Ben Gurion University of the Negev, Israel. Her work spans American, Hebrew, and Brazilian modernisms, and she has also translated between the three languages, most recently translating Shimon Adaf's *Aviva-No* from Hebrew to English (Alice James Books, 2019), and Clarice Lispector's *A via crucis do corpo* from Portuguese to Hebrew (Ha-kibbutz ha-me'uchad, 2016). Her book in progress uncovers the global circulation of the New Critical practice of close reading. It follow 'close reading' as it travels from North America to Brazil and Israel, and demonstrates how, in all three locations, this reading method is mobilized by local intellectuals as a technique of the self, meant to conjure a new national subject. Her articles on such issues as psychoanalysis and modernism, identity politics in Israeli poetry, and the history of close reading have been published in venues including *Arizona Quarterly*, *CLCWeb*, and *Modern Fiction Studies*.

Carlos Mendes de Sousa is Associate Professor at the Escola de Letras, Artes e Ciências Humanas at the Universidade do Minho (ELACH), Portugal. His areas of research are Brazilian literature and modern and contemporary Portuguese poetry. He has published several studies on Clarice Lispector in journals and collections of essays, as well as the following monographs: *Clarice Lispector: figuras da escrita* (CEHUM, 2000), which was awarded the Essay Prize by the Associação Portuguesa de Escritores, and which came out in Brazil in 2012; and *Clarice Lispector: Pinturas* (Rocco, 2013). He is co-director of the Fundação Luís Miguel Nava and the poetry journal *Relâmpago*.

Paloma Vidal is a writer, academic and translator. She teaches Literary Theory at the Universidade Federal de São Paulo. She has published novels, plays, short story collections and poetry including *Algum lugar* (7 Letras, 2009), *Mar azul* (Rocco, 2012), *Três peças* (Dobro, 2014), *Dupla exposição* (Anfiteatro, 2016; images by Elisa Pessoa), *Wyoming* and *Menini* (both 7 Letras, 2018) and *Pré-história* (7 Letras, 2020). In literary criticism she has published *A história em seus restos: literatura e exílio no Cone Sul* (Annablume, 2004), *Escrever de fora: viagem e experiência na narrativa argentina contemporânea* (Lumme, 2011) and *Estar entre: ensaios de literaturas em trânsito* (Papéis Selvagens, 2019). She edits the journal *Grumo* (<salagrumo.com>) and has translated Latin American authors such as Clarice Lispector, Adolfo Bioy Casares, Margo Glantz, Tamara Kamenszain and Silviano Santiago.

Nelson H. Vieira is Emeritus Professor of Portuguese and Brazilian Studies and Judaic Studies at Brown University and the North American founding co-editor of the literary journal, *Brasil/Brazil* (1988 to present). Besides articles on Brazilian literature and culture, from late nineteenth- through twenty-first-century Brazilian fiction, his recent research includes a book-length study on the short story writer Dalton Trevisan. Some of his major publications include: *Jewish Voices in Brazilian Literature: A Prophetic Discourse of Alterity* (University Press of Florida, 1995) and *Contemporary Jewish Writing in Brazil* (University of Nebraska Press, 2009), as well as the edited volume *Roads to Today's Portugal* (Gávea-Brown, 1983), *Brasil e Portugal: a imagem recíproca* (Instituto de Cultura e Língua Portuguesa, 1991), and *Construindo a imagem do judeu: algumas abordagens teóricas* (Imago, 1994); and translations of *The Prophet and Other Stories* by Samuel Rawet (University of New Mexico Press, 1998) and *Anonymous Celebrity* by Ignácio de Loyola Brandão (Dalkey Archive Press, 2009).

Claire Williams is Associate Professor in Brazilian Literature and Culture at the University of Oxford and a Fellow of St Peter's College. She has been a reader of Clarice Lispector for thirty years, publishing her doctoral thesis *The Encounter between Opposites in the Works of Clarice Lispector* (University of Bristol, 2006), and numerous articles and book chapters on the author, as well prefacing her interviews with celebrities of the 1960s and 1970s, collected in *Entrevistas* (Rocco, 2007).

Kelli D. Zaytoun is Professor and Director of Graduate Studies in the Department of English at Wright State University in Dayton, Ohio, USA. Her scholarship and teaching focus on identity and narrative, multi-ethnic American literature, and the writings of Gloria Anzaldúa, María Lugones, and Clarice Lispector. Her 2022 book, *Shapeshifting Subjects: Gloria Anzaldúa's Naguala and Border Arte*, is part of the University of Illinois Press series 'Transformations: Womanist, Feminist, and Indigenous Studies', edited by AnaLouise Keating.

INTRODUCTION: AFTERTHOUGHTS AND AFTERWORDS

'After', the *Oxford English Dictionary* tells us, is a very versatile word. It can be a noun, an adjective, a preposition, a conjunction, an adverb, and a prefix. It can indicate both time, place, manner and order, denoting one specific event occurring in immediate succession to another, or everything subsequent, and it can even give a sense of the future. Those following after may be in pursuit of something, or in search of it, awaiting or resulting from it, in accordance with, in imitation or memory of it; or even resembling it.

After Clarice: Reading Lispector's Legacy in the Twenty-First Century, echoes the multiple meanings and functions of this kaleidoscopic term in the ways it addresses the legacies of the life and works of Ukrainian-born naturalized Brazilian writer Clarice Lispector (1920–1977), one of the great Latin American writers of the twentieth century. Chronologically, its contributions discuss the publishing history, critical fortunes, growing internationalization and wider cultural impact *after* her death, but also her influence on other writers. Translators and biographers fascinated with her words and her experiences, not to mention archivists, literary critics and researchers of all kinds, have pursued the woman and the meaning/s of what she wrote. Her works and her image have been re-visioned in different media (film, theatre, dance), fragmented or caricatured and circulated on social media, co-opted for a self-help agenda, and used as the inspiration for new literary creations, *après* Clarice. For many readers, the impact of their first encounter with the writer and the intimacy her work seems to represent a watershed moment in their lives, marking out the periods 'before' and 'after' Clarice.[1]

We, the editors, Adriana X. Jacobs and Claire Williams, have brought together a deliberately diverse and eclectic range of scholarly articles, works of fiction and poetry, personal essays and archival material in order to reassess how Lispector's wide-ranging *oeuvre* is read today. Many of these contributions developed in the months following an international conference on Lispector that we co-organized, and which took place on 17–18 November 2017, at St John's College, Oxford. This conference, also called *After Clarice*, commemorated the fortieth anniversary of Lispector's death, but also aimed specifically to analyse her legacy and influence as it has developed in the decades since.

The volume highlights the fluctuations and swerves in Clarice Lispector's critical fortunes, focusing on the way her works have circulated through translation into other languages, genres, media and cultures. Our conference was committed to reaching out to international scholars and translators working in non-Western languages, for example Israeli Hebrew (Chapters 9 and 24) and Mandarin (Chapter 28). We also wanted to acknowledge the ways that Lispector is read beyond academia, reflected here in the inclusion of poems, personal essays and song lyrics. Some chapters venture beyond the grave — literally, in the case of Giovanni Pontiero's 'lost' translation of *The Besieged City* (Chapter 7), and more figuratively, in Magdalena Edwards' discussion of Lispector's only TV interview (Chapter 21), and the posthumous conversations imagined by other authors as examined by Claire Williams (Chapter 14). Other contributions further explore Lispector's status as a Jewish writer, issues of identity, class, race, gender and sexual identity in her work, translation and reception, as well as the politics of publishing and marketing Lispector — or Clarice, as many of our contributors prefer to address her — for international readerships.

Clarice Lispector is one of the most widely translated and re-translated Portuguese-language writers of the twentieth century. Internationally acclaimed authors from Brazil and further afield, from Elena Ferrante and Colm Tóibín to Jhumpa Lahiri and Tommy Orange, have acknowledged the transformative influence of her writing on their own work. But addressing the place and status of Lispector in twentieth- and twenty-first-century configurations of world literature requires that we challenge and move beyond the tendency to read her global status within the context of anglophone translation and rewriting. Given that this is a volume published in English by a UK press, the present editors decided early on to take care in the editing process to keep the structure and style of the academically oriented chapters open and fluid. We acknowledge that what constitutes an academic argument can differ between different academic cultures and languages. For instance, academics in Brazil tend to approach Lispector's work with greater intimacy — this is evident, in part, in the tendency to refer to her simply as Clarice, a convention that a number of her anglophone translators have adopted. Although we initially encouraged contributors to go with 'Lispector', in keeping with academic conventions in the United States and United Kingdom, at a later stage, we decided to give contributors the choice of their preferred mode of address. The name of the conference and this present volume also reflect the intimacy with which we ourselves approach her writing. The inclusion of works of fiction, experimental essays, archival material, song lyrics and poetry acknowledges that much of the academic research on Lispector is both indebted to these creative approaches and shaped by them. The participation of early career and advanced graduate students amplifies the next generation of Lispector scholarship.

Any consideration of Lispector's legacy builds on the work that has come before. This volume would not exist without the studies, translations, and creative re-imaginings of her work that preceded our own investigations. In an analysis of the ebbs and flows of Lispector's critical fortunes, Nádia Battella Gotlib (following Benedito Nunes) identified three waves: 1943–60, when her works were read and studied by a small group of intellectuals; 1960–77, when the author's journalism, especially her Saturday column in the *Jornal do Brasil*, had brought her to the attention of a wider audience, keen to read more of her work; and after 1977, when the unexpected form and content of the last two works enthused and inspired new readers.[2] We might add a fourth wave, representing the international interest in Lispector enabled by her translation into other languages. The twenty-first century has been distinguished by a boom of anglophone translations and retranslations of Lispector's writing, which arguably has sparked renewed interest in her work both in Brazil and abroad. But where is this interest in Lispector taking us? What new approaches to reading and remixing her work are in formation? In the visual, musical and literary arts, a creation that is 'after' someone or something indicates a relation of influence. Possibly thanks to the German 'nach', this 'after' can also signal a translational relation. But often implicit in relations of influence are uneven power dynamics. The anglophone influence on her work notwithstanding, one of the challenges of the present volume has been to lay the groundwork for future engagements with her work that decentre anglophone influence and translation. We were proud to welcome five of her published translators to the Oxford conference, where, in a memorable session, they each read a paragraph of one of Lispector's stories in translation into their own languages. In the book, we are delighted to include contributions from seven translators of Lispector — Vidal has translated her into Latin American Spanish; Min into Mandarin Chinese; Segalovitz into Hebrew; Dodson, Edwards, and Novey into US English; and Pontiero into UK English — either reflecting on their encounters with her words or reflecting critically on her work.

The structure of *After Clarice* highlights one of various ways of reading and interpreting Lispector's legacy. For ease of navigation, we have divided the volume into seven parts, each part consisting of interrelated chapters. Of course, other constellations are possible, and we have included within each chapter cross-references to other chapters in the volume. Part I, 'Maps and Places', sets the scene by introducing the reader to Lispector's world, from the familiar and intimate to the strange and exotic. We begin, in Chapter 1, with an excerpt from Teresa Montero's *O Rio de Clarice: passeio afetivo pela cidade* (2018), a work that blends biography, history and geography as it maps locations significant to Lispector in the city of Rio de Janeiro. In the section we have included in this volume, Montero invites readers to visit the streets of Leme, the neighbourhood to which Lispector returned after almost two decades abroad and where she spent the remaining eighteen years of her life. In Chapter 2, Laís Botler evaluates Lispector's relation to place through a close reading of her correspondence with friends and family during the years she lived outside of Brazil. During this period, Lispector travelled widely, and her letters are replete with descriptions of the places she visited and inhabited. But Botler is also interested in the role 'non-places' (e.g., hotel rooms, train stations, roads) played in shaping, unsettling, and even suspending Lispector's sense of self and belonging in these critical years before her return to Brazil, leaving their mark in the works that followed. In Chapter 3, Dafna Hornike reads *The Passion According to G.H.* through its references to the Middle East. Although Lispector never visited that part of the world, and the novel is largely set in one small room, the text is 'haunted' by what

Hornike calls 'Holy Land imagery', which informs the protagonist's sense of spatial awareness and growing realization of (and negotiating to find) her place in the world; what could be called her personal 'journey' towards subjectivity.

Part II, 'Archives and Manuscripts', brings together chapters that address with manuscripts, archive material, little-studied texts and a (once) lost translation. The former head of the Literature Department of the Instituto Moreira Salles, Elvia Bezerra, presents some of the more surprising items in the Institute's Clarice Lispector Archive in Chapter 4. Lispector was not, as Bezerra shows, the most meticulous or consistent saver of her own work. This makes organizing her archive a challenge, but also lends an exciting unpredictability to the collection. Each item has its story, some answer lingering questions about Lispector's life and work, others raise new questions, ensuring that the archive remains, in Bezerra's words, 'unsettling'. The magical experience of visiting the IMS archive is evoked in Paloma Vidal's *crônica* 'And now', which first appeared in a special manuscript-edition of *The Hour of the Star* (Rocco, 2017).[3] Vidal — who has translated Lispector's *Um sopro de vida* and *A legião estrangeira* into Latin American Spanish — describes the encounter with Lispector's notes and drafts for *A hora da estrela* as a 'surgical operation'. Like many other archives, the IMS closed during the Covid-19 pandemic, and months of lockdown and social distancing resonate poignantly in Vidal's intimate account of the time she spent 'in a small glass room' with Lispector's manuscripts. In Chapter 6, Nádia Battella Gotlib revisits Lispector's 1963 conference paper on avant-garde Brazilian literature, a rarely-studied piece that the author delivered on multiple occasions. Though not published in her lifetime, the lecture illuminates Lispector's wrestling with her place in the Brazilian vanguard and her own understanding of the vanguard as a movement of liberation and self-knowledge. Gotlib reads this lecture alongside Lispector's novels *The Passion According to G.H.* and *The Hour of the Star*, focusing on how she applied and further developed her theory of the vanguard in her own writing. This section closes with Giovanni Pontiero's 'Afterword' to his translation of *A cidade sitiada*, which he appears to have completed in 1994. In her preface, Claire Williams recounts the detective work involved in determining what happened to this translation, long thought lost or non-existent. Following a trail of footnotes and ISBN numbers, Williams's search ends with a printout of the novel and the continued mystery of why this translation of one of Lispector's eminent translators remained unpublished at the time of his death.

For years, Lispector's works have found their way into a wide range of theoretical frameworks, perhaps most notably in the writing of French feminist and philosopher Hélène Cixous. In Section III, Theorizing Clarice, we bring together chapters that read Lispector's work in light of more recent theoretical approaches, while also acknowledging how earlier theoretical readings continue to inform appraisals of her work in academia. In Chapter 8, Marta Peixoto turns to affect theory to describe the nature of the encounter in Lispector's work. Noting a tendency to read the Claricean encounter (between people, objects and creatures) as moments of revelation and epiphany, Peixoto asks why these moments nonetheless feel inconclusive, mysterious and unresolved. Focusing on Lispector's short stories, and specifically two stories from the 1964 collection *The Foreign Legion*, Peixoto calls attention to how Lispector stages and describes these encounters as an unconscious and even contradictory affective process. In Chapter 9, Yael Segalovitz locates in Lispector's writing, and specifically in the short story collection *A via crucis do corpo* [The Via Crucis of the Body] (1974), a 'rhetoric of mistakes'. Through a close scrutiny of Lispector's citational practices and her 'highly calculated' modifications of Jewish texts, including the Hebrew Bible, Segalovitz — who has also translated this collection into Hebrew — sees these instances of error and mistake as politically charged, resisting 'the crushing force of the law'. Rather than things to be dismissed and discarded, these 'mistakes' have the potential to forge an anti-hierarchical, feminist intertextuality.

In Chapter 10, Julie Côté retraces Cixous's interest in Lispector and the extent to which Lispector's work shaped the development of Cixous's theory of *écriture féminine*; in fact, Côté asserts emphatically that 'Lispector made *écriture féminine* happen for Cixous'. Weighing up the early reception of Cixous's readings of Lispector, Côté asks what it means to go 'too far' when reading a text and what kind of errors and misreadings are permissible, if at all. Despite potential asymmetries between author and reader, Côté cites Lispector's own error-prone protagonists as evidence that the author herself invited a fearless engagement with her texts, even one that was excessive and prone to mistakes, as a form of collaborative reading. Closing this section, in Chapter 11, Nelson Vieira makes the case for including Lispector's work in the category of 'world literature'. Alongside recent theories of world literature, he offers a close reading of Lispector's own work and the late novel *The Hour of the Star* in particular. It is here — in the narrator's grappling with the material conditions of Macabéa's daily life — that Vieira locates and elaborates Lispector's own thinking about the (asymmetrical) relation between the local and global, the individual and the collective, author and readership.

Lispector's life and words have had a rich textual afterlife in the works of other writers. In Part IV, 'Writing and Rewriting', we bring together literary works and scholarship that highlight these engagements, which can range from inspiration and allusion to a radical remixing and rewriting of her work. Two of these chapters republish material that have appeared in other contexts; by including them here, we wish to show how they are a vital part of an important and ongoing conversation on Lispector's legacy. The writer Idra Novey translated *The Passion According to G.H.* for New Directions in 2012, an experience that shaped her 2014 poetry collection *Clarice: The Visitor*. For this volume, we have selected poems from this book that evoke the transformative experience of translating a beloved author, as well as the complicated economy of debt and inheritance that persists in our own writing. In her introduction to this selection, Novey addresses the legacy of Lispector and the intimacy her translators, editors, and readers feel towards her work. But Clarice, Novey cautions 'doesn't belong to us'.

Hélia Correia's short story 'Captura' [Capture] recasts Lispector's 'A imitação da rosa' [Imitation of the Rose] from a different angle, perhaps more disturbing than the original. Correia's story first appeared in her 2014 collection *Vinte degraus e outros contos* [Twenty Steps and Other Stories], and we have included it here in Annie McDermott's translation, along with an introduction Correia prepared for this volume. Here, Correia describes the 'fear and fascination' that grips her as a reader of Lispector's works. Laura, the protagonist of Lispector's 'Imitation of the Rose', is likewise and simultaneously transfixed and troubled by a vase of roses she has purchased earlier in the day. As she gazes obsessively at the flowers, we sense that Laura is in the grips of some affliction that is never directly named. Correia's story assumes a different, surprising perspective, one that brings Laura's mental and physical conditions into sharper relief, while also elucidating how our own gazes limit and delimit our ways of reading.

Claire Williams's analyses of literary afterlives, in Chapter 14, shows how Lispector's influence has haunted writers in recent decades. She detects these 'spectres of Clarice' in 'different kinds of textual relationships' that have emerged in English, French, Spanish, and Portuguese-language prose and poetry published between 1989 and 2017. Reading is key to the alchemical process of keeping Lispector and her works alive, and the writers gathered here — among them Erín Moure, Natalia Carrero, and José Eduardo Agualusa — are first and foremost readers of her work. As Williams shows, these 'haunted readers' wrestle with the ways in which they remain haunted by Lispector's words and legacy and are thereby compelled to reincarnate, worship and even exorcize her through their own writing and rewriting. In Chapter 15, Karyn Mota assesses the popularity of Lispector's words and persona, often taken out of context, and their proliferation online, primarily via social media platforms. Drawing on a rich trove of memes, Mota shows how participants of digital culture forge new meanings and narratives out of Lispector's language. At the same time, Lispector's words — and images of Lispector herself — circulate in ways and in contexts that can contribute to misreadings or misattributions of her work, thereby raising crucial questions about authorship, accessibility and copyright.

Lispector's writing is impressively open to reading through any number of theoretical frameworks, including, as previous chapters illustrate, feminist and affect theories. As Part V, 'The Posthuman', explores, her work has a levelling quality that treats animal, vegetable, mineral and thing equally, making it eminently applicable to theories of the posthuman and eco-criticism. The encounter between cockroach and narrator in *The Passion According to G.H.* (1964) has long fascinated posthuman theorists, but in Chapter 16, Kelli Zaytoun looks to Lispector's late works to gauge how these accord with, but also challenge posthumanism's understandings of the relation between subjectivity and death. For Zaytoun, Gloria Anzaldúa's theory of the shapeshifter/*la naguala* links productively to Lispector's tropes and characters, while also attending to the ways that Lispector's writing, particularly in her late and posthumous works, suggests a decolonizing turn away from Western models and theories of the human. In Chapter 17, Ami Schiess draws our attention to the wardrobe described in Lispector's 1973 novel *Água Viva*, and specifically to its *porta-espelho* (mirrored door). Charting the appearance and descriptions of this piece of furniture, Schiess asks how we as readers are meant to reconcile Lispector's detailed and insistent representations of such objects alongside her tendency to resist realism and mimesis. At the heart of Lispector's 'theory of the object' is an understanding of the object as vital and, in the case of the *porta-espelho*, as more than a reflection of our Self. Recognizing this carries ethical stakes, as Schiess shows in her study of Lispector's *The Hour of the Star*, a text that grapples openly with 'the complexities and ambivalences inherent in making an Other the object of representation'. Martin MacInnes's 2016 novel *Infinite Ground* opens with a line from *The Passion According to G.H.*, and although this is the novel's only direct reference to Lispector, this line sets a dramatic tone — and raises a question — that resonates throughout the book. In a conversation with Clare Archibald, which took place around the time the novel came out, MacInnes acknowledged the influence Lispector's understanding of nature had on his work. Against a 'stable' view of nature, Lispector approaches the natural world in a way that, in MacInnes's words, 'really challenged her own ego, risked losing herself'.[4] In Chapter 18, he expresses his admiration for Lispector's awareness of the inaccessibility of the body, her view of the human as 'something that is larger, stranger'.

Part 6, 'Transmediality and Performance', demonstrates how Lispector's texts can be productively 'read' by and even transformed and transfigured into other media. In Chapter 19, musician Kiran Leonard introduces the lyrics to his song 'The Mute Wide-Open Eye of All Things', which was inspired by several Lispector texts. He explains her appeal as a non-hierarchical writer whose words can speak to anyone, describing his own experience of reading her work as 'instinctive'. The title comes from Lispector's first novel *Perto do coração selvagem*, published in 1943, but the song itself gestures to other works by Lispector and 'the nausea / and the resplendence' of her visions. It seemed appropriate to follow Leonard's song lyrics with Carlos Mendes de Sousa's discussion of music across Lispector's *oeuvre* in Chapter 20. Lispector's letters to family and friends testify to the constant presence of music in her life, one that permeates her literature, as Sousa shows. But music was not just in the background; rather, musical references and scenes in her writing reveal how Lispector understood the art of composition and how these ideas developed across her many novels and short stories. In this wide-ranging analysis, Sousa shows how Lispector's interest in dissonance, 'tuneless singing', and the spontaneous compositions made from quotidian sounds fuelled her experimentations in writing.

The following three chapters address visual media, starting with Magdalena Edwards's critical viewing of Lispector's famous and infamous television interview with the journalist Júlio Lerner, which took place a few months before her death. At our Oxford conference, Edwards, an acclaimed actress and also a translator of Lispector's *The Chandelier* (New Directions, 2018), performed the lecture 'The Body Speaks: Clarice Lispector's *The Chandelier*', where she played the roles of translator, the protagonist Virginia and Lispector herself. She watched the interview repeatedly in preparation for her performance, discerning in the process powerful connections between this recording and Lispector's own interest in performance and theatre. Placing this interview in the context of 1970s Brazilian video art, Edwards shows how Lispector turns the Lerner interview into an 'anti-interview', one that calls attention to her discomfort and illness. But, more importantly, her refusal to play the part of the 'the author' proves to be transformative, allowing her to forge a radical relation to her protagonists and freeing her own readers and audience to be 'other'.

Chapter 22 by Mariela Méndez proposes a queer reading of the TV series *Correio feminino* [Ladies' Mail], a glamorous adaptation, directed by Luiz Fernando Carvalho, of a series of lifestyle columns that Lispector wrote under the pseudonym Helen Palmer. Méndez asks why the series did not prove popular with Brazilian audiences and suggests that the reason may lie in the way that the show, influenced by Lispector's own columns, unsettles gender and sex categories. Méndez argues that Lispector's destabilizing of heteronormative expectations responded to Brazil's developing consumer culture in ways that continue to resonate with and trouble viewers in the present day. This section ends with Sara Costa's chapter on Suzana Amaral's prize-winning 1985 film adaptation of Lispector's novel *A hora da estrela*. Comparing the film and novel, Costa evaluates the transcreative potential of film, the way it advances a 'poetic language' that derives from the literary text but also expands its semiotic range. This is particularly evident in how the film incorporates the novel's narrator, a figure who is never seen or described in the novel. She shows how Amaral conveys and translates — through sound, imagery, camera work and editing — the presence of the novel's narrator in ways that transcend Lispector's text.

Our seventh and last section, 'Translating Clarice', addresses the global engagement with Lispector's work via translation. Most of Lispector's works are now available in English, a phenomenon that has undoubtedly led to the last decade's 'tidal wave' of interest in her. Nevertheless, the chapters in this section also acknowledge that this interest is motivated by her translation into multiple other languages, not just English. In Chapter 24, Jacobs returns to the moment of Lispector's death and the attention to her Jewish background that it provoked, using this scene to consider how a Jewish reading of Lispector's *oeuvre* is activated by her translation into Hebrew. Reading *A hora da estrela* alongside Miriam Tivon's translation *She'at ha-kokhav*, Jacobs shows how the translation of 'compassion', from the Portuguese *piedade* to the Hebrew *rachamim*, allows for the formation of new intertextual relations that support and complicate a Jewish framing of Lispector's work.

As is to be expected with a writer who is canonical *and* popular, garnering interest for living an extraordinary life as well as for the literature she wrote, an enormous amount of critical and biographical material is available, including numerous *depoimentos* or personal accounts by those who knew her. The first 'sketch for a biography', published four years after her death, was written by Olga Borelli, her close companion in later years.[5] This unapologetically personal and subjective account has been followed by more traditional biographies, which Júlia Braga Neves explores in Chapter 25. Here she examines the techniques of life writing used in the three major literary biographies of Lispector — Nádia Battella Gotlib's *Clarice: uma vida que se conta* [Clarice: A Life that Tells Itself] (1995), Teresa Montero's *Eu sou uma pergunta: uma biografia de Clarice Lispector* [I am a Question: A Biography of Clarice Lispector] (1999) and Benjamin Moser's *Why This World: A Biography of*

Clarice Lispector (2009) — discerning in each text evidence of 'the entanglement between Lispector's life and work'.[6] In the case of Moser's biography, Neves also identifies small but meaningful differences between the English version and its Brazilian Portuguese translation. Although readers have long turned to Lispector's work for clues about her life (and vice versa), Neves shows how autobiographical readings of her fiction have increased and intensified in recent years, in no small measure due to these biographies.

Luana Freitas and Cynthia Costa provide a comprehensive list of all existing published translations of Lispector into English and compare translators' styles and methods in Chapter 26. Their comparison of translations by Giovanni Pontiero and Katrina Dodson highlights the ways in which translation (in this case, into English) can offer the Portuguese reader of Lispector new perspectives on her work. Translation, they show, is not only for those who do not read the original language. In Chapter 27, Katrina Dodson shares her experiences of the 'mystical journey' that was translating *The Complete Stories* for New Directions (published in 2015). Dodson, who was also completing a dissertation on Lispector at the time, deals sensitively with the shift of priorities and expectations between translator and scholar and those moments when the line between translator and author begin to blur. Closing this section, and the volume, is Chapter 28 by Min Xuefei, who is gradually translating all of Lispector's books into Mandarin Chinese, which is spoken by seventy percent of the Chinese population. Min describes her translation process as intimate and, like Dodson, mystical. In her translation, she has followed Lispector's style closely, allowing her repetitions and ambiguities to find their way into Chinese. In her approach, she has taken inspiration from translators like Fu Lei and Ezra Pound whose translations — however contested then and now — nonetheless showed how translated literature can cross national borders and become absorbed by another literary culture and tradition.

Finally, a few afterthoughts. On 10 December 2018, on what would have been her ninety-eighth birthday, the daily Google Doodle was dedicated to Clarice Lispector. It featured a collage by the artist Mariana Valente, Lispector's granddaughter. Valente's collages of her celebrated grandmother contain a number of references to Lispector's literary texts, but also, in Valente's words, 'represent her epiphanies coming from everyday scenes'.[7] This collage is one of several that Valente has created about her grandmother, and we are grateful that she agreed to let use one of these images for both our conference poster and the cover of this volume. The collage we selected brings together flora and fauna of Brazil, the typewriter that Lispector preferred to hold in her lap as she typed, and her interest in astrology and the occult, but we also want to call attention to the ship climbing down her neck. In Valente's collages, the ship is a figure of immigration, a reference to the ship that brought the Lispector family from what is now Ukraine to the shores of Brazil. The ship appears to be moving out of the frame, but the full image reveals that it is sailing towards a keyhole at the base of her neck.

After Clarice gestures to the future readers and scholars of Clarice Lispector, but it also recognizes the many ways that our own thinking about life and literature has been shaped by our encounters with her texts. Many of the contributors to the volume could tell you the first time they read Lispector, which exact text pulled them in. For Adriana, it was reading Giovanni Pontiero's translation of *The Hour of the Star* in her freshman year of college, a copy that is still on her bookshelf, full of marginalia and (double, triple) underlined words and phrases. For Claire, too, it was *A hora da estrela*, read in amazement and delight after being intrigued by hearing, in a lecture on French Twentieth Century Women's Writing, about Cixous's assertion that Lispector was the greatest practitioner of *écriture féminine*. She teaches the text every year and it still surprises her.

In December 2020 Clarice scholars around the world were marking the centenary of Lispector's birth in a wide range of media and genres. The many commemorative events, launches, exhibitions, film premieres and publications, planned to be held in locations as far afield as Princeton and Macau, had to adjust to the challenges of a global pandemic, but they still went ahead, adapting to new formats.[8] Our birthday present was an online preview of this volume, reuniting the contributors to the book in virtual form, since it was not possible for us to celebrate in person.[9] Each contributor presented a condensed version of their chapter in three minutes and was instructed not to let slip any spoilers. During the pandemic we have all learned to work and talk and communicate in new ways, and one silver lining was the technology enabling colleagues in Rio, São Paulo, Montreal, New York, Oxford, Sintra, Jerusalem and Beijing to participate in events simultaneously. This sense of togetherness and collaboration, despite great distances, was very important to us as we worked on the book, liaising with our contributors, and watching it progress while so much else was halted and interrupted, was truly a marvellous experience. Carlos Mendes de Sousa aptly described the sense of camaraderie and shared enthusiasm for Lispector that we all recognized that day as 'amizade com Clarice ao fundo' [friendship with Clarice in the background]. Her open, writerly texts enable multiple readings by multiple readers, which makes us confident that there are many more readings to come: with Clarice and after Clarice.

Works Cited

ALMEIDA, HUGO (ed.), *Feliz aniversário Clarice* (Belo Horizonte: Autêntica, 2020)
ARCHIBALD, CLARE, 'In Conversation with Martin MacInnes', *Envirohum* <https://envirohum.wixsite.com/home/single-post/2016/10/11/in-conversation-with-martin-macinnes> [accessed 1 October 2021]
BORELLI, OLGA, *Clarice Lispector: esboço para um possível retrato* (Rio de Janeiro: Nova Fronteira, 1981)
CORREIA, HÉLIA, *Vinte degraus e outros contos* (Lisbon: Relógio d'Água, 2014)
GOTLIB, NÁDIA BATTELLA, *Clarice: uma vida que se conta* (São Paulo: Ática, 1995)
—— 'Readers of Clarice, Who Are You?', in *Closer to the Wild Heart: Essays on Clarice Lispector*, ed. by Cláudia Pazos Alonso and Claire Williams (Oxford: Legenda, 2002), pp. 182–97
MACINNES, MARTIN, *Infinite Ground* (London: Atlantic Books, 2016)
MÉNDEZ, MARIELA, CLAUDIA DARRIGRANDI and MÀCARENEA MALLEA (eds), *El arte de pensar sin riesgos*, ed. by (Buenos Aires: Corregidor, 2021)

MERCADÉ, ISABEL (ed.), *Clarice Lispector: alguién dirá mi nombre* (Santander: Shangrila, 2020)
MONTERO, TERESA, *Eu sou uma pergunta: uma biografia de Clarice Lispector* (Rio de Janeiro: Rocco, 1999)
—— *O Rio de Clarice: passeio afetivo pela cidade* (Belo Horizonte: Autêntica, 2018)
MONTES, RAFAEL, *Perfect Days*, trans. by Alison Entrekin (London: Harvill Secker, 2016)
MOSER, BENJAMIN, *Why This World: A Biography of Clarice Lispector* (London: Haus, 2009)
NOVEY, IDRA, *Clarice: The Visitor* (London: Sylph, 2014)
RODRIGUES, JOSÉ MÁRIO (ed.), *O que eu escrevo continua: dez ensaios no centenário de Clarice Lispector* (Recife: Cepe, 2021)

Notes to the Afterword

1. The impact is literal in Rafael Montes's dark thriller *Dias perfeitos* (2014), where a 'beautifully bound' five-hundred-page hardback edition of Lispector's short stories is used as a weapon, against a woman called Clarice; *Perfect Days*, trans. by Alison Entrekin (London: Harvill Secker, 2016), p. 28.
2. Nádia Battella Gotlib, 'Readers of Clarice, Who Are You?', in *Closer to the Wild Heart: Essays on Clarice Lispector*, ed. by Cláudia Pazos Alonso and Claire Williams (Oxford: Legenda, 2002), pp. 182–97 (p. 183).
3. The *crônica* is a journalistic genre popular in Latin America, similar to an op-ed article, or regularly appearing column. The *cronista*, or columnist, reflects on current events from a personal perspective, often developing an idiosyncratic style. In European Portuguese the word is accented differently: *crónica*.
4. Clare Archibald, 'In Conversation with Martin MacInnes', *Envirohum*, <https://envirohum.wixsite.com/home/single-post/2016/10/11/in-conversation-with-martin-macinnes> [accessed 1 October 2021].
5. Olga Borelli, *Clarice Lispector: esboço para um possível retrato* (Rio de Janeiro: Nova Fronteira, 1981).
6. Nádia Battella Gotlib, *Clarice: uma vida que se conta* (São Paulo: Ática, 1995); Teresa Montero, *Eu sou uma pergunta: uma biografia de Clarice Lispector* (Rio de Janeiro: Rocco, 1999); Benjamin Moser, *Why This World: A Biography of Clarice Lispector* (London: Haus, 2009).
7. <https://www.google.com/doodles/clarice-lispectors-98th-birthday> [accessed 2 October 2021].
8. *Clarice Lispector: alguién dirá mi nombre*, ed. by Isabel Mercadé (Santander: Shangrila, 2020); *Feliz aniversário Clarice*, ed. by Hugo Almeida (Belo Horizonte: Autêntica, 2020); *O que eu escrevo continua: dez ensaios no centenário de Clarice Lispector*, ed. by José Mário Rodrigues (Recife: Cepe, 2021); *El arte de pensar sin riesgos*, ed. by Mariela Méndez, Claudia Darrigrandi and Màcarenea Mallea (Buenos Aires: Corregidor, 2021) are just some of the publications released to commemorate the centenary of Lispector's birth. Her French publishers, des femmes, put together a 'Coffret Anniversaire', with new translations of *The Passion According to G.H.* and *The Hour of the Star*. A collection of all known correspondence, *Todas as cartas*, was launched by Rocco, which in 2021 published *À procura da própria coisa*, an expanded edition of Teresa Montero's 1999 biography. In addition, New Directions brought out a commemorative edition of *The Hour of the Star*, with an afterword by Lispector's son Paulo Gurgel Valente. Two critically acclaimed film adaptations of novels by Lispector came out in 2020, but could not be widely distributed to cinemas: *A paixão segundo G.H.* [*The Passion According to G.H.*] (directed by Luiz Fernando Carvalho) and *O livro dos prazeres* [*The Book of Pleasures*] (directed by Marcela Lordy).
9. The event took place on 12 December 2020 and was generously hosted by the Oxford University Brazilian Society, with invaluable technical support from José Inácio da Costa Filho. It was recorded and is still available online: <https://www.youtube.com/watch?v=JPYImR-GmJk> [accessed 2 October 2021].

PART I

Maps and Places

CHAPTER 1

A Walk through Clarice's Leme: One of the 'O Rio de Clarice' Guided Tours

Teresa Montero

The neighbourhood of Leme runs alongside the Avenida Atlântica as it sets off towards Copacabana.[1] Two neighbourhoods were built alongside the thoroughfare, parted by the Avenida Princesa Isabel, but at first sight they look like one. Some say that Leme is the glorious starting point of Copacabana beach, since the Avenida Atlântica begins there, at the Pedra do Leme, a rock formation in the shape of a rudder ('leme').[2] But others are convinced that it is the finishing line for those arriving from Posto 6, at the other end of the beach.[3]

Leme has been important to the city of Rio de Janeiro since colonial times due to its strategic location for defence against pirate attacks, particularly the Fort. Leme and Copacabana share the same coastline and were discovered and developed at the same time. It all began with a royal picnic in 1858, when the emperor, Dom Pedro II (1825–1891), and his family went to see two beached whales, and to take the healthy sea air. The area later became linked to the city centre by public transport, and started to grow and prosper. When trams arrived in the Brazilian capital in the last decade of the nineteenth century, public spaces were deemed necessary between Leme and Igrejinha, as the other end of the beach was known.

It was here in this safe harbour, with the Atlantic Ocean lapping at the shore, that Clarice Gurgel Valente (not officially separated from her husband until 1964), and her sons Pedro, aged ten, and Paulo, aged six, dropped anchor in 1959. The small knot of streets squeezed between the beach and the hills of Babilônia and Chapéu Mangueira, with their favela communities, became their home for the next eighteen years. Clarice made many friends in the neighbourhood, which was popular with artists and writers, but she also relished her solitude and the calm of an early morning, gazing out of her penthouse apartment over the sea.

> De repente acordar no meio da noite e ter essa coisa rara: solidão. Quase nenhum ruído. Só o das ondas do mar batendo na praia. E tomo café com gosto, toda sozinha no mundo. Ninguém me interrompe o nada. É um nada a um tempo vazio e rico. E o telefone mudo, sem aquele toque súbito que sobressalta.

Depois vai amanhecendo. As nuvens se clareando sob um sol às vezes pálido como uma lua, às vezes de fogo puro. Vou ao terraço e sou talvez a primeira do dia a ver a espuma branca do mar. O mar é meu, o sol é meu, a terra é minha. E sinto-me feliz por nada, por tudo. Até que, como o sol subindo, a casa vai acordando e há o reencontro com meus filhos sonolentos.

[To wake up suddenly in the middle of the night and feel this rare thing: solitude. Scarcely a sound to be heard. Only the sea waves beating against the shore. And I drink my coffee with pleasure, all alone in the world. No one interrupts this void. A void so empty and yet so rich. And the telephone silent. No sudden ringing to give one a fright. Then the first glimmer of light. The clouds lighten beneath the sun, sometimes pale as the moon, sometimes burning like fire. I go onto the terrace, probably the first person that morning to contemplate the sea's white spume. The sea is mine, the sun is mine, the earth is mine. And I feel happy for nothing and everything. Until the house awakens like sunrise and I am reunited with my sleepy children.][4]

A well-travelled woman, Clarice had been away from Brazil for sixteen years. It took her thirty-nine years, crossing four countries, two capital cities and numerous neighbourhoods of Rio de Janeiro, but when questioned about her travels around the world she answered categorically: 'Agora, minha terra é o Leme' [Leme is my land now]. What was it that enchanted her about Leme and meant that she stayed in the neighbourhood for the rest of her life when she separated from her husband and returned definitively to Brazil? It was by no means easy for a woman of her generation, and with two small children. Leme represented the start of a new phase in her life: a return to Brazil and to writing. She had not written a line in almost three years, since she put the final full stop to *A maçã no escuro* [The Apple in the Dark], in Washington, in 1961.

The 'land of Leme' had its own life, and Clarice could find all she needed just a few steps away from her front door. Over the next eighteen years, she lived at two addresses: from 1959 to 1965 at no. 2, Rua General Ribeiro da Costa and from 1965 to 1977 at no. 88, Rua Gustavo Sampaio. Leme was the neighbourhood where Clarice wrote most of her works, twelve books out of the seventeen published over four decades. She was leaving behind the image of a shadowy figure mentioned every now and then in the newspapers and becoming a key player in carioca culture and Brazilian literature.

In the early 1960s, Clarice's typewriter keys tapped away alongside voices clamouring for social reform in the hillside communities. Renée Delorme, a Dominican missionary, had set up a clinic in Chapéu Mangueira and, in collaboration with Asaleme, won support from the Archbishop of Rio de Janeiro, Dom Hélder Câmara, in her campaign to get running water installed in the favela.

North American poet Elizabeth Bishop, who translated a few of Clarice's short stories, and also a selection of contemporary poets in *An Anthology of Twentieth Century Brazilian Poetry* (1972), lived just round the corner.[5] Bishop and her partner Lota de Macedo Soares (an architect and urban planner who worked on the reclaiming and landscaping of Rio's beachfront area) resided in Edifício Mandori at no. 5 Rua Antônio Vieira.[6] It was from her window in this apartment that Bishop watched the bandit known as Micuçú chased by police through the favela, an event she would later turn into the poem 'The Burglar of Babylon', first published in the *New Yorker* in 1964.

Actors and cameramen were to scale the hill in 1967 to film *Una Rosa Per Tutti* [A Rose for Everyone/Every Man's Woman], directed by Franco Rossi and starring Claudia Cardinale. Many teenage boys, including Clarice's son Paulo, were thrilled to hear that the beautiful actress would be visiting their neighbourhood.

Clarice would often climb the side road leading uphill, Ladeira Ary Barroso, to see her friends at no. 26: the Pernambucan designer Aloiso Magalhães and his wife Solange. And there were many more artists living beyond the block formed by Rua General Ribeiro da Costa and Ladeira Ary Barroso. Painter Candido Portinari lived at no. 900 Avenida Atlântica and the studio of sculptor Bruno Giorgi (married to Clarice's friend Mira Engelhardt), was on Rua Gustavo Sampaio, beside the Edifício Montese.[7]

The soundtrack to Leme at that time was eclectic: lots of samba and bossa nova, the latter ready to move to Ipanema in the 1960s. Leme was a bohemian neighbourhood which, together with Copacabana, was home to 80% of Rio's nightclubs. There is no way of knowing whether Clarice was a habitué, but she certainly visited some, including the most famous one, at the corner of Rua Antônio Vieira and the Avenida Atlântica: 'Sacha's Seven to Seven', where pianist Sacha Rubin performed for artists, journalists, intellectuals and politicians. In the Rua Gustavo Sampaio was 'Arpège', owned by the pianist Waldir Calmon, whose tunes on the solovox (an early form of synthesizer) were the background music for several generations of courting couples. Many young musicians who were just starting out played sets in the club, including the godfathers of bossa nova, João Gilberto, Tom Jobim, Vinicius de Moraes and singer-songwriter Chico Buarque.

Local businesses were able to provide everything she needed to fill her cupboards. They were mostly concentrated in Rua Gustavo Sampaio, the main thoroughfare running through the neighbourhood, with a few shops located round the corner on Rua Anchieta. Although Clarice makes hardly any references to shops or local businesses in her short stories and *crônicas*, another new arrival to Leme at the time, newspaper columnist Elsie Lessa wrote a full portrait of the neighbourhood in one go, in a *crônica* called 'A nova moradora do Leme' [A new resident in Leme].[8] In it she spots a nice hunk of meat, 'vermelha e úmida, pendendo ricamente dos ganchos do teto' [red and moist, hanging richly from the hooks in the roof],[9] at Sr. João's butcher's shop, which had a set of scales so large that lots of his customers used it to weigh their children. Cereals and dairy products? Easy to find at the general stores run by Sr. Avelino and Sr. Porto, or at the Casas Gaio Marti, where purchases were recorded in a notebook, for payment at the end of the month.

Lessa's *crônica* continues, describing Sr. Tobias Timovski's 'LemeFar' pharmacy: 'Pode-se ficar doente em paz nesta rua, que a farmácia tudo provê e prevê. Balança na porta, luz fluorescente, perfumarias, drogas e artigos de toucador' [Don't worry about falling ill in this street, because the pharmacy provides everything you need right now, and anything you might need later. There are scales by the door, fluorescent lights, perfumes, medicines and cosmetics].[10] Indeed, when she wanted medicine, eye drops, or to cash a cheque, that's where Clarice went.

If she was running out of Hollywood cigarettes (filter), or there was no Coca-Cola in the fridge, when she could not listen to Rádio MEC or Rádio Relógio because she needed new batteries for the radio, she would go downstairs, cross the entrance hall and head to the *botequim* on the other side of the street, where the Portuguese proprietor, Manuel Constantino, would supply the items immediately.

Elsie Lessa wrote evocatively about the smell of fresh bread wafting down the streets: 'Só isto bastaria para fazer o orgulho de qualquer bairro' [This in itself would be the pride and joy of any neighbourhood].[11] Leme was full of the aromas of 'broa de milho, pão sovado, brioches, empadas e pastéis' [cornbread, sourdough, brioches, pies and pastries][12] produced by bakers and confectioners such as 'Rio Leme', 'Duque de Caxias' and 'A Nossa Padaria'. It also boasted the 'Alvorada' shoe shop, two dry cleaners ('Tio Sam' and 'Elisa'), a tiny cinema, the 'Danúbio', above the 'Alpino': 'Grande bar, bem começo do século, bem bávaro, bem antes da era melancólica das boates' [A great bar, very 'turn of the century', very Bavarian, very pre- the melancholy era of nightclubs],[13] lamented the columnist, in the heart of nightclub territory. As the mother of school-age children, Clarice was probably aware of the Alpino. According to Elsie Lessa, the orchestra played only until midnight, because 'este bairro é honesto, familiar e deita cedo. Um grande bairro' [this is an honest neighbourhood, a family neighbourhood, and we go to bed early. A great neighbourhood].[14]

We do not know whether or not Clarice read this *crônica*, but we do know that she liked Elsie Lessa. When she realized how much she was loved by the readers of her own column, in the *Jornal do Brasil*, she wanted to share the news with her neighbour: 'Vou telefonar para Elsie, que faz crônica há mais tempo do que eu, para lhe perguntar que faço dos telefonemas maravilhosos que recebo, das rosas pungentes de tanta beleza que me oferecem, das cartas simples e profundas que me mandam' [I must telephone Elsie, who has been writing a column for much longer than me, to ask her what I should do about the marvellous telephone calls I receive, the lovely, sweet-smelling roses people give me, and the simple yet profound letters people send in].[15]

Clarice's Leme was well catered for in terms of transport links. In the 1960s, a tram ran along Rua Gustavo Sampaio and terminated at Praça Júlio de Noronha. There were also buses known as 'lotações'. Once, when Clarice was waiting for a bus, she spotted Elsie Lessa's son, Ivan, one of the editors of *Senhor* magazine which had published some of her short stories.[16] They watched a man walk past with 'o seu tranquilo cachorro puxado pela correia' [with his placid little dog on a lead].[17] Except it was not a dog, but a coati. This event became the *crônica* 'Um amor conquistado' [Conquered Love], first published in *A legião estrangeira* [*The Foreign Legion*].[18]

But there is no doubt that Clarice's preferred means of transport was the taxi, and there were four taxi ranks at her disposal. Her taxi rides were the subject of many *crônicas*. She loved listening to classical music during the journey and if the piece had not finished by the time they arrived at their destination, she would stay in the car until it had.

> Com a minha mania de andar de táxi, entrevisto todos os chofores com quem viajo. Uma noite dessas viajei com um espanhol ainda bem moço, de bigodinho e olhar triste. Conversa vai, conversa vem, ele me perguntou se eu tinha filhos. Perguntei-lhe se ele também tinha, respondeu que não era casado, que jamais se casaria. E contou-me sua história.
>
> [With my mania for taxis, I started interviewing all the taxi-drivers. One night, the driver was a young Spaniard with a tiny moustache and sad expression. Chatting about this and that, he asked me if I had any children. I asked him the same question whereupon he told me that he was not married and had no intention of marrying. Then he told me his story.][19]

With so few streets, Leme could be crossed in a matter of minutes. And although Elsie Lessa wrote about the smell of bread perfuming the neighbourhood, for Clarice it was the smell of the sea. There is, however, only one existing photo of her on Leme beach, where she so often took her children.[20] Numerous references to the sea can be found in her *crônicas*, short stories and novels. One of them tells of a trip to Leme beach and an unexpected encounter with three nuns, which she shared with the readers of the *Jornal do Brasil*:

> Numa dessa manhãs fui muito cedo à praia. Era um dia de calor insuportável, mês de março, mas a praia ainda estava deserta, pelo menos essa foi a primeira impressão que tive. Logo desfeita pela visão de quatro freiras, duas de prêto e duas de branco, todas apanhando alguma coisa na areia. Pareciam, as de branco, duas pombas. Estavam as quatro descalças. Não aguentei a curiosidade, fui para uma delas. E perguntei: 'Posso ajudar em alguma coisa? O que é que as senhoras estão procurando?' 'Nada, só conchas, estamos só brincando, enquanto esperamos que nos venham buscar'. Uma era do Rio mesmo e mora na Rua Oriente, as três outras são de Belo Horizonte e vieram aqui para se tratar: devem ir à praia todos os dias, embora lhes seja proibido entrar no mar.
>
> [One morning, not so long ago, I went to the beach very early. It was an unbearably hot day in March, but the beach was still deserted, at least, that was my first impression. Soon disproved by the sight of four nuns, two dressed in black and two in white, all searching for something in the sand. The two in white looked like a pair of doves. All four had bare feet. I could not rein in my curiosity so I went over to one of them and asked: 'Can I help you at all, Sisters? What are you looking for?' 'Nothing, just shells. We're just playing while we wait for someone to come and pick us up'. One was from right here in Rio and she lives in Rua Oriente; the other three are from Belo Horizonte and came here for their health. They must go to the beach every day, although they are forbidden from going into the sea.][21]

Clarice had no intention of making do with the allowance she received from her ex-husband to look after herself and their children, nor with the scant royalty payments from her first three books. Her solution was to go back to journalism. Before she had even returned to Brazil she had started to collaborate with *Senhor* magazine, where she had been publishing short stories since 1959. They were received so positively that she continued sending material until 1962, when she contributed her own column, 'Children's Corner' (the title was in English), which included short stories, thoughts and *crônicas*.[22]

Clarice certainly needed stamina and courage during her first years living in Leme. She was determined that her children would receive a first-class education. So we should not be surprised to hear that she supplemented her income writing women's pages in daily newspapers. The first, under the pseudonym Helen Palmer, was entitled 'Correio Feminino' [Ladies' Mail] and ran in the *Correio da Manhã* in 1959 and 1960. From 1960 to 1961 she worked as a ghost writer for actress Ilka Soares, producing the 'Só para Mulheres' [Women Only] page for *Diário da Noite*. Ilka had not been invented by the newspaper's editor, Alberto Dines. The actress and model, married to the actor Anselmo Duarte, was Clarice's neighbour. She lived in Edifício Cáceres, no. 16, Rua Aurelino Leal. While Ilka gave Clarice fashion tips to go in the newspaper, her children Anselmo Jr. and Lídia played with Paulo, Clarice's youngest. Their favourite place to play was the street.

An intense day of working as a journalist robbed Clarice of time she could have dedicated to literature. Nonetheless, after just one enquiry from publishers Francisco Alves about whether she had any original works lying forgotten in a drawer, her work started coming out in Brazil again, in the form of the thirteen short stories brought together as *Laços de família* [Family Ties] (1960). Seven of them were new, and the others had been published by the Ministry of Education and Health as *Alguns contos* [Stories] (1952) and in *Senhor*.

During her first ten years living in Leme, Clarice's works diversified into other modes of artistic expression. The publication of *Laços de família*, and *A maçã no escuro* and Fauzi Arap's adaptation of her texts for the theatre in 1965 led to a certain amount of fame and she could no longer count on anonymity within the neighbourhood.[23] Maria Bethânia read Clarice's texts aloud as part of her show *Comigo me desavim* [I'm at odds with myself] (1967),[24] and there were incursions into children's literature with *O mistério do coelho pensante* [The Mystery of the Thinking Rabbit] (1967) and *A mulher que matou os peixes* [The Woman who Killed the Fish] (1968). Nonetheless, nothing generated so great an impact as her Saturday column in the *Jornal do Brasil*. She started her collaboration with the newspaper in August 1967 and it brought her many new readers. In her *crônicas* she reflected on all sorts of things, including impressions of Leme and Rio de Janeiro. Her popularity increased even further when she started interviewing celebrities for *Manchete* magazine in May 1968.

Anyone who read the 'Caderno B' supplement on a Saturday, and the residents of Leme certainly did, knew just how much the writer Clarice Lispector felt uncomfortable with so much popularity: 'Todos querem me conhecer. Pior para mim. Não sou domínio público [...] O *Jornal do Brasil* me está tornando popular. Ganho rosas. Um dia paro' [Everyone was anxious to meet me. All the worse for me. I am not public property. [...] My articles in the *Jornal do Brasil* are bringing me fame. Readers send me roses. One day I shall stop writing].[25]

The residents of Edifício Tietê, on Rua Gustavo Sampaio, were among the first to learn of the drama taking place on 14 September 1966, when a fire caused by an unextinguished cigarette destroyed Clarice's bedroom. Clarice smoked, and she needed medication to help her sleep; this may explain how the accident happened.

The residents of Edifício Tietê, which backs onto the front of Edifício Macedo, shouted out when they saw the fire. The porter on duty, João Medeiros Farias, heard them and ran to put out the flames, with the help of Sr. Saul, who lived in the apartment next door to Clarice.

There were several operations, skin grafts, and even the threat of amputation to her right hand (the hand she used to write), but Clarice overcame these challenges and continued to produce her texts. The support of her family, her friends and her readers — some of whom lived in Leme — was crucial to her recovery.

> o que você escreveu hoje no jornal foi exatamente como eu sinto; e então eu, que moro defronte de você e assisti o seu incêndio e sei pela luz acesa quando você tem insônia, eu então trouxe um polvo para você.
>
> [The things you wrote in your column today sum up exactly how I feel. I live opposite and I was at my window the night your apartment caught fire, and whenever I see your light on I know that you are having a sleepless night. So I've brought you an octopus.][26]

In the early 1970s, artistic expression was subject to censorship by the military dictatorship and the publishing market had cooled down, at least when it came to Clarice's books. Her former publisher, Sabiá, was bought by José Olympio in 1973, and this meant that the most powerful publisher of Brazilian literature would finally publish her works. It began by re-issuing the books that had already come out with Sabiá.

In the same period, Artenova, run by Álvaro Pacheco, brought out a paperback to be sold at newspaper kiosks; something completely new in Brazil. It was the short story anthology *A imitação da rosa* (1973) which brought together texts selected by Clarice herself. He was bold enough to publish *Água viva* (1973), an original manuscript which Clarice had hesitated about publishing because the narrative was so experimental. Pacheco went on to commission the volume of erotic stories *A via crucis do corpo* [The Via Crucis of the Body] (1974) and *De corpo inteiro* [The Whole Body/Full Size] (1975), which collected some of the interviews Clarice had done for *Manchete* and included three new ones.

The decade continued to be full of obstacles for Clarice. A serious blow came when she was sacked from the *Jornal do Brasil* in 1974, but she managed to find a new income from translating international bestsellers into Portuguese for publishers Artenova and Imago. Fortunately, the head of Imago was her neighbour. Pedro Paulo Sousa Madureira lived in the Edifício Maracati, in Rua General Ribeiro da Costa.[27] He and Clarice became firm friends who breakfasted together at least once a week. The early bird would arrive very early, when her friend was still asleep. No problem: Babá, Pedro Paulo's maid, kept Dona Clarice happy with delicious northeastern delicacies which the two women would enjoy together.

The 1970s was fated to be one which produced short stories. When Clarice published novels, like *Água viva*, they were often confused with novellas because of their length. Francisco Alves published a selection of forty-five *crônicas* from the *Jornal do Brasil* in a volume entitled *Visão do esplendor: impressões leves* [Vision of Splendour: Brief Impressions] (1975).

Clarice returned to journalism in December 1976, when she started interviewing for the magazine *Fatos e fotos: gente*, carrying on until October 1977. After she stopped publishing her columns in the *Jornal do Brasil*, Leme appeared less often in her literary works. It is still detectable, however: in the market stalls and Sr. Manuel Constantino's bar opposite the Edifício Macedo; the deserted beach, early in the morning; the taxi rank; the almond trees of Rua Gustavo Sampaio; and the maids working in her building. In the *crônicas* there were frequent references to her daily life, to her maid, her dog Ulisses, and her sons. In 1971, Paulo moved to a small apartment on the same street, where he lived for the next five years, until he got married. He was eighteen and studying Economics at the Federal University of Rio de Janeiro, so he needed his own space, but did not want to be too far from his mother. Indeed, they had lunch together every day. In 1974, Pedro went to live with his father, Maury Gurgel Valente, and his new wife Isabel, in Montevideo, where Maury was Brazilian Ambassador to Uruguay. Once her sons had moved out, Clarice bought a dog which was a basset mongrel cross. Ulisses stayed with her to the end of her life — she could no longer live without him. Her love for dogs dated back to her time in Naples, when she had adopted a stray and called it Dilermando.

In 1977, the year of her death, she collaborated with the newspaper *Última Hora*, republishing *crônicas* from the *Jornal do Brasil*, and in October she launched her last novel, *A hora da estrela* with José Olympio Editora. There was no time to find out what her readers thought about it. Also in October, Clarice went to hospital with an intestinal obstruction of unknown cause. On 28 October, she underwent an operation at the Casa de Saúde São Sebastião, in the neighbourhood of Catete and was diagnosed with cancer.

That last day, the 26th? the 27th?, she started to say goodbye to Leme. Though her body was failing her, there was nothing wrong with Clarice's imagination and she suggested to her friend Olga Borelli and her assistant and nurse Siléa Marchi that they play a game of 'let's pretend' in the taxi on the way to hospital. Clarice made up a story that they were not going to hospital, that she was not ill and that they were actually on their way to Paris. The driver asked if he could tag along, and Clarice told him that he could bring his girlfriend too. When he confessed that he did not have enough money for the trip and that his girlfriend was elderly, Clarice told him to pretend that he had won the lottery.

Let us pretend that Clarice went to 'Paris' listening to the samba by Alcyr Pires Vermelho and Alberto Ribeiro: 'Que lindas mulheres de olhos azuis, tu és a cidade luz / Paris, Paris, *je t'aime*, mas eu gosto muito mais do Leme' [What beautiful women with blue eyes, you are the city of light, Paris, Paris, *je t'aime*, but the place I love the most is Leme].

The Casa de Saúde São Sebastião was very expensive. Clarice's friends Nélida Piñon and Rosa Cass decided to save her the expense and got her transferred to a public hospital: Hospital da Lagoa on the Rua Jardim Botânico. She saw Leme for the last time in November, from the ambulance which took her and Paulo to the Hospital da Lagoa. And it was in the neighbourhood named after the Jardim Botânico [Botanical Garden], which had inspired her writing as she wandered down its avenues, that she passed away. She was buried on 11 December 1977 in the Cemitério Comunal Israelita do Caju, the Jewish cemetery in the North Zone of Rio, close to her very first home in the city.

In 2016, thirty-nine years after she 'went to Paris', she returned to Leme in the form of a bronze statue by Edgar Duvivier. Clarice and her dog Ulisses no longer reside at no. 88 Rua Gustavo Sampaio but on Leme beach.

Paths through Clarice's Leme

2 — Rua Gustavo Sampaio[28]

Gustavo Sampaio was an army lieutenant and supporter of President Floriano Peixoto. He was fatally wounded by shrapnel during the revolt known as Revolta da Armada (1893–94), and died at the age of twenty-two. Nobody knows why the main street in Leme, the first to be built, and the one where Clarice lived for fourteen years, was named after the young military martyr. She used to go to the famous Monday market, which still operates today. There would be stalls along part of Rua Gustavo Sampaio and in front of her building. Olga Borelli commented that Clarice used to complain about the noise made by the stallholders putting their stalls up at dawn. Another resident of the street, who was a student of journalism at the time and a loyal reader of Clarice's *crônicas* remembers occasionally seeing her: 'de lenço na cabeça, linda no seu tipo eslavo, comprando legumes, verduras e peixe' [wearing a headscarf, beautiful with her Slavic looks, buying vegetables, salad and fish].[29]

4 — Igreja Nossa Senhora do Rosário (Rua General Ribeiro da Costa no. 164)

This is the only church in Leme and it belongs to the Dominican Order. The building was completed on 4 August 1939. Frei [Father] Rolim and Frei Marcos Mendes de Faria were well-known personalities working at this church which, from the mid-1950s up until the early twenty-first century achieved a great deal of social work in collaboration with the residents of Leme. They integrated themselves in the life of the neighbourhood and became members of the residents' association, Asaleme.

One Leme resident and regular churchgoer mentioned to Frei Bruno Palma that she had seen Clarice on a few occasions sitting there in an empty pew. Indeed, this was apparently something she liked to do, because in the *crônica* 'Quase' [Almost] she wrote about a visit to the Santa Teresinha do Menino Jesus Church in Rua Lauro Sodré: 'Meu táxi aproximava-se do túnel que leva para o Leme ou para Copacabana, quando olhei e vi a igreja de Santa Teresinha. Meu coração bateu forte: reconheci dentro da carne da alma, que sentia na dor, reconheci que seria na igreja que eu poderia encontrar refúgio' [My taxi was approaching the tunnel which goes to Leme and Copacabana when I saw the Church of St Teresa of Lisieux. My heart beat faster: I recognized in the depths of my suffering soul that I might be able to find refuge in that church].[30]

Clarice liked talking about Christianity with her friends Nélida Piñon and Olga Borelli. She was impressed by Christ's entreaty to 'love one another as I love you'. This idea terrified her: loving someone to the point of giving one's life for them. There were some saints she prayed to, especially St Anthony, of whom she had a small statue. She was fond of him for the humanity he represented, but without religious connotations, according to her son Paulo. When she interviewed Zagallo, the Brazilian national football team coach, she admitted that in moments of crisis she held tight to St Anthony, St Rita de Cássia and St Judas Tadeu.[31]

5 — Rua Aurelino Leal

Aurelino Leal was a politician, journalist and district attorney, but he became famous in Rio when, as chief of police of Distrito Federal, he inspired Donga and Mauro de Almeida to compose what is known as the first samba to be recorded in Brazil: 'Pelo telefone' (1917). Leal told his subordinates to inform offenders 'over the telephone' about the seizing of items used in gambling. The unofficial version of the lyrics even mentioned 'Chefe Aureliano'.

At no. 16, in Edifício Cáceres, lived Justino and Lucinda Martins with their son Carlitos. Lucinda was the sister of Mafalda Veríssimo, the wife of Érico Veríssimo.[32] Clarice had become very friendly with the Veríssimos during her time in Washington D.C. and they were the godparents to her sons. She worked for *Manchete*, run by Justino Martins, who was responsible for developing the magazine into what became its iconic format: colour photos and entertaining content. Érico and Mafalda's son, the writer Luis Fernando Veríssimo, fondly remembers the time when he was living at Aunt Lucinda's apartment: eating out at Fiorentina, celebrating the 1962 World Cup and doing a job that Clarice arranged for him, at an advertising agency. It is Lucinda who appears beside Clarice and her sons in the only known photo of the family on Leme beach.

Clarice mentioned the death of Lucinda's son Carlito in the *crônica* 'Desculpem, mas se morre' [Inevitable Death].[33] Other residents of the Cáceres were Ilka Soares and Anselmo Duarte and their children, and Ronaldo Salermo, a friend of Paulo's referred to in the *crônica* 'Come, meu filho' [Eat Up, My Son].[34]

6A — Ladeira Ary Barroso

Originally, this road which slopes up the hillside was known as Ladeira da Babilônia and was built by Wilhelm Marx, father of landscape gardener Roberto Burle Marx, on his own land. Its name was changed to Ladeira Ary Barroso in homage to the composer of 'Aquarela do Brasil',[35] by Mayor Marcos Tamoyo in 1975. The musician lived in the neighbourhood from the 1930s, firstly at no. 74 Rua Gustavo Sampaio, where the Edifício Montese now stands. Barroso bought land that was part of a plot belonging to the Burle Marx family (some say it was a gift from his friend Roberto), and he built a three-storey house at no. 9, moving there in 1948. During the period when he was a local councillor (from 1947), he had the road asphalted. From the mid-1950s onwards, basic sanitation and urban infrastructure were installed in the

Fig. 1.1. Paulo Gurgel Valente, Clarice Lispector, Pedro Gurgel Valente and Lucinda Martins, on Leme Beach, June 1959. Photographer unknown. Acervo Clarice Lispector, Instituto Moreira Salles.

area, the project backed by the Church, a committee of residents from the favela community, and members of Asaleme.

The first residents on the hillside were soldiers who had worked at the Fort and construction workers who had helped to build the so-called 'New Tunnel' which joins the neighbourhoods of Copacabana and Botafogo. They had moved to Rio from all over the country in search of work. In time, they were joined by people working on other nearby building projects, like the Hotel Vogue (the location of the most famous nightclub in the city in the 1950s, before it was destroyed by a fire).

At the time, those who lived on the asphalted streets, like Clarice, felt no threat of violence.[36] Even so, she was no stranger to the troubles of her less privileged neighbours. As soon as she moved to Leme she 'mostrou-se interessada pelo assunto "favela" e qualquer dia destes pretende dar um pulo lá para ver a coisa de perto' [showed interest in the favela question and one of these days she plans to visit and take a closer look].[37] Elsewhere, she wrote:

> Se tomar conta do mundo dá muito trabalho? Sim. Por exemplo, obriga-me a lembrar-me do rosto terrivelmente inexpressível da mulher que vi na rua. Com os olhos tomo conta dos favelados costa acima.
>
> [Is taking care of the world a lot of trouble? Yes. For example, it forces me to remember the terribly expressionless face of a woman I saw in the street. With my eyes I take care of the favelados living up the hill.][38]

In the *crônica* 'Minheirinho', she demonstrates her concern for the same cause.[39] By all accounts, Minheirinho was one of those bandits considered by the residents of the favela as a carioca Robin Hood, but to the tabloid press he was public enemy number one. They reported his death with gusto and his story was made into a film by Aurélio Teixeira in 1967.

6B — no. 23 Ladeira Ary Barroso — Home of Aloisio and Solange Magalhães

Aloisio Magalhães (1927–1982) was one of Brazil's first professional graphic designers. As well as being President of IPHAN (Instituto do Patrimônio Histórico e Artístico Nacional) [National Institute of Historic and Artistic Heritage] and its sister organization the Fundação Pró-Memória [Pro-Memory Foundation], he was also appointed Secretary of Culture at the Ministry of Culture and Education. According to Clarice Magalhães, her father moved up the hill in around 1959–60. The house was both home and headquarters; from here he ran the design firm Magalhães, Noronha and Pontual (MNP). His wife, Solange, was also an artist, and their children Clarice and Carolina were born in 1963 and 1964. The text for the catalogue for Solange Magalhães's first solo exhibition, at the Galeria Bonino in 1968, was written by Clarice Lispector.

In the 1960s, the Ladeira Ary Barroso was a kind of paradise. It was lush and green, bordered by *pitanga* trees, with only a few houses but a fantastic view, from right by the Magalhães house. There were practically no shops nearby, so the baker delivered milk and bread. Electricity blackouts and water shortages were common. Since the house had an enormous cistern, Solange distributed water to her neighbours, who queued up holding various receptacles. But when the rain was torrential, the Magalhães house flooded.

When she went up the hill to visit them, Clarice liked to go to the library, where there was a collection of records, Aloisio's desk and a hammock. On one of these visits, Solange painted a portrait of her friend. When the Magalhães family went to Rua Gustavo Sampaio, Clarice regaled them with stories. She loved reading aloud what she had just finished writing to her junior readers, Carolina and Clarice. The latter remembers particularly well listening to the writer's slow and rather husky voice, and that some of her fingers had no nails, because she had lost them in the fire. After the stories came *casadinhos* and Coca-Cola.[40] Every get-together was memorable, for Clarice too: she wrote about one of them in 'Três encontros que são quatro' [Three Meetings Make Four]:

> O terceiro encontro — como nos *Três mosqueteiros* que na verdade são quatro — foi duplo: revi as duas filhas de Aloísio e Solange Magalhães. Uma tem meu nome e é engraçado a gente se falar. Parece que se está tendo o diálogo perfeito. Deu-me dois quadros por ela desenhados e em um deles escreveu: 'Para Clarice de Clarice'. E havia a quarta mosqueteira que era Carolina. São o que se pode esperar de uma criança: limpidez e pureza e criatividade e afeto e naturalidade. Foi um encontro feliz.
>
> [The third meeting — as in *The Three Musketeers* who are, in fact, four — was a double meeting. I bumped into the daughters of Aluísio and Solange Magalhães. One of them is called after me, and having a chat with her greatly

amuses me. It is like having the perfect dialogue. She made me a gift of two of her drawings and on the back she had written: 'For Clarice from Clarice'. And there was a fourth musketeer called Carolina. These girls are everything one could hope for in children: transparent and pure, creative, affectionate and natural. It was a happy meeting].[41]

7 — Praça Almirante Júlio de Noronha

Located at the very beginnings of both the Avenida Atlântica and Rua Gustavo Sampaio, this square, also known as Praça do Leme, landscaped by Roberto Burle Marx, was designated important cultural heritage by the City Hall in 2009. It is named after Admiral Júlio César de Noronha (1845–1932), a military hero who fought in the Paraguayan War, and became Minister for the Navy and Minister for the Supreme Military Court.

From Clarice's time onwards, the Forte Duque de Caxias (aka Forte do Leme), now the Centro de Estudos de Pessoal [Centre for Personnel Studies], a training centre run by the Brazilian Army, has been the dominant building in the square. But it was only in 1987 that the Centre started collaborating with local residents to support Asaleme and promote reforestation of the hills of Urubu and Babilônia. The success of these ventures led to the establishment of an Area of Environmental Protection in 1990.

Another important building in the square is the Escola Municipal Santo Tomás de Aquino [St Thomas of Aquinas Municipal School]. It is the only school in the neighbourhood and was founded in 1960, an initiative led by Asaleme. In 1945, the Sociedade Pestalozzi do Brasil, founded by educational psychologist Helena Antipoff, established its headquarters at no. 29 Rua Gustavo Sampaio, on the corner of the square. It was a pioneering institution in the area of specialist education, supporting children with disabilities and from underprivileged backgrounds.

Olga Borelli remembered that Clarice liked walking her dog in this square:

> Quando a visitava no correr da semana, saíamos ao entardecer, para um passeio com Ulisses na praça do final do Leme. Sentávamo-nos sob as amendoeiras; ficávamos horas ali. Ela mergulhada em si mesma, em silêncio, mas atenta a tudo, às conversas de mães e babás, às crianças brincando, à felicidade de Ulisses.

> [When I visited her during the week, in the early evening we would take Ulisses for a walk in the square at the end of the neighbourhood. We would sit under the almond trees and stay there for hours. She would be immersed in her own thoughts, in silence, but attentive to everything around her: mothers and nannies chatting, children playing, how happy Ulisses was.][42]

They would stay until the street lights came on, when Clarice stood up to indicate that she wanted to leave.

8 — Edifício Visconde de Pelotas (ap. 301, no. 2 Rua General Ribeiro da Costa)

Clarice lived in this twelve-storey building (of 48 apartments), between 1959 and 1965. She rented no. 301 on 8 July 1959 for 16,000 cruzeiros. According to her son Paulo, the apartment had three bedrooms and she used the one beside the living room as her office. It appeared in several photos used to accompany interviews she gave to newspapers and magazines. In these photos she stands or sits in front of the bookshelves and a lampshade. The beach was partly visible from the window. The other room overlooking the street was the boys' bedroom and Clarice's bedroom was at the back.

The living room, with its large window, can be seen partially in some photos, one of them in a piece for *Realidade* magazine, in 1961. The photographer, Claudia Andujar, captured Clarice sitting at her typewriter, on the sofa, the curtain (with its Piet Mondrian print) in the background. The idea for the photo was Clarice's own: when she was photographed she let herself become absorbed by the act of writing, as if she did not notice the photographer was present.

The utility room was spacious and opened onto the kitchen. Paulo always thought that the description of the maid Janair's room in *A paixão segundo G.H.* was based on the utility room in this apartment, and, indeed, the novel was written while they were living here.

9 — Edifício Macedo (ap. 701, no. 88 Rua Gustavo Sampaio)

Clarice lived in this thirteen-storey building (of 26 apartments) between 1965 and 1977. Her apartment, no. 701, has three bedrooms, a spacious living room, a kitchen and a utility room. In the corner of the living room, by the window, is a space she used to call the terrace, and that is where she sat to have her make-up done by Gilles (João Roberto Pereira) every month. He noticed that in that part of the room there were lots of magazines, papers, the typewriter and a framed photograph of Ulisses in a hat, with a cigarette in his mouth. It was also Clarice's workspace, furnished with a two-seater sofa, where she worked with her Olympia on her lap, beside a table with some books, her typescripts, an ashtray, cigarettes, and so on. There was also a rocking chair, where she placed manuscripts.

The wall from the front door to the kitchen was lined with panels of Scotch pine, upon which hung a photo by Humberto Franceschi of the Açude da Solidão.[43] On the wall opposite her workspace were three bookshelves, a sofa and an armchair. A journalist who visited this room in the 1970s to interview her mentions 'Dois santos numa redoma, algumas conchas sob uma mesinha. O retrato dos filhos quando tinham um ano, ou mesmo meses' [Two statuettes of saints in a domed glass case, some shells on a little table. Photographs of her sons when they were a year, or just a few months old].[44] Heloisa Azevedo also remembers indigenous arts and crafts were used to decorate the room.

Heloisa was Clarice's next-door neighbour, from no. 702, and she was the only one in the building with whom Clarice got along. The writer visited her often, at around three in the afternoon, for a coffee and a cigarette. She would ask her neighbour's opinion about clothes and domestic issues, like how to mend the keys

FIG. 1.2. Clarice and Ulisses in the living room of her apartment, no. 88, Rua Gustavo Sampaio. The block used to print Maria Bonomi's *A Águia* is visible in the upper right-hand corner. Arquivo-Museu de Literatura Brasileira, Fundação-Casa Rui Barbosa.

on her typewriter. Heloisa, who lived in Recife before moving to Rio, always brought Clarice things back from her trips there, making her very happy and giving her living room a northeastern flavour. She described herself as someone who lives to help others and it was she who came to Clarice's aid on the night of the fire and took her to Miguel Couto Hospital.

One thing the newspapers always mentioned were the paintings in this room, especially the portraits of Clarice by Italian modernist Giorgio de Chirico (1945), Brazilian artists Alfredo de Ceschiatti (1947) and Carlos Scliar (1972), and Ukraine-born Dimitri Ismailovitch (1974). Other items in her collection were works by the Italian painter Angelo Savelli and Brazilian artists like Iberê Camargo, Grauben, Fayga Ostrower, Djanira, Lúcio Cardoso and her friend Maria Bonomi.[45] 'Clarice's Gallery' was commented upon in her own *crônicas* and in articles about her, two pictures in particular. One was Savelli's 'A anunciação' [The Annunciation] (1944) which hung in pride of place behind the sofa; she wrote a *crônica* about it in which she said 'todo ser humano é responsável pelo mundo inteiro' [each of us is responsible for the entire world].[46] The other is the engraved wooden block used by Maria Bonomi to print '*Águia*' (1967).

When Bonomi asked her friend (who was also godmother to her son) to choose a print, Clarice made an unexpected request: she asked for the block instead, and hung it on her living room wall. The gift became another *crônica*: 'E o livro que eu estava tentando escrever e talvez publique corre de algum modo paralelo com a sua xilogravura [...] Maria escreve meus livros e eu canhestramente talho a madeira' [And the book I was trying to write and may publish was somehow moving in parallel with her engravings. Maria writes my books and I clumsily carve the wood].[47]

According to Olga Borelli, Clarice's bedroom, opposite the bathroom, was quite sparsely decorated:

> Uma cama espaçosa, um armário embutido ocupando toda a extensão da parede, uma estante com seus livros, uma escrivaninha antiga, uma estante pequena sob a janela com caixinhas de cremes, maquiagem, e sempre um copo cheio de água.
> De cor verde-claro, o quarto tinha duas janelas. Uma, ampla, dava para a rua Gustavo Sampaio; a outra, menor, para as quadras de tênis de um clube, o Leme Ténis Clube, acima das quais se estendia a vegetação dos morros do Forte do Leme.
>
> [A built-in wardrobe that ran the whole length of the wall, a big bed, a shelf with her books, an antique writing desk, a small shelf under the window with pots of cosmetics, her make-up and always a full glass of water.
> The pale green bedroom had two windows. The larger one looked out over the Rua Gustavo Sampaio, the other, smaller one over the tennis courts of Leme Tennis Club, and above them the vegetation of the hillsides surrounding the Fort].[48]

Pedro's bedroom was next-door to Clarice's. Paulo's was at the other end of the hall and was larger, with an en suite bathroom.

She liked to have lunch at midday, usually something light, according to Borelli. She ate no dessert, except occasionally fruit that was in season, and she did not usually eat dinner. At around six o'clock she would have a snack of coffee and bread and butter, or cheese and biscuits.[49]

The apartment currently belongs to actress and singer Zezé Motta.

12 — Hotel Luxor Continental (no. 320, Rua Gustavo Sampaio; now Novotel)

The Luxor Group, managed by Walter Ribas, owned the Hotel Regente and the Luxor Hotel, both in Copacabana, when the Hotel Luxor Continental was built in Leme. According to the manager, Pedro Lima, the building was erected between the late 1960s and the early 1970s. Clarice used to stay in this hotel when she needed time to herself, an escape from routine or to proofread a book. She stayed here when she was writing *Uma aprendizagem ou o livro dos prazeres* (1969), as reported by Remy Gorga Filho[50] and confirmed by this note to Olga Borelli.

> 8 January 1975
> Olga, senti necessidade de maior concentração e de isolamento, longe do telefone, necessidade de 'ir embora' e sozinha. De modo que estou no Hotel Continental, onde ficarei até sábado, ao meio-dia. Se eu descansar logo, interrompo a estada e volto antes para casa. Até sábado. Abraços da Clarice.
>
> [Olga, I feel the need for greater concentration and isolation, far from the telephone, the need to get away and be by myself. So I'm at the Hotel

Continental, where I'll stay until midday on Saturday. If I can rest straight away, I'll cut my stay short and go home earlier. See you on Saturday. Love, Clarice.][51]

14 — *Restaurante La Fiorentina (no. 454, Avenida Atlântica)*

Clarice first started eating at La Fiorentina when she lived in Rua General Ribeiro da Costa. It was five minutes away from her apartment: all she had to do was walk along Rua Aurelino Leal towards the sea. Her friends Maria Bonomi, Nélida Piñon and Rosa Cass fondly recall eating there with her. Paulo remembers that her favourite dish was prawn cocktail. Clarice would drink Coca-Cola, or sometimes a glass of red wine, and she always had a coffee.

Rosa Cass remembers going there for lunch on Saturdays, when they would share a plate of chicken with *noisette* potatoes. When Maria Bonomi was in Rio, she would always drop by to visit her friend. Whatever the time of day or night, they would go out to eat, snack or sup and to talk about everything under the sun. If the diners sitting nearby bothered them, Clarice would suggest moving to the beach. They would take their pizza out in a disposable tray, sit in the sand, looking at the sea, and eat with their hands, 'nos matando de rir' [killing ourselves laughing], Bonomi recalls.[52]

The restaurant has an unusual feature that is unique to Rio, and maybe Brazil as a whole: pillars covered with autographs and walls full of photos of the celebrities who were or are part of the city's cultural scene since the 1960s. There are hundreds of autographs on the ornamental pillars: from *bossa nova* muse Nara Leão to beloved comic actress Dercy Gonçalves, from Oscar-nominated actress Fernanda Montenegro to ballet dancer Ana Botafogo. Clarice's autograph was lost in a fire which damaged the restaurant in 1987. To make up for its loss, two photographic prints have been hung on the wall. The first, donated by Teresa Montero in 2005, shows the writer in her twenties. The other was given by the owner, Omar Peres, and it shows Clarice with her two sons, when they were small, at an unidentified beach that some say is Leme.

The story behind the restaurant's decorations has become a legend. According to Peres, once, when his stepfather, the former owner, Sylvio Hoffman, was visiting Europe, he had bought dinner for Picasso. To show his gratitude, the artist drew a picture on his napkin. With the proceeds from selling the napkin, Hoffman bought the restaurant. One of Omar Peres's initiatives when he took over the restaurant was to consult specialist restorer Lucia Teles who worked on it from November 2011 to August 2013. The restoration of the columns was done in several stages, which involved removing layers of accumulated dirt: grease, sea air, customers' interventions (leaving signatures, drawings or comments in pen, footprints and scratches). The walls with the most recent signatures have been covered with transparent acrylic sheets to protect them.

15 — Restaurante Veneziana (Store C, no. 410 Rua Gustavo Sampaio)

The Veneziana has been a confectioner's, a pizzeria and an ice-cream parlour. In the 1970s, Paulo Gurgel Valente, who lived next door, was a regular customer. Clarice accompanied him on more than one occasion to share a pizza with him.

16 — Casas Gaio Marti (no. 361 Rua Gustavo Sampaio; now Pizzaria Vezpa)

This grocery store is present in the memories of many residents. Purchases were recorded in a notebook and paid at the end of the month, according to Paulo Gurgel Valente.

17 — Padaria Duque de Caxias (no. 508 Rua Gustavo Sampaio)

This bakery supplied the delicious snacks enjoyed by Clarice and Babá, the maid of her friend Pedro Paulo Sena Madureira, who lived in the Edifício Maracati.

18 — Sorveteria e Confeitaria Gatão (no. 528 A Rua Gustavo Sampaio)

The bohemians of Leme frequented this ice-cream parlour and confectioners, which sold snacks, beer, sandwiches and coffee. In Clarice's time, it was an ice-cream parlour popular with the residents. It is mentioned in the *crônica* 'Come, meu filho', first published in the 'Children's Corner' column in the magazine *Senhor*, and later in *A legião estrangeira* (1964). The text reproduces a dialogue between mother and son, during a meal:

> 'Onde foi inventado feijão com arroz?'
> 'Aqui.'
> 'Ou no árabe, igual que Pedrinho disse da outra coisa?'
> 'Aqui.'
> 'Na Sorveteria Gatão o sorvete é bom porque tem gosto igual da cor. Para você carne tem gosto de carne?'
> 'Às vezes.'

> ['Where did they invent beans and rice?'
> 'Here.'
> 'Or at that Arabian place, like Pedrinho said about something else?'
> 'Here.'
> 'At the Sorveteria Gatão the ice cream tastes good because it tastes just like the color. Does meat taste like meat to you?'
> 'Sometimes.'][53]

19 — Newspaper Kiosk owned by Salvador Vanzillotta and his sons Santo and Francisco (Rua Gustavo Sampaio, opposite the Duque de Caxias Bakery)

This is the most popular kiosk in the neighbourhood. In Clarice's time, there were morning and evening editions of newspapers. Santo Vanzillotta remembers Clarice buying both newspapers (*Correio da Manhã, Diário de Notícias,* and *Jornal do Brasil*) and magazines (*Manchete* and *O Cruzeiro*). He called her 'a mulher lua' [the moon lady] because she was not always cheerful but his father told him he should always be nice to her. She stood out because she was beautiful and dressed so elegantly.[54]

21 — Seu Zé's Newspaper Stand (no. 223 Rua Gustavo Sampaio)

José Leôncio (known to his customers as Seu Zé) ran this business for forty-five years. He moved to Rio from the northeastern state of Ceará in 1971. It was a meeting point for a chat between residents, such as Colonel Dulcídio do Espírito Santo Cardoso (Mayor of Rio between 1950 and 1954, who lived in the Porto Mar Porto Sol apartment building) and playwright Nelson Rodrigues.

Seu Zé remembered that Clarice bought newspapers from him on several occasions, sometimes on her own, sometimes with Ulisses. At other times it was her maid Geni who bought the paper when walking the dog. In the last few years, this newspaper stand started to sell second-hand books, and, at Teresa Montero's suggestion, it was renamed 'Sebo Clarice Lispector' to commemorate eight years of the 'Rio de Clarice' guided tours.

22 — Farmácia LemeFar (no. 323 Rua Gustavo Sampaio; now Bar Gaia Arte & Café)

The proprietor was Tobias Timovski. Chicão (Francisco Nunes), who worked there as a delivery boy in the 1970s, remembers Clarice buying eye drops and medicine.

23 — Salão New York (Store C, no. 576 Rua Gustavo Sampaio; now Atual Unidas Material de Construção)

Hairdresser Pedro Estevão remembers seeing Clarice having her hair cut there. At the time he was very young and worked at the salon serving coffee. In her telephone book, Clarice noted: 'Salão New York — cabeleireiro Toledo' [New York Salon — hairdresser Toledo].

Forty years later, the establishment was turned into a hardware store selling construction materials, owned since 2000 by José Mario Valro. It was in this shop that Edgar Duvivier ended up buying one of the tins of Sikadur glue he used to stick down the statues of Clarice and Ulisses when they were installed on 14 May 2016.

24 — Statue of Clarice and her dog Ulisses (Caminho dos Pescadores Ted Boy Marino)

On 14 December 2014, this pathway round the rock was named after wrestler and actor Ted Boy Marino (1939–2012). Located at the foot of Leme hill, it provides a space for fishing and leisure activities from where one can look up the whole of Copacabana beach. When Clarice lived in Leme, there was no street lighting here, or railings; fishermen had to balance on the rocks. In December 1986 the path was built as a form of sea protection.

The statue of Clarice Lispector and her dog Ulisses, by sculptor Edgar Duvivier, was financed from the sale of four small models of the monument for R$ 2,500 each. The choice of setting and the idea of selling the models were the sculptor's own, after numerous attempts to find sponsorship had failed. The idea of erecting a statue to celebrate Clarice's long association with Leme and mark its importance as one of the main guided visits on the 'O Rio de Clarice' tour, dates back to 2012. But it was only after an article called 'No Leme de Clarice Lispector' [In Clarice Lispector's Leme], published in O Globo in 2013, that a campaign was started by actress Beth Goulart, Niura Antunes (who lives in the Edifício Macedo), Teresa Montero and Mariana Muller, who wrote the piece. The initiative was supported by Clarice's readers who signed petitions, one collected during the run of the play *Simplesmente eu, Clarice Lispector* (starring Goulart), and the other in the La Fiorentina restaurant on 7 June 2014.

The statue was unveiled on 14 May 2016 and alongside it a plaque was put up, engraved with some lines from the *crônica* 'As três experiências', chosen by Paulo Gurgel Valente: 'Há três coisas para as quais eu nasci e para as quais eu dou a minha vida. Nasci para amar os outros, nasci para escrever, e nasci para criar meus filhos. O "amar os outros" é tão vasto que inclui até perdão para mim mesma, com o que sobra' [There are three things for which I was born and for which I am prepared to give my life. I was born to love others and to raise [my] children. To 'love others' is something so momentous that it even includes forgiving myself with what love remains].[55]

Works Cited

Borelli, Olga, *Clarice Lispector: esboço para um possível retrato* (Rio de Janeiro: Nova Fronteira, 1981)

Boyd, William, 'Must we dream our dreams?', *The Guardian*, 11 September 2010, <https://www.theguardian.com/books/2010/sep/11/william-boyd-elizabeth-bishop-brazil> [accessed 12 September 2019]

Filho, Remy Gorga, 'Clarice Lispector: eu não sou um monstro sagrado', *Revista do Livro*, 13.41 (1970), 112–15

Lamare, Germana, 'Clarisse Lispector esconde um objeto gritante', *Correio da Manhã* (Anexo), 5 March 1972, p. 4

Lessa, Elsie, *Dama da noite* (Rio de Janeiro: José Olympio, 1963)

Lispector, Clarice, *A legião estrangeira* (Rio de Janeiro: Editora do Autor, 1964)

—— 'Por falar em banho', *Jornal do Brasil*, 24 April 1971, Caderno B, p. 2

—— 'Carta sobre Maria Bonomi', *Jornal do Brasil*, 2 October 1971, Caderno B, p. 2

—— *A paixão segundo G.H.*, critical edn, ed. by Benedito Nunes (Florianópolis: ALLCA, 1988 [1964])

—— *A descoberta do mundo* (Rio de Janeiro: Rocco, 1999); *Discovering the World*, trans. by Giovanni Pontiero (Manchester: Carcanet, 1992)

—— *Entrevistas*, ed. by Claire Williams (Rio de Janeiro: Rocco, 2007)

—— *The Complete Stories*, trans. by Katrina Dodson (London: Penguin, 2015)

Méndez, Mariela, 'O sucesso do inacabado: Clarice Lispector e sua "Children's Corner" na revista *Senhor*', *Journal of Lusophone Studies*, 4.2 (2019), 117–37

Montero, Teresa, *O Rio de Clarice: passeio afetivo pela cidade* (Belo Horizonte: Autêntica, 2018)

Solberg, Helena, 'Os dois mundos de Clarice: livros e filhos', Supplement 'Revista Mundo Ilustrado', p. 40, *Diário de Notícias* (n.d.)

Sousa, Carlos Mendes de, *Clarice Lispector: pinturas* (Rio de Janeiro: Rocco, 2013)

Notes to Chapter 1

1. This chapter, edited, translated, and with notes by Claire Williams, is an abridged version of the last chapter in Teresa Montero's *O Rio de Clarice: passeio afetivo pela cidade* (Belo Horizonte: Autêntica, 2018). The book is based on the Lispector-themed guided visits around seven different neighbourhoods in Rio, designed and run by Montero. It commemorates ten years since her first 'Clarice's Rio' tour, which took place on 28 September 2008. This text has been reproduced exclusively for the present volume.
2. There are several explanations for the name of the neighbourhood. The shape of the rock is one. But historians have pondered the fact that in the eighteenth century a certain Francisco Pereira Leme owned a plantation there.
3. TN: Rio's beaches are divided into *postos* (lifeguard stations), numbered 1–12. Posto 6 is the furthest from Leme.
4. Clarice Lispector, 'Insônia infeliz e feliz', in *A descoberta do mundo* (Rio de Janeiro: Rocco, 1999), p. 69; 'Accursed and blissful insomnia', in *Discovering the World*, trans. by Giovanni Pontiero (Manchester: Carcanet, 1992), p. 93.
5. TN: Bishop's translations were hugely influential in promoting Brazilian literature in the United States.
6. TN: See William Boyd on Bishop's Brazil in 'Must we dream our dreams?', *The Guardian*, 11 September 2010, <https://www.theguardian.com/books/2010/sep/11/william-boyd-elizabeth-bishop-brazil> [accessed 12 September 2019].
7. TN: Candido Portinari (1903–1962) is considered one of Brazil's most important modernist painters, who sought to portray his land and its people in all their diversity. His murals adorn the Library of Congress in Washington D.C. and the United Nations Headquarters in New York. Bruno Giorgi (1905–1993) was a Brazilian sculptor perhaps best known for his monumental public works in Brasília.
8. Journalist and columnist Elsie Lessa (1912–2000) started working as a reporter for O Globo newspaper in 1946 and stayed there for the rest of her life: she was the paper's longest serving writer. This *crônica* featured in the volume *Rio de Janeiro em prosa e verso*, edited by poets Carlos Drummond de Andrade and Manuel Bandeira (Rio de Janeiro: José Olympio, 1965), but it had also appeared, as 'Descoberta do bairro' [Discovering the neighbourhood], in a collection of Lessa's *crônicas* called *Dama da noite* (Rio de Janeiro: José Olympio, 1963), pp. 85–86. Page numbers refer to the latter version.
9. Lessa, *Dama da noite*, p. 85.
10. Ibid., p. 86.
11. Ibid., p. 85.
12. Ibid.
13. Ibid., p. 85.
14. Ibid.
15. Lispector, *A descoberta do mundo*, p. 94; *Discovering the World*, pp. 126–27.
16. TN: Ivan Lessa (1935–2012) was a writer, editor and journalist. He lived in London for many years and worked for the BBC.
17. Lispector, *A descoberta do mundo*, p. 200; *Discovering the World*, p. 493.
18. Lispector, *A legião estrangeira* (Rio de Janeiro: Editora do Autor, 1964), p. 200; *Discovering the World*, pp. 493–94.
19. Ibid., p. 30; ibid., p. 43.
20. This family photo, from the archives held at the Instituto Moreira Salles, appears on the cover of *O Rio de Clarice*.
21. Clarice Lispector, 'Por falar em banho', *Jornal do Brasil*, 24 April 1971, Caderno B, p. 2. TN: this *crônica* was not included in *A descoberta do mundo* and therefore not translated by Pontiero for *Discovering the World*.
22. TN: For more on this series, see Mariela Méndez, 'O sucesso do inacabado: Clarice Lispector e sua "Children's Corner" na revista *Senhor*', *Journal of Lusophone Studies*, 4.2 (2019), 117–37.
23. TN: Fauzi Arap (1938–2013) was a highly respected and multiple prize-winning director, playwright and actor.

24. TN: Maria Bethânia (b. 1946) is a singer-songwriter also known for performing dramatized readings of literature at her concerts. 'Comigo me desavim' is a poem by the Portuguese Renaissance poet Francisco Sá de Miranda.
25. Lispector, *A descoberta do mundo*, p. 53; *Discovering the World*, p. 73.
26. Ibid., p. 86; ibid., p. 116.
27. In the 1980s, Pedro Paulo became Editorial Manager of Nova Fronteira publishers, which acquired the rights to Clarice's works immediately after her death.
28. These numbers match points marked on the map on pp. 96-97 of *O Rio de Clarice* (also available online: <bit.ly/LemeClarice> [accessed 1 February 2022]).
29. Personal telephone interview with Teresa Montero (6 June 2016).
30. Lispector, *A descoberta do mundo*, p. 167; *Discovering the World*, p. 221.
31. 'Zagallo', in Clarice Lispector, *Entrevistas*, ed. by Claire Williams (Rio de Janeiro: Rocco, 2007), pp. 219–23 (p. 221).
32. TN: Érico Veríssimo (1905–1975), was a prolific writer from Porto Alegre, in southern Brazil. From 1953 to 1956 he was director of the Department of Cultural Affairs of the Organization of American States, in Washington, D.C., where he met Clarice and their families became good friends.
33. Lispector, *A descoberta do mundo*, p. 346; *Discovering the World*, p. 454.
34. First published in *Senhor*, then included in Lispector, *A legião estrangeira*, pp. 176–77; *The Complete Stories*, trans. by Katrina Dodson (London: Penguin, 2015), pp. 377–78.
35. TN: One of the most famous Brazilian songs of all time, often called the unofficial national anthem, it has been recorded by international musicians and singers, from Frank Sinatra to Kate Bush. Terry Gilliam's 1985 film *Brazil* was named after it, it appears in the score of *Star Wars: The Last Jedi* (2017), and it was sung at the opening ceremony of the 2014 FIFA World Cup, in Rio de Janeiro.
36. TN: The distinction between 'o asfalto' [asphalted streets] and dirt roads is a shorthand for middle-class residential areas and less-privileged communities, sometimes called 'favelas'.
37. This was reported in an interview with Helena Solberg, who is now a prize-winning documentary film director, 'Os dois mundos de Clarice: livros e filhos', *Diário de Notícias*, 40 (no date), 'Revista Mundo Ilustrado', p. 40.
38. From the typescript of *Água viva*.
39. 'Minheirinho' was first published in her column 'Children's Corner' in *Senhor* magazine in 1962, and in Lispector, *A legião estrangeira*, pp. 252–57; *The Complete Stories*, pp. 362–66. For more on this *crônica*, see the chapter by Magdalena Edwards in this volume.
40. TN: *casadinhas* are little biscuits sandwiched together with guava paste.
41. Lispector, *A descoberta do mundo*, p. 372; *Discovering the World*, p. 490.
42. Olga Borelli, *Clarice Lispector: esboço para um possível retrato* (Rio de Janeiro: Nova Fronteira, 1981), p. 97.
43. TN: Humberto Franceschi (1930–2014) was a photographer, and a specialist in popular Brazilian music. O Açude da Solidão [The Weir of Solitude] is a picturesque spot in Tijuca Forest that Clarice liked to visit. See also the chapter on Tijuca in *O Rio de Clarice*, especially p. 25.
44. Germana Lamare, 'Clarisse Lispector esconde um objeto gritante', *Correio da Manhã*, 5 March 1972, Anexo, p. 4.
45. TN: She interviewed Scliar, Ostrower, Djanira and Bonomi for magazines *Manchete* and *Fatos e Fotos* (included in *Entrevistas*) and wrote a *crônica* about Grauben. For more on Lispector's relationship to painting and paintings, see Carlos Mendes de Sousa, *Clarice Lispector: pinturas* (Rio de Janeiro: Rocco, 2013).
46. Lispector, *A descoberta do mundo*, p. 158; *Discovering the World*, p. 209.
47. Lispector, 'Carta sobre Maria Bonomi', *Jornal do Brasil*, 2 October 1971, Caderno B, p. 2.
48. Borelli, *Clarice Lispector*, pp. 94–95.
49. Ibid., p. 95.
50. Remy Gorga Filho, 'Clarice Lispector: eu não sou um monstro sagrado', *Revista do Livro*, 13.41 (1970), 112–15 (p. 113).
51. Note from Clarice to Olga Borelli. Published in Clarice Lispector, *A paixão segundo G.H.*, critical edition ed. by Benedito Nunes (Florianópolis: ALLCA, 1988), p. xi.

52. Email correspondence between Teresa Montero and Maria Bonomi (25 January 2014).
53. Lispector, *A legião estrangeira*, p. 177; *The Complete Stories*, pp. 377–78.
54. Personal interview with Teresa Montero, Leme (19 February 2014).
55. Lispector, *A descoberta do mundo*, pp. 101–02; *Discovering the World*, pp. 134–35; TN: Pontiero's translation omits the possessive pronoun 'my'.

CHAPTER 2

In Search of Belonging: Places and Non-places in *Correspondências* and *Minhas queridas*

Laís Maria Rosal Botler

'Do you believe that space can give life, or take it away, that space has power?'
— bell hooks[1]

Living in a period when moving to different places in a short time span was not as common as it is nowadays, the Brazilian writer Clarice Lispector found herself, most notably in the period she lived abroad — from 1944 to 1959 — in a state of physical instability and displacement due to the Second World War and to her diplomat husband's profession, which required continuous travel. Letters written in these years to her sisters and several friends, and later published in the books *Correspondências*[2] and *Minhas queridas*,[3] contextualize her relation to place, but also reveal Clarice's dynamic experience of non-place, a term coined by anthropologist Marc Augé to describe transient spaces like hotel rooms and airports. In what follows, I examine how issues related to belonging are experienced, represented and described by Clarice in her correspondence from this period, particularly with regard to relations she established with the places and non-places in which she sojourned and resided.

In his landmark 1995 study, *Non-places: Introduction to an Anthropology of Supermodernity*, Augé argues for the possibility of an anthropological look at the facts of the present, specifically in the postmodern world, which he calls 'supermodernity'.[4] In this supermodernity, one finds excesses of time, space and ego, which are further contextualized through an overabundance of facts, spaces and individualization of references. These three pervasive aspects evolve rapidly and modify the physical characterization of space. Certainly, the way space is defined and approached has changed; it is no longer considered to be an Edenic and passive entity as it was generally regarded up until the beginning of the twentieth century, but instead it is dynamic and shapes people's lives.[5] According to Doreen Massey, the following essential aspects define space: first, it is a result of interrelations and is formed from interactions; second, it is connected to the plurality that characterizes the contemporary world (in her words, 'without space, no multiplicity; without multiplicity, no space')[6]; third, space is always in a process of construction, and thus, never finished. Moreover, the definition of space does not allow for a simplistic view; since it is so complex, it demands deep reflection in order to avoid misreading.

Along with the complexity found in the meaning and configuration of space in the contemporary world, the failure of dichotomic views in dealing with this configuration has generated new concepts in relation to space, such as the concept of non-places.[7] This concept, as proposed by Augé, best describes one of these changes: the multiplication of spaces in which there is an accelerated circulation of people. For Augé, 'if a place can be defined as relational, historical and concerned with identity, then a space which cannot be defined as relational, or historical, or concerned with identity will be a non-place'.[8] Consequently, non-places, such as airports, hotels, roads, or even large commercial centres or refugee camps, are the spaces designed to allow for and accommodate this accelerated circulation of people.

Non-places are, therefore, spaces that maintain their own specific aims, along with the particular, subjective relation people establish with them: an indistinguishable presence, meaningless to its temporary residents or passengers. In the words of Zygmunt Bauman, non-places 'discourage the thought of "settling in", making colonization or domestication of space all but impossible'.[9] The travellers maintain the corresponding specific habits and behaviour rules of the non-place, but those prove irrelevant to their stay: 'everyone there should feel as if *chez soi*, while no one should *behave* as if truly at home'.[10] Despite non-places being a contemporary critical concept, according to Augé some aspects of supermodernity (and its excesses) have already been anticipated in the modern era by people who confront this new stage of society with an avant-garde attitude, thus enabling this experiential phenomenon to grow more common over time. This seems to have been the case for Clarice, who was born into displacement and experienced numerous spatial changes in a relatively short amount of time.

After the First World War and the Russian Revolution, a hostile environment and constant anti-Semitic attacks led her parents, Pinkhas and Mania, to flee Ukraine and emigrate to Brazil. On their way, the couple stopped in the small village of Tchechelnik, where Mania gave birth to Clarice (Haya) in 1920.[11] In 1922, Clarice and her family arrived in Maceió, Brazil, and relocated three years later to Recife, where she spent most of her childhood. At the age of fourteen, after her mother's death, the entire family moved to Rio de Janeiro. It was in Rio that Clarice studied, worked, and got married in 1943. This marriage brought with it new experiences in and perspectives on geographic displacement, as determined by her husband's career as a diplomat. During her marriage, Clarice lived in many cities throughout the world: Belém do Pará (Brazil), Naples (Italy), Berne (Switzerland), Torquay (the United Kingdom) and Washington, DC (United States). Across a sixteen-year period she split her travels between Brazil and residencies abroad and maintained regular correspondence with her two sisters and her friends. According to her biographer Nádia Battella Gotlib, given the time in which Clarice was living, without the luxury of current communication technology, these letters served as an outlet for releasing tension and nurturing family ties.[12]

Motifs of uprooting and nostalgia fill her letters and are intrinsically related to the concept of belonging, which itself cannot be dissociated from notions of place, where roots are usually more stable, and of non-place, where such roots do not exist. In this context, when analysing the representation of places and non-places in Clarice's letters, the concept of non-place, as previously defined, emerges as central, especially in relation to interactions between the two concepts: how a traditional place — a place of belonging — can come to be seen and experienced as a non-place and vice versa.

Letters are a textual genre typically characterized by linguistic features denoting privacy. These characteristically private and pervasive features, such as informality and spontaneity, are evidence of letters being one of the written genres most closely related to oral language.[13] The subjectivity and intimacy of her letters lead us to a deeper understanding of how Clarice saw her relationships with the world and which questions relating to life — either everyday life or existentialist problems — concerned her more directly. Moreover, by reading these letters, it is possible to better contextualize these questions as part of her creative process. In some cases, the creative process itself is the focus of the letters, which may be of interest in an analysis of her fictional texts.

When addressing letters, especially those written by famous people, it becomes necessary to define the borders between public and private spheres. Despite their private nature, letters written by renowned writers sometimes become public upon their passing. Clarice reveals her awareness of these peculiarities of the genre in the following extract from a letter written to her sisters in January 1942, while still in Brazil:

> Tenho recebido cartas formidáveis do Maury. Houve uma briga entre nós porque ele interpretou como literária uma carta que eu mandei. Você bem sabe que isso é a coisa que mais me pode ofender. *Eu quero uma vida-vida e é por isso que desejo fazer um bloco separado da literatura. E além do mais, eu tinha escrito a carta com uma espontaneidade integral.*
>
> [I have received wonderful letters from Maury. There was an argument between us because he interpreted a letter that I had sent him as literary. You know very well that that is the thing which I find most offensive. *I want a life-life and that is why I wish to keep it separate from literature. Besides, I had written the letter with complete spontaneity.*][14]

Clarice's reference to spontaneity is in fact a sign that not all her letters are as spontaneous as she tries to make them seem. Her husband's perception of the 'literary' quality of the letter also serves to highlight Clarice's difficulty in separating life from literature. Gotlib emphasizes that, while she agrees with Maury about the literary nature of the letters, she also understands Clarice's perspective due to her natural directness and honesty; she asserts that both perspectives can coexist due to Clarice's failure to separate literature from life.[15] As Gotlib affirms, Clarice was naturally a 'literary' author, and therefore her husband understood her better than she understood herself in this case.

Scholars of the epistolary genre have often addressed the question of literary quality, particularly as it concerns letters penned by writers. With respect to literary correspondences, Sophia Angelides asserts that letters written by writers have the peculiar characteristic of falling between non-literary and literary language.[16] In their reading of Clarice's letters, Adalberto Rafael Guimarães and Ilca Vieira de Oliveira highlight the relevance of correspondence in the study of her fiction, arguing that letters can be a rich source for the analysis of literary texts.[17] But with regard to the correspondence between artists, Ligia Dabul claims that it also can interfere with the creative process, since artists sometimes offer a sketch of what they plan to write and exchange ideas and opinions about their work in progress.[18] Dabul further argues that emotional proximity (due to friendship or kinship) and a lack of formality between correspondents can facilitate the introduction of topics related to artistic creation, although this is more common in exchanges between friends who share the same profession. This can be observed in Clarice's letters, mainly in her correspondence with the writers Lucio Cardoso and Fernando Sabino.[19]

Clarice seemed aware of the potential visibility of these letters and their importance for her own creative process. Teresa Montero, who prepared Clarice's letters for publication, observes that, in contrast to her handling of the manuscripts of her literary texts, Clarice demonstrated care in the safeguarding of her correspondence, motivated by a 'preocupação em guardar a memória de um tempo em que viveu longe do Brasil' [concern to preserve the memory of a time in which she lived far from Brazil].[20] In an interview, Clarice emphasized that she 'hated' diplomatic life and, in fact, letters written in this period confirm that it was not an easy time for her, possibly due to frequent uprooting in a relatively short period of time. On the other hand, these letters express, as highlighted by Gotlib, a relationship of complicity between the sisters, expressed through tenderness, friendship, love and nostalgia.[21]

For Michel Foucault, the letter is a genre of writing the self and therefore plays a role in the constitution of being.[22] Writing is a way of digesting the different discourses to which a person is exposed, an exercise in self-reflection. Indeed, the letters' demand for constant self-reflection could influence the way writers perceive themselves. As Foucault himself highlights, the letter is a reciprocal act, influencing both the sender and the recipient. While abroad, letters were a way of keeping in touch with her sisters, but Clarice also recognized the role they played in the constitution of her being.[23] In the excerpt below, from September 1948, Clarice explains the hope and expectation surrounding the moment of receiving the letters, the difference between her feelings and those of her sisters with regard to their correspondence, as well as some contradictory feelings she had concerning the letters:

> Preparei, num momento de febre e raiva, uma carta para vocês que felizmente não mandei. Eu avisava que só escreveria muito raramente, que estava cansada de ser o cachorrinho da família. Que durante 4 anos implorou uma notícia para recebê-la apenas depois de 5 ou 6 cartas vazias de vocês.
>
> [I prepared, in a moment of fever and anger, a letter for you that I fortunately did not send. I was going to warn you that I would only write very rarely, and

that I was tired of being the puppy of the family. Who begged for news for four years and only received it after 5 or 6 empty letters from you.]²⁴

The hope of receiving letters was part of Clarice's daily life. While living far from her friends and family, she was the one who most needed to receive news and answers from them. She used letters as a way of expressing what she felt, learned and saw abroad and expected an answer as a validation to these experiences. However, sometimes these answers did not arrive as fast as she hoped, which caused reactions such as the one described in the letter above, where she expresses anger towards her sisters. These letters constituted a support network, where love and tenderness were frequently expressed, but the absence of letters could bring on a feeling of taking a back seat, a shattering of this connection.

Her correspondence with the writer Fernando Sabino, who also lived abroad for many years, had the appearance of a more stable connection, given their similar circumstances. Clarice herself acknowledged this: 'Me escrevam, agora que vocês sabem o quanto pode valer uma carta e sobretudo certas cartas' [Write to me, now that you know how much a letter can be worth and especially certain letters].²⁵ Their letters reflect a relationship of trust, one in which they could share their inner conflicts as foreigners and writers. As Guimarães and de Oliveira note, they both used these letters as a way of writing about themselves and of working towards self-understanding:²⁶

> De repente me pareceu que eu devo continuar a trabalhar, que tudo está ruim, mas que é assim mesmo, que as coisas são desconhecidas até que rebentam numa conhecida, a pessoa está só no mundo de modo que deve tomar certas providências urgentes de silêncio e meditação, já que não se sabe nem se pode agir, e que de vez em quando a gente pode receber este presente gratuito que é a palavra amiga de um amigo [...].
>
> [It suddenly seemed to me that I should continue working, that everything is bad, but that's how it is, things are unknown until they burst into being known, a person is alone in this world so she must take certain urgent steps of silence and meditation, since we do not know, nor can we act, but from time to time we can receive this free gift that is the friendly word of a friend.]²⁷

The habit of maintaining a correspondence also enables a person to make herself present, to share information about her life, failures and successes. In her letters, Clarice describes her day or the city where she lived in great detail and at different moments,²⁸ thereby making herself more present to her sisters and, at the same time, bringing them closer to her foreign, daily life: 'Querida, como você vê, estou contando mil fatos pequenos sem importância mas que dão uma ideia da vida em Berna...' [Honey, as you can see, I'm telling you a thousand little unimportant facts but they give you an idea of life in Berne...].²⁹ As Esther Milne has shown, 'little unimportant facts' like these 'are often used by letter writers to convey and invoke a sense of immediacy, intimacy and presence'.³⁰ These descriptions played, therefore, an important role in maintaining Clarice's relationship with her sisters, reducing the feeling of physical absence and working as a kind of replacement for her presence. Moreover, Clarice's letters to her sisters offer an important perspective on her understanding of space and of her conflicts with the places and non-places in which she lived and with which she interacted.

During her first period abroad, Clarice lived with the expectation that the end of the war would bring her travels to an end and with it the possibility of returning to Brazil and to her sisters: 'Espero tremendamente que a guerra acabe, por todos os motivos. E o mais egoísta é esse, o de permitir que eu faça essa viagem [para o Brasil]' [I very much hope that the war will end, for all sorts of reasons. And the most selfish one is this, that of allowing me to make this trip [to Brazil]].[31] In the meantime, moving constantly was unavoidable, and with it the exposure to the extraordinary number of turbulent events and changes occurring in the world at that time. In a letter written to her sister Tania, Clarice reflects on this overwhelming situation in relation to her creative process, particularly when writing *A cidade sitiada* (1949):

> Estou trabalhando, mal ou bem; falta ainda o sentido do livro, uma razão mais forte para ele existir — aos poucos é que está subindo à tona, à medida que eu for trabalhando. O que tem me perturbado intimamente é que as coisas do mundo chegaram para mim a um certo ponto em que eu tenho que saber como encará-las, quero dizer, a situação de guerra, a situação das pessoas, essas tragédias. Sempre encarei com revolta. Mas ao mesmo tempo que sinto necessidade de fazer alguma coisa, sinto que não tenho meios.
>
> [One way or another, I've been working; the book is still missing a meaning, a stronger reason for it to exist — little by little, as I work, it starts to rise to the surface. What has troubled me deeply is that things that happen in the world reached me at a point when I have to know how to face them, I mean, the war situation, people's situations, those sorts of tragedies. I've always faced them with outrage. But at the same time I feel the need to do something, I feel I have no means to do it.][32]

In these two excerpts, Clarice illustrates how impossible it was to feel indifferent towards current events around the world, and how they affected her both on a personal level and on a greater scale, since the humanitarian issues mattered to her profoundly. Clarice lived the consequences of the world's developments in her daily life abroad and she focuses on this very progress and its correlation with space when writing *A cidade sitiada*. In this novel, the importance of space is also especially highlighted, as reflected in the very title. The suburb itself takes a leading role and, though inanimate, plays one of the main characters. The novel develops from the connection the protagonist Lucrécia feels with the surrounding suburban space, and her relationships with other characters are directly affected and intertwined with her relation to different spaces. This rings true particularly in the suburb, but also in the city, where she lives for a short period after getting married.

In the letters, Clarice deliberates with her sister Tania over the use of the word 'suburb' to characterize the city of São Geraldo. She also discusses the relationship between one of the characters and the city and its development, along with the potential feelings of loss and *saudade*[33] which may arise as a consequence of this progress — feelings similar to those she herself experienced while living in Europe, a place supposedly more developed than Brazil.

IN SEARCH OF BELONGING   45

> Também o fato de eu chamar S. Geraldo de subúrbio, vou estudar. [...] Mas vejo que você entendeu bem o que eu queria pelo fato de você ter falado em 'cidadela'. — Quanto ao fato de Efigênia ser invejada como pessoa, apesar de ser rústica, etc. — é mesmo pelo fato de ela não tomar parte no progresso de S. Geraldo que ela adquire importância aos olhos dos outros. Os outros sentiam o perigo em S. Geraldo progressista, e já tinham um pouco a nostalgia da 'volta' à rusticidade.
>
> [I will also think about the fact that I call S. Geraldo a suburb [...] But I see you really understood what I meant since you talked about a 'citadel'. — As for the fact that Efigênia is envied as a person, despite being rustic etc. — it's because she doesn't take part in S. Geraldo's progress that she acquires importance in the eyes of others. The others felt the danger in progressive S. Geraldo and were already a little nostalgic for the 'return' to rusticity.][34]

The relationship between character and space, present in the passage above, is revisited in Clarice's letters throughout her creative process composing *A cidade sitiada*, and she highlights the suburb and its progress as the most important part of the book. Her questioning about the book is combined in the aforementioned letters with differing descriptions of the city of Berne: some of which are positive and heartening ('Continuo a achar a cidade muito bonitinha. Há passeios deliciosos à beira do rio Aar' [I still find the city very cute. There are delicious walks along the river Aar]),[35] but most reflect her dispiritedness and discouragement ('De minha prisão em Berna, mando-lhes minhas lembranças comovidas' [From my imprisonment in Berne, I send you my heartfelt memories]).[36] A number of critics highlight how Clarice's often dismal opinion of the city may have influenced her work to a degree, partially correlating her writing to these feelings. Varin, for example, wonders: 'Um pouco da monotonia de Berna introduz-se sub-repticiamente nele?' [Does a little bit of Berne's monotony surreptitiously introduce itself into it?].[37] Along the same lines, Pontieri conflates the two realities: 'Esse — o olhar da escritora-pintora vivendo e vendo Berna, (d)escrevendo e pintando uma cidade que se chamaria S. Geraldo' [One — the gaze of the writer-painter living and seeing Berne, writing/describing and painting [the other], a city that would be called S. Geraldo].[38]

As in her literary texts, Clarice constantly describes and reflects in her letters on the real places and spaces she encounters. Moving from one place to another, by ship or by plane, Clarice herself can be characterized as the traveller whose space is, in Augé's words, the archetype of non-places. As described in her letters, she is frequently in transit, passing by (and through) places that do not mean anything in particular to her. The uninterrupted and constant speed with which she appears almost to float through these places, as if she could not touch or feel them, is represented by descriptions just as fleeting, which demonstrate, through emphasis and repetition, how she attempts to gain a sense of connection — she needs to tell herself where she is in order to have some reaction to these spaces:

> No dia 30 domingo de julho, embarquei às duas horas da tarde. Viajei com muitos missionários e olhando para uma mulherzinha santa que dormia frente a mim, eu mesma me sentia fraca e horrivelmente espiritual [...]. Na manhã

> seguinte chegamos a Fisherman's Lake, na Libéria, onde passamos um dia e uma noite. Eu precisava me repetir: isso é África — para sentir alguma coisa. Nunca vi ninguém menos turista. (Vi muitas coisas mas não só tenho preguiça de contar, como de lembrar.)
>
> [I boarded at 2 o'clock in the afternoon on Sunday the 30th of July. I travelled with many missionaries and looking at a holy little woman who was asleep opposite me, I myself felt weak and dreadfully spiritual [...]. On the following morning we arrived at Fisherman's Lake, in Liberia, where we spent a day and a night. I needed to keep telling myself: this is Africa — so I could feel something. I never saw anyone who was such a bad tourist. (I saw lots of things but I am too lazy to tell you, or even remember them.)][39]

Her depiction of her trips resembles a fast-paced modern movie, in which images overlap and many details are missing. She goes on to describe her travels through many cities: Bolama, Dakar, Lisbon, Casablanca, and Algiers. She realizes that the more places she visits, the more alike they appear: 'As coisas são iguais em toda a parte — eis o suspiro da mulherzinha viajada' [Things are the same everywhere — hear the sigh of the well-travelled woman].[40] This uniformity and lack of differentiation of built spaces is underscored by Augé as one of the features of supermodernity related to the abundance of non-places.[41] In other letters, Clarice comments on the sameness of cinemas worldwide ('Os cinemas do mundo inteiro se chamam Odeon, Capitólio, Império, Rex, Olímpia' [Cinemas the whole world over are called Odeon, Capitol, Empire, Rex, Olympia]),[42] and similarities between US cities like Miami and Los Angeles ('As mesmas casas baixas, o mesmo ar meio devastado e meio bagunça, sem graça' [The same low houses, the same half-devastated air and a bit messy, dull]).[43] This sameness and this lack of particularization disturb her; they fail to add new perspectives to her world view.

The Second World War, which some consider as a landmark of postmodernity, also contributed to the greater presence of non-places in Clarice's life during this period, due in part to the succession of places she is compelled to pass through in an abbreviated period of time as a result of security considerations or the availability of transport. In the passage below, she highlights the speed with which she blows past various places, without there being any deepening in their meaning:

> Fiz uma viagem complicada e demorada do Brasil até Roma. Chegando em Casa Blanca não havia avião para Roma — tive que ir ao... Cairo, onde passei dois dias e pouco; de lá fui a Roma, almoçando em Atenas... Vi as pirâmides, vi a esfinge. *São umas belezas, infelizmente tão exploradas que diante delas a gente só pode ter uma sensação já descrita no almanaque da Saúde da Mulher.* [...]. *Almocei comida americana* e enquanto o avião se aprontava para partir, entrei no *jeep* de um americano que 'voou' até a Acrópole e eu pude ver de longe o Partenon. *A visão foi igual à que eu teria se olhasse uma fotografia, porque foi rápida.* [...] O maometano disse que eu tinha 'white heart', coração puro... O que eu tenho na verdade é um coração pequeno onde já não cabem coisas, tão cheio de amor guardado ele é. Várias vezes eu tenho tido uma vontade aguda de abraçar, por exemplo, a Marcinha.
>
> [I made a long and complicated trip from Brazil to Rome. When I arrived in Casablanca there was no plane to Rome, so I had to go to... Cairo, where

I spent two and a bit days; from there, I travelled to Rome, having lunch in Athens... I saw the pyramids, the Sphinx. They are such beautiful sights, unfortunately so used up[44] that when we stand before them we can only feel a sensation already described in Women's Health magazine. [...] I ate American food for lunch and while the plane was being prepared to leave, I got into the jeep belonging to an American who 'flew' to the Acropolis and I was able to see the Parthenon in the distance. The view was the same as if I had looked at a photograph, because it was fast. [...] The Mohammedan said that I had a 'white heart', a pure heart... What I have in truth is a small heart with no space left, because it is so full of saved-up love. On several occasions, I've felt a sudden wish to hug, for example, Marcinha.][45]

In the course of several days, Clarice visits at least four countries, using three different means of transport (plane, jeep and train). Once again, the speed of these events leads her to compare real places like the Parthenon to a photograph, as something static without a profound meaning for her, or, alternately, to something fluid, in Zygmunt Bauman's sense, as a slippery instability one cannot fully embrace.[46]

For Clarice, there is a consequence to traversing so rapidly places of significance to humankind, like the Egyptian pyramids. As transience begins to shape her perspective, such prominent destinations become non-places. The places which she simply passes through, without feeling any sense of identification or belonging, are emptied of their meaning. Hence, even extremely renowned sites are transformed from meaningful places into homogeneous non-places when approached by people, particularly tourists, whose sole interaction might be limited to the taking of a photograph.

It is not incidental, therefore, that in the above passage she abruptly discontinues her description of these (for her) non-places to talk about private issues, such as the purity of her heart and the sudden desire to hug her niece. It is as if, noticing her own lack of grounding and familiar references, she feels the need to grab onto something that might fortify her being and sense of belonging. In a similar vein, Elspeth Probyn points out how the idea of belonging is connected to the act of desiring, especially when related to people, places or ways of being.[47] For Probyn, being an outsider is one of the conditions that leads a person to the need to belong. bell hooks corroborates this viewpoint in attesting to how she only became conscious of how Kentuckian she was once she left her homeland. hooks also highlights that this awareness prevented her from ever truly leaving her birthplace, since internally she was always searching for references she could only recover at home, namely her place of origin.[48] Likewise, the implications of being an outsider become clear to Clarice, who laments: 'Eu sou uma pobre exilada. Você não imagina como longe do Brasil se tem saudade dele. Sou capaz de escrever um novo Brasil, país do futuro...' [I am a poor exile. You have no idea how much one misses Brazil when one is far away. I am capable of writing a new Brazil, the country of the future].[49]

When navigating her situation abroad, it is apparent that Clarice experiences the feeling of being exiled. As Cláudia Nina points out, in the case of Clarice 'o termo exílio não é visto aqui como punição, mas simplesmente em referência ao sentimento de saudade, ou melhor, de nostalgia, que expressa a separação de um indivíduo de sua pátria, e ainda o desejo de retornar a ela algum dia' [The term exile is not seen here as punishment, but simply in reference to the feeling of longing, or rather, of nostalgia, which expresses the separation of an individual from their homeland, and yet the desire to return to it someday].[50] In the previous quote from Clarice's letter, it becomes evident that being exiled was a pre-condition of *saudade* and of feeling the importance of belonging. However, this Brazil she was missing was not a concrete place, but rather an imagined one. According to Ernst van Alphen, after leaving it, a place can only be felt through the lens of the present, 'framed by the historical dimension of the place where the imagining act takes place'.[51] It is therefore through the lens of her life abroad that Clarice maintains her connection to Brazil and its culture. This lens will be responsible, then, for the new view Clarice builds of Brazil.

Thus, even when settling in a specific city, Clarice remains unable to see herself as belonging to these places:

> Assim não tenho gostado verdadeiramente da Itália, como não poderia gostar verdadeiramente de nenhum lugar; sinto que há entre mim e tudo uma coisa, como se eu fosse daquelas pessoas que têm olhos cobertos por uma camada branca.
>
> [So I have not really liked Italy, just as I could not really like any place; I feel that there is something between me and everything else, as if I were one of those people whose eyes are covered by a white layer.][52]

This feeling of disconnection followed her to other cities, such as Berne. Despite recognizing the city's positive aspects, she nonetheless could not feel totally happy there, and this embarrassed her:

> Embora agora mesmo esteja envergonhada de ser assim, porque enquanto escrevo a catedral está batendo os sinos; fico envergonhada de não viver bem em qualquer lugar onde uma catedral bata sinos, onde haja um rio, onde as pessoas trabalhem e façam compras; mas é assim mesmo.
>
> [Although I am ashamed to be so now, because as I write the cathedral bells are ringing; I am ashamed of not living happily in a place where cathedral bells ring, where there is a river, where people work and shop; but that's how it is.][53]

There are two reasons potentially underlying and justifying such lack of identification and belonging: first, the assurance that she would not live in that particular city forever, an assumption compounded by the inherent, persistent sensation of exile that accompanies her throughout her travels; and, second, the twofold internal and external absence of 'home'.

In part due to the war and high rental prices, Clarice and her family resided either at the Brazilian consulate in whichever country she lived or in hotels:

> Todos têm pena da gente porque estamos morando há mais de um ano no Consulado; ninguém entende como principalmente eu suporto, que nem trabalhar posso. Casa é impossível achar. Estou tão cansada de certas mesquinharias que acho que de volta das férias vamos morar numa pensão (hotéis são destruídos ou requisitados para militares ou civis em trânsito) se não acharmos mesmo casa.

> [Everyone pities us because we have been living in the Consulate for over a year; nobody understands how we (me in particular) can bear it, since I can't even work. It is impossible to find a house. I am so tired of certain petty things that I think that upon returning from vacation we will live in a guest house (hotels are destroyed or requisitioned for the military or civilians in transit) if we really can't find a house.][54]

Hotels are, per se, an excellent example of a non-place. Despite attempts at creating a familiar, personal environment, the guest is compelled to live intimately among people with whom he or she has no connection, while also abiding by a specific set of rules prescribed by the site. Similarly, the Brazilian consulate can be interpreted as a type of non-place, in spite of its intended function to 'stand in' for Brazil while nationals are abroad. Clarice was still surrounded by strangers, living daily among many others, who, despite their good nature (as she affirms in a letter), were not members of her family. [55] Thus, she approximates the resulting environment of the consulate to that of any ordinary hotel, as opposed to a comforting place like home.

Throughout her letters, this category of the non-place often emerges as a concern for Clarice. In many instances, she draws attention to efforts to find a house or apartment, despite exorbitant prices, because she is aware of the influence of a home on her well-being. This concern becomes even more persistent after the birth of her first child, Pedro, when the instabilities of hotel living and interactions with unfamiliar people begin to affect her son.

> Por outro lado, o hotel onde estávamos [...] era caro demais e sem comodidade para uma criança. Mudamos para outro, onde simplesmente gelamos. Pedrinho dorme na nossa cama para se esquentar. Então já andamos procurando outro hotel e mudaremos na quinta-feira. A comida é, de um modo geral, bem ruinzinha e pouca.
>
> [On the other hand, the hotel where we were staying [...] was too expensive and not set up for a child. We moved to another one, where we simply froze. Pedrinho sleeps in our bed to get warm. So we have already been looking for another hotel and we will move on Thursday. The food, in general, is really quite terrible and there is very little of it.][56]

Gaston Bachelard stresses the importance of home as a human being's first microcosm, the place where he or she finds grounds for illusions of stability, and where he or she can derive a sense of value and also dream in peace. Without a house or home, 'man would be a dispersed being'.[57] Clarice seems to subscribe to this perspective: she recognizes and acknowledges the influence of a home in the construction of her own identity. Despite associating this place called home with Brazil, she realized that home not only needed to be a physical place, but also one related to people, more specifically to her sisters:

> Gostaria de estar aí com vocês ou com Maury. O mundo todo é ligeiramente chato, parece. O que importa na vida é estar junto de quem se gosta. Isso é a maior verdade do mundo. E se existe um lugar especialmente simpático é o Brasil.
>
> [I would like to be there with you two or with Maury. The whole world seems slightly boring. What matters in life is being with the ones you love. This is

the greatest truth in the world. And if such an especially friendly place exists, it is Brazil.][58]

Later, living in Torquay, she complained about having to move so much and, as a consequence, missing stable points of reference, such as familiar people and places. She felt hopeless, aware that lacking a home could be her lifestyle for years to come:

> Agora vou terminar porque tenho que começar a arrumar as malas. Vocês não podem imaginar como estamos cansados de viagens e mudanças. Estamos espiritualmente cansados, fisicamente cansados. Para decidirmos ir a Londres, foi um problema. Imagina que daqui a uns anos estaremos exaustos. O corpo e a cabeça ficam constantemente procurando uma adaptação, a gente fica fora de foco, sem saber mais o que é e o que não é. Nem meu anjo da guarda sabe mais onde moro.

> [Now I'll finish because I have to start packing. You cannot imagine how tired we are of travelling and moving. We are spiritually tired, physically tired. Just deciding to go to London was a problem. Imagine that in a few years we will be exhausted. Our bodies and minds are used to constantly having to adapt, we are out of focus, without knowing if we're coming or going. Not even my guardian angel knows where I live any more.][59]

In the middle of this plethora of places and non-places, Clarice comprehends how her identity and understanding of self are affected. In the realm of supermodernity, identity becomes refracted, but in non-places there is a suspension and deconstruction of identity. This latter phenomenon is what Clarice describes in her letters: alongside her search for a home, she invariably underscores the sensation of being rootless in her experience of exile, which develops in the face of needing to adapt and pretending to feel at home.

Clarice connects her need for deeper belonging to her 'immediate community', in terms put forward by Lynn Pearce.[60] For Clarice, belonging means feeling part of her place of origin, as well as being close to people she loves and values; it means finding and cultivating a space where she can put down roots, a place she can identify with, a community where she can speak her own language and, ultimately, truly feel at home. In other words, Clarice searches, in bell hooks's words, for a 'culture of place'.[61] In a letter to her friend Lúcio Cardoso, she asserts:

> E você tem bem razão de não querer sair do Brasil. Se sair, que seja por pouco tempo, só para dar uma espiada, e voltar. É ruim estar fora da terra onde a gente se criou, é horrível ouvir ao redor da gente línguas estrangeiras, *tudo parece sem raiz* [...]. Para mim, se foi bom, como um remédio é bom para saúde, ver outros lugares e outras pessoas, já há muito está passando do bom, está no ruim nunca pensei ser tão indatável [sic], nunca pensei que precisava tanto das coisas que possuo.

> [And you are quite right about not wanting to leave Brazil. If you leave, let it be only for a short while, just to take a peek, and come back. It is awful to be outside the land where one grew up, it is horrible to hear foreign languages around one, *everything seems rootless* [...]. To me, although seeing other places and other people was good, as medicine is good for one's health, for a long time now that goodness has been slipping away and turning bad, I had never thought I was so undatable [sic], I never thought I needed my possessions so much.][62]

An absence of roots translates into a lack of belonging, as she ascertains that these lacks are inter-connected, and increasingly perceives how her roots (her sisters, her language, her friends) are not there with her. She feels exiled and incapable of fully integrating into a 'foreign' society, which she sometimes compares to her parents' migration:

> Mas acho que em grande parte, isso vem do desenraizamento dessa vida no estrangeiro. Nem todos são bastante fortes para suportar não ter ambiente propriamente, nem amigos. Cada vez mais, admiro papai e outros que, como ele, souberam ter 'vida nova'; é preciso ter muita coragem para ter vida nova.
>
> [But I think that for the most part this comes from the uprooting of this life abroad. Not everyone is strong enough to put up with not having a proper environment, or friends. More and more, I admire Daddy and others who, like him, knew how to start 'a new life'; it takes a lot of courage to start a new life.][63]

Unlike Clarice's situation, her parents' migration to Brazil (along with Clarice and her sisters) was imposed by war. Thus, her parents were, in a certain way, obliged to discover a new life in order to survive and forget about the idea of returning to their original country. Clarice, however, always maintained the expectation of going back to Brazil, the place where she felt she most belonged, even if at times she feared the way she would be received by her loved ones upon her return, after all the changes she had undergone. Consequently, she consciously remained a foreigner, an exile, and from her point of view, this existence prevented her from achieving a fulfilling life abroad — in the end, she divorced her husband and relocated to Brazil. Just like 'the passenger through non-places' who, according to Augé, 'retrieves his identity only at Customs, the tollbooth, at the check-out counter',[64] Clarice seems to understand that she would only have a chance to recover her identity, suspended in this excess of spaces, once she returned to Brazil.

During her years overseas, Clarice seemed to be aware of how she had changed due to her time abroad and through experiences as a diplomat's wife. In different letters, from Berne to Washington, she expresses how insecure she felt in anticipation of meeting her sisters after a long period of separation:

> Pretendia apenas lhe contar o meu novo caráter, ou falta de caráter, um mês antes de irmos para o Brasil, para você estar prevenida. Mas espero de tal forma que no navio ou no avião que nos levar de volta eu me transforme instantaneamente na antiga que eu era, que talvez nem fosse necessário contar. Querida, quase quatro anos me transformaram muito. Do momento em que me resignei, perdi toda a vivacidade e todo interesse pelas coisas.
>
> [I just wanted to tell you about my new personality, or lack of personality, a month before we go to Brazil, so you are forewarned. But I'm hoping so much that on the ship or plane that takes us back I will instantly become my old self, that perhaps it was not even necessary to tell you. My dear, almost four years have transformed me a lot. From the moment I resigned myself to it, I lost all my vivacity and all interest in things.][65]

Despite her insecurity, she still expresses the hope of recovering the person she had left behind, especially with the support and the presence of her sisters, in a place she used to know so well. Her eventual return to Brazil is not that simple. Suddenly, the place she knew so well seems new to her, albeit in a positive way: 'Ainda não absorvi o Rio, sou lenta e difícil. Precisaria de mais alguns meses para entender de novo a atmosfera. Mas que é bom, é. É selvagem, é inesperado, e salve-se quem puder' [I still have not absorbed Rio, I'm slow and difficult. I would need several more months to understand the atmosphere again. But it is certainly good. Oh yes. It is wild, it is unexpected, and it is every man for himself].[66] According to bell hooks, in order to completely belong to a place, a full self-understanding is necessary, as well as a full comprehension of the environment to which we belong.[67] In this new step after returning to Brazil, Clarice must reinvent herself to recover her place of belonging.

The subject of places and non-places is deeply linked to personal issues in Clarice's letters. The only letters in which there are references to spaces and places are the ones addressed to her sisters and to her close friends Lúcio Cardoso and Fernando Sabino. This presents convincing evidence of how intimate the matter of place/space is for her, as she feels the urge to express her feelings about it privately and solely to people she trusts. The interrelationship between the tense environment in which Clarice lived while abroad and the core concept of belonging also play an important role in the letters. This correlation is expressed on numerous occasions through the many non-places described in the correspondences she maintained during this period. Moreover, the act of writing letters seems to assume a role in providing a sense of belonging, since it is through her letters that Clarice finds her place in the world. This sense is also connected to her writing process during this period, as evidenced in some of the letters. The suspension of her identity while abroad, a suspension associated with non-places, shapes the literature Clarice produces during this period and is made manifest in her search to uncover a feeling of belonging.

Works Cited

ALPHEN, ERNST VAN, 'Imagined Homelands', *Intersecting*, 9 (2002), 53–70
ANGELIDES, SOPHIA, *Carta e literatura: correspondência entre Tchekhov e Gorki* (São Paulo: Editora da Universidade de São Paulo, 2001)
AUGÉ, MARC, *Non-places: Introduction to an Anthropology of Supermodernity*, trans. by John Howe (London: Verso, 1995 [1992])
BACHELARD, GASTON, *The Poetics of Space*, trans. by Maria Jolas (Boston, MA: Beacon Press, 1984 [1958])
BAUMAN, ZYGMUNT, *Liquid Modernity* (Cambridge: Polity Press, 2000)
DABUL, LIGIA, 'Correspondência e poesia: apontamentos sobre criação, interações e disseminação da arte', *Revista Maracanan*, 12 (2016), 97–106
FOUCAULT, MICHEL, 'A escrita de si', *Ética, sexualidade, política*, ed. by Manoel Barros da Motta, trans. by Elisa Monteiro and Inês Autran Dourado Barbosa (Rio de Janeiro: Forense Universitária, 2004), pp. 144–62
GOTLIB, NÁDIA BATTELLA, *Clarice: uma vida que se conta* (São Paulo: Editora da Universidade de São Paulo, 2009)
—— 'Clarice Lispector y las cartas a sus Hermanas', *Tierra Adentro* (January–February 2018), 14–19

GUIMARÃES, ADALBERTO RAFAEL, and ILCA VIEIRA DE OLIVEIRA, 'Cartas perto do coração: a construção da identidade na escrita de si de Fernando Sabino e Clarice Lispector', *Revista Araticum*, 7 (2013), 1–15
HOOKS, BELL, *Belonging: A Culture of Place* (New York: Routledge, 2009)
JONES, ELIZABETH H., *Spaces of Belonging: Home, Culture and Identity in 20th Century French Autobiography* (Amsterdam and New York: Rodopi, 2007)
LISPECTOR, CLARICE, *Correspondências*, ed. by Teresa Montero (Rio de Janeiro: Rocco, 2002)
—— *Minhas queridas*, ed. by Teresa Montero (Rio de Janeiro: Rocco, 2007)
MARCUSCHI, LUIZ ANTÔNIO, *Da fala para a escrita: atividades de retextualização* (São Paulo: Cortez, 2010)
MASSEY, DOREEN B., *For Spaces* (London: Sage, 2005)
MILNE, ESTHER, *Letters, Postcards, Email: Technologies of Presence* (New York: Routledge, 2010)
MOSER, BENJAMIN *Why This World: A Biography of Clarice Lispector* (New York: Oxford University Press, 2009)
NINA, CLÁUDIA, *A palavra usurpada: exílio e nomadismo na obra de Clarice Lispector* (Porto Alegre: EDIPUCRS, 2003)
PEARCE, LYNN, 'The Place of Literature in the Spaces of Belonging', *European Journal of Cultural Studies*, 5 (2002), 275–91
PONTIERI, REGINA, *Clarice Lispector: uma poética do olhar* (São Paulo: Ateliê, 1999)
PROBYN, ELSPETH, *Outside Belongings* (New York: Routledge, 1996)
SABINO, FERNANDO, *Cartas perto do coração: dois jovens escritores unidos ante o mistério da criação* (Rio de Janeiro: Record, 2011)
VARIN, CLAIRE, *Línguas de Fogo: Ensaio sobre Clarice Lispector*, trans. by Lúcia Peixoto Cherem (São Paulo: Limiar, 2002 [1990])

Notes to Chapter 2

1. bell hooks, *Belonging: A Culture of Place* (New York: Routledge, 2009), p. 120.
2. Clarice Lispector, *Correspondências*, ed. by Teresa Montero (Rio de Janeiro: Rocco, 2002).
3. Clarice Lispector, *Minhas queridas*, ed. by Teresa Montero (Rio de Janeiro: Rocco, 2007).
4. Marc Augé, *Non-places: Introduction to an Anthropology of Supermodernity* (London: Verso, 1995).
5. See Elizabeth H. Jones, *Spaces of Belonging: Home, Culture and Identity in 20th Century French Autobiography* (Amsterdam and New York: Rodopi, 2007); Doreen B. Massey: *For Spaces* (London: Sage, 2005); and Linda McDowell: *Gender, Identity and Place: Understanding Feminist Geographies* (Minneapolis: University of Minnesota Press, 1999).
6. Massey, *For Spaces*, p. 9.
7. For a detailed discussion of this theme, see Jones, *Spaces of Belonging*, pp. 40–45.
8. Augé, *Non-places*, p. 77.
9. Zygmunt Bauman, *Liquid Modernity* (Cambridge: Polity Press, 2000), p. 102.
10. Ibid.
11. The dates and facts of this short biography were mainly based on the following works: Nádia Battella Gotlib, *Clarice: uma vida que se conta* (São Paulo: Editora da Universidade de São Paulo, 2009) and Benjamin Moser, *Why This World: A Biography of Clarice Lispector* (New York: Oxford University Press, 2009).
12. Nádia Battella Gotlib, 'Clarice Lispector y las cartas a sus Hermanas', *Tierra Adentro* (January–February 2018), pp. 14–19.
13. Luiz Antônio Marcuschi, *Da fala para a escrita: atividades de retextualização* (São Paulo: Cortez, 2010), p. 41.
14. Lispector, *Minhas queridas*, p. 23 (my emphasis). All translations into English are mine, unless otherwise noted.
15. Gotlib, 'Clarice Lispector y las cartas a sus Hermanas', pp. 14–19.

16. Sophia Angelides, *Carta e literatura: correspondência entre Tchekhov e Gorki* (São Paulo: Editora da Universidade de São Paulo, 2001), p. 23.
17. Adalberto Rafael Guimarães and Ilca Vieira de Oliveira, 'Cartas perto do coração: a construção da identidade na escrita de si de Fernando Sabino e Clarice Lispector', *Revista Araticum*, 7 (2013), 1–15.
18. Ligia Dabul, 'Correspondência e poesia: apontamentos sobre criação, interações e disseminação da arte', *Revista Maracanan*, 12 (2016), 97–106.
19. See Lispector, *Correspondências* and Fernando Sabino, *Cartas perto do coração: dois jovens escritores unidos ante o mistério da criação* (Rio de Janeiro: Record, 2011). Fernando Sabino (1923–2004) was a Brazilian writer and journalist who published many novels and collections of short stories, such as *O homem nu* and *O grande mentecapto*. He met Clarice in 1945, and between 1946 and 1969 they exchanged letters, which were later published in *Cartas perto do coração*.
20. Lispector, *Correspondências*, p. 12.
21. Gotlib, 'Clarice Lispector y las cartas a sus Hermanas', pp. 14–19.
22. Michel Foucault, 'A escrita de si', *Ética, sexualidade, política*, ed. by Manoel Barros da Motta, trans. by Elisa Monteiro and Inês Autran Dourado Barbosa (Rio de Janeiro: Forense Universitária, 2004), pp. 144–62.
23. Lispector, *Minhas queridas*, pp. 108; 113; 158–59; 170; 200.
24. Letter dated 21 September 1948. Lispector, *Minhas queridas*, p. 200.
25. Lispector and Sabino, *Cartas perto do coração*, p. 23.
26. Guimarães and de Oliveira, 'Cartas perto do coração', p. 14.
27. Lispector and Sabino, *Cartas perto do coração*, p. 48.
28. Lispector, *Minhas queridas* p. 205; *Correspondências*, pp. 64; 91.
29. Letter dated 19 October 1948. Lispector, *Minhas queridas*, p. 205.
30. Esther Milne, *Letters, Postcards, Email: Technologies of Presence* (New York: Routledge, 2010), p. 14.
31. Letter dated 18 December 1944. Lispector, *Minhas queridas*, p. 64.
32. Letter dated 8 May 1946. Lispector, *Minhas queridas*, p. 114. I would like to thank Magdalena Edwards for her comments on this translation.
33. *Saudade* is usually considered a very hard word to translate; it may even be 'untranslatable'. It is defined by Tim Lomas as 'a melancholic longing or nostalgia for a person, place or thing that is far away either spatially or in time — a vague, dreaming wistfulness for phenomena that may not even exist'. David Robson, 'The untranslatable emotions you never knew you had', *BBC*, 26 January 2017 <https://www.bbc.com/future/article/20170126-the-untranslatable-emotions-you-never-knew-you-had> [accessed 27 October 2019].
34. Letter dated 5 November 1948. Lispector, *Correspondências*, pp. 177–78.
35. Letter dated 12 May 1946. Lispector, *Minhas queridas*, p. 118.
36. Letter dated 30 June 1946. Lispector, *Minhas queridas*, p. 124.
37. Claire Varin, *Línguas de fogo: ensaio sobre Clarice Lispector*, trans. by Lúcia Peixoto Cherem. (São Paulo: Limiar, 2002), p. 122.
38. Regina Pontieri, *Clarice Lispector: uma Poética do Olhar* (São Paulo: Ateliê, 1999), p. 14.
39. Letter dated 5 October 1944. Lispector, *Correspondências*, p. 54.
40. Ibid., pp. 54–55.
41. Augé, *Non-places*, p. 77.
42. Ibid., p. 55.
43. Letter dated 13 August 1957. Lispector, *Minhas queridas*, p. 290.
44. The word 'exploradas' could be translated either as explored or exploited. Since none of them fully satisfy the meaning in Portuguese, in this case, 'used up' seemed a better choice. I would like to thank Magdalena Edwards once more for her help with this translation.
45. Letter dated 14 April 1946. Lispector, *Minhas queridas*, p. 103. My emphasis.
46. Bauman, *Liquid Modernity*, p. 2.
47. Elspeth Probyn, *Outside Belongings* (New York: Routledge, 1996).
48. hooks, *Belonging*, p. 13.
49. Letter dated 21 November 1944. Lispector, *Minhas queridas*, p. 63.

50. Cláudia Nina, *A palavra usurpada: exílio e nomadismo na obra de Clarice Lispector* (Porto Alegre: EDIPUCRS, 2003), p. 11.
51. Ernst van Alphen, 'Imagined Homelands', *Intersecting* 9 (2002), 53–70 (pp. 66–67).
52. Undated letter. Lispector, *Correspondências*, p. 63.
53. Letter dated 13 August 1947. Lispector, *Correspondências*, p. 145.
54. Letter dated 26 November 1945. Lispector, *Minhas queridas*, p. 101.
55. 'Quero também não morar com tanta gente. Estamos num apartamento grande, com todos do consulado, que são ótimas pessoas; mas eu nunca precisei de ótimas pessoas' [I also do not want to live with so many people. We are in a big apartment, with everyone from the consulate, who are great people; but I never needed great people]. Undated letter. Lispector, *Correspondências*, p. 56.
56. Letter dated 3 October 1950. Lispector, *Minhas queridas*, p. 227.
57. Gaston Bachelard, *The Poetics of Space*, trans. by Maria Jolas (Boston, MA: Beacon Press, 1984), p. 7.
58. Letter dated 7 August 1944. Lispector, *Minhas queridas*, p. 40.
59. Letter dated 28 November 1950. Lispector, *Minhas queridas*, p. 234.
60. Lynn Pearce, 'The Place of Literature in the Spaces of Belonging', *European Journal of Cultural Studies*, 5 (2002), 275–91.
61. hooks, *Belonging*, p. 2.
62. Letter dated 13 August 1947. Lispector, *Correspondências*, p. 145. My emphasis.
63. Letter dated 22 October 1947. Lispector, *Minhas queridas*, p. 176.
64. Augé, *Non-places*, p. 103.
65. Letter dated 6 January 1948. Lispector, *Correspondências*, p. 164.
66. Letter dated 14 August 1954. Lispector, *Correspondências*, p. 202.
67. hooks, *Belonging*, p. 220.

CHAPTER 3

Bridging the Imaginary Gap between Distant Cartographies: The Visit that Never Was

Dafna Hornike

In March 1947 the young and already published Jewish Brazilian author Clarice Lispector was planning her upcoming international travels as a diplomat's wife. Her journeys would take her to Libya, Egypt, Italy, Switzerland, the United States, and beyond, travelling by train, aeroplane, and even camel. Not surprisingly, Lispector has often been associated with nomadic readings, mainly focusing on the impact of her personal life on her writing. Her diplomatic passport frequently appears in biographies, so as to prove she was well travelled and informed about other cultures. Benjamin Moser's biography even goes so far as to depict her international origins in a map using a Tolkien-like font, evoking *Lord of the Rings* mythology as part of reconstructing Lispector's own movements through space.[1] Nevertheless, what interests me in my research is triggered by the commonly overlooked Palestinian visa Lispector was issued in 1946 (which can be seen in the Casa Rui Barbosa archive), as well as by numerous references to the Middle East in her texts: the Galilee, Constantinople, and Damascus to name just a few. As a writer dedicated to the depiction of the subjective experience of the multiple connections between subject and space, Lispector's usage of spatial allusions is not to be taken lightly. Indeed, her texts are haunted by Middle Eastern imagery, calling for a closer look at these meaningful spaces and their function for the reader.

The avid reader of her works can trace an insistence on these spaces, a continuous usage of what I call Holy Land imagery: spatial tropes of a land Lispector never even visited. The author maintained a conflicted relationship with this imaginary cartography that influenced her writing, a land she only knew from other accounts. What follows, therefore, is an examination of the points of departure Lispector imagined when writing. In other words, this non-existent visit to the real land of Palestine/Israel may be the event that enabled the author's usage of the imaginary space as a focal point in her literature. I wish to go through the open door that lies between the tangible and historical facts and the fictive, imaginary depiction of the same space. How does Lispector construct spatial imagery in her writing, and what is the impact of the geographical landscape of this unknown land on her texts?

What is the place of the imagined Palestinian space on the writer's exploration of subjectivity? Does this space hold an orientalist function for Lispector, or does it open a promising portal into a more nuanced understanding of the author's work?

As Claire Williams notes in 'Cidadã do mundo: as viagens de Lispector', the characters in her books possess a remarkable sense of awareness to space, as well as to travelling through it.[2] *A paixão segundo G.H.* [*The Passion According to G.H.*] (1964) is one such text, a powerful and unique exploration of an inner journey, depicted through a dichotomist insistence on extended and enclosed spaces. According to Cláudia Nina in *A palavra usurpada, exílio e nomadismo na obra de Clarice Lispector*, *The Passion* is a transitional text that lies at the end of *ciclo do exílio* [the exile cycle]: texts written when the author was living abroad that share a strong sense of being away.[3] The following cycle is the 'nomadic' one, which is characterized by a strong first-person narrator immersed in an ontological quest. This change in the author's writing positions *The Passion* at the cusp of an inward turn for which Lispector is widely known, marking it as both the turning point in the author's *oeuvre* and a pathway to a more attuned understanding of the function of space in her literature. *The Passion*, with its insistence on a subjective inner journey, will therefore be at the centre of my exploration of the multiple connections between far away spaces and their function in Lispector's works.

The Passion is a fine example of the author's economy of language which can be read as a representation of a breaking down of subjectivity itself. The narration is triggered by absence, though not in the traditional gendered analysis that deciphers the location of Woman in Western thought as symbolized by lack.[4] After her black maid quits, the protagonist, G.H., decides to venture into the deserted room in the back of her otherwise familiar apartment under the pretence of reclaiming her private space. In the maid's empty room G.H. is confronted with her own racial stereotypes, which set her on a nomadic journey inwards. She is obsessively focused on the most subtle specifics of her own thoughts and inner feelings, making her confrontation with the limits of race a call for crossing borders. The text focuses on the subjective experience of the protagonist, while being saturated with spatial images that make the inner journey a road into subjectivity itself. G.H.'s perception of the actual physical space around her keeps getting smaller and more confined: from the apartment to the maid's room, from the room to the (empty) closet where she encounters a cockroach. These ever-shrinking spatial circles echo the protagonist's concentration on her own subjective experience, suggesting that a confined space enables and opens up a view onto the inner realms of the subject. While there is a growing focus on the subject and the processes it experiences, this focus is accompanied by a diminished space so that going inward is both metaphorical and spatial. *The Passion* takes us on an inner journey, a nomadic transgression of boundaries that culminates in a sense of expansion of the self. This process is built upon numerous spatial references and tropes, in such a way that space becomes the privileged metaphor to articulate change and growth.

The text opens in the middle of the page with six consecutive hyphens: '– – – – – – estou procurando, estou procurando' [I keep looking, looking].[5] The graphic symbols create a sense of continuation, as if we were entering the text *in medias res*, jumping into an ongoing motion that had started prior to reading (or writing) itself. The gerund verb form that follows emphasizes the search as a primordial part of being; the first thing we learn of this first-person narration is that it is in process. The object of this search is unknown to us and will remain undefined. And precisely because it is undefined, it is a nomadic search, although it is not deprived of a sense of place since there are certain stops along the way. One of these stops is the reference to being:

> Se eu me confirmar e me considerar verdadeira, estarei perdida porque não saberei onde engastar meu novo modo de ser — se eu for adiante nas minhas visões fragmentárias, o mundo inteiro terá que se transformar para eu caber nele.
>
> [If I go ahead with that grounding and consider myself true, I'll be lost because I won't know where to set up my new way of being — if I go forward with my fragmentary visions, the whole world will have to change for me to fit in it.][6]

This still unnamed protagonist draws our attention to her fictiveness, or at least to her questioning of the realness of her being. If she were to consider herself 'real', whatever that means in this case, she would be lost, disoriented, without knowing how to encase herself in the world. The world will therefore have to change in order to fit her in, as if it were an exterior form containing special material. Nevertheless, this questioning of the reality of the subject is not necessarily related to the nature of the text (usually read as fiction), but rather to the fictive nature of the subject. What we usually understand as the subject, or subjectivity, is not real, in the sense that it is not unified. As Judith Butler affirms in *The Psychic Life of Power*: 'the subject ought to be designated as a linguistic category, a placeholder, a structure in formation'.[7] Following Lispector, if the narrator were to consider herself 'real' in the sense of a unified existence, she would be lost, would be unable to find her place and would therefore have to question how the world relates to her. This is, indeed, a text about the search for reciprocity between subject and world, a search that entails a transformation for both.

This process of change and search takes form in writing, and thereby maintains a strong connection between movement through space and the self. When talking about beginning her narration, this is how the narrator chooses to relate her efforts: 'Entender é uma criação, meu único modo. Precisarei com esforço traduzir sinais de telégrafo — traduzir o desconhecido para uma língua que desconheço, e sem sequer entender para que valem os sinais' [Understanding is a creation, my only way. I shall have to force myself to translate telegraph signals — translate the unknown into a language I do not know, without even understanding what the signals amount to].[8] The act of telling is merely the translation of an experience into a language the narrator does not even know. Thus, understanding is not really possible but is still the only way to travel this road, following signals that are strange and unfamiliar. The telegraph (*tele*, 'far' and *graph*, 'writing') is an appropriate metaphor in this context since it draws an image of a writing that is transferred through space, divided into lines that trace a determined place. Having to translate the staccato signs of the telegraph is, indeed, like translating the unknown into a foreign language, bridging languages as well as spaces. With the metaphor of the telegraph we can consider language as a code that is transmitted across space along a cartographic line of meaning, a delicate connection that can be severed or lost at any point.

Travelling through space and the futile attempt to connect distant cartographies can also be seen in the following example: 'O resto era o modo como pouco a pouco eu havia me transformado na pessoa que tem o meu nome. E acabei sendo o meu nome. É suficiente ver no couro de minhas valises as iniciais G.H., e eis-me' [The rest was the way in which, little by little, I have transformed into the person who bears my name. And I ended up being my own name. It is sufficient seeing my name on the leather of my suitcases, and it is I].[9] This wonderful image of the suitcases with the narrator's name inscribed on them stresses two aspects of the text that are of interest: on the one hand we witness the process the subject goes through in order to be transformed into the person who bears a certain name. The monogram on the suitcases places the protagonist within a determined social discourse and by doing so it functions as the binding act of a name, a way to claim a unified and easily read subjectivity. A woman of a certain economic class is characterized and expected to be a person of means, someone who travels with the right luggage.

On the other hand, the transformation into oneself that Lispector suggests is inscribed on the narrator's suitcases, containers that hold her belongings when travelling. G.H. is, therefore, not only an artistic middle-class woman who has the means to travel; she is also a subject that questions the relation between the name and what it holds. In this manner, the subject is depicted as a continuous and disrupted being that struggles to fit into the way it is labelled and named, a subject that carries a precarious connection with travelling. These are sedentary suitcases that constantly serve as reminders of a nomadic negotiation of being. Although these suitcases remain closed in the text, every other aspect of the outer shell of the subject is being unravelled. In spite of our conscious effort to avoid conflating Lispector with G.H., writer with protagonist, one cannot help but imagine the former reflecting on the relationship between traveller and belongings when writing this passage.

Nomadic journeys continue to be a key theme in the text, accompanied by a complex structure of imposing limits and then transgressing them. Throughout the text Lispector depicts a series of physical limits on the narrator: she is located within her apartment and will move into smaller and smaller spaces. Our attention is directed towards the importance of limits in the captivating metaphor of the photo: 'Essa imagem de mim entre aspas me satisfazia, e não apenas superficialmente. Eu era a imagem do que eu não era, e essa imagem do não-ser me cumulava toda: um dos modos mais fortes é ser negativamente' [That image of myself between quotation marks satisfied me, and not just superficially. I was the image of that which I wasn't, and that image of not being summarized me — one of the strongest ways of being is to be negatively].[10] The image of the self, placed within the frame of a photo brings to mind the limits upon the image, the visible borders that satisfy the narrator. This frame functions like quotation marks in the sense that it marks a beginning and an end to the image, while helping tie together the photographic image — the visual aspect of the protagonist — with the act of writing and the materiality of punctuation marks. In other words, before embarking on her journey, the narrator calls our attention to borders through the emphasis on the limit of the photographed subject, and the quotation marks that encase the self. With our attention drawn to boundaries we continue reading and encounter more space.

The apartment in which G.H. lives is similar to the quotation marks on the edge of the photo, as well as to the suitcases with her initials, since it provides the physical setting and the actual borders for the subject. Space has specific descriptions and a determined location: it is an apartment, on the thirteenth floor of a building in Rio de Janeiro:

> Olhei para baixo: treze andares caíam do edifício. [...] Olhei a área interna, o fundo dos apartamentos para os quais o meu apartamento também se via como fundos. Por fora meu prédio era branco, com lisura de mármore e lisura de superfície. Mas por dentro a área interna era um amontoado oblíquo de chuvas, janela arreganhada contra janela, bocas olhando bocas.
>
> [I looked down: thirteen flours of building below [...] I looked at the inside area, the backs of all the apartments, for which my own apartment too existed as a back. On the outside, my building was white, with the smoothness of marble and the smoothness of finished surface. But on the inside, the inside area was a chaotic jumble of square blocks, windows, dark streaks and blotches from the rain, window snarling at window, mouths looking into mouths.][11]

This seemingly descriptive paragraph depicting an urban building — an apartment that overlooks a patio in a construction with surfaces of marble and glass — takes on a different meaning through the reflective narrating voice. The movement of looking outside and downward as if from a tower marks the first steps taken in the protagonist's journey. This grid of urban scenery is a mixture of man-made surfaces that seem smooth and even, but when seen from the inside are in fact an assembly of organic openings, mouths facing each other. This view of the building, wherein the protagonist is located, is a mixture of interiority and exteriority, closed and open surfaces, beginning to destabilize our understanding of space. Thus, even the view outside directs the reader's attention to the symbolic nature of space, in which windows can seem like open mouths, gaps opened on the border of an actual wall.

Back inside the apartment, the maid's deserted room is the setting for the rest of the nomadic journey the protagonist undergoes. Crossing the threshold into this room triggers a physical feeling of inconvenience since G.H. was expecting to find that the maid had left it messy, not clean and tidy. Lispector is subtle in the way she portrays the protagonist's stereotypes of the maid; however, there is no doubt that the main element that sets in motion the intense process she will go through is the encounter with her perception of otherness: 'Na minha casa fresca, aconchegada e úmida, a criada sem me avisar abrira um vazio seco' [Without telling me, the maid had opened up a dry, empty space in my fresh, cozy, moist home].[12] G.H. opens the door onto another space, this different space inside the protagonist's apartment in which there are other conditions and another kind of weather. Contrary to the humidity desired by G.H., one that is so characteristic of Rio de Janeiro's tropical climate, the room is now dry and empty. In other words, the maid has managed not only to clean and organize the room, but also to change its climate, and in a way that has become challenging and dangerous for G.H.

From this moment on, a portal is opened here to other climates, different spaces. Following the transgression into this modified room, space becomes coded with alternative meanings, evoking other cultures. At this moment even the physical location of the room now seems transformed: 'estar em nível incomparavelmente acima do próprio apartamento. Como um minarete' [The room seemed to occupy a level much higher than that of the rest of the apartment. Like a minaret.].[13] Space, or the experience of space, is altered. This reference to the minaret is the first of many that carry the weight of other cultures, exotic places and faraway lands. As is the case for the suitcases, the text constantly alludes to travelling to other places without the protagonist's physical dislocation, as if echoing Michel Foucault's heterotopias, those spaces are superimposed on common places. G.H. experiences this space as different, oriental: 'Não ser inteiramente regular nos seus ângulos dava-lhe uma impressão de fragilidade de base como se o quarto-minarete não estivesse incrustado no apartamento nem no edifício' [Its not being entirely regular in its angles gave it an appearance of basic fragility, as though this minaret of a room were not attached to either the apartment or the building].[14] This classic Lispectorian subjunctive phrase cannot be taken lightly, since the journey that G.H. begins in this space traverses precisely the most foreign and strange lands of her own being. The author's 'as if' brings together two kinds of spaces at the same time: the reader realizes the room is part of the apartment but also that it is experienced as being elsewhere. In this way, the same space is part of two different sets of meaning: the here and the there. The physical space of the room in relation to the apartment and in relation to G.H.'s own experience of space has changed, and so have the rules inside it.

In a way, the dual meaning of this space functions here as an impossible meeting between two different cultures as represented by two distinct women: a middle-class, presumably white woman and her usually quiet black maid. Preceding this encounter, her descriptions of the maid utilize adjectives such as 'dark', 'invisible', 'quiet', 'with features of an African queen' — all stereotypical ways of looking at otherness in relation to the protagonist.[15] At the same time, following the discovery of the drawings, Janair is named for the first time, becoming 'a primeira pessoa realmente exterior de cujo olhar eu tomava consciência' [Janair was the first outside person whose gaze I really took notice of].[16] This is a powerful meeting between the two, one that is enabled only through absence. The drawing on the wall, which G.H. interprets as hieroglyphs, is the first step in an impossible dialogue between two women who used to share the same space and never, we assume, broke the social standards of a relationship between an employer and an employee. G.H. imagines Janair's message to be one of hate, something that may very well be true when one considers the power relations between the two, although we, of course, never find out. Nevertheless, here Lispector sets up a charged encounter between subject and other, one that for G.H. becomes the first time she acknowledges that her maid is a subject in her own right. In other words, this is an example of what lies between the subject and what she perceives as an exterior, exotic object (as we saw in the references to the oriental minaret), inviting the consequential transformation of that Other into subject.

The otherness of the black maid, who had recreated the room as a dry desert in contrast to humid Rio de Janeiro, brings me to rethink the category of Other as personified through the spatially characterized concept of Orientalism. Working through texts by Edward Said and Frantz Fanon, Sara Ahmed offers a fresh and relevant insight into the term: 'The Orient is the "not Europe" through which the boundaries between Europe and what is "not Europe" are established as a way of "locating" a distinction between self and other'.[17] Ahmed is talking here about an otherness that is established through space, as well as the production of whiteness on the cultural and corporal level. The other, then, is what establishes the boundary of the speaking subject, assuming that the definition is generated in 'Europe'. The Orient is that faraway land that lies beyond the boundaries of what is perceived as centre, so that the distinction between self and other is constituted in space. In addition, according to Ahmed, Otherness is associated with the mobility and directionality of bodies, such that the 'Orient' is a horizon, a potentiality for an action, something to reach or from which to distance oneself. In this sense, othering is not simply a form of negation (the Orient is everything that Europe is not), but a form of extension I can reach with my body.[18] The Other, in Ahmed's definition, is linked to the construction of race and the distinction between 'white' and 'non-white' subjects; however, it can of course be understood according to many different categories that are based on the distinction between self and other. For example, Ahmed's assertion: 'Whiteness is only invisible for those who inhabit it, or for those who get so used to its inhabitants that they learn not to see it, even when they are not it'.[19] The same can be said about the invisibility of gender when one inhabits or is accustomed to passing as the dominant gender; when one does not inhabit the 'proper' body or gender performance, normative gender categories become visible through processes of othering. In any case, inhabiting the right body, according to Ahmed, is what allows an individual to have social mobility: moving 'up' in the world depends on what is below.[20] Since a 'black, quiet, and invisible' body like Janair's serves as the Other to G.H.'s body, it is no surprise that Lispector's protagonist does not provide any details as to her own appearance. Being the speaking subject and presumably white, she only needs to mention the maid's otherness in order to distinguish herself.

The otherness of this maid is even more difficult for G.H. to encounter since it is located and even encased within her own home. As Ahmed affirms when speaking of the experience of traveling as an Other: 'While the stranger may not be "at home", the stranger only becomes a stranger by coming too close to home. The politics of mobility, of who gets to move with ease across the lines that divide spaces, can be re-described into inhabitable spaces, as spaces that are inhabitable as they extend the surfaces of such bodies'.[21] In other words, certain bodies feel more at home than others in certain spaces when referring to race, and strangers become Other when they are close enough to be different, to be a threat to the inhabitants of a certain space. Janair's lingering existence in the apartment is a threat to G.H. because it is so close, affecting the protagonist's own space. Her body, silent or not, reflects otherness by simply extending itself into space, a process that also accounts for G.H.'s powerful reaction to the charcoal drawings: black markings on her white wall. Nevertheless, G.H. specifically says that through the encounter with Janair she experiences for the first time the existence of someone external to herself. G.H.'s acceptance of otherness is positive but also convenient, in so far as Janair, the only other person who might benefit from the white woman's acknowledgement of her being, is not even present. In this sense, Janair functions as an intermediary agent, allowing the nomadic journey to take place without being able to benefit from its results.

Olga de Sá analyses further this absent character: 'A empregada, pelo nome (Janair/Janaína, outro nome de Iemanjá) e por seus traços, leva o leitor a associá-la a ritos africanos. Por outro lado, nomeando as múmias do Egito, os hieróglifos, os sarcófagos, o deserto, as salamandras e os grifos, o texto fornece-nos elementos de ambiência oriental' [The maid, from her name (Janair/Janaina, another name for Iemanjá), and from her features, leads the reader to associate her with African rituals. On the other hand, naming Egypt's mummies, hieroglyphs, sarcophagi, the desert, salamanders and gryphons, the text provides us with elements of an oriental nature].[22] Janair is marked as Other through two spatial belongings: on the one hand she is of African descent, and on the other she is associated with 'the Orient'. This duality of belonging also manifests in the name Lispector chooses for her: Janair, or Iemanjá in the Afro-Brazilian tradition, is of course the female deity or *orixá*, the mother of the ocean and the patron saint of shipwreck survivors, as well as the feminine principle of creation. Janair also echoes the word 'Janeiro', the month of January in Portuguese, named after Janus, the Roman male deity responsible for beginnings. Janus is depicted in Roman art as having two faces that point to the east and west, symbolic of past and the future. Janair is therefore not only a combination of two spaces — Africa and the Orient — but also a mixture of religions and genders. She is the hybrid Other that is in charge of creation and new beginnings, facing east and west, orientalized and 'westernized' at the same time. As Ahmed's work on the concept of Orientalism asserts: ' "The Orient" is a horizon, a potentiality of an action, something to reach or from which to distance oneself. In this sense, othering is not simply a form of negation (the Orient is everything that Europe is not), but a form of extension I can reach with my body'.[23] The deserted room marks the horizon for the narrator's self-exploration, orienting her journey towards other spaces as well as pointing our attention to the centrality of the Other space.

Recognizing the protagonist's positionality in space and her directionality in relation to Janair is part of the process G.H. undergoes: 'Eu me preparara para limpar coisas sujas mas lidar com aquela ausência me desnorteava' [I had been prepared to clean up a mess, but this struggle with its absence disoriented me].[24] In Portuguese the word for 'oriented' is 'norteada', as if the Other by which one positions oneself is the north and not the east as it is in the English language. Choosing to reference disorientation by the north is telling here, especially since Portuguese does use 'desorientada' as well. One could say that speaking from a peripheral location that was 'discovered' late in world history, Portuguese marks 'otherness' as what lies over there, in the north, possibly North America. Following Ahmed's logic, the north functions here as a directionality of the body, a horizon of possibilities as well as a conceptual boundary. As the main trigger for the nomadic transformation that G.H. experiences, Janair has a complex role as the character that represents corporeal and spatial otherness. Though not even present, Janair is the first Other that becomes personified for the protagonist, the first one to become an (imagined) subject.

Finally, we must not overlook the first impression that Janair's name conjures up, referring us back to the name of the actual city where this nomadic process takes place: Rio de Janeiro. In spite of the alternative spelling, Janair refers to Janeiro in a way that links the maid's presence to the physical place of narration. Lispector's choice of name brilliantly portrays a union of faraway otherness and an inherent connection to both the space of narration and of writing itself. The other-turned-subject can be seen, in fact, as a personification of the city, and in this sense Lispector endows the disenfranchised inhabitants of Rio de Janeiro a key role in her text. The many possibilities that this name proposes for the reader turn the missing maid into the only subject that G.H. recognizes, as well as a multiple and layered being with contradicting histories and nomadic belongings.

Once inside Janair's room, G.H.'s gaze is directed (oriented) into the closet. Inside it she finds the cockroach, the most extreme representation of otherness the protagonist can imagine: 'É que eu olhara a barata viva e nela descobrira a identidade de minha vida mais profunda. Em derrocada difícil, abriam-se dentro de mim passagens duras e estreitas' [I had looked upon the live cockroach and had discovered in it my deepest life identity. In a difficult demolition, hard, narrow passages were opening inside me].[25] G.H. discovers in the cockroach a reflection of her innermost life, thus establishing a solid connection between the two beings. The discovery of her inner life, a subjective awakening, described as a series of passages opening inside the self that recall the mythological implications of Janair's name. For Lispector, the journey inside the apartment and into the smallest space that her protagonist can find is a way to direct our attention and the narration's focus to the inner space of the self.

It is there, in the smallest of spaces correlating with the protagonist's inner journey, that G.H. finally reaches a place of expansion, where space itself opens up: 'Levantei-me antes mesmo de decidir, e, mesmo inutilmente, procurei escancarar ainda mais a janela já toda escancarada, e procurava respirar, ainda que fosse respirar de uma amplidão visual, eu procurava uma amplidão' [I got up before I had really decided to and, even though it was useless, tried to throw open even wider the already fully opened window, and I tried to breathe, even though it might be breathing from a visual vastness, I sought a vastness].[26] This moment lies almost at the centre of the novel, forming a bridge between the protagonist's physical movement into the maid's room and the experience of an intense and mystical revelation. G.H. is about to experience an epiphany triggered by her confrontation with otherness, and the way this moment is described is not only spatial, but also uses a very particular set of spatial imagery. From the window she now sees an extension of roofs larger than Spain, as the familiar Rio de Janeiro is transformed into a hybrid space punctuated by oriental references.[27] Looming over the favela she sees from her window are the plateaus of Asia Minor, as the edges of the familiar fade into the faraway landscape of the Mediterranean. In the following pages G.H. lists a number of European and Mediterranean places stretching out from the margins of the favela: the Dardanelles, Syria, Athens, Constantinople, and the Black Sea.[28] She is trying to draw a map that is superimposed on the familiar space of Rio de Janeiro, as if spaces were images that can be pressed together; what this city needs, she actually says, is cartographic work.[29] G.H.'s view onto the urban scenery stretching from her window weaves together the Brazilian cartography with that of other spaces, convoluted Mediterranean imagery seen from a carioca bird's eye view.

From now on, the spaces of Rio de Janeiro and the Middle East are fused together: 'Mentalmente tracei um círculo em torno das semi-ruínas das favelas, e conheci que ali poderia ter outrora vivido uma cidade tão grande e límpida quanto Atenas no seu apogeu, com meninos correndo entre mercadorias expostas nas ruas' [I mentally traced a circle around the semiruins of the favelas, and I realized that a city as large and limpid as Athens at its zenith could once have lived there, with children running through merchandise set out along the streets].[30] This is a mental map drawn by the protagonist, who sees the potentiality of another city existing on top of the common favelas — and the city she chooses to evoke is Athens. G.H. takes on a mental task, as she says, following a method of seeing that is not seeing, or double seeing, following residues or imprints of other spaces. Following Ahmed's line of analysis, for the protagonist 'the orient' is not a specific and empirical set of coordinates, but a grid of potentialities, a possible direction towards which the self can be extended. This is, indeed, the not-so-distant Orient that lingers just beyond the protagonist's perception, the presence of the Other space as connected to the known location of Home. At the centre of G.H.'s internal journey is the *axis mundi* that bridges Rio de Janeiro and Middle Eastern cartography.

Following G.H.'s feeling of inner expansion we are now able to see the bridge constructed over favelas, minarets, a carioca residential building, and the Galilee. The superimposed spaces of Rio de Janeiro and the Middle East may not be so different after all:

> Para sustentar sem quedas meu ânimo de trabalho, eu procuraria não esquecer que os geólogos já sabem que no subsolo de Saara há um imenso lago de água potável, lembro-me de que li isso; [...]. O deserto tem uma umidade que é preciso encontrar de novo.

[To keep my work spirit from flagging, I would try not to forget that geologists now know that in the Sahara's subsoil there is a huge lake of potable water, I remember reading that; [...]. The desert has a humidity that must be found again.][31]

When G.H. speaks of this remote space, she refers, in fact, to the way even the most extreme example of oriental otherness can still be similar to the humidity at the centre of the narration. One space can have two meanings, sustain two different ways of life, and sustain different meanings for different inhabitants. In a way, G.H. depicts a cartography of otherness, of a specifically oriental otherness that is superimposed upon the place from which she narrates this story. Her experience of Rio de Janeiro does not only carry the weight of the faraway and unfamiliar spaces she has only read about; it also bridges and alters both the place of enunciation and the 'other' place. The presence of this othered space mirrors the impossible encounter between subject and other, a subject obsessed with her own subjectivity, an 'other' whose difference is so challenging that the author chooses to represent it through absence. The workings of space, the portal between the here and the there, is established through the encounter between two unequal protagonists, thus forming a bridge between spaces and subjects.

The boundaries that G.H. explores and transgresses, as well as her relation with otherness, are not external to the self, but rather quite internal. While the space that surrounds the protagonist unlocks the process she undergoes, it is the personal and subjective experience that influences her transformation. Speaking of the human part of her soul in reference to the cockroach's proximity, G.H. explains: 'Toda a parte mais intangível de minha alma e que não me pertence — é aquela que toca na minha fronteira com o que já não é eu, e à qual me dou' [The most unreachable part of my soul, the one not belonging to me, is the part that touches on my border with what is not me and the part to which I give myself over].[32] There is a clear boundary here that marks the line between the self and the non-self, or, we might say, the subject and other. In this intimate journey of proximity to the other, G.H. is getting close to the parts of her self that are unattainable, inner parts that are perhaps the substructure of the subject. The becoming G.H. experiences has driven her as close to this boundary as possible, so much so that she is now experiencing an inner frontier between her own self and the other. This is a risky process in which the protagonist crosses to the other side in her quest, the same one alluded to in the novel's epigraph. On the other side of this boundary lies the Other, but also the otherness that she experiences, the other she becomes: 'Que podia eu oferecer de mim — eu, que estava sendo o deserto, eu, que o havia pedido e tido?' [What did I offer? What could I offer of myself — I who was becoming the desert, I who had sought and held it?].[33] The protagonist encounters otherness, as we have seen, and by doing so she also becomes the other space, the desert. This becoming is described with a continuous gerund — was being the desert — as an undefined process that never quite ceases. As Rosi Braidotti explains: 'The nomadic tense is the imperfect: it is active, continuous; the nomadic trajectory is controlled speed'.[34]

Towards the end of the text, G.H. discovers — through her infamous act of physically and intimately touching the abject cockroach — that she is transforming herself, expanding her own limits. This transformation, as she specifically says in the penultimate paragraph, is into a new self, a place where conventional boundaries are altered:

> Eu estava agora tão maior que já não me via mais. Tão grande como uma paisagem ao longe. Eu era ao longe. Mas perceptível nas linhas mais últimas montanhas e nos meus mais remotos rios: a atualidade simultânea não me assustava mais, e na mais última extremidade de mim eu podia enfim sorrir sem nem ao menos sorrir.
>
> [Now I was so big that I could no longer see me. As large as a distant passage. I was the distance. More perceptible in the lines of my most remote mountains and in my remote rivers: the simultaneous present no longer frightened me, and in my most remote limbs I could finally smile without even smiling.][35]

In a religious tone the protagonist narrates the transgression of the final boundary. She has surpassed the threshold of the taboo, broken into the suitcase, violated the margins of the photo and expanded them. As she says, this is an I that is as large as a landscape, perhaps the same one she imagined seeing over the rooftops of Rio de Janeiro. The new self is this distant horizon; the bridge extending between faraway landscapes and cultures. Lispector's protagonist utilizes spatial imagery as a way to represent not only an inner journey in the traditional and common way, but as a symbolic union between self and other, an other that is charged with oriental attributes. As such, Lispector's insistence on a Mediterranean cartography makes these superimposed places closer than ever, suggesting a proximity that is beyond language barriers. The telegraphic mission, as well as the nomadic journey across bridges and through passages, comes to an end in the protagonist's newfound self. This self is made up of spaces, transcending boundaries in a way that piques our curiosity. In *The Passion*, Lispector sketches an imagined cartographic unity between Middle Eastern spaces and Brazilian ones, as if filling in the enormous gap between two cultures. In this way, the Middle East is not merely an imaginary, Orientalized space that haunts the text, but rather a structural and active participant in the articulation of the innermost parts of the protagonist. While Lispector is clearly dedicated to the articulation of subject and other in this complex piece of work, her usage of Middle Eastern spaces to articulate parts of the subject that are othered, orientalized, or westernized, shows an insistence on that space by the writer. *The Passion* is forever stamped with a faded visa to a land Lispector never physically visited and nonetheless impacted her work. At the end of the text we are left with this imaginary union, wondering whether we can also reside in this mesmerizing location where the Galilee stretches over Rio de Janeiro.

Works Cited

AHMED, SARA, *Queer Phenomenology: Orientations, Objects, Others* (Durham, NC: Duke University Press, 2006)

BRAIDOTTI, ROSI, *Nomadic Subjects: Embodiment and Sexual Difference in Contemporary Feminist Theory* (New York: Columbia University Press, 1994)

BUTLER, JUDITH, *The Psychic Life of Power: Theories in Subjection* (Stanford, CA: Stanford University Press, 1997)

IRIGARAY, LUCE, *This Sex Which Is Not One* (Ithaca, NY: Cornell University Press, 1985)

LISPECTOR, CLARICE, *A paixão segundo G.H.* (Rio de Janeiro: Rocco, 1998); *The Passion According to G.H.*, trans. by Ronald W. Sousa (Minneapolis: University of Minnesota Press, 1988)

MOSER, BENJAMIN, *Why This World: A Biography of Clarice Lispector* (New York: Oxford University Press, 2009)

NINA, CLÁUDIA, *A palavra usurpada: exílio e nomadismo na obra de Clarice Lispector* (Porto Alegre: EDIPUCRS, 2003)

SÁ, OLGA DE, "Paródia e metafísica', in Clarice Lispector, *A paixão segundo G.H.*, critical edn, ed. by Benedito Nunes (Florianópolis: Editora da UFSC, 1988), pp. 213–21

WILLIAMS, CLAIRE, 'Cidadã do mundo: as viagens de Lispector' in *Clarice Lispector: novos aportes críticos*, ed. by Cristina Ferreira Pinto and Regina Zilberman (Pittsburgh: Instituto Internacional de Literatura Iberoamericana, Universidad de Pittsburgh, 2007), pp. 129–50

Notes to Chapter 3

1. Benjamin Moser, *Why This World: A Biography of Clarice Lispector* (New York: Oxford University Press, 2009), pp. ix–x.
2. Claire Williams, 'Cidadã do mundo: as viagens de Lispector', in *Clarice Lispector: novos aportes críticos*, ed. by Cristina Ferreira Pinto and Regina Zilberman (Pittsburgh, PA: Instituto Internacional de Literatura Iberoamericana, Universidad de Pittsburgh, 2007), pp. 129–50 (p. 129).
3. Cláudia Nina, *A palavra usurpada: exílio e nomadismo na obra de Clarice Lispector* (Porto Alegre: EDIPUCRS, 2003), pp. 122–23.
4. See the works of Luce Irigaray, specifically *This Sex Which Is Not One* (1985).
5. Lispector, *A paixão segundo G.H.* (Rio de Janeiro: Rocco, 1998), p. 11; Clarice Lispector, *The Passion According to G.H.*, trans. by Ronald W. Sousa (Minneapolis: University of Minnesota Press, 1988), p. 3.
6. Lispector, *A paixão*, p. 11; *The Passion*, p. 3.
7. Judith Butler, *Psychic Life of Power: Theories in Subjection* (Stanford, CA: Stanford University Press, 1997), p. 10.
8. Lispector, *A paixão*, p. 21. My translation.
9. Lispector, *A paixão*, p. 25. My translation.
10. Lispector, *A paixão*, p. 31. My translation.
11. Lispector, *A paixão*, p. 35; *The Passion*, p. 27.
12. Lispector, *A paixão*, p. 38; *The Passion*, p. 30.
13. Ibid., p. 38; ibid., p. 30.
14. Ibid., p. 38; ibid., p. 30.
15. Lispector, *The Passion*, p. 33.
16. Lispector, *A paixão*, p. 40; *The Passion*, p. 32.
17. Sara Ahmed, *Queer Phenomenology: Orientations, Objects, Others* (Durham, NC: Duke University Press, 2006), p. 114.
18. Ibid., p. 115.
19. Ibid., p. 133.

20. Ibid., p. 138.
21. Ibid., p. 142.
22. Olga de Sá, 'Paródia e metafísica', in Clarice Lispector, *A paixão segundo G.H.*, critical edn, ed. by Benedito Nunes (Florianópolis: Editora da UFSC, 1988), pp. 213–21 (p. 219). My translation.
23. Ahmed, *Queer Phenomenology*, p. 115.
24. Lispector, *A paixão*, p. 43; *The Passion*, p. 35.
25. Ibid., p. 57; ibid., pp. 49–50.
26. Ibid., p. 104; ibid., p. 96.
27. Lispector, *A paixão*, p. 105.
28. Ibid., pp. 106–11.
29. Ibid., p. 107.
30. Ibid., p. 108; Lispector, *The Passion*, p. 100.
31. Ibid., p. 109; ibid., p. 101.
32. Ibid., p. 123; ibid., p. 116.
33. Lispector, *A paixão*, p. 131. My translation.
34. Rosi Braidotti, *Nomadic Subjects: Embodiment and Sexual Difference in Contemporary Feminist Theory* (New York: Columbia University Press, 1994), p. 25.
35. Lispector, *A paixão*, p. 179. My translation.

PART II

Archives and Manuscripts

CHAPTER 4

Clarice Lispector's Unsettling Archive

Elvia Bezerra

Clarice Lispector began putting aside personal papers as far back as the start of her relationship with Maury Gurgel Valente, the future diplomat whom she would marry in 1943.[1] The letters from her beau, who was head-over-heels for the twenty-one-year-old, are the first items in a collection of documents that she would preserve for the rest of her life, despite fifteen years spent crisscrossing the world as she followed her husband's career postings.

By 'saving papers' I do not mean archiving them devotedly like the great Brazilian poet and musicologist Mário de Andrade, who systematically organized not only his own manuscripts but also more than eight thousand letters.[2] Quite the opposite: Clarice tended to destroy her drafts, or early versions, but, fortunately, from 1959 onwards, she kept her literary papers in a steel filing cabinet. Her younger son, Paulo Gurgel Valente, remembers the cabinet standing four or five drawers high.

She kept on saving her work, although somewhat sporadically, and by no means systematically, right up to her death on 9 December 1977. That very month, Paulo — then aged twenty-four — was contacted by Plínio Doyle, a lawyer and bibliophile who was also the director (and co-founder) of the Arquivo-Museu de Literatura Brasileira (AMLB) housed at the Fundação Casa de Rui Barbosa, an institution which had done pioneering work in preserving the personal papers of Brazilian writers. Clarice's son sent the bulk of his mother's work to the AMLB, but held back a small, priceless collection that would eventually come to the Instituto Moreira Salles (IMS).

Anyone who has worked on a writer's archive is intimately familiar with the surprises that may present themselves amidst the many thousands of pages. Of course, this assortment may include the complete originals of a given author's life's work. But there are also loose sheets, apparently meaningless, that may, nevertheless, provide some future researcher with the key to an investigation, change the course of a project, or refute some previously held belief. Of course, part of the power of a collection lies in the multiplicity of the visions it may offer. A single annotation can be used as evidence to serve various, even contradictory hypotheses. Depending on the researcher's point of view, one seemingly banal observation can come to illuminate some aspect of the author's life or works. It is precisely because we know that Clarice did not preserve her original papers with great care that the collection under the protection of the IMS is so precious. It contains her only known book manuscripts, including letters, notebooks, short stories and the fragments from which her last two novels were compiled.

It is both a duty and a privilege to leaf through pages written in such a haphazard fashion, to come across notes dashed down in shaky handwriting — as if written in haste so as not to let an idea escape — to touch these papers and witness their uniqueness. In the case of Clarice's archive, unpredictability manifests itself in the form of valuable notes found on seemingly worthless scraps of paper, or the germs of future short stories or novels, identified amidst the entries of a rather disorganized travel journal. As the coordinator of the IMS's Literature Department until the end of 2019, and as a researcher myself, I cannot deny the glee with which I have delved into archival material and supervised its organization before it is made available for consultation.

Clarice Lispector's papers came to the IMS in several batches, each one a wonderful surprise. In April 2004, Paulo Valente brought us the unique and original manuscripts of two novels, *A hora da estrela* [*The Hour of the Star*] and *Um sopro de vida* [*A Breath of Life*], a few typescripts of short stories with the author's handwritten annotations and corrections, and a few letters to and from her husband-to-be. This rare collection was initially kept at the IMS's Photography Department, a building erected adjacent to the house originally built in the 1950s as the family home of diplomat and banker Walther Moreira Salles. Since 1999, the house has served as the headquarters of the IMS, in the Gávea neighbourhood of Rio. And that is how Clarice's papers found a new home, shared between the IMS and the AMLB. From then on, the Reading Room at the IMS would never lack scholars, who come from all over the world to peruse the originals.

But Paulo Valente was still holding back a few treasures. In 2012, he brought us a 17 by 10.5 cm notebook, dated 1944: the travel journal mentioned above.[3] Its fifty-eight pages are filled with handwritten notes, jottings and scribbles made by Clarice on her trip to Naples, where she went to join her husband at his first diplomatic posting. Still more documents, which I will mention briefly in due course, arrived later. For now, though, I would like to linger on just two: the notebook in question and a lone sheet of paper found in the middle of the manuscript of *Um sopro de vida*. Both documents refer to Clarice's love life, a matter of no small importance in the life of such a fascinating personality.

The Travel Journal

It fell to Rui Ribeiro Couto (1898–1963), the Brazilian diplomat, poet, and writer, to welcome Clarice to Lisbon, where she stayed 2–14 August 1944, during a stop en route to Naples. Clarice, who had married Maury on 23 January 1943, left the port of Natal in Rio Grande do Norte on 19 July 1944. She was to set foot in Portugal as the fêted author of *Perto do coração selvagem* [*Near to the Wild Heart*], which had been published the year of her wedding. From Lisbon she went on to Casablanca, her last stop before arriving on Neapolitan shores. Here, on 16 July, 5081 Brazilian soldiers of the First Expeditionary Infantry Division, under the command of General

CLARICE LISPECTOR'S UNSETTLING ARCHIVE 75

Fig. 4.1. 'Chegamos a Natal...' [Arriving at Natal], Ribeiro Couto's sketch of Clarice Lispector from her travel journal *Caderno de bordo* (1944). Acervo Clarice Lispector, Instituto Moreira Salles.

Mascarenhas de Moraes, had disembarked in order to join the United States Fifth Army and help drive the Germans from Monte Castello.

Her stay in the Portuguese capital made for lively entries in the notebook. These accounts have been examined from a literary angle by Elizama Almeida in her essay 'Caderno de Bordo' [Travel Journal][4] published on the IMS website. There, she identifies the genesis of the 1946 novel *O lustre* [*The Chandelier*], as well as notes from the trip that Clarice would later develop into the short story 'A menor mulher do mundo' [The Smallest Woman in the World].[5]

On 2 August, the day she arrived in Lisbon, Couto noticed three aspects of his guest's personality, which she jotted down at the time: 'infância, vida profunda e alguma coisa áspera' [childhood, deeply profound life, and something harsh]. He went further, describing her 'animalidade banhada de luar' [moonlight-bathed animality], a quality that comes through in the sketch he did of her, dated the very same day.

Evidently unsettled by the suggestive interest of the forty-four-year-old diplomat, Clarice concluded the entry with a plea: 'Deus meu me perdoai, me dai real paz' [Forgive me, God, and grant me true peace].

While carrying out his duties as her host, Couto confessed that he had been fascinated with her since the days when he used to walk down Rua Silveira Martins (where she had lived with her sister Tânia after their father's death), just to try to catch a glimpse of her. Couto was explicit. He spoke of the overwhelming spell that had been cast over him ever since her arrival, as well as the poems that she had inspired him to write. 'Me desagrada, horrível esse derrame lírico' [I can't stand this horrible lyrical outpouring], she confessed to her notebook.

The notes indicate that the future ambassador set his mind to the task of winning over his guest with undisguised desire, which very nearly led to disaster. Despite his 'lyrical outpouring' and attempts to control her movements, he was unsuccessful. The journal reveals that Clarice had a firm grasp on the situation and was able to extricate herself from her host's advances, as we can see from the entry dated 8 August:

> Que coisa desagradável, desagradável, desagradável. Ribeiro Couto jantou comigo na casa dele, já pela segunda ou terceira vez. Não vi nada demais nisso, ele me tratava como camarada, e eu até ficava com medo que ele estivesse saindo comigo de má vontade, só por dever de ser delicado. Fez duas poesias sobre mim, e disse que fez muitas outras por causa de mim. Que há muito tempo isso não sucedia. Que ele ia sentir minha falta. Que eu era estranha e curiosa. Mil vezes, a propósito de tudo, me dizia como ele era discreto, como o principal era a reputação. Que o fato de eu ter ido à casa dele, aos olhos dos outros, era como se eu tivesse dormido com ele. Por isso era melhor não dizer a ninguém. [...] No carro, segurou minha mão, beijou-a muitas vezes, encostou-a ao rosto. Eu fiquei fria de aborrecimento. Eu disse: que explosão. Ele disse: só interna e mais coisas. Que ele não tinha dormido por minha causa (ele tinha antes contado apenas a insônia). Depois de outras tentativas, que eu repelia vexada, ele disse que sentia muita ternura por minha vida, uma vida difícil. Depois viu mesmo o meu silêncio, e disse: mais tarde você vai ver, vou me vingar. Eu disse: como?! Ele disse: sem gestos.

[How dreadful, dreadful, dreadful. Ribeiro Couto dined with me at his home, that's the second or third time now. I didn't think too much of it; he was treating me like a colleague, and I had even worried that he might be taking me out against his will, only because it was his duty to be polite. He wrote two poems about me and said he'd written many more because of me. That that hadn't happened in a long time. That he was going to miss me. That I was strange and curious. A thousand times, apropos of anything, he'd say how discreet he was, how reputation came first. That in the eyes of some people, the mere fact of my having gone to his house was as good as sleeping with him. And so it was best not to tell anyone. [...] In the car, he held my hand, kissed it again and again, and held it to his face. I went cold with disgust. I said: what an outburst. He said: only on the inside, and other things. That he hadn't slept because of me (he'd mentioned it before, but only the insomnia). After I warded off more advances, irritated, he said that he felt great tenderness towards my life, that it had been a difficult life. Then he realized I was keeping silent and said: you'll see, later on I'll get my revenge. I said: how?! And he said: without gestures.]

Torn between good manners and revulsion, as her notes suggest, she remained polite, but in her notebook she records the discomfort that Ribeiro Couto's forwardness caused her. 'Esquivar-me sem ofendê-lo' [to dodge away without offending him] was her goal.

On 11 August, during a long phone call in which Couto, still bent on seduction, expressed a wish for her to stay in Lisbon for 'thirty thousand days', waiting for her flight, he returned to the issue of his passionate 'explosão' [outburst]. But her host had underestimated Clarice's experience and determination: 'O tolo pensa que eu não sei nada sobre explosão, nem me conhece como me espera' [The silly man thinks I don't know anything about outbursts of passion. He doesn't even know me the way he thinks he does].

Having survived the Portuguese 'earthquake', Clarice went on to Casablanca. From what we can glean from her fragmentary notes, she seemed to feel safer in the air than on terra firma. Far away from her admirer, she could finally see the other side of things. During the flight, she picked up her notebook again, with a sense of relief but at the same time contradicting herself, to write: 'R.C. é uma das melhores pessoas que conheço. [...] É bom que eu esteja casada e feliz — senão ele se apaixonava. Fiquei com pena de embarcar, com pena dele, se bem que não haja motivo' [R.C. is one of the finest people I know. [...] It's just as well that I'm happily married, or he might fall in love with me. I almost felt bad about leaving; I felt sorry for him, although there's no reason to]. Up in the clouds, and at a distance, she was more understanding.

What we know about the aftermath of this encounter is that from 24 August 1944 to 2 December 1945, Ribeiro Couto started corresponding with Clarice. These short letters, which can be found among her papers at the AMLB, reveal that he was following the still-ongoing coverage of *Perto do coração selvagem*. Having read excerpts of the manuscript in Lisbon, he was also eager to hear about *O lustre*, which would finally be published in 1946.

Judging from the letters held in the Ribeiro Couto archive at the AMLB, one can surmise that Clarice did not write back. If that was the case, then she truly managed to 'dodge without offending him', and their encounter in Lisbon, so electric for him and unpleasant for her, left no more fallout than a few entries in her travel journal. Broadly speaking, these entries reflect Clarice's life as a writer, attesting to her intellectual curiosity, vanity, and fascination with the mystical. And there is no lack of resolutions, written down so as to be observed: 'Todos os dias — trabalhar, ir ao cinema, ler policial, procurar costureira segunda-feira, indagar cartomante' [Every day: work, go to the movies, read detective novels, go to seamstress on Monday, question fortune-teller]. On one page of the journal she attributes a quote to André Gide: 'Oser être soi même'. Was 'daring to be oneself' really a risk for a diplomat's wife? Was she truly ready for the role? One gets the impression that she is aware of what awaits her and is still determined to 'dare'.

The Clarice files have grown dynamically, and almost organically. On 27 May 2015, we received yet another bundle: the manuscript originals of 154 letters that Clarice sent to Tânia and Elisa. Of the total, 48 have yet to be published in book form. The rest were included in the collection edited by Teresa Montero, *Minhas queridas* [My Dears].[6] Unsurprisingly, these letters to her sisters reveal her disenchantment and outright irritation at the rigid social duties she was expected to perform in the role of diplomat's wife.

After a few small donations, 20 February 2018 brought the IMS a remarkable bequest: the second half of the manuscript of *Um sopro de vida*, 349 pages that followed on from the 293 previously held by the institution. The manuscripts and fragments which eventually made up this novel, begun in the last year of Clarice's life, had to be deciphered by her friend and collaborator Olga Borelli.[7] Interpretations of Clarice's handwriting diverge, and the novel itself may be altered by new studies of the originals. Indeed, Portuguese academic Carlos Mendes de Sousa has been invited by the IMS to prepare a new edition of the novel for publication.

A Page and a Prayer[8]

Among the documents in the file named *Um sopro de vida*, archivists came across a page that did not belong to the novel: a short, dashed-off but meaningful 'to-do' list on a page torn from a notebook. In between reminders of the times of her manicure and make-up appointments, Clarice, who intermingled literary composition with the records of her daily life, wrote at the top of the page:

> Santo Antônio, pelo amor de Deus,
> ache o PMC para mim, para sempre,
> mesmo que só como amigo. Amém
>
> [St Anthony,[9] for the love of God,
> find PMC for me, forever,
> even if only as a friend. Amen.]

The man she was searching for was Paulo Mendes Campos, the poet and journalist with whom she had had an affair in the 1960s just after separating from her husband. Paulo (1922–1991) had moved to Rio de Janeiro from Belo Horizonte, in the state of Minas Gerais, in 1945. He and his fellow journalists Otto Lara Resende, Fernando

Sabino, and the psychoanalyst Hélio Pellegrino, became known as the 'quarteto de Minas' [the four men from Minas]. They made history while writing for the best papers in Rio in the 1950s, and they frequented the best bars in the city at a time when whisky reigned supreme. Their group of talented bohemians included the poet and composer Vinicius de Moraes and the *cronista* Rubem Braga. Clarice slipped into their midst during her stay in the city from January to March of 1946, having come to Rio to promote *O lustre*.

Clarice's romance with Paulo Mendes Campos would take place nearly two decades later, when, at the age of forty, she was free to pursue a relationship. The same was not true for the married Paulo. On 25 October 1951, the very day that his first book of poetry, *A palavra escrita* [The Written Word], came out, he had sworn at the altar to eternally love and cherish Joan Abercrombie, an Englishwoman with whom he would go on to have two children.

Paulo and Clarice's affair in 1962 was brief but passionate. It was an important year for both writers: Paulo had just published *Homenzinho na ventania* [Little Man in a Gale] and had taken LSD, as an experiment, under the supervision of a doctor. Clarice, meanwhile, had received the Carmen Dolores Prize for her novel *A maçã no escuro* [The Apple in the Dark], which had been published the year before, and was establishing herself as a writer of short stories with weekly contributions to *Senhor* magazine.

It so happened that St Anthony did not answer Clarice's prayers. When Joan Abercrombie threatened to go back to England and take their children with her, Mendes Campos left his lover and chose his family. The author of the famous *crônica* 'O amor acaba' [Love Comes to an End][10] died surrounded by his family in 1991, at the age of sixty-nine.

Even so, the timeline drawn up by Clarice's biographer, Nádia Battella Gotlib, for the special double issue of the IMS *Cadernos de Literatura Brasileira* series on the writer, indicates that Mendes Campos was there for his erstwhile lover in 1967, when she underwent a series of operations to recover from burns suffered during a fire at her home.[11] His presence must have been discreet, since the notebook page with the prayer to St Anthony also includes a reminder about an appointment with Dr Jacob David Azulay, a psychoanalyst with whom she had begun therapy in 1968. It seems likely that the prayer, at least, is from that year.

Clarice and Mendes Campos had complementary temperaments. In their youths, before crossing paths, they had each experienced considerable happiness; but they were drawn together by a certain shared vision of the world. The Mendes Campos of the poem 'Relógio de Sol' [Sundial] — 'o meu coração arbitrário / girando em sentido contrário / à parábola do poente' [my arbitrary heart / spinning away in the opposite direction from / the parabola of the setting sun][12] — shows clear parallels with Clarice's unusual attitude towards literature and life. Although he was not a pessimist, Paulo did write: 'Nada do que é humano me é estranho, a não ser *a joie de vivre*' [Nothing human is alien to me, except *joie de vivre*],[13] an aphorism that could easily have been penned by Clarice, who felt the suffering of others with intensity and claimed to absorb 'as dores do mundo' [the burden of the world's sorrows].[14]

While the Clarice Lispector collection at the IMS includes letters, complete drafts and typescripts, and loose papers, the bulk of it is manuscript originals, comprising 330 items in total.[15] Later additions to the original set have strengthened it over the years, increasing the value of this relatively small collection. Details like the scribbled prayer can reveal a great deal about the writer's life, and fragmented manuscripts, like that of *Um sopro de vida*, can point to alternative versions of a familiar text.

Next, I will make a few comments about Clarice's library, and the remarkable and unusual story of how it came to be housed at the IMS. Like the fragments that can be composed in different ways to produce different texts, we can surmise that the writer's books reflect the multiple aspects of her personality.

Do Books Mirror their Owners?

Whereas most of Clarice's papers have come — and continue to come — directly from her son Paulo, the arrival of her library at the IMS was orchestrated by another noteworthy protagonist, the scholar and biographer Nádia Battella Gotlib. In 2004, at Paulo's request, she sought out Antonio Fernando De Franceschi, the then director of the IMS, and arranged for the transfer of Lispector's library, which previously had been kept at Té-Kinfim, the country home of Gisel Kauffmann, Paulo's mother-in-law, in the mountaintop town of Teresópolis, not far from Rio. In this task, Gotlib was aided by another Clarice specialist, Aparecida Maria Nunes, a university professor and researcher who has worked closely on Lispector's journalistic writings and has explained that these works planted the seeds for some of her most remarkable novels.[16] Arriving at the IMS accompanied by two illustrious professors made this donation even more special, signalling yet again the uniqueness of the Lispector collection.

It is rare for a writer's library to be delivered to a host institution from outside the family, and by such expert hands. Families tend to hold on to these book collections but, when they, entirely understandably, want to free up space in their homes, they take steps to ensure that they are kept together in an archive, library or museum, where they can be accessed by researchers. This was the case with the more than four thousand books that make up the library of the poet Carlos Drummond de Andrade.[17] They were preserved by his grandchildren and brought to the IMS twenty years after his death. The same thing happened to books belonging to Otto Lara Resende, although they were donated to the IMS, along with his immense archive, less than two years after his death. Obviously, although more unusually, there are also examples of one or more heirs looking after the archive themselves, as has happened with the eighteen thousand letters comprising the correspondence of the lawyer Sobral Pinto, meticulously curated by his nephew Roberto Sobral Pinto.[18] What makes Clarice's library unique among all those in the IMS's Literature Department is the way it came to us.

Bringing the library to the IMS headquarters proved to be a much more complex task than the two academics had imagined. They were taken aback by the number of books: close to nine hundred volumes stored in a room that was scheduled to be emptied by two removal men in one day. Gotlib and Nunes did their utmost to ensure the safety of the collection. They were present as every volume was taken off the shelves, taking care to make sure that the books were stored in order. Thanks to their hard work, the IMS received the 896 books on 14 July 2004. Upon arrival, they were stored in the vault, which had previously housed the library of Walther Moreira Salles. Archivist and librarian Manoela Purcell D'Oliveira, who also assists visiting researchers, soon began the cataloguing process.

It is natural to want to see writers' libraries as the reflection of their tastes, a projection of their interests, or the confirmation of their aesthetic practices. For example, it is not surprising to find a considerable selection of French literature amongst the books of poet Carlos Drummond de Andrade, which are also housed at the IMS. He was born in 1905, part of a generation strongly influenced by the poets who hailed from the land of Baudelaire. Likewise, we do not find remarkable the preponderance of Spanish works on the shelves of another modernist, Manuel Bandeira, some of whose books are stored at the Academia Brasileira de Letras. The poet of Pasárgada,[19] curious, cultured, and dutiful, acquired a wealth of works to prepare for his lectures on Hispanic-American literature at the Federal University of Rio de Janeiro (UFRJ), as his library affirms.

Of course, there is no way to prove that Clarice herself purchased all of the books in her library. What we have before us is a collection of the volumes she acquired during her lifetime, no matter their provenance. With that disclaimer in mind, we might ask: what does Clarice Lispector's library reflect about her? How much does it speak to her literary tastes and her interests in life? I would say that it is a curious, even entertaining, array of texts, and certainly an intriguing one. To start with, there are no obvious surprises. As a cultured woman with a keen mind (how clichéd it seems to put it that way!) she was not given to flaunting her erudition. She preferred to say, not without a dash of irony, as she did in the *crônica* 'Conversas' ['Conversation']: 'Adoro ouvir coisas que dão a medida da minha ignorância' [I love to hear things that give me the measure of my ignorance.].[20] Moreover, in 'Intelectual? Não' [Intellectual? No!] she wrote:

> Ser intelectual é também ter cultura, e eu sou tão má leitora que, agora já sem pudor, digo que não tenho mesmo cultura. Nem sequer li as obras importantes da humanidade. Além do que leio pouco: só li muito, e lia avidamente o que me caísse nas mãos, entre os treze e quinze anos de idade. Depois passei a ler esporadicamente, sem ter a orientação de ninguém. Isto sem confessar que — dessa vez digo-o com alguma vergonha — durante anos eu só lia romance policial. Hoje em dia, apesar de ter muitas vezes preguiça de escrever, chego de vez em quando a ter mais preguiça de ler do que de escrever.
>
> [To be an intellectual is to be cultured, and I am such a poor reader that I can say with no compunctions that I really am uncultured. I have yet to read the great works of civilization. What's more, I read very little: the only time I read avidly, reading everything that came into my hands, was between ages thirteen and fifteen. From then on I've read only sporadically, without guidance from anyone. And I'll confess – now with a hint of shame – that for years I only read

detective novels. These days, though I'm often lazy about writing, at times I find myself even lazier when it comes to reading.]²¹

While the library does not indicate an in-depth investigation into one given topic or field, it does reveal a robust curiosity, taking in everything from composer Aaron Copland's *What to Listen for in Music* (1939) to *Les Pages immortelles de Spinoza, choisies et expliquées par Arnold Zweig* [The Living Thoughts of Spinoza Selected and Presented by Arnold Zweig] (1940). It includes Shakespeare and Proust in their original languages. Thomas Mann and Gide can also be found, alongside around twenty books on philosophy, and even a copy of British humanist author Hector Hawton's *Philosophy for Pleasure* (1949). Clarice's taste for detective novels is clear: Agatha Christie is here, along with a healthy selection of the works of Georges Simenon (indeed, the Belgian writer has a slight numerical edge).

The sheer variety of topics is striking. Among these, the question of sex did not escape Clarice's interest. The books within this category range from the Kama Sutra, in Portuguese translation, to Maurice Caullery's *Les Problèmes de la sexualité* [Problems of Sexuality] (originally published in 1920), and Marie N. Robinson's *The Power of Sexual Surrender* (1959) (several sections were underlined in this volume). Gotlib writes in *Clarice: uma vida que se conta* that the book was a gift from Maury, sent from Washington D.C. along with a letter dated 28 July 1959.²² Clarice's husband was trying to save his marriage; his letter is full of words of understanding and affection, humility and love, but there was no going back. Clarice stayed in Rio, and the relationship came to an end.

The author is well known for her connection to the strange and supernatural, which can be seen in *crônicas* such as 'O milagre das folhas' [Miraculous Leaves], short stories like 'Onde estivestes de noite' [Where You Were at Night] and novels such as *A paixão segundo G.H.* [*The Passion According to G.H.*].²³

There are a number of books in Clarice's library that reflect her interest in spirituality and the 'miracle' of everyday phenomena. They include a 1961 Brazilian edition of D. T. Suzuki's *An Introduction to Zen Buddhism* and a copy of *The I Ching or Book of Changes*, published that same year. In the latter, we come across a loose diary page, dated 10 December 1974: Clarice's 54th birthday. Written on it is the question: 'Qual é o meu futuro de um modo geral?' [What is my future, in general terms?] On another piece of paper, another question: 'Quero saber se ainda vou amar alguém que me ama' [I want to know if there's still a chance I will love someone who loves me]. Here, the words 'love' and 'loves' are scratched out, but legible. Clarice also asked the *I Ching*: 'Pergunto se devo ir a uma sessão espírita pedir e se serei atendida' [I ask whether or not I should go to a spiritist session to ask for this, and if my wish will be granted].

Clarice clearly took her health and physical appearance seriously; a copy of Adelle Davis's *Let's Eat Right to Keep Fit* (1954) seems to confirm that. Of course, it was not enough to simply dress elegantly, hold oneself the right way, and master the art of makeup. She was drawn to other realms of femininity, which may explain the presence of Leon Bopp's *L'Art de vouloir, d'aimer et comprendre: nouveaux exercices spirituels* (1946) [The Art of Wanting, Loving and Understanding: New Spiritual Exercises], and Alma Archer's *Your Power as a Woman: How to Develop and Use It*

(1957). She had a few resources at hand, therefore, when she accepted Alberto Dines's invitation to write a weekly column for the newspaper *Jornal do Brasil*, which she did from 1967 to 1973. Before *Jornal do Brasil*, she had contributed women's pages under the pen name Helen Palmer for *Correio da Manhã*, and also had been actress Ilka Soares's ghostwriter in the *Diário da Noite*, in addition to writing for *Comício*.[24]

In her library there are, as we have already seen, publications in a number of different languages, which must have been picked up on her travels abroad, such as an Italian edition of Katherine Mansfield's letters (*Lettere*, 1941, translated by Milli Dandolo).[25] There is also a copy of Dino Buzzati's stunning *Il deserto dei Tartari* (The Tartar Steppe, 1957), in French rather than Italian: *Le Désert des tartares* (translated by Michel Arnaud).

Of her own published work, in Portuguese and other languages, one highlight is the first edition of *A legião estrangeira* [*The Foreign Legion*], from 1964, with marginalia. Before the title of the *crônica* 'Berna', for example, she added, in pen, *Lembrança de*, thus changing it to 'Remembrance of Berne.' However, she later published it in *Jornal do Brasil* on 14 February 1970 as 'Lembrança de uma Fonte, de uma Cidade' [Remembrance of a Fountain, of a City], the same name with which it was reproduced in *A descoberta do mundo* (1984) [*Discovering the World*] and in the recently published complete anthology *Todas as crônicas* (2018). Incidences like these prove useful for practitioners of genetic criticism or the editors of subsequent editions.

The still uncut pages of *Près du cœur sauvage*, the French edition of *Perto do coração selvagem*, her international debut, are a reminder of the fraught story of its translation into French. The novel was published by Plon in 1954, with a preface by none other than Paulo Mendes Campos. It is no secret that Clarice was seriously displeased with this translation. In a letter from 10 May of that year to Tania and Elisa, her indignation at the solutions devised by the translator Denise Moutonnier is clear:

> Quando escrevo a palavra 'porcaria' ela traduz por 'excrementos', mesmo quando não é o caso. Sem falar em liberdades engraçadas que ela tomou. Eu escrevo: 'a criada' e ela traduz: 'a criada preta' — sendo que em nenhum pedaço do livro se fala em nenhum criado negro.
>
> [When I write the word 'filth' she translates it as 'excrement', even when that's not the case. To say nothing of the odd liberties she has taken. I write 'the maid', and she translates it as: 'the black maid' — when nowhere in the book is there any mention of a black servant.][26]

Clarice seems to have taken a fine-toothed comb to the French edition, and it appears that her efforts did bring about the desired result: the comments and corrections she sent were heeded. Three years later, she wrote to Pierre de Lescure, the editor at Plon, and praised the translation, according to Cecília Himmelseher in 'A tradução do indizível' [Translating the Unsayable], published on the IMS blog on 15 October 2011.[27]

In interviews, Clarice spoke about the way she worked, and how she tended to take notes on any scrap of paper that came to hand. She only started keeping them at the end of her life, but this practice of notetaking did become a habit, as documented by Paulo Mendes Campos in his preface to the abovementioned French translation of *Perto do coração selvagem*. There he mentions the author's 'pudeur un peu sauvage' [rather wild shame], explaining how, from the very start, she would hide her originals and then destroy them.

In 1958, de Lescure sent her a letter informing her that a thousand copies of the book would have to be burned to free up space in their stockroom. This meant condemning to the flames a cover designed by none other than Henri Matisse, who had turned to publishers for work as a graphic artist in the last years of his life.

A look at Clarice in group photos reveals an attentive woman, more given to simply grasping what was before her, especially when she did not understand it, than to explaining or exposing it. For her, heaven and hell were to be found within the self. They did not come from without, or above, as they did for Gaston Bachelard, who raised the library to celestial heights in this remarkable excerpt from *The Poetics of Reverie*:

> I would like a basket full of books telling the youth of images which fall from heaven for me every day. This desire is natural. This prodigy is easy. For, up there, in heaven, isn't paradise an immense library?[28]

No, a library was certainly not Clarice's idea of paradise, although it was a heavenly encounter when she discovered the stories of Katherine Mansfield, an author present on her shelves, alongside Virginia Woolf. And even so (ah, the contradictions), we find only two books of Mansfield's: *Lettere*, the Italian translation of her correspondence mentioned above, and *The Doll's House and Other Stories*.

My reflections on these documents, and on Clarice's library, seek to illustrate the surprising nature of the collection and offer the reader of the present volume a taste of the diversity of material in the archive. These books and documents are part of the legacy of a writer who, upon her death, on 9 December 1977, was evoked in *O Globo* (the following day), in a subtle observation by her friend Otto Lara Resende: Clarice was 'um exemplo brutal da singularidade da pessoa humana' [a raw example of the singularity of the human being].

Works Cited

ALMEIDA, ELIZAMA, 'Caderno de bordo', 2012, <https://site.claricelispector.ims.com.br/acervo/caderno-de-bordo/> [accessed 31 May 2019]

BACHELARD, GASTON, *The Poetics of Reverie: Childhood, Language and the Cosmos*, trans. by Daniel Russell (Boston, MA: Beacon, 1971)

BEZERRA, ELVIA, 'Caderno de Lisboa: Clarice Lispector' (16 July 2020), <https://ims.com.br/por-dentro-acervos/caderno-de-lisboa-clarice-lispector/> [accessed 6 August 2021]

BORELLI, OLGA, *Clarice: um esboço de retrato* (Rio de Janeiro: Nova Fronteira, 1981)

CAMPOS, PAULO MENDES, 'O amor acaba', *Manchete*, 630 (16 May 1964), p. 28

—— *Transumanas* (Rio de Janeiro: Codecri, 1977)

—— *Diário da Tarde*, commemorative edition (Rio de Janeiro: Instituto Moreira Salles, 2013)

GOTLIB, NÁDIA BATTELLA, 'A descoberta do mundo', *Cadernos de Literatura Brasileira*, 17–18 (2004), 8–43

HIMMELSEHER, CECÍLIA, 'A tradução do indizível', Instituto Moreira Salles blog (15 October

2011), <https://blogdoims.com.br/a-traducao-do-indizivel-por-cecilia-himmelseher-elizama-almeida-e-marcela-isensee/> [accessed 6 June 2019]

LISPECTOR, CLARICE, *A descoberta do mundo* (Rio de Janeiro: Francisco Alves, 1994 [1978]); *Discovering the World*, trans. by Giovanni Pontiero (Manchester: Carcanet, 1992)

—— *Correio feminino*, ed. by Aparecida Maria Nunes (Rio de Janeiro: Rocco, 2006)

—— *Minhas queridas*, ed. by Teresa Montero (Rio de Janeiro: Rocco, 2007)

—— *Só para mulheres*, ed. by Aparecida Maria Nunes (Rio de Janeiro: Rocco, 2008)

Clarice Lispector website, Instituto Moreira Salles, <https://ims.com.br/titular-colecao/clarice-lispector/> [accessed 6 August 2021]

Notes to Chapter 4

1. Translated by Flora Thomson-DeVeaux.
2. EN: Mário de Andrade's archive is housed at the Instituto de Estudos Brasileiros (IEB), at the Universidade de São Paulo.
3. EN: The journal can be consulted in facsimile and transcribed versions on the IMS website: <https://claricelispectorims.com.br/caderno-de-bordo/> (accessed 31 May 2019). See also Elvia Bezerra, 'Caderno de Lisboa: Clarice Lispector' (16 July 2020), <https://ims.com.br/por-dentro-acervos/caderno-de-lisboa-clarice-lispector/> [accessed 6 August 2021].
4. Elizama Almeida, 'Caderno de Bordo' (2012), <https://site.claricelispector.ims.com.br/acervo/caderno-de-bordo/> [accessed 31 May 2019].
5. First published in *Senhor* magazine in 1959, this story was later included in the collection *Laços de família [Family Ties]* (1960).
6. Clarice Lispector, *Minhas queridas*, ed. by Teresa Montero (Rio de Janeiro: Rocco, 2007).
7. Borelli describes their friendship and working relationship in *Clarice: um esboço de retrato* (Rio de Janeiro: Nova Fronteira, 1981).
8. An earlier version of this section was published on the IMS website on 31 July 2018: <https://ims.com.br/por-dentro-acervos/santo-antonio-nao-ouviu-clarice-elvia-bezerra/>.
9. EN: In Brazil, Spain, and Portugal, St Anthony of Padua (Santo Antônio) is not only the patron saint of lost things; he is also traditionally the saint to pray to if one wishes to get married, to a specific person or at all. He was one of Clarice's favourite saints: see Teresa Montero's chapter in this volume, p. 000.
10. Paulo Mendes Campos, 'O amor acaba', *Manchete*, 630 (16 May 1964), p. 28, <https://cronicabrasileira.org.br/cronicas/7153/o-amor-acaba> [accessed 3 June 2019].
11. Nádia Battella Gotlib and the IMS Team, 'A descoberta do mundo', *Cadernos de Literatura Brasileira*, 17–18 (2004), 8–43 (p. 30); <https://issuu.com/ims_instituto_moreira_salles/docs/clb_clarice_lispector> [accessed 17 August 2021].
12. Paulo Mendes Campos, *Transumanas* (Rio de Janeiro: Codecri, 1977), p. 63.
13. This quotation comes from 'Coriscos na floresta', a section of an imaginary newspaper entitled *Diário da Tarde* first published in book form by Civilização Brasileira in 1981, and later by the Companhia das Letras in 2014. The IMS brought out a version in tabloid format in 2013, in which the quotation appears on p. 32.
14. Clarice Lispector, 'Ao correr da máquina (14 April 1971)', *A descoberta do mundo* (Rio de Janeiro: Francisco Alves, 1994 [1978]), pp. 367–68 (p. 367); 'To the Rhythm of My Typewriter', trans. by Giovanni Pontiero, *Discovering the World* (Manchester: Carcanet, 1992), pp. 446–48 (p. 446).
15. The components of the archive can be found at: <https://ims.com.br/titular-colecao/clarice-lispector/> [accessed 6 August 2021].
16. See Nunes's introduction to *Clarice na cabeceira: jornalismo*, one of four volumes in the 'bedside table' box set published by Rocco in 2012. Nunes's research into Clarice's writing for the press would also lead to the publication of *Correio feminino* (Rio de Janeiro: Rocco, 2006) and *Só para mulheres* (Rio de Janeiro: Rocco, 2008).
17. EN: Carlos Drummond de Andrade (1902–1987) was a Modernist poet and *cronista*.
18. EN: Heráclito Fountoura Sobral Pinto (1893–1991) was a human rights lawyer and activist.

19. EN: One of Bandeira's best-loved poems is entitled 'Vou-me embora p'ra Pasárgada' [Off to Pasárgada], from the collection *Libertinagem* (1930). An English translation can be found in *This Earth, That Sky: Poems by Manuel Bandeira*, trans. by Candace Slater (Berkeley: University of California Press, 1989), p. 104.
20. Lispector, *A descoberta do mundo*, pp. 137–38; translated by Flora Thomson-DeVaux.
21. Lispector, *A descoberta do mundo*, pp. 152–53; translated by Flora Thomson-DeVaux.
22. Gotlib, *Clarice: uma vida que se conta*, pp. 317–20.
23. Clarice Lispector, 'O milagre das folhas', in *A descoberta do mundo*, pp. 169–70; 'Miraculous Leaves', in *Discovering the World*, pp. 217–18.
24. EN: For more on Lispector's contributions to women's pages of newspapers, see Mariela Méndez's chapter in this volume.
25. EN: After being greatly influenced by Mansfield's writings while composing *Perto do coração selvagem*, Clarice 'renewed her acquaintance' with the New Zealand author when she arrived in Naples, writing to Lúcio Cardoso about reading her 'extraordinary' letters. Benjamin Moser, *Why This World: A Biography of Clarice Lispector* (New York: Oxford University Press, 2009), pp. 143–44.
26. Clarice Lispector, *Minhas queridas*, ed. by Teresa Montero (Rio de Janeiro: Rocco, 2007), pp. 254–55.
27. Cecília Himmelseher, 'A tradução do indizível' (15 October 2011), <https://blogdoims.com.br/a-traducao-do-indizivel-por-cecilia-himmelseher-elizama-almeida-e-marcela-isensee/> [accessed 6 June 2019].
28. Gaston Bachelard, *The Poetics of Reverie: Childhood, Language and the Cosmos*, trans. by Daniel Russell (Boston, MA: Beacon, 1971), p. 25.

CHAPTER 5

And Now:
A *Crônica* about My Encounter with the Manuscripts of *The Hour of the Star*

Paloma Vidal

for Tatiana Salem Levy

A pair of plastic gloves, a box so white it shines, in a small glass room with artificial lighting.[1] All this reminds me of a surgical operation. That's what I noted down. Followed by a question about how to trigger an emotion there. I noted that down and lifted my head, trying to avoid being seen as I looked at J., busy and vigilant, sitting at the desk facing mine. It was she who offered me the sheets of paper, also white, and a pencil, which she sharpened first, in a deliberately anachronistic gesture. She spends hours in this room, with breaks for lunch and coffee, watching as people open and close the white boxes, which look like presents, less for their inherent properties, than the anticipation felt by those who open them. She has already seen this gesture so many, many times that she could compile a list of common types: those who laugh, those who cry, the disdainful and the exasperated, those whose eyes widen, those whose eyes narrow. There are some suspicious ones, like me. Everything is more or less predictable. I wonder how many of them accept the sheets of paper she offers so kindly with the sharpened pencil, since the use of computers is allowed. Notebooks and pens, no, computers, yes.

This is just how it was the only other time I've seen manuscripts up close. Notebooks and pens were forbidden, and photos were not allowed. But there were no gloves, and the boxes were grey. When I came face to face with the files for *Mourning Diary* written by Roland Barthes between 1977 and 1979, after the death of his mother, I cried, and I felt ridiculous. Perhaps that's why, this time, I have come forearmed with a question. Or perhaps it is the glass room. Or the proximity of J. The first time, in the Richelieu Room of the French National Library in Paris, I looked around me and was surprised that nobody else was crying. Earlier, that morning, I had dropped off my children at school. It was the last day before the holidays. Something was being left behind and I wanted to remember absolutely everything. At every step, I took a photo. The photos I took on 5 July 2016 show the two children at the front door of the apartment, in the hall of the apartment block, in the yard, our steps towards the front gate, them opening the gate, them at the corner of the street leading to their school, a few steps further on, at the school gate, waving goodbye, my steps along the street where the school was, on the way to the bus stop. After these images, on my cellphone camera, come some smuggled shots of Barthes's diary, which are there to register a continuity that justifies my emotion.

This time, there was no need to take and smuggle photos and I should have made this clear from the outset: when I got to the little room in the Moreira Salles Institute in Rio de Janeiro, and before opening the white box, I had already seen scanned copies of Clarice Lispector's notes for *The Hour of the Star*. Together with the request to write a *crônica* about my encounter with the manuscripts for a commemorative edition, in 2017, marking forty years since the book was first published, came images of the documents, which I insisted upon seeing in the flesh, nonetheless.[2] Why? If I had asked myself that question before I opened the white box, I would have replied that it was because of my previous experience, with Barthes' diary. I wanted that emotion, but I doubted that it would come to me in the same way, since the encounter had already taken place.

This is my second encounter, then, in this small room, wearing gloves, in the company of J., who holds out sheets of white paper and a pencil, and I accept them, although I have brought my computer with me. I accept out of courtesy, because I usually find it hard to refuse something offered to me so politely. But it isn't just that: it is an invitation to write by hand. J. is making me an unusual invitation. An invitation that could, in turn, make sense of this encounter. I want her gesture in me. That's what I noted down next, before I finally decided to open the white box.

I must also make it clear that I was preparing myself for this encounter, even with the fear that, as well as having already seen scanned copies of the notes, preparation would distance me from what I was looking for, following up on the proposition that had been made, which I repeated, to myself and others: to write an essay about my encounter with the manuscripts. An essay about my encounter with the manuscripts of *The Hour of the Star*, the last book published by Clarice in her lifetime, in October 1977. There was no other way. In the days leading up to this moment, I had needed to talk about it: furthermore, I had needed to hear from others, possible future readers, what they expected me to do when I got here. S. told me about his own wish to write something about the last years of Clarice's life. T. teased me, saying that, since she was born in 1979, she might be a reincarnation of the author. G. suggested that I copy the book out by hand. J.P. asked me if I remembered how old I was when I read *The Hour of the Star* for the first time. In their own way, each of them showed me possible ways to proceed and came along with me. Even J.. I didn't open the box alone. They all opened it with me.

Inside we find 34 folders, all cream, of different sizes, numbered on the right, in pencil: 1/34, 2/34, 3/34, and so on. We will soon discover that the size of the folders corresponds to the size of the sheets of paper they hold — smaller folders for loose notes, larger ones for sheets from standard notepads — and we will wonder if somebody has made them by hand. We will also discover that the titles written in the middle of the cover of the folders, also in pencil, correspond to the first words of the first page of the manuscripts contained within. All this points to somebody having done the work by hand. 'An archive presupposes an archivist, a hand that collects and classifies', writes Arlette Farge in *The Allure of the Archives*.[3] I think about those hands while I run mine over the folders, before I open them. I think that lots of hands have touched this archive before mine. And many more will come, in search of this survival, this vestige of the real, as vivid as it is inaccessible.

I think about this as I open folder 34/34, the last one, which has caught my attention because it contains another folder, an orange, cardboard one, standard size, which was probably used to store and transport these papers. I did not see this reproduced among the scans. I therefore try to be precise in my description, because it is all I'll be able to count on when I leave the room. On the folder is a note in red pen, 'OLGA'S WORK', and under that, in black, 'Clarice's manuscripts'. These notes are a record of the hands in action. Someone makes notes about something someone else noted down before. In blue, on a small scrap of paper, I read: 'LAST Note by Clarice / Written in the Hospital da Lagoa / On 7–12–77'.[4] This is the note that opens the manuscripts, in folder 1/34, which I open now, going backwards, obeying the order dictated by the archive. The note must have been written by Olga Borelli, as part of her work (which will be continued by that of archivists, ordering, numbering and annotating), when the manuscripts arrived at the Institute in 2004, brought by Paulo Gurgel Valente, the son who is letting go, bit by bit, of his mother's writings, so that others can handle them. The last item he donated, in 2012, was the 'Caderno de Bordo' [Log Book], a small notebook with notes about a journey made by Clarice between July and August 1944.[5]

While I'm noting down 'before' and 'after' I realize that this way of describing the way things move around the archive does absolutely no justice to its comings and goings, its hesitations, a to and fro that should be less linear and more overlapping, like the game of piling up and pulling away hands, in which the pile is made and unmade at the same time. But it's not by chance that my description turns out this way: the relationship between the archive and the origin is narrow, even etymologically speaking, leading us to think in terms of something which came first, which was involved in the creation of another thing, like, in this case, the manuscripts which came before the book. We are seduced by thinking in a linear fashion, even though the archive contradicts as much as reinforces this linearity. How can you help but think like this when the first word is 'LAST'? When we are forced to think about the end when we are only just beginning? I see this as a sign that as far as this encounter is concerned, there's no point trying to reveal before or after a beginning or an end. Time frames are going to overlap. Unexpected contiguities will arise.

I'm getting ahead of myself, I know. It's just that I, myself, am here, in the little room, and I'm already no longer here. I'm making notes by hand on the white sheets of paper that J. gave me, and I'm no longer there, as I copy my notes onto the computer screen. I'm getting ahead of myself in order to disobey the archive, wanting to be true to it. 'The geneticist's task is to try to put these times, dispersed in space, into a temporal order — not a perfect order, not an indestructible chain

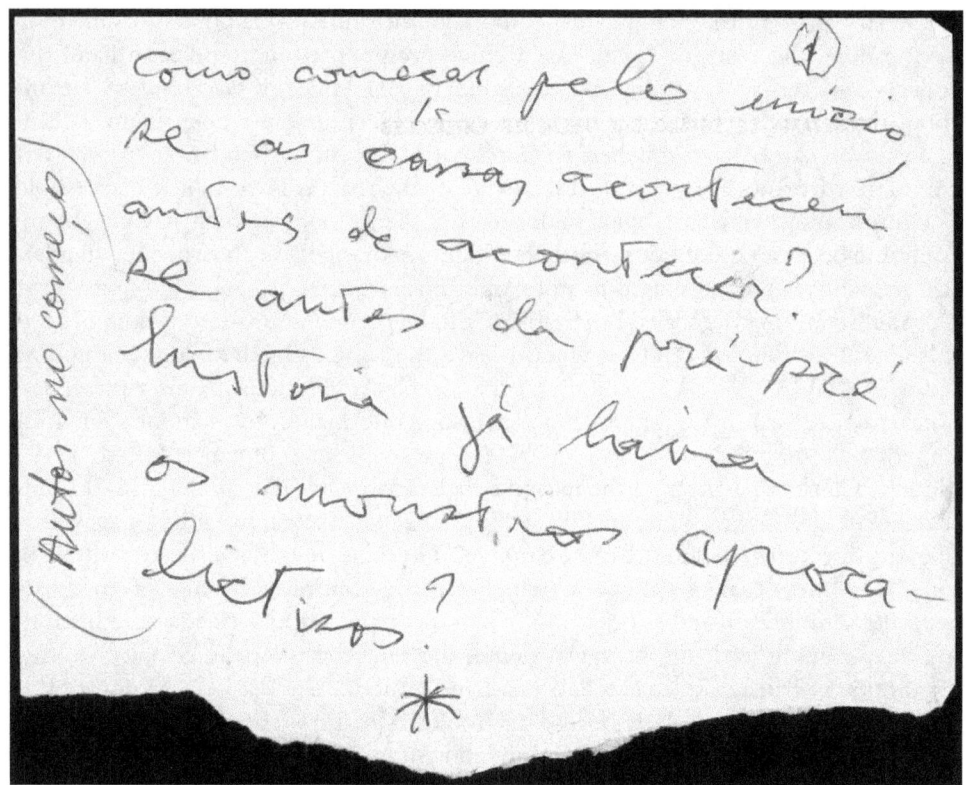

Fig. 5.1. "Como começar pelo início' [How does one start at the beginning]. Fragment, MS *A hora da estrela* 3/34. Acervo Clarice Lispector, Instituto Moreira Salles.

— but a movement which goes in a certain direction', write Claudia Amigo Pino and Roberto Zular about a kind of genetic criticism that seeks to reconstruct the creative process, in the belief that it is possible to reach the origin of a work.[6] They are critical of this idea, proposing that we focus on the performative aspect of literature, which, when it doubles over on itself problematizes the process, and they cite the questions Rodrigo S.M. asks at the beginning of *The Hour of the Star*: 'Como começar pelo início, se as coisas acontecem antes de acontecer? Se antes da pré-pré história já havia os monstros apocalípticos?' [How does one start at the beginning, if things happen before they happen? If before pre-prehistory apocalyptic monsters already existed?].[7] They are the same ones we'll find in folder 3/34.

On the cover of this folder, only the beginning of the sentence is copied out, followed by ellipses, using a ruler to create an imaginary line, in very flowery handwriting, which reminds me of old school exercise books, that primary school combination of care and control. I copy what the archivist copied onto my blank page, but without a ruler, taming the writing myself, because it comes out irregular and wobbly for lack of recent practice. I want to maintain this gesture of mine, to get a little closer to the manual work of the archivist. I see that J.'s invitation gave me this as well: the opportunity to be a little closer to what the archivist gives us

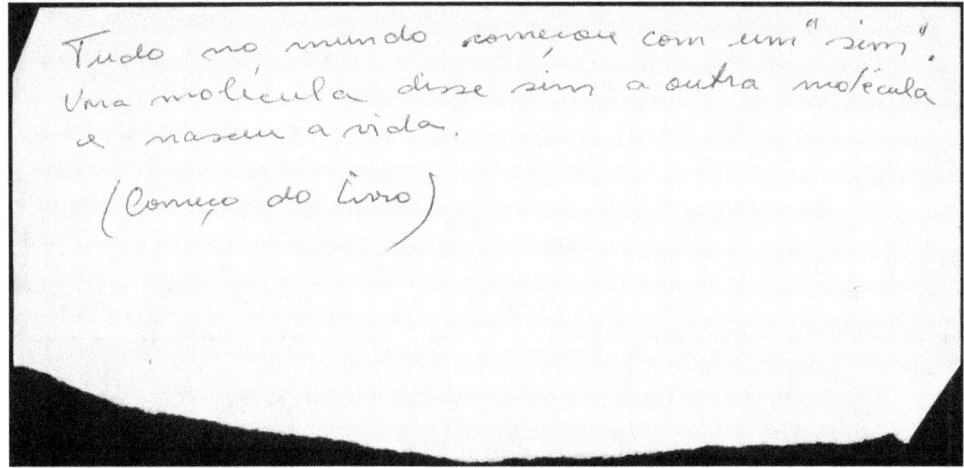

Fig. 5.2. 'Tudo no mundo começou com um "sim"' [Everything in the world began with a 'yes']. Fragment, in Olga Borelli's handwriting, MS *A hora da estrela* fol. 5, p. 1. Acervo Clarice Lispector, Instituto Moreira Salles.

when they recapture a fragment of text by copying it, guaranteeing the survival of so many texts over so many centuries. 'The allure of the archives passes through this slow and unrewarding artisanal task of recopying texts, section after section, without changing the format, the grammar, or even the punctuation. Without giving it too much thought. Thinking about it constantly. As if the hand, through this task, could make it possible for the mind to be simultaneously an accomplice and a stranger to this past time and to these men and women describing their experiences'.[8]

Simultaneously an accomplice and a stranger — that's how I think of Olga Borelli, noting down pointers to situate the notes, which would provide the basic structure for the book, work she had been helping Clarice with since *Água viva* (1974). In the manuscripts in folder 5/34, the opening line of the book appears in her handwriting: 'Tudo no mundo começou com um "sim". Uma molécula disse sim a outra molécula e nasceu a vida' [Everything in the world began with a 'yes'. One molecule said yes to another molecule and life was born].[9]

Clarice met Olga in late 1970. On 11 December that year she wrote her a letter which opens by saying: 'Olga, datilografo esta carta porque minha letra anda péssima' [Olga, I'm typing this letter because my handwriting is terrible at the moment].[10] In these folders, however, everything is written by hand. Clarice's handwriting meets up with Olga's, complicit here and different there. In almost all the drafts there are notes by her, like 'descrição de Maca' [description of Maca] or 'morte de Maca' [death of Maca], sometimes doubtful: 'Autor?' [Author?]

I forge ahead. I realize I cannot linger too long, waiting for every one of these notes to reveal something to me. I start to go through the notes and folders more quickly, making small piles that alarm J.: 'will you be alright putting them back in the correct order?', she asks me, pulling the headphones from her ears and interrupting the silence that seemed to have been agreed between us since our roles

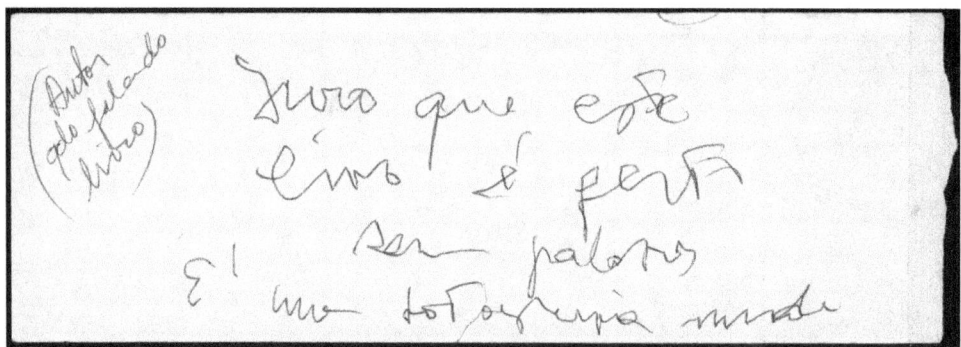

Fig. 5.3. 'Juro que este' [I swear that this]. Fragment, MS *A hora da estrela* fol. 8, p. 1. Acervo Clarice Lispector, Instituto Moreira Salles.

were handed out. I answer what she already knows: that the folders are numbered and yes, yes, everything is under control. She must have noticed my anxiousness. My feeling of being unprepared. It's not the first time this has happened. Some people know what they are looking for and some just look, without knowing where to start. 'How does one start at the beginning, if things happen before they actually happen?' J. might very well have told me that I could start wherever I wanted to. That she is there to make sure that I maintain the order of the archive but that when I'm writing, being, who knows, unfaithful to that order, I could, careless of the intentions of the archivist, become an accomplice of these manuscripts.

I jump. The complicity I'm looking for might be found in a note in folder 8/34. With very shaky handwriting, in four lines, with no punctuation, Clarice writes on the back of a cheque stub: 'Juro que este / livro é feito / sem palavras / É uma fotografia muda' [I swear that this / book is made / without words / It is a mute photograph].[11]

The image of the back of the cheque stub was not among the scans of the pages of notes I had received, and had it not been for this later encounter, I might not have discovered the origin of the paper upon which those lines were written. In the image, you can see that it is textured, fine beige stripes covering creamy-coloured paper, with a slightly darker border. I think about the frequency of these notes in Clarice's handwriting, when the sentences come unexpectedly, when she feels the need to jot them down, at any moment, in any place. In these folders there are envelopes, pages torn from notebooks, loose sheets, this scrap of cheque. I see the fascination exerted when recording writing that comes without warning and cannot be contained. The registering of an instant. The instant in which something is created. Not to mention witnessing a method, which only later, after opening a few more folders, will I be able to glimpse more clearly.

For the time being, I linger over this note. The encounter between these sentences and this paper. Any kind of paper would have done to note these words down, I know, including this one, which, nonetheless, unlike the others, has a date printed on it: 15/9/76. An account number, a name: 'Lido', a branch office of the Banco Nacional. In this specific case writing comes into existence in time and space in a relationship much more concrete with the reality of which it is part and of which it has become a remnant. It makes visible a body, the body of someone who passes through and inhabits a specific place in the city, at a certain time, with its own distinguishing marks. Whereas the text itself speaks of the wish to make visible, photograph, as I imagine it now: a woman slowly crosses the Avenida Princesa Isabel towards Avenida Prado Júnior; she halts, distracted, looking through her dark glasses at the sparkling windows of the shops in Avenida Nossa Senhora de Copacabana, but she is not really interested in the clothes, which look too shiny, as much as in the mute mannequins, which reflect back solitude shared with a crowd of people who, like her, are walking along the street barely able to stand the heat. Photograph that woman, keep her, and then try to speak her, knowing that there will not be an encounter between the words and the woman.

There will be another encounter, an unexpected one, hard to talk about here. In 1976, Argentina and Brazil were both living under dictatorships. In June 1977, when I was two years old, my parents arrived in Brazil from Buenos Aires, and set up home in a rented apartment on the ninth floor of a block in the Avenida Nossa Senhora de Copacabana, opposite the Praça do Lido. I know that this *crônica* shouldn't be about me. About where I was in October 1977. Or between June and December 1977. Or in July 2016. The first person is pretty much excluded from the request to write 'a *crônica* about your encounter with the manuscripts'. It should be an encounter, to a certain extent, as far as the *crônica* itself permits, that is impersonal, almost anonymous. Except that an encounter is made up of coincidences that cannot be foreseen or avoided. And not even the scanned pages of notes I saw before I came here could have foretold the word 'Lido' marking out a shared space on the map of Rio de Janeiro. I notice that there is something about the simultaneity of places and times that might reveal a fragment of common history. That what we have in common can enable other voices to speak, as well as mine, and hers.

I return to the note. I am also lingering on it because it draws my attention to a relationship which is not unlike what this book, of all Clarice's writings, does with such force, as those who have read it over the course of the last four decades have stated: making an appeal to the external, to what is outside the self, outside literature itself, even, taking a risk that other writers would not undertake lightly. 'Transgredir, porém, os meus próprios limites me fascinou de repente. E foi quando pensei em escrever sobre a realidade, já que essa me ultrapassa' [However, the idea of transcending my own limits suddenly appealed to me. And it was at the moment when I decided to write about reality, since reality exceeds me],[12] writes the author at the beginning of the book. The word written on the cheque stub draws my attention to the profane dimension of this text, which in so many ways questions the place of who is writing and what is being written in the world. 'Estou absolutamente cansado de literatura; só a mudez me faz companhia' [I am absolutely fed up with literature; only silence keeps me company],[13] the author continues, in an echo of the 'fotografia muda' [mute photograph].[14] Furthermore: 'Se ainda escrevo é porque nada mais tenho a fazer no mundo enquanto espero a morte. A procura da palavra no escuro. O pequeno sucesso me invade e me põe no olho da rua' [If I'm still writing, it's because I have nothing else to do in this world while I'm waiting for death. Searching for the word in the dark. Small achievements invade me and put me on display to all and sundry].[15] This passage appears towards the end of the book, set apart from the rest, and it is not in the manuscripts. Some parts jump out at me: 'waiting for death', 'searching for the word in the dark', 'on display to all and sundry'. Literature made at the limits, of life and of itself.

    I don't want to get ahead of myself. 'Só não inicio pelo fim que justificaria o começo — como a morte parece dizer sobre a vida — porque preciso registrar os fatos antecedentes' [I'm only not starting with the end that would justify the beginning — just as death seems to comment on life — because I feel the need to record the preceding facts],[16] the author explains. I also, in the search for complicity, want 'uma visão gradual' [a gradual vision][17] of these manuscripts. And that's what happens at that very moment. What comes out of the white box, folder 10/34, to be precise, is no longer loose sheets, but a notepad, with writing on both sides of standard sized sheets of paper, numbered by Clarice herself: pages 1 to 14 are here, then 23 to 43, and two page 39s, making a total of 36 pages of manuscript with relatively few crossings out. There are some pages with no amendments at all and several have only small corrections. They begin with the title 'Quanto ao futuro' [As for the Future], followed by 'Registro de fatos antecedentes' [A Record of Preceding Facts], two of the thirteen titles that open the published book.[18] I am trying to be precise in describing them, because I would like people to be able to see what appears to me to be a discovery: on these pages, with a beginning, middle and 'gran finale', Clarice copied out Macabéa's story.

    She begins with: 'Eu já acabei de escrever o fim desta história singela' [I have just finished writing the end of this simple story],[19] a sentence absent from the published text, which gives us a clue to what will be at stake on the pages of this handwritten notebook. After a short preamble of two pages, in contrast to the fourteen which open the book, Clarice writes at the top of the third page: 'Vou começar pelo meio dizendo que' [I am going to start in the middle by saying that],[20] followed by a long dash and a line from one side of the page to the other. That is when we start living with Maca: 'Que ela era incompetente. Incompetente para a vida' [that she was incompetent. Incompetent for life],[21] we read, as it will go on to say in the book. Then comes the scene with her boss when she almost gets the sack. Maca goes to the bathroom 'porque estava um pouco atordoada com a notícia' [because she felt rather shaken after hearing the news].[22] Then Clarice writes that she 'conseguiu enxergar-se toda deformada pelo espelho ordinário' [she managed to glimpse herself entirely distorted by the plain old mirror],[23] whereas in the book this line reads 'enxergou a cara toda deformada pelo espelho ordinário' [she glimpsed her face entirely distorted by the plain old mirror].[24] Without the addition of 'cara' [face], the image in the mirror leads more directly into the story told in the following pages: a sickly baby born in the backlands of Alagoas; the death of her parents when she was two; moving to Maceió with her religious aunt; the violence she suffered during her childhood and another move, to Rio de Janeiro; living in a room shared with four other girls in an old two-storey house in Rua do Acre; working as a typist in Rua do Lavradio — as I turn the pages I follow the story, which I already know, which we all already know. Except here we read it with fewer interventions from the author, for example, fewer of the bracketed comments that interrupt the book, even in the first paragraph of the 'fatos antecedentes' [preceding facts]:

> (Vai ser difícil escrever esta história. Apesar de eu não ter nada a ver com a Maca, terei que me escrever todo através dela por entre espantos meus. Os fatos são sonoros mas entre os fatos há um sussurro. É o sussurro o que me impressiona).[25]
>
> [It's going to be hard to tell this story. Even though I have nothing to do with Maca, I shall have to write everything through her, amid my own fears. The facts sound sweet but among the facts there is a whisper. It's the whisper that makes an impression on me.]

This highlights something already suggested by Vilma Arêas: 'Clarice illuminates the text from within, making Macabéa stand out sharply and emphatically'.[26] Here, Maca standing out more sharply reminds me of the film directed by Suzana Amaral,[27] which foregrounds her actions, in her brief passage through a most un-marvelous city 'toda feita contra ela' [that was completely against her],[28] its quayside, its viaducts, its empty squares, its streets with paving stones and squat houses, its gutters. Maca without her author? Not completely, because he has already made his presence felt: 'Quando penso que eu poderia ter nascido ela — e por que não? — estremeço. E parece-me uma fuga covarde o fato de eu não ser ela, sinto uma espécie de estranha culpa' [When I think that I could have been born her — and why shouldn't I have? — I shudder. And the fact that I am not her feels to me like a cowardly escape, I feel a kind of strange guilt].[29] But an author who observes from a distance, who takes a step back, so that the reader can 'embeba dessa moça assim como um pano todo encharcado' [soak up this young woman like a sodden wet cloth].[30] This image is all too real, even more so in the book, where Clarice adds 'de chão' to the 'pano', making it a 'cloth' for wiping 'the floor'. A cloth that becomes saturated with water. Clarice becoming saturated with her Maca, copying her out on these pages, 'pois todos nós somos um' [for all of us are one],[31] forging a unity that will later break into fragments during the assembly process. Clarice, who gets so close, only to pull away. The manuscripts bring out the way the text was tacked together piece by piece, which gradually creates a character, 'uma pessoa inteira' [a whole person][32] as the author puts it, while he makes a point of flagging up the tensions involved in the process.

As I read the handwritten notebook, I think about the role humour plays in these movements. I wonder if Clarice laughed when she was writing those lines. Because beyond the 'estranha culpa' [strange guilt] — in fact, just before it, in the pages I am reading right now — there appears the taste for the futility of feminine beauty sold in magazines and for the commonplace language of advertising, clearly beyond Maca's reach, from which Clarice, copying her out, distances herself. This is what happens with the image of the face cream 'tão apetitoso que se tivesse dinheiro para comprá-lo não seria boba: que pele, que nada, ela o comeria, isso sim, às colheradas no pote mesmo' [so appetizing that, if she ever had the money to buy it, she would never be so silly: forget using it on her skin, no way, she would eat it, yes sir, whole spoonfuls straight out of the jar].³³ On the following page, separation — guilt, because it is not her. But first comes humour.

In a 1927 essay Freud wrote that humour 'is not resigned; it is rebellious'; in other words, no matter how unfavourable real circumstances may be, the self that is capable of humour rebels against them: 'The ego refuses to be distressed by the provocations of reality, to let itself be compelled to suffer. It insists that it cannot be affected by the traumas of the external world; it shows, in fact, that such traumas are no more than occasions for it to gain pleasure'.³⁴ At the moment Maca's story is being told, pleasure and suffering are walking side by side in a narrative that insists on rejecting the commonplaces of victimization, exploding — literally, too, with its disconcerting bracketed 'explosions', which interrupt the manuscripts just as they do the book — the borders between 'low' and 'high', sublime and grotesque, comic and tragic, sacred and profane. Humour and death walking side by side, as in the example Freud uses as a guide, in which a condemned man, led to the scaffold on a Monday morning, remarks 'Well, the week's beginning nicely'.³⁵

On the last pages of the handwritten manuscript in the notepad, we reach Maca's death. The author prevaricates and the brackets appear:

> (Eu ainda poderia voltar atrás e recomeçar do ponto em que Macabéa está em pé na calçada — e talvez dizer que um homem alourado olhou-a com olhos de não-importa-de-que-cor. Mas — mas agora fui longe demais e não posso retroceder. Mas pelo menos não falei em morte e sim apenas em grave atropelamento).³⁶

> [I could still go back and start again at the point when Macabéa is standing on the pavement — and maybe say that a fair-haired man looked at her with it-doesn't-matter-what-colour eyes. But — but now I've gone too far and I can't turn back. But at least I didn't say anything about death, just a serious hit-and-run accident.]

One of the questions the manuscripts forces us to face, in shock, is how to narrate death. Here comes the 'gran finale' announced by the author, meticulously disavowed by the interruptions which, when putting the book together, Clarice made throughout the body of the text, many of them noted down on the scraps of paper inside these folders. Their presence, disturbing the narrative flow, means that the book contradicts the truth about life being on a trajectory from a beginning to an end. The 'linha fatal' [fatal line] will be cut short. Between brackets, in the book, these words from the opening pages are taken up again: 'A verdade é sempre um contato interior inexplicável. A verdade é irreconhecível' [The truth is always an inexplicable inner contact. The truth is unrecognizable].³⁷

Whether or not Clarice knows the end of the story — death, inevitably — the writing needs to do something else with it. What can it do? It slows down, interrupts, immobilizes even, by repeating procedures: it adds reflections and questions, parentheses, paragraphs cut short, long dashes, like the one that appears in the manuscript at the moment of the hit and run, which in the book are reduced to hyphens: 'E enorme como um transatlântico o Mercedes amarelo pegou-a — e neste mesmo instante em algum único lugar do mundo um cavalo como resposta empinou-se em gargalhada de relincho' [And, enormous as an ocean liner, the yellow Mercedes hit her — and at that very moment, in one single place somewhere in the world, in response, a horse reared up in a series of neighs].[38] Looking from the manuscript to the book, and then back again, I can see the desire to deal with time in a new way, non-linear, simultaneous, made up of overlapping instants, which signifies another meaning for writing. This meaning does not proceed in one direction only, but spreads out, through the house, into drawers, handbags, folders, occupying the unexpected space afforded by the notes dispersed by Clarice, later collected by the hands of archivists.

We have reached the end, but we must begin again. I have already reached the end, but I begin again when I copy out what I wrote on the blank sheets of paper that J. gave me. There are still several folders to go. I open 11/34. Inside, a fragment of the ending, copied down by Olga Borelli, with a note, between brackets: '(Quando Maca morre)' [When Maca dies].[39] In the next one, 12/34, a fragment of the beginning: 'Antes da pre-história houve também a pre-história da pre-história' [Before prehistory there was also the prehistory of prehistory].[40] And in the next one, 13/34, at the beginning, still, Olga writes in the corner of the page: 'Autor antes de entrar na história de Macabéa' [Author before getting into Macabéa's story].[41] The note goes on: 'Sei que estou adiando a história e que brinco de bola sem a bola' [I know I am holding up this story and that I am playing ball without the ball].[42] On one corner of this note, Clarice writes: 'O fato é um ato?' [Is the fact an act?].[43]

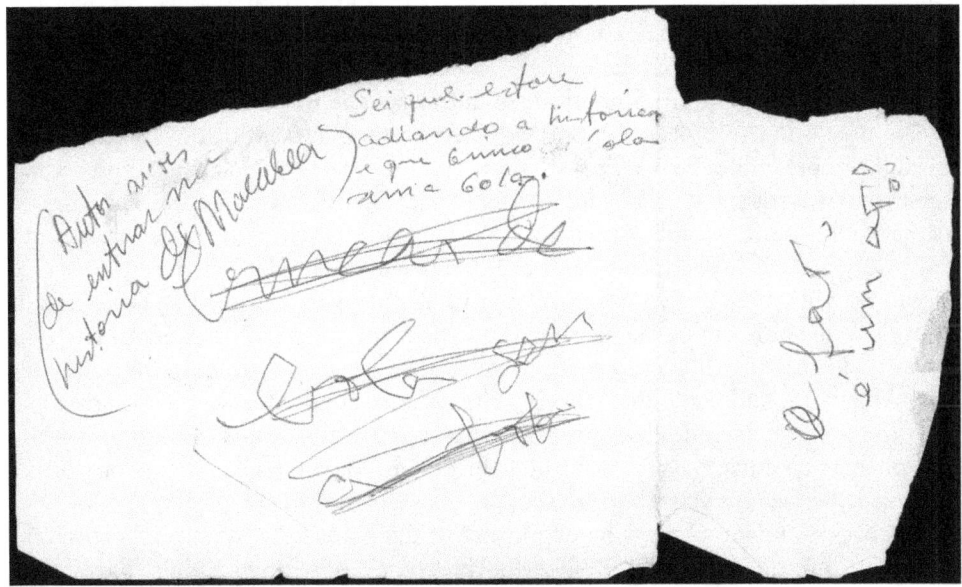

FIG. 5.4. 'O fato é um ato?' [Is the fact an act?]. Fragment, MS *A hora da estrela* fol. 13, p. 1. Acervo Clarice Lispector, Instituto Moreira Salles.

In folders 11 to 31, there are various notes, fragments of text; some ended up in the book, others did not.[44] What do these fragments prove? Much the same as my encounter with them — here, up to here, before and after folder 10/34, following the order of the archive — much like a contrast between the sequence of pages and loose scraps of paper, between the continuous and the discontinuous, a structure created from the tension between the two, following a temporal thread and yet wanting to clash with itself, creating continuities and undoing them.

In folder 25/34, there is an example I love: two sentences, separated by a line and an asterisk. The first reads: 'A morte é o encontro consigo' [Death is an encounter with oneself].[45] The second: 'Deitada, morta, era tão grande como um cavalo morto' [Prone, dead, Macabéa was as great as a dead horse]. They appear right at the end of the book, on page 86. Maca is already dead. First comes the aphorism, then the description; separated in the manuscript, they will be adjacent in the book, highlighting a process which creates a correspondence between ways of writing, in order to cross the border between reflection and narrative. And, furthermore, the correspondence between everybody's death — including, obviously, that of the person who is writing — (the 'encounter with oneself'), and the death of the character. Continuous yet discontinuous, once again, because there is no hour more solitary than the hour of our death, and yet the book attempts, perplexed, to share it: 'Meu Deus, só agora me lembrei que a gente morre. Mas — mas eu também?!' [My God, I've only just remembered that people die. But — but, me too?].[46] At this moment, then, I start crying, finding myself ridiculous again, lowering my head to hide from J., pointlessly, it turns out, because she is absorbed: eyes on the screen, headphones in her ears.

Maca dies several times in the manuscript, in several of the fragments: on the last pages of the notepad in folder 10/34; in 33/34, in a long, drawn-out way over the ten pages upon which Clarice copied out her death scene, starting from the point when Maca leaves the fortune-teller's house. But, hold on. Not yet. Because in folder 32/34 there is another notepad, smaller than the one in folder 10. There are twelve pages, numbered by Clarice, which correspond, with a few variations, to the author's preamble, before he starts to narrate the 'fatos antecedentes' [preceding facts]. As I'm writing this, an idea comes to me: there are many different ways to read a book, many ways to visualize it in the space in which its pages are set out and to organize it in our heads, and each reader undoubtedly has their own. This encounter with the archive organizes the book for us in a particular fashion and, from then onwards, the book acquires a specific form, our reading contaminated for good. At least that is how it is turning out for me, and what I am doing with this text, when all is said and done, is trying to contaminate the reading of other people with the order of these folders, just like when a character from a book acquires the face of their cinematic avatar, for good, in our minds. Perhaps, for lots of people, Maca has the face of Marcélia Cartaxo.[47]

I go back to folder 32/34. The beginning of the manuscript does not correspond to the beginning of the book, but to the fourth paragraph, when the author begins to deal more directly with how to write the story that is to come. The three previous paragraphs, which do not appear here are, nonetheless, present in the manuscript, like the note in 18/34: 'A verdade é sempre um contato interior e inexplicável. A minha vida a mais verdadeira é irreconhecível, extremamente interior e não tem uma só palavra que a signifique. Meu coração se esvaziou de todo desejo e reduz-se ao próprio último ou primeiro pulsar' [The truth is always an inexplicable inner contact. My truest life is unrecognizable, extremely deep inside me and its meaning cannot be captured in a single word. My heart has emptied itself of every desire and reduces itself to its final or initial pulsing].[48] Clarice copies into this notepad the words of the author 'esquentando o corpo para iniciar' [warming up my body before I start],[49] preparing himself, preparing the readers: first, she writes 'Esta história será o resultado de uma visão gradual' [This story will emerge from a gradual vision].[50] 'É visão na iminência de. De quê. Mais tarde verei' [It is vision in the imminence of. Of what. Perhaps I shall find out later].[51] And in the book she would add: 'Como que estou escrevendo na hora mesma em que sou lido' [Just as I am writing at the very same time I am being read].[52] I think of Barthes, who in 1978 began his course on 'The Preparation of the Novel'.[53] I think of his wish to prepare the novel alongside his students, challenging, session after session, his ability to fulfill that wish. In some ways he is heading in the same direction as Clarice is in these pages: line by line, she is wondering whether she will be able to write this book, which demands persistence and madness from her, which modifies her way of writing, which makes her abandon all she knows, launching herself into the unknown.

Preparing is a form of beginning: it is what Clarice is doing, and possibly what Barthes wanted to do, with the novel he never got to write. Preparing, preparing themselves, doubling back on themselves, these pages do, nonetheless, advance, line by line, scrutinizing the difficult act of writing. I think of this act, which the manuscripts enable us to see, the palpable effort involved. 'Não é fácil escrever' [It is not easy to write],[54] Clarice writes. One has to copy and re-copy, make notes, assemble, in order for the text to finally start to emerge. It is in the preparation demonstrated in these pages, which Clarice will put at the beginning of her book, that various challenges overlap, challenges that whoever writes is forced to confront. The impossibility of the task is overwhelming. I think of Clarice's hand forming every one of the small letters on the lines, at the same time watching the ink advance on the paper and the text pause to consider itself: 'É. Parece que estou mudando de modo de escrever. Mas acontece que só escrevo o que quero — e preciso falar sobre a moça senão sufoco. Escrevo em traços ríspidos' [Yes. It seems that I am changing the way I write. But the thing is, I only write what I want — and I need to write about this girl otherwise I will choke. I write in bold strokes].[55]

Clarice advances, towards 'alguma coisa viva' [something alive]. 'Não é pesca submarina de arpão, nem de anzol: é com as mãos de dedos duros que apalpo o que quero na lama' [It's not fishing underwater with a harpoon, or fishing with bait: it's with stiff fingers that I feel around for what I want in the mud].[56] She halts. Once again, she hesitates before starting. And she wonders several times: why do I write? 'Escrevo porque sou um desesperado? E estou cansado: não suporto mais a rotina de me ser e suicido-me todos os dias. Preparado para ir-me discretamente pela saída da porta dos fundos' [Do I write because I'm desperate? And I'm tired: I can no longer bear the routine of being me and I kill myself every day. Prepared to leave discreetly through the back door].[57] Life and death meet. It is, simultaneously, writing about melancholy and against it. It is writing sponsored by Coca-Cola and accompanied from beginning to end by a 'levíssima e constante dor de dente' [very faint but constant toothache].[58] 'E mais: afianço que esta história é também acompanhada por um violino que um homem magro de paletó puído toca bem na esquina. A cara do homem é estreita e amarela como se ele tivesse morrido' [There's more: I guarantee that the story will also be accompanied by a violin played by a thin man in a threadbare jacket right on the corner of the street. His face is gaunt and yellow as if he were dead].[59]

We already know the violin player, from folder 10. I take another look. When, at the end of this block of text, Clarice reaches Maca's death, she finds the apex of her character's life, which becomes art in the form of melodrama: 'Apareceu portanto o fantasma do homem magro de paletó puído tocando violino na esquina' [But then there appeared the ghost of the thin man in the threadbare jacket playing the violin on the street corner].[60] The apparition harks back to her childhood: 'Este homem, eu o vi uma vez ao anoitecer quando eu era criança' [That man, I saw him once, at dusk, when I was a child].[61] There are several crossings-out in this passage in the manuscript: for example, she adds 'em Recife' [in Recife] and then crosses it out, although it is maintained in the book. Further on, she writes, in brackets: '(Quando eu morrer vou ouvir de novo o violino na esquina)' [When I die I will hear once again the violin on the street corner],[62] which is different from what appears in the book, where the brackets are erased and we read: 'Sei que quando eu morrer vou ouvir o violino do homem' [I know that when I die I will hear the man's violin].[63] What I see here, in the manuscript, is how Clarice's encounter with her Maca is intensified. I can see it also in the encounter between what is written and what is erased, in the indecision which deepens the intensity of the moment, in which she imagines her own death, simultaneously creating a link between the beginning and the end of life, overlapping times and spaces.

I remember the scene described twice by Benjamin Moser, at the beginning and the end of his biography of Clarice, when, in a taxi to the hospital where she's to be admitted, the writer says to Olga Borelli: 'Let's pretend that we're not going to the hospital, that I'm not sick, and that we're going to Paris'.[64] It's also where I read about Clarice's last journey abroad, a few months before the publication of *A hora da estrela*. On 19 June 1977, Clarice and Olga disembarked in Paris, where they planned to spend a month, but stayed only five days: 'The city was full of painful memories — of her lost friends Bluma Wainer and San Tiago Dantas, of her years with Maury, of her departed beauty and youth'.[65] Clarice smoked her way round the streets of Paris, overwhelmed by the heat and the tourists. She was already tired when she left Rio de Janeiro, after getting ready for the journey. Everything around her was a source of vexation. The city which had once enchanted her was now expelling her. At the end of each excursion, anguish made her turn to Olga and ask: 'What now?'

It is hard to think of a better effect writing can have than its power to transport you to another place. Paris, in a taxi in Rio de Janeiro. Rio de Janeiro, which would always be a little bit like Recife. Or Maceió. Or Buenos Aires. 1977, and forty years later, in this small glass-panelled room, in the company of J., who reminds me that it is almost six o'clock, when she will have to leave, and so will I. Shall we open the last folder? We can turn the pages and be with Maca one more time. Because although there is no hour more solitary than this one, Clarice copies, and recopies, in handwriting that no longer keeps to the lines, which gets more and more wobbly, as each page is filled. 'Sim, foi este o modo como eu quis dizer que — que Macabéa morreu' [Yes, this was the way I wanted to announce that — that Macabéa had died].[66] Yes, she died, one more time. 'E agora — agora só me resta acender um cigarro e ir para casa. É tempo de morangos' [And now — now all that's left for me to do is light a cigarette and go home. It's strawberry time].[67]

Works Cited

ARÊAS, VILMA, *Clarice Lispector: com a ponta dos dedos* (São Paulo: Companhia das Letras, 2005)

BARTHES, ROLAND, *The Preparation of the Novel: Lecture Courses and Seminars at the Collège de France (1978–1979 and 1979–1980)*, trans. by Kate Briggs (New York and Chichester: Columbia University Press, 2011)

BORELLI, OLGA, 'Liminar: a difícil definição', in *A paixão segundo G.H.*, critical edition edited by Benedito Nunes (Paris: ALLCA XX, 1988), pp. xx–xxiii

FARGE, ARLETTE, *The Allure of the Archives* (1989), trans. by Thomas Scott-Railton (New Haven, CT, and London: Yale University Press, 2013)

FREUD, SIGMUND, 'Humour' (1927), in *The Standard Edition of the Complete Psychological Works of Sigmund Freud*, ed. and trans. by James Strachey (London: The Hogarth Press, 1961), pp. 159–66

LISPECTOR, CLARICE, *A hora da estrela* (Rio de Janeiro: Rocco, 1998 [1977])

—— *A hora da estrela: edição especial com manuscritos e ensaios inéditos* [special edition with manuscripts and unpublished critical essays] (Rio de Janeiro: Rocco, 2017)

—— MS *A hora da estrela*, Instituto Moreira Salles, Rio de Janeiro: <https://site.claricelispector.ims.com.br/acervo/notas-de-a-hora-da-estrela/>

MOSER, BENJAMIN, *Why This World: A Biography of Clarice Lispector* (New York: Oxford University Press, 2009)

PINO, CLAUDIA AMIGO, and ROBERTO ZULAR, *Escrever sobre escrever: uma introdução crítica à crítica genética* (São Paulo: Martins Fontes, 2007)

Notes to Chapter 5

1. Translated by Claire Williams.
2. Clarice Lispector, *A hora da estrela: edição especial com manuscritos e ensaios inéditos* [special edition with manuscripts and unpublished critical essays] (Rio de Janeiro: Rocco, 2017).
3. Arlette Farge, *The Allure of the Archives* [1989], trans. by Thomas Scott-Railton (New Haven, CT, and London: Yale University Press, 2013), p. 3.
4. Rio de Janeiro, Instituto Moreira Salles, MS *A hora da estrela*, fol. 1, p. 1.
5. TN: There are images of the notebook and more details about it on the pages devoted to Clarice Lispector on the Instituto Moreira Salles website: <http://claricelispectorims.com.br/caderno-de-bordo>. See chapter 4 by Elvia Bezerra in this volume.

6. Claudia Amigo Pino and Roberto Zular, *Escrever sobre escrever: uma introdução crítica à crítica genética* (São Paulo: Martins Fontes, 2007), p. 28.
7. Clarice Lispector, *A hora da estrela* (Rio de Janeiro: Rocco, 1998), p. 11.
8. Farge, *The Allure of the Archives*, p. 17.
9. MS *A hora da estrela*, fol. 5, p. 1.
10. Olga Borelli, 'Liminar: a difícil definição', in *A paixão segundo G.H.*, critical edition edited by Benedito Nunes (Paris: ALLCA XX, 1988), pp. xx–xxiii.
11. MS *A hora da estrela*, fol. 8, p. 1.
12. Lispector, *A hora da estrela*, p. 17.
13. Ibid., p. 70.
14. Ibid., p. 17.
15. Ibid., p. 70.
16. Ibid., p. 12.
17. Ibid.
18. Manuscript, folder 10/34, p. 1.
19. Ibid.
20. Ibid., p. 3.
21. Ibid.
22. Ibid., p. 4.
23. Ibid.
24. Lispector, *A hora da estrela*, p. 24.
25. Ibid.
26. Vilma Arêas, *Clarice Lispector: com a ponta dos dedos* (São Paulo: Companhia das Letras, 2005), p. 84.
27. TN: Amaral's adaptation of *A hora da estrela* premiered in 1985 to great critical acclaim in Brazil and on the international circuit. It was Brazil's entry for Best Foreign Language Film at the 59th Academy Awards. For a detailed reading of the film, see Sara André da Costa's chapter in this volume.
28. Lispector, *A hora da estrela*, p. 15.
29. MS *A hora da estrela*, fol. 10, p. 11.
30. Ibid., p. 12.
31. Lispector, *A hora da estrela*, p. 12.
32. Ibid., p. 19.
33. Ibid., p. 10.
34. Sigmund Freud, 'Humour' (1927), in *The Standard Edition of the Complete Psychological Works of Sigmund Freud*, ed. and trans. by James Strachey (London: The Hogarth Press, 1961), pp. 159–66 (p. 162).
35. Freud, 'Humour', p. 161.
36. MS *A hora da estrela*, fol. 10, p. 34.
37. Lispector, *A hora da estrela*, p. 80.
38. Ibid., p. 79.
39. MS *A hora da estrela*, fol. 11, p. 1.
40. MS *A hora da estrela*, fol. 12, p. 1.
41. MS *A hora da estrela*, fol. 13, p. 1.
42. Ibid.
43. Ibid.
44. TN: These can be seen on the IMS website dedicated to Clarice Lispector, with notes about their relationship to the final version of the book: <https://site.claricelispector.ims.com.br/acervo/notas-de-a-hora-da-estrela/> [accessed 18 August 2021].
45. MS *A hora da estrela*, fol. 25, p. 1.
46. Lispector, *A hora da estrela*, p. 87.
47. TN: Marcélia Cartaxo is the actress who played Macabéa in the 1985 film adaptation. Her performance won her the Silver Bear for Best Actress at the 36th Berlin International Film Festival.

48. MS *A hora da estrela*, fol. 18, p. 1.
49. Lispector, *A hora da estrela*, p. 14.
50. Ibid., p. 12.
51. MS *A hora da estrela*, fol. 32, p. 2.
52. Lispector, *A hora da estrela*, p. 12.
53. Roland Barthes, *The Preparation of the Novel: Lecture Courses and Seminars at the Collège de France (1978–1979 and 1979–1980)*, trans. by Kate Briggs (New York and Chichester: Columbia University Press, 2011).
54. MS *A hora da estrela*, fol. 32, p. 5.
55. Ibid., p. 4.
56. Ibid., p. 5.
57. Ibid., p. 8.
58. Ibid., p. 8.
59. Ibid., p. 11.
60. MS *A hora da estrela*, fol. 10, p. 36.
61. Ibid.
62. Ibid.
63. Lispector, *A hora da estrela*, p. 82.
64. Benjamin Moser, *Why This World: A Biography of Clarice Lispector* (New York: Oxford University Press, 2009), p. 61.
65. Moser, *Why This World*, p. 371.
66. MS *A hora da estrela*, fol. 33, p. 10.
67. MS *A hora da estrela*, fol. 10, p. 8.

CHAPTER 6

Clarice Lispector the Conference Speaker: The Vanguard and the Right to Narrate

Nádia Battella Gotlib

Innovation, According to Antonio Candido Adventure, risk, search, and approach[1]

One of the first articles about Clarice Lispector's first novel, *Perto do coração selvagem* [*Near to the Wild Heart*], was written by Antonio Candido, sadly missed professor at the University of São Paulo.[2] It was published in two parts in the *Folha da Manhã* newspaper (later to become the *Folha de São Paulo*), in 1944, in the months of June and July respectively; therefore, five and six months after the novel's release. In the version of this article which appeared in the collection *Vários escritos* [*Selected Writings*], it acquired the appropriate and even prescient title: 'No raiar de Clarice Lispector' [In the dawning of Clarice Lispector].[3]

With the novel hot off the press, Candido essentially delineated avenues of analytical and critical reading which would come to be borne out by Clarice's subsequent works and backed up by other critics who followed him. One of the reasons it was so apposite lies in Candido's prediction of a promising future for Clarice, who up until then had been completely unknown to him and to other readers, with the exception of those who were already her close friends. Among the latter were Lêdo Ivo, Lúcio Cardoso and Antônio Callado, who had been colleagues of the then-journalist on the editorial team of the *Agência Nacional* and *A Noite*, in the early 1940s. She was also known to the critics who had ventured to write reviews of the novel in the newspapers of the day, including — in addition to Cardoso — Lauro Escorel, who wrote two reviews, and Sérgio Milliet.[4]

His encouraging prediction is inherent in the title itself — 'No raiar de Clarice Lispector' — which suggests not only the beginning of the novice's literary fame, but also the appearance of the first 'dawn rays' illuminating the whole field, auguring the brilliance and impact of a light that would spread across time and space, covering Brazilian territory and other continents.[5] In his article, he highlights the innovative quality of the novel, against a backdrop of a certain 'conformismo estilístico' [stylistic conformism] then in vogue in Brazilian literature of that era, and of a lack of what he refers to as a 'verdadeira aventura de expressão' [genuine adventure in expressivity], that could succeed in 'estender o domínio da palavra sobre regiões mais complexas e mais inexprimíveis' [extending the domain of the word over more complex, inexpressible regions].[6] By way of example, he cites the achievements of *Memórias sentimentais de João Miramar* [*The Sentimental Memoirs of João Miramar*] (1924), by Oswald de Andrade, and *Macunaíma* (1928), by Mário de Andrade. He concludes:

> Com efeito, este romance é uma tentativa impressionante para levar nossa língua canhestra a domínios pouco explorados, forçando-a a adaptar-se a um pensamento cheio de mistério, para o qual sentimos que a ficção não é um exercício ou uma aventura afetiva, mas um instrumento real do espírito, capaz de nos fazer penetrar em alguns dos labirintos mais retorcidos da mente.
>
> [In fact, this novel is an impressive attempt to take our clumsy language into seldom explored domains, forcing it to adapt itself to a thought process full of mystery, making us feel that fiction is not merely a technical exercise or an emotional adventure, but rather a genuine instrument of the spirit, enabling us to penetrate some of the most twisted labyrinths of the mind.][7]

Candido affirms that Clarice's literature 'é *performance* da melhor qualidade' (author's emphasis) [is a *performance* of the highest quality].[8] Moreover, and this is the aspect which I would like to focus on here, it seems to belong, still in the critic's words, to those people who prefer 'o risco da aposta à comodidade do ramerrão' [the risk of gambling to the comfort of humdrum routine].[9] In relation to Clarice's debut novel, this is an opportune and pertinent reading, due to considerations that may extend to her other novels and texts. In fact, in Clarice's fiction — in this novel and in a number of others, and even in her non-fiction texts which are more journalistic in character — one unequivocally observes, in Candido's words, a thought process full of 'mystery', in which literature is constructed in a strange atmosphere of instability. This happens at the precise moment when the narrator presents the character plunging into the depths of their own mind, in risky situations, surprising the reader.

The narrator does this through attempts to undo the mere binaries of subject/object, author/character, through a process which Candido finds in what he calls 'romances de aproximação' [novels of approach]:[10] novels in which one seeks identification with the other. Such novels achieve an unusual sense of 'tensão psicológica' [psychological tension].[11] On one hand, he carefully characterizes his interpretation of this novel as an attempt at renewal, at a moment in time when the work, her first to reach publication, had yet to establish its place within a context of critical reception. On the other, he goes so far as to define the basic ingredients constituting this renewal.

In order to be reassured of the specificity, but also the uniqueness, of Clarice's debut, one need go no further than examining work by other women writers of the day who were considered important social-realist novelists. One example would be Rachel de Queiroz and her novels *O quinze* (1930) [*The Year Fifteen*] or *Caminho de pedras* (1937) [*The Stone Path*]. Another is Lúcia Miguel-Pereira, with her three novels from the 1930s: *Maria Luíza* (1933), *Em surdina* (1949, but written in 1932) [*Secretly*] and *Amanhecer* (1938) [*Dawn*]. Then there is Pagu (the pen-name of Patrícia Galvão), whose *Parque industrial* (1933) [*Industrial Park*] is innovative in formal terms, but whose world-view was derived directly from the modernist tradition of the 1920s, and centred on the discussion of the disparity between social classes, so characteristic of the 1930s in Brazil. These were not, however, concerns upon which Clarice's first novel were based.

In *Perto do coração selvagem*, the focus shifts. The narrator (whose gender is unknown) seems to delve into the characters' interior goings-on from a third-person perspective, focusing his or her attention on the protagonist Joana. The other characters in the triangle — Otávio, the husband, and Lídia, the other woman — only exist insofar as they interact with Joana, who *experiments* with life and all of its challenges from infancy to maturity. Dissatisfaction characterizes her journey through life and generates a kind of search or seeking. This will be the basic pattern underpinning the literary embroidery of the novels to come. Joana, at the end of *Perto do coração selvagem*, finds herself on the cusp of new horizons as she glimpses the prospect of a journey. In *A cidade sitiada* [*The Besieged City*], Lucrécia, who lives in the city of São Geraldo, undergoes a number of experiences while looking for others, until, just like Joana, her goal becomes the prospect of a new encounter. Of the three protagonists who feature in Clarice's 1940s output, only Virgínia (*O lustre* [*The Chandelier*], 1946) meets a definitive end: after a series of encounters with a number of different partners, she dies. In death she is surrounded by others, seen by others, in anticipation of what happens to Macabéa in the tragic final scene of *A hora da estrela* [*The Hour of the Star*].[12]

On the one hand this thematic framework comes from a long tradition: a woman's quest for romantic partners, each with his own respective characteristics or 'meanings'. On the other hand, such novels possess a specific feature: the translation of a woman's intimate experiences into words, while maximizing the capacity for extending or testing language's ability to translate, in a detailed way, the movements, the 'labyrinths of the mind' to which Candido referred. This begs the question: in light of the adventurous, risk-taking and anti-conformist character of Clarice's writing, is it still possible to fit her innovative tendencies into the category of vanguard literature?

The Vanguard, According to Clarice Lispector

Clarice's innovative style certainly qualifies as vanguardist, if we are mindful of her own conception of the vanguard, as she formulated it in a conference lecture entitled 'Literatura de Vanguarda no Brasil' [Vanguard Literature in Brazil]. This lecture was first given at the University of Texas, in Austin, in 1963, and published by the publishing house Rocco in the book *Outros escritos* [*Other Writings*] in 2005.[13] Furthermore, it was the only lecture Clarice ever wrote, and one she delivered numerous times. She used it when she accepted speaking invitations from people and institutions in a number of cities, recording the names by hand on the last page of the typed manuscript: Texas, Brasília, Vitória de Espírito Santo, Belo Horizonte, Campos, Belém do Pará.[14]

Anxious to fulfil her assignment of lecturing on the Brazilian vanguard, Clarice 'the lecturer' opens her remarks by confessing her weaknesses and inability to tackle the theme.

> Nunca tive, enfim, o que se chama verdadeiramente de vida intelectual. [...] Apesar de ocupada, desde que eu me conheço, com o escrever — eu já escrevia quando tinha sete anos de idade — , apesar disso infelizmente faltou-me encarar também a literatura de fora para dentro, isto é, como uma abstração.
>
> [I have never led what is properly called an intellectual life. [...] Despite dedicating myself, ever since I can remember, to writing — I was already writing at the age of seven — in spite of this, I have unfortunately failed to approach literature from the outside in, in other words, as an abstraction.][15]

Nevertheless, she then proceeds to set out her conception of what literature is: 'Literatura para mim é o modo como os outros chamam o que nós, os escritores, fazemos' [Literature, for me, is the name other people give to what we writers do].[16] Just as the reader is almost convinced that Clarice 'the person' is completely unable to make headway with this task, Clarice 'the lecturer' goes ahead and does it. She makes successive attempts at defining what the concept of vanguard could mean to her, but every time she puts forward a new definition, she immediately negates it.

Could it be defined as experimentation? Apparently so: 'Vanguarda seria, também para mim, é claro, experimentação' [For me, too, clearly, the vanguard would be experimentation].[17] However, it is not quite so straightforward:

> O que me confundiu um pouco a respeito de vanguarda como experimentação, é que toda verdadeira arte é também uma experimentação, e, lamento contrariar muitos, toda verdadeira vida é experimentação, ninguém escapa.
>
> [What confused me a little with respect to the vanguard as experimentation is that all true art is also experimentation, and, I regret contradicting lots of people, all true life is experimentation too, there's no escaping it.][18]

By broadening the meaning of vanguard, Clarice also verifies that the object of her presentation, the vanguard, thereby loses the opportunity of finding its specificity through definition. Her method is to feel for the meaning, herself 'experimenting' with new possible directions in her path of reflection. This is why her search moves forward by asking questions. Could it be seen as going against the formal values in vogue at the time? Yes, but...

> Por que então uma experimentação era vanguarda e outra não? Vanguarda seria aquela que revertesse valores formais e tentasse, por assim dizer, um oposto ao que se estivesse no momento sendo formalmente feito?
>
> [Why, in that case, would one form of experimentation qualify as the vanguard and another one not? Might the vanguard be whichever one inverts formal values and tries, in a manner of speaking, to do the opposite of that which is presently the done thing, in terms of form?][19]

That, she asserts, would be 'simplório demais, além de que tão raso quanto as modas' [too simplistic, as well as being as superficial as the fashion trends themselves].[20]

It is interesting to observe that, in a way, by rejecting the idea of the vanguard as simply taking the opposite direction to what was done previously, she is able to insert a vehement criticism of radicalism in terms of both the superficial nature of its vision and its status as an easy option, lacking a basis of solid and trustworthy discussion. And her reference to fashion trends, although not in direct relation to her analysis of the sense of vanguard, does not seem to be random: it reminds the reader that fashions pass, just like — and this is up to the reader — fleeting vanguards that set themselves up simply in opposition to what went before.

Could the vanguard have something to do with introducing a new aesthetic element? Could it be a new way of breaking up antiquated, stratified forms and making way for a new vision?

> Qualquer verdadeira experimentação levaria a maior autoconhecimento, o que significaria: conhecimento. Vanguarda seria, pois, em última análise, um dos instrumentos de conhecimento, um instrumento avançado de pesquisa.
>
> [Any true experimentation would lead to greater self-knowledge, which would be equivalent to: knowledge itself. The vanguard would thus be, in the final analysis, one of the instruments of knowledge, a refined research tool.][21]

Curiously, here Clarice uses almost the same term as that employed by Antonio Candido when he refers to her literature as being 'um instrumento real de espírito capaz de nos fazer penetrar em alguns dos labirintos mais retorcidos da mente' [a genuine instrument of the spirit, enabling us to penetrate some of the most twisted labyrinths of the mind].[22]

For Clarice, therefore, the vanguard is experimentation, self-knowledge, knowledge and searching. It implies 'renovações formais' [renewals in form] which would lead to the 're-exame de conceitos' [re-examination of concepts].[23] And on the basis of these premises she adopts a concept, which she goes on to develop, as a consequence of the preceding ones: of the vanguard as a form of liberation. By way of example, she invokes the 1922 Modernist movement, a movement characterized by profound liberation, as being 'sobretudo um novo modo de ver' [above all, a new way of seeing], concluding that: 'libertação é sempre vanguarda' [liberation is always the vanguard].[24]

At this point in her reflections, her concept reaches, I think, its maximum elasticity, because by accepting the Modernist movement of 1922 as a movement of liberation, and extending this condition of liberation to all vanguard acts, she ends up dismantling the possibility of a conceptualization founded on the condition that the vanguard is produced by a group. She relativizes the concept of vanguard, which thence becomes dependent on the experience of each individual. That is what she proposes next.

But, we might ask, liberation for whom? And then she raises another interesting issue: 'libertação é às vezes avanço apenas para quem se está libertando, e pode não ter valor de moeda corrente para os outros' [liberation is sometimes only a step forward for the one who is liberating themselves, and may not have the same currency value for others].[25] The vanguard is only liberation, therefore, for the person who is liberating themselves. Here we have an individualist conception of what 'the vanguard' is, which does not factor in the progress made by the frontline troops, advancing new ways of being (and, therefore, of acting) artistically.

In her lecture, Clarice names writers and works according to her own tastes. It is an unusual selection of writers who are not usually grouped together, but they are all significant figures in the history of Brazilian literature. She refers to particular poems in order to illustrate how each featured poet may be considered an artist of the vanguard. She transcribes poems by Mário de Andrade ('Ode ao burguês' [Ode to the bourgeois man]), Carlos Drummond de Andrade ('Poema das sete faces' [Seven Sided Poem]),[26] João Cabral de Melo Neto ('Psicologia da composição' [The Psychology of Composition]), Manuel Bandeira ('O anjo da guarda' [The Guardian Angel]). And she quotes prose writers too: Adonias Filho, Dalton Trevisan, Murilo Rubião, Rubem Fonseca, Marina Colasanti, Sérgio Sant'Anna, Luiz Vilela, Mora Fontes, Marly de Oliveira, Nélida Piñon.[27] I will linger here over Carlos Drummond de Andrade, whom Clarice reads with exceptional sensitivity. Recognizing the rupturing quality of Drummond's declamations, with reference to his 'Poema de sete faces', she asserts:

> Drummond é a palavra nua, coberta somente por uma tênue camada: a da contenção da nudez. Drummond não se permite o êxtase, nem mesmo o do sofrimento — e nessa autoprivação ele nos dói ainda mais.
>
> [Drummond is the naked word, covered only by a tenuous layer: that which contains the nudity. Drummond does not permit himself ecstasy, not even the ecstasy of suffering — and in that self-deprivation we feel his hurt all the more.][28]

Her solution to this is to relinquish any attempt to analyse Drummond: 'por não poder analisá-lo, é que fico com todo ele' [since I am not able to analyse him, I am left with all of him].[29]

Once again Clarice the conference speaker frustrates the expectations of her listeners who, I believe, would have been anticipating some sort of analytical considerations of the poem, no matter how minimal. She frustrates them not only because she confesses her 'inability' to analyse, but because this very inability is, for Clarice as reader, a reason to rejoice, because it grants her a certain freedom by providing close, direct contact with the poem. This shows, therefore, that analysis, according to Clarice, can be seen as distancing the reader from the work, instead of bringing them closer.

Now, let us turn to her conclusion, which is inspired by Drummond's poem:

> Que será que faz com que certos rostos sejam inominavelmente a face verdadeira de um homem? E não apenas uma face? O que quer que seja, o olhar o vê e reconhece, o inominavelmente. Lendo Drummond, não um poema, mas acompanhando a sua obra, acompanha-se a profunda respiração de um homem. Ele é um guia, sem que eu saiba dizer em quê — e isto é vanguarda para mim.
>
> [What is it that makes certain faces unnameably the true face of a man? And not just one face? Whatever the reason, the gaze recognizes and perceives this unnameableness. Reading Drummond, not merely a poem by him, but rather accompanying his whole work, one accompanies closely the very breath of a

man. He is a guide, without my knowing in what sense precisely — and that, to me, is the vanguard.][30]

Here, by way of a reading of Drummond, we have a new concept of the vanguard: according to Clarice Lispector, the vanguard is that which matters most, that which most aptly translates an artist and their art, and for that reason would go in front (avant-garde), of any other resource. This is why it becomes a guide for the reader, even without our knowing in what sense.

This way of reasoning is rather strange to those accustomed to an academic discourse founded in various concepts of the vanguard upholding theoretical and critical reflections. Clarice takes another route, just as she does in her literary texts, which evade categorization and even narrative genre. In *Água viva* she asserts: 'Inútil querer me classificar: eu simplesmente escapulo não deixando, gênero não me pega mais' [No use trying to pin me down. I simply slip away and won't allow it, no label will stick].[31] It is a book she considered to be not a novel but simply 'ficção' [fiction], in the way that she declared *Um sopro de vida* to be 'pulsações' [pulsations]. Likewise, her conclusion about the vanguard eschews conceptual norms: for her, the vanguard becomes what the reader is able to apprehend in the author as being the 'face verdadeira' [true face] or 'a profunda respiração de um homem' [the deep breathing of a man].[32] This being the case, she bases her characterization of the vanguard on her own experience as a reader, revealing how daring she is by applying such eminently personal criteria.

The Hour of the Star and the Vanguard

At this point, deciding whether or not Drummond is a vanguard artist is irrelevant (she asserts that it is a question of semantics, in any case), because what really matters is that his poetry is 'uma reflexão profundamente vivida sobre a pungência de se estar no mundo' [a deeply lived reflection on the intense emotional disturbance of being in the world].[33] Here, Clarice emphasizes the idea that being in the vanguard consists of having a new point of view, 'mesmo que às vezes levasse apenas a mais um milímetro de visão' [even if this only results in the extension of one's vision by a single millimetre], and being able to bring about change.[34] Thus, Clarice arrives at the last feature of the vanguard, the one to which all of its other features relate: the political. And it is at this point that she finally turns to the traditional, military concept of the vanguard, invoking a front-line atmosphere where the political and aesthetic converge:

> o nosso crescimento íntimo está forçando as comportas e rebentará com as formas inúteis de ser ou de escrever. Estou chamando o nosso progressivo autoconhecimento de vanguarda. Estou chamando de vanguarda 'pensarmos' a nossa língua.
>
> [our personal growth is straining at the floodgates and will burst through, and sweep away useless ways of being and writing. I am calling our progressive acquisition of self-knowledge a form of vanguard. I am calling 'thinking through' our language a form of the vanguard.][35]

This is precisely the way Rodrigo S.M. writes his novel about Macabéa, 'em estado de urgência e de calamidade pública' [during a state of emergency and public calamity].[36] Here is a new way of reading Clarice's final novel, or the last to be published in her lifetime. In fact, *The Hour of the Star* constitutes a moment of extreme tension, to my mind comparable only with *The Passion According to G.H.*, published in 1964, thirteen years earlier. Furthermore, in both novels the structure takes the form of a sequence founded on an 'approach': of the narrator towards his character, and of the character towards another character.

In the 1964 novel, the 'other' who is being sought takes the shape of Janair, the maid, who in turn becomes transfigured into an African queen, and, ultimately, into the cockroach. This vile insect is then transfigured into a precious and horrifying vital substance, vital insofar as it is wild archaic matter, forever being massacred, an inhabitant of the 'escombros' [ruins], which nonetheless manages to resist, pulsating.[37] This process involves a difficult confrontation with the other, one in which, step by step, a gamut of prejudices and myths deeply ingrained in our *machista* culture are deconstructed. G.H. actually sees Janair, her former maid, for the first time. Until this point she has failed to notice the woman who used to work for her in the penthouse apartment. In other words, 'the other', the poor person, gains visibility. This is how G.H. comes to experience (to her very core) another side of life, the other side of life, which is more humanized, more authentically hers. She experiences the inside of the cockroach, which is her own inside, up to now repressed, emerging there in the fullness of her femininity, sexuality, and liberty. She finally and effectively becomes a being in the act of being. Interestingly, G.H. experiences what Macabéa already is in her neutral innocence and impartiality. Macabéa experiences without being conscious of experiencing. Despite having nothing in a world founded on the principle of having, she succeeds in resisting and, to a certain extent, surviving, until she is run over by the yellow Mercedes Benz. The logo of this brand of luxury car, ironically, is a star, in this case a star that lacerates the entrails of the Northeastern girl, opening up, figuratively, into a thousand murderous spikes.

In *The Passion According to G.H.*, the bursting open is mediated by the act of devouring, or self-devouring. It takes place during a scene of autophagy: the protagonist perceives what she had previously not seen, and experiences the terrible and delicious flavour of a life free from prejudice, open to sensations without limits. In *The Hour of the Star*, this bursting open occurs in destruction, disaster, annihilation. Macabéa has her hour of glory, finally being seen by those who crowd around her as she finds herself on the verge of death, having been knocked over while crossing the road, and tossed onto the pavement.

In both cases, something attacks the body's insides, causing the material inside the character to emerge, already modified by the intimate experience of liberation. In the first case this involves transplanting the cockroach's sap into G.H.'s body; in the second, the thousand spikes of a star piercing Macabéa's skin. In both novels, a gradual sequential development is brought to a halt by the final scene, in which the 'other' (the cockroach's sap, the star on the front of the luxury vehicle) is incorporated, bringing each of the characters the experience of liberation.

In *The Hour of the Star*, the plot is limited to three occurrences or characters: the author, the narrator and the character. It is no coincidence that they are distributed into the categories of feminine, masculine, and a kind of neuter that eludes the exigencies ruling our socio-political consciousness. In other words, insofar as it escapes the system (which we might judge to consist of the aforementioned unreachable territory of the unnameable), it manifests itself to us in the uncertain space wherein a life of poverty entails neither revolt nor revenge. The character Macabéa simply floats 'beyond the reach of thought'.[38] The novel embraces different cultural strata, including the stratum that is 'cultured' (in the widest sense) or that has the power to narrate (Clarice Lispector), and who delegates that function to another, who is equally cultured (Rodrigo S.M.), and narrates the life of the one who is uncultured (Macabéa). Insofar as the author (Clarice Lispector) divides the characters into three different social classes and problematizes this social situation, the novel provokes us to think about who has the right to narrate.

The question of human rights was not new to Clarice, who wanted to study Law because she had a thirst for justice and prison reform. While she was a student at the Universidade do Brasil, as it was formerly known (it is now the Universidade Federal do Rio de Janeiro), she wrote an article for a student magazine entitled 'Observações sobre o direito de punir' [Observations on the Right to Punish], in which she asked: who has the right to punish?[39] I wonder whether the question, in *The Hour of the Star*, to paraphrase Clarice, might not be: who has the right to narrate? How can I comprehend the other, if, as I write or use the power of words, bread turns into gold (to use one of Clarice's own images)?[40]

Here we have a topic that is intimately related to Brazil's culture and language. Thinking through language is in itself a politicizing act and consolidation of citizenship that enables the act of 'seeing the other', and, thereby, to question class difference and the rights of each citizen towards each other, to narrate 'the other'. What matters at this stage in the author's deliberations is how this turning the focus back on oneself, from multiple angles, leads to a comprehension of the self. This is what happens in the final part of her lecture, when Clarice asserts that: '"Pensar" a língua portuguesa do Brasil significa pensar sociologicamente, psicologicamente, filosoficamente, linguisticamente sobre nós mesmos' [To 'think through' the Brazilian Portuguese language implies thinking about ourselves sociologically, psychologically, philosophically, and linguistically].[41] This section puts forward a political analysis of our language.

> É maravilhosamente difícil escrever em língua que ainda borbulha; que precisa mais do presente do que mesmo de uma tradição; em língua que, para ser trabalhada, exige que o escritor se trabalhe a si próprio como pessoa. Cada sintaxe nova é então reflexo indireto de novos relacionamentos, de um maior aprofundamento em nós mesmos, de uma consciência mais nítida do mundo e do nosso mundo.
>
> [It is fantastically difficult to write in a language which is still new, still bubbling; which is in greater need of the present than of a tradition; in a language which, in order to be shaped, demands that the writer first shape themselves as a person. Therefore every new piece of syntax obliquely reflects

new relationships, a delving-deeper into ourselves, a clearer awareness of the world and of our world.][42]

By this point in the conference speaker's argument, her extreme awareness of language and the craft of literature can be seen from the form of the presentation. It has been present as one of the ingredients of a long narrative project which, to my mind, began with her first texts in the 1940s: the quest for and conquest of an awareness of self and construction of liberty through the use of language, as she goes on to explain:

> Cada sintaxe nova abre então pequenas novas liberdades. Não as liberdades arbitrárias de quem pretende 'variar', mas uma liberdade mais verdadeira, e esta consiste em descobrir que se é livre. Isto não é fácil: descobrir que se é livre é uma violentação criativa. Nesta se ferem escritor e linguagem, pois, qualquer aprofundamento é penoso: ferem-se, mas reagem vivos. [...] A linguagem está descobrindo o nosso pensamento, e o nosso pensamento está formando uma língua que se chama literária e que eu chamo, para maior alegria minha, de linguagem da vida.

> [Every new piece of syntax makes way for slight new freedoms. Not the inconsequential freedoms of those who merely 'fancy a change', but a truer freedom, which consists in discovering that one is free oneself. This is not easy: discovering that one is free oneself is a creative act of violation. By committing this act, the writer and their language wound one another, because any delving-deeper is painful: they wound one another but come alive. [...] Our language is discovering our thought, and our thought is forming a language that is typically referred to as 'literary' but which I call, to my great personal joy, a language of life.][43]

Here we have the vanguard in its most wide-ranging sense. This is why Clarice considers Guimarães Rosa[44] to be a vanguard writer and renovator of the novel, a claim she justifies by saying:

> Pois criou uma linguagem que é subjacente à nossa, algumas vezes como se fosse um substrato de nossa língua, e que, por isso mesmo, na sua aparente estranheza, nós reconhecemos como tocando na nossa maior intimidade. Ele é de vanguarda porque se adiantou e precipitou nossa consciência de uma verdade que não é apenas linguística, mas da pessoa brasileira. Somos, por enquanto, falsos cosmopolitas, e o interior do Brasil revelado por Guimarães Rosa está em cada um de nós, e tão bem revelado que atinge a altura de uma invenção.

> [Because he created a language that lies beneath our own, sometimes as though it were the substratum of our own language, and for that reason, in its apparent strangeness we recognize how it touches us in our most intimate selves. He is a vanguard writer because he anticipated and hastened our realization of a truth that is not merely linguistic but rather has to do with the Brazilian people. We are, for the time being, false cosmopolitans, and Brazil's hinterlands are revealed by Guimarães Rosa to be within every one of us, and they are indeed revealed with such aplomb that they attain the status of an invention.][45]

And she concludes: 'Temos fome de saber de nós, e grande urgência, porque estamos precisando de nós mesmos, mais do que dos outros' [We are hungry to know ourselves, and feel it as an urgent need, because presently we need ourselves, more than others].[46] Clarice does not overlook the problem of what she calls 'false vanguards' (passing fads, intellectualism, contrived art and copying), and criticizes them because 'Não vão diretamente à fonte, seguem o resultado já atingido por outros escritores' [They do not go directly to the source, but instead reproduce the results already obtained by other writers].[47] She goes on to quote the academic and critic José Guilherme Merquior, who 'fala das obras de vários poetas [...] que exprimem o desespero do mundo sem ter desespero nem mundo' [speaks of the works of a number of poets [...] who express the despair of the world, while they themselves have neither despair nor world].[48]

Finally, she returns to herself, donning her writer's cap. She explains that she is disillusioned, has not found peace, may no longer write, or may return to writing. Above all, she states, she likes to paint. And then she recounts some brief comments made by writers and critics who attended a conference on literature in Brasília (Benedito Nunes, Affonso Romano de Sant'anna, Mário Chamie, José Guilherme Merquior, Autran Dourado, Silviano Santiago, Elias José).[49] She asked them about the future of literature, the relationship between literature and journalism, the enduring nature (or otherwise) of literature. These are pressing and current themes which feed into today's discussions about culture, intensified, obviously, by globalization. I mean discussions about the future of the book and the role of literature on a new cultural horizon, because of the strong competition it faces from the many forms of digital circulation of information. But also discussions about the relationship between literature and journalism, which have actually been taking place since the nineteenth century, but have opened up to include new means of communication and their role in culture. Clarice the conference speaker acts, therefore, as an interviewer, asking her friends and colleagues questions which she brought together opportunely to develop as the subject of her conference presentation.

It is also important to consider how careful she clearly was, in her speech and in her fiction, when referring to literature and the Portuguese language as powerful cultural tools. Clarice's undertaking in *The Hour of the Star* is to think through the Portuguese language and Brazilian culture. The fact that Rodrigo the narrator tells us that Macabéa asks, precisely, 'o que é cultura?' [what is culture?] is no coincidence. Nor is the fact that this semi-literate girl misspells the word 'designar' [designate] as 'desi**gui**nar', adding a syllable between the 'g' and the 'n'; just as the word is pronounced in Brazilian Portuguese.[50] Here we have a star with a thousand spikes, a fictional constellation extracted from Macabéa's entrails, a cry of indignation in the face of the misery of the human condition, which only in the hour of agony gains any visibility.

The Hour of the Star continues to shine alone, and for this reason cannot be affiliated with any other texts, either by Clarice or anyone else, because of its originality and daring. Nevertheless, due to the way it uses inspiration as an instrumental mode of seeking to penetrate the aforementioned labyrinths of the mind, it does indeed appear to constitute a vanguard work, in accordance with

Clarice's definition. It does so because it advances and catalyses the production of so many other such labyrinths, radiating light onto the stage of writing that tries out and expresses pain and injustice. As a guiding light of the vanguard (and here I paraphrase the writer herself, when describing Carlos Drummond de Andrade, declaring: 'He is a guide, without my knowing in what sense precisely — and that, to me, is the vanguard'), I declare: 'She, Clarice, is a guide, without my knowing in what sense precisely'. Who can say whether it is not precisely in that gap between knowledge and uncertainty that the most authentic manifestation of the vanguard lies? According to Clarice.

Works Cited

CANDIDO, ANTONIO, 'No raiar de Clarice Lispector', *Vários Escritos* (São Paulo: Duas Cidades, 1970), pp. 125–31
LISPECTOR, CLARICE, *Água viva* (Rio de Janeiro: Artenova, 1973); *Água Viva*, trans. by Stefan Tobler (New York: New Directions, 2012)
—— *A paixão segundo G.H.* (Rio de Janeiro: Francisco Alves, 1991 [1964]); *The Passion According to G.H.*, trans. by Idra Novey (New York: New Directions, 2012)
—— *A hora da estrela* (Rio de Janeiro: Rocco, 1998 [1977])); *The Hour of the Star*, trans. by Giovanni Pontiero (Manchester: Carcanet, 1992 [1986])
—— 'Literatura de vanguarda no Brasil', in *Outros escritos*, ed. by Teresa Montero and Lícia Manzo (Rio de Janeiro: Rocco, 2005), pp. 95–111

Notes to Chapter 6

1. Translated by Andrzej Stuart-Thompson.
2. Translator's note (TN): Antonio Candido (1918–2017) was a hugely influential writer, university professor and sociologist, and one of the biggest names in Brazilian literary criticism.
3. Antonio Candido, 'No raiar de Clarice Lispector', in *Vários escritos* (São Paulo: Duas Cidades, 1970), pp. 125–31.
4. (TN): Ivo, Cardoso and Callado became well-known literary figures in Brazil. Escorel was a professor of literature who later became a diplomat, and Milliet was a poet and essayist whose reviews were very influential at the time the novel came out. For more on early reviews of Lispector's work, see, for example, Neli dos Santos, 'A crítica jornalística sobre Clarice Lispector (1943–1997)' (unpublished Master's dissertation, Universidade de Campinas, 1999).
5. All translations from the Portuguese are by Andrzej Stuart-Thompson, unless otherwise attributed.
6. Candido, 'No raiar de Clarice Lispector', p. 126.
7. Ibid., p. 127.
8. Ibid. p. 128.
9. Ibid., p. 127.
10. Ibid., pp. 128–29.
11. Ibid., p. 129.
12. See chapter by Magdalena Edwards in this volume.
13. The manuscript is held at the AMLB archive at the Fundação Casa de Rui Barbosa in Rio de Janeiro (Arquivo Clarice Lispector, Produção intelectual, CL/pi 27). It is included, under the title 'Literatura de vanguarda no Brasil', in *Outros escritos*, ed. by Teresa Montero and Lícia Manzo (Rio de Janeiro: Rocco, 2005), pp. 95–111. References to the text are taken from this edition.
14. I presented some of these considerations under the title 'Clarice Lispector and the Vanguard of Women's Writing' at the '100 Years of Futurism' event, which took place at the Federal

University of Rio de Janeiro (UFRJ) and the Federal Fluminense University (UFF) on 28 October 2017.
15. Lispector, 'Literatura de vanguarda', p. 96.
16. Ibid., p. 96.
17. Ibid., p. 97.
18. Ibid., p. 97.
19. Ibid., p. 97.
20. Ibid., p. 97.
21. Ibid., p. 97.
22. Candido, 'O raiar de Clarice Lispector', p. 127.
23. Lispector, 'Literatura de vanguarda', p. 96.
24. Ibid., p. 99.
25. Ibid., p. 99.
26. (EN): One of the poet's best-known poems, first published in 1930, it has been translated many times, including by Elizabeth Bishop in 1969. A 2014 version by Richard Zenith can be found at <https://modernpoetryintranslation.com/poem/seven-sided-poem/> [accessed 6 August 2021].
27. Mário de Andrade (1893–1945) was one of the founding members of the Modernist movement in Brazil. He was a poet, critic, researcher into popular culture and the author of many literary works. As well as writing *crônicas*, Carlos Drummond de Andrade (1902–1987), was one of the greatest Brazilian poets of the twentieth century, along with João Cabral de Melo Neto (1920–1999), and the poet and *cronista* Manuel Bandeira (1886–1968). Adonias Filho (1915–1990) wrote novels portraying the cacao plantation culture of Bahia (in the north east of Brazil). Clarice also quotes Murilo Rubião (1916–1991), known for his fantasy stories, and Dalton Trevisan (1925–), author of numerous erotic tales. Marly de Oliveira (1935–2007) was another well-known poet and a good friend of Clarice's, in the company of whom the latter wrote fragments of *A paixão segundo G.H.* [*The Passion According to G.H.*]. She also mentions contemporary authors whose work spans her era and our own, like Rubem Fonseca (1925–), whose novels and short stories portray urban violence, Marina Colasanti (1937–), who has published works mainly for children and young adults, and Nélida Piñon (1937–), a writer of Iberian descent, who is one of Brazil's best-known novelists. She includes authors born in the 1940s, like poet, short story writer and novelist Sérgio Sant'Anna (1941–), and Luiz Vilela (1942–), a journalist and writer of short stories and novels. Mora Fuentes (1951–2009) was a writer (known for his short stories) and artist, Spanish by birth, who settled in Brazil.
28. Lispector, 'Literatura de Vanguarda', p. 101.
29. Ibid., p. 101.
30. Ibid., p. 101.
31. Clarice Lispector, *Água viva* (Rio de Janeiro: Artenova, 1973), p. 14; *Água Viva*, trans. by Stefan Tobler (New York: New Directions, 2012), p. 7.
32. Lispector, 'Literatura de vanguarda', p. 101.
33. Ibid., p. 102.
34. Ibid., p. 105.
35. Lispector, 'Literatura de vanguarda', p. 109.
36. Clarice Lispector, *A hora da estrela* (Rio de Janeiro: Rocco, 1998 [1977]), p. 8; *The Hour of the Star*, trans. by Giovanni Pontiero (Manchester: Carcanet, 1986), p. 8.
37. Clarice Lispector, *A paixão segundo G.H.* (Rio de Janeiro: Francisco Alves, 1991 [1964]), p. 67; *The Passion According to G.H.*, trans. by Idra Novey (New York: New Directions, 2012), p. 58.
38. (EN): This is an allusion to 'Atrás do pensamento', one of the titles considered for what became *Água viva*, and quoted within the text.
39. (EN): The text is also included in *Outros escritos*, pp. 45–49.
40. The image comes from Lispector, *A hora da estrela*, p. 19; *The Hour of the Star*, p. 15.
41. Lispector, 'Literatura de vanguarda', p. 106.
42. Ibid., p. 106.
43. Ibid., p. 106.
44. João Guimarães Rosa (1908–1967) was the author of, among other things, one of the best Brazilian novels of the twentieth century: *Grande sertão: veredas* (1956) [*Bedeviled in the Backlands*,

trans. by Alison Entrekin, forthcoming in 2021]. He is known for the creative language skills with which he translated the world of the 'sertão' [backlands] of Minas Gerais, in the Southeast of the country.
45. Lispector, 'Literatura de vanguarda', pp. 106–07.
46. Ibid., p. 107.
47. Ibid., p. 109.
48. Ibid., p. 109. José Guilherme Merquior (1941–1991) was a literary critic, diplomat, sociologist and political scientist who published books in all these fields of knowledge.
49. Benedito Nunes (1929–2011) was a Professor of Philosophy and one of the great specialists in Clarice Lispector's literature. He began publishing critical essays on her work in 1965 and some of them were collected in *O drama da linguagem: uma leitura de Clarice Lispector* (São Paulo: Ática, 1989). Affonso Romano de Sant'Anna (1937–), is a Professor of Literature, a poet, *cronista* and literary critic, and was also a friend and compadre of Clarice. He has published widely on her work and their friendship. Mário Chamie (1933–2011) was a lecturer and poet associated with the Poesia-Praxis movement, which he founded in 1961. He published several books of poetry and essays on literature. Autran Dourado (1926–2012) published short stories, essays, memoirs and important novels, in which he portrayed family life in the closed and repressive society in Minas Gerais. Silviano Santiago (1936–), is a poet, Professor, one of Brazil's most important cultural critics and essayists, and he has published many works of fiction in the form of both short stories and novels. Elias José (1936–2008), as well as writing novels, short stories, poetry and *crônicas*, is best known for his many works for children and young adults.
50. Lispector, *A hora da estrela*, p. 20; *The Hour of the Star*, p. 15.

CHAPTER 7

Afterword to
The Besieged City

Giovanni Pontiero

Introduction by Claire Williams

An internet search for *The Besieged City*, Professor Giovanni Pontiero's translation into English of Clarice Lispector's third novel *A cidade sitiada* (1948) quickly provides the curious reader with the information that it was published by Carcanet in 1995 (or 1997, or 1999). The hardback has an ISBN number and the price given on the Waterstones website is £14.95, yet it is 'currently unavailable'.[1] Multiple copies are available from Amazon and AbeBooks (usually from third-party sellers), yet, on further investigation, when one clicks through to make a purchase, it becomes clear that these are, in fact, the 2019 translation by Johnny Lorenz for New Directions and Penguin.

In *The Translator's Dialogue*, a book of essays written in tribute to Pontiero, Robyn Marsack discusses her experience of working with him as an editor on several projects and focuses particularly on their last book together, *The Besieged City*.[2] As well as providing a fascinating account of Pontiero's working process, there is a tantalizing footnote: 'Giovanni Pontiero's translation is awaiting publication'.[3]

So what happened to this Pontiero/Carcanet collaboration? I continued my search by consulting the catalogues of the UK copyright libraries, where publishers are legally obliged to deposit a copy of every book published in the country. But *The Besieged City* could not be found in the British Library, Cambridge University Library or the Taylorian Library in Oxford. Carcanet told me that the book definitely existed, but nobody had a copy they could send me. I mentioned my frustration to my friend and colleague Hilary Owen (Professor Emerita in Portuguese and Luso-African Studies at the University of Manchester and Research Fellow in the Sub-Faculty of Portuguese at Oxford), who worked with Pontiero at the University of Manchester. She vaguely remembered that he had given her a printout of a Lispector translation not long before his death (in 1996); and she promised to take a look on her bookshelves.

In June 2020, with the first UK lockdown easing and the chance of going on holiday looking like a distinct probability, Hilary sent me the printout, and I was able to see that Pontiero's translation was print-ready, complete with an Afterword dated Summer 1994. Through Hilary, I got in touch with Professor Juan Sager, Pontiero's partner and executor of his estate, to ask permission to reproduce this precious lost text in *After Clarice*. He was more than happy to grant it, but was surprised to learn that the book had never actually been published.

Now I had a copy of the manuscript, the next stage in my detective work was to try to find out why it had not come out in print. This involved consulting the Carcanet archive held by the John Rylands Library at the University of Manchester. That was easier said than done under Coronavirus restrictions. The Creative Arts Archivist, Jess Smith, kindly dug through the correspondence relating to *The Besieged City* and discovered that in 1993 and 1994 Pontiero had applied for a grant from the Brazilian Government's 'Programa de Apoio à Tradução e à Publicação de Autores Brasileiros no Exterior' [Programme of Support for the Translation and Publication of Brazilian Authors Abroad]. This funding scheme, which has been running since 1991 through the National Library Foundation (Fundação Biblioteca Nacional), has been extremely important for the promotion of Brazilian literature in translation around the world.[4] In the Carcanet archive there is a letter from the Head of the Cultural Section of the Brazilian Embassy in London, dated 13 July 1993, explaining that, regrettably, the fund was not able to support the publication of *The Besieged City*. There was no response to the 1994 application; at least, nothing appears in the archive.

This lack of funding for the same book project, two years in a row, may explain why a small 'enterprising' press (to use Pontiero's own words) like Carcanet was unable to go ahead with the book.[5] All of Pontiero's previous translations of Lispector's works for the Manchester-based publishing house — *Family Ties* (1985); *The Foreign Legion* (1986); *The Hour of the Star* (1986); *Near to the Wild Heart* (1990); and *Discovering the World* (1992) — received support from the UK Arts Council, as did his translation of Lya Luft's *The Red House* (1993, originally *Exílio*, 1988). But he also accessed funding from Brazil. On the copyright page of *Near to the Wild Heart*, a note reads: 'The publisher thanks Vitae — Apoio à Cultura, Educação e Promoção Social — and — INL — Instituta [sic] Nacional do Livro/Ministério da Cultura, Brazil, for their translation grant'.[6] By 1992, the acknowledgement has been translated: 'The publisher thanks the Vitae Foundation and the National Book Institute for their translation grant'.[7] The grant, in both cases, was an early incarnation of the 'Programa de Apoio' mentioned above. Why was it not awarded in the following year to support the publication of the translation of a lesser-known work by a canonical writer done by a prize-winning translator? It may come down to historical and economic circumstances. During this period, Brazil was recovering from high inflation and the 1992 impeachment of the president on corruption charges. It is not surprising that cuts were made to cultural initiatives, as is often the case in times of financial crises.

Giovanni Pontiero retired in 1995 and passed away in 1996. Thirty years later, *The Besieged City* is still awaiting publication. We hope this status changes, but in the meantime Adriana and I are very proud to include him among the contributors of *After Clarice* and to give readers a small taste of his last, no longer lost, translation in the Afterword which follows.

Afterword to *The Besieged City*

by Giovanni Pontiero

Clarice Lispector's third novel, *The Besieged City*, was completed in Berne, where her husband was posted to the Brazilian Embassy in 1946. The manuscript underwent numerous drafts but was finally ready for submission in May that same year. As we know from the author's correspondence, however, finding a publisher proved far from easy and it took three years of patient negotiations before the novel finally appeared. Its completion coincided with the birth of the couple's first child and, by the following year, Lispector would be celebrating her thirtieth birthday.

In retrospect, she described the drafting of *The Besieged City* as both awkward and frustrating. In her own words: 'This was the book I found most difficult to write. It demanded interpretation, something of which I am incapable'. When asked what had inspired her to write the book, she explained:

> It was the formation of a city, the formation of a human being within the city, a suburb growing, with horses. Everything so vital, and growing. And then it was no longer a suburb. And the protagonist escaped.

When the book was finally published in Brazil in 1949, the puzzled reactions of the critics caused her deep disappointment. In a chronicle which appeared many years later in the *Jornal do Brasil*, she recalled the gloom and despondency of those years in the Swiss capital:

> It was in Berne that I wrote my least popular novel, *The Besieged City*, which people sometimes grow to like on a second reading. I owe an enormous debt of gratitude to this book. The sheer effort of writing it kept me occupied and helped me to ignore the eerie silence in the streets of Berne... an open city, so why did I feel trapped and isolated? I used to go to the cinema every afternoon, no matter what film was being shown. And I can remember how I would often come out of the cinema to find that it had started snowing. As dusk fell and I walked home alone in the medieval city beneath a flurry of snowflakes, I felt worse than a beggar-woman. For I had no idea what I should beg for.

She found Switzerland 'a cemetery of sensations' and struggled to write in a constant state of apathy and despair. Those reactions undoubtedly account for the tone of the novel, and the daily trips to the cinema almost certainly influenced the fragmented nature of the book and its episodic structure.

The Besieged City focuses on the dramatic changes which transform São Geraldo, a bustling suburb in provincial Brazil in the 1920s, as seen through the eyes of the main protagonist, Lucretia Neves. Progress shapes a new reality and Lucretia rapidly grows in self-awareness as she struggles to adapt to new circumstances and surroundings: 'Everything Lucretia Neves could know about herself was outside herself: she saw'.

The destiny mapped out for Lucretia in a social environment fettered by tradition and prejudice is in conflict with her inner desires and inclinations. Her rebellious spirit challenges all restraints. She confides: 'I can feel in my flesh a law that contradicts the law of my spirit', and human relationships, whatever their nature, are seen as a potential threat to her inner freedom. Domestic life with a widowed, self-pitying mother is reduced to a tiresome game of emotional blackmail, with Lucretia stubbornly refusing to play the dutiful daughter. Friendships outside the family home are no less discouraging. Brief contact with a religious association for young women is enough to convince Lucretia that she lacks their sense of commitment and has no real interest in feminine solidarity. And, although the inevitable adolescent attachments to young men can be equally troublesome, the men of São Geraldo are 'more innocent and loyal' than the women, and somehow easier to manipulate. Tentative flirtations with Felipe, a young soldier, and Perseus, a handsome but somewhat vacuous student, bring out the best and worst in Lucretia, who searches in vain for 'a point of neutrality' in these relationships. Like the female protagonists in Lispector's two earlier novels, Lucretia would rather die than surrender her freedom, and there is no more knowing writer than Lispector when it comes to showing how sexuality can be exploited to mask one's deepest insecurities. The question of emotional commitment is still unresolved when Lucretia finally marries Mateus, an affluent businessman who can offer her a new life and social status in a more sophisticated milieu. The farcical clichés of this new identity are not lost on Lucretia and the novelty of married life with its bourgeois routine soon wears thin. The husband–wife relationship is summed up with naked contempt: 'He was masculine and servile. Servile without humiliation, like a gladiator on hire. And she, being a woman, served him'. It takes a short-lived affair with the family doctor — who is married — to give her some foretaste of 'sweet evil', but she is finally persuaded that: 'Love always brings a desire to hate and hate a desire to love'. Things, places, people, are simply unable to fill the void and an increasingly disenchanted Lucretia is beginning to feel nostalgic about the backward suburb of her childhood when the unexpected death of her husband leaves her free at last to return to São Geraldo. But the place has changed beyond recognition and soon she is preparing to escape once more. As she makes her final exit, she is still asking herself what she has learnt from life, her determination to defy fate much chastened.

As with so many of Lispector's women characters, Lucretia is emotionally fragile, her moods fluctuating between wrath and humility, between compassion and cruelty. Her perceptions of the world around her shift back and forth between things real and imagined, between moments of acute awareness and alienating somnolence. The instrument of her own troubled existence, she can be perversely obsessive in her tenacious pursuit of that elusive thing vaguely defined as 'happiness', and there is a savage irony in her inner thoughts as she moves through a world of unpredictable objects and disturbing presences. A mistress of disguise, she has mastered various roles: wayward adolescent, unresponsive daughter, fawning bride, rebellious spouse, femme fatale, only to find all of these stereotyped roles ultimately futile. Timid and aggressive in turn, she discovers she has two faces: 'One that is almost pretty, one that is almost ugly'. Like her native São Geraldo, she, too, has progressed and changed, but is ever restless and dissatisfied, and anxious to move on and confront some new challenge before familiarity and stagnation can begin their destructive process. She finally concedes that it has been much easier to live her story than actually narrate it.

In retrospect, *The Besieged City* remains one of Lispector's most dense and hermetic novels. As a location, São Geraldo lies somewhere between desert and civilization, a setting both real and oneiric with its echoes of mythology (even in the characters' names), with its majestic horses, 'noble, proud and rebellious', its dark omens, reflecting mirrors, and chiaroscuro effects created by a continuous interplay of revelation and concealment.

Building on the intuitive approach to fiction she pursued in her first novel, *Near to the Wild Heart*, Lispector stretches her 'knowing sensibility' even further in *The Besieged City*. By making Lucretia both protagonist and spectator, she shows how a perceptive mind can absorb, transform and wholly personalize the external world. This is the slender thread the author would have us pursue in order to grasp the book's meaning. In an open letter to the critics she refuted any suggestion of mystifying her readers and clarified her objectives:

> So what was I trying to express through Lucretia — this woman who is without the weapons of intelligence yet who aspires to that kind of spiritual integrity one associates with a horse which does not **communicate** what it sees, which has no **verbal or mental** vision of things, which feels no need to complete an impression by expressing it — the horse which is capable of this miracle whereby the impression is **total** and so **real** that any impression on the horse's part is already expression? I thought I had made it abundantly clear that Lucretia Neves' real story was independent of her personal details. The struggle to achieve reality — that is the most important thing about this character who tries to adhere to what exists by means of a total vision of things.

I also tried to show how that vision — that way of seeing or point of view — can change reality even while creating it.

Reality, as observed by Lucretia, is in a state of constant transformation. Anxious to assert her individuality and dominate external reality by spiritual means, she establishes subtle relationships between seeing, being and thinking: between the inherent nature of humans, animals, and things — interdependent and often interchangeable. These deeper philosophical questions weaving in and out of the narrative find the author at her most enigmatic and ambivalent. Lucretia lives her life in a state of constant vigilance; in avid pursuit of the 'whole fruit' yet fearful that it might be better 'not to understand', and the frequent aphorisms in the novel convey similar ambiguities, alerting the reader to the fact that: 'What one is unable to think, one sees', or that: 'To lose oneself is also a path'.

Intrigued by the experimental nature of Lispector's prose with its endless pursuit of 'the instantaneous and ever elusive moments of tangible existence', critics somehow misrepresented her objectives and she tried to put the record straight. With admirable clarity and an unmistakable note of irritation, she explained:

> Critics tend to go on, or at least they used to, about my **vocabulary** and **syntax** as if these were purely verbal. Yet at no point in *The Besieged City* do I play with words... what I was striving for — and have achieved, damn it — was to communicate through words and not simply to invent phrases for their

own sake. To hear critics defining the painful process of matching words to emotions as 'purely verbal' fills me with horror. And it is further proof of the great divide between what one gives and what one receives.

'Matching words to emotions' and 'with invisible stitching', as she once described the process, neatly sums up one of her greatest achievements in this novel, where each person, animal and thing responds to its own secret and fiercely individual rhythm.

Manchester, Summer 1994

Notes to Chapter 7

1. <https://www.waterstones.com/book/the-besieged-city/clarice-lispector/giovanni-pontiero/9781857540611> [accessed 20 August 2021].
2. Pilar Orero and Juan Sager, eds, *The Translator's Dialogue: Giovanni Pontiero* (Amsterdam: John Benjamins, 1997).
3. Robyn Marsack, 'Discovering the Word', in Orero and Sager, eds, *The Translator's Dialogue*, pp. 99–106 (p. 100). Confusingly, the translation is the last one listed in the Bibliography, as a 1997 Carcanet publication; ibid., p. 179.
4. See <https://www.bn.gov.br/explore/programas-de-fomento/programa-apoio-traducao-publicacao-autores> [accessed 20 August 2021]. The history of the Programa is described in Lilia Feres Baranski and Valéria Brisolara, 'A literatura brasileira em tradução: o caso do Programa de Apoio à Tradução e à Publicação de Autores Brasileiros no Exterior', *Revista da Anpoll*, 1. 44 (2018), 331–45, <https://revistadaanpoll.emnuvens.com.br/revista/article/view/1157/956> [accessed 7 September 2021].
5. The term is Pontiero's: see Patrícia Bins, 'Interview with Giovanni Pontiero', in Orero and Sager, pp. 165–72, (p. 169).
6. Clarice Lispector, *Near to the Wild Heart*, trans. by Giovanni Pontiero (Manchester: Carcanet, 1990), n.pag.
7. Clarice Lispector, *Discovering the World*, trans. by Giovanni Pontiero (Manchester: Carcanet, 1992), n.pag.

PART III

Theorizing Clarice

CHAPTER 8

'Prender um inefável':
Affect in Clarice's Fictions

Marta Peixoto

Gosto de intensidades. [I like intensities]
— *Água viva*

Eu vivo em êxtases provisórios.
[I live in provisional ecstasies]
— *Um sopro de vida* [*A Breath of Life*][1]

Clarice's prolific and varied *oeuvre* ranges, as we know, from the disarmingly straightforward conversational style of some of her newspaper columns, her Sunday chats ('conversinhas de domingo'), to the ambitious philosophical reflections in *A paixão segundo G.H.* [*The Passion According to G.H.*], and have been the object of equally diverse critical approaches.[2] This essay, drawing on affect theory, will reflect on certain recurring moments in her work where characters, encountering an external object or creature or person, abandon their everyday selves through no conscious choice of their own, and are gripped by sensations and mental processes they struggle to put into words. These moments, termed epiphanies by critics of her work, have, however, a markedly inconclusive quality.[3] If an epiphany consists of a revelation or sudden insight, Clarice's are peculiar, in that her characters often remain in the dark about what the epiphany actually reveals to them, despite the intense and disorienting impact of the experience. Their too-ample, partly unconscious and inaccessible responses may remain mysterious. No lasting understanding results from those states of altered consciousness. The characters more or less settle back into their normal lives or take off in directions that seem unrelated to what they've just undergone. The challenge Clarice often seeks out is to render the impact on her characters, wordless and evanescent, with her instrument of choice or necessity, words. These signature moments can profitably be considered in light of affect theory. From this ample and complex theoretical field that has touched many disciplines and has roots in neuroscience and philosophy (Spinoza, Bergson, Deleuze), one can identify some concepts that offer useful resonances with Clarice's writing, illuminating aspects of her literary endeavour.

The term affect, in the sense widely used in affect theory, relies on but also departs from its two primary dictionary meanings: 'a feeling or emotion as distinguished from cognition, thought, or action', and 'a strong feeling having active consequences' (American Heritage College Dictionary)'. As non-cognitive states or processes, affects, while affecting the body, are not available to the conscious mind in the way feelings or emotions are commonly thought to be. Ruth Leys, in her useful overview and critique of affect theory, maintains along with other scholars that 'affects must be viewed as independent of, and in an important sense prior to ideology, meanings, reasons, and belief — because they are non-signifying autonomic processes that take place below the threshold of conscious awareness and meaning'.[4] For Brian Massumi, the influential affect theorist, affects encompass a plurality of latent feelings, registered by the body but outside consciousness; as they move from this virtual sphere into consciousness they are drastically reduced to become a recognizable emotion or to generate an action. As Massumi states, 'the virtual is a cresting in a liminal realm of emergence, where half-actualized actions and expressions arise like waves on a sea to which most no sooner return.'[5] Most of these proto-actions or proto-sensations are never enacted, never emerge into consciousness; they remain virtualities, with their unrealized potential for feeling or action.

It is important to emphasize, as do Massumi and other theorists, the difference between affect and emotion. Emotion, for Massumi, emerges and becomes distinguished from these waves of the virtual. As he maintains, '[e]motion is a qualified intensity, the conventional, consensual point of insertion of intensity into semantically and semiotically formed progressions, into narrativizable action-reaction circuits, into function and meaning. It is intensity owned and recognized.'[6] So affects, which Massumi uses as a synonym for intensity, can't be qualified, recognized, put into words. For Eric Shouse '[a]ffect is the body's way of preparing itself for action in a given circumstance by adding a quantitative dimension of intensity to the quality of an experience. The body has a grammar of its own that cannot be fully captured in language [...]'.[7] Affects are intensities that have no name and can't have a name; when one tries to name them, something always escapes. But an indistinct sensation of this escape remains, along with the perception or emotion that proved dominant and that limits, reduces or transforms affect, making a portion of it recognizable. Affect is something that persists without capture, without actualization, that remains always open, so that Massumi characterizes it as 'autonomous to the degree to which it escapes confinement in the particular body whose vitality, or potential for interaction, it is.'[8]

These formulations of affect theory resonate with crucial moments of Clarice's texts, so often focused on the grammar of the body, and riveted by that which escapes cognition and capture by words. There is always a difference, which Clarice underlines, between the sense the narrator makes of their experiences (usually with more or less subtle interventions in their free indirect discourse) and what the characters themselves understand. They sometimes don't get far in the process of transforming affect into recognizable and motivated emotions, or they might register their wordless bodily intensity as rapidly shifting, incompatible emotions. Several well-known stories — such as 'Devaneio e embriaguez de uma rapariga'

[Daydreams and Drunkenness of a Young Lady], 'Amor' [Love], 'A imitação da rosa' [The Imitation of the Rose], from *Laços de família* [*Family Ties*]; 'A legião estrangeira' [The Foreign Legion] and 'Os desastres de Sofia' [The Disasters of Sofia] from *A legião estrangeira*) — could provide examples of such characters; they occur in her novels as well.[9] But in what follows I will consider this affective process in two texts from *A legião estrangeira*: 'Desenhando um menino' [Drawing a Boy] — a title Clarice later changed to 'Menino a bico de pena' [Boy in Pen and Ink] — and 'A Mensagem' [The Message].

In these stories, the protagonists, an infant and two adolescents, are in transition in their grasp of language: the boy just learning to speak and the youths, ambitious writers-to-be, coming to an expanded realization of all that words can and cannot express. In both stories it's the conversion of nameless sensations into recognizable verbal formulations, and therefore emotions, that matters. The infant in 'Menino a bico de pena' struggles to enter a community made possible by speech, shaped by cause and effect, the interplay of presence and absence of the objects named, and the effective power of words. His consciousness and unconsciousness of himself Lispector terms 'de um real que tenho de chamar de vegetativo para poder entender' [of a reality that I must call vegetative to understand].[10] Understanding the sensations and affects of this being who does not know himself is the impossible objective that generates the text.

> Como conhecer jamais o menino? Para conhecê-lo tenho que esperar que ele se deteriore, e só então ele estará ao meu alcance. Lá está ele, um ponto no infinito. Ninguém conhecerá o hoje dele. Nem ele próprio. Quanto a mim, olho e é inútil. Não consigo entender coisa apenas atual, totalmente atual.
>
> [How can you ever know a little boy? To know him I have to wait until he deteriorates, and only then will he be within reach. There he is, a dot in the infinite. No one will ever know his today. Not even he himself. As for me, I look, and it's no use: I can't manage to understand something that's solely in the present, completely in the present.][11]

The infant exists in an 'atualidade absoluta' [absolute present] that eludes capture in words and even in a graphic instrument of the most delicate and subtle precision: 'Não sei como desenhar o menino. Sei que é impossível desenhá-lo a carvão, pois até bico de pena mancha o papel para além da finíssima linha de extrema atualidade em que ele vive' [I don't know how to sketch the boy. I know it's impossible to sketch him in charcoal, for even pen and ink bleed on the paper beyond the incredibly fine line of extreme presentness in which he lives].[12] Yet the boy himself focuses on learning to capture and transform his intensities into words, 'prender um inefável' [pin down something ineffable].[13] And he begins to realize that words can bring about presence but can also mark an absence, as they recall but don't necessarily summon the desired object. The violent effort to create presence out of absence visits him even 'em pesadelo súbito' [a sudden nightmare]: 'uma das palavras que ele aprendeu lhe ocorre: ele estremece violentamente, abre os olhos. E para o seu terror, vê apenas isso: o vazio quente e claro do ar, sem mãe' [one of the words he's learned occurs to him: he shudders violently, opens his eyes. And in terror sees only this: the hot, bright emptiness of the air, without his mother].[14] It is perhaps not surprising that Clarice frames the efforts of the infant as a betrayal of the ample wordless realm he will forever leave behind as his primary mode of existence, a necessary though tainted bargain he must make to enter human society of verbal communication: 'sua segurança é saber que tem um mundo para trair e vender, e que o venderá' [his security is knowing he has a world to betray and sell out, and that he will sell it].[15] He abdicates from a mode of existence that nevertheless persists as an impossible yearning in the later narratives, such as *Água viva* where the protagonist seeks to capture o 'instante-já' [instant-now]: 'captar o presente, que pela sua própria natureza me é interdito, o presente me foge, a atualidade me escapa, a atualidade sou eu, sempre no já' [to capture the present, forbidden to me by its very nature: the present slips away and the instant too, the instant is me, forever in the now].[16]

'A Mensagem' offers a different dramatization of the incommensurability of words and intense bodily sensations, which is to say, the impossibility of capturing all of conscious and unconscious experience in words. The two protagonists, male and female adolescents, begin to suspect that words are inadequate to convey the full scope of their complex thoughts, inner processes and sensations. The project of becoming writers energizes their somewhat hostile friendship, devoid of sexual desire and shot through with competition and doubts they both harbour about whether or not a woman might be capable of serious intellectual adventures. Their friendship arose when they discovered that both suffered from 'angústia', [anguish] which they deem a marker of a special sensibility. They also share the certainty that words, in their everyday usage, are insufficient, deceptive. The visual confrontation with an object that crystalizes, transforms and eventually ends their friendship, leaves them mute and astounded. As they wander aimlessly in a residential neighbourhood, they find themselves suddenly standing on a narrow sidewalk between the buses that go rushing by and a large house — massive, old, ugly — set close to the sidewalk. 'Se recuassem seriam atingidos pelos ônibus, se avançassem esbarrariam na monstruosa casa. Tinham sido capturados. [...] A casa era angústia e calma. Como palavra nenhuma o fora' [If they backed away they'd be hit by the buses, if they stepped forward, they'd hit the monstrous house. They'd been captured [...] The house was anguish and calm. As no word had ever been].[17]

What exactly happens to leave them mute and stopped in their tracks? The narrator interprets the impact that renders them speechless with an understanding that far surpasses that of the characters. As Claire Williams argues in her insightful analysis, the story 'presents the moment when the adolescent man and woman suddenly become conscious of the weight of their gender identity'.[18] The narrator frames with irony the characters' conventional notions of what is appropriately masculine and feminine, as the young woman ends up feeling diminished while the young man becomes triumphantly aware of his masculine strength. Yet the association between the house, gender identity and the word 'angústia' remains mysterious. Clarice underlines the wordless confusion that is their first reaction to the visual impact of the old house, the grammar of the body that cannot be fully captured in words. Readings, including those of the narrator, seek to tie loose threads into coherent interpretations, but Clarice's texts often point to their less than complete adequacy.

The impact of the house at first deprives the characters of speech:

> A moça olhava adormecida. Quanto ao rapaz, seu sétimo sentido enganchara-se na parte mais interior da construção e ele sentia na ponta do fio um mínimo estremecimento de resposta. Mal se movia, com medo de espantar a própria atenção. A moça ancorara-se no espanto, com medo de sair deste para o terror de uma descoberta. Mal falassem, e a casa desabaria.
>
> [The girl looked on sleepily. As for the boy, his seventh sense snagged on the building's innermost part and he felt the slightest tug of a response at the end of the line. He barely moved, fearful of frightening off his own watchfulness. The girl had become anchored in her alarm, afraid to emerge from it into the terror of a discovery. At their slightest word, the house would collapse.][19]

The momentary trance they undergo occludes normal perception and impedes cognition:

> A moça desviou subitamente o rosto com uma espécie de grunhido. Quanto ao rapaz, ele rapidamente perdia pé na vaguidão como se fosse ficando sem um pensamento. [...] Verdes e nauseados, eles não saberiam exprimir. A casa simbolizava alguma coisa que eles jamais poderiam alcançar, mesmo com toda uma vida de procura de expressão.
>
> [The girl suddenly averted her face with a kind of grunt. As for the boy, he quickly lost his footing in the vagueness as if mired without a thought. [...] Green and nauseated, they didn't know how to express. The house symbolized some thing they could never attain, even after a lifetime spent seeking expression.][20]

The narrator, who doesn't lose the power of words, seeks to make them adequate to the character's inner processes by paradoxes, hyperboles and at times extravagant, even macabre, metaphors that suggest the house's impact. In the indeterminacy of free indirect discourse, however, with its characteristic back and forth movements between the narrator's complete identification with the character's sensations and thoughts, and a pulling back for evaluation from an external perspective, it can remain unclear whether the metaphors are the characters' or the narrator's: 'aquela catedral do medo solidificado' [that cathedral of solidified fear] with 'aquele ar de estrangulamento, aquele silêncio de enforcado tranquilo' [that strangled look, the silence of a tranquil hanged corpse], 'a nua angústia' [naked anguish], 'a casa sem olhos com a potência de um cego' [the eyeless house, with the power of a blind man].[21]

The narrator does not elucidate completely the reason for the sudden shock that the old house inflicts upon the adolescents. It perhaps has something to do with the weight of the past, including traditional notions of gender identity, perceived as limit and obstacle to the dream they each have of becoming writers (it is not irrelevant that the house is located near a cemetery), or the ready-made world, already encoded, that distorts deceptive words such as poetry, 'essa palavra constrangedora' [that embarrassing word], 'poesia era a palavra dos mais velhos' [poetry was the word older people used].²² In any case, the adolescents come out of the trance not freer from the past but more stuck in the gender roles that their intellectual and platonic friendship had transgressed. As the young man feels himself to be more of a man than ever, he looks at the young woman with traditional male lasciviousness and disdain, but also, strangely, as disparagingly animal-like, 'como um macaco de saia curta' [like a monkey in a short skirt], as he sees her climb onto the bus that will take her home.²³ The young woman, in turn, feels diminished by her female condition, resenting the awkwardness of just at that moment having breasts and a necklace. In her own silent estimation, with which the young man silently concurs, 'ela não era nada' [she was nothing].²⁴ And the friendship, instead of gaining strength through the shared, mysterious and intense experience, ends on an uncertain note, when the young man feels deceived by the young woman, thinking it would be best to have a male and loyal friend. But as though to confound any neat interpretation the reader might have been constructing and to point back to the ample realm of unconscious and contradictory affects, Clarice ends the story by having the young man say to himself, enigmatically: 'Mamãe' [Mama].²⁵

What the frightened young man asks himself: 'Que é! Mas afinal que é que está me acontecendo?' [What! but what after all is happening to me?], is indeed a question that resonates in the dénouement of many of Clarice's texts.²⁶ Characters often express what they don't understand by physical gestures of distress. The young woman in 'Preciosidade' [Preciousness] in *Laços de família* becomes paralyzed and mute after an incident of being sexually touched by strangers on the street. She interrupts her brisk walk and leans against a wall until dawn. The girls in the stories 'Mistério em São Cristóvão' [Mystery in São Cristóvão] (*Laços de família*) and 'Os desastres de Sofia' (*A legião estrangeira*), as well as G.H. in the apex of her passion, are overtaken by fits of vomiting. Often, characters that undergo intense crises pointedly fail to reach new and lasting levels of self-understanding. They may, as in 'A Mensagem', attain a new and not necessarily positive self-awareness that never reveals its connection to their intense experience. Or they simply return after their crises to their preceding situations, or yet take off in new directions, without reaching a completely satisfactory interpretation of the relationship between crisis and consequence. Ana, in the final words of 'Amor' in *Laços de família*, distances herself from her momentous experience: '[a]ntes de se deitar, como se apagasse uma vela soprou a pequena flama do dia' [before going to bed, as if putting out a candle, she blew out the little flame of the day].²⁷ At the end of 'A legião estrangeira', Lispector dispatches Ofélia back to a desiccated world of appearances and repression, from which the wrenching experience of desiring the little chick had momentarily freed her: 'Ofélia é que não voltou: cresceu. Foi ser a princesa hindu por quem no deserto a sua tribo esperava' [Ofélia is the one who didn't return: she grew up. She went off to become the Hindu princess her tribe awaited in the desert].²⁸ One may well conclude that what interests Lispector is not so much the results but the unfolding of the intense experience whereby affects become reduced to emotions that can be named, without ever denying all that escapes in the process. Her texts famously resist interpretation, even the interpretations that the narrator provides, by suggesting — and perhaps this is the point — that the affect of the characters, overly abundant, cannot be completely grasped by their consciousness or accommodated by the narrator into the domain of words. The leftovers or residues that can't be completely assimilated or interpreted make Clarice's texts always enigmatic and provocative, calling out for renewed efforts of interpretation.

Clarice's narrators often note that they must rely on an ultimately inadequate medium for the task at hand. Words may be slippery, uncontrollable:

> Não, talvez não seja isso. As palavras me antecedem e ultrapassam, elas me tentam e me modificam, e se não tomo cuidado será tarde demais: as coisas serão ditas sem eu as ter dito.
>
> [No, maybe that wasn't it. Words precede and surpass me, they tempt and alter me, and if I am not careful it will be too late: things will be said without my having said them.][29]

Or they may be likened metaphorically to stones, dense, obdurate, incommensurable to the sensations they seek to express: 'As palavras nada tem a ver com sensações. As palavras são pedras duras e sensações delicadíssimas, fugazes, extremas' [Words have nothing to do with sensations. Words are hard stones and sensations are ever so delicate, fleeting, extreme].[30]

Clarice may have sensed early on that pursuing inexpressible sensations with words would be a direction she would take in her literary work. In a 1973 chronicle, she describes as a kind of epiphany the impact and shock of identification she felt when she first read Katherine Mansfield. At age fifteen, with the first money she earned for herself, she went into a bookstore to buy a book and browsed for a while:

> [D]e repente, um dos livros que abri, continha frases tão diferentes que fiquei lendo, presa, ali mesmo. Emocionada, eu pensava: mas esse livro sou eu! E, contendo um estremecimento de profunda emoção, comprei-o.
>
> [Until I opened a book which contained phrases so different from anything I had ever read before that I remained there, my eyes glued to the page. In my excitement I thought to myself: but this book *is me*! And struggling to control my emotions, I bought it.][31]

Only later would she find out that the author was the renowned Katherine Mansfield. Teresa Montero points out that this important literary encounter would likely have occurred later, as the Portuguese translation of the collection *Bliss* (*Felicidade*) came out in 1940, when Clarice was already twenty.[32] While Clarice doesn't specify in what way Mansfield's sentences struck her as 'tão diferentes' [so different] it is plausible to imagine that they describe moments such as the one we find in the story 'Bliss', where the protagonist Bertha is suddenly invaded by a powerful, unmotivated feeling that seems excessive, almost overwhelming, unconnected to her daily life.

> What can you do if you are thirty, and, turning the corner of your own street, you are overcome, suddenly, by a feeling of bliss — absolute bliss! — as though you'd suddenly swallowed a bright piece of that late afternoon sun and it burned in your bosom, sending out a little shower of sparks into every particle, into every finger and toe?[33]

Although Bertha unmistakably identifies her surge of emotion as 'bliss', the story turns on her efforts to understand its origin, as it recurs throughout the day, not unlike what Clarice sums up in *Um sopro de vida* as 'Vivo em êxtases provisórios' [I live in provisional ecstasies].[34] Bertha realizes that her life has reached a moment of perfect plenitude, then finds, in another surge of bliss, an equivalent plenitude in a lovely pear tree in her back yard: 'a tall, slender pear tree in fullest, richest bloom; it stood perfect, as though becalmed against the jade-green sky. Bertha couldn't help feeling, even from this distance, that it had not a single bud or a faded petal.'[35] Later in the evening, she shares what she feels as a moment of joyful understanding with a new woman friend, as they both gaze together at the pear tree. But all this perfection, which includes the certainty that she and her husband 'were as much in love as ever', comes crumbling down when she catches her husband and her new friend engaged in a passionate kiss.[36] This story, cruel to its protagonist as Clarice's often are, could have been the one that attracted her attention. In addition to the deceptive symbol of the pear tree (deceptive in a way similar to the perfect roses that lure Laura back into another bout of psychosis in a story Clarice wrote much later, 'A imitação da rosa'), it might have been the significance given to surges of seemingly unmotivated emotions that caught her eye.[37]

Often in Clarice's fictions, when characters become speechless, the writer struggles, and displays herself struggling, to register the turbulent and often failed efforts towards understanding and cognitive grasp. In 'Menino a bico de pena' and 'A mensagem', the 'extrema atualidade' [extreme presentness] of the boy in a lived reality not yet shaped by words, unknowable to himself and to the writer, or the reasons for the vertiginous and unfathomable shock the two adolescents undergo while facing the old house, the characters can't fully understand and Clarice doesn't or can't explain (a move no doubt advantageous to the literary quality of her texts). The reader, puzzled and provoked, may echo the young man when he asks: 'Que é! Mas afinal que é que está me acontecendo?' [What! but what after all is happening to me?].[38] What was **that** all about?

The intention of making her text suggest what has no name, what refuses to be captured in words, was, for Clarice, the object of repeated reflection. In *Água viva* and later, such reflections gain in urgency, and the characters are often shown considering the limit of what language can name, even while living through an experience they can't put into words. Always alert to the insufficiencies of language, and in this way in tune with other writers of the nineteenth and twentieth centuries, such as Stéphane Mallarmé, Paul Valéry, Carlos Drummond de Andrade and João Cabral de Melo Neto, among others, who made of the impasses of writing the motive for writing, Clarice, in her own voice and in those of her characters, accepts that this fallible and dubious instrument is also indispensable and she proposes that success may emerge from these very failures. 'Eu tenho na medida que designo' [I have to the extent I designate], G.H. writes:

> [...] e este é o esplendor de se ter uma linguagem. Mas eu tenho muito mais à medida que não consigo designar. [...] O indizível só me poderá ser dado através do fracasso da minha linguagem. Só quando falha a construção é que obtenho o que ela não conseguiu.

> [...and this is the splendor of having a language. But I have much more to the extent I cannot designate. [...] The unsayable can only be given to me through the failure of my language. Only when the construction fails, can I obtain what it could not achieve.]³⁹

This miracle of transforming failure into success is made explicit as such in the brief chronicle 'A pesca milagrosa' [Miraculous Fishing] in which a word is useful as bait for that which lies beyond words. Here is the complete, well-known, chronicle:

> Então escrever é o modo de quem tem a palavra como isca: a palavra pescando o que não é palavra. Quando essa não palavra morde a isca, alguma coisa se escreveu. Mas aí cessa a analogia: a não palavra, ao morder a isca, incorporou-a. O que salva, então, é ler distraidamente.
>
> [To write, therefore, is the way in which someone uses the word as bait: the word fishes for something that is not a word. When this non-word takes the bait, something has been written. Once what lies between the lines has been caught, the word can be discarded with a sense of relief. But here the analogy ends: the non-word, upon taking the bait, has assimilated it. Salvation, then, lies in [reading] *without thinking*.]⁴⁰

It is worth noting that what occurs outside of consciousness and can't be expressed in words determines not only writing but the way Clarice proposes that her texts be read. 'O que salva então é ler distraidamente' [Salvation, then, lies in reading *without thinking*]. In the moment of reading what saves us — saves, Clarice says, provocatively, emphatically — is what we assimilate while distracted and is more than what we consciously apprehend.

As one of the remarkable accomplishments of her long writing career, Clarice brought to Brazilian literature, with persistence and luminous intensity, something that resonates with certain formulations of affect theory: the foregrounding of non-conscious processes in the experience of her characters, in her own writing methods and even in designating what lies beyond consciousness as an essential component of the act of reading. Clarice seeks out pre-verbal psychic states that can't be reduced to words, insisting, however, as is inevitable, on suggesting them in the words of her texts. Suggesting but not explaining, for what often matters most are the moments of unknowable, inapprehensible intensities, which escape capture and definitions.

Works Cited

CESAR, ANA CRISTINA, 'O conto *Bliss* anotado', in *Escritos da Inglaterra* (São Paulo: Brasiliense, 1988), pp. 9–84

GOTLIB, NÁDIA BATTELLA, *Clarice: uma vida que se conta*, 6th edn (São Paulo: Edusp, 2009)

FERREIRA, TERESA CRISTINA MONTERO, *Eu sou uma pergunta: uma biografia de Clarice Lispector* (Rio de Janeiro: Rocco, 1999)

LEYS, RUTH, 'The Turn to Affect: A Critique', *Critical Inquiry*, 37.3 (Spring, 2011), 434–72

LISPECTOR, CLARICE, *Laços de família*, 2nd edn (Rio de Janeiro: Francisco Alves, 1961)

—— *A legião estrangeira* (Rio de Janeiro: Editora do Autor, 1964)

—— *A paixão segundo G.H.*, 3rd edn (Rio de Janeiro: Sabiá, 1972); *The Passion According to G.H.*, trans. by Idra Novey (London: Penguin, 2012)

—— *Visão do esplendor: impressões leves* (Rio de Janeiro: Francisco Alves, 1975)

—— *Um sopro de vida* (Rio de Janeiro: Nova Fronteira, 1978); *A Breath of Life*, trans. by Johnny Lorenz (London: Penguin, 2012)
—— *Água viva*, 5th edn (Rio de Janeiro: Nova Fronteira, 1980); *Água viva*, trans. by Stefan Tobler (London: Penguin, 2012)
—— *A Descoberta do Mundo* (Rio de Janeiro: Nova Fronteira, 1984); *Discovering the World*, trans. by Giovanni Pontiero (Manchester: Carcanet, 1992)
—— *The Complete Stories*, trans. by by Katrina Dodson (London: Penguin, 2015)
MASSUMI, BRIAN, 'The Autonomy of Affect', *Cultural Critique*, 31 (1995), 83–109
NUNES, BENEDITO, *Leitura de Clarice Lispector* (São Paulo: Quíron, 1973)
SÁ, OLGA DE, 'O conceito e o procedimento da epifania', in *A escritura de Clarice Lispector* (Petrópolis: Vozes, 1974), pp. 129–65
SANTA'ANNA, AFFONSO ROMANO DE, 'Laços de família e Legião estrangeira', in *Análise estrutural de romances brasileiros* (Petrópolis: Vozes, 1973), pp. 180–212
SHOUSE, ERIC, 'Feeling, Emotion, Affect', *M/C Journal*, 8.6 (December 2005), <http://journal.media-culture.org.au/0512/03-shouse.php> [accessed 19 October 2019]
WILLIAMS, CLAIRE, *The Encounter Between Opposites in the Works of Clarice Lispector* (Bristol: HiPLAM, 2006)

Notes to Chapter 8

1. Clarice Lispector, *Água viva*, 5th edn (Rio de Janeiro: Nova Fronteira, 1980), p. 62; *Água viva*, trans. by Stefan Tobler (London: Penguin, 2012), p. 54; Clarice Lispector, *Um sopro de vida* (Rio de Janeiro: Nova Fronteira, 1978), p. 170; *A Breath of Life*, trans. by Johnny Lorenz (London: Penguin, 2012), p. 140.
2. Lispector, *A paixão segundo G.H.*, 3rd edn (Rio de Janeiro: Sabiá, 1972); *The Passion According to G.H.*, trans. by Idra Novey (London: Penguin, 2012).
3. From the early critical analyses by Affonso Romano de Santa'Anna, 'Laços de família e Legião estrangeira', in *Análise estrutural de romances brasileiros* (Petrópolis: Vozes, 1973), pp. 180–212 and Benedito Nunes, *Leitura de Clarice Lispector* (São Paulo: Quíron, 1973) to Olga de Sá's detailed and probing discussion 'O conceito e o procedimento da epifania', in *A escritura de Clarice Lispector* (Petrópolis: Vozes, 1974), pp. 129–65, and to Claire Williams's book-length study of 'the interaction of the self with the Other in an epiphanic encounter between opposites', *The Encounter Between Opposites in the Works of Clarice Lispector* (Bristol: HiPLAM, 2006), p. xvi, critics have singled out these epiphanies as crucial to Clarice's literary endeavour.
4. Ruth Leys, 'The Turn to Affect: A Critique', *Critical Inquiry*, 37.3 (Spring 2011), 434–72 (p. 437).
5. Brian Massumi, 'The Autonomy of Affect', *Cultural Critique*, 31 (1995), 83–109 (p. 92).
6. Ibid., p. 88.
7. Eric Shouse, 'Feeling, Emotion, Affect', *M/C Journal*, 8.6 (December 2005), <http://journal.media-culture.org.au/0512/03-shouse.php <accessed 19 October 2019>
8. Massumi, p. 96.
9. Clarice Lispector, *Laços de família*, 2nd edn (Rio de Janeiro: Francisco Alves, 1961) and *A legião estrangeira* (Rio de Janeiro: Editora do Autor, 1964).
10. Lispector, *A legião estrangeira*, p. 206; Lispector, *The Complete Stories*, trans. by Katrina Dodson (London: Penguin, 2015), pp. 397–400 (p. 397).
11. Lispector, *A legião estrangeira*, p. 206; *The Complete Stories*, p. 397.
12. Ibid; ibid.
13. Lispector, *A legião estrangeira*, p. 208; *The Complete Stories*, p. 399.
14. Ibid; ibid.
15. Lispector, *A legião estrangeira*, p. 209; my translation.
16. Lispector, *Água viva*, pp. 9–10; my translation.
17. Lispector, *A legião estrangeira*, p. 43; *The Complete Stories*, p. 270.
18. Williams, *The Encounter Between Opposites*, p. 22.

19. Lispector, *A legião estrangeira*, p. 44; *The Complete Stories*, p. 271.
20. Ibid., p. 45; ibid., p. 272.
21. Ibid., pp. 43–44; ibid., pp. 270, 271.
22. Ibid., pp. 43–44; ibid., pp. 266.
23. Ibid., pp. 48; ibid., p. 275.
24. Ibid., p. 47; ibid., p. 274.
25. Ibid., p. 50; ibid., p. 276.
26. Ibid., p. 50; ibid., p. 276.
27. Lispector, *Laços de família*, p. 33; *The Complete Stories*, p. 131.
28. Lispector, *A legião estrangeira*, p. 124; *The Complete Stories*, p. 336.
29. Ibid., pp. 10–11; ibid., p. 236.
30. Lispector, 'Brasília', in *Visão do esplendor: impressões leves*' (Rio de Janeiro: Francisco Alves, 1975), p. 27; *The Complete Stories*, p. 596.
31. Lispector, 'O primeiro livro de cada uma de minhas vidas', in *A descoberta do mundo* (Rio de Janeiro: Nova Fronteira, 1984), pp. 722–23; 'The First Book of Each of My Lives', in *Discovering the World*, trans. by Giovanni Pontiero (Manchester: Carcanet, 1992), pp. 598–99 (p. 599).
32. Teresa Montero, *Eu sou uma pergunta: uma biografia de Clarice Lispector* (Rio de Janeiro: Rocco, 1999), p. 75, note 1. The translation of Katherine Mansfield's *Bliss* would have been *Felicidade*, trans. by Érico Veríssimo (Porto Alegre: Livraria do Globo, 1940).
33. Katherine Mansfield, 'Bliss', in Ana Cristina Cesar, 'O conto *Bliss* anotado', in *Escritos da Inglaterra* (São Paulo: Brasiliense, 1988), pp. 9–84 (p. 23).
34. Lispector, *Um sopro de vida*, p. 170; *A Breath of Life*, p. 140.
35. Mansfield, 'Bliss', p. 31.
36. Ibid., p. 32.
37. See Nádia Battella Gotlib, *Clarice: uma vida que se conta*, 6th edn (São Paulo: Edusp, 2009), pp. 170–74. Gotlib compares 'Bliss' to 'Amor' in her perceptive discussion of Mansfield's importance to Clarice, especially in relation to 'a flagrância do êxtase' [the capturing of ecstasy] which she links to feminine experiences in the fiction of both writers.
38. Lispector, *A legião estrangeira*, p. 50; *The Complete Stories*, p. 268.
39. Lispector, *A paixão segundo G.H.*, p. 213; *The Passion According to G.H.*, p. 186.
40. Lispector, *A legião estrangeira*, p. 143; *Discovering the World*, pp. 508–09. Pontiero translates it as 'writing' without thinking, rather than reading. My emphasis.

CHAPTER 9

'My Error Is My Mirror':
Clarice Lispector's
Jewish Rhetoric of Mistakes

Yael Segalovitz

> [The epigraph] is a doormat inviting readers to linger at the door, hoping they won't wipe their feet with it — Nana Ariel and Uri Yoeli, *Epigraph*[1]

This essay takes its cue from an epigraph, a seemingly modest paratext liable to be overlooked, but one that often holds the key to the text, putting the reader's 'hermeneutic capacity [...] to the test', as Gerard Genette puts it.[2] Indeed, Clarice Lispector's epigraph to her 1974 short story collection, *A via crucis do corpo* [*The Via Crucis of the Body*], reveals a fundamental facet not only of this collection, but of Lispector's *oeuvre* more generally.[3] As I will show, this epigraph suggests that Lispector engages in her writing with a specific aspect of the Jewish exegetical tradition: she adopts and rethinks the citational practice of the *midrash* (i.e. the basic interpretation method of the Talmud and rabbinical literature), which is characterized by 'repetition with change', in Chana Kronfeld's terms.[4] More specifically, Lispector sophisticatedly modifies the citational Jewish practice in order to develop what I call her 'rhetoric of mistakes'.[5]

The thematics of *A via crucis* focuses on female sexuality, but also explores various other forms of marginalized desire. The collection follows, among other characters, a nun overtaken by sexual appetite to the point of 'arder' [burning], a woman whose face is 'anulado' [annulled] by a man who competes with her over the sexual attention of an older businessman, and a pious virgin who finally encounters bodily joy through a sexual interaction with an alien.[6] These characters move (or try to) within a specifically Brazilian diegetic world, confined by strict heteronormativity; and they are constantly supervised by agents embodying patriarchal authority (the priest, the officer, the doctor), who strive to normalize desire, or punish these characters for their ostensible transgressions. But against all odds, Lispector's humorous and compassionate language always grants the body its final word, even though it is frequently a sigh of pain.

A via crucis's provocative, forceful stories do not carry any definite Jewish mark. In fact, the collection's title reaches right into the heart of Christianity, echoing Jesus's agonizing journey in Jerusalem towards his crucifixion (in a street still called today *Via Dolorosa*), and Christian preoccupation with the flesh overflows the collection.[7] My claim nevertheless is that the volume adopts the Jewish traditional attitude towards the Bible — which grants the interpreter the right, or even obligation, to intervene in the text of authority — and leverages this approach for her own engagement with the patriarchal law of heteronormativity. As Daniel Boyarin demonstrates, the midrash, the hermeneutical practice at the core of Jewish rabbinic literature, is intertextual in nature. A typical midrash — which Boyarin describes as 'a dialogical encounter' between rabbis around the interpretation of a specific passage — will bring together various verses from across the Bible, quoted by the rabbis in question in order to strengthen their own view of a local passage; a written conversation which thus receives a 'mosaic structure'.[8] What is exceptional about this hermeneutical practice, Boyarin notes, is that it 'both continues and breaches the tradition'.[9] That is, the rabbis undoubtedly accept the authority of the biblical text and follow its ideology, but at the same time they quite liberally use biblical citations in order to renew the understanding of the scriptures: the midrashists commonly use a verse in a sense opposite to its original meaning, or create a mosaic structure out of quotations unrelated to each other. These 'disruptive' quotations, Boyarin makes clear, do not work to annihilate the authoritative quoted text, but on the contrary, they work to open a dialogue about it and extract new meanings from within it.[10] Elaborating on Boyarin's point, Kronfeld accounts for the modern poetic tradition of radical intertextuality to grow out of this Jewish exegetical tradition. As she writes, 'In the Jewish textual tradition, and the theories of allusion produced by it [...], the norms, as well as the source of aesthetic pleasure have always resided in the radical rewriting of the authoritative "sources".'[11]

Lispector's epigraph to *A via crucis* points to her reliance on this Jewish intertextual practice, though this dialogue has so far gone unnoticed by scholarship. It is the only place in Lispector's *oeuvre* where the Hebrew Bible is quoted with full citational details; in fact, the five quotations that open the book include not only references to the Hebrew Bible but to Jewish liturgy specifically. And Lispector engages with these Jewish sources via a radical form of 'repetition with change': she takes the midrashic attitude to the extreme and allows herself to mis-cite the Bible in her epigraph. Her manipulations of the biblical text are highly calculated, yet they take on the appearance of mistakes, namely, they lend themselves to be understood as the outcome of carelessness or ineptitude. This rhetorical move permits Lispector to leverage exegetical practices in order to communicate a feminist message through the authoritative biblical text, which upholds the violent Brazilian patriarchal law governing her diegetic world.[12] This same move also advances the mistake, more generally, as a potential form of resistance; through her ostensibly accidental distortions, Lispector hints to her readers that she is willing to endure her perception as incompetent for the sake of disobeying the law right under the radar of censorship: the mistake, after all, can always be said to have occurred unawares.

Lispector continues to explore the potentiality of 'mistakes' in the body of the collection as well. She depicts women characters who are able to escape violence, if only momentarily, by disguising themselves as mistaken, and by paying proper attention to what presents itself as an error. This is especially true in the short story 'A língua do "p"' [Pig Latin], where Lispector also strains to train her readers in identifying and engaging with the rhetoric of mistakes.[13] However, nowhere in the collection does Lispector depict the mistake as an easy or all-encompassing solution to the problem of patriarchal violence and its regulatory restriction of non-normative desire. Strategies, gaps, and loopholes notwithstanding, women's tragic 'destiny' in Lispector's diegetic world remains 'implacável' [implacable].[14]

In referring to Lispector's 'rhetoric', then, I gesture at her concrete attempt to masquerade her subversion under the guise of an innocent mistake, and at her more general poetics of mistakes, that is, her focus in *A via crucis* on the multilayered functions of the mistake as a political vehicle of both oppression and resistance. My use of 'mistake' might seem improper, given that dictionary definitions of the term align it with unintentionality, while I discuss orchestrated distortions. But, as Lispector makes clear in her *crônica* 'Mineirinho' (1964), it is not the motivation for conducting a mistake that interests her, but the matrix of power that defines when and under what conditions an utterance or action will be marked a 'mistake' (or an 'error' in her terms).[15] For Lispector, the label 'mistake' functions as a political tool for demarcating boundaries between correct and incorrect, acceptable and impermissible; but it can also be manipulated to destabilize these boundaries. In this fashion, for example, labelling someone's actions as 'mistaken' can, by way of metonymy, mark them more generally as incapable, while self-presenting an action as an 'error' can function both as a way of concealing responsibility and of flying under the radar of authority.[16]

In 'Mineirinho', Lispector reflects on the overdetermined nature of the 'error' as she rethinks the murder of a twenty-eight-year-old 'thug' from Minas Gerais, who 'já matara demais' [had already killed too many], and is consequently shot thirteen times by the police, and dies: '[E]le é o meu erro. E de uma vida inteira, por Deus, o que se salva às vezes é apenas o erro, e eu sei que não nos salvaremos enquanto nosso erro não nos for precioso' [He is my error. And out of a whole lifetime, by God, sometimes the only thing that saves a person is error, and I know that we shall not be saved as long as our error is not precious to us].[17] Lispector marks 'Mineirinho' himself an 'error', which is to say that his violent way of life is likely to be perceived as an arbitrary error in the system, or the result of Mineirinho's innate incompetence (his 'mistaken' life choices). This conception allows one, as she writes, to carry on 'fingirão que estamos todos certos e que nada há a fazer' [pretend[ing] that we are all in the right and that there is nothing to be done].[18] However, for Lispector, Mineirinho's 'mistakes' are not accidental or personal, they were enforced upon him by a social order that would end up violently terminating his life. In this sense, thinking of Mineirinho's life and subsequent killing as 'erroneous' exposes this term's potential function as a tool of disavowing responsibility. As a countermove, Lispector explicitly acknowledges her complacency in the social order that brought about Mineirinho's violent desperation, and identifies him as *her* error: 'Meu erro é o meu espelho, onde vejo o que em silêncio eu fiz de um homem' [My error is my mirror, where I see what in silence I made of a man].[19] Paradoxically, the 'error' as a 'mirror' also draws the outline of a possible escape, as it 'disrupts' the system by exposing social and psychic realities. For Lispector, de-neutralizing ostensible 'errors' holds the power to disclose power structures and facilitate self-reflection; and leveraging the rhetoric of mistake can enable the subject to safeguard herself from violent oppressive forces. Indeed, in *A via crucis*, Lispector follows characters who are all socially condemned as 'errors', but within this universe, they, along with their creator, utilize mistakes to try and evade a destiny not unlike Mineirinho's.

Though Lispector lays down a nuanced theorization of mistakes in her fictional writings, she does so implicitly. Surprisingly, one can find a more explicit vocabulary for Lispector's bold poetic-political moves in Judith Butler's generative theory of performativity, published from the other side of the continent two decades after *A via crucis*.[20] Glossing Lispector's rhetoric of mistakes via Butler's theory of performativity and Kronfeld's interpretation of it forces to the fore the threads *A via crucis* spins between citational errors, feminist resistance, and Jewish textual tradition. As is well known, Butler suggests disobedient reiterations of canonical cultural gestures as a gap through which the subject may leave herself the possibility of reappropriating the texts of authority. As she famously argues, 'what we might call "agency" or "freedom" or "possibility" is always a specific political prerogative that is produced by the gaps opened up in regulatory norms, in the interpellating work of such norms, in the process of their self-repetition'.[21] Within this framework, Butler understands gender identity as the linguistic repetition of authoritative utterances forced upon the subject (such as 'It's a girl!' and 'I pronounce you man and wife'), which is why 'citation' (and mis-citation) forms a central concept for her. However, Butler uses 'citation' in a semi-metaphorical manner.[22] She borrows from the textual practice of intertextuality to reflect on social (and linguistically, mostly oral) gender negotiation. Kronfeld boldly suggests, nevertheless, that Butler borrows her sociopolitical metaphor from a concrete Jewish practice of exegetical citation:

> [Butler] herself uses the language of intertextuality [...] in order to both describe the constitution of the subject by the authority and to analyze the possibility of a [...] resistant response to interpellation. [...] Butler's description applies with surprising accuracy to the critical intertextual practices that are the hallmark of the Hebrew Poetry of Dalia Ravikovitch and Yitzhak Laor, who in turn provide a secular twist on an age-old religious — but no less radical — Jewish exegetical tradition of rewriting and textual reappropriation.[23]

Lispector, I believe, makes literal Butler's theory *avant la lettre*, relying herself on the 'Jewish exegetical tradition' Kronfeld mentions. Lispector takes the idea of mis-repetition of regulatory norms at face value, and mis-cites the Bible in order to insert her feminist voice into this key patriarchal text. Through the 'gaps opened up' in this authoritative work, she tries to conjure a feminist 'agency' or 'possibility' within the restricting heteronormative universe she depicts in *A via crucis*.[24] But Lispector is highly aware, like Butler, that the practice of mis-citation does not necessarily operate as 'subversive'. As Butler insists: 'femininity is thus not the product of a choice, but the forcible citation of a norm, one whose complex historicity is indissociable from relations of discipline, regulation, punishment'.[25]

And Lispector's characters are indeed continually disciplined for their 'mistaken' desires: an older woman who actuates her desire for a younger man is deserted and robbed of all her money, and an erotic dancer who enjoys her sexual encounters is being denied her very sense of femininity.[26] In fact, Lispector herself, who not only literally mis-cites the Bible but also mis-cites literary norms by centring her work on queer sexuality, is being punished as well: to this day very little has been written about *A via crucis*, a critical neglect, as I will show in the following section, that is inseparable from the perception of her collection as improper and 'trashy'. Yet, as Lispector will hint through her rhetoric of mistakes, at times being called 'trash' allows one the freedom to exercise a 'political prerogative', limited and fragile as it might be. Ultimately, Lispector's and Butler's political conceptualization of mis-reiteration urges us to re-examine the politics of citation: who represents the authoritative text in an intertextual dialogue, and who has the authority to question its claims.

'Yes, Trash'

A via crucis was written by Lispector at a time of need. After losing her main source of income in 1974 (as a columnist at the *Jornal do Brasil*), she agreed to write a commissioned book about women's sexuality ('E era assunto perigoso' [And it was a dangerous subject], she writes).[27] In the introduction to her collection, titled 'Explicação' [Explanation], Lispector claims that all thirteen stories came gushing out of her immediately upon ending the conversation with her editor, so that the book was ready for print in just a few days. Notwithstanding the accuracy of this account (Lispector is known for conflating fiction and reality), this collection does exhibit a change in style perhaps due to a different writing process.[28] While her previous novels and short stories figured highly metaphorical language, saturated with oxymorons, which followed the minutest changes in the characters' stream of consciousness, the sentences in *A via crucis* are short, frequently repetitive, and written in a much lower register of Portuguese. This is accompanied by a characterological change: the protagonists of *A via crucis* are no longer the heterosexual bourgeois women of Lispector's previous books, but characters who inhabit the social margins of Brazilian society.[29] In addition, the voice leading the collection drifts away from grave self-reflection to a provocative and ironic narration, a playfulness Vilma Arêas claims will eventually bring about the unique combination of modernist experimentalism and gallows humour to be found in Lispector's final work (and for many, her masterpiece), *A hora da estrela* (1977).[30]

Lispector's freer hand had its price. Just a year before publishing *A via crucis*, she received rave reviews for her previous novel, *Água viva*, which was described in *Veja*, the leading weekly news magazine at the time, as elevating Brazilian literature 'to a level of universal perennity and perfection'.[31] *A via crucis*, on the other hand, was met with resounding silence by the academic community, and with open disdain by reviewers.[32] 'Sim, lixo' [Yes, Trash] was the degrading title of a review that appeared in the same magazine, where Bruna Becherucci claimed that the book was 'no more than a half-pathetic, half-shocking gallery of the most melancholic human bodily convulsions'.[33] In the *Jornal do Brasil*, Lispector's former workplace, Emanuel de Moraes wrote in the same vein: 'This is one of those books that should not have been written. It does not befit an author so venerated for her previous books'.[34] These critics denounced both the book's style and theme, claiming that its plots were unsophisticated, obscene anecdotes verging on pornography, and that the language used to portray them was coarse and in bad taste. Publishing *A via crucis*, they insisted, was a mistake.

Lispector was not surprised by such harsh criticism; in fact, she had predicted it well in advance. In her introduction to the collection, she states that both her critics and her readers will punish her gravely for writing this book: 'Vão me jogar pedras. Pouco importa. Não sou de brincadeiras, sou mulher séria' [They will throw stones at me. It doesn't matter. I'm a serious woman, I don't play games].[35] As Moser points out, it is significant that Lispector refers to stoning as her imagined punishment, given that this was the biblical punishment meted out to sinful promiscuous women.[36] Lispector marks herself as yet another character in her collection, whose sexuality (inextricable from her creativity) is being delegitimized and reproved. But Lispector not only predicts the critical reception of her book, she also incorporates in the text itself a well-formulated and premeditated answer to these critics' attack on her book as 'lixo'. She answers them back through what can be thought of as a *trashy* literary practice.

Lispector begins articulating this nuanced response towards the end of her introduction: 'Uma pessoa leu meus contos e disse que aquilo não era literatura, era lixo. Concordo. Mas há hora para tudo. Há também a hora do lixo' [Someone read my stories and said they were not literature, they were trash. I agree. But there is a time for everything. There is also a time for trash].[37] This statement is in intertextual dialogue with the famous verse in Ecclesiastes: 'Everything has a season, and a time for every matter under the heavens. A time to be born and a time to die. A time to plant and a time to uproot what is planted. A time to kill and a time to heal' (3. 1–3). There is also, according to Lispector, a specific time for trash, a moment or circumstance in which the recourse to 'lixo' is requisite. This biblical allusion beckons to the citations that open her collection. There, trash, female desire, mistakes, and patriarchal violence are all discussed and acted out.

Of the five quotations that function as the epigraph to *A via crucis*, three are taken from the Hebrew Bible: two from Psalms, and one from Lamentations:

> A minha alma está quebrantada pelo teu desejo. (Salmos 119. 12)

> Eu, que entendo o corpo. E suas cruéis exigências. Sempre conheci o corpo. O seu vórtice estonteante. O corpo grave. (Personagem meu ainda sem nome)

> Por essas cousas eu ando chorando. Os meus olhos destilam águas. (Lamentações de Jeremias)

> E bendiga toda a carne o seu santo nome para todo e sempre. (Salmo de David)

> Quem viu jamais vida amorosa que não a visse afogada nas lágrimas do desastre ou do arrependimento? (Não sei de quem é)

> [My soul breaketh for your desire. (Psalms 119. 12)

> I, who understand the body. And its cruel demands. I have always known the body. Its dizzying vortex. The grave body. (A still-unnamed character of mine)
>
> For these things I weep. Mine eye runneth down with water. (Lamentations of Jeremiah)
>
> And let all flesh bless his holy name for ever and ever. (Psalms of David)
>
> Who has ever seen a love life and not seen it drowned in tears of disaster or regret? (I don't know who said this.)][38]

Lispector inserts two quotations of her own into this holy list. One is attributed to a 'still-unnamed character', and the other to an anonymous author, 'I don't know who said this'. According to Arêas, this move works to appraise the reader of the book's sacrilegious attitude right off the bat: '[In the epigraph], biblical discourse is being degraded, intermingled with words by an anonymous character and by a character of dubious standing. We are thus informed, from the outset, that no organizing principle will uphold any traditional morals in these stories, and will not guarantee us the privilege to exclude specific voices from this space'.[39] Arêas is undoubtedly correct, but I believe that Lispector's freedom in placing her unknown characters alongside such biblical narrators as David of Psalms and Jeremiah of Lamentations is also indicative of an intimacy with the biblical text. This coalescence insinuates that Lispector imagines the biblical characters as flawed, and her own characters as heroes. In fact, Lispector's arrangement of quotations can be taken to express the precise combination of intimacy, wordplay and admiration that traditionally characterizes the Jewish commentators of the Hebrew Bible, as mentioned above.

Per Lispector's promise, *A via crucis* indeed occupies a 'time of trash'; that is, from the outset, Lispector presents her narrative as following a chronotope littered with mistakes. The quotations opening the collection appear to be sloppy. They entertain various 'mistakes', varying in gravity, which suggest that Lispector mishandles the conventions of citation: she refers to the same work by two different titles, she 'forgets' to indicate chapter and verse numbers, she specifies the wrong verse number, and she misquotes the verses themselves. In directing this theatre of mistakes, Lispector takes into consideration her readers and their knowledge. In the predominantly Christian Brazilian context, Lispector had expected a reader less familiar with the Hebrew Bible, who would disregard these mistakes and take in her distorted citations along with their engraved feminist message — and indeed, these mistakes have so far gone unnoticed by criticism altogether. On the other hand, these citations can function as another proof that the book is 'trash' for those who consider a collection on female sexuality to be 'pornographic'. But there are also those readers whose social position as 'unnamed' or 'unknown' had already taught them that errors are 'precious'. Those readers will sense Lispector's subversive gesture; in fact, Lispector will attempt to educate all of her readers into identifying and taking mistakes seriously through the stories themselves.

Lispector makes the boldest and most iconoclastic mistake in her first quotation of the epigraph. This quotation, the text declares, is taken from the book of Psalms, chapter 119, verse 12, but tellingly, this verse is in fact number 20. It might have been possible to dismiss this misidentification as a typo, or even an editorial mistake, but Lispector not only gets the verse number wrong, she also misquotes the verse itself. Lispector's quotations suggests that she is using the *Sociedade Bíblica Britânica e Estrangeira* Portuguese translation of the Bible, where the verse reads: 'A minha alma está quebrantada pelo desejo' [My soul breaketh from desire], but Lispector adds to this verse an extra word of her own: 'A minha alma está quebrantada pelo *teu* desejo' [My soul breaketh from/for *your* desire]. What is going on here?

The verse in the original Hebrew is '*garsa nafshi le-ta'ava el mishpatekha bekhol 'et*'; a verse rendered by the King James version as: 'My soul breaketh for the longing that it hath unto thy judgments at all times'. The verse in Hebrew describes the soul as being literally shattered or broken by the desire, the longing, for God's laws.[40] Lispector, in her version, however, cuts off the verse's final part and adds the possessive pronoun '*teu*' before the noun 'longing'. Since the omitted final part which pertains to divine Law still hovers above the text, we are in fact impelled to read Lispector's version as: 'My soul breaks under *your* desire, *your* longing, for the Law, at all times' (emphasis mine). In Lispector's mistaken version, then, the relations between the speaker, the addressee, desire, and the law are utterly changed, so that two interpretations present themselves. The speaker is no longer a subject overladen with desire for the law to the point of pain, but is either a subject tormented as a consequence of someone else's violent desire for divine law or, in the extremely sacrilegious version, a subject tormented by God's own desire for God's law. This final proposition is not only bold due to its corporealization of divinity, imbuing it with desire, but it is also linguistically imprudent, addressing God with the highly intimate possessive pronoun '*teu*' instead of the venerating '*vosso*'. Interestingly, verse number 12, to which Lispector sends us, is much more proper than number 20, mentioning neither desire nor the flesh: 'Blessed art thou, O Lord: teach me thy statutes' (Psalms 119. 12). By conducting her subversive act under the guise of a mistake, Lispector can always answer accusations by pointing to the verse that she has meant to quote but 'unintentionally' mis-cited.

Lispector's distortion — brazenly injected into the space bounded by quotation marks without signalling it with the conventional square brackets — manipulates the biblical verse to assert that she, as well as her characters, is being crushed by a society obeying patriarchal Law. She is drawing an affinity (not an identity) between divine and patriarchal authority in their demand, or better yet desire, for complete obedience. However, as her practice of mistakes evinces, Jewish tradition presents divine law as inviting interpretation and as open to continuous change, while the Brazilian patriarchy that Lispector will go on to describe in her stories is vehemently resistant to modification. Through this mistake, Lispector is also able to predict the condemnation of her book as 'trash': her critics' desire for the law of 'proper' language and themes, predicated on heteronormative values, will crush her. Yet her malpractice of translation not only works to depict the violence she and her characters are subject to, it also functions as a potential retort to that violence. By distorting the quotation from Psalms, Lispector carves her own problem as a subaltern into the text of tradition: she inserts a feminist voice into the heart of a constitutive patriarchal text. That is to say, Lispector sophisticatedly leverages the Jewish textual practice of repetition with change in order to react against a patriarchal system undergirded by the biblical text itself.

Other inaccuracies in the epigraph jump more readily off the page. Lispector uses two different titles to refer to the same biblical book. She first refers to Psalms as 'Salmos', the conventional title in Portuguese, and then, in the fourth quotation, she shifts to 'Salmo de David'. Moreover, in this second mention of Psalms, Lispector neglects to mention a chapter and verse number. Seemingly negligent, this inconsistency in fact testifies to her deep acquaintance with the specifically Jewish-practised version of Psalms. Lispector quotes from psalm 145, which is not an incidental choice; this is a chapter of such significance in Jewish tradition that Tractate Berachot in the Mishna states: 'Said Rabbi Elazar b. Abina: Anyone who recites *T'hillah l'david* (Psalms 145) three times every day is guaranteed to enter the world-to-come' (4b). Indeed, psalm 145 constitutes one of the central prayers in Jewish daily liturgical practice, recited three times a day, and named after the chapter's opening words: 'A David Song of Praise', or in Portuguese, *Salmo de David* (also frequently referred to by its first word in Hebrew, *'Ashrei'*). Lispector refers in her epigraph, then, to the liturgical version of Psalms, which explains why she does indicate a chapter or verse number, unnecessary when quoting a prayer. Lispector leaves this shift in genre unspecified as part of her rhetoric of mistakes, granting her citational practice a semblance of negligence.

Against this backdrop, Lispector's additional manipulation of this quotation receives new meaning. Both the biblical chapter of Psalms and its liturgical version are centred on the praise of God as metaphysical and superior to human existence in benevolence and generosity, such as with the famous verse: 'Thou openest thine hand, and satisfiest the desire of every living thing' [abres a mão, e satisfazes o desejo de todos os viventes] (145. 16). Similarly, the full verse that Lispector is working with asserts: 'My mouth shall speak the praise of the Lord: and let all flesh bless his holy name for ever and ever' (145. 21). The word 'flesh' in the Hebrew (*basar*) is anything but central to this psalm. In fact, the Hebrew term does not signify the body specifically, but functions as a metonymy for a 'human being' which is why in different translations of Psalms into Portuguese, the Hebrew 'flesh' is translated as 'todo ser vivo' [all living beings].[41] Lispector, however, truncates the verse and through this omission makes 'flesh' the subject of the quoted text. Now the biblical text appears to depict the human body as the dwelling place for God's blessings, in contrast with its initial emphasis on God's praise. Lispector suggests that nothing is more blessed, worthier of attention than the decaying flesh, which will stand at the centre of the collection; she stealthily turns a text about the disembodied God into a panegyric on the embodied human.

In the third epigraph, Lispector's manipulation of the biblical text fits more readily with the conventional midrashic move of placing a quotation in a new context that imbues it with meaning radically foreign to its original one. She extracts a verse from a misogynist context *par excellence*, but makes her selection such that the woman at its centre is suddenly granted the opportunity to protest her condition and make her voice heard. More specifically, Lispector turns here to one of the harshest allegories of the Hebrew Bible, the first chapter of Lamentations. There, Jeremiah the prophet provides an explanation for the exile of the Israelites from Jerusalem and the destruction of kingdom of Judah by the Babylonians: he wrathfully condemns the Israelites for worshiping other gods and, in order to abash them for their disloyalty, compares them to a sexually transgressive woman. In this allegory, the Israelites are represented by a personified Jerusalem who is said to have betrayed her husband and consequently been brutally punished, thus finding herself abandoned by her lovers and forsaken by her sons: 'An offense did Jerusalem commit, therefore she became despised. All who honoured her degrade her, for they have seen her nakedness' (Lamentations 1. 8). The Hebrew term for 'she became despised', *nidah*, is associated with a menstruant woman, considered unclean, and is generally used to refer to taboo sexual relations and their shamefulness, thus that the phrase 'they have seen her nakedness' extends the overall sexual metaphor of the chapter. The resulting image, as Robert Alter puts it, is 'of Zion as a woman flung down, her skirt pulled up, her nakedness exposed'.[42]

There is hardly a biblical text as misogynist as Lamentations 1, and yet it is one of the very few biblical portions (along with The Song of Songs, for example) that grants the voice of narration, if only for a few verses, to a woman. Though the majority of the chapter is narrated in the third person by Jeremiah, verses 12–22 of this chapter are spoken in the first person by the feminized Jerusalem. Lispector shrewdly picks a verse from this section and takes advantage of its unique narratological feature to turn the biblical allegory on its head. By placing the cry of the socially condemned and sexually abused Jerusalem at the opening of a collection populated with other characters similarly punished for their desires (erotic dancers, prostitutes, neglected mothers, and frustrated nuns), Lispector extracts Jerusalem from her enforced isolation ('how she sits alone, the city once great with people' [1. 1]). She also concretizes and embodies the allegorical fallen woman, such that a voice of feminist protest surprisingly emerges from the Bible: 'For these things I weep. Mine eye runneth down with water'. In her epigraph, then, Lispector diligently chooses verses, or parts and distortions thereof, which would give voice to the 'weep[ing] I' and her flesh, while also thematizing a response to the Law under which this flesh is 'crushed': if mistakes in the (only available) language of authority allow one to speak her voice, then the price of being labelled 'trash' is worth paying.

Mistakes as Self-Defence

'A lingua do "p"', the eleventh story of *A via crucis*, corresponds to the eleventh station of the mythic route to Jesus's crucifixion, the nailing on the cross. It is hence, unsurprisingly, the most violent of the collection. In the story, a young English teacher called Maria Aparecida (nicknamed Cidinha) catches a train to Rio. Two men board the same, almost empty, car and begin talking in a strange language. It sounds familiar to Cidinha but she cannot recognize where from. Suddenly she realizes: the two men are speaking the 'P' language, which is the Brazilian version of the schoolboy code known as Pig Latin. Cidinha quickly understands that the two men are planning to rape her at the next tunnel. If she tries to resist, they will kill her. Frightened, she frantically tries to think of ways to save herself until she finally decides to pretend to be a prostitute, realizing that they would not want to rape a whore. So, Cidinha raises her skirt, opens her blouse and starts behaving provocatively. It works: the two men decide that she is a fool and cannot stop laughing at her. Meanwhile, the ticket collector reports her to the driver, who stops at the next station so she can be arrested. There, a policeman brutally forces Cidinha to disembark. Outside, she catches a quick glimpse of another young woman boarding her car. That young woman looks at her in contempt. Cidinha is then taken to jail and kept there for three long days. When she is finally set free, she wanders the streets of Rio exhausted and humiliated. Then, at a small stand she sees a newspaper headline: a woman was raped and killed on a train. She realizes it was the young woman who looked at her so scornfully.

According to Carlos Magno Gomes, 'A lingua do "p"' follows the mechanism of the sadistic 'masculine desire to possess'.[43] It is also, Earl Fitz briefly suggests, among the stories in which Lispector 'involve[s] the reader more directly than she had ever done before in the creation and interpretation of a text's meaning'.[44] Fitz does not elaborate on his intriguing statement, but in the context of her rhetoric of mistakes one can certainly identify how Lispector strives in 'A lingua do "p"' to educate her reader in noticing and manipulating the workings of mistakes in the service of, and as a pushback against, the oppressive power Gomes points to.[45] In that sense, Lispector points through fiction to the political strategy of resistance to be later theorized by the abovementioned Butler.

As in the case of 'Mineirinho', the multiple meanings of 'mistake' are refracted through 'A lingua do "p"'. As we learn as early as the first sentence, Cidinha is an expert at keeping up appearances, an expertise inscribed in her very name, 'Aparecida' (from *aparecer*, 'to appear'). Cidinha directs her performative skills at conforming to social expectations, gender norms included. Though she is 'Nem rica nem pobre' [neither rich nor poor], Cidinha struggles to appear well-off and proper: 'vestia-se com apuro. Parecia rica. Até suas malas eram de boa qualidade' [she dressed impeccably. She looked rich. Even her suitcases were high quality].[46] She is also a translator, a professional trainer in transforming one thing into looking and sounding like another, a skill she aims to 'perfect' (*aperfeiçoar-se*) in the U.S., very much as she likes to see 'perfection' (*perfeição*) in her students. As in English, *perfeição* suggests a bar so high as to be achieved only in appearances, so that one can say that Cidinha knows how to lead people to mistake her for what she not altogether is in order to elevate her social status: she labours to be mistaken for a 'perfect', 'rich' teacher. The men on the train, however, presume that Cidinha will be inattentive to their linguistic 'mistakes' or will count as mistaken her own intuition, which she almost does: 'No começo Cidinha não entendeu palavra. Parecia brincadeira' [at first Cidinha didn't understand a word. It seemed like a game].[47] Yet Cidinha's proclivity for distortions allows her to grasp the men's violent plans over and above their expectations, though the politics of mistakes also works against her. Cidinha well knows that if she reports the men's plan to the authorities they could always respond that she simply misunderstood — was mistaken — and carry out their violent act as planned (this is also why, when Cidinha is later taken to the police, she does not tell her side of the story). She realizes that within the dynamic of a patriarchal gender hierarchy — she being conceived as a prostitute, and the two men as law-keeping citizens — 'A língua do "p" não tinha explicação' [there was no explanation for Pig Latin]).[48] Cidinha must pretend to mistake the men's language for gibberish: 'Cidinha fingiu não entender: entender seria perigoso para ela' [Cidinha pretended not to understand: understanding would be dangerous for her].[49] The same verb, 'fingir' [pretend], will be later used to describe Cidinha's own manipulation of performative mistakes as a move of self-defence: 'se eu me fingir de prostituta, eles desistem' [If I pretend I'm a prostitute, they'll change their minds].[50] In this case, Cidinha cites social convention with the aim of lowering rather than elevating her status, saving herself while bringing about her imprisonment. Lispector herself, we recall, like Cidinha, was called 'dos piores nomes' [by the worst names] for publishing her book, as she had predicted, very much like Jerusalem of Lamentations, who has been made a whore through violent metaphorical language.[51] However, through her distorted citations, and via Cidinha's story, Lispector hints that being mistaken for 'trash' — 'trash' being for Lispector a social rather than an essentialist category — is at times the only way out.

It is significant that Lispector mentions twice in the story that the other woman looks upon Cidinha 'with scorn' when she is thrown off the train. This is a reminder of the danger involved in completely identifying with and perfectly citing the law, without even realizing its citational quality (as Butler will later warn, the law operates precisely by concealing its citationality).[52] This young woman, by looking at Cidinha as trash — like the men on the train, and like the policemen — repeats the gestures of patriarchy to perfection, those gestures that are a moment later directed against her. Lispector, on the other hand, wants to emphasize the importance of identifying and manipulating mistakes, distortions, and wrong repetitions — these practices, slippery and elusive, nevertheless hold for Lispector the potential of enabling the survival and even creativity of society's 'others'. The price they entail is being labelled trash, but this label only forces to the fore what is in fact an ongoing labour of a law that constantly controls and manipulates the economy of social value. Being labelled trash is a confirmation that one is indeed fighting against the system that is threatening to crush her.

Lispector makes sure that her readers, too, practice their ability to read 'mistakes'. She does so by portraying the two men's conversation in the form of the 'P language'. She writes, for instance:

> Sepe repesispistirpir popodepemospos mapatarpar epelapa.
> Se resistisse podiam matá-la. Era assim então.
>
> [Ifway eshay utspay upway away ightfay eway ancay illkay erhay
> If she puts up a fight they could kill her. So that's how it was.]⁵³

This formal presentation forces the reader to join Cidinha in her excruciating, crucial attempts at translation. Each exchange is first presented in the P language, urging the reader, who engages with the text diachronically, to pause and attempt to decipher the logic of these systematic distortions. Only after the reader encounters the utterance in its coded form (and perhaps senses the anxiety accompanying unintelligibility as well) is the reader presented with a translation, not of the sentence as is, but as it is understood by Cidinha herself, once again forcing the reader to experience the decoding process alongside the protagonist. In the fragment of the conversation above, for example, one of the men says: 'If she puts up a fight we can kill her', a sentence which Cidinha processes in the third person, 'If she puts up a fight *they* could kill her'. Cidinha desperately concludes, 'So that's how it was', and consequently hurries herself 'to think fast, fast, fast' ('Tinha que pensar depressa, depressa, depressa').⁵⁴ From a narratological perspective, the repetition of the conversation in both forms — grammatical and distorted — is redundant. However, it works to create a reading experience that thrusts the reader, along with Cidinha, into the space controlled by those within the circle of power, those who manipulate language such that it is comprehensible for them while appearing to be a series of random mistakes to subjects excluded from it.

A via crucis, from its epigraph, through the introduction, to the stories, offers readers a glimpse into Lispector's alternative logic of mistakes, a logic which emanates from within the sphere of violent power, but, in a Foucauldian manner, can also function as a form of resistance, fragile as it might be. The act of citation, Lispector implicitly claims, is at the core of the individual's interaction with authority: the citation of norms, the citations of authorial texts. In addition, as Butler would explicitly claim, given that identity formation functions on the basis of repetition of interpellation gestures, the subject always holds the prerogative to misquote. And Lispector concretizes this practice textually by misquoting specifically the biblical text. She thus insinuates that Jewish exegetical tradition has already set the foundation for this form of subversion via repetition with change; a counter-practice that can even work to undermine the patriarchal values upholding the scriptures themselves. Indeed, through the radical manipulation of repetition with change to the extent of appearing mistaken, Lispector, as well as the characters that inhabit the diegetic world of *A via crucis*, are able to create a place, within an oppressive patriarchal sphere, for their continually degraded bodily desires, a place for their flesh. However, the strategy proposed by Lispector is not, in any way, utopian. The deliberate distortions of cultural and textual tradition, she predicts, will be perceived and labelled by authority as resulting from incapacity, such that the lives associated with these 'mistakes' will stand the risk of being marked worthless as well. In this vein, Lispector is labelled 'trash' and is in danger of 'stoning' for making the 'mistake' of publishing a book about delegitimized pleasures; and Cidinha is humiliated, insulted, and put in jail for deceiving others into mistaking her for a trashy woman, a prostitute. But as Lispector insists through her biblical mis-citation, these errors hold the potential to save one from the crushing force of the law. There are moments of danger — like Lamentation's Jerusalem, her skirt pulled up, her nakedness exposed — where mistakes are necessary: 'there is also a time for trash'.

Works Cited

'The Writings [Ketuvim]', in *The Hebrew Bible: A Translation with Commentary*, trans. by Robert Alter, vol. III (New York, London: Norton, 2019)
ARÊAS, VILMA, *Clarice Lispector: com a ponta dos dedos* (Rio de Janeiro: Companhia das Letras, 2005)
ARIEL, NANA, and URI YOELI, *Epigraph* [אפיגרף] (Tel Aviv: Home-Press, 2019)
BECHERUCCI, BRUNA, 'Sim, lixo', *Veja*, 31 July 1974, p. 101
BOYARIN, DANIEL, 'Placing Reading: Ancient Israel and Medieval Europe', in *The Ethnography of Reading*, ed. by Jonathan Boyarin (Berkeley: University of California Press, 1993), pp. 10–37
—— 'Reciting the Torah: The Function of Quotation in the Midrash', in *Intertextuality and the Reading of Midrash* (Bloomington: Indiana University Press, 1994), pp. 22–38
BUTLER, JUDITH, 'Critically Queer', *GLQ*, 1 (1993), 17–31
—— *Gender Trouble* (New York: Routledge, 2007 [1990])
—— *Bodies that Matter: On the Discursive Limits of Sex* (New York: Routledge, 2011 [1992])
FITZ, EARL, 'A Writer in Transition: Clarice Lispector and *A via crucis do corpo*', *Latin American Literary Review*, 16.32 (1988), pp. 41–52
FREUD, SIGMUND, *Psychopathology of Everyday Life*, trans. by A. A. Brill (New York: Macmillan Company, 1914), in *Bartleby.com, Great Books Online* <http://www.bartleby.com/284/5.html> [accessed 15 October 2019]
GENETTE, GERARD, *Paratexts: Thresholds of Interpretation* (Cambridge: Cambridge University Press, 1997)
GOMES, CARLOS MAGNO, 'Marcas da violência contra a mulher na literatura', *Diadorim*, 13 (2013), 1–11
GOTLIB, NÁDIA BATTELLA, *Clarice: uma vida que se conta* (São Paulo: Ática, 1995)
KRONFELD, CHANA, *The Full Severity of Compassion: The Poetry of Yehuda Amichai* (Stanford, CA: Stanford University Press, 2015)
LISPECTOR, CLARICE, *Soulstorm*, trans. by Alexis Levitin (New York: New Directions, 1989)
—— *A via crucis do corpo* (Rio de Janeiro: Rocco, 1998 [1974])
—— *The Complete Stories*, trans. by Katrina Dodson (New York: New Directions, 2015)
—— *Todos os contos* (Rio de Janeiro: Rocco, 2016)
MORAES, EMANUEL DE, 'A via crucis de Clarice', *Jornal do Brasil*, 17 August 1974, p. 4
MOSER, BENJAMIN, *Why This World: A Biography of Clarice Lispector* (New York: Oxford University Press, 2009)
RASHI, *Rashi on Psalms* <www.sefaria.org.il/Rashi_on_Psalms.119.20.1 > [accessed 13 August 2019]
RIBEIRO, LEO GILSON, 'Auto-inspeção', *Veja*, 19 September 1973, p. 113
SALIH, SARA, *Judith Butler* (New York: Routledge, 2002)

Notes to Chapter 9

1. Nana Ariel and Uri Yoeli, *Epigraph* [אפיגרף] (Tel Aviv: Home-Press, 2019), p. 1. All translations from the Portuguese and Hebrew are mine unless otherwise noted.
2. Gerard Genette, *Paratexts: Thresholds of Interpretation* (Cambridge: Cambridge University Press, 1997), p. 158.
3. Clarice Lispector, *A via crucis do corpo* (Rio de Janeiro: Rocco, 1998 [1974]); Clarice Lispector, 'The Via Crucis of the Body', in *The Complete Stories*, trans. by Katrina Dodson (New York: New Directions, 2015), pp. 503–68.
4. Chana Kronfeld, *The Full Severity of Compassion: The Poetry of Yehuda Amichai* (Stanford, CA: Stanford University Press, 2015), p. 169.
5. The term 'practice' is central to Jewish tradition, which was always centred in praxis; even linguistically one does not refer to a 'believing Jew' but a 'practising Jew', one who repeatedly performs a set of action and adopts a certain manner of living and being in the world.
6. Lispector, *The Complete Stories*, pp. 563, 573; *A via crucis*, pp. 71, 43.
7. Earl Fitz takes 'flesh' to play such a key role in *A via crucis* that he translated the collection's title as 'The Via Crucis of the Flesh', 'A Writer in Transition: Clarice Lispector and *A via crucis do corpo*', *Latin American Literary Review*, 16.32 (1988), 41–52. This was prior to the first translation of the collection into English as 'The Stations of the Body', in Clarice Lispector, *Soulstorm*, trans. by Alexis Levitin (New York: New Directions, 1989).
8. Daniel Boyarin, 'Placing Reading: Ancient Israel and Medieval Europe', in *The Ethnography of Reading*, ed. by Jonathan Boyarin (Berkeley: University of California Press, 1993), pp. 10–37 (p. 18); Daniel Boyarin, 'Reciting the Torah: The Function of Quotation in the Midrash', in *Intertextuality and the Reading of Midrash* (Bloomington: Indiana University Press, 1994), pp. 22–38 (p. 25).
9. Boyarin, *Intertextuality and the Reading of Midrash*, p. 24.
10. Ibid., p. 25.
11. Kronfeld, *Full Severity*, p. 160.
12. Berta Waldman argues that the subtly Jewish quality of Lispector's writing can be detected through her biblical references, which work to bring about a discussion concerning the law, 'Clarice e Elisa Lispector: caminhos divergentes', *WebMosaica*, 6.1 (2014), 10–17 (p. 14).
13. Lispector, *A via crucis*, pp. 67–70; *The Complete Stories*, pp. 558–61.
14. Lispector, *A via crucis*, p. 70; *The Complete Stories*, p. 561.
15. Clarice Lispector, 'Minheirinho', in *Todos os contos* (Rio de Janeiro: Rocco, 2016), pp. 386–90; *The Complete Stories*, pp. 362–66. The *crônica* is a Brazilian genre of short writings at the intersection of literature, autobiography, and journalism. It is usually published in newspaper or magazine columns, and discusses daily topics from a personal perspective. As for terminology, I will use 'mistake' and 'error' interchangeably.
16. Lispector's explicitly political understanding of the 'mistake', both in 'Mineirinho' and in *A via crucis*, distances her from Freud's key conceptualization of 'slips of the tongue'. For Freud, 'mistakes in speech' are a result of an 'inner [unconscious] conflict that is betrayed to us through the disturbance in speech' (Sigmund Freud, *Psychopathology of Everyday Life*, trans. by A. A. Brill (New York: Macmillan Company, [1914]), in *Bartleby.com, Great Books Online* <http://www.bartleby.com/284/5.html> [accessed 15 October 2019]. For Freud, then, the mistake is an unintentional expression of an unconscious individual conflict, while for Lispector it is a tool intentionally used within political relations of power.
17. Lispector, *Todos os contos*, pp. 386, 387; *The Complete Stories*, pp. 362, 363. For an extensive exploration of the historical events behind Lispector's 'Mineirinho' and the *crônica*'s ethical valence see, Yudith Rosenbaum, 'A ética na literatura: leitura de "Mineirinho" de Clarice Lispector', *Estudos Avançados*, 24.69 (2010), 169–82.
18. Lispector, *Todos os contos*, p. 388; Lispector, *The Complete Stories*, p. 365.
19. Ibid., p. 363; ibid., p. 387.
20. For Butler's formative work on gender performativity, see *Gender Trouble* (New York: Routledge, 2007 [1990]).

21. Judith Butler, 'Critically Queer', *GLQ*, 1 (1993), 17–31 (p. 22).
22. Ibid., p. 23.
23. Kronfeld, *Full Severity*, pp. 161–62.
24. Interestingly, Butler herself has been accused of lack of rigour for mis-citing Freud and inserting the 'body' into his discourse; see Jay Prosser, *Second Skins* (New York: Columbia University Press, 1998), p. 4. It is a criticism I believe Lispector behoves us to rethink with the matrix of gender power structure in mind.
25. Butler, 'Critically', pp. 22–23.
26. See 'But it's going to rain' [Mas vai chover] and 'Praça Mauá' (Lispector, *A via crucis*, pp. 75–78, 61–65; *The Complete Stories*, pp. 565–68, 553–57).
27. Lispector, *A via crucis*, p. 11; *The Complete Stories*, p. 505. We cannot know for sure what this 'subject' was. The content of the story strongly implies women's sexuality, but Benjamin Moser, for example, claims that it is 'motherhood' rather than 'sex' that is the governing principle of the book. See Moser, *Why This World: A Biography of Clarice Lispector* (New York: Oxford University Press, 2009), p. 348.
28. Lispector's conflation of fiction and reality is especially evident in her *crônicas*. Yet, among the more provocative examples of Lispector's ongoing push against the binary 'fact' vs. 'fiction' is her manipulation of her own biography: only after her death was it revealed that she had fictionalized her birthdate, which was a year earlier than she reported, see Moser, *Why This World*, p. 8.
29. For more on sexual diversity in *A via crucis*, see, Moser, *Why This World*, p. 346; Earl Fitz, 'A Writer in Transition', p. 43; Claudiana Gois dos Santos, 'A emergência lésbica em Clarice Lispector', *Criação & Crítica* 20 (2018), 89–107.
30. Vilma Arêas, *Clarice Lispector: com a ponta dos dedos* (Rio de Janeiro: Companhia das Letras, 2005), p. 58.
31. Leo Gilson Ribeiro, 'Auto-inspeção', *Veja*, 19 September 1973, p. 113.
32. An exception to this rule is Hélio Pólvora's review of *A via crucis*, 'Da arte de mexer no lixo', mentioned in dos Santos, 'A emergência', p. 104.
33. Bruna Becherucci, 'Sim, lixo', *Veja*, 31 July 1974, p. 101.
34. Emanuel de Moraes, 'A via crucis de Clarice', *Jornal do Brasil*, 17 August 1974, p. 4.
35. Lispector, *A via crucis*, p. 11; *The Complete Stories*, p. 505.
36. Moser, *Why This World*, p. 347.
37. Lispector, *A via crucis*, p. 12; *The Complete Stories*, p. 506.
38. Ibid., p. 503; ibid., p. 7. I was fortunate to have been in dialogue with Katrina Dodson as she was working on her translation into English of *A via crucis*, a conversation which resulted in her incorporation of Lispector's 'mistake' into *The Complete Stories* (via a distortion of the King James Version of the Bible), the first critical engagement, to date, with Lispector's manipulation of her epigraph. Dodson leaves out Lispector's quotation marks, which I took liberty of reinserting into the English iteration in order to underscore Lispector's explicit reliance on citational practices in her epigraph.
39. Arêas, *Com a ponta dos dedos*, p. 60.
40. This is the only time in the biblical corpus that the Hebrew verb in this verse, *garas* [גרס], occurs; hence, its meaning is uncertain. However, various commentators trace this verb back to the act of grinding wheat into flour. Rashi writes, for example: 'My soul breaks because of longing, as (Leviticus 2. 14) "crushed kernels of the fresh ears." Menachem, however, associated "from longing" with (Amos 6. 8) "I destroy the pride of Jacob," and both are an expression of breaking', *Rashi on Psalms*, <https://www.sefaria.org.il/Rashi_on_Psalms.119.20.1> [accessed 20 August 2021].
41. For Portuguese translations of the Hebrew '*basar*' into 'ser vivo' see, for example, the *Bíblia King James Atualizada* and the *Nova versão internacional*. As for the biblical meaning of the Hebrew '*basar*', see for instance the Book of Job, where it is said: 'In whose hand is the soul of every living thing, and the breath of all mankind' (KJV 12. 10). In this verse, the Hebrew '*basar*' is the equivalent of the English 'mankind', and it is also, by way of parallelism, the equivalent of the 'soul of every living thing' (in Hebrew: *nefesh kol ḥay*). The biblical '*basar*', in other words, has no necessary connection to the flesh.

42. 'The Writings [Ketuvim]', in *The Hebrew Bible: A Translation with Commentary*, trans. by Robert Alter, vol. III (New York; London: Norton, 2019), p. 649.
43. Carlos Magno Gomes, 'Marcas da violência contra a mulher na literatura', *Diadorim*, 13 (2013), 1–11 (p. 7).
44. Fitz, 'A Writer in Transition', p. 41.
45. Gomes notes that the role newspapers play in the story places it, in terms of genre, in between fiction and journalism, which underlines the story's social and political facet, 'Marcas da violência', p. 7.
46. Lispector, *A via crucis*, p. 67; *The Complete Stories*, p. 558.
47. Ibid., p. 68; ibid., p. 559.
48. Ibid., p. 69; ibid., p. 561.
49. Ibid., p. 68; ibid., p. 559.
50. Ibid., p. 69; ibid., p. 560.
51. Ibid., p. 69; ibid., p. 561.
52. Sara Salih, *Judith Butler* (New York: Routledge, 2002), p. 95. Salih reaches this conclusion while discussing Judith Butler's *Bodies that Matter: On the Discursive Limits of Sex* (New York: Routledge, 1992), p. 12.
53. Lispector, *A via crucis*, p. 68; *The Complete Stories*, p. 559.
54. Ibid., p. 69; ibid., p. 560.

CHAPTER 10

'The error had often become my path': Lispector, Cixous and Ways of Reading

Julie Côté

Anyone with a scholarly interest in Clarice Lispector's work will most likely encounter the name of Algerian-born French author Hélène Cixous, whose work is widely associated with *écriture féminine*. While *écriture féminine* may seem to refer to writing by women only, it should be understood as an approach to the text, as 'textual ways of spending'.[1] This understanding of writing may be summarized, albeit partially, as an encounter with something or someone else that allows for questioning and undoing 'the hierarchies and oppositions that determine the limits of most conscious life'.[2] At first glance, *écriture féminine* may not seem to have much to do with Lispector, but Cixous's contribution to *écriture féminine* was shaped by Lispector's long-lasting effect on her work. In fact, as Cixous herself acknowledged, Lispector holds a unique, incomparable place in her 'space of references'.[3]

Cixous's interest in sexual difference in writing preceded her encounter with Lispector. Not only was it the topic of her famous text 'Le Rire de la Méduse' [The Laugh of the Medusa], where she addresses *écriture féminine* and most specifically '*ce qu'elle fera*'[4] [what it will do], but she also mentions it in interviews prior to 1977. That said, after being introduced to Lispector's work, in 1977,[5] Cixous's conception of *écriture féminine* became much more clearly defined.[6] Only after this decisive encounter — which occurred through reading *Água viva* — did it appear that Cixous had changed her perspective on *écriture féminine*. She no longer talked about what it was going to do, for she had found in Lispector the perfect example to express what it was already doing. No longer relegated to a mere theoretical concern, Lispector made *écriture féminine* happen for Cixous. In the years following her first reading of Lispector, many of the latter's books were translated and published by Éditions des femmes[7] (also Cixous's publisher); additionally, Cixous wrote many texts openly inspired by Lispector and discussed them in her seminars.[8] Regardless of the medium, Cixous's reading often emphasized how the Lispectorian text was written in a feminine way, an approach critics did not find palatable, charging her with imposing her own interests on Lispector's texts.[9] For example, according to Anna Klobucka, through Cixous's reading, 'Lispector [is] becoming in effect more "Cixousian" than Cixous herself has been "Lispectorian"'.[10] The fact that Cixous was learning Portuguese while reading Lispector did not go unnoticed either, and critics sometimes dismissed completely the interpretations that she had offered of Lispector's texts (or even her whole project) because she misunderstood some part of the original text. Some went as far as to charge Cixous with acting as a colonizer in relation to Lispector's work, in contradiction to the ethos of her feminist reading.[11] In short, critics found that Cixous became so deeply involved with Lispector's writing that she risked losing her individuality in the process and becoming incorporated by the Brazilian writer. And to some extent, Lispector's global reception indeed bears the mark of Cixous's reading in the Francophone world and in feminist criticism, or at least it did until more recently. But despite the critics' gloomy prophecy, Lispector, or at least her work, did not vanish, and nor did Cixous. The impact was in some ways mutual, with Lispector also profoundly influencing Cixous and her thinking.

At the basis of this conflict between Cixous and her critics lie different conceptions of the text and of the ways we must engage with it. How far should one go in the act of reading? Is the text to be read at a distance, like an object, as a critic would? Or should we let it affect us the same way that we modify it through our reading? This second approach is obviously the one adopted by Cixous; it contradicts the very task of criticism.[12] Feminine writing seeks to undo the limitations that prevent an encounter with another (be it a being, a text or something that can be experienced) from happening, a process that also means that the risk of going too far is heightened by such a reading (or writing). Therefore, in order to read in a feminine way, some risks have to be accepted. If we consider Lispector's words, if we read her carefully, we will find out that we must take the risk; actually, we have to go too far and make the error — at least this is what she suggests in *A paixão segundo G.H.* [*The Passion According to G.H.*] through her protagonist, who considers the error as one of her 'modos [...] de trabalho' [ways of working] and the 'caminho' [path] in her endeavour.[13] While Cixous's critics have condemned her approach, deeming it disrespectful, they have overlooked Lispector's writing while doing so. In the process of defending her from possible annihilation at the hands of Cixous, they have hazarded silencing her even further.

In what follows, I revisit the narrative Cixous constructed of her first encounter with Lispector and thereby examine how Clarice — as she comes to call her — shaped her thinking with regard to *écriture féminine* and the different ways relationships can be experienced, both through the text and in life. Cixous's understanding of reading and relationships is irreconcilable with that of her critics, particularly with regard to the role that power plays in relationships. Finally, and perhaps most importantly, I revisit *A paixão segundo G.H.*, a text that taught Cixous how to find her own way in writing while following in Lispector's footsteps.

Cixous Meets Clarice

Cixous tells the story of her first encounter with Lispector in *Vivre l'orange* [To Live the Orange], first published in French in 1979 and then in a French-English bilingual edition as *L'Heure de Clarice Lispector* [The Hour of Clarice Lispector] in 1989. According to her narrative, it occurred on 12 October 1978, which means that Lispector was already dead by the time Cixous first read her. The encounter had an astounding effect on Cixous and put her in a state of elation. Before reading Lispector, Cixous had never found the friendly voices she was looking for in literature; therefore, this encounter put an end to a long period of loneliness:

> Une écriture est venue à pas d'ange, — quand j'étais si loin de moi-même, seule à l'extrémité de mon être-finie, j'avais l'être d'écriture qui se désolait d'être si seule, qui envoyait des lettres sans adresse de plus en plus tristes: *«J'ai erré dix ans dans le désert des livres sans rencontrer une réponse»*, des lettres de plus en plus courtes *«mais où sont les amies?»* [...]
> [U]ne écriture m'a trouvée quand j'étais introuvable à moi-même.
>
> [A writing came with an angel's footsteps, — when I was so far from myself, alone at the extremity of my finite being, my writing-being was grieving for being so lonely, sending sadder and sadder unaddressed letters: *'I've wandered ten years in the desert of books — without encountering an answer'*, its letters shorter and shorter *'but where are the amies?'*
> [A] writing found me when I was unfindable to myself.][14]

Lispector's voice not only reconnects Cixous with herself but also allows her to engage with other women; it is precisely her voice that reminds all women, including Cixous, of their need to go back to their common source, *'[their] need to go further into the birth-voice'*[15], *'[b]ut too often [they] forget'*[16]; they need the voice to remind them what they are forgetting. Therefore, through the voice she heard in Lispector's text, Cixous could engage with this invisible community of women who walk together towards this source. In Cixous's narrative, Clarice hands her an orange, which represents women, *les amies* [female friends], as well as 'savoirs', those things that are known through the senses or instinctively that Clarice returns to the memory of Cixous and the other women. Reminding them that they used to know how to do these things, she teaches them how to pick the orange, how to smell and taste it. For Cixous, the orange also echoes the apple in Lispector's own work, namely in *A maçã no escuro*, and articulates what she calls 'libidinal economies', which are central to her understanding of *écriture féminine*. To explain the distinction between masculine and feminine economies, she provides her own take on Eve's eating of the proverbial apple in Genesis 3, recounting this episode in 'L'Auteur en vérité' [The Author in Truth], also published in *L'Heure de Clarice Lispector*:

> La première fable de notre premier livre a pour enjeu le rapport à la loi. [...] C'est un combat entre la Pomme et le discours de Dieu. [...] L'Histoire commence par la Pomme: au commencement de tout il y a une pomme, et cette pomme quand il en est parlé, il est dit que c'est un fruit-à-ne-pas. Il y a pomme, et aussitôt il y a la loi.

> [The first tale of our first book talks about the relationship to the law. [...] It is a struggle between the Apple and God's word. [...] History begins with the Apple: in the beginning of everything there is an apple, and this apple, whenever something is spoken about it, it is said to be a fruit-not-to. There is apple, and right away there is the law.][17]

According to Cixous, the law forbidding Eve from eating the apple was unintelligible. Why should she fear God's threat if she did not know what death was in the first place? Since Eve could not make sense of the law, the apple must have seemed all the more exquisite. When she takes the first bite, she discovers:

> [L]'intérieur de la pomme, et cet intérieur est bon. [...] Ève n'a pas peur de l'intérieur, ni du sien, ni de l'autre. Le rapport à l'intérieur, à la pénétration, au toucher du dedans est positif.
>
> [[T]he inside of the apple, and this inside is good. [...] Eve is not afraid of the inside, neither hers or another's. The relationship to the inside, to the penetration and to the touch from the inside is positive.][18]

This is how Cixous defines the feminine economy, which may refer to the way a text is read or how the world is experienced without fear of the law; alternately, the masculine economy is linked to the law and obedience to it.[19] The reason why Lispector made such an impression on Cixous is that never before had she encountered writing that depicted so well the feminine economy that she had in mind, as she says here:

> Clarice Lispector [...] arrives from the opposite side with her body, her torments, with her life, with her sorrows, and she says that to live is sufficient. I need nothing else but to live; living produces living. [...] She affirms life in a pure affirmation; that is 'feminine,' that is the source itself [...]. She is a woman who says things as closely as possible to a feminine economy, that is to say, one of the greatest generosity possible, of the greatest virtue, of the greatest spending.[20]

In a feminine economy, things are to be experienced at their fullest, without being inhibited by the fear of the law, which does not mean that there is no law at all, as we will see later. In some ways, the apple becomes the depiction of this economy for Cixous, considering its importance in the Bible (since Eve was not afraid to eat it) and in Lispector's work.

Cixous, however, does not simply emulate Lispector; she considers that she has to make her own voice heard in order to recognize Clarice's voice, and that is why she chose to identify with the orange, not the apple.[21] As she writes, '[d]ans la traduction de la pomme (en orange), [elle] essaie de [se] dénoncer. [...] Loin de l'orange, [elle ne se] pardonne pas d'écrire' [In the translation of the apple (into orange) I try to denounce myself. [...] Far from the orange, I do not forgive myself for writing].[22] Since it would betray Lispector (and herself) to hide behind the former's voice without recognizing her own, she chooses to highlight their individuality. She also mentions that Lispector's words are sometimes needed to shape her own thinking, acknowledging that she is guilty of leaning on her when necessary. Clarice gives her the courage and strength to write a particular sentence, and at times Cixous cannot seem to do it without her.[23] In some respects, Clarice is writing Cixous's words just as much as Cixous is writing her own. The fact that Cixous needs Clarice so much might explain why she is reluctant to talk about her. Doing so risks objectifying her and, ultimately, annihilating Clarice's voice by covering it with her own. That is why she wants to approach her texts in a gentle manner, while keeping silent, so that Clarice's voice can come and whisper sentences to her. If she is talking, she won't hear them.

Even though Cixous expresses concern over concealing Clarice's voice in *Vivre l'orange*, she did not, in fact, remain silent about Lispector in real life. There is no doubt that at some point she felt the need to talk about Clarice at length. Cixous mentions that her approach to Lispector, and to the literary text in general, is to let the author speak through her, to let herself be invaded by the text. Cixous actually views the way she reads not as a method that needs to be applied to a text, but more like a long process of multiple readings in which the text will reveal its various meanings to the reader, in due course. This is not to say that the reader has absolutely no power over the text, but rather that Cixous envisions reading as a relationship with the author (as she does with Lispector) and with the text as well. As a matter of fact, the text also guides the reader, telling her how it should be approached and read, but only if the reader accepts being 'carried off' by the text, as Cixous puts it:

> When we read a text, we are either read by the text or we are in the text. Either we tame a text, we ride on it, we roll over it, or we are swallowed up by it, as by a whale. There are thousands of possible relations to a text, and if we are in a nondefensive, nonresisting relationship, we are carried off by the text.[24]

While the critic will keep a distance between the text and herself, Cixous considers reading as a relationship in which each component affects the other, be it the text itself, the reader or the author. The distance between these entities varies greatly and changes constantly; through its various readings, the text will reveal how it should be read. But reading this way implies perceiving the text as more than a mere literary object that can be studied and mastered; Cixous views the text as carrying something, voices for instance, that may be revealed to us through glimpses, but cannot be possessed or recreated. In order to adhere to this view of the text, one must accept that the text holds something greater than what the reader can experience, the way a being cannot fully be known by someone else. Therefore, in a feminine way of reading, no one component exerts its power over another. But Cixous's critics did not deem this possible, arguing that her own reading overpowered Lispector's voice.

In fact, critics who opposed Cixous's approach to Lispector — Arrojo, Carrera, Klobucka, for example — did so primarily through a postcolonial reading. In other words, Cixous's attempt at thinking through relationships that are devoid of a power struggle could only be met with disbelief by those whose own reading aims to highlight power inequality in all types of encounters. This does not mean that the dissenting critique of Cixous's work was any less valid, but it has to be acknowledged that a project like Cixous's is most likely irreconcilable with a postcolonial reading. Postcolonialism and *écriture féminine* constitute opposing views about reading and about the world; while the former stresses the power that is unfairly asserted by one entity over the other one in an unequal relationship, the latter suggests the possibility of an equal relationship that maintains individuality. Therefore, it is not surprising that Cixous's critics would characterize her reading of Lispector as domineering, but it sometimes led them to an unfair assessment of Cixous's work. For instance, whenever Cixous's critics rightfully criticize some of her interpretations of Lispector's texts, they discredit her entire reading, even when parts of it are faithful to Lispector. It is particularly obvious when Cixous's limited knowledge of Portuguese skewed her analysis of Lispector's texts. She offers this interpretation of the short text 'É para là que eu vou' [That's Where I'm Going], in which the narrator goes back and forth, as if she was drifting in the wind: 'Clarice writes in order to dissolve through a certain chemistry, through a certain magic and love that which would be retention, weight, solidification, an arrest of the act of writing. That is why she ends by dropping the subject pronoun and saying: 'What am I saying? Am saying love."[25] Some critics, like Carrera, have remarked that Cixous was undoubtedly not aware that omitting the pronoun before the verb is common in Portuguese. Even with her misunderstanding of the use of pronouns in Portuguese, the remainder of Cixous's reading depicts Lispector's text quite faithfully, something the critics have not mentioned. It is of course the task of criticism to question interpretations, but since Cixous regards reading as an equal relationship with the text, mastering it is not her aim; rather, she wants to engage with it, even if this means that she will sometimes misread it. Therefore, it seems that both Cixous and her critics are simply at an impasse: they strongly disapprove of her 'domineering' reading, yet they command her to master the text better. How is this reconcilable?

Indeed, some of these critics appear more preoccupied with defending Lispector's integrity than in listening to what she has to say through her own writing. In their defence of Lispector, they did not let her speak for herself and seldom offer a counter-reading of her texts to justify their criticism of Cixous. Take, for instance, Arrojo's claim that Cixous turned Lispector into a 'ghostly guest that is rarely invited to the scene of interpretation'.[26] Here Arrojo alludes to Barthes's 'death of the author' to underline the detrimental impact of Cixous's reading, but it also could be said that Cixous is so haunted by Lispector that she carries the author within herself. The same cannot be said of the critics, who not only forget to invite Lispector 'to the scene of interpretation', to borrow Arrojo's words, but do not attempt to respect what she has expressly written, as I will show in the section that follows, using *A paixão segundo G.H.* as a case study.

Toward the Error

While the importance of the error might not be what most readers remember from *A paixão segundo G.H.*, I would like to argue that it is in this book that Lispector teaches her readers that there is no way to avoid it. It is necessary to go too far, since the error has to be made for the truth to be known. It is only when G.H. eats the substance that comes out of the roach that she realizes that she was wrong all along in her quest to transcend her humanity. Before that decisive moment, G.H. affirms that 'o erro básico de viver era ter nojo de uma barata' [the basic error in living was being disgusted by a roach].[27] She thinks like this because she considers kissing the roach as a loving gesture equivalent to that of Jesus kissing the leper: in order to love it the same way, she has to master her disgust. But shortly after tasting the white matter that is leaking out of the insect, she realizes that the way she was envisioning love was wrong since she had neglected to take herself into consideration:

> Só parei na minha fúria quando compreendi com surpresa que estava desfazendo tudo o que laboriosamente havia feito, quando compreendi que estava me renegando. E que, ai de mim, eu não estava à altura senão de minha própria vida.
>
> [I only halted in my fury when I understood with surprise that I was undoing everything I had laboriously done, when I understood I was renouncing myself. And that, alas, I was only up to my own life.][28]

What she discovers afterwards is that she cannot escape her own humanity, she cannot pretend to be like God as she was aiming to; instead, she finds out that she can only expect to be a human and to act as such, with the limitations accorded to each species:

> Mas a vida é dividida em qualidades e espécies, e a lei é que a barata só será amada e comida por outra barata; e que uma mulher [...] está vivendo a sua própria espécie. Entendi que eu já havia feito o equivalente de viver a massa de barata — pois a lei é que eu viva com a matéria de uma pessoa e não de uma barata.
>
> [But life is divided into qualities and kinds, and the law is that the roach shall only be loved and eaten by another roach; and that a woman [...] is living her own kind. I understood that I had already done the equivalent of living the paste of the roach — for the law is that I must live with the matter of a person and not of a roach.][29]

By tasting the roach, G.H. discovers that she cannot simply make herself equal to it, since they belong to different species, which is what the law, of which she becomes aware, stipulates. By transgressing it, she was disrespecting her own and the roach's individuality. A roach must generate disgust in mankind, refusing to feel this disgust goes against the law. There is a parallel to be drawn here with what Cixous wrote about the law, since Lispector portrays a law that is not meant to engender fear but is simply a truth that needs to be discovered. Just like Eve and the apple, G.H. is not to be stopped by the law — only the gesture of eating the substance allows her to know the truth about her humanity. Therefore, neither the error nor the law are perceived as negative, because the first one is what enables the second one to be revealed; therefore, the law does not serve a prohibitive purpose. And because it is experienced, the law is acceptable for G.H., since it is intelligible.

However, it is not because the error is considered in a positive light that reaching this point is easy; rather, Lispector shows that the opposite is the case, given that most people will not succeed in failing:

> Nem todos chegam a fracassar porque é tão trabalhoso, é preciso antes subir penosamente até enfim atingir a altura de poder cair — só posso alcançar a despersonalidade da mudez se eu antes tiver construído toda uma voz. [...] É exatamente através do malogro da voz que se vai pela primeira vez ouvir a própria mudez e a dos outros e a das coisas, e aceitá-la como a possível linguagem. Só então minha natureza é aceita [...]. E é aceita a nossa condição como a única possível, já que ela é o que existe, e não outra.
>
> [Not everyone manages to fail because it is so laborious, one first must climb painfully until finally reaching high enough to be able to fall — I can only reach the depersonality of muteness if I have first constructed an entire voice. [...] It is exactly through the failure of the voice that one comes to hear for the first time one's own muteness and that of others and of things, and accepts it as the possible language. Only then is my nature accepted [...]. And our condition is accepted as the only one possible, since it is what exists, and not another.][30]

We can take from this excerpt that there is no possible shortcut to the truth; not only does the error have to be made, but to even get to this point a long path must be followed, which makes failing hard to achieve. What is going to be proved wrong must first be built, and the law that will be found in the end cannot be anticipated. Therefore, G.H. realizes that she cannot aim for depersonality — that is, getting rid of one's individuality — without first accepting that she is a person:

> [...] é inútil procurar encurtar caminho [...], já começando por ser despessoal. Pois existe a trajetória, e a trajetória não é apenas um modo de ir. [...] Em matéria de viver, nunca se pode chegar antes.
>
> [[...] it is no use to try to take a shortcut [...], starting straightaway with being depersonal. For the journey exists, and the journey is not simply a manner of going. [...] In the matter of living, one can never arrive beforehand.][31]

This is similar to the efforts of the writing subject in *Água viva*, who also concludes that humility implies recognizing one's own presence. But because it is necessary for the voice to be constructed in order to be mute, we can find here an answer to Cixous's critics, who wanted her voice to be less present in her own text, a presence accentuated by her use of the first-person pronoun, among other things. The fact that her voice is heard does not necessarily mean that it cannot be silent at times. Maybe it was still in the process of being constructed, a process that required Clarice's help, as we have seen. G.H. also seems to reveal that the use of the first-person pronoun can be a means to achieve depersonality, when she remarks, 'respondo cada vez que alguém disser: eu' [I reply whenever someone says: I].[32] I suggest that by using the first-person pronoun, Cixous followed Clarice's teachings; she built her own voice first, for she understood that there was no use in trying to silence it until it could be heard. Though she may have made the mistake of going too far in her reading of Lispector by taking over Clarice's voice, one could say that she followed a path similar to that of G.H., who at first believes she can think of the roach as her equal. While it could be argued that the relationship between G.H. and the roach does not compare with that of Cixous and Lispector, there is nonetheless an encounter in both cases. If we follow Lispector's logic, as articulated in *A paixão segundo G.H.*, we can say that going too far is not intrinsically negative, for it allows the truth to be known.

Of course, Lispector does not consider things as either feminine or masculine — these are Cixous's words. That being said, Lispector's writing allowed Cixous to better define her ideas of the feminine economy and *écriture féminine* in general, especially with regard to the law and relationships. Maybe G.H. and the roach cannot be equals, but Lispector nonetheless suggests that humans can be, so that a relationship is possible between humans without one overpowering the other. This does not mean that there is no power at all, but it shows the possibility for relationships to be thought of in terms of equality. At least, this is the truth as G.H. found it. As for Cixous, we cannot know with certainty the truth she discovered through her reading of Lispector. What we can know is that she found in Lispector's work the means to shape and deepen her own thinking and develop a 'way of working'. And just as she required Clarice to whisper the sentence to her, maybe Lispector needed Cixous to give her thinking a new shape, and thereby keep it alive.

Conclusion

The fact that some of Cixous's critics were so adamant about depicting her as a colonizer shows how her work demands that we consider anew relationships in general, but more specifically, in this case, a relationship between two authors. While we usually accept that authors influence one another, this influence is sometimes perceived in negative terms as a burden or an expectation for the author on the receiving end.[33] Even though Cixous envisioned Lispector's influence on her work in positive terms, critics nonetheless raised the question of appropriation and loss of individuality. Conversely, Lispector and Cixous open the door to the possibility that two writers, writing in different times, can work together, in a collaboration that we could deem *feminine*, to borrow Cixous's wording.

Lispector herself often invites her reader to engage in the text and to respond to her, as if wanting to put an end to her loneliness. In some of her novels, like *A hora da estrela*, these calls are made directly, while elsewhere they are subtler. For instance, in *Um sopro de vida*, before the author creates Ângela, he addresses the great difficulty of being oneself: 'eu que escrevo para me livrar da carga difícil de uma pessoa ser ela mesma' [I who write to free myself from the difficult burden of a person being himself].[34] To put an end to his unbearable solitude, he creates Ângela, but the author also reaches out to the reader, instructing them how the text should be read: 'Não ler o que escrevo como se fosse um leitor. A menos que esse leitor trabalhasse, ele também, nos solilóquios do escuro irracional' [Do not read what I write as a reader would do. Unless this reader works, he too, on the soliloquies of the irrational dark].[35] Such moments constitute Lispector's invitation to her reader to work with her on the text.

In fact, the last sentence of *Um sopro de vida* is left to be completed and can be read as an invitation to carry on her work after she could no longer do it herself (the work was actually published posthumously). Similarly, the end of *Água viva* suggests that the author's writing should be continued, even through reading: 'O que te escrevo é um "isto". Não vai parar: continua. [...] O que te escrevo continua e estou enfeitiçada' [What I'm writing you is a 'this.' It won't stop: it goes on. [...] What I'm writing to you goes on and I am bewitched].[36] Just as Cixous found comfort in the voice of Clarice, Lispector herself needed to hear friendly voices in the text, including those of her readers. Like G.H., who needs to invent a hand to hold while she discovers the truth about her humanity, Lispector's writing makes room for those who may engage with her later on. Their presence, even if only imagined, was necessary to alleviate her solitude and to continue the difficult task of writing; therefore, she left some space for them to fill, a space they should not be afraid to make their own. Like Cixous, Lispector saw the text as the place where relationships can take shape in a way that makes loneliness more tolerable. She needed to think that someone would someday respond to her invitation, and Cixous did.

There is no doubt that Lispector's legacy greatly exceeds what I am about to suggest, but I think that she encourages us, her readers, not to be afraid of the laws that regulate the world and the text and instead to engage with it deeply, courageously, so that the law can be discovered and then — and only then — accepted. The truth that is to be found might not be intelligible to everyone, just as Cixous's approach was misunderstood by her critics, but she did as the protagonist of *A paixão segundo G.H.* did: she took the risk of going too far, of making the error, and in return, she shaped her thinking based on what Lispector taught her. What is paramount is what Lispector's and Cixous's works teach us: that the error is the only right path to follow, that we should not refrain from engaging personally with the text. Only by going too far in our reading will it reveal its truth to us.

Works Cited

ANDERMATT CONLEY, VERENA, 'Appendix: An Exchange with Hélène Cixous', in *Hélène Cixous: Writing the Feminine* (Lincoln and London: University of Nebraska Press, 1984)

ARROJO, ROSEMARY, 'Interpretation as Possessive Love: Hélène Cixous, Clarice Lispector and the Ambivalence of Fidelity', in *Post-colonial Translation: Theory and Practice*, ed. by Susan Bassnett and Harish Trivedi (London and New York: Routledge, 1999), pp. 141–61

BLOOM, HAROLD, *Kabbalah and Criticism* (New York: The Seabury Press, 1975)

——— *The Anxiety of Influence* (Oxford and New York: Oxford University Press, 1997 [1973])

CARRERA, ELENA, 'The Reception of Clarice Lispector via Hélène Cixous: Reading from the Whale's Belly', in *Brazilian Feminisms*, ed. by Solange Ribeiro de Oliveira and Judith Still (Nottingham: University of Nottingham, 1999), pp. 85–100

CIXOUS, HÉLÈNE, *L'Heure de Clarice Lispector* (Paris: Éditions des femmes, 1989)

——— *Reading with Clarice Lispector*, ed. and trans. by Verena Andermatt Conley (Minneapolis: University of Minnesota Press, 1990)

——— *Le Rire de la Méduse: et autres ironies* (Paris: Galilée, 2010)

——— *White Ink: Interviews on Sex, Text and Politics*, ed. by Susan Sellers (New York: Columbia University Press, 2008)

KLOBUCKA, ANNA, 'Hélène Cixous and The Hour of Clarice Lispector', *SubStance*, 23.1, Issue 73, (1994), 41–62

LISPECTOR, CLARICE, *Água viva* (bilingual edition), trans. by Regina Helena de Oliveira Machado (Paris: Éditions des femmes, 1981); *Água Viva*, trans. by Stefan Tobler (New York: New Directions, 2012)

—— *A paixão segundo G.H.* (Rio de Janeiro: Rocco, 2009 [1964]); *The Passion According to G.H.*, trans. by Idra Novey (New York: New Directions, 2012)

—— *Um sopro de vida* (Rio de Janeiro: Rocco, 1999 [1978]); *A Breath of Life*, trans. by Johnny Lorenz (New York: New Directions, 2012)

Notes to Chapter 10

1. Verena Andermatt Conley, 'Introduction', in Hélène Cixous, *Reading with Clarice Lispector*, ed. and trans. by Verena Andermatt Conley (Minneapolis: University of Minnesota Press, 1990), p. vii.
2. Ibid.
3. Hélène Cixous, *White Ink: Interviews on Sex, Text and Politics*, ed. by Susan Sellers (New York: Columbia University Press, 2008), p. 82.
4. Hélène Cixous, 'Le Rire de la Méduse', in Hélène Cixous, *Le Rire de la Méduse: et autres ironies* (Paris: Galilée, 2010), p. 37; 'The Laugh of the Medusa', trans. by Keith Cohen and Paula Cohen, *Signs*, 1.4 (Summer 1976), 875–93. Italics in the original.
5. In some interviews, Cixous says she started reading Lispector in 1977, the year of her death, while in her text 'Vivre l'orange', she writes that this first encounter occurred on 12 October 1978.
6. In a 1976 interview, Cixous was asked to talk about feminine writing, which she did mostly by mentioning what it was not (she did not consider Nathalie Sarraute's work as feminine, for instance). Her writings on this topic in the years that follow succeed in articulating what *écriture féminine* is, and use Lispector's works as the basis to consider this different approach. This interview appears in English in Cixous, *White Ink*, pp. 58–78.
7. Most of Lispector's works translated into French were published by Éditions des femmes from 1978 to 1995, and they brought out the complete collection of her *Contos* [*Nouvelles*] in 2017, translated by Jacques and Teresa Thiériot, Claudia Poncioni and Didier Lamaison, Sylvie Durastanti and Claude Farny, and Geneviève Leibrich and Nicole Biros. Only *A maçã no escuro* was published by a different publisher, Gallimard, in 1970, under the title *Le Bâtisseur de ruines* [literally, The Builder of Ruins], translated by Violante Do Canto.
8. These seminars were held at Université de Paris VIII–Vincennes at Saint-Denis and at the Collège International de Philosophie.
9. Elena Carrera observes that 'Lispector has provided Cixous with a frame, a name and a voice, an external authority, within with to speak of her own ideas, obsessions and dreams', 'The Reception of Clarice Lispector via Hélène Cixous: Reading from the Whale's Belly', in *Brazilian Feminisms*, ed. by Solange Ribeiro de Oliveira and Judith Still (Nottingham: University of Nottingham, 1999), pp. 85–100 (p. 86). Similarly, Rosemary Arrojo argues that Cixous transformed Lispector into 'an exemplary sample of feminine writing', the latter being used by Cixous to illustrate her feminine ways of spending, 'Interpretation as Possessive Love: Hélène Cixous, Clarice Lispector and the Ambivalence of Fidelity', in *Post-colonial Translation: Theory and Practice*, ed. by Susan Bassnett and Harish Trivedi (London and New York: Routledge, 1999), pp. 141–61 (p. 149).
10. Anna Klobucka, 'Hélène Cixous and The Hour of Clarice Lispector', *SubStance*, 23.1, Issue 73 (1994), 41–62 (p. 44).
11. This claim is actually at the core of Rosemary Arrojo's critique of Cixous's work: 'From this perspective, we could say that Cixous's reading of Lispector is also a form of "colonization", in which whatever or whoever is subject to foreign domination not only has to adopt the interests of the colonizer but also comes under the latter's complete control.' Arrojo, 'Interpretation as Possessive Love', p. 156.
12. Klobucka, comparing Cixous's reading to a 'intrauterine experience' similar to that had by the prophet Jonah in the whale's belly, asserts that Cixous reads Lispector in a solely personal way, leaving out anybody else and therefore refusing any discussion about her readings: 'She does not need to engage with other critics of Lispector, since she is not interested in finding an objective

truth about Lispector, but in exploring her own subjectivity through the reading. She can simply go on speaking of herself, her own obsessions from inside the belly of Lispector's texts, inside the belly of her seminars'. Klobucka, 'Hélène Cixous and The Hour of Clarice Lispector', p. 100.

13. Clarice Lispector, *A paixão segundo G.H.* (Rio de Janeiro: Rocco, 2009 [1964]), pp. 116, 113; *The Passion According to G.H.*, trans. by Idra Novey (New York: New Directions, 2012), pp. 115, 111.
14. Hélène Cixous, *Vivre l'orange/To Live the Orange*, in Hélène Cixous, *L'Heure de Clarice Lispector* (Paris: Éditions des femmes, 1989), pp. 10–13. Cixous's English text draws from a translation by Ann Liddle and Sarah Cornell. Italics in original.
15. Hélène Cixous, *Vivre l'orange/To Live the Orange*, p. 16.
16. Ibid., p. 74.
17. Hélène Cixous, 'L'Auteur en vérité', in Hélène Cixous, *L'Heure de Clarice Lispector* (Paris: Éditions des femmes, 1989), pp. 137–38. All translations into English are mine, unless otherwise indicated.
18. Ibid., pp. 138–39.
19. While Cixous recognizes that a woman is more likely to 'adopt' a feminine economy than a man, neither of these economies is attached to a specific gender or sex.
20. Verena Andermatt Conley, 'Appendix: An Exchange with Hélène Cixous', in *Hélène Cixous: Writing the Feminine* (Lincoln and London: University of Nebraska Press, 1984), p. 154.
21. I thank Adriana X. Jacobs for bringing to my attention that the Hebrew text of Genesis does not specify which fruit is eaten — it is only referred to as the fruit of the tree (*'pri ha-ets'*), which allows for many possibilities. Interestingly, on the back cover of *L'Heure de Clarice Lispector*, Cixous invites her reader to choose her own fruit: 'Pomme le sien. Orange le mien. Et le tien? Quelle couleur? Quelle douloureuse joie?' [Apple, hers. Orange, mine. And yours? What colour? What painful joy?].
22. Hélène Cixous, *Vivre l'orange/To Live the Orange*, pp. 40–41.
23. She calls what she manages to write, with the help of Clarice, a 'voluntary translation' in which she wants to acknowledge Clarice's input. Cixous, *Vivre l'orange*, p. 38.
24. Cixous, *Reading with Clarice Lispector*, p. 3.
25. Ibid., p. 69.
26. Arrojo, 'Interpretation as Possessive Love', p. 154.
27. Lispector, *A paixão segundo G.H.*, p. 163; *The Passion According to G.H.*, p. 171.
28. Ibid., p. 167; ibid., p. 175.
29. Ibid., p. 169; ibid., p. 178.
30. Ibid., p. 175; ibid., p. 185.
31. Ibid., p. 176; ibid., p. 186.
32. Ibid., p. 175; ibid., p. 185.
33. Harold Bloom's work on influence is particularly enlightening in this context, because it shows how negatively it is usually perceived. He considers reading to be a defensive process, comparing it to warfare. *Kabbalah and Criticism* (New York: The Seabury Press, 1975), p. 103. In fact, for Bloom, any reading is actually a misreading, which he calls misprision; similar to what Lispector suggests in *A paixão segundo G.H.*, the error is necessary to every reading, to the extent where he suggests that there are no such things as good readings, only misreadings. According to him, '[s]trong poets *must* be misread' (p. 103). That being said, it seems to me that Lispector and Cixous depict both influence and the error much more positively in their respective works than Bloom does. See also Bloom, *The Anxiety of Influence* (Oxford and New York: Oxford University Press, 1997 [1973]).
34. Clarice Lispector, *Um sopro de vida* (Rio de Janeiro: Rocco, 1999 [1978]), p. 17; Clarice Lispector, *A Breath of Life*, trans. by Johnny Lorenz (New York: New Directions, 2012), p. 8.
35. Lispector, *Um sopro de vida*, p. 21; Lispector, *A Breath of Life*, p. 12.
36. Clarice Lispector, *Água viva*, trans. by Regina Helena de Oliveira Machado (Paris: Éditions des femmes, 1981), p. 258. This is a bilingual (Portuguese-French) edition; Clarice Lispector, *Água Viva*, trans. by Stefan Tobler (New York: New Directions, 2012), p. 88.

CHAPTER 11

Clarice Lispector and World Literature: Is *The Hour of the Star* a Global Novel?

Nelson H. Vieira

> ... and clearly the story is true even though invented — let everyone see it reflected in himself for we are all one and the same person, and he who is not poor in terms of money is poor in spirit or feeling — Clarice Lispector[1]

Clarice Lispector's writing occupies a heralded pedestal in Brazilian letters, affording her a special *hors de concours* standing that has transformed her into a national literary and cultural icon. This study argues that Clarice's rich body of work transcends Brazilian boundaries and merits recognition within the theatre of world literature, the currently much contested *Weltliteratur*, interpreted as the coveted imprimatur of literary prestige. The above epigraph constitutes a possible pathway toward achieving a critical global reading of Clarice, that is, her deserving a spotlight on the world stage of literature since her writing orients readers to navigate the multiple labyrinths of life that complicated her own and her protagonists' feelings about belonging, dislocation and identity.

Permeating all her narratives, these feelings as themes reveal a preoccupation with deep-rooted anxieties of uncertainty, lack, itinerancy, and displacement, visible in lives residing in the arenas of the local as well as the global. This span of ontological concerns serves as common universal ground for explaining the ever-increasing reception of Clarice's writing, undoubtedly enhanced by varied translations, diverse readerships, and international media. The above epigraph serves as an inroad towards a critical perception into (1) her wide optic of the world and the meaning of belonging; (2) her predisposition toward alterity beyond egoism; and (3) her engaging form of dialogicality.[2] Recent attention to theories, definitions and concepts of *Weltliteratur* have led Claricean scholars to assess the global expanse of her reception, given the international spectrum of her translated publications into more than twenty foreign languages. In other words, how extensive is the span of her readership? While translation may be one barometer used to measure her international reception, this study will focus primarily upon the literary and humanistic features of her writing to argue why one can read Clarice via a global optic.

In view of the many theories applied to the concept of world literature, how can one approach Clarice's fiction internationally as well as nationally? To begin this inquiry into the global, an initial and relevant cue can be found in Héctor Hoyos's meaning of 'globality', defined in his recent book, *Beyond Bolaño: The Global Latin American Novel*, as an 'understanding of the literary representation of a "broadening consciousness" of the world as a whole'.[3] This definition relates to Clarice's voice, especially because in *A hora da estrela* [*The Hour of the Star*] (1977) the narrative embodies and encompasses a broadening consciousness from the local to the global. In this novella, the expanding consciousness emerges from local middle- to lower-class gender tensions to the commercial and globalized features of mass culture ingested vicariously by the indentured and marginalized protagonist Macabéa, whose sparse social existence subsists on emblems of Coca-Cola, Marilyn Monroe, red lipstick, melodic music, radio, fan magazines, and other world-wide media. Clarice casts Macabéa's fractured and quasi-destitute life of abandonment from multiple social points of view and in so doing keenly ensnares and awakens her diverse readers to Macabéa's plight of migration, marginalization and poverty by deftly inducing the narrative with literature's gift for conveying what is humanly and thus ontologically relatable to all readers.

The broadening consciousness emanating from *The Hour of the Star* also lies in its evocation of the 'world on the move' initiative, in this case, the internal migration from Brazil's North to South which echoes other internal and external movements across all types of borders to alert the reader that the world, then and now, is undergoing another intense 'age of migration.'[4] This social and world phenomenon is metaphorically expressed by the anthropologist James Clifford in his book *Routes: Travel and Translation in the Late Twentieth Century*, where the first word in the title, 'routes', stands in opposition to roots.[5] Macabéa's northeastern roots migrate to and wither in Rio's world of blatant capitalism and urban culture, leaving her to survive barely in a lower social world of quasi-poverty.

The super-consciousness generated by the novella's focus upon how its characters think or act propels readers to shed their inveterate will or propensity for certainty, happy endings and definitive answers. The novel's potential for stirring a myriad of critical readings can also be attributed to its against-the-grain narrative formation of exasperating but sly and defiant meta-fictional intrusions; its play with the ironic special and august naming of the lowly protagonists — recalling the Maccabees, Olympian gods, and divine Glory, as well as by mounting a narrative sequencing of life's disorder. This disarray or unevenness is made manifest via the novella's dramatization of Brazilian/Latin American variegated and hybrid particularities, its mixing of spiritism with Catholicism, and its production of a regional northeast singsong accent and vocabulary in contrast to standard Portuguese from southern Brazil.[6] Moreover, the novella's selectively humane but frequently sarcastic intonation is melancholically played out against a consumerist background of capitalism, commercialization, Coca-Cola, the kitsch of plastic flowers and furniture coverings, lipstick, and Mercedes-Benz, all part of a ubiquitous and aggressive form of globalization.

Specifically, and as an appropriate Claricean example, I contend that *The Hour of the Star*, published in 1977, prior to the current literary hullabaloo driving the dialogue about the internationalization of Brazilian literature, is indeed roundly emblematic of the above-referenced broadening consciousness.⁷ With the threatening socio-economic background of a New World Order, one trenchantly crafted by the implied author, but not dogmatically, there appear insertions within the narrative of intermittent and simulated explosions or shocks that jar the protagonist's naïve outlook and actions. Furthermore, by inhibiting Macabéa's already poor communication skills with these rhetorical explosions of doom or fear into the body of the narration, Clarice employs a simple grammatical tool to underscore the very problematic reality of one being able to escape unscathed and to belong easily to the world and to life itself.

David Damrosch provides balanced insights on world literature as offering 'multiple "windows on the world"' and also as a 'mode of circulation and of reading'.⁸ On the other hand, my approach is more aligned with Adam Kirsch's view in *The Global Novel: Writing the World in the 21st Century* that 'sees humanity on the level of the species [...] [enabling] the capacity of fiction to reveal humanity to itself'; and, concomitantly, with Roger D. Sell's *Communicational Criticism: Studies in Literature as Dialogue* which argues for an interpersonal dialogicality between writer and reader in reference to literature's dramatization of the other, that is, engaging the contradictory and sometimes unfamiliar values and thoughts of another individual and another society.⁹ This dialogicality, nonetheless, is to be accompanied by ethical deliberations around fairness, non-condescension, equality, and generosity.¹⁰

In view of the above critical considerations, our focus will not examine the contentious polemics of literary histories and rigid rubrics evoked by Pascale Casanova in *The World Republic of Letters* with her mapping of a centre–periphery model around prestige vs. lesser-known literatures.¹¹ Nor will we argue for exploring the implications of cosmopolitan vs. parochial literatures. Nor will we deliberate much upon the issues of circulation and translation as modes of prestige for all literatures; except, that is, for my next reference to the Japanese writer and critic Minae Mizumura and her controversial but provocative study about translation in *The Fall of Language in the Age of English*.¹² Mizumura's study harbours implications for Clarice and particularly for a multi-dimensional understanding and appreciation of her work on its way to achieving a critical mass of transnational readership. Implications about reading her in the original Portuguese or via translation arise especially when Mizumura underscores the 'asymmetrical relationship between the universal and particular' or international and national literatures:

> Those who live only in the universal temporality [of English] can make their voices heard by the world. Those who simultaneously live in the universal and particular [Portuguese] temporalities may hear voices from the other side, but they cannot make their own voices heard. [...] novels written in English are increasingly dominating the world and can only continue to do so. [...] English no longer belongs to this or that group of people but to everyone who wishes to use it. [...] English is no longer a national language, and texts written in English are no longer national literature.¹³

How do Mizumura's sobering pronouncements relate to what the Brazilian poet Lêdo Ivo referred to in Clarice's original Portuguese as 'the foreignness of her prose'?[14] Will translation into English be the most efficient and only mode for acknowledging Clarice's literary globality? Or, in a perfect scenario, does the world have to become bilingual in order to feel the full linguistic range and impact of her words? These considerations also beg the obvious question: how much is lost via translation of Clarice's prose? These queries are not meant to represent a libel against translation per se, but perhaps a call for multiple translations of a single text as complementary side roads to more enriched readings, which in turn call attention to the creative alternatives gleaned from the application of comparative translations. Interestingly, in this case, a comparative translation approach can be applied since there already exist two English translations of *The Hour of the Star*.

While comparative translation may not serve as the most expeditious way of capturing the fullness of a Brazilian or Latin American text, a global lens can promote and appreciate its other worldliness dimensions such as its self-declared 'asymmetry,' recalling Mizumura's pronouncement, in order to show Latin America's uniqueness in imaging and understanding the interconnected world or the global condition by being 'both site-specific and [one that] that looks for common ground'.[15] Or for that matter to apply Casanova's term of 'double positionality' in order to define world consciousness as operating 'in the region and elsewhere'.[16] Along these lines, at one point Hoyos imagines a 'scholar of world literature, who regards novels as part of a broader ensemble, relatively unbound from its provenance yet open to a potentially global community of readers'.[17] In what follows, I will show how *The Hour of the Star* takes part in the broader ensemble imagined by Hoyos.

By supporting Kirsch's argument on 'the capability of fiction to reveal humanity to itself', I also applaud Hoyos's application of Borges's short story 'The Aleph' as a metaphor for works that generate an effect on how we as readers see the world as well as how literary texts may impart meaning beyond their national contexts. In Borges's story, the Aleph represents 'one of the points in space that contain all points [...] the place where, without admixture or confusion, all the places of the world, seen from every angle, coexist'.[18] The felicitous use of the Aleph as a metaphor for global coexistence (of cultures) challenges a hegemonic view, that is, one envisioning the world from a position of dominance. According to Hoyos:

> the Aleph is an objectification of the idea of much in little, carried to its final logical consequences. Not only is it a world in miniature, but it is also an infinitude of points of view, where recursiveness is unavoidable and where time and space — succession and distance — lose their meaning.[19]

Hoyos's use of the concept of *multum in parvo* (much in little), reflective of Borges's 'The Aleph', dialogues technically and philosophically with Clarice's multifaceted novella *The Hour of the Star* not only due to its muted Jewish resonance, but also to the compelling yet conflicting points of view, subtle cultural inflections and media tropes that surface to challenge the readers' often staid interpretation or misguided stereotyping about the Other, gender, faith, migration, love, class, writing, G-d, and, above all, existence.[20] For example, this novella contributes to how we may see the world of class conflict and gender asymmetry as well as its narrative place on the world stage of literary performance. Hoyos draws upon Borges's short story to elaborate on how the concept of the Aleph

> grounds the experience of globality. Note that this is not just a smaller version of the world we think we know. It would be one thing to describe a world from one point of view and then imagine its miniature; here there is an infinitude of points of view. This paradoxical transfiguration of parts and whole collapses the logic of synecdoche. It depicts a world rich in possibilities, in the full dimension of its becoming.[21]

The Hour of the Star exudes many possible points of view on life itself because it shakes the reader into seeing outside his or her own space of existence as well as how others see and think differently, and thereby wonder where the centre of the universe is actually located or not. The juggling of points of view within a meta-fictional frame that challenges a traditional narrative structure makes way for an uncertain, interrogative and, at times, uncomfortable stance that the reader experiences as self-questioning about their own existence and beliefs. An anecdotal confirmation of Clarice's incisive literary and dialogical commitment to existential and metaphysical questions appears in her *crônica*, 'Idle Chatter', dated 14 September 1968, where she proudly cites João Guimarães Rosa's reading of her writing, 'not for literature but for life', thus zeroing in on her preference for primary big-picture questions on the meaning of life and the fragility of existence.[22]

While underscoring the reader's intense dialogue with the text and the writer, in his *Where I'm Reading From: The Changing World of Books*, Tim Parks speaks of the reader's important engagement with art and 'the need for readers to counter the experience of art [as] something that might correct our normally reductive and rapacious ways of thinking'.[23] This observation extends not only to a perspicacious, conscientious and empathetic sense of alterity, as alluded to above, but also to the reader's own sense of selfhood, the extent of his or her own degree of self-knowledge. Parks further proposes: 'The challenge [...] is to be aware of one's habits, to be ready to negotiate, even to surprise oneself. Perhaps it's the books that very slightly shift an old position, or at least oblige you to think it through again, that become most precious'.[24] *The Hour of the Star* is such a book.

The universal themes of life, God, the void, and world in one way or another permeate all of Clarice's writing, particularly the novels that follow *The Apple in the Dark* (1961) and *The Passion According to G.H.* (1964), but in *The Hour of the Star* these themes are vibrantly echoed on a planetary and quantum scale as expressed in its famous beginning of breadth and breath: 'All the world began with a yes. One molecule said yes to another molecule and life was born', thereby setting the stage for a 'much in little' vision of life as illuminated by a cast of vulnerable characters who barely function as they struggle within a particular, consumerist and urban scenario of displacement and abandonment.[25] Speaking of life's puzzling inscrutability yet familiar existential angst, the smart-alecky and sometimes angry or at least grumpy narrator alludes condescendingly to a human commonality: 'Everyone alive knows, even if they don't know they know'.[26] But what does such a statement mean to a sparse figure like the uneducated and inexperienced Macabéa who has to scrape through life randomly? How distant, unaware and unreliable is the male narrator as he constructs Macabéa? How ironic is his role as male narrator, perhaps a masculine alter ego, when the reader senses the paratextual presence of the female implied author — Clarice? Does this duel of narrators also destabilize and displace the authority of the male narrator while simultaneously challenging and blurring the line between fiction and reality, thereby giving a real face to the social and economic depravity victimizing migrants within Brazil and elsewhere in the world?

The ironic invocation of an everyman version of poverty conflates with the dialogical bent or communication embedded in Clarice's text between narrator and reader. According to Roger D. Sell, 'a communicator can explore general or moral truths which go beyond the detail of particular empirical cases, or can probe feelings and opinions which have yet to be stabilized into constant attitudes'.[27] These feelings and opinions also involve those of the reader particularly in how the narrator addresses or treats the reader. The use of the behind-the-scenes narrator (Clarice) purposely complicates even more the novella's dialogical features because the somewhat dyspeptic meta-fictional male narrator Rodrigo, who does not always act ethically, as well as the implied author's muted holographic female presence, uncomfortably position the reader as receiver of two voices or two points of view. This narrative set-up recalls what Sell refers to as the literary device of addressivity: the narrators/addresser(s) treat the reader/addressees as personae (not as passive narratees/interlocutors). This addressivity or dialogicality differs from Bakhtin's dialogic imagination because it invites the real readers 'to try on for size' psychological masks from a personal wardrobe of feelings, beliefs, prejudices, attitudes, and moods.[28] While addressing the reader about Macabéa, the cranky and unconsciously irresponsible Rodrigo dismissively states: 'Take care of her because all I can do is show her so you can recognize her on the street, walking lightly because of her quivering thinness'.[29] By having readers respond/react to the text interpersonally, this engineered textual experience incites acceptance or rejection just as we negotiate our responses in everyday conversation.

Given the broad concept of addressivity cogently manifested in *The Hour of the Star*, it behoves one to switch temporal positions in order to recognize that the universal takes in the global while being influenced by the particular. Even though Mizumura sees the particular as frequently participating in an asymmetrical relationship with dominant literary canons, another approach would be to recognize that the world and Latin American literary poles can incite mutual 'cross-pollination'.[30] Just as Borges's Aleph questions where the centre of the universe lies, Clarice's novella, as her own *multum in parvo* Aleph, in turn challenges the idea that the world's centrality reverberates only from a well-known dominant temporality and, what's more, usually via English.

Defining world literature 'as an affiliation of the different', Sell proposes that literatures can also serve as a balanced dialogue in relation to 'communicational ethics, both in the world at large and within literary writing and literary discussion in particular'.[31] This critic refers to communicational ethics as the ethics of address and response. Communicational ethics resonate continually in Clarice's 'formative fictions'[32] as in her showcasing of how 'a writer's way of entering into human relationships, both with individual readers and with readers in larger groupings [...] [can be achieved] by fostering a new self-consciousness about the connections between language use and human relationships'.[33] Notice how the male narrator arrogantly dictates what feelings a passive reader should adopt or of course reject: 'Anyway, it's true that I too have no pity for my main character, the northeastern girl: it's a story I want to be cold. But I have the right to be sadly cold and you don't'.[34] Consequently, the argument here implies that in *The Hour of the Star* Clarice maps out a dialogical architecture that engages the reader via an ethics of address and response; ethics which can also be defied. Clearly, CL is not the sole author to dramatize addressivity but she positions this device deftly and ardently in *The Hour of the Star*.

The backstage 'mechanics of the theatre', a metaphor employed by Colm Tóibín in his introduction to Ben Moser's translation, further fuels the argument on the novella's formative tools of narration and what they do for all types of readers' apprehensions and emotions.[35] In other words, narrative form serves here as an insidious and infectious mode to help the Brazilian and non-Brazilian readers connect with the affect arising from the frustration and anxiety generated by the unsayable. This awareness of 'what a text does instead of what a text says', according to Landy, drops the reader into the arena of artifice, however, moving way beyond narrow moralizing or the mere transfer of information:

> What [transformative fictions] give us is *know-how*; rather than transmitting beliefs, what they equip us with are *skills*; rather than teaching, what they do is *train*. They are not informative, that is, but formative. They present themselves as spiritual exercises (whether sacred or profane), spaces for prolonged and active encounters that serve, over time, to hone our abilities and thus, in the end, to help us become who we are.[36]

In this manner, *The Hour of the Star* primarily forms, but does not inform, readers by helping them to unlearn certain ways of thinking, reading, speaking or judging and perhaps even to acquire more self-knowledge. The novella's puzzling ambiguity and daunting uncertainty about many things, like how to create art or a fictional character, are articulated via the unsteady and ambivalent male narrator who speaks both sympathetically and haughtily about Macabéa. This treatment further complicates and unsettles the readers' opinions about this woman's harsh poverty and peculiar innocence or potential halo. Thus, this narrative situation propels the reader into wondering whose voice you can actually trust, especially when the reader intuits the subterranean voice of Clarice as skilful ventriloquist or ambiguous cross-dresser. Can a writer's voice be both male and female? This question immediately expands the potentialities of the gender spectrum. The novella's penetrating uncertainty also pulls the reader to the point of having to rethink their stance toward gender, the uneducated *povo* [people, masses], migrants, marginality, lifestyles, and low dialects versus high vernacular forms delineating class distinctions. These uncomfortable scenarios usually lead to the inevitable question first coined by Gayatri Spivak — can the subaltern really speak through voice(s) of intellectually sophisticated and economically stable writers? These questions transcend Brazil's national culture, for they relate in different ways to all cultures. Clarice's own privilege as a well-translated nationally iconic Brazilian writer who had lived and closely witnessed as a child the experience of the northeastern plight of subalternity and marginality, coupled with her plangent and ironic voice (paratextually echoing her family's refugee history), in addition to references to international consumerist products (like Coca-Cola), affords this Brazilian novella a transnational aura. At the same time this work evokes an authentic subaltern voicing via a holographic narration of the author's stated past experience as a female voice of subaltern identification which insidiously counters the narrator Rodrigo's privileged male voice. In so doing, this narrative set-up challenges the male narrator's voice as sole authority. Clarice's unique family history, her international recognition via translation and her aforementioned literary ingenuity place her and this novella on the cosmopolitan stage of world conditions and mounting globalization.

The novel does 'inform' the readers about Brazil's particular national and regional North/South social experiences alongside universal issues like migration, economic injustice, male superiority, female submission, racial and social prejudices, combined with the local flavour of the Northeast *literatura de cordel*'s codes of *firmeza* and *falsidade* [steadfastness and deceitfulness], codes that in themselves may be seen as universal or global.[37] Nonetheless, it is with a well-crafted dialogical focus upon the form(ation) of readers via visions of the particular reverberating global ramifications that Clarice's novella forms and touches readers so that they will be able to acknowledge and handle conflicting views or beliefs. For example, how does the reader characterize the male narrator's attitude or stance when he proclaims: 'Actually I'm more of an actor because with only one way to punctuate, I juggle with intonation and force another's breathing to accompany my text'?[38] Such pronouncements raise the question of the sincerity of the male narrator's stance, ergo the sly insertion of another perspective, a ghostly one, as a humane counterbalance.

Obviously, the narrator's attempt to carve a true picture of Macabéa's thin existence is not without prejudice and thus suggests his ambiguous feelings about Macabéa and her class. These in turn unmask his authorial performance as a form of Pygmalion-manqué, incapable of honest loving-kindness toward his non-exalted muse, Macabéa, and remind the reader of certain masculine blunders and behaviours that stretch across the universe. Therefore, the narrative's deft sleight of hand in having subtle input from the implied female author contributes to the reader's ability to weigh up both behaviours and perspectives. Rodrigo is for most emblematic of a lack of cultural sensitivity evident in both genders and many world cultures, but here primarily manifested in the novella's male protagonists, including the narrator himself. Therefore, the implied author's choice of using a male narrator becomes profoundly ironic because it ultimately subverts Rodrigo's declared intent of producing a cold, factual and straightforward story but instead renders a tale of conflicting cultural attitudes and social paradoxes in a disturbingly meta-fictional, gender-driven and worldly consciousness that places the reader in the dubious role of judge as well as jury.

In this novella's process of 'forming' readers who must interact and grapple with its non-linear narrative in order to appreciate the breadth of the book's indirect call for interpersonal humanity, as well as its global inferences relatable to international audiences or readerships, close attention must be paid to its peculiar form of preface consisting of thirteen subtitles listed with the original author's authentic signature — Clarice Lispector — inserted between the fourth and fifth subtitle. This unusual construct at the beginning of the novel, besides confirming Clarice's presence as paratext, also underscores one of the unique ways of approaching or announcing a story. This list of subtitles does not conform to any sense of a national or broader brand of preface or genre; their placement is not necessarily Brazilian or Latin American in style and content in a way that would preclude their being applied to other cultures. The list of subtitles serves as a prime example of Clarice's freedom from rigid literary rubrics or national literature genres.

Although the thirteen subtitles generate a sad tone prior to the narrative, they may also relate as a contrast to the luminous thousand-pointed star, the halo of stardom aspired to by Macabéa, a fantasized destiny, a daydream floating above her lowly self and conferring a positive note to her being. Even an imagined lit candle for mourning at the time of her hit-and-run evokes a type of sanctity: 'The luxury of the rich flame seemed to sing glory'.[39] But the subtitles primarily reflect the actual features of Macabéa's life: abandonment, shame, shock, empathy, irony, perplexity, pity. While her dream of stardom does appear in the list of subtitles, it is overshadowed by most of the other more melancholic subtitles. Ironically, she imaginatively achieves stardom vicariously just prior to her death when she feels herself becoming someone with a happy fate, a promising subject instead of cast-aside object. On the other hand, the special attributes of Macabéa's dogged resistance and life affirmation are hinted at indirectly and intermittently by the surprised narrator who invariably employs a sardonic tone: 'I forgot to say that it was really alarming that from Macabéa's almost parched body so vast was her almost unlimited breath of life and as rich as of that of a pregnant maiden'.[40] Despite Macabéa's tragic plight, her story implies the existence of a special something, an unsayable humane quality that transcends the materialistic and cold world she faces.

The intermittent burst of explosions, alluded to earlier, can also represent crescendo drumrolls for the narrator to increase mockingly the suspense of a kitschy melodrama, unconsciously unmasking his insidious compulsion to treat her story as a B-movie or second-rate TV novella: 'Is this a melodrama? What I know is that melodrama was the summit of her life, all lives are an art and hers inclined toward the great uncontrollable weeping like rain and lightning'.[41] The irony in this statement contradicts an earlier statement: 'And even what I'm writing somebody else could write. A male writer, that is, because a woman would make it all weepy and maudlin'.[42] In this way, Rodrigo exhibits a masculine aporia that suggests a clichéd form of a Brazilian or Latin American patriarchal attitude. Furthermore, his particularity co-exists with other but different worldwide, interconnected codes of cultural masculinity and, in so doing, awakens any reader, not just a Brazilian, to the pitfalls of unjust gender behaviour.

The gender conundrums emanating from the narrative voice(s) spark multiple re-readings because the text evokes more than a sociological interpretation of cruel poverty and social inequities in its challenge to the reader to recognize the nuances and subtleties of hegemonic and subaltern behaviours and emotions. Hoyos defends a broad focus on such social behaviours and injustices through the lens of world literature by interpreting this view as a result of adopting a global stance, in the spirit of the transformation toward wider world views: 'the intensified interconnection [...] [called] [...] globality'.[43] Since Hoyos believes that 'Latin America should effectively become a literary pole that can stimulate the transnational field, rather than a locale ancillary to the workings of metropolitan centers', he also calls attention to the very 'strong tradition in Brazil and Spanish America of negotiating particularity with universality, specificity with generality, all within complex transactions among national, regional and global realms'.[44] This stance is very much in line with his strong belief in cultural cross-pollination. This negotiation occurs in *The Hour of the Star* by shaking up the readers' ideologies, obliging them to rethink their own philosophies of and situations in life, hopefully generating a more humanistic or ethical way of 'reading' the world.

To conclude, one can appreciate Clarice's novella alongside today's emphasis upon world literature because it furnishes the reader with a refreshingly broad communicative encounter with the world of different affiliations. The reader can discover, even identify with, many parallel lives, experiencing and behaving in similar ways. Consequently, it bears repeating that Clarice expressed and dramatized local/global awareness via her own *multum in parvo*, her much-in-little novella which preceded today's celebratory but often disputed definitions of world literature, a literary polemic and challenge that came AFTER CLARICE.

Works Cited

CASANOVA, PASCALE, *The World Republic of Letters*, trans. by M. B. DeBevoise (Cambridge: Harvard University Press, 2007 [1999])

CLIFFORD, JAMES, *Routes: Travel and Translation in the Late Twentieth Century* (Cambridge, MA: Harvard University Press, 1997)

COUTINHO, EDUARDO, ed., *Brazilian Literature as World Literature* (New York: Bloomsbury Academic, 2018)

DAMROSCH, DAVID, *What is World Literature?* (Princeton, NJ: Princeton University Press, 2003)

HOYOS, HÉCTOR, *Beyond Bolaño: The Global Latin American Novel* (New York: Columbia University Press, 2017)

KIRSCH, ADAM, *The Global Novel: Writing the World in the 21st Century* (New York: Columbia Reports, 2016)

LANDY, JOSHUA, *How to Do Things with Fictions* (Oxford: Oxford University Press, 2012)

LISPECTOR, CLARICE, *A hora da estrela*, 19th edn (Rio de Janeiro: Francisco Alves, 1992 [1977]); *The Hour of the Star*, trans. by Benjamin Moser, intro. by Colm Tóibín (New York: New Directions, 2011); *The Hour of the Star*, trans. by Giovanni Pontiero (Manchester: Carcanet, 1986)

—— *Discovering the World*, trans. by Giovanni Pontiero (Manchester: Carcanet, 1992)

Mizumura, Minae, *The Fall of Language in the Age of English*, trans. by Mari Yoshihara and Juliet Winters Carpenter (New York: Columbia University Press, 2017 [2008])

Parks, Tim, *Where I'm Reading From: The Changing World of Books* (New York: New York Review Books, 2015)

Resende, Beatriz, *Contemporâneos: expressões da literatura brasileira no século XXI* (Rio de Janeiro: Casa da Palavra, 2008)

Santiago, Silviano, *O cosmopolitismo do pobre* (Belo Horizonte: Editora UFMG, 2008)

Sell, Roger D., *Communicational Criticism: Studies in Literature as Dialogue* (Amsterdam: John Benjamins, 2011)

Vieira, Nelson H., *Jewish Voices in Brazilian Literature: A Prophetic Discourse of Alterity* (Gainesville: University Press of Florida, 1995)

Notes to Chapter 11

1. Clarice Lispector, *The Hour of the Star*, trans. by Giovanni Pontiero (Manchester: Carcanet, 1986), p. 12.
2. Here, 'dialogicality' refers to the writer's ability to engage the reader into understanding the values and culture of the protagonist as Other vis-à-vis the reader's own values and thereby to go beyond the boundaries of one's self, enabling the reader to know how to see more openly, instead of only seeing what he or she already knows. This experience of reading simulates a dialogue between the reader, the protagonist and even the narrator.
3. Héctor Hoyos, *Beyond Bolaño: The Global Latin American Novel* (New York: Columbia University Press, 2017), p. 2.
4. 'World on the Move' is a current national public education initiative developed by the American Anthropological Association (AAA) aimed at changing the public conversation on the issues of migration and displacement. Clarice's novella from 1977 evokes an age-old migratory phenomenon that contributes to today's public discussions on this world movement via literature.
5. James Clifford, *Routes: Travel and Translation in the Late Twentieth Century* (Cambridge, MA: Harvard University Press, 1997).
6. The northeastern manner of speaking is mentioned and illustrated in the English translation by the following example: 'He came up to her with a singsong northeastern voice that moved her, asked her: "And I beg your pardon, missy, can I invite you for a stroll?"' Lispector, *The Hour of the Star*, p. 34. In standard Portuguese from the south, the word 'miss' instead of 'missy' would be used. In the original Portuguese text 'senhorinha' is used instead of the more standard 'você' or 'senhora'. Clarice Lispector, *A hora da estrela*, 19 edn (Rio de Janeiro: Francisco Alves, 1992 [1977]), p. 59.
7. Examples of Brazilian criticism related to the internationalization of Brazilian literature are: Silviano Santiago, *O cosmopolitismo do pobre* (Belo Horizonte: Editora UFMG, 2008); Beatriz Resende, *Contemporâneos: expressões da literatura brasileira no século XXI* (Rio de Janeiro: Casa da Palavra, 2008); and Eduardo Coutinho, ed., *Brazilian Literature as World Literature* (New York: Bloomsbury Academic, 2018).
8. David Damrosch, *What is World Literature?* (Princeton, NJ: Princeton University Press, 2003), pp. 15, 5.
9. Adam Kirsch, *The Global Novel: Writing the World in the 21st Century* (New York: Columbia Reports, 2016), p. 26.
10. Sell, *Communicational Criticism*, p. 18.
11. Pascale Casanova, *The World Republic of Letters*, trans. by M. B. DeBevoise (Cambridge, MA: Harvard University Press, 2007 [1999]).
12. Minae Mizumura, *The Fall of Language in the Age of English*, trans. by Mari Yoshihara and Juliet Winters Carpenter (New York: Columbia University Press, 2017 [2008]).
13. Mizumura, *The Fall of Language in the Age of English*, pp. 58, 61.
14. Benjamin Moser, 'Translator's Afterword' in Lispector, *The Hour of the Star*, p. 80.

15. Hoyos, *Beyond Bolaño*, p. 29.
16. Ibid., p. 23.
17. Ibid., p. 31.
18. Ibid., p. 2.
19. Ibid.
20. For commentary on Clarice's Jewish identity see, Nelson H. Vieira, *Jewish Voices in Brazilian Literature: A Prophetic Discourse of Alterity* (Gainesville: University Press of Florida, 1995), pp. 100–50. See also chapters by Adriana X. Jacobs and Yael Segalovitz in this volume.
21. Hoyos, *Beyond Bolaño*, p. 3.
22. Clarice Lispector, 'Idle Chatter', in *Discovering the World*, trans. by Giovanni Pontiero (Manchester: Carcanet, 1992), pp. 180–81.
23. Tim Parks, *Where I'm Reading From: The Changing World of Books* (New York: New York Review Books, 2015), p. 78.
24. Parks, *Where I'm Reading From*, p. 45.
25. Lispector, *The Hour of the Star*, p. 3.
26. Ibid., p. 4.
27. Sell, *Communicational Criticism*, p. 13.
28. Ibid., p. 14.
29. Lispector, *The Hour of the Star*, p. 11.
30. Hoyos, *Beyond Bolaño*, p. 9.
31. Sell, *Communicational Criticism*, p. 4.
32. See Joshua Landy's introduction 'Formative Fictions', in *How to Do Things with Fictions* (Oxford: Oxford University Press, 2012), pp. 8–11.
33. Sell, *Communicational Criticism*, pp. 5–6.
34. Lispector, *The Hour of the Star*, p. 5.
35. Colm Tóibín, 'A Passion for the Void,' in Lispector, *The Hour of the Star*, p. x.
36. Landy, 'Formative Fictions', p. 10.
37. *Literatura de cordel*, literally stories on a string, is a popular and inexpensive genre of booklets, produced mainly by local northeastern poets and storytellers or modern day troubadors, that via poems, folk tales and songs address universal themes of good and evil, love and hate, honour and shame, honesty and steadfastness. These pamphlets are produced and sold in street markets and by street vendors who hang the booklets on strings to display them for potential customers.
38. Lispector, *The Hour of the Star*, p. 14.
39. Ibid., p. 72.
40. Ibid., p. 51.
41. Ibid., p. 72.
42. Ibid., p. 6.
43. Hoyos, *Beyond Bolaño*, p. 31.
44. Ibid., pp. 30, 31.

PART IV

Writing and Rewriting

CHAPTER 12

Clarice: The Visitor

Idra Novey

In the Brazilian anthology *Clarice at My Bedside*, singer-songwriter Maria Bethânia describes reaching at night for 'minha Clarice', my Clarice. I think many of us who connect deeply with Clarice's books refer to her as if speaking of a beloved aunt. Her work produces in us an almost bodily sense of connection. Her candor is so radical you finish her sentences convinced that they were written for you, that the profound questions she poses belong to you, and you belong to her.

Of course, Clarice doesn't belong to any of us. Her words and her legacy belong to no one. Not to those of us in the English-speaking world who re-translated her books for New Directions and Penguin UK, and not to those who will hopefully go on to retranslate her work in the future. She doesn't belong to any of her critics or to her biographers.

A writer's legacy can't, and shouldn't, be possessed by any other writer or translator. And yet it is hard to resist as a reader, when you reach for the same writer on your bedside for years, that some particle of that author's spirit might belong to you. When Maria Bethânia evokes 'minha Clarice', it is an evocation of the singular kind of intimacy many of us have found in Clarice's writing, and continue to find in it, as writers trying to stay true to our own voices in what is still very much a patriarchal world.

I first read Lispector twenty years ago as an undergraduate at Barnard College. In my first year as a comparative literature major, I was convinced nothing would impact my ideas of the kind of writing I wanted to do more than Julio Cortázar's *Cronopios and Famas* did, or not until I read Clarice's *The Passion According to G.H.* The depth of self-questioning in G.H., Clarice's willingness to push a sentence to a point of extreme vulnerability, felt profoundly in sync with my internal state as a college student. It astounded me that a writer this extraordinary could be absent from the crew of must-read Latin American canonical authors like Borges and Cortázar. How could a novel this accomplished, reckoning with racism and moral complacency in such an audacious way, with a narrator deciding to bite into a cockroach, not be a canonical book?

Even twenty years later, with her work finally gaining the overdue canonical status it indisputably deserves, the political questions fuelling *The Passion According to G.H.* and many of Clarice's books remain underacknowledged, as so often the politically charged aspects of novels by women still do. In the epistolary poems to

Clarice that I wrote while completing my translation of G.H. I kept thinking about the convergence of the domestic and the political, on what insect lurks there for all of us. That sequence of epistolary poems to Clarice led to a first novel that might be read as a *roman-à-clef* on my experience translating G.H.

I owe a significant debt to Clarice for my second novel as well. Every day, whether I am writing my own sentences or translating those of someone else, G.H. continues to echo, *when even then I can't find the courage, then I dream.*

I

> *At three in the afternoon, I'm the most demanding woman in the world... When it's over, six in the afternoon comes, also indescribable, in which I turn blind.*
>
> Lispector to Fernando Sabino, 1946

Dear C, I'm turning from.
Have been syntaxed and stirred into a purple.
Blurred to blind.
I made a mess of page twenty-two,
couldn't resurrect what you left unsaid
into words that wouldn't.
Do you believe in grieving?
I mean for language, the endangered
animal of, fleeing into caves.
I can only keep after it in fits
or I get trapped
in the keeping after. That,
and bliss.
Your spinning but devoted
I.N.

II

> *I know I'm using words that perhaps sound*
> *too strong (I had a night of insomnia,*
> *believe me...)*
>
> Lispector to Fernando Sabino, 1957

C, I dropped your sequence
in hot water. I talked
to the boil. I said Here
is my thumb for you to burn.
Here is the soft heart
of my hand and my arm
and the nape of my wreck.
I said vapor, just take me.
I'm done burning
with these pages. Being invisible
doesn't mean a person
won't blister, doesn't mean
the blisters won't fill
with pockets of water
or when lanced the rawest flesh
won't emerge. First the word
then the leak of water,
what another mind
may never skin.

III

> *Fernando, this is a ghost named Clarice*
> *writing to you.*
>
> Lispector to Fernando Sabino, 1956

Dear author ghost,
dear desk, I've left you
for a man. The body
has its callings
after all.

Your mortal
but abiding

I.N.

IV

> ...*in a small daily life, in which a person risks herself more deeply, with greater threats.*
> Lispector to Fernando Sabino, 1953

If a woman translates a woman who writes a woman who sculpts a pleasant something out of small clutches of bread.

If the clatter of earrings.

If the clutches become less pleasant, can no longer be called the tender

rendering of bread.

If a woman translates a woman writes a woman who is less and less.

If the flesh of bread.

If folded between fingers.

If the word for deadline and rolling and oratorio.

If collapsing under.

If the matter with the clatter of earrings is.

V

> *this is a letter for sharing news and complaints.*
> Lispector to Fernando Sabino, 1953

These letters, C,
are my geese to you.
They come backward
in the formation of a letter
from an alphabet
that can only be flown.

So much geese-work
leaves me fat and baffled,
my vocabulary slack
with Latinates.

I miss my sleek years, slender
with the certainty of what I knew.

What's terrifying about you, C,
is that you know
what you don't know, what
none of us do.

But I have to go — my sons
want me to speak in puppet.
And so it is performing your words:
I'm a blue-faced creature
with seams between her fingers.
A being with no eyelids
who cannot blink.

VI

> *nearly eight months since Paulinho was born...*
> *I drink fewer milkshakes and carry on*
> *a vacant, agitated daily life.*
>
> Lispector to Fernando Sabino, 1953

A fantasy:
We are standing by a sandbox,
both lost
in the camouflage of those hours
and their boxes.
I ask about the pronoun you often place
before God
and you go on smoking.
The sun now
above the playground begins to burn
and then
the snow burns. My sons are grown.
At last
you turn to answer and I
am listening.

These poems first appeared in Idra Novey, *Clarice: The Visitor* (London: Sylph Editions, 2014).

CHAPTER 13

Capture

After 'The Intimation of the Rose'
by Clarice Lispector

Hélia Correia

I don't remember the night Clarice came into my life. All I know is that she never left it. I am speaking as a reader, never a writer, since the crafting of a text cannot abide when another more formidable text overshadows it, suffocates it and makes it yield. As a reader, fear and fascination for Clarice's text has stayed with me to this day. Fear and fascination for the power of those words, and their ability to say the unsayable. Theirs is a diabolical power, a Faustian power, which jars; a power that, forgive me, scholars, is not something that is ever studied, that it is not even within our reach to summon. That is why it comes as no surprise that I do not read her often. Some people can get used to living under a volcano. I cannot.

When I was invited to write a short story based on one of Clarice's characters, a whole complex forest within my memory parted to render visible those small creatures: the roses bought at the market. It is a very commonplace thing to say, but, in fact, they were the ones who shined the light of choice upon me. I couldn't even stop to think about whether I ought to put my hand into that world which had always seemed to me to be another place, out of reach. It was the roses: they did not give me time. The roses and my fingers understood each other, for some fanciful reason unknown to me, even now.

They are innocent figures in all their predatory nature. In them there is something like redemption, a need to absorb, to give the individual the peace of wholeness.

I can say that now, speculating, because I am not at all aware what they wanted.[1]

I

Yes: in spite of the terrible shock, our mission is accomplished.[2] The woman has been delivered. And now we can turn our efforts to dying, to the details of a sumptuous death, the sort of death that happens in drawing rooms. Maybe even tonight, or by sunrise tomorrow at the latest. Dona Carlota's maid will cry out when she sees the petals on the floor. A little cry, the kind that is merely an announcement of itself, that finds the hand already there to cover the mouth and muffle its sound. Because Dona Carlota needs to wake up slowly. With a cup of coffee and only the usual cautious morning murmurings, without any fuss, without the slightest domestic upset. She's an easy woman to understand. There's no mystery about her; to see one side of her is to see the whole person. From the way she received the news over the phone and then announced it to the maid and her husband, we could tell straight away that she's one of those people who know, that she belongs to the species of human most akin to thistles, those highly protected organisms who know how to keep themselves alive and well-nourished. If any jealousy surfaces within them they dismiss it. 'Ridiculous!' they say. 'After all, what does beauty really matter?' But the truth is that they, too, produce rare, beautiful, magnificent flowers, the kind of flowers humans tend not to pick, not because they're afraid of the prickles — after all, they pick us, don't they? — but because they make them feel awkward, self-conscious, as if they were attending a dinner party where they don't understand the social norms. Dona Carlota is, in a sense, a social norm transfigured. Beautiful and resilient, beautiful and tough, taking care of the house rules and routines, and pronouncing her verdicts of 'I don't like that' and 'I rather like that', which so rarely match those of anyone else.

She put down the phone and said: 'She's had a relapse. She's not coming after all.' The other two looked over at the table, which was immaculately laid, though no wine had yet been served, craning their necks to see how the plan was falling apart without a speck of dust being disturbed. Dona Carlota said: 'I thought the roses were a bad sign.'

'Which roses?'

'Those ones.' And she pointed at us.

II

Yes, in spite of this wholly unexpected move. Carried into Dona Carlota's living room by a maid who hated having to do it, because it meant spending her night off going out of her way, maybe even into a different neighbourhood — it seemed to us like a very long walk — with the tissue paper disintegrating in her tightly-clasped left hand, and her right hand holding the basket of leftover food that was essentially stolen: redirected, you might say. And there we were, sticking our thorns into skin so calloused it fought back and we didn't even draw blood. For shame! A bouquet of frightened roses. Launched into the unknown, like a litter of cubs from their mother's womb. With our work still to be done. When Dona Carlota saw us, she didn't understand why Laura had sent us, or how a few bright little things could make her shudder like that in disgust. Maybe because the journey and the shock had left us feeling fragile. Maybe because the scent given off by an agitated rose contains a trace of the bacteria from the rotting earth in which it was born, and the promise of its own decay. Whatever it was, she didn't look at all pleased, as if a problem had arisen at a most inconvenient moment. Why had Laura, going out for dinner for the first time since her illness, asked the maid to bring us over beforehand? Dona Carlota was the sort of person who enjoys that kind of mystery. We are not. Because Laura, and everything to do with Laura, needed careful deliberation. More care than anyone happy could possibly take. You had to be psychic — which Dona Carlota was not — to see that sending us here was really an act of war. And it looked as if we'd been defeated. As if we hadn't completed our mission.

III

We had always kept a close watch on her. Or at least we had since her school days, when neat, methodical Laura would almost send the nuns mad with her submissive arrogance. They thought that only the pope was allowed an oxymoron like that. However, even then, the girl was never where she seemed to be. Those good, hard-working hands of hers did things without anyone noticing, without giving any assurances. Which meant that she often used to look back over her shoulder to make sure the thing had really been done. Because her attention, and everything else there was in Laura, didn't accompany her working body anywhere, and nor was it there with her when she studied. It remained hidden, waiting, nothing but eyes. Our eyes, which never miss an opportunity. Which hover like flies, suspended in the afternoon air. Us, pure organism. Primitive. Our particles spread through different creatures: flies, roses. We're as alert as guard dogs. Trying to collect, to gather up once again, those who have escaped us. The humans. Some humans, at least, like Laura, whom it might be possible to get back. The ones who are all flesh. The ones whose dreams still contain a vague memory of the forest. And who, because of this, combine disaster with perfect manners. Never tiring of washing, of tidying, of filling in the gaps so that neither ants nor unformed thoughts can get through. Tiny disconnected thoughts as resplendent as gods.

We are a little like witch doctors, always on the lookout for symptoms that might prove profitable. Wandering through villages in search of them. In fact, they sometimes reveal themselves very early on in the child who should be walking by now but who hesitates, hesitates because the space ahead looks empty, but is nothing of the sort, because she sees in it the little crowd, celebratory and menacing: the entities waiting to devour her. In cases like this, the light and the floating flecks of dust halfway down a corridor sketch out a whole destiny. So we take the child into our care, stand her back up, and from then on she will never put a foot right. She trips over and one day will get run down, or fall into a ravine, and all because she couldn't see properly. Because she could see too much.

Laura also used to lose her balance when she was a little girl, but this was because of her short, fat legs. Legs that might lead her body into the most seductive of wiggles or the worst of inelegancies. Although in fact they did neither, because Laura, with her methodical bent, began wearing a corset the moment her body showed its first sensual curves. And so she became an old-fashioned lady, ramrod stiff and short of breath.

As for us, when it came to Laura, we were very patient. We knew the day would come when we could reclaim her, because it was only her will-power that held her together, like the corset binding her hips. The stitches would eventually have to burst. And the Laura inside, like her suffocated silhouette, would spill out in the wrong direction, the undomesticated direction, the direction that is loose and mysterious. She sensed our presence in the atmosphere, sensed a fault in the structure of space, like a hole in a mosaic, and she was afraid. She was afraid of any kind of untidiness. She was afraid of her own apertures, from which bad smells emerged and babies were meant to be born. She was afraid that stray, out of control words would pour from her mouth, and that she would struggle to swallow something in a public place and choke, making everyone else feel sick. As a result, eating out became a tragedy about which she never spoke. People saw a kind of spiritual refinement in the way she carefully cut up and chewed her vegetables.

She grew up side by side with her secrets, which were nothing like the usual vulgar teenage secrets, although she was insecure and shy. What worried her parents most of all was her lack of vivacity, of charm. Her feminine qualities, like her cleanliness and enjoyment of routine tasks, were not apparent to all. They required a kind of publicity that was difficult to achieve. And when her father led his daughter to the altar, that daughter who never gave them the slightest cause for concern, but who nevertheless concerned them a great deal, he did not dare to smile for fear of revealing how pleased he was. The father approaching the altar with his mousy, rather clumsy daughter, who, for that moment, was transformed into a lovely shimmer of satin.

Back then, no one guessed it was to be a marriage that would not continue the family line. Not a single child. The husband, however, remained perfectly agreeable. As men sometimes do, he gave Laura various roles. The natural one, that of wife; the others, such as that of a daughter in need of protection; and the nocturnal ones, at which she proved surprisingly adept.

IV

We watched Laura adjust to married life, finding it an easy enough garment to wear. Armando did not even seem like a real man; more than anything, he seemed like a function being fulfilled. He probably was a function; a force in the struggle against us. A perfect match, with his liking for fatty meat, whether at the dinner table or between the sheets. He had no taste for the finer things. Only for peace and quiet. A provider of the perfect conditions for his little lady. Who was lucky, everybody said. Who was very lucky indeed, considering her lack of qualities. And considering that the first child was long overdue. A child was necessary proof of masculinity. If infertility was caused by some dark divine curse, its consequence was shame and people avoiding the couple's eyes. But Laura was fine, just fine. She saw her friends having babies and felt slightly sad, sorry she couldn't give her husband the same gift, the same recompense. But what she never told anyone was that children scared her. That perhaps she would feel glorious when the thing was taking shape in her belly, but that afterwards, oh, afterwards... 'Instinct will guide you,' she often heard people say. But what instinct? The instinct to nurse the baby, perhaps, but the instinct to bring the child up? To wash it, and comb its hair, and comfort it in the darkness? Laura wouldn't know what to do shut away with an incomprehensible creature, twenty-four hours a day. Children were strange, very strange. Laura observed them closely and noticed how their heads were abnormally large, out of proportion with their bodies. Were they even monstrous? She buried this thought deep within herself, crushed it, and shuddered. Thoughts must come from the same place as snakes. Slippery, silent and cold. She crushed them beneath her heel, as the Bible told her to do.

We never stopped letting her know that we were with her. Waiting for her. And she never doubted it. That there was a plan, a desire to conquer. Or rather, to reclaim. For hadn't Laura been ours all along? Oh, yes. As much as any human could be. Those humans who are always trying too hard, who look around themselves and scrub, and go on scrubbing, without ever making the primordial disappear.

We called to her time and again and she turned to listen, and it was the rain. We called to her, and it was a river that didn't even pass nearby, a river in her mind. Colourful little accidents, sweets that filled with bacteria and went bad. Defenceless animals collapsing outside her back door and exchanging meaningful glances with her in their dying moments. She gave herself instructions: what a wife should and shouldn't do. A wife shouldn't look at an animal in such a familiar way. A wife shouldn't lean out of the window thinking about everything that still needed to be cleaned. A mousy wife. Not even much given to flights of fancy.

In her case, there was no doubt about it: it wasn't her imagination, it was an illness. That's what they said, and her mother wept, and Armando tried to calm the panic that gripped the household and left even the maid unable to pack the mistress's possessions into a suitcase, along with suitable clothing, for her stay at the clinic. Laura was sitting in the visitors' room, perfectly composed. But she wasn't visiting. She was gone. Because we had taken her away.

V

They call it medicine. The thing charged with taking care of Laura's remains. The portion of Laura that heard and saw nothing, and that held a great emptiness within. However, medicine doesn't care about the state of the body it receives; it uses the body to regain its hold on a person's essence. It moves through the veins, along the digestive tube, with its chemical powers, or worse: with its offer to interpret. 'A case,' they say. 'We have here a case.' In the clinic, with Laura's outer layer, with the laboratorial part of her subject to analyses and tests, everyone was pleased. 'We have here a case,' they said. 'We have here an absolute coherence of symptoms.' Sterility, obsession, obesity, irregular menstrual cycles, all deriving from a single origin, a sudden release of hormones, as happens with diabetes. Something to be treated once and for all, in a white room that no one would enter without wearing an encouraging smile on their face. A very clean room, as if it were being used for the first time, disinfected of all its previous inhabitants.

Medicine is a very powerful thing. It has its victories over us, although it's been proven that, in the end, or, at the very least, at the moment of death, everything is returned into our hands.

With Laura, for example, the injections and pills began to hunt down all the bad things in her body. Bad things, from the point of view of medicine, are defects in the workings of the organism. Science can't accept that the problem isn't material; that the problem is us. We are the problem. We, the unsaid. The untold. The unquantifiable. We who had taken Laura, the true Laura, to places where the individual no longer exists.

However, medicine gradually managed to get close to her, to put her back together into a whole, a consciousness. Which is not surprising, because in a way it had ventured into our territory and studied what it found there, learning to interfere with microscopic elements, invisible to the human eye, which can only be detected when they combine with others. When Laura was discharged, she got a pat on the back. It was what the clinic did to patients to show them how robust they were, as if they were on the same sports team. Victory. It knew it had won, and it knew which weapons it had taken into battle. It just didn't know who it had beaten.

VI

Laura tried so hard, poor thing. It was painful to see how hard she tried, how carefully she followed the doctor's instructions. She did everything she could to make Armando forget, once and for all, about waiting for catastrophe to strike again.

Dona Carlota invited everyone over for dinner. Oh yes, everyone, with no exceptions. They knew this would be the final test, the proof that Laura had been cured. That she would take her husband's arm and travel with him on public transport, her hand resting on his arm and strong enough to remove, first from people's eyes and then from their hearts, the unbearable anxiety with which they constantly watched her.

That dinner posed great risks. It was a frontier, and if Laura crossed it she would escape us for good. For good, that is, as long as she lived. Because the other side belongs indisputably to us. It's a restitution. Earth to earth, and everything else that has been written on the subject. Where there is particular beauty or particular deformity, we act quickly, and immediately reabsorb the creature. Not with Laura, though. Laura was a conquered territory we had defended in battle after battle. We mobilized our troops on her behalf.

VII

The insistence of the man at the market, the forceful way he pressed the stems of the roses into her hand, would have aroused suspicion in a woman more used to the tricks of commerce. The roses must have been old or stolen. But Laura wasn't surprised to see those wild flowers there, flowers picked from beside some crumbling wall. The man was persistent, she worried he was going to start shouting, and that the market crowd would turn its face to look at her, a single face, ready to watch the scene unfold. The man was opening and closing his mouth, moving his fleshy, chapped lips, a poor man's lips. It was all getting rather frightening, Laura thought. The only way to put an end to things was to hand over some money and be done with it. She stuffed the stiff stems into her bag. That was us.

Yes, we had taken the form of flowers. Not just any flowers: wild roses, which have the most potent sap. What was our mission? To take Laura and carry her back to the place humans call madness. Or perhaps not to madness, exactly, but to the blessed state of belonging.

She arrived home, filled the vase with water and arranged our stems inside. You could see she was paying us less attention than she usually paid to any new addition to her living room. She always had to turn intruders into old friends right away. To make sure they didn't clash. Laura wanted the different elements of her house to be in harmony. But today she was barely listening to her own advice. Because she was going out, with her husband, to have dinner in the house of some friends. And this was no simple matter, particularly since it ought to have been. She had the tormented air of someone cooking with a recipe, measuring the flour out so meticulously that she begins to doubt the accuracy of her scales. Time and again she examined her gestures and poses, sometimes, in her confusion, forgetting where she was. There even came a point when we thought our intervention would be unnecessary, that the pressure of going out to dinner would take care of everything by itself. That medicine would lose Laura simply because it had been so merciless in its advice to her.

But then, in the middle of the afternoon, the light changed. Overturning all of Laura's good intentions, as if the light coming from the west, being more concentrated, had actually given them a push. The same light that had taken the trouble to alter our texture and appearance. This light knew how to get its message across. It pointed to our flowers' apparently innocent perfection, pointed and said 'Look, look over here.' Almost shouting. And Laura looked. Just in time for us to get to work.

What happened next is written on two separate sheets of paper, in different coloured inks. On one sheet the words used are bright, and on the other they are dark. One sheet is legible. The other less so.

Thoughts were slipping through Laura's brain in single file, forming their sentences with beginnings and endings. Every now and then, they broke apart in their rusty mechanism and were left hanging, unfinished, so that she had to keep starting again. And all they did was address the subject of beauty, which is a very easy subject to address.

But written on the sheet of paper underneath were the words we ourselves had murmured. A purple text. An insistent text: 'Turn around. Come over here.' A text that was already angry, already impatient, losing its cool like any text with a mission. With our insolent beauty, we demanded Laura for ourselves. On the sheet of paper that does not contain her thoughts, it said that beautiful things and horrible things are one and the same, that passion and death are alike, and that we had come looking for Laura, that charmless, obsessive woman, to bring her back to the point of origin where water, animals and roots carry out their never-ending work, opening and closing the pathway of light like dancers.

Laura, who saw both badly and too well, noticed that the form we had adopted — red buds about to open, held up by a little stem — concealed our true form: outstretched hands, with claws, ready to drag her down to the depths where wild animals feast. She didn't want to go with us. No one does. Human understanding trembled in the face of a threat that was nothing but a sprig of wild roses. That's when she said: 'I'll send them to her.' The sheet of paper on top said this would be an elegant thing to do, a polite gesture, one woman to another. On the page below, you could read that Laura was terrified by the soulless beauty of a few roses and wanted them out of her living room. That this woman had a vague inkling of what we wanted from her. We, in the form of roses, cried out, making our case. 'We're yours! We've come for you!' while she removed our stems from the central branch and made a bouquet, which she then imprisoned in some tissue paper. Laura was still hesitating. She said: 'They're mine.' 'Mine,' she said again. Meanwhile, the maid gathered us up and took us straight downstairs. It was as if she'd decided which side she was on. Had medicine won, then? It seemed so.

VIII

On Dona Carlota's dresser, we were doomed to indifference. Our function reduced, essentially, to decorating a grand room that was clearly meant for grand flowers. Nature was taking its leave of us, with a last farewell, a last breath of scent. When Laura arrived, all she would see would be a bunch of roses. And we, by then, would have forgotten as well. A woman with her husband, paying a visit, and a few rosebuds about to open.

Then the telephone rang. 'She's had a relapse.'

'She's not moving, she's not speaking, Armando says,' explained Dona Carlota, who had answered the phone. She looked at her husband, and at the maid, and then said: 'We have to go over there.'

And she shot us a rather hostile look.

Notes to Chapter 13

1. Translated from the Portuguese by Claire Williams.
2. Translated by Annie McDermott. First published as 'Captura', in *Extra-textos 1: Clarice Lispector, personagens reescritos*, ed. by Mayara R. Guimarães and Luiz Maffei (Rio de Janeiro: Oficina Raquel, 2012), pp. 33–42. Published in English, as 'Capture', trans. by Annie McDermott, in *Take Six: Six Portuguese Women Writers*, ed. by Margaret Jull Costa (London: Dedalus, 2018), pp. 229–41.

CHAPTER 14

Spectres of Clarice: Lispector's Literary Afterlives

Claire Williams

'Ao que parece venho trabalhando muito desde que desencarnei' [It looks as though I have been doing a lot of work since I disincarnated].[1] This sarcastic comment purportedly comes from Clarice Lispector, decades after her death in 1977. The author (in truth Portuguese-Angolan novelist José Eduardo Agualusa) imagines the deceased's perplexed reaction to the publication of Benjamin Moser's biography of her in Brazil and Portugal; perplexed because 'she' considers that, in contrast to the potential effects of her fiction, 'Uma biografia [...] não me resgata, não me explica' [A biography cannot rescue me, does not explain me].[2] Her surprise at being so busy despite not having a body is an allusion to Moser's assertion that she frequently speaks to the living through mediums and spiritists.[3] Nonetheless, it can equally be applied to the number of spectral Clarices brought to life (almost one per year), in literary texts of varying lengths and styles, in different languages, from different countries; what we might call Lispector's literary afterlives.[4]

In this chapter I engage with examples from prose and poetry published in print between 1989 and 2017 (the fortieth anniversary of her death).[5] Writers from around the world have channelled their responses to Lispector's life and work into fictional representations of the writer, varying from a vague presence (including memories of encounters with her), to imaginary dialogues, and creative biofiction (reconstructions of events documented in, or tantalizingly absent from existing biographies), not to mention characters clearly based on her. After all, she led an extraordinary and eventful life, travelled the world, was a pioneer in the careers she chose, and she knew great joy and great tragedy.[6] The afterlives are expressed in poems, impressionistic *crônicas*, published online or in newspapers or journals, standalone texts or part of a series, short stories and fully fledged novels. Her writing also inspires different kinds of textual relationships. Rather than taking an oppositional stance towards their predecessor, most writers of afterlives establish something more symbiotic, through metafictional presences, issues of translation and by expressing themselves in a different genre: poetry rather than prose, for example. The real person, Brazilian writer Clarice Lispector, is long departed, but her readers who are (or who become) writers still feel the need to communicate with her, and thus she keeps coming back to life in literary form.

These spectral encounters evoke and invoke the 'original' Lispector in a variety of ways. Some are based on (and acknowledge) biographical sources, but they raise questions more interesting than just how true to life the stories are. Others take characters, phrases or even a single word from her writing to spin a new web that enriches the meaning of the original.[7] Though some take liberties with recorded facts, the Clarices they imagine complement the existing biographies and critical material in unexpected ways, also drawing out nuances present in her writing. They are unequivocal proof she has achieved classic status. They tell us how others understand her legacy and they also function as examples of that legacy: her inheritors follow her example by putting into practice the audacity to express themselves in writing, challenge conventions and overflow rigid categorizations. They also manifest more widely ways of thinking about the relationship between author and text, fact and fiction, history and literature, life and death. And they reflect developments in biographical writing and theories about life-writing over a forty-year period; as it has become more metabiographical or experimental, it has moved further and further from the idea that a definitive biography can be achieved.[8]

In their collection of essays on Jane Austen's afterlives, Gillian Dow and Clare Hanson posit that these sorts of literary invocations and rewritings 'engage too with the history of [the author's] literary reputation and with her construction as a canonical author, and examine the long-standing tension between the responses of her "common readers" (to borrow Virginia Woolf's term) and the views of the literary-critical establishment, a tension that has been strongly marked by gender'.[9] Although Austen and Lispector are not obviously comparable, the effects on their readers are, and so are the resulting texts. The tension between male critic and female writer is dramatized specifically in a short story by Claudia Lage, discussed below, but it is also noticeable that the majority of these fictional texts about Lispector are by women; indeed, she can be seen to function as 'a common point of reference and a unifying signifier', or, indeed, a role model for women writers in particular.[10]

Abigail Derecho's concept of 'archontic literature' (from the 'archontic principle' postulated by Jacques Derrida in his article on 'Archive Fever'[11]) is useful here to describe the way certain entities and bodies of work attract fans and compel admirers to engage with and expand upon them.[12] In her words:

> archontic texts are not delimited properties with definite borders that can be transgressed. So all texts that build on a previously existing text are not lesser than the source text; rather, they only add to the text's archive, becoming a part of the archive and expanding it. An archontic text allows, or even invites, writers to enter it, select specific items they find useful, make new artifacts using those found objects, and deposit the newly made work back into the source text's archive.[13]

Lispector's 'archive' certainly 'allows' and 'invites' readers and writers in; it now includes a significant amount of biographical and anecdotal material, and, of course, literary criticism but also caricatures, graffiti and memes, film/theatre/dance adaptations and anthologies of short stories like *Extratextos 1: Clarice Lispector* —

Personagens reescritas (2012), in which authors from the Portuguese-speaking world re-imagine Lispector's characters, and *Feliz aniversário, Clarice* (2020), twenty-seven stories inspired by Lispector's own *Laços de família* [*Family Ties*].[14]

In this chapter I will analyse a series of texts in which the emphasis falls on the characters' or narrators' reactions to Lispector's writing. In these prosopopeic texts she usually takes the form of a benevolent spirit or tutelary figure, administering advice, or overseeing their work, though she can manifest as a ghostly character within it.[15] She continues to 'haunt' such authors long after their first, often life-changing, encounter with her words; a spectral presence overseeing their literary endeavours and often summoned to appear from beyond the grave and engage directly with them, to answer questions or accept their grateful tributes.

St Clarice, Patron Saint of Writers

By focusing my attention on the 'haunted'/reader rather than the 'ghost'/Lispector, I am following the lead of Canadian literary critic Marie-Ange Depierre, in her 1993 study *Paroles fantomatiques et cryptes textuelles* [Phantomatic words and textual crypts].[16] Depierre's collection of short, poetic fragments, interspersed with photographs, 'Dire oui à Clarice Lispector', is the earliest published literary text about Lispector that I have been able to find.[17] In it, Depierre dialogues with quotations from the Brazilian writer's works and expresses awe and gratitude at what they have taught, shown, revealed to her, and enabled her to write:

> L'écriture de Clarice me projette dans la joie. [...] En lisant Clarice j'écris. Je trace une voie, un sillon dans la parole. [...] Le regard de Clarice m'accompagne dans ma découverte. Je perçois l'état brut des choses, comme la rose regardée par Clarice.
>
> [Clarice's writing projects me into joy. As I'm reading Clarice, I'm writing. I'm tracing a path, a furrow in the word. Clarice's gaze accompanies me in my discovery. I perceive the raw state of things, like the rose gazed at by Clarice].[18]

Reading Lispector becomes a turning point in the author's life: there is a before (like a long, serene coma) and an enlightened after. Lispector is painted as a compassionate Mary venerated by the poet: 'Clarice s'est tenue debout près de moi que agonisais pour entrer dans une autre vie. Un *Stabat Mater* suivi de la déportation de mon corps qu'elle a pris dans ses bras' [Clarice stood close to me as I was agonizing to start a new life. A *Stabat Mater* followed by the deportation of my body, which she had taken in her arms].[19] This emotional, enthusiastic appreciation of sentences from Lispector's writing applied to 'real life' has also been used in self-help material.[20] The use of religious analogies and language is not at all uncommon in her literary afterlives and finds parallels in Hélène Cixous's rhapsodic close readings and interpretations. Indeed, the similarities between fandom and religious devotion and use of language such as 'cult', 'icon', 'worship', 'conversion' (which I signal in my choice of title for this section), is often discussed by cultural critics.[21]

Poet and translator Erín Moure, also based in Quebec, has acknowledged the powerful influence of Lispector's writing on her work, in both theory and practice.²² Moure incorporates into her poetry concepts explored by the Brazilian writer, most notably the idea of 'aproximação' [approach], from *A paixão segundo G.H.* [*The Passion according to G.H.*], which becomes fundamental to her thinking-through of the meaning of 'citizenship' in *O cidadán* (2002).²³ Moure's multilingual stretching of words underpins the discussion, adapting the writer's name into 'A kind of movement, [...] *lisp-ecto-real*' and asserting that 'the voice in Lispector is Lispectoral, spectral'.²⁴ The overlapping, porosity and 'intersolubility' of borders also applies to the relationship between writer and reader:

> Whatever else, Clarice Lispector does not construct her reader as a receptacle of authorial direct speech but engages readers in the word's enactment/folding: 'What I write you is a *this*. [...] As such she shows us what a "perturbance of locale" might be. Perhaps, first, a disturbance of the body. A sudden (or not) shift into "foreignness"'.²⁵

Moure's incorporation of Lispector into her poetry turns the Brazilian writer into a philosophical spokesperson who expands concepts and language. This can be seen as both a homage and a collaboration, almost a conversation in which the poet learns from, comments on and then redeploys the words of the novelist.

Lispector has fulfilled a similar function for legions of readers and fans who channel their admiration into writing. She blazed trails as a woman writing at a time and in a country where women writers were in the definite minority, and she wrote in a way that challenged ideas about what constituted literary content and form. As Idra Novey puts it in the introduction to her poems in this volume, readers empathize viscerally with her words and become devoted to the point of obsession: 'Her work produces in us an almost bodily sense of connection. Her candor is so radical you finish her sentences convinced that they were written for you, that the profound questions she poses belong to you, and you belong to her'.²⁶

But Lispector's originality has also caused problems for younger generations of writers, especially experimental and women writers. Brazilian novelists Adriana Lisboa and Tatiana Salem Levy have both written about the problem of what Lisboa terms 'fictional traps':

> as armadilhas do *pós-Clarice*, do *anti-Clarice*, ou do meramente *assim-como-Clarice*. Nesse cenário, a tessitura da escrita, o magnetismo da autora canônica e a necessidade de situar as novas vozes formam uma espécie de tríade a apontar quase que irresistivelmente à categorização 'literatura feminina'. [...] Christiane Tassis afirma: 'Penso que a figura de Clarice [...] paira sobre a literatura brasileira; às vezes como um fantasma, às vezes como uma pluma'.

> [the traps of being labelled *post-Clarice*, *anti-Clarice*, or merely *just-like-Clarice*. In such a scenario, the texture of the writing, the magnetism of the canonical writer and the need to situate new voices form a kind of triad that points almost irresistibly to the categorization 'women's literature'. In Christiane Tassis's words: 'I think that the figure of Clarice hovers above Brazilian literature; sometimes like a ghost, sometimes like a feather.]²⁷

In a text which takes the form of a letter to Lispector, Levy agrees that the older writer, addressing her directly, is a kind of monument or benchmark against which Brazilian writers, particularly women, feel they are being measured:

> Readers would sometimes share their impressions with me, and some would say, *You sound like Clarice — are you a fan of hers?* Gradually I came to understand that this was not an exclusive privilege of mine. Through conversations with female writer friends I learned that they underwent the same comparison, as if all Brazilian female writers suffered the same influence; as if it were impossible for us to avoid writing *like* you, no matter how different our texts were from yours.[28]

What can writers do when 'in a sense, each of us ends up coming across the enormous moment that is you [...]. Ignore it? Embrace it? Destroy it? Swerve around it?'[29] Levy decides to embrace the powerful effects of her own experiences of reading Lispector. An early version of her letter appeared in literary magazine *Rascunho*, in a feature ironically entitled 'As Vítimas de Clarice' [The Victims of Clarice], alongside five other authors' confessions of influence, indebtedness and their first, transformative encounters with Lispector.[30]

Lispector's name is still used in reviews and merchandising material for new books as shorthand for experimental, psychological fiction, and not just in Brazil. Blurbs (often anonymous) on book covers bracket her with other (usually women) writers, in order to endorse and sell new writers (often female, often Luso-Hispanic). A quick internet search garnered examples from the anglophone publishing world such as: 'Juxtaposing fantastic imagery and brutal depictions of violence, Somers will resonate with readers of Clarice Lispector, Angela Carter, and Djuna Barnes';[31] 'With the fierce emotional and intellectual power of such classics as Jean Rhys's *Good Morning, Midnight*, Sylvia Plath's *The Bell Jar*, and Clarice Lispector's *The Hour of the Star*, Kate Zambreno's novel *Green Girl* is a provocative, sharply etched portrait of a young woman navigating the spectrum between anomie and epiphany';[32] and 'If Jean Baudrillard, Hélène Cixous, and Clarice Lispector had collaborated on a novel, *Girl Imagined by Chance* would be the result'.[33]

Living up to comparisons with Lispector is not easy, but there are strategies for asserting one's self and style: writing *with* or *to* her, rather than *like* her.[34] Indeed, plots portraying her as a foremother, a guardian angel, a benevolent saint who answers the prayers of confused and conflicted women writers comprise another form of literary afterlife. In the article quoted above, Adriana Lisboa analyses 'Clarice', a short story by Adriana Lunardi, from *Vésperas*, an elegiac collection about the lives and deaths of nine women writers.[35] In Lunardi's story, a seventeen-year-old girl is striking out for independence, testing her distracted father's love and paying her respects to Lispector, to whom she feels a close bond, by visiting her grave and placing a stone on it, following the Jewish custom. There are nods here to Lispector's life and fiction. According to Lisboa, Lunardi's tale escapes the aforementioned traps:

> pela via do abraço: deliberadamente filiando-se a Clarice Lispector, sem abdicar de sua própria personalidade autoral e escrevendo (inscrevendo-se) em sua própria contemporaneidade. O gesto mesmo da reescritura, não como oposição, mas como suplementação, fortalece seu lugar.
>
> [by choosing the route of the embrace: deliberately affiliating herself[36] with Clarice Lispector, without abdicating her own authorial personality and writing (inscribing herself) in her own contemporaneity. The very gesture of

rewriting, not in opposition but supplementing the original, strengthens her place.]³⁷

The story can also be seen as emblematic of what many people describe as their experience of reading Lispector and becoming seduced, taught, healed and liberated by her words:

> Clarice me era tão familiar do que qualquer outro ser no mundo. Com ela eu tinha finalmente uma coisa parecida. Uma coisa fundamental. Ela era alguém que me olhava nos olhos, e nesse olhar estava o segredo que compartilhávamos. [...] E me encorajava a ser o que eu era, a gostar de sê-lo. Assumia a minha estranheza, apontava-me a beleza que havia nela e, sobretudo, cercava-a de dignidade.
>
> [Clarice was as familiar to me as any other being in the world. With her I finally had something in common. Something fundamental. She was someone who looked me in the eye, and in that gaze was the secret we shared. And she encouraged me to be what I was, to enjoy being what I was. She accepted my strangeness, she pointed out the beauty in it and, above all, she surrounded it with dignity.]³⁸

Even though the writer is physically absent, the girl feels a deeper connection to Lispector than she does to her father. For the girl, she is still very much alive, and comes back to life in fiction, to engage with them and even offer advice.

Claudia Lage's short story 'Near to the Heart of Language' works on a number of levels, including the personal and the theoretical.³⁹ In the story, based on documented fact, Lage imagines Lispector moving into a new apartment in Berne, Switzerland, where her husband took up a diplomatic posting in 1946. Lage quotes excerpts from the correspondence between Lispector and her good friend, the writer and editor Fernando Sabino, in which they discussed the creative process.⁴⁰ Interrupting the process of unpacking, 'Clarice' eagerly opens a letter from a friend, only to find it contains a newspaper cutting of a very unsympathetic review of her first two novels by influential literary critic Álvaro Lins. The character is 'devastated', 'drowning in the emptiness of the apartment and the depths of the boxes'.⁴¹ She is dismayed that the critic was unable to understand what she was trying to do in her writing and the feeling of rejection temporarily halts her plans to write. The narrator then explains that Lins was a conservative reader who saw what he called 'incompleteness' as her greatest defect when, in fact, as 'Clarice' realizes at the end of the story, it is actually 'the most important feature of her writing', because it marks her originality.⁴² This is obviously a story about the reception of women writers in the patriarchal world of publishing, but its self-referential format, in strident defence of Lispector, also undercuts the rigidity of conventional criticism. For the English translation, Lage added seventeen footnotes to the story, in which her narrator addresses Lispector (and Lins) directly and informally:

> (7) That's the feeling I have when I read you, Clarice. That you bring to the surface hidden treasures. Sometimes delicately, other times with a terrifying brutality. I can't understand how Álvaro, the reader, didn't make out the glow, even if it was hazy or opaque, amid what he called the mutilated and incomplete pieces of novels and characters.

(8) [...] When I started writing this text, I didn't think I'd write about the act of writing. In this text I'm writing about you, I see you shaken up after getting a bad review. [...] You, Clarice. For decades considered one of our greatest writers. At the same time, I know that writing is about the here and now. Past and future don't exist. One is always at risk, always midleap. And you, like few others, risked many leaps. Was that how you felt? Struck during flight?[43]

There is no anxiety of influence here from the narrator, but sympathy for and empathy with a woman at the beginning of her career who was brave enough to write in a different way from her peers and was criticized as a result. Fortunately, the young Clarice was not deterred, went on to write many more books and is now positively celebrated for her idiosyncratic style.

The ghost of Clarice is perhaps most vivid when she appears to the narrator and protagonist of *Soy una caja* [I am a Box], by Catalan novelist Natalia Carrero.[44] This text is hard to categorize, incorporating autobiography, biography, research diary, literary criticism and anthology of quotations, but the underlying plot tells how Nadila, a young woman searching for a purpose in life, managed to become a writer, thanks to Clarice Lispector.[45] The Brazilian writer is portrayed, variously, as saint, tormentor, role model and life coach. There are serious points being made (about body image and mental illness, for example), but the overall tone is playful, self-deprecating and ironic, as are the cartoons, emojis and photographs dotted throughout it. The stylistic experiments (drama, short story, poetry, interview, emails; parodies of advertising discourse and women's pages) show Nadila's self-imposed apprenticeship to Lispector, which passes through several phases, including attempted assimilation (through the copying out of whole short stories) and rejection; she even imagines a cowboy-style face-off.[46] The symmetry of the relationship between teacher and pupil changes as Nadila gains in confidence and learns how to bring her writing (and her sense of self) under control, fulfilling the challenge she set at the beginning: 'I WILL WRITE MYSELF'.[47] By the end, the pupil/reader has become a writer: indeed, the proof is in our hands. But Lispector remains elusive: 'Who was Clarice? [...] Was I really paying homage to her? / No, if I was honest. Under the guise of talking about my favorite writer, I was really just exhibiting myself'.[48]

Carrero's 'novel' recreates the magical process by which readers become enchanted by a particular writer, and inspired to write themselves, by themselves.[49] The first encounters with Lispector's name, image and words are shocks to Nadila's system. There is no going back: her life is divided into before and after Clarice.[50] She uses different sets of metaphors to describe the process, some alluding to religious devotion (the 'miracle' by which she encountered the writer, whose writing is like 'sacred apocryphal scriptures'; she is now an 'idol' to 'the devoted Clarician that I am'),[51] others to the violent and transformative physical and internal disturbances that reading Lispector caused her at first:

> Who had put a washing machine inside me? I suddenly wondered. A woman in there had turned it on. Instead of clothes it was washing thoughts, words, ideas, dreams, desires. And oh, how it hurt when it was time to spin-dry.[52]

Nadila's obsession becomes so extreme that she believes Lispector is speaking to her, consoling, counselling and advising. When she first encounters the author's image, it appears to be directly challenging her:

> On the back cover I saw Clarice's face for the first time, or she saw me for the first time. Her heavily painted, slanting eyes — framed by a broad forehead, which undoubtedly held a thousand thoughts at once, and a pair of excessively pronounced cheekbones — regarded me defiantly. *So you think you're going to read me, little girl?*[53] (original emphasis)

A ghostly presence then appears in the bathroom mirror (surely a nod to a similar moment in *A hora da estrela* [*The Hour of the Star*]), and they hold a conversation about how Nadila can improve her writing. Lispector raises the issue of the overlap between autobiography and fiction:

> The only ghost here is me. Please don't try to rob me of my [leading role] any more than you already have. You claimed to be writing a speculative biography about me (you invoked me and I appeared) and look what you're doing: you, you and only you all over the place. Maybe you haven't heard, literature about 'me' is dead. Where do you intend to go by spinning on your own axis?[54]

Like the tutors at the creative writing workshops Nadila has attended (including the novelists Laura Freixas and Roberto Bolaño),[55] Lispector gives her specific tips, even about the text that is appearing in front of the reader's eyes. Nadila absorbs Lispector's words as if they were intended just for her, as her sense of intimacy with the writer intensifies until she believes they have an exclusive relationship. She rewrites a letter Lispector sent to her sisters in 1948, addressing it to herself, confident that 'Over time, using serendipity as a vehicle, the letter had finally reached its true recipient'.[56]

Lispector's last 'apparition' is sparked when Nadila reads *Um sopro de vida* [*A Breath of Life*] and they discuss the relationship between Author and Character (of course, ironically, both of them are simultaneously authors and characters, who write about authors and characters, and death). By the end of this last staged conversation, it seems that Lispector has talked Nadila out of ending her life: she has literally and literarily saved her reader's life.

Lispector's epigrammatic sentences have often been co-opted and used out of context on websites and in memes, as Karyn Mota shows, often with a personal improvement or self-help agenda.[57] José Eduardo Agualusa has parodied this phenomenon and the obsessiveness of Lispector fans in an affectionate *crônica* entitled 'If nothing else helps, read Clarice' (2003), in which it is Clarice Lispector, not the Virgin Mary, to whom an old fisherman from Pernambuco prays when 'humanity' and 'other people's mistakes' become too much to bear.

> People on the island said that the old man had been lost at sea for three weeks. He'd had a miraculous rescue. On his thirteenth day at sea Our Lady had appeared to him on his skiff, bringing him a leg of pork and a liter bottle of Coke. He himself flatly denied the miracle, sounding a little annoyed.
> 'Our Lady?! Rubbish! It was Clarice Lispector who appeared to me!...' [...]
> He told me that Clarice had appeared to him at daybreak holding *The Apple*

in the Dark, and read the entire novel to him. Afterward, when she saw that he felt better, she taught him to dream up fish.[58]

Agualusa's fisherman worships Lispector like a saint or goddess who possesses the power to work miracles and save lives, both literally (in his case) and metaphorically, through her writing. His saintly Clarice also offers up her book like a sacred text, reminiscent of Moses or Joseph Smith.

As well as salvation through the word, a sense of intimacy keeps coming back in writing about Lispector and gives authors a sense of legitimacy in texts where they not only address her directly (in the second person), but *she answers them*. This interactive strategy functions as an alternative to the reverent and respectful approach whereby the author holds Lispector at a distance, or perhaps puts her on a pedestal. Carrero, Agualusa (in the text I quoted at the beginning of the chapter) and Lage construct interviews and conversations in which they or their protagonists speak to Clarice Lispector from beyond the grave. These emotions and strategies are channelled by Canadian poet Laura Broadbent in her collection *In on the Great Joke* (2016), which contains 'Posthumous Interviews' with writers, after a preface ironically entitled 'What a Relief not to Meet you in Person: An Homage to the Alchemy of Reading'.[59] Broadbent reflects on the reading process as being highly collaborative, dependent on empathy, 'radical receptivity', listening and collaboration in order to achieve the goal of 'contact between souls'.[60] Readers, she admits, also have a certain amount of control over the intensity of the reading experience and can choose when to interrupt it or halt altogether. The 'Posthumous Interviews' are her way of engaging with authors through specific texts; in Lispector's case it is *Água viva*. The authors 'speak' through allusions to their works, but Broadbent controls the overall dialogue expressing their poetic collaboration as immersive, shared love: 'Of course, their answers sound like both them and me combined, but that is what happens when one reads, not unlike what happens when one loves — you cannot feel where you begin and the other ends'.[61]

Once again the shock of the poet's encounter with Lispector's words is foregrounded, alongside her originality, daring, intensity and virtuosity. The Brazilian writer is like an alchemist who transforms the 'ugliest' raw human material into smooth, clear emotions and words:

> Clarice Lispector's words violently kick up the fine dust of my dreaming self. She evokes the female id/it/unconscious... or something. That is, she manages to write the unsayable. She is unleashed, horrifying eroticism and she embraces the ugliest human mess because this is her material and she renders the mess as graceful and natural and pure as a mountain stream, right into the unified field of pure blissful emptiness. Home run.
>
> *Can you name a first impulse to write?*
>
> A kind of crazy, crazy harmony. [...]
> I like intensities. Fury of impulses. [...]
> I just end up knowing what the world is like. [...]
>
> You who read me help me to be born.
> Marvellous scandal
> I is.

> *Thank you for taking the time from being dead.*
> YOU ARE
> A WAY
> OF BEING
> ME
> AND I
> OF BEING
> YOU.[62]

Here, a phantom Lispector takes 'the time from being dead' to answer Broadbent's questions with lines that pulse with energy, uttering strange and oxymoronic metaphors ('crazy harmony', 'marvellous scandal'). The magical, alchemical process of reading not only affects the poet, but her interlocutor too, helping her 'to be born', in a renovated language in which it is grammatically acceptable to say 'I is'. Broadbent's poem emphatically conveys the passionate identification readers feel when reading Lispector and their wonder that, to paraphrase Hélène Cixous, she is so strangely them.[63]

Another set of poems which share this intimacy and engage with Lispector across the threshold of death, as if in conversation, is *Clarice: The Visitor* by Idra Novey.[64] The US poet's experience of what she calls 'the haunting handiwork' of translating *A paixão segundo G.H.* into English was so overwhelming ('stunned alive') that she needed to process it by expressing it in poetry: 'I found she took up residence in my life with such intensity that it was impossible to forget her breath-altering sentences even as I was sitting down to eat with actual house-guests in my home'.[65] In a series of eleven 'Letters to C.', the poet, 'Your spinning but devoted I.N.' confides in her addressee the exasperating wait for the right word, how to intuit 'the left unsaid' and how to deal with the 'gluing of impossibilities' and the sense of failure that 'makes a person feel so irremediably alive'.[66] The imagery blends painful physical experiences with anecdotes of everyday awkwardness. The translator is in thrall to C's unsettling superior knowledge: 'What's terrifying about you, C, / is that you know / what you don't know, what / none of us do'.[67] In comparison, I.N. feels herself to be a clumsy puppet, incapable of controlled and nuanced movements, like her children's toys, 'performing your words: / I'm a blue-faced creature / with seams between her fingers. / A being with no eyelids / who can bow but cannot blink'.[68] Ironically, it is the absent, dead C whose visitations invigorate the living poet, in spite of I.N.'s self-deprecating analysis of her reactions. This spectral Lispector manages to dominate the poet's thoughts, yet remain tantalizingly out of reach, their relationship a vivid dramatization of the collaborative process of translation. She is a visitor who stayed longer than expected, exhilarating I.N. yet quietly intimidating her, and who still has not left.

Conclusion: 'Dear author ghost'[69]

Ghosts (figures, appearing in narratives, whom the other characters and the reader know to be deceased) may have a number of purposes, not just the standard horror premise of unfinished business: the revelation of a repressed secret, delivery of a warning, the taking of revenge. Rather than vampirishly threatening, Lispector is almost always a benign spirit. She is re-incarnated fictionally so frequently because she is very real, and alive, to her readers, who want, indeed, to engage with her, speak to and interview her through the process of writing her. Her own texts are open, archontic; not just in their receptiveness to multiple interpretations, but also because her narrators give the impression of exposing their deepest selves. This process is dramatized in the afterlives when she answers back.

In 'real life' she was a person who valued her privacy and often rebuffed interviewers, which gave her the reputation of being difficult and mysterious. Her texts are full of references to and examples of death, fate, coincidence, intuition trumping the rational. She was superstitious, she read the I Ching and consulted fortune-tellers, and she interviewed the specialist in parapsychology Padre Azevedo.[70] Her attendance at a Witchcraft Conference in Colombia in 1975 appeared to confirm her supernatural qualities.

In his pseudo-autobiographical short story 'A bruxa' [The Witch] (2016), veteran Brazilian author Sérgio Sant'anna recalls sitting next to Lispector, the witch of the title, at a dinner party.[71] She gives him practical advice about his love life, but by the end of the story, the narrative becomes fantastical and metafictional:

> Fui impelido, então, a aproximar meu rosto ao espelho, onde estivera a grande mariposa negra, ou Clarice, e vi que ela deixara atrás de si um pozinho, como um pólen, fertilizando talvez outras bruxas, mas fertilizando, com toda a certeza, o meu conto.
>
> [Then I felt compelled to bring my face closer to the mirror, where the big black butterfly, or Clarice, had been, and I saw that she had left behind her a fine dust, like pollen, perhaps fertilizing other witches, but, no doubt about it, definitely fertilizing my short story.][72]

This last quotation brings together elements that recur in the literary afterlives I have examined: the text acting as a permeable mirror between writer and subject, writer and reader; and Lispector's almost supernatural power to 'fertilize' other writers. The sheer number, international reach, and variety (in form and content) of literary responses to Clarice Lispector, the woman and the writer, in the forty years since her death are testimony to the power of her impact on readers and her legacy. They show a desire to extend and enhance her life because the meaning of her writing and her life go beyond the limits of her fifty-seven-year-long life-span. They complement the existing biographies and literary critical research on her work, offering glimpses of what might have been, adding to the Lispector archive. In fact, the very act of reading can be considered a form of afterlife, if we equate the initial act of writing to 'life'; and we readers have the power to reincarnate her. As poet and art critic Ferreira Gullar wrote, remembering his friend:

Não obstante, isso era tudo o que valia a pena fazer na vida, conforme afirmou: 'Quando não escrevo, estou morta.'
Em compensação, quando a lemos, ressuscita.

[Nonetheless, that was all it was worth doing in life, as she asserted: 'When I'm not writing, I'm dead.'
To make up for that, when we read her, she comes back to life.][73]

Works Cited

AGUALUSA, JOSÉ EDUARDO, 'Se nada mais der certo, leia Clarice', *Catálogo de sombras* (Lisbon: Dom Quixote, 2003), pp. 97–101; 'If nothing else helps, read Clarice', trans. by Stefan Tobler, *Words without Borders* (January 2010), <https://www.wordswithoutborders.org/article/if-nothing-else-helps-read-clarice> [accessed 15 September 2020]

—— *O lugar do morto* (Lisbon: Tinta da China, 2011)

BROADBENT, LAURA, *In on the Great Joke* (Toronto: Coach House Books, 2016)

CARRERO, NATALIA, *Soy una Caja* (Madrid: Caballo de Troya, 2008); *I am a Box*, trans. by Johanna Warren (Las Vegas: Amazon Crossing, 2011)

CIXOUS, HÉLÈNE: *Coming to Writing and Other Essays*, trans. and ed. by Deborah Jenson (Cambridge, MA: Harvard University Press, 1991)

DE MAN, PAUL, 'Autobiography as De-facement', *Modern Language Notes*, 94 (1979), 919–30

DEPIERRE, MARIE-ANGE, *Une petite liberté (récits), suivi de Dire oui à Clarice Lispector* (Montreal: Triptyque, 1989)

—— *Paroles fantomatiques et cryptes textuelles* (Seyssel: Champ Vallon, 1993)

DERECHO, ABIGAIL, 'Archontic literature: A Definition, a History, and Several Theories of Fan Fiction', in *Fan Fiction and Fan Communities in the Age of the Internet*, ed. by Karen Hellekson and Kristina Busse (Jefferson, NC: McFarland, 2006), pp. 61–78

DERRIDA, JACQUES, 'Archive Fever: A Freudian Impression' (1994), trans. by Eric Prenowitz, *Diacritics*, 25.2 (1995), 9–63

—— *Spectres of Marx: The State of the Debt, the Work of Mourning and the New International*, trans. by Peggy Kamuf (London: Routledge, 2006 [1993])

DOW, GILLIAN, and CLARE HANSON (eds), *Uses of Austen: Jane's Afterlives* (London: Palgrave, 2012)

GULLAR, FERREIRA, 'Apresentação do conto "O caso do caneta de ouro"', in Clarice Lispector, *Clarice na cabeceira: crônicas*, ed. by Teresa Montero (Rio de Janeiro: Rocco, 2010), pp. 57–59

HILLS, MATT, *Fan Cultures* (London: Routledge, 2002)

HOWARTH, CLAIRE, 'Q&A: Biographer Benjamin Moser on the Elusive Clarice Lispector', *Vanity Fair*, 18 August 2009, <https://www.vanityfair.com/news/2009/08/why-this-world-benjamin-mosers> [accessed 15 September 2020]

LAGE, CLAUDIA, 'Perto do coração da linguagem', *Rascunho*, 103 (2008), <https://rascunho.com.br/noticias/perto-do-coracao-da-linguagem/> [accessed 13 August 2020]; reprinted in *O labirinto da palavra* (Rio de Janeiro: Record, 2013), pp. 115–18; reprinted and revised as 'Near to the Heart of Language', trans. by Ana Fletcher, *Music & Literature*, 4 (2014), 92–95

LEVY, TATIANA SALEM, 'A Letter to Clarice', trans. by Ana Fletcher, in *Music & Literature*, 4 (2014), 3–8

LISBOA, ADRIANA, 'Escrever no Brasil depois de Clarice Lispector: armadilhas ficcionais', *Journal of Iberian and Latin American Studies*, 14.2–3 (2008), 141–45

LISPECTOR, CLARICE, 'Provocado por Clarice Lispector, o parapsicólogo Padre Quevedo afirma que não há milagre fora de Deus. Mas, afinal, o que é milagre?', *Fatos e Fotos: Gente*, 819 (2 May 1977), 42–43

LUNARDI, ADRIANA, *Vésperas* (Rio de Janeiro: Rocco, 2002)
MILLER, LUCASTA, 'Lives and Afterlives: The Brontë Myth Revisited', *Brontë Studies*, 39.4 (Nov 2014), 254–66
MOURE, ERÍN, *O cidadán* (Toronto: House of Anansi Press, 2002)
—— *My Beloved Wager: Essays from a Writing Practice* (Edmonton: NeWest Press, 2009)
NOLASCO, EDGAR CÉZAR, 'Espectros Críticos de C.L.', *Revista de Letras (Universidade Federal do Ceará)* 1/2.29 (2007–08), 45–50, <http://www.periodicos.ufc.br/revletras/article/view/2340> [accessed 26 May 2021]
NOVEY, IDRA, *Clarice: The Visitor* (London: Sylph, 2014)
—— *Ways to Disappear* (New York: Little, Brown & Co., 2016)
PAULINO, SIMONE, *Como Clarice Lispector pode mudar sua vida* (São Paulo: Buzz, 2017)
RASCUNHO, 'As Vítimas de Clarice', *Rascunho*, 118 (2012), <https://rascunho.com.br/wp-content/uploads/2012/01/Book_118.pdf> [accessed 28 January 2022]
SABINO, FERNANDO, and CLARICE LISPECTOR, *Cartas perto do coração* (Rio de Janeiro: Record, 2001)
SÉRGIO SANT'ANNA, *O conto zero e outras histórias* (São Paulo: Companhia das Letras, 2016)
WILLIAMS, CLAIRE, 'Clarice Lispector: The Star of the Hour', in *The Oxford Handbook of the Latin American Novel*, ed. by Juan DeCastro and Ignacio Lopez Calvo (Oxford: Oxford University Press, forthcoming)
WORD ON THE STREEP, 'Wish list entry #5: Clarice Lispector' (5 July 2017), 'Word on the Streep' blog, <http://www.wordonthestreep.com/2017/07/wish-list-entry-5-clarice-lispector.html> [accessed 20 March 2019]

Appendix: Clarice Lispector's Literary Afterlives, 1989–2017

1989   Marie-Ange Depierre, *Une petite liberté (récits), suivi de Dire oui à Clarice Lispector* (Montréal: Triptyque, 1989) (poetic fragments)

1992   Vilma Arêas, 'Sobre os espelhos', in *A terceira perna* (São Paulo: Brasiliense, 1992), pp. 17–20 (memoir-short story)

1996   Ana Miranda, *Clarice Lispector: o tesouro de minha cidade* (Rio de Janeiro: Relume Dumará: Prefeitura, 1996), Série Perfis do Rio, no. 3 (biofiction)

2000   Flávio Carneiro, *Lalande* (São Paulo: Global, 2000), Coleção Aventura Radical (Young Adult fantasy fiction)

2002   Adriana Lunardi, 'Clarice', in *Vésperas* (Rio de Janeiro: Rocco, 2002), pp. 65–78 (short story)
       Erín Moure, *O cidadán* (Toronto: House of Anansi Press, 2002) (poetry)
       Lygia Fagundes Telles, 'Onde estiveste de noite?', in *Durante aquele estranho chá: perdidos e achados*, ed. by Suênio Campos de Lucena (Rio de Janeiro: Rocco, 2002) (memoir)

2003   José Eduardo Agualusa, 'Se nada mais der certo, leia Clarice', *Catálogo de sombras* (Lisbon: Dom Quixote, 2003), pp. 97–101; 'If nothing else helps, read Clarice', trans. by Stefan Tobler, *Words without Borders* (January 2010), <https://www.wordswithoutborders.org/article/if-nothing-else-helps-read-clarice> [accessed 15 September 2020] [originally published in *Revista Pública*] (crónica)
       Claire Varin, 'Hommage au jour du souvenir', in *Le Carnaval des fêtes* (Laval: Trois, 2003), pp. 131–46 (short story)

2004	Braulio Tavares: 'Claríssimo espectro', *Jornal da Paraíba*, 14 November 2004, also on Blog Mundo Fantasma. Also published in *Histórias para lembrar dormindo* (Casa da Palavra, 2013), <http://mundofantasmo.blogspot.com/2008/08/0517-clarssimo-espectro-14112004.html> (11 August 2020) (*crônica*)
2005	Jorge Miguel Marinho, *Lis no peito: um livro que pede perdão* (São Paulo: Biruta, 2005) (novel)
2006	Edgar Cézar Nolasco and Lucilene Machado, *Claricianas* (Rio de Janeiro: 7 Letras, 2006) (short stories and *crônicas*).
2008	Natalia Carrero: *Soy una caja* (Madrid: Caballo de Troya, 2008); *I am a Box*, trans. by Johanna Warren (Las Vegas: Amazon Crossing, 2011) (novel) Cláudia Lage, 'Perto do coração da linguagem', *Rascunho*, 103 (November 2008), <https://rascunho.com.br/noticias/perto-do-coracao-da-linguagem/> [accessed 13 August 2020]; reprinted in *O labirinto da palavra* (Rio de Janeiro: Record, 2013), pp. 115–18; revised version 'Near to the Heart of Language', trans. by Ana Fletcher, in *Music & Literature*, 4 (2014), 92–95 (short story)
2011	José Eduardo Agualusa: 'Morrer é a gente se alhear', in *O lugar do morto* (Lisbon: Tinta da China, 2011), pp. 113–16 [originally appeared in *Leia* magazine] (book review) Sonia Coutinho, 'Orquídeas para Clarice', in *La palabra según Clarice Lispector — aproximaciones críticas / A palavra segundo Clarice Lispector — aproximações críticas / The Word According to Clarice Lispector — Critical Approaches*, ed. by Luciana Namorato and César Ferreira (Lima: Universidad Nacional Mayor de San Marcos, 2011), pp. 21–29; reprinted in Sonia Coutinho, *Toda a verdade sobre a tia de Lúcia* (Rio de Janeiro: 7Letras, 2011), pp. 47–56 (short story)
2013	Marina Colasanti: 'Por que a pena', in Affonso Romano de Sant'Anna and Marina Colasanti (eds), *Com Clarice* (São Paulo: Editora UNESP, 2013), pp. 41–47 (short story/memoir)
2014	Edgar Cézar Nolasco, *Quem tem medo de Clarice Lispector?* (São Paulo: Intermeios, 2014) (short stories and *crônicas*) Idra Novey, *Clarice: The Visitor* (London: Sylph, 2014) (poetry)
2015	Carla Guelfenbein, *Contigo en la distancia* (Santiago: Alfaguara, 2015); *In the Distance with You*, trans. by John Cullen (New York: Other Press, 2018) (novel) Tatiana Salem Levy, 'A Letter to Clarice', trans. by Ana Fletcher, *Music & Literature*, 4 (2014), 3–8; 'Querida Clarice,' in *O mundo não vai acabar* (Rio de Janeiro: José Olympio, 2017), pp. 155–59 (*crônica*) Gustavo Álvarez Núñez, 'Clarice Lispector: en mi comienzo está mi fin', *Vidas epifánicas* (Buenos Aires: Mansalva, 2015), pp. 11–15 (short story)
2016	Laura Broadbent, 'Posthumous Interview with Clarice Lispector', in *In on the Great Joke* (Toronto: Coach House Books, 2016), pp. 55–60 (poetry) Idra Novey, *Ways to Disappear* (New York: Little, Brown, 2016) (novel) Sérgio Sant'anna, 'A Bruxa', in *O conto zero e outras histórias* (São Paulo: Companhia das Letras, 2016), pp. 148–55 (short story/memoir)

| 2017 | Conceição Evaristo, *Poemas da recordação e outros movimentos* (Rio de Janeiro: Malê, 2017) (poetry) |
| | Noemi Jaffe, 'O que vou fazer eu?', in *Não está mais aqui quem falou* (São Paulo: Companhia das Letras, 2017), pp. 100–04 (*crônica*) |

Notes to Chapter 14

1. José Eduardo Agualusa, 'Morrer é a gente se alhear' [Dying is when one becomes oblivious], in José Eduardo Agualusa, *O lugar do morto* (Lisbon: Tinta da China, 2011), pp. 113–16 (p. 115). All translations into English are mine, unless otherwise attributed.
2. Ibid.
3. Claire Howarth, 'Q&A: Biographer Benjamin Moser on the Elusive Clarice Lispector', *Vanity Fair*, 18 August 2009, <https://www.vanityfair.com/news/2009/08/why-this-world-benjamin-mosers> [accessed 15 September 2020].
4. In the words of Brontë scholar Lucasta Miller: 'Afterlife study is, in the end, a form of critical enquiry which can interrogate the intersection between real lives and their cultural construction, both within the lifetime of the subject and posthumously. It looks beyond and beneath the inherently fascinating qualities of iconic lives [...] to explain its grip on the posthumous imagination in terms of the historical contingencies through which the narrative of those lives entered the public arena', 'Lives and Afterlives: The Brontë Myth Revisited', *Brontë Studies*, 39.4 (Nov 2014), 254–66 (p. 263). Although there are immense differences between the biographies of the Brontë sisters and the Lispector sisters, the ways their afterlives have evolved and been studied can be compared usefully.
5. See Appendix. Mine is not an exhaustive survey and I am sure there are many more literary afterlives in languages and formats I have been unable to access.
6. There was a rumour circulating on the internet that Meryl Streep was going to play Lispector in a biopic: 'Wish list entry #5: Clarice Lispector', 5 July 2017, 'Word on the Streep' blog, <http://www.wordonthestreep.com/2017/07/wish-list-entry-5-clarice-lispector.html> [accessed 20 March 2019].
7. In *Lalande* (São Paulo: Global, 2000), Brazilian writer Flávio Carneiro picked up on a single word coined by Lispector's character Joana in *Perto do coração selvagem* [*Near to the Wild Heart*], 'Lalande', and used it as the inspiration for a tale for young adults.
8. Miller, 'Lives and Afterlives', pp. 255–56.
9. Gillian Dow and Clare Hanson, 'Introduction', in *Uses of Austen: Jane's Afterlives*, ed. by Gillian Dow and Clare Hanson (London: Palgrave, 2012), pp. 1–18 (p. 1).
10. Ibid., p. 13.
11. Jacques Derrida, 'Archive Fever: A Freudian Impression' (1994), trans. by Eric Prenowitz, *Diacritics*, 25.2 (1995), 9–63.
12. Abigail Derecho, 'Archontic Literature: A Definition, a History, and Several Theories of Fan Fiction', in *Fan Fiction and Fan Communities in the Age of the Internet*, ed. by Karen Hellekson and Kristina Busse (Jefferson, NC: McFarland, 2006), pp. 61–78 (p. 64).
13. Ibid.
14. Luis Maffei and Mayara R. Guimarães (eds), *Extratextos 1. Clarice Lispector: personagens reescritas* (Rio de Janeiro: Oficina Raquel, 2012); Hugo Almeida (ed.), *Feliz Aniversário, Clarice: contos inspirados em 'Laços de família'* (Belo Horizonte: Autêntica, 2020). Along the same lines, in February 2020 the Brazilian Embassy in London launched a competition for university students of Portuguese to write a short story inspired by Lispctor, either from the point of view of one of her characters, or engaging thematically and intertextually with one of her stories. The winning entries can be found at <http://londres.itamaraty.gov.br/en-us/concurso_brasilidades.xml> [accessed 15 September 2020].
15. Paul de Man defines prosopopeia as 'the fiction of an apostrophe to an absent, deceased or voiceless entity, which posits the possibility of the latter's reply and confers upon it the power of speech', 'Autobiography as De-facement', in *Modern Language Notes*, 94 (1979), 919–30 (p. 926).

I discuss fictional Clarice Lispectors in 'Clarice Lispector: The Star of the Hour', in *The Oxford Handbook of the Latin American Novel*, ed. by Juan DeCastro and Ignacio Lopez Calvo (Oxford: Oxford University Press, forthcoming).

16. Marie-Ange Depierre, *Paroles fantomatiques et cryptes textuelles* (Seyssel: Champ Vallon, 1993). Although Lispector is not one of the main authors studied by Depierre in this book, she is quoted.
17. Marie-Ange Depierre, *Une petite liberté (récits), suivi de Dire oui à Clarice Lispector* (Montréal: Triptyque, 1989).
18. Depierre, 'Dire oui', pp. 71, 73. This could be a reference to the rose longed for and then stolen by the young Clarice in the *crônica* 'Cem anos de perdão', from *Felicidade clandestina* (1971).
19. Ibid., p. 91.
20. For more on the ways Lispector's writing has been deployed as 'self-help', see Karyn Mota's chapter in this volume and Simone Paulino, *Como Clarice Lispector pode mudar sua vida* (São Paulo: Buzz, 2017).
21. See, for example, Matt Hills, *Fan Cultures* (London: Routledge, 2002), particularly Chapter 5.
22. Erín Moure, *My Beloved Wager: Essays from a Writing Practice* (Edmonton: NeWest Press, 2009). See in particular 'The Public Relation: Redefining Citizenship by Poetic Means', pp. 163–77 and 'Subjectivities: An Approach through Clarice and Fernando', pp. 179–86.
23. Erín Moure, *O cidadán* (Toronto: House of Anansi Press, 2002). This is the third volume in a ten-year-long trilogy about citizenship. In Moure's words: 'The idea of the incommensurability of "approximation" (to make an estimate, a guess, but to fail to coincide) in English and "aproximação" in Portuguese ("proximidade no espaço ou no tempo; avizinhamento" [proximity in space or time; bordering on]) struck me as key [...] that something surged for me for relations in language, and through language, with others', email interview with Claire Williams, July 2020.
24. Ibid., pp. 21, 97.
25. Ibid., p. 121.
26. See Idra Novey's chapter in this volume.
27. Adriana Lisboa, 'Escrever no Brasil depois de Clarice Lispector: armadilhas ficcionais', *Journal of Iberian and Latin American Studies*, 14.2–3 (2008), 141–45 (pp. 142, 143). Lisboa quotes from an article by Tassis that is no longer available online.
28. Tatiana Salem Levy, 'A Letter to Clarice', trans. by Ana Fletcher, in *Music & Literature*, 4 (2014), 3–8 (pp. 6–7).
29. Ibid., p. 7.
30. 'As Vítimas de Clarice', *Rascunho*, 118 (2012), <https://rascunho.com.br/wp-content/uploads/2012/01/Book_118.pdf> [accessed 28 January 2022].
31. Armonía Somers, *The Naked Woman*, trans. by Kit Maude (New York: Feminist Press at the City University of New York, 2018 [1950]).
32. Kate Zambreno, *Green Girl* (2011) (New York: Harper Collins, 2014).
33. Lance Olsen, *Girl Imagined by Chance* (Tallahassee, FL: Fiction Collective Two, 2002).
34. I am alluding here to Derrida's exhortation to 'speak *of the* ghost, indeed *to the* ghost and *with* it', in *Spectres of Marx: The State of the Debt, the Work of Mourning and the New International*, trans. by Peggy Kamuf (London: Routledge, 2006 [1993]), p. xviii. Levy quotes from the same study in her letter to Lispector and Edgar Cézar Nolasco engages closely with it his article 'Espectros críticos de C.L.', *Revista de Letras (Universidade Federal do Ceará)* 1/2.29 (2007–08), 45–50, <http://www.periodicos.ufc.br/revletras/article/view/2340> [accessed 26 May 2021].
35. Adriana Lunardi, 'Clarice', in *Vésperas* (Rio de Janeiro: Rocco, 2002), pp. 65–78. Dorothy Parker and Virginia Woolf are among the other writers portrayed in Lunardi's stories.
36. 'Filiação' is also the legal term used on documents for people to record the names of their parents.
37. Lisboa, 'Escrever no Brasil', pp. 142–43.
38. Lunardi, 'Clarice', p. 76.
39. Lage's story was first published in the online literary journal, 'Perto do coração da linguagem', *Rascunho*, 103 (2008), <http://rascunho.com.br/perto-do-coracao-da-linguagem/> (13 August

2020); reprinted in *O labirinto da palavra* (Rio de Janeiro: Record, 2013), pp. 115–18; then published as 'Near to the Heart of Language', trans. by Ana Fletcher, in *Music & Literature*, 4 (2014), 92–95.
40. The excerpts are taken from Sabino's *Cartas perto do coração* (Rio de Janeiro: Record, 2001).
41. Lage, 'Near to the Heart', p. 92. Lage states clearly that these events really took place.
42. Ibid., p. 95.
43. Ibid., pp. 93, 94. I am grateful to Claudia Lage for explaining how the story evolved. Email correspondence, 20 September 2020.
44. Natalia Carrero, *Soy una caja* (Madrid: Caballo de Troya, 2008); *I am a Box*, trans. by Johanna Warren (Las Vegas: Amazon Crossing, 2011).
45. In the last chapter, Nadila tries to sum up what she has created: 'It's not a novel, it's not a biography, it's not an adventure, it's not a shoe, it's not a plate of spaghetti, it's not a joy or a sesame seed', ibid., p. 159. The title emphasizes the function of the text as a receptacle for holding diverse and sometimes surprising words, fragments and ideas. Email correspondence with Natalia Carrero, 23 July 2020.
46. Ibid., p. 141.
47. Ibid., p. 29 (author's emphasis).
48. Ibid., p. 141.
49. 'Falling in love' is a form of words often chosen by fans in general and readers of Lispector to express their first encounter with her work.
50. Ibid., p. 157.
51. Ibid., pp. 1, 14, 55, 56.
52. Ibid., pp. 25–26, p. 77.
53. Ibid., p. 24.
54. Ibid., p. 42. NB: Warren's translation of the original 'el protagonismo' is 'my distinction'.
55. Nadila, like Natalia Carrero herself, was encouraged to read Lispector at a writers' workshop in Cadaqués, in 1990, by María Laura, a barely disguised version of novelist and editor Laura Freixas. Freixas is a great advocate for Lispector, having authored two biographical works, commissioned translations of her fiction into Spanish, and consistently promoted Lispector's writing to Spanish readers. Carrero does not provide bibliographical data within her text, but she does name authors and critics whose work on Lispector influenced her novel.
56. Ibid., p. 87.
57. See Karyn Mota's chapter in this volume. See also Paulino, *Como Clarice Lispector pode mudar sua vida*.
58. José Eduardo Agualusa, 'Se nada mais der certo, leia Clarice', *Catálogo de sombras* (Lisbon: Dom Quixote, 2003), pp. 97–101; 'If nothing else helps, read Clarice', trans. by Stefan Tobler, *Words without Borders* (January 2010), <https://www.wordswithoutborders.org/article/if-nothing-else-helps-read-clarice> [accessed 15 September 2020].
59. Laura Broadbent, *In on the Great Joke* (Toronto: Coach House Books, 2016).
60. Ibid., pp. 43, 44.
61. Ibid., p. 45.
62. Ibid., pp. 55, 60.
63. 'Who are you, who are so strangely me?' Hélène Cixous, 'The Author in Truth', in *Coming to Writing and Other Essays*, ed. and trans. by Deborah Jenson (Cambridge, MA: Harvard University Press, 1991), p. 169.
64. Idra Novey, *Clarice: The Visitor* (London: Sylph, 2014).
65. Ibid., pp. 18, 5, 5. Novey's debut novel, *Ways to Disappear* (New York: Little, Brown & Co., 2016), further explores the translation process, the publishing industry and the deeply intimate relationship between translator and author.
66. Novey, *Clarice: The Visitor*, pp. 9, 18.
67. Ibid., p. 19.
68. Ibid., p. 19.
69. Ibid., p. 14.
70. 'Provocado por Clarice Lispector, o parapsicólogo Padre Quevedo afirma que não há milagre

fora de Deus. Mas, afinal, o que é milagre?', *Fatos e Fotos: Gente*, 819 (2 May 1977), 42–43. Lispector's last question to the priest is 'Eu, uma simples mulher, poderia provocar estados parapsicológicos?' [Could I, a simple woman, provoke parapsychological states?], to which the answer is 'yes! You and everybody else'.

71. Sérgio Sant'anna, 'A bruxa', in *O conto zero e outras histórias* (São Paulo: Companhia das Letras, 2016), pp. 152–55.
72. Ibid., p. 155.
73. Ferreira Gullar, 'Apresentação do conto "O caso do caneta de ouro"', in Clarice Lispector, *Clarice na cabeceira: crônicas*, ed. by Teresa Montero (Rio de Janeiro: Rocco, 2010), pp. 57–59 (p. 59).

CHAPTER 15

Rewriting Clarice Lispector in the Digital Age

Karyn Mota

The digital age has turned Clarice Lispector into a social media phenomenon. Appropriations of Lispector's literary works by online users have led to new creations based on her ideas and imparted different meanings to her words. In this chapter, I will identify how Lispector's narratives and persona create a discursive impact in digital culture[1] and analyse the unique compatibility of her literary creations and her image with the contemporary digital world, as encapsulated in the form of internet memes.[2] I argue that far from being mere copying, the act of rewriting Lispector through internet memes coalesces with the idea of building narratives on social media as a new form of meaning-making in light of human creativity. What can be considered narrative in the realm of internet memes and social media? How do online users — members of participatory digital culture — use Lispector memes discursively?

In 2014, Fábio Malini published an article which explored the impact of social media on the production, consumption, distribution, and exchange of Brazilian literary works, a relatively unstudied area at the time.[3] In the first stage of his research, he examined the social media presence of canonical Brazilian writers and poets: Machado de Assis (1839–1908), Guimarães Rosa (1908–1967), Graciliano Ramos (1892–1953), Mário de Andrade (1893–1945), Carlos Drummond de Andrade (1902–1987), Paulo Leminski (1944–1989), Caio Fernando de Abreu (1948–1996) and Clarice Lispector (1920–1977), the only female author in Malini's case study. His most interesting finding was that academic interest in an author did not translate into social media popularity.

In order to put Lispector's social media reach into perspective, it is essential to understand the state of readership in Brazil. The Instituto Pró-Livro [Institute for the Book] conducts the systematic analysis of reader behaviour and habits in Brazil, using data collected by IBOPE [Brazilian Institute of Public Opinion and Statistics]. Compared to the results of the previous survey (undertaken in 2011), the findings of the 2016 report were positive, showing a significant increase in numbers of readers, from 50% to 56% (104.7 million).[4] This averaged to at least one book read in the last three months for each Brazilian. The data also revealed that each Brazilian reads, on average, 2.43 books per year. Additionally, most of the books that people chose to read did not fall under the category of canonical literature. The report also highlighted the need to encourage more extensive reading habits and 'to focus efforts on increasing the number of readers from an essential tripod formed by the family, the state and civil society' to draw in the remaining 44% of non-readers.[5]

Given Brazilian society's struggles with readership as a consequence of profound economic, social and cultural inequalities ranging from recurrent problems with the quality of the educational system to high rates of illiteracy, Lispector's pop star status, which is due in part to her social media presence, is impressive. Lispector's success on social media is part of a contemporary cultural movement that was already evident in academia, literary events, publications, translations, newspapers, magazines, television programmes, movies, theatre, music, and the visual arts. Nevertheless, now, a female canonical author known for her challenging writing has not only grabbed the spotlight in contemporary Brazilian digital culture, but also attained status as an international literary figure. The latter increased her social media popularity, since the general Brazilian audience, for whom she has served as a national muse, now sees her as a global phenomenon.

Take for example the widespread proliferation of internet memes, primarily image-based memes that represent visual-verbal expressions, to create meaning with quotes and images drawn from Lispector's life and work. A simple Google search for 'Clarice Lispector memes' yields over a million and a half results. Online users that engage with social media activities and interact with thematic social media communities (Facebook communities, or Instagram pages dedicated to literature and/or famous authors) generate memes, often spreading them on social media through individual profiles that identify and connect with Lispector-related content. Recent theories can provide valuable insights into how internet memes, such as those featuring Lispector, mediate the cultural transmission of practices and modes of behaviour. In *The Discursive Power of Memes in Digital Culture: Ideology, Semiotics, and Intertextuality* (2019), Bradley E. Wiggins argues that internet memes are discursive units of digital culture, intended for rapid consumption and sharing, that designate an ideological practice.[6] He discusses the transformation of the concept through the history of the term 'meme', which was introduced in Richard Dawkins's *The Selfish Gene* (1976) as 'a cultural corollary to the gene'.[7] In a 2013 performance piece, Dawkins himself commented on the transformation of the term:

> [T]he very idea of the meme, has itself mutated and evolved in a new direction. An internet meme is a hijacking of the original idea. Instead of mutating by random chance, before spreading by a form of Darwinian selection, internet memes are altered deliberately by human creativity. In the hijacked version, mutations are designed — not random — with the full knowledge of the person doing the mutating.[8]

In other words, the meme is an appropriation by definition, and therefore Lispector memes represent the appropriation of an appropriation, since fragments of her literary works and image have been used to create multiple types of memes. Dawkins's use of the word 'hijack' implies the idea of taking something, in this context, a creative work, for one's own use, and typically without the owner's permission. However, the transformation of this creative work through human and machine agents also results in a new creation that goes beyond the mere act of copying. Lispector memes, through appropriation, inherit meaning from her literary works, but they also generate a new discourse through the new meanings they acquire at the hands of online users.

Wiggins debates the value of memes as a cultural commodity with regard to social relationships with and through memes.[9] Individuals use memes to voice their opinions, views, and desires through the acquisition, display, and reaction to these 'discursive units of digital culture'.[10] As Wiggins explains, digital culture '[...] acknowledges a departure from earlier forms of media largely dominated by print, radio, and television and a movement toward personalization, user-generated content, algorithmic news feed, and a fear of missing out'.[11] This statement contextualizes how the Lispector phenomenon has been forged on social media. In this context, internet memes about her illustrate the relationship between appropriation and human creativity. A simple Google search for 'Clarice Lispector frases' or 'Clarice Lispector memes' often turns up the popular Brazilian website *Pensador*,[12] a repository of quotations by well-known authors and celebrities which online users can easily share on social media (Facebook, Twitter, Pinterest) and other platforms (WhatsApp) to celebrate their favourite writers. *Pensador*'s home page displays an opening section entitled 'Top Autores' [Top Authors], where Lispector is at the top of the list, followed by Albert Einstein, Machado de Assis, William Shakespeare, Luís de Camões, and others. Notably, Lispector is the only female writer or celebrity mentioned in this section.[13]

A search for quotations by Lispector in *Pensador*'s repository yields more than 2000 results, ranking them by number of shares and comments. The highest-ranking quote, with more than 50,000 shares, is drawn from a 1948 letter from Lispector, in Switzerland, to her sister Tania Kaufmann, back in Rio. In the first paragraph, she states, 'Até cortar os próprios defeitos pode ser perigoso. Nunca se sabe qual é o defeito que sustenta nosso edifício inteiro' [Even fixing one's flaws can be dangerous — you never know which flaw is holding up your entire building].[14] In fact, this quote has been transformed into a popular meme that circulates widely in social media and on the web (see Fig. 15.9).

Another example comes from Lispector's début novel *Perto do coração selvagem* [*Near to the Wild Heart*]: 'Liberdade é pouco. O que eu desejo ainda não tem nome' [Freedom isn't enough. What I desire doesn't have a name yet].[15] Like the example above, this quote features in a meme currently circulating on the web, and is alluded to in the preface of the 2020 edition of *Perto do coração selvagem*, which was reissued in celebration of the 100th anniversary of Lispector's birth. On the jacket copy of this volume we find the observation that this particular sentence has acquired 'o peso de uma verdadeira palavra de ordem para muitos leitores de Clarice' [the weight of a real slogan for many of Clarice's readers].[16] What would Lispector have made of the broad audience that has been appropriating fragments of her novels on social media? In her own view, her chronicles and short stories, which were mainly published between 1967 and 1973, appealed to a much wider readership:

> Escrevi nove livros que fizeram muitas pessoas me amar de longe. Mas ser cronista tem um mistério que não entendo: é que os cronistas, pelo menos os do Rio, são muito amados. E escrever essa espécie de crônica aos sábados tem me trazido mais amor ainda. Sinto-me tão perto de quem me lê.
>
> [I have published nine books which have made people love me from afar. But writing a weekly column has confronted me with a mystery I fail to understand: journalists who write them, at least here in Rio, have a wide readership. And writing these articles every Saturday has certainly brought me more love than I have ever known. I feel so close to those who read my articles.][17]

Lispector's chronicles may have made her more accessible to a diverse audience, but these memes demonstrate that contemporary digital culture has made available an array of material that reached even further any communication medium. At the same time, Lispector memes do not always acknowledge their source text and pull these quotes out of context. The words in the quote from *Perto do coração selvagem* mentioned above were retrieved from the beginning of the novel when Joana's aunt and uncle decide to send her to a boarding school after catching her stealing a book in a bookstore. The narrator, Joana, finds herself in her dorm, and starts daydreaming about the sky and the stars — she wants to be a star in the sky. Joana's stream of consciousness takes her to a glimpse of her image in a mirror. She is frightened by her own reflection, but through her image's stare she dives into a profound dialogue with herself about the importance of being alive or knowing that she is living. Joana's reflections about life are treasured deep inside her being, and she waits for her true-self to emerge from this dive. But she actually finds herself prisoner of her ideas about life, and consequently the feeling of solitude arises as a physical loneliness, as she describes. Joana feels divided between captivity and freedom, but she finally declares: 'Liberdade é pouco. O que eu desejo ainda não tem nome' [Freedom isn't enough. What I desire doesn't have a name yet].[18]

This sentence is transformed in the memes presented here, replacing 'Liberdade' [Freedom] with a range of different concepts, mainly for the purpose of making jokes about her introspective tone and existentialist approach. While Lispector is making a comment on her character's quest towards freedom in which she seeks a level of freedom beyond the definition (or lack of definition) of freedom itself, the following memes drop 'freedom' used as a leitmotif for Lispector's character's existential approach. Instead, online users appropriate the same rationale for a more prosaic activity, like hunger or heat — far away from any elaboration as used for freedom. These memes also fit within another category of Lispector memes which attach superficial statements to images of the author looking intense or serious:

These two examples show how 'discursive units of digital culture' construct meaning through the appropriation of Lispector's literary work, while also telling us something about the meme's imagined audience[19]. These memes have an encoded meaning that is directed to an imagined audience that is on the joke. They can be split into two groups: 1) Lispector fans who are familiar with her writings and understand her frequent use of stream of consciousness and existential

FIG. 15.1. 'Fome é pouco. O que eu tenho ainda não tem nome'
[Hunger isn't enough. What I have doesn't have a name yet.]

FIG. 15.2. 'Calor é pouco. O que eu sinto ainda não tem nome'
[Heat isn't enough. What I feel doesn't have a name yet.]

material; 2) online users who know Lispector as a Brazilian muse and the epitome of a poetic intellectual. Both groups would understand the comedy in twisting Lispector's words in this way. In both cases, these are not actual Lispector quotes but are clearly inspired by the aforementioned popular quote from *Perto do coração selvagem*. These two memes illustrate how appropriations of Lispector's writing sets the stage for online user's own creative interpretation of her words, resulting in the creation of different meanings, as well as a whole new discursive contribution to Brazilian digital culture. The meme's imagined audience also situates the purpose of 'discursive units of digital culture' as an element of discursive power in digital culture by allowing a diverse array of expressions related to Lispector's works to take place. For the meme to be 'complete' the imagined audience must fill in the blanks of the internet meme's message. Further analysing the meme's thematic aspects and its imagined audience can tell us something about how the identities of online users are constructed in this virtual environment.

As Wiggins explains:

> Internet memes exist in a large part because agents are involved in the recursive production and reproduction of memes but also because the structures enacted by the agential creation of memes lead to the further production of memes. Memes continue to be created as long as agential practical consciousness is defined by a desire for memetic content to be remixed, iterated, and distributed further.[20]

The memes I have gathered fall under the definition of an 'unstated but known structure', in other words, the memes themselves invite online users to appropriate and remix Lispector's quotes and her image accordingly with their creative investment, interpretation and desire to create different meanings to her words resulting in the production of new memes. The structure followed by this first category of Lispector memes that I just shared showcases a degree of creativity motivated by participatory digital culture through the remixing of Lispector's words in ways that challenge their original place in her narratives and also situate them within an alternate discourse. Online users who create Lispector memes are interacting with Lispector's status as a Brazilian muse who has reached an international audience. They are constructing and deconstructing her works and image as a way of collaborating with this phenomenon — but also making fun of this status — by creating their very own social media phenomenon.

I would like to turn now to another category of Lispector memes based on her words and image. In one group of memes, Lispector is praised as a deep thinker and an intellectual, which is part of the joke. These memes are targeting online users who employ Lispector's words for their own intellectual credibility by associating their online identities with her works. When Lispector's writing and image are connected to superficial topics and her words are used as bywords for deep emotion, introspection, and epiphany, the target of the joke is precisely people posing as profound, smart intellectuals. The critical intent of these memes is conveyed by using Lispector's words and image contrary to expectations, or parodying her persona. For example, see Figs. 15.3–15.5.:

These memes critique the dualities of depth and shallowness, eloquence and inarticulateness, introspection and openness. The last one in particular addresses directly the Lispector social media phenomenon. Here the joke is about Lispector's massive presence on Facebook, suggesting that the author herself is 'consumed' by social media, possibly because she is kept busy updating 'her' social media profile. As a result, she does not have time to do anything else. This meme acknowledges the environment in which digital culture is formed (Facebook) and the enormous amount of data that overflows through virtual channels, multiplying into different versions of the same data. Lispector is also 'consumed', that is, devoured or

Fig. 15.3. 'Hoje acordei meio Clarice Lispector: só no monólogo interior esperando uma epifania para salvar meu dia' [Today I woke up feeling a bit Clarice Lispector: alone in an inner monologue waiting for an epiphany to save my day.]

Fig. 15.4. 'Cita frase minha em momento de recalque, mas nunca leu um livro meu. Muita pós-modernidade para o meu gosto' [You quote my words when things get tough, but you've never read one of my books. Too postmodern for my taste.]

Fig. 15.5. 'Não tenho tempo para mais nada. O Facebook me consome muito' [I do not have time for anything else. I spend a lot of time on Facebook (literal translation: Facebook consumes me a lot).]

Fig. 15.6. 'Eu sou mansa mas minha função de viver é feroz' [I am meek but my function in living is fierce.]

Fig. 15.7. 'E eu não aguento a resignação. Ah, como eu devoro com fome e prazer a revolta' [I cannot bear resignation. Ah, how I swallow my disgust with greed and pleasure].

appropriated by others. At the same time, stating that she does not have time for anything else implies a critique of online users' social media diet.

This kind of meme also opens up questions related to literacy. The quotations, which are a key feature in these appropriations and remixings of Lispector's words by online users, do not necessarily draw from any direct knowledge of her literary works. In fact, I would argue that images used by online users to create these memes would appear to corroborate this claim, since they often feature actresses who have played Lispector on stage, most commonly Beth Goulart and Rita Elmôr (see Fig. 15.3 and Fig. 15.5 above).[21] In a 2016 article entitled 'A autora mais citada (e confundida) da internet' [The most quoted (and misquoted) author on the internet], published in O Povo online portal, the scholars Nádia Battella Gotlib and Teresa Montero shared their thoughts about Lispector's presence on the web. Gotlib asserts that social media took Lispector to the next level of success, but she points out two sides of this social media phenomenon:

> Há que considerar também que, se a rede, por um lado, divulga a literatura de Clarice, por outro faz trabalho contrário, na medida em que divulga textos de uma falsa Clarice, textos que ali aparecem como se fossem de Clarice mas que, na verdade, não são. E isso é péssimo.
>
> [We mustn't forget that, while, on the one hand, the internet publicizes Clarice's literature, on the other hand, it is counterproductive, insofar as it publicizes texts by a false Clarice, that appear there as if they were Clarice's texts but, in fact, are not. And that is terrible.][22]

Montero highlights a complex element of the Lispector social media phenomenon that this chapter also aims to disentangle:

> Logo quando a comunicação online ficou acessível no Brasil, houve um boom de Clarice Lispector. No Orkut existiam comunidades com mais de um milhão de leitores. E eu indagava: como uma escritora pode ter tantos seguidores em um país onde o acesso à literatura ainda é mínimo?
>
> [As soon as online communication became accessible in Brazil, there was a Clarice Lispector *boom*. On Orkut,[23] there were virtual communities with more than one million readers. And I asked myself: how can a writer have so many followers in a country where access to literature is still minimal?]

In answer to Montero's question, I contend that this could be due, firstly, to the internationalization of Lispector through translations and recognition of her from abroad; and secondly to the presence of her works in different media such as newspapers, magazines, cinema, theatre, TV shows, and social media. These two facts contribute to Lispector's status as a pop star in contemporary Brazilian culture which has enabled her to become a social media phenomenon, as Montero has pointed out. Her ubiquity across various platforms and in different media has increased her accessibility, which suggests to me that people don't really read Lispector's works, rather they 'consume' her as a brand that marks consumers as smart, thereby enhancing their status. A third category of Lispector memes redeploys lines from her works as self-help advice, most often using material that deals with identity, belonging, life experience, sadness, womanhood, and love:

Fig. 15.8. 'No Impossível é que está a realidade'
[It's in the Impossible that you find reality.]

Fig. 15.9. 'Até cortar os próprios defeitos pode ser perigoso. Nunca se sabe qual é o defeito que sustenta nosso edifício inteiro' [Even fixing one's flaws can be dangerous — you never know which flaw is holding up your entire building.]

This self-help aspect reaches beyond contemporary digital culture. Rocco, Lispector's publishing house since 1999, has developed an editorial strategy, perhaps influenced by this social media activity, of using fragments of her works out of context as self-help messages. The volumes *As palavras* (2013) [Words][28] and *O tempo* (2014) [Time], edited by Roberto Corrêa dos Santos, and Simone Paulino's *Como Clarice Lispector pode mudar a sua vida* (2018) [How Clarice Lispector Can Change your Life] are examples of how the publishing world has learned from online users' behaviour.[29]

The dissemination of fragments of her work through virtual communities raises issues about authorship or about who owns the text. Lispector is not just massively quoted on social media, but phrases attributed to her are shared widely by online users. There is also another significant group of Lispector memes that could be read as standing up for authors' rights, as a comment on copyright infringement. Some of the Lispector memes directly acknowledge the problem of correctly corroborating her authorship: see for example Figs. 15.10, 15.11, and 15.12.

Yet another group of memes attributes random nonsense quotes to Lispector, making an obvious joke about the authorship issue. One meme even used an image of Steve Jobs giving a presentation that shows him quoting Lispector joking about her authorship appropriation.[30] This genre of memes relies heavily on the absurdity of the phrase attached to Lispector's image, particularly her intense gaze. The intention behind them is not to imitate her style or voice, but to take to task online users who appropriate her name as a byword for credibility, almost calling them out for their misattributions.

Dr Paulo Gurgel Valente, Lispector's son and the executor of her estate, has raised concerns about copyright infringement related to this social media activity.[31] He himself has no social media profile and is not aware of what is happening in the virtual communities dedicated to his mother. The only information he has accessed consists of newspaper articles on the subject. He knows that she is often misquoted and that the viral aspect of social media has made it possible for several misattributions to spread through the web. He has raised concerns about texts that are ultimately the creations of social media users and could harm the reception of her work. He has indicated that what is happening on social media could be pursued as a legal case regarding copyright infringement. However, ensuring Lispector's intellectual property and copyright are properly respected on social media would entail a complicated and lengthy legal battle that, in his estimation, is not worth pursuing. He is also aware of the positive relationship between his mother's social media presence and publications and sales of works by and related to Lispector, including Rocco's editorial projects and her internationalization through the New Directions/Penguin English-language translations.[32]

Lispector's importance in Brazilian digital culture is a significant element of the afterlives of Lispector. Understanding the process that has made Lispector a social media phenomenon can provide evidence for lines of interpretation about her reception, particularly the adaptability of her work. Lispector memes and their virtual environment also reveal how online users view and present themselves, how they negotiate their identity in relation to the material they are adapting.

Fig. 15.10. 'Apenas observando você usar citações incríveis com créditos falsos'
[Simply watching you using amazing quotes with false credits.]

Fig. 15.11. 'Sai já dessa citação que não te pertence'
[Get out of this quote, right now: it does not belong to you.]

Fig. 15.12. 'Meu saco já está explodindo de ver tanta porcaria que vocês postam em meu nome nesta merda' [My balls burst when I see all the crap that you post in my name].

This process shows how appropriations of Lispector's words and her persona are discursively connected to Brazilian digital culture.

In order to understand the scale of Lispector's presence and writing on social media, it is necessary to explore the narrative transformations that this technological environment has made possible. Digital media are flexible and dynamic, promoting interaction among online users. This legitimizes their existence as a cultural form in their own right and as a new symbolic value. Lev Manovich's argument on the non-narrative logic of the web and the creative process in the computer age illuminates the narrative transformations that these Lispector memes catalyse:

> Many new media objects do not tell stories; they don't have beginning or end; in fact, they don't have any development, thematically, formally or otherwise which would organize their elements into a sequence. Instead, they are collections of individual items, where every item has the same significance as any other.[33]

Manovich seeks to untangle the non-narratives produced in the digital age. He applies the term 'new media objects' to items in a constantly expanding database. Such contributions comprise a collection, but not a story. Since content on social media continues to accumulate, how can a coherent narrative be established? According to Manovich, the database itself is considered a cultural form and therefore becomes the centre of the creative process in the computer age. In the world of new media, hyper-narrative as an 'interactive narrative' has displaced the conceptual space of 'the word *narrative* that is often used as the all-inclusive term'.[34]

Online users, often concerned with managing their online identity, have established a new way of relating to the past and sharing their experience of the present. Fragments of Lispector's works circulating on social media call into question the idea of authorship as new media facilitate the selection, re-creation, and recombination of what already exists on social media, forming a repository of *Claricean* micronarratives, or what we might call a Lispector database. Manovich's principle of variability states that it is 'possible to create different interfaces to the same material',[35] meaning that the cultural objects created through social media from fragments of Lispector's literary works can be seen to follow intertwining trajectories through a vast number of database records that can be linked together.

The interactive aspect of online social media fosters a participatory culture that develops online users' activity in a way that is only possible on the internet. A reader's/user's connection with Lispector's writing is made more complex by the various virtual actions — like, follow, share, tag, update, post, publish — that platforms such as Facebook, Twitter and Instagram offer. While this creates more ways of establishing a relationship with her writings and builds new meanings for her words, this kind of interaction may compromise Lispector's original works. The point here is not about a right way to read Lispector's works — as some readers, and especially scholars may claim a specific interpretation of her words. The iconic Lispector's interview for the TV programme 'Panorama Especial' [Special Panorama], aired by TV Cultura and hosted by the journalist Júlio Lerner in 1977, reveals Lispector's perspective on how readers understand her works:

> LERNER. Dos seus trabalhos, qual é aquele que você acredita que mais atinja o público jovem?
> LISPECTOR. Depende, depende inteiramente. Por exemplo, o meu livro *A paixão segundo G.H.*, um professor de português do Pedro II veio lá em casa e disse que leu quatro vezes o livro e não sabe do que se trata. No dia seguinte, uma jovem de dezessete anos, universitária, disse que este livro é o livro de cabeceira dela. Quer dizer, não dá pra entender.
> LERNER. E isso aconteceu em relação a outros dos seus trabalhos?
> LISPECTOR. Também em relação a outros dos meus trabalhos. Ou toca, ou não toca. Quer dizer, eu suponho que entender não é uma questão de inteligência, e sim de sentir e de entrar em contato. Tanto que o professor de português e literatura que deveria ser o mais apto a me entender, não me entendia e a moça de dezessete anos lia e relia o livro. Parece que eu ganho na releitura, né? O que é um alívio.
>
> [LERNER. Of all your writings, which one do you think most speaks to young people?
> LISPECTOR. It depends. It entirely depends. For example, my book *The Passion according to G.H.*, a Portuguese teacher from Pedro II [an elite Rio high school] came to my house, said he'd read it four times, and he didn't know what

it was all about. The next day a young girl, seventeen years old, came over and said that the book was her very favourite. I mean, you can't understand it.
LERNER. Has this happened with your other books as well?
LISPECTOR. It has. It either touches people or it doesn't. I mean, I guess the question of understanding isn't about intelligence, it's about feeling, about entering into contact. So the Portuguese and literature teacher, who ought to be the one most prepared to understand me, didn't, and the seventeen-year-old girl read and reread the book. It seems I gain by rereading, which is a relief.][36]

Lispector's anecdote about her readers give us valuable insights on how there are no rules to interpret her words, as she mentioned. Therefore, the only stake related to her original works implicated by the appropriations of decontextualized micronarratives in social media is about preserving the investment that publishers, agents, executors, and translators have in her work. Online users often use social media tools to chart a new, distinctive narrative path for Lispector's writing and to cast their intention to rewrite Lispector; this is evident through the critical and ironic tone of online memes creatively misquoting her literary works.

Lispector has become a 'brand' that conveys intelligence and high-brow literary taste, and social media users in Brazil are continuously adding her name to posts for credibility, even when what they are quoting is not actually her work, as the memes discussed above show. Some famous cases of quotes being misattributed to Lispector have been compiled in a website that has set itself the quest to identify whether certain phrases were penned by Lispector or not, such as: 'Ainda bem que sempre existe outro dia. E outros sonhos. E outros risos. E outras pessoas. E outras coisas' [Thankfully, there is always another day. And other dreams. Other laughs. Other people. Other things] (unknown author)[37], and 'Não se preocupe em entender, viver ultrapassa qualquer entendimento' [Don't worry about understanding, living surpasses any understanding], which appears on the back covers of the 1990s Francisco Alves editions of her works.[38] In this scenario, the issue of authorship is problematized because such posts from these online users, who have not necessarily read her work, are, in effect, creating a new persona for Lispector.

A close look at the Lispector memes provides examples of Manovich's observation that the randomness of this activity hinders narrative coherence.[39] The obsessive path of micronarratives created in the realm of virtual communities on social media takes advantage of the vast amount of information and data available at the mere click of a button. Online users are confronted with the writer's recirculating motifs of existentialism, introspection, class conflict, and identity and reproduce this content, in some cases creating unexpected connections or no connections at all.

Paulo Gurgel Valente was unable to explain the reasons behind the Lispector social media phenomenon, or the motivations behind online users' appropriation of her words. But at the end of our interview, he shared some of Rocco's new editions of Lispector's books as a present, including a bookmark with a phrase attributed to Lispector: 'Em todas as frases um clímax' [In every sentence a climax].[40] This aphorism gave me a new perspective on Lispector's creative process and made me reflect on how to approach the connection between her work and online users. My initial focus had been on the aspects that distinguished Lispector's literary works from social media users' creations or appropriations, but after encountering this quotation, I started to consider their similarities.

On the website of the Instituto Moreira Salles, which houses much of the author's personal and literary archive, the page reproducing the fragmented notes that were eventually pieced together to make *A hora da estrela* (1977) [*The Hour of the Star*] is accompanied by Fábio Frohwein's text describing some of the stages involved in Lispector's creative process, which he divides into two stages: 'inspirations' and the concatenation, or putting together, of those inspirations.[41] The writer herself coined these terms in an interview:

> Quando eu estou escrevendo alguma coisa, eu anoto a qualquer hora do dia ou da noite coisas que me vêm... O que se chama inspiração, né? Agora quando estou no ato de concatenar as inspirações, aí eu sou obrigada a trabalhar diariamente.
>
> [When I'm writing something, I take notes at any hour of the day or night, things that come to me. What's called inspiration, right? But when I'm actually putting those inspirations together, then I have to work every day].[42]

Lispector began her 'inspirations' with small ideas and short phrases, revealing a fragmentary creative writing technique. Given that she herself began her works with fragments, as can be seen from the manuscripts available on the IMS website, then online users are sharing her writing in a way that corresponds with her own practice.[43] Among many examples of quotations from Lispector that trend on social media, the following could be used to aptly describe online users' main motivation for appropriating her texts: 'Escrever é tentar entender, é tentar reproduzir o irreproduzível' [To write is to seek to understand, it is to seek to reproduce the irreproducible].[44] However, her fragments were used as building blocks to create a narrative; its completion was achieved through the 'concatenation of inspirations' stage. That is what is missing from these online creations. Thus, in order to understand the full power of Lispector's literary production, the linking of context, scenario, and plot is required.

Taking into account the aspect of cultural commodity related to the process of rewriting Lispector in the Digital Age and the reception and afterlives of the writer in the context of digital culture, it becomes a real challenge to distinguish what is 'interpretation' and what is 'use' when faced with the virtual storehouse of Lispector quotations available in contemporary times. I have highlighted the relevance of the Lispector phenomenon for literary, cultural, and new media studies, but it also points to potential work that can be undertaken in the global landscape of the Digital Humanities.

The digital reverberation of Lispector's words and images unveils and illustrates broader questions for contemporary times, for example, how can the digital milieu challenge the limits of print knowledge? How can literary theory and criticism be used to collect and give meaning to born-digital material containing a multitude of objects and voices that reshape the concept of narrative? How can the innovative approach to new digital collections and repositories impact and transform research in the Humanities through the concepts of openness and collaborative work present in Digital Humanities? Moreover, how can digital tools transform the interpretation of works of literature created in the past in comparison to born-digital material? These questions contribute to a new way of approaching Lispector's *oeuvre* through critical reflection on the internet meme as a unit that encapsulates their written and visual nature, and also as key elements of contemporary digital culture which corresponds, in this case, to a connection between the literary world and the digital world. The rewriting of Lispector in the Digital Age reflects the discursive power that enables online users to enact different ways of meaning and expressions as a response to Lispector's literary contributions while creating their own online discourse about her life and works.

Works Cited

ALIBERTI, ROSANGELA, 'Falsas atribuições: Clarice Lispector e o que é mesmo dela,' Recanto das Letras <https://www.recantodasletras.com.br/artigos-de-literatura/3560471> [accessed 16 August 2021]

ATHAYDE, MANAÍRA AIRES, and REJANE CRISTINA ROCHA, 'The Circulation of Literature in the Online World: The Cases of Clarice Lispector and Caio Fernando Abreu', *Estudos de Literatura Brasileira Contemporânea*, 59 (2020), 1–25

BORELLI, OLGA, *Clarice Lispector, esboço para um possível retrato* (Rio de Janeiro: Editora Nova Fronteira, 1981)

COSTA, ISABEL, 'A autora mais citada (e confundida) da internet,' *O Povo* <https://blogs.opovo.com.br/leiturasdabel/2016/12/07/com-memes-e-citacoes-clarice-lispector-e-a-autora-mais-querida-da-internet/> [accessed 16 August 2021]

DAWKINS, RICHARD, *Just for Hits*, video recording, The Saatchi & Saatchi New Directors' Showcase (22 June 2013)

FAILLA, ZOARA (ed.), *Retratos da leitura no Brasil*, 4 (Rio de Janeiro: Sextante, 2016), <http://cbl.org.br/upload/reading-portraits-in-brazil.pdf> [accessed 11 April 2021]

Frases e pensamentos: mais de 1 milhão de frases e pensamentos para compartilhar, Pensador, <https://www.pensador.com/clarice_lispector/> [accessed 16 August 2021]

FROHWEIN, FÁBIO, 'Inspirações ou Notas?', <https://site.claricelispector.ims.com.br/acervo/notas-de-a-hora-da-estrela/> [accessed 11 April 2021]

LISPECTOR, CLARICE, *Perto do coração selvagem* (Rio de Janeiro: Rocco, 2020 [1943]); *Near to the Wild Heart*, trans. by Alison Entrekin (New York: New Directions, 2012)

—— *A paixão segundo G.H.* (Rio de Janeiro: Rocco, 2019 [1964]); *The Passion According to G.H.*, trans. by Idra Novey (New York: New Directions, 2012)

—— *Uma aprendizagem ou o livro dos prazeres* (Rio de Janeiro: Francisco Alves, 1994 [1969]); *An Apprenticeship or the Book of Pleasures*, trans. by Stefan Tobler (London: Penguin, 2021)

—— *A descoberta do mundo* (Rio de Janeiro: Rocco, 1999 [1984]); *Discovering the World*, trans. by Giovanni Pontiero (Manchester: Carcanet Press, 1992)

—— *Correspondências*, ed. by Teresa Montero (Rio de Janeiro: Rocco, 2002)

—— 'The Last Interview', trans. by Benjamin Moser, *Music & Literature*, 4 (2014), 13–22

MALINI, FÁBIO, 'A economia dos Likes e do RTs dos usuários-fãs de literatura brasileira nas redes sociais: Leminski, Clarice, Machado e Caio F. Abreu' (2014), <https://www.labic.net/publicacao/a-economia-dos-likes-e-do-rts-dos-usuarios-fas-de-literatura-brasileira-nas-redes-sociais-leminski-clarice-machado-e-caio-f-abreu/> [accessed 11 April 2021]

MANOVICH, LEV, *The Language of New Media* (Cambridge, MA: MIT Press, 2015)

Montagens no Facebook criam mistura surreal de frases falsas e personalidades improváveis, web image, UOL, <https://noticias.uol.com.br/tecnologia/album/2012/04/03/internautas-fazem-montagens-envolvendo-frases-falsas-e-personalidades-fora-de-contexto.htm?foto=9> [accessed 16 August 2021]

MOTA, KARYN DE PAULA, 'Clarice Lispector na era digital: a apropriação da escritora na rede' (unpublished master's dissertation, PUC Rio, 2018), <https://www.maxwell.vrac.puc-rio.br/38676/38676.PDF> [accessed 11 August 2020]

PAULINO, SIMONE, *Como Clarice Lispector pode mudar sua vida* (São Paulo: Buzz, 2017)

PEREIRA, MARCOS DA VEIGA, 'Transforming the Reading Portrait in Brazil: A Challenge for Brazilian Society', *Retratos da leitura no Brasil*, 4, ed. by Zoara Failla (Rio de Janeiro: Sextante, 2016) <http://cbl.org.br/upload/reading-portraits-in-brazil.pdf> [accessed 11 April 2021]

ROCHA, EVELYN, *Encontros: Clarice Lispector* (Rio de Janeiro: Beco do Azougue, 2011)

SANTOS, ROBERTO CORRÊA DOS, 'As palavras de Clarice: quatro perguntas para Roberto Corrêa dos Santos', Blog IMS <https://blogdoims.com.br/as-palavras-de-clarice-quatro-perguntas-para-roberto-correa-dos-santos/> [accessed 16 August 2021]

SILVA, EMILY FIDELIX DA, 'Entre achados e perdidos: o arquivo pessoal de Clarice Lispector' (unpublished master's dissertation, Universidade Federal de Santa Catarina, 2017), <https://repositorio.ufsc.br/xmlui/bitstream/handle/123456789/177778/346986.pdf> [accessed 16 August 2021]

WIGGINS, BRADLEY E. *The Discursive Power of Memes in Digital Culture: Ideology, Semiotics, and Intertextuality* (New York: Routledge, 2019)

Notes to Chapter 15

1. My use of the term 'digital culture' draws from Bradley Wiggins, *The Discursive Power of Memes in Digital Culture: Ideology, Semiotics, and Intertextuality* (New York: Routledge, 2019).
2. Wiggins also suggests a specific definition for this term: 'The *internet meme is hereby defined* as a remixed, iterated message that can be rapidly diffused by members of participatory digital culture for the purpose of satire, parody, critique, or other discursive activity. An *internet meme* is a more specific term for the various iterations it represents, such as image macro memes, GIFs, hashtags, video memes, and more. Its function is to posit an argument, visually, in order to commence, extend, counter, or influence a discourse', *The Discursive Power*, p. 11.
3. Fábio Malini, *A economia dos Likes e do RTs dos usuários-fãs de literatura brasileira nas redes sociais: Leminski, Clarice, Machado e Caio F. Abreu* (2014), <https://www.labic.net/publicacao/a-economia-dos-likes-e-do-rts-dos-usuarios-fas-de-literatura-brasileira-nas-redes-sociais-leminski-clarice-machado-e-caio-f-abreu/> [accessed 11 April 2021].
4. Zoara Failla, ed., *Retratos da leitura no Brasil*, 4 (Rio de Janeiro: Sextante, 2016), <http://cbl.org.br/upload/reading-portraits-in-brazil.pdf> [accessed 11 April 2021].
5. Marcos da Veiga Pereira, 'Transforming the reading portrait in Brazil — a challenge for Brazilian society', in Failla, *Retratos*, np. <http://cbl.org.br/upload/reading-portraits-in-brazil.pdf> [accessed 11 April 2021].
6. Wiggins, *The Discursive Power*, p. xv.
7. Ibid., p. 7
8. Richard Dawkins, *Just for Hits,* video file, The Saatchi & Saatchi New Directors' Showcase (22 June 2013).
9. Wiggins, *The Discursive Power*, pp. 6–7.
10. Ibid., p. xv.
11. Ibid., p. 22
12. *Frases e Pensamentos: mais de 1 milhão de frases e pensamentos para compartilhar*, Pensador, <https://www.pensador.com/clarice_lispector/> [accessed 11 April 2021].
13. This result was displayed when the website was last accessed on 10 July 2020.

14. Clarice Lispector, *Correspondências*, ed. by Teresa Montero (Rio de Janeiro: Rocco, 2002), p. 132.
15. Clarice Lispector, *Perto do coração selvagem* (Rio de Janeiro: Rocco, 2020 [1943]), p. 67; *Near to the Wild Heart*, trans. by Alison Entrekin (New York: New Directions, 2012), p. 61.
16. Lispector, *Perto do coração selvagem*, jacket copy.
17. Clarice Lispector, *A descoberta do mundo* (Rio de Janeiro: Francisco Alves, 1994 [1984]), p. 93; *Discovering the World*, trans. by Giovanni Pontiero (Manchester: Carcanet Press, 1992), p. 126.
18. Lispector, *Perto do coração selvagem*, p. 67; *Near to the Wild Heart*, p. 61.
19. For a fuller discussion on the concept of the imagined audience, see Wiggins *The Discursive Power*, p. 112.
20. Wiggins, *The Discursive Power*, p. 50.
21. See Katrina Dodson's chapter in this volume.
22. 'A autora mais citada (e confundida) da internet', *O Povo*, <https://blogs.opovo.com.br/leiturasdabel/2016/12/07/com-memes-e-citacoes-clarice-lispector-e-a-autora-mais-querida-da-internet/> [accessed 11 April 2021].
23. Orkut was a social networking service created by Google and launched in 2004. Orkut's largest audience was in Brazil, and in 2008 Google decided that Orkut would be managed and operated from Brazil. In 2014, Google announced that Orkut would be closed.
24. Clarice Lispector, *A paixão segundo G.H.* (Rio de Janeiro: Rocco, 2019 [1964]), p. 75; *The Passion according to G.H.*, trans. by Idra Novey (New York: New Directions, 2012), p. 119.
25. Clarice Lispector, *A Descoberta do Mundo*, p. 23; *Discovering the World*, p. 33.
26. Lispector, *Uma aprendizagem ou o livro dos prazeres* (Rio de Janeiro: Francisco Alves, 1994 [1969]), p. 125; *An Apprenticeship or the Book of Pleasures*, trans. by Stefan Tobler (London: Penguin, 2021), p. 75.
27. Lispector, *Correspondências*, p. 132.
28. For more information about how Roberto Corrêa dos Santos organized these texts, see: 'As palavras de Clarice: quatro perguntas para Roberto Corrêa dos Santos', *Blog do IMS*, <https://blogdoims.com.br/as-palavras-de-clarice-quatro-perguntas-para-roberto-correa-dos-santos/> [accessed 11 April 2021].
29. Simone Paulino, *Como Clarice Lispector pode mudar sua vida* (São Paulo: Buzz, 2017).
30. *Montagens no Facebook criam mistura surreal de frases falsas e personalidades improváveis*, UOL, <https://noticias.uol.com.br/tecnologia/album/2012/04/03/internautas-fazem-montagens-envolvendo-frases-falsas-e-personalidades-fora-de-contexto.htm?foto=9> [11 April 2021].
31. This interview was conducted in July 2018, as part of my master's dissertation. Karyn da Paula Mota, 'Clarice Lispector na era digital: a apropriação da escritora na rede' (unpublished master's dissertation, PUC-Rio, 2018).
32. Paulo Gurgel Valente talked about the plans to celebrate the 100th anniversary of Lispector's birth, on 10 December 2020, when Rocco released special editions of all Clarice Lispector's books with cover artwork by Victor Burton and academic introductions. The commemorative edition of *Água Viva* (originally published in 1974) includes facsimiles of the manuscript drafts of the novel.
33. Lev Manovich, *The Language of New Media* (Cambridge: MIT Press, 2001), p. 218.
34. Ibid., p. 228.
35. Ibid., p. 227.
36. Clarice Lispector, *The Last Interview of Clarice Lispector*, February 1977 [video file]. Retrieved from <https://www.youtube.com/watch?v=ohHPI12EVnU&t=12s> [accessed 11 April 2021]. The interview is transcribed in *Encontros: Clarice Lispector*, ed. by Evelyn Rocha (Rio de Janeiro: Beco do Azougue, 2011), pp. 172–85 (pp. 182–83); 'The Last Interview', trans. by Benjamin Moser, *Music & Literature*, 4 (2014), 13–22 (p. 20).
37. *Falsas atribuições: Clarice Lispector e o que é mesmo dela*, Recanto das Letras, <https://www.recantodasletras.com.br/artigos-de-literatura/3560471> [accessed 11 April 2021].
38. This is a mis-citation of a sentence from *Uma aprendizagem ou o livro dos prazeres*: 'Não entender era tão vasto que ultrapassava qualquer entender — entender era sempre limitado' ['Not understanding' was so vast that it surpassed all understanding — understanding was always limited]. Lispector, *Uma aprendizagem*, p. 52; *An Apprenticeship*, pp. 32–33.

39. Manovich, *The Language of New Media*, pp. 227–28.
40. Olga Borelli, *Clarice Lispector, esboço para um possível retrato*. (Rio de Janeiro: Nova Fronteira, 1981), p. 86.
41. Fábio Frohwein, *Inspirações ou notas?*, Clarice Lispector IMS <https://site.claricelispector.ims.com.br/acervo/notas-de-a-hora-da-estrela/> [accessed 11 April 2021]. See also Paloma Vidal's chapter in this volume.
42. Interview with Júlio Lerner, 'A última entrevista', pp. 177–78; Lispector, 'The Last Interview', p. 16.
43. One illustration of her practices is the webpage on *Caderno de bordo* [Travel Journal] on the Instituto Moreira Salles website, which presents digitalized copies of Lispector's personal notebook from July to August 1944. Nádia Battella Gotlib was invited to transcribe and annotate these texts, which illustrate the stages of Lispector's process of composition: <https://site.claricelispector.ims.com.br/en/archive/logbook/> [accessed 11 April 2021]. See also Emily Fidelix da Silva's, 'Entre achados e perdidos: o arquivo pessoal de Clarice Lispector' (unpublished master's dissertation, Universidade Federal de Santa Catarina, 2017), <https://repositorio.ufsc.br/xmlui/bitstream/handle/123456789/177778/346986.pdf> [accessed 11 April 2021].
44. Lispector, *A descoberta do mundo*, p. 134; *Discovering the World*, p. 179.

PART V

The Posthuman

CHAPTER 16

Writing Life beyond the Humanist Subject in *The Hour of the Star* and *A Breath of Life*

Kelli D. Zaytoun

'It was quite alarming to observe how the breath of life surged within Macabéa's parched body; expansive and diffused [...], she experienced the weirdest dreams with visions of immense prehistoric animals, as if she were living in some more remote age of this violent territory.' — Clarice Lispector[1]

'Life is passing and we do not own it; we just inhabit it.' — Rosi Braidotti[2]

The academy's late twentieth-century theoretical turn from liberal humanism's privileging of the disembodied, disembedded subject and rational thought gave way to, among other approaches, a critical posthumanism that seeks to rethink subjectivity as radically relational and expansive. Although Clarice Lispector's work, by way of themes, characters, and form, easily lends itself to critiques of humanism, posthumanist readings of Lispector in English are few, and refer mostly to the 1964 novel *A paixão segundo G.H.* [*The Passion According to G.H.*]. A first mention of the posthuman in Lispector, specifically the intimacy in and limits of the human–insect relationship in *The Passion According to G.H.*, is seen in Steven Shaviro's 'Two Lessons from Burroughs' in Jack Halberstam and Ira Livingston's 1995 edited book *Posthuman Bodies*.[3] Rosi Braidotti, in her 2002 study *Metamorphoses: Towards a Materialist Theory of Becoming*, offers an early critique of humanist traditions in the first, what she terms, 'new materialist' analysis of Lispector's work in her reading of *The Passion According to G.H.*[4] More recently, critics have used poststructuralist theory to explore aspects of the posthuman in *The Passion According to G.H.*, building on Gilles Deleuze's concept of becoming-animal (Jutta Ittner, Anne Schillmoller) and Jacques Derrida's 'tout autre est tout autre' [every other is totally other] (Irving Goh).[5] Rodolfo Piskorski has provided what he calls a 'zoogrammatological' reading, grounded in Derrida's 'supplementarity', of *A maçã no escuro* [*The Apple in the Dark*] (1960), linking animality and textuality.[6] In 2016, both Goh and Mattias Kärrholm examined the arguable line between animal, thing, and human in *The Passion According to G.H.* as well as Lispector's posthumously published *Um sopro de vida (pulsações)* [*A Breath of Life (Pulsations)*] (1978), Goh with an emphasis on the concept of touch (he also explores *Água viva* [1974]), and Kärrholm with a focus on animism.[7] Recently, Elisabeth Friis identified, working with theories of Braidotti and Hélène Cixous, what she refers to as 'post humanist life writing' and the 'anti-anthropocentric willpower' that ultimately results in an undoing of the singular subject in *Água viva*.[8] Similarly, in 2018, Fernanda Negrete took up a number of Deleuze's concepts to demonstrate how the unitary self dissolves in Lispector's work, focusing on *Água viva*.[9]

These analyses demonstrate that reading Clarice Lispector with critical posthumanist lenses illuminates one of the richest and most unique aspects of her work: the writing's awareness of how human life is steeped in an immensely vigorous material context that escapes reason, a context in which forces of nature and a variety of living and non-living things not only co-exist but are co-constitutive and deeply enmeshed. Expanding these revelations in Lispector, this chapter turns the reader's attention to an understudied topic, namely the relationship between subjectivity and death, returning Braidotti's theorizing, in this case her work on the posthuman and posthuman death theory, to readings of Lispector, particularly what the author was working on as she herself approached death: *A hora da estrela* [*The Hour of the Star*] (1977) and *A Breath of Life*. The chapter also connects Gloria Anzaldúa's late-in-life theory of the shapeshifter/*la naguala* to Lispector's characters and themes, indicating links between Lispector and theorizing beyond modern, Western thought. Because Anzaldúa's approach does not depend on European philosophical traditions for its foundation, unlike other theories of the posthuman, including Braidotti's, my reading suggests that Lispector's work can be considered as not only deconstructive and posthumanist but decolonial as well.[10]

Lispector's late works reveal an acute awareness of and particular take on dying: that a single human death marks neither a transcendent nor an inanimate state, but a 'radical empirical immanence', a participating and becoming with a broad, persistent, concrete, yet beyond-human generative force, what Lispector describes in *The Hour of the Star* as 'an inflexible geometry [that] vibrates behind everything'.[11] Lispector's existential and mystical anxieties and pursuits, for which she is widely known and which are particularly intense in her final two novels, can be better mapped and appreciated if read alongside what Braidotti refers to as a type of posthumanism or 'pan-humanity' that 'work[s] hard to free us from the provincialism of the mind, the sectarianism of ideologies, the dishonesty of grandiose posturing and the grip of fear', a pan-humanity that is aware of the 'power that each and every one of us exercises in the everyday network of social relations, at both the micro- and macro-political levels'.[12] This chapter seeks to establish that, at the end of her life, Lispector was communicating intently, imaginatively, and critically about the expansive materiality of self, writing, and death, particularly in her articulation of the characters of Macabéa (*The Hour of the Star*) and Ângela (*A Breath of Life*). Both protagonists can be read as calling into question liberal humanism's lines between thought and sensation, subject and object, the animate and inanimate, and life and death. As they serve to situate the chapter's central argument, explanations of Braidotti's and Anzaldúa's theories begin this chapter's investigation of the relational, posthuman subject and death scenes in the two novels.

Braidotti's critical posthumanism put forth in *The Posthuman* has many influences, mostly Spinoza's vitalism and her rereading of it through Deleuze and Guattari, Foucault, and numerous feminist and postcolonial thinkers. She posits, as the epigraph to this chapter highlights, that living subjects are not strictly unitary; they participate in 'a relational vitality', in a self-organizing, material, empirical life force — *zoe* — that persists within but also outside, and beyond the demise, of a human life.[13] Informed by an 'embedded and embodied' condition, posthuman subjects, therefore, are 'framed by embodiment, sexuality, affectivity, empathy, and desire as core qualities'.[14] Braidotti also emphasizes, following Foucault, the role of power and discourse, which she says is 'polycentric and dynamic' and neither stable nor coherent nor rational, in the posthuman condition.[15] She states that 'power formations not only function at the material level but are also expressed in systems of theoretical and cultural representation, political and normative narratives and social modes of identification'.[16] Power and systems of meaning, including scientific ones, are complex: 'nothing [is] neutral or given'.[17] Her posthumanism, like many of the broader new materialisms of which Braidotti is a part, rejects, therefore, the dualisms in humanism and modernism, including a natural distinction between matter and discourse, and rethinks the human subject — its stability and superiority among other actants, in the Latourian sense.[18] Braidotti suggests that new, affirmative and creative ethics can develop within the posthumanist understanding of subjects as radically and deeply relational.

Of particular interest to this chapter is Braidotti's take on death, which argues that the boundaries between living and dying are blurred because both are a part of *zoe*, the same generative life force, which is neither human nor divine. Human life becomes imperceptible in death but the human is still 'becoming' in the larger sense of its participation in 'the great animal-machine of the universe, beyond personal individual death'.[19] Braidotti's 'death as impersonal' stance does not, however, diminish the importance of a single person; instead she suggests that one person's life, and death, have implications for the universe as a whole because of the intricate ways in which human life is connected to its context.[20] Death, therefore, is an immanent rather than transcendent state, a 'merging with the web of non-human forces that frame him/her, the cosmos as a whole', in other words, 'the grounding totality of the moment when we coincide completely with our body in becoming at last what we will have been all along: a virtual corpse'.[21] Lastly, according to Braidotti, the move from the unitary, self-interested humanist subject to the 'environmentally bound' and 'interdependent' posthuman makes possible an inclusive, affirmative politics and ethics.[22] Macabéa's and Angela's subjectivity and deaths, and on some level Lispector's, are interpreted here with attention to the qualities of posthuman subjects and the meaning of death that Braidotti proposes.

This chapter also works with Gloria Anzaldúa's theory of *la naguala*, the feminine form of *nagual*, which is Nahuatl, or Uto-Aztecan, for 'shapeshifter'.[23] In keeping with the mythological traditions of her Indian *curandera* [healer] ancestors, Anzaldúa, the daughter of sixth-generation Mexican-American farmers, invoked shapeshifting characters in addition to Mesoamerican deities in her fiction and also non-fiction writing. Toward the end of her life, *la naguala* took on new meaning for Anzaldúa, a United States-based feminist activist who supported coalition work across race, gender and other categories of 'non-dominant' difference.[24] In her final essays, particularly, Anzaldúa began to refer to *la naguala* as a practice of consciousness in which a person merges, temporarily, with another person or with one's surroundings in order to develop empathy and compassion for that person or situation. One does not fully become another in shapeshifting consciousness; it is an emotional, energetic movement from self to other, 'a hyperempathetic perception'.[25] Like Braidotti's posthuman subject, a person maintains a sense of self, but the borders between subject and surroundings are expansive. Anzaldúa's descriptions of *nagualan* practice begin with the importance of the imagination, which stimulates even physical change in the body. The acts of reading and writing, therefore, for Anzaldúa, were potentially *nagualan* activities with concrete implications and transformative potential. Anzaldúa's theory attempts to rethink the subject, using not only the shamanism-inspired concept of the shapeshifter but of indigenous deities as well, in part to resist western, humanist constructions of self and the disembodied unitary subject. In my earlier work I map the similarities between Anzaldúa's and Lispector's fiction with respect to shapeshifting subjectivity.[26] Their works are very similar in writing style, subject matter, including death scenes, and the subjective practice of characters, and both writers call on readers to rethink the potentials of language unfettered by humanism's boundaries. In this chapter, however, I extend that analysis, most substantially by including *A Breath of Life* and a comparison of it with *The Hour of the Star*.

To compare Anzaldúa with Lispector is an unexpected and complicated endeavour. Although both share the designation of Latin American writer, Anzaldúa was from the U.S./Mexico border, her worldview steeped in the Mesoamerican heritage to which she overtly made mention, while Lispector, born in Western Ukraine to Jewish parents who immigrated to northeast Brazil when she was an infant, evaded reference to her family roots, particularly her Jewish culture, in her work. Scholars, most notably and comprehensively Nelson Vieira, have noted, however, the parallels between Jewish thought and cultural traditions and Lispector's writing. Vieira's early work links Lispector's Jewish family background and concepts of Jewish mysticism to Lispector's themes; he later refers to Lispector as having honed 'a literary approach with a universal vision that also incorporated Jewish particularities', recognizing that Lispector also pulled from the Christianity and other multiethnic religious influences and 'alternative cults' of her Brazilian audience.[27] Importantly, although she praises Vieira for his thorough work, Naomi Lindstrom warns scholars against finding a Jewish 'attitude or vision' in Lispector's writing without specific textual evidence, so it is with caution that I point out the similarities, with respect to what inspired them, in Anzaldúa's take on and use of language as a creative, constitutive force with Lispector's.[28] Although Anzaldúa was explicit about the influence of shamanism on her conception of language, Lispector's links to Jewish mysticism, which, like shamanism, lends a significant amount of power to language, might not be responsible for, certainly not solely so, Lispector's fascination with and treatment of the written word.[29] A well-developed and supported theory that Anzaldúa's and Lispector's similar styles and themes are linked by an adherence to traditions in their heritages and worldviews is beyond the scope of this chapter. However, that Anzaldúa and Lispector were motivated by and took seriously the relationships between language, story, and bodies is clear. As Lispector states, for example, 'In every word a heart beats', and Anzaldúa, 'When I write it feels like I'm carving bone'.[30] For the purposes of this chapter, the similarities in the radically embodied and embedded subjects that show up in both authors' works are of particular interest and what will be the focus of comparison. Anzaldúa's *nagualan* subject proves useful in helping to describe the depth of complexity in the relationships between Lispector's characters as well as in Lispector's drive to write.

As the remainder of the chapter turns to the posthuman in Lispector with a focus on the similarities in *The Hour of the Star* and *A Breath of Life*, the differences in these two texts are also worth noting. Although Lispector was working on both novels simultaneously, *The Hour of the Star* was completed and published the October before her December 1977 death, while the more abstract and disjointed *A Breath of Life* was left unfinished. Her close friend Olga Borelli organized and published the book the following year. Her more well-known *Hour of the Star* has what Nelson Vieira calls a 'sociological message', which is 'not typical of her writing' in the narrator's self-reflexive struggle to represent the other, in this case, a young, barely skilled typist named Macabéa, who has fled from poverty in the rural northeast to metropolitan Rio de Janeiro, Brazil.[31] The novel is as overly sentimental and comic as it is dark, ironic, and gritty, a reflection in part of the narrator's anguished, impossible attempts to accurately tell his protagonist's story. The even less conventional *A Breath of Life* is virtually plotless, a series of intense, philosophical exchanges between narrator and protagonist, what looks like a dialogue but is not, as the protagonist is unaware of the narrator's existence. This text is, even more overtly than *The Hour of the Star*, a deep look at the relationship between writer, narrator, and character. The themes in both texts relate to the impossibilities of representation and, like many of Lispector's works, the struggle to understand the unpredictability of the human condition, including death. Indeed, these two novels, especially *The Hour of the Star*, are rich with absurdist motifs. However, Lispector's musings on chaos, violence, and meaninglessness reveal an underlying consistency about life: the human participates in a vast materiality that's larger than the rational mind conceives, a condition in which the boundaries between nature and culture, and humans, animals, and things, are blurred. As protagonist Ângela Pralini says in *A Breath of Life*, 'I am a part of the great energy of the world [...] I see luminosity without theme, without story, without facts'.[32] Mattias Kärrholm described *A Breath of Life*, like *The Passion According to G.H.*, as an example of Lispector's use of animistic strategies in writing, where protagonist Ângela Pralini 'opens up for a symmetry between all beings'.[33] He says, 'Lispector animates the world and makes it her equal.'[34] This ability is ever present in her final two novels.

As Lispector herself faces the final months of her life, her protagonists and stories of their deaths complicate humanist expectations of subjects in multiple ways. Neither protagonist is largely motivated by mastery of a skill or rational thought, or by attaining a distinct, autonomous personhood and economic wealth in order to make meaning or to live fully. From page to page these characters develop by way of imagination and a deep awareness of the moment and their vastly embedded and embodied circumstances. Their existence as subjects is bound to others and material context, but in ways that expand, not diminish them. *The Hour of the Star*'s Macabéa is sickly, homely, and lives a 'sparse' existence.[35] However, she displays an odd contentment with her simple life, cutting and pasting together colourful newspaper advertisements in an album by candlelight. She desires the face cream in the ad not for what it would do for her skin but because it looks so good she wants to eat it. She meditates while she types, and daydreams out loud on her bus ride to work. 'She was nourished by her own entity' according to the male narrator, Rodrigo S.M., who is completely perplexed and transformed by Macabéa's behaviour.[36] She lives in the moment, pondering over such things as the speed of a fly, while her short-time boyfriend Olímpico is obsessed with his future. Macabéa says she has 'no worries' or any need for wealth or achievement.[37] He thinks that 'the good life is only for the privileged' while she thinks '[i]t's wonderful to be alive'.[38] Macabéa, compared to her well-educated, anxious narrator and her self-conscious and self-absorbed boyfriend is happy and resilient. Indeed, as her narrator observes and as mentioned in the opening epigraph, 'the breath of life surge[s] within Macabéa's parched body'.[39] The above focus might be read as dismissive of the concrete, material deprivation that Macabéa faces as a poor young girl, a situation that warrants a critique of the capitalism and colonialism that dominated Brazil during Macabéa's time and has continued to do so since; this critique is indeed found in the story, but I want to focus here on how characters like Macabéa, and others in Lispector's texts, like Ruth in 'Miss Algrave,' (*A via-crucis do corpo* [*The Via Crucis of the Body*] (1974)) are written in ways that resist their being read as weak and unimportant despite their lack of wealth, the marker of success in the modern world. And in the cases of Macabéa and Ângela, their seemingly tragic deaths do not simply represent a tragic end to their lives. In other words, although these characters' deaths are unexpected, even gruesome in Macabéa's case, and importantly, the result of their lack of power and control, they appear to embrace their deaths, and the meanings in them, for the broad-ranging materiality of, not transcendence beyond, the experience, which I return to in the last part of this chapter. Before turning to those death scenes, I will explore the relational subjectivity present in the narrator–protagonist–thing interaction in *The Hour of the Star* and *A Breath of Life*.

A Breath of Life highlights, even more so than *The Hour of the Star*, the relationship between a male narrator, simply called 'Author', and a female protagonist, Ângela, whom we don't know much about, except that like Macabéa, her work, as a journalist, depends on her writing. Ângela's narrator is frustrated with her because she is inconsistent and doesn't finish what she starts.[40] She is writing a book called *The Story of Things* about 'things and objects and their aura' and for a full twenty-six pages of this brief book, Ângela describes the force of and power in everyday objects, from bottles to elevators, a folding screen, a silver box, a clock, an iron guardrail, a car, a record player, and a trash can.[41] 'More mysterious than the soul is matter' she says, '[t]he thing that is miraculously concrete in your hands' and she is fascinated by the 'shape, shadow, aura, function' of things, and the idea that '[t]he thing in itself has a plan' of which she becomes a part.[42] Ângela falls in love with things, feels sorry for them, ascribes magic to them, says they are 'worth the very air'.[43] A round table is sly and 'smiles', a brooch is 'serious' in its weight, and an elevator 'sulky' and 'rude'.[44] Comments like, 'You feel in the clock time vibrating' and 'I don't put anything inside the box so that it won't be burdened' demonstrate Ângela's peculiar awareness and expansive sense of relationship to her surroundings.[45] Ângela's anthropomorphic descriptions are curious as a literary device here; she is describing a relationship between herself and the objects, not simply assigning human characteristics to them. Ângela seems to be saying, like theorist Jane Bennett argues in *Vibrant Matter*, that objects, inanimate things, have animating power: they can produce effects.[46] 'Sensation is the soul of the world', our narrator tells us, then asks: 'Is intelligence a sensation? In Ângela it is', directly confronting the mind/body divide.[47] Of course, Ângela is only a character, but this character teaches our narrator, who is arguably closer to 'Clarice the writer' than even Rodrigo S.M., that the permeable, radically embedded body is the vehicle to knowing and meaning in a vastly alive world.

The relationship between narrator and protagonist is particularly prominent and critically noted in *The Hour of the Star* and *A Breath of Life*. Both narrators try desperately to become their characters, to shapeshift in the Anzaldúan sense, and their narrating is the vehicle through which their subjectivity transforms. For example, Rodrigo S.M., Macabéa's narrator, reveals that '[t]he action of this story will result in my transfiguration into someone else and in my ultimate materialization into an object. Perhaps I might even acquire the sweet tones of the flute and become entwined in a creeper vine'.[48] Similarly, the Author in *A Breath of Life* states, 'My own life has an actual plot. It would be the history of the bark of a tree and not of the tree. A bunch of facts that only the senses would explain.'[49] Both narrators articulate an expansive, sensorial existence, one that is part of a larger force, becoming something entirely other-than-human yet intensely embodied subjects, but such transformation is dependent on their protagonists and the stories that they tell. Their characters depend on them as well. In the case of Macabéa, who is uneducated and ignorant of her lack of power, she depends on Rodrigo to not only write her story but to explain the story's political concerns, or to write her into a particular realm of existence. However, she surprises her narrator by her resilience despite the oppression she faces, and she offers a view into her existence that the narrator cannot. The coming together of these two subjects creates another within the text — one with the sensibilities, awareness, and knowledge of both. Ângela, who lives squarely in the moment and in her 'urgent and emergent' desires, needs her narrator or she wouldn't finish anything, while her narrator needs her because she is the result of his creative output, the 'daydream' that he needs to have in order to exist.[50] Lispector, the writer, needs them both; all three become intensely entangled in *A Breath of Life*, as critics have commented.[51] She said in an interview, filmed the year of her death, referring to the purpose of writing: 'At the end of the day we're not trying to change things, we are trying to open up somehow', which suggests that for her, the narrators and characters in both novels extend her own struggling and fragmented, yet expansive subjectivity, as a writer.[52] 'When I'm not writing I'm dead', she says, when the interviewer asks, in reference to a question Rilke posed to a young aspiring writer: 'If you could no longer write, would you die?' These comments might imply that for Lispector writing was a critical part of her being, not just an occupation, but an intense practice of enlarging herself, not just in the act and result of writing, but by way of narrator and character.

The complex relationship between narrator and protagonist in *The Hour of the Star* and *A Breath of Life* also reveals the difficulties of fully becoming one with as well as representing the other. As Rodrigo S.M. says, telling Macabéa's story is like 'attempt[ing] to extract gold from charcoal. [...] holding up the narrative and playing at ball without a ball'.[53] He also ponders, 'Is it possible that in penetrating the seeds of her existence, I am violating the secrets of the Pharaohs?'[54] Rodrigo S.M. is conscious of and tormented by his responsibility as narrator, and Macabéa resists and perplexes him. The Author in *A Breath of Life* expresses similar tensions; he doesn't wish to describe Ângela but wants to 'lodge [him]self temporarily within her way of being'[55]. The key word here is 'temporarily' (in the original Portuguese 'temporariamente') demonstrating the narrator's awareness of his ability to become one with his character yet shift back to his separate role as storyteller.[56] Lispector's writing of the narrator–protagonist relationship, particularly the narrators' self-awareness, offers an unusual look at the problems and anxieties of representation and of subjects' permeability — how they are profoundly affected by their relationships and contexts. Anzaldúa describes in detail a process of shapeshifting subjectivity that can be traced in the narrators' commentaries above: she refers to a person's core consciousness as a 'knower' that has several 'functions', including the function 'that arouses the awareness that beneath individual separateness lies a deeper interrelatedness', which she calls *la naguala*.[57] After a person 'empathize[s]' with the other, one 'shifts to a less defensive, more inclusive identity' and 'compassion', where transformation, individuality and collectivity take place.[58] Subjects are always in flux, in a process of integration with and differentiation from other subjects; even those we, and others, have invented; those we read and those we write. Lispector demonstrates an intense awareness of, and creates and participates in, a radical shapeshifting subjectivity in her work. Macabéa is written in a way that puzzles her narrator and that says that despite her meagre circumstances, Macabéa will not be broken, neither by patriarchy nor political power. In the more philosophical *A Breath of Life*, Ângela exists for desire, sensation, and wholeness; she is an achievement created by a narrator in spite of his own suspiciousness, reservation and melancholy. Ângela, as a character, and as imagination, resists being appropriated by reason or by her creator/narrator.

Braidotti's posthuman theory of death provides a foundation for reading the death scenes in these texts as destabilizing humanist, anthropocentric assumptions about the characters and the meanings associated with their demise. At the end of *The Hour of the Star*, Rodrigo S.M.'s descriptions of Macabéa, who has been struck by a car, focus on her perishing body in all its physicality and mortality. For several pages of this short novel, the reader sees the blood from Macabéa's head and mouth, her effort to breathe, her curling into the foetal position 'grotesque as ever', and 'look[ing] as imposing as a dead stallion'[59]. Yet, Lispector somehow makes this gruesome scene seem joyful, and not for the relief or transcendence that Macabéa achieves, but for the physical transformation itself, a participation in 'zoe in all its powers', as if Macabéa is answering Braidotti's call to 'catch the wave of life's intensities in a secular manner and ride on it, exposing the boundaries or limits as we transgress them'.[60] Peace seems to take over Macabéa: as she lies in the road, seeing sprouts of green grass, she thinks, '[T]oday is the dawn of my existence: I am born.'[61] Consider Ângela as well, in the other novel's last words: 'It's dawning; I hear roosters. I am dawning.'[62] Macabéa is not looking toward the sky and Ângela does not hear angels: they are focused on their very plant-and-animal earthliness. Even references to God involve situational irony: when Macabéa searches for God, she looks into 'the deep black essence of her own being' and refers to God's grace as '[a] sensation as pleasurable, tender, horrifying, chilling and penetrating as love'.[63] Ângela similarly finds God in 'the wind in the leaves' and 'fear[s] the *natural law* that we call God'.[64] Both characters turn towards the physical experience and context of the body in death, and the narrators turn toward this transformation as well, as the novels come to a close.

The value of both lives, and Lispector's too, however, is far from diminished in their expiring physical states. Narrator Rodrigo S.M.'s comment that 'in some remote corner of the world, a horse reared and gave a loud neigh, as if in response' to Macabéa's death brings attention to the breadth of the experience, involving the cosmic 'roar' as Braidotti calls it, the enduring persistence of zoe.[65] Macabéa's last words are '[a]s for the future,' indicating that her life is about something larger than her individual existence, perhaps other girls like her at the novel's particular historical moment, or the continuation of 'the radical immanence of "just a life"', or both.[66] *A Breath of Life*'s Author reveals his understanding of his own life that lingers after death, but in its empirical, expansive, material way: 'I occupy a place and even after death I shall continue to occupy the earth.'[67]

Lispector's awareness of her own expansive legacy is prominent in *A Breath of Life*, without a fictional storyline to distract the reader from the links between writer, narrator, character, and themes. When Borelli is left to structure the unfinished text after Lispector's death, authorship shapeshifts from Lispector to Borelli. Lispector seems to predict this outcome, as Author says of the text, 'This I suppose will be a book made apparently out of shards of a book.'[68] Lispector's consciousness of her own closeness to death lurks in plain sight in the conversation between the narrator and Ângela. Ângela states, 'Oh human face that should be mine and is yours. I'm still alive though close to death.'[69] Author then says, 'Note: I want to see if I won't forget to give Ângela a face.'[70] Lispector's legacy seems to be on display here as she, by way of narrator and character, struggles with death's meaning. Says Author, 'Death is beyond human measure... It sometimes seems to me that death is not a fact it's a sensation that must already be with me. But I still haven't reached it.'[71] Braidotti says that death is always with us, part of 'our psychic and somatic landscapes' and 'has already taken place as a virtual potential that constructs everything we are,' which helps to explain arguably the best-known of all the statements in this text, 'Life is a madness that death makes'.[72] I read Lispector's madness here in a posthumanist way — as desire that 'aims at expressing itself' — in that there is no dialectical tension between Eros and Thanatos, because they are 'really just one force'.[73]

A logical story with a traditional, definitive narrative arc is not what Lispector leaves for us in *A Breath of Life* as she comes into her own time of death. Instead, our narrator admits to cutting half of the book, only leaving, he says, 'what provokes and inspires [him] for life: a star lit at dusk'[74]. Lispector seems to be stretching language to tell a story beyond language, a mystery beyond reach, like a star. She demonstrates in this pervious relationship between herself as writer, the narrator, and Ângela Pralini the character, that although language falls short, her determination does not, in her attempts to share with her readers her struggle with the body and with language to make meaning of her life and ever-approaching death. The 'star lit as dusk': a single life that matters despite its randomness and smallness against a vast, dark backdrop. The star metaphor here has some obvious links to *The Hour of the Star,* which wins out as title of the book over Lispector's thirteen other possibilities. The metaphor's usage here is similar: Macabéa's star status, like Ângela's, becomes most evident as she is dying. Macabéa wants to become a film star, and our narrator tells us that 'one day she would surely die as if she had already learned by heart how to play the starring role. For at the hour of death you become a celebrated film star, it is a moment of glory for everyone, when the choral music scales the top notes'.[75] Interestingly, both Ângela and Macabéa are described by their narrators as film stars in their moments of death. Their existence is amplified by the attention they are receiving from witnesses to their death, including their readers. *A Breath of Life*'s narrator announces Ângela's death by, unexpectedly, switching his position to that of a film's cameraperson. He states: 'I pull back my gaze my camera and Ângela starts getting small, small, smaller — until I lose sight of her.'[76] Ângela, like Macabéa, fades away like a star at dawn or an actress's role that ends when the film does, but like both, Ângela and Macabéa revive, albeit in a different form. Stars shine again when night-time comes, as a film actress does when she is cast in her next role.

Curiously, and perhaps even ironically, given a star's construction as 'unearthly', death for these characters is associated not with a transcendence beyond the body, but with a delving into an even more concretely embedded material existence. For example, after Ângela's narrator loses sight of her in his camera lens, he says, 'Ângela interrupted life by going into the earth. But not the earth in which one is buried but the earth in which one is revived. With abundant rain in the forest and the whisper of the winds.'[77] Instead of moving onto an ethereal plane, Ângela, like Macabéa, becomes one with her physical context, and the reach of her decomposition extends beyond the dirt. Ângela and Macabéa are like stars even in a material sense: 'stars are so large and have so much matter in them [technically a nuclear fusion of hydrogen and helium] that it will take billions of years for the explosion to use all the "fuel" in the star'.[78] To the human eye a star's presence fades and resurfaces, but in a material sense, it persists, like Macabéa and Ângela in their beyond-human yet material, posthuman forms.

Macabéa and Ângela's deaths are important not because they, at last, escape life but because of how they live it, how they open to it, as Lispector might say. Lastly, I want to extend the shapeshifting writer, narrator, character relationship to include the reader. Considering that Lispector's characters are more than representations; a posthumanist, particularly Anzaldúan reading of tropes, is that they have a vibrant relationship with their readers that can create, in emotional and physical ways, personal and collective experiences. The boundaries of the porous posthuman subject are limitless, and I close with a quote from *A Breath of Life* that supports my suspicion that Lispector may have felt this way as well: 'It's when the self no longer exists, no longer makes demands, that it joins the tree of life — and that's what I struggle to attain. To forget oneself and yet to live so intensely.'[79]

Works Cited

ANZALDÚA, GLORIA, 'now let us shift...the path of conocimiento...inner work, public acts', in *this bridge we call home: radical visions for transformation*, ed. by Gloria Anzaldúa and AnaLouise Keating (New York: Routledge, 2002), pp. 540–79

—— *Borderlands/La Frontera*, 4th edn (San Francisco, CA: Aunt Lute Books, 2012 [1987])

BENNETT, JANE, *Vibrant Matter: A Political Ecology of Things* (Durham, NC: Duke University Press, 2010)

BRAIDOTTI, ROSI, *Metamorphoses: Towards a Materialist Theory of Becoming* (Cambridge: Polity, 2002)

—— *The Posthuman* (Cambridge: Polity Books, 2013)

ELIOR, RACHEL, *The Mystical Origins of Hasidism* (Oxford: Liverpool University Press, 2006)

FRIIS, ELISABETH, 'In My Core I have the Strange Impression that I don't Belong to the Human Species: Clarice Lispector's *Água Viva* as Life Writing?' in *Narrating Life: Experiments with Human and Animal Bodies in Literature, Science and Art*, ed. by Stefan Herbrechter and Elisabeth Friis (Leiden: Brill-Rodopi, 2016), pp. 31–54

GOH, IRVING, 'Blindness and Animality, or Learning How to Live Finally in Clarice Lispector's *The Passion According to G.H.*', differences: *A Journal of Feminist Cultural Studies*, 25 (2012), 113–35

—— 'Le Toucher, le cafard, or, On Touching: The Cockroach in Clarice Lispector's *Passion According to G.H.*', *MLN*, 131 (2016), 461–80

—— 'Writing, Touching, and Eating in Clarice Lispector: *Água Viva* and *A Breath of Life*', *MLN*, 131 (2016), 1347–69

KÄRRHOLM, MATTIAS, 'The Animistic Moment: Clarice Lispector, Louis Kahn and a Reassembling of Materialities', *Lo Squaderno*, 39 (2016), 71–77

LINDSTROM, NAOMI, 'Judaic Traces in the Narrative of Clarice Lispector: Identity Politics and Evidence', in *Latin American Jewish Cultural Production*, ed. by David William Foster (Nashville, TN: Vanderbilt University Press, 2009), pp. 83–96

LISPECTOR, CLARICE, *A hora da estrela* (1977); *The Hour of the Star*, trans. by Giovanni Pontiero (New York: New Directions, 1992 [1986])

—— *Um sopro de vida (pulsações)* (Rio de Janeiro: Rocco, 1998 [1978]); *A Breath of Life (Pulsations)*, trans. by Johnny Lorenz (New York: New Directions, 2012)

LUGONES, MARÍA, 'Radical Multiculturalism and Women of Color Feminisms', *Journal for Cultural and Religious Theory*, 13 (Winter 2014), 68–80

Moser, Benjamin, *Why this World: A Biography of Clarice Lispector* (New York: Oxford University Press, 2009)

Negrete, Fernanda, 'Approaching Impersonal Life with Clarice Lispector', *Humanities*, 7.55 (2018) <https://doi.org/10.3390/h7020055> [accessed 31 January 2022]

Piepenbring, Dan, 'It Changes Nothing' *The Paris Review* (10 December 2014), <https://www.theparisreview.org/blog/2014/12/10/it-changes-nothing/> [accessed 12 July 2018]

Piskorski, Rodolfo, 'The Light That Therefore I Give (to): Paleonymy and Animal Supplementarity in Clarice Lispector's *The Apple in the Dark*', in *What Is Zoopoetics?: Texts, Bodies, Entanglement*, ed. by Kári Driscoll and Eva Hoffman (New York: Palgrave Macmillan, 2018), pp. 103–28

Qualitative Reasoning Group, 'What are Stars Made Of?', Northwestern University <http://www.qrg.northwestern.edu/projects/vss/docs/space-environment/2-what-are-stars-made-of.html> [accessed 9 July 2018]

Shapiro, Steven, 'Two Lessons from Burroughs', in *Posthuman Bodies*, ed. by Judith Halberstam and Ira Livingston (Bloomington: Indiana University Press, 1995), pp. 38–54

Vieira, Nelson H., *Jewish Voices in Brazilian Literature: A Prophetic Discourse of Alterity* (Gainesville: University of Florida Press, 1995)

—— 'Clarice Lispector (1920–1977): A Woman of Spirit', in *Makers of Jewish Modernity: Thinkers, Artists, Leaders, and the World They Made*, ed. by Jacques Picard, Jacques Revel, Michael P. Steinberg, and Idith Zertal (Princeton, NJ: Princeton University Press, 2016), pp. 552

Zaytoun, Kelli D., 'Resistance as Shapeshifter: A Posthumanist Reading of Subjectivity and Death in the Fiction of Gloria Anzaldúa and Clarice Lispector', *Contemporary Women's Writing*, 10.3 (2016), 394–410

Notes to Chapter 16

1. Clarice Lispector, *The Hour of the Star*, trans. by Giovanni Pontiero (New York: New Directions, 1992 [1986]), pp. 59–60.
2. Rosi Braidotti, *The Posthuman* (Cambridge: Polity Books, 2013), p. 131.
3. Steven Shapiro, 'Two Lessons from Burroughs', in *Posthuman Bodies*, ed. by Judith Halberstam and Ira Livingston (Bloomington: Indiana University Press, 1995), pp. 38–54.
4. Rosi Braidotti, *Metamorphoses: Towards a Materialist Theory of Becoming* (Cambridge: Polity, 2002).
5. Jutta Ittner, 'Who's Looking? The Animal Gaze in the Fiction of Brigette Kronauer and Clarice Lispector', in *Figuring Animals: Essays on Animal Images in Art, Literature, Philosophy, and Popular Culture*, ed. by Mary Sanders Pollock and Catherine Rainwater (New York: Palgrave Macmillan, 2005), pp. 99–118; Anne Schillmoller, 'Gaining Ground: Towards a Discourse of Posthuman Animality: A Geophilosophical Journey', *Southern Cross University Law Review*, 14 (2012), 41–73; Irving Goh, 'Blindness and Animality, or Learning How to Live Finally in Clarice Lispector's *The Passion according to G.H.*', *differences: A Journal of Feminist Cultural Studies*, 25 (2012), 113–35.
6. Rodolfo Piskorski, 'The Light That Therefore I Give (to): Paleonymy and Animal Supplementarity in Clarice Lispector's *The Apple in the Dark*', in *What Is Zoopoetics?: Texts, Bodies, Entanglement*, ed. by Kári Driscoll and Eva Hoffman (New York: Palgrave Macmillan, 2018), pp. 103–28.
7. Irving Goh, 'Le Toucher, le cafard, or, On Touching: The Cockroach in Clarice Lispector's *Passion according to G.H.*', *MLN*, 131 (2016), 461–80, and 'Writing, Touching, and Eating in Clarice Lispector: *Água Viva* and *A Breath of Life*', *MLN*, 131 (2016), 1347–69; Mattias Kärrholm, 'The Animistic Moment: Clarice Lispector, Louis Kahn and a Reassembling of Materialities', *Lo Squaderno*, 39 (2016), 71–77.
8. Elisabeth Friis, 'In My Core I have the Strange Impression that I don't Belong to the Human Species: Clarice Lispector's *Água Viva* as Life Writing?', in *Narrating Life: Experiments with Human and Animal Bodies in Literature, Science and Art*, ed. by Stefan Herbrechter and Elisabeth Friis (Leiden: Brill-Rodopi, 2016), pp. 31–54 (p. 53).

9. Fernanda Negrete, 'Approaching Impersonal Life with Clarice Lispector', *Humanities*, 7.55 (2018) <https://doi.org/10.3390/h7020055> [accessed 31 January 2022].
10. I use the term decolonial instead of pre- or post-colonial to emphasize the specific project of decoloniality as discussed by Latin American scholars like Walter Mignolo, María Lugones, and Anibal Quijano. Decolonialism works to uncover and resist the coloniality of power, in its broadest reaches, from the construction of knowledge and modernity to constructions of gender, sex, and race. Focusing on the specifically decolonial potential of Lispector's writing is beyond the scope of this chapter, but it is mentioned here as a possible avenue for future scholarly investigations.
11. Braidotti, *The Posthuman*, p. 136; Lispector, *The Hour of the Star*, p. 82.
12. Braidotti, *The Posthuman*, pp. 11–12.
13. Ibid., p. 188.
14. Ibid., p. 102, 26.
15. Ibid., p. 27, 26.
16. Ibid., p. 26.
17. Ibid., p. 27.
18. Jane Bennett, *Vibrant Matter: A Political Ecology of Things* (Durham, NC: Duke University Press, 2010), p. 9. Bennett takes up Latour's term and discussion of 'actant' to refer to 'a source of action', which can be 'human or not, or most likely, a combination of both', complicating traditional understandings of agents and subjects.
19. Braidotti, *The Posthuman*, p. 136.
20. Ibid., p. 194.
21. Ibid., p. 136.
22. Ibid., p. 139.
23. Gloria Anzaldúa, 'now let us shift...the path of conocimiento...inner work, public acts', in *this bridge we call home: radical visions for transformation*, ed. by Gloria Anzaldúa and AnaLouise Keating (New York: Routledge, 2002), pp. 540–79.
24. In 2014, María Lugones revived Audre Lorde's language of 'nondominant differences' from Lorde's 1984 essay 'The Master's Tools Will Never Dismantle the Master's House'. Lugones says, 'Lorde is not celebrating a coalition that arises from a denial of power differentials, but one that arises from within resistances to power at all levels of oppression' (p. 77). I use the term here with respect to Lugones' interpretation. See Lugones, 'Radical Multiculturalism and Women of Color Feminisms', *Journal for Cultural and Religious Theory*, 13 (Winter 2014), 68–80.
25. Anzaldúa, 'now let us shift', p. 577.
26. See Kelli D. Zaytoun, 'Resistance as Shapeshifter: A Posthumanist Reading of Subjectivity and Death in the Fiction of Gloria Anzaldúa and Clarice Lispector', *Contemporary Women's Writing*, 10.3 (2016), 394–410. In this article, I offer my initial Braidotti-informed, posthumanist reading of *The Hour of the Star* in relation to the theories and fiction of Gloria Anzaldúa. I expand that reading in this chapter and extend the analysis to include *A Breath of Life*.
27. Nelson H. Vieira, *Jewish Voices in Brazilian Literature: A Prophetic Discourse of Alterity* (Gainesville: University of Florida Press, 1995); 'Clarice Lispector (1920–1977): A Woman of Spirit', in *Makers of Jewish Modernity: Thinkers, Artists, Leaders, and the World They Made*, ed. by Jacques Picard, Jacques Revel, Michael P. Steinberg, and Idith Zertal (Princeton, NJ: Princeton University Press, 2016), pp. 552. In this chapter, Vieira also documents Lispector's direct engagement with Spinoza and the influence of his philosophy on her texts as early as the writing of her first novel *Near to the Wild Heart* and sees a connection between modern Jewish thinkers like Leo Strauss and Emmanuel Levinas.
28. Naomi Lindstrom, 'Judaic Traces in the Narrative of Clarice Lispector: Identity Politics and Evidence', in *Latin American Jewish Cultural Production*, ed. by David William Foster (Nashville, TN: Vanderbilt University Press, 2009), pp. 83–96.
29. Rachel Elior, *The Mystical Origins of Hasidism* (Oxford: Liverpool University Press, 2006), p. 46.
30. Clarice Lispector, *Um sopro de vida (pulsações)* (Rio de Janeiro: Rocco, 1978), p. 17; *A Breath of Life (Pulsations)*, trans. by Johnny Lorenz (New York: New Directions Books, 2012), p. 8; Gloria Anzaldúa, *Borderlands/La Frontera*, 4th edn (San Francisco: Aunt Lute Books, 2012 [1987]), p. 95.

31. Vieira, 'Clarice Lispector (1920–1977): A Woman of Spirit', p. 559.
32. Lispector, *A Breath of Life*, p. 195.
33. Kärrholm, 'The Animistic Moment', p. 72.
34. Ibid., p. 72.
35. Lispector, *The Hour of the Star*, p. 23.
36. Ibid., p. 37.
37. Ibid., p. 49.
38. Ibid., p. 52.
39. Ibid., p. 59. This quote presents an obvious opportunity to link mentions of 'the breath of life' in *The Hour of the Star*, which occur more than once, and Lispector's posthumous novel *The Breath of Life*, pointing to her fixation on linking life-force and the body, which will be discussed later in the chapter.
40. Lispector, *A Breath of Life*, pp. 98–99.
41. Ibid., p. 98.
42. Ibid., p. 101, 103.
43. Ibid., p. 111.
44. Ibid., p. 117, 119, 122.
45. Ibid., p. 113, 112.
46. Bennett, *Vibrant Matter*, p. 6.
47. Lispector, *A Breath of Life*, p. 23.
48. Lispector, *The Hour of the Star*, p. 20.
49. Lispector, *A Breath of Life*, p. 11.
50. Ibid., p. 76.
51. See Benjamin Moser, *Why this World: A Biography of Clarice Lispector* (Oxford: Oxford University Press, 2009), p. 356, and Irving Goh, 'Writing, Touching, and Eating in Clarice Lispector'.
52. Cf. Dan Piepenbring, 'It Changes Nothing', *The Paris Review*, <https://www.theparisreview.org/blog/2014/12/10/it-changes-nothing/> [accessed 12 July 2018]. Embedded in this article is Lispector's first and only TV interview given in February 1977 with TV Cultura in São Paulo.
53. Lispector, *The Hour of the Star*, p. 17.
54. Ibid., p. 39.
55. Lispector, *A Breath of Life*, p. 103.
56. Lispector, *Um Sopro de Vida*, p. 106.
57. Anzaldúa, 'now let us shift', pp. 569.
58. Ibid., pp. 569.
59. Lispector, *The Hour of the Star*, pp. 79, 85.
60. Braidotti, *The Posthuman*, p. 131.
61. Lispector, *The Hour of the Star*, p. 80.
62. Lispector, *A Breath of Life*, p. 163.
63. Lispector, *The Hour of the Star*, p. 83.
64. Lispector, *A Breath of Life*, p. 150, emphasis mine.
65. Lispector, *The Hour of the Star*, p. 79. Braidotti refers to this passage as her favourite in the English language, from George Eliot's *Middlemarch*: 'If we had a keen vision and feeling of all ordinary human life, it would be like hearing the grass grow and the squirrel's heart beat, and we should die of that roar which lies on the other side of silence. As it is, the quickest of us walk around well wadded with stupidity'. Quoted in Braidotti, *The Posthuman*, p. 55.
66. Lispector, *The Hour of the Star*, p. 84; Braidotti, *The Posthuman*, p. 132.
67. Lispector, *A Breath of Life*, p. 157.
68. Ibid., p. 10.
69. Ibid., p. 152.
70. Ibid., p. 152.
71. Ibid., p. 153.
72. Lispector, *A Breath of Life*, p. 31; Braidotti, *The Posthuman*, pp. 131–32.
73. Braidotti, *The Posthuman*, p. 134.
74. Lispector, *A Breath of Life*, p. 12.

75. Lispector, *The Hour of the Star*, p. 28.
76. Lispector, *A Breath of Life*, p. 163.
77. Ibid., p. 163.
78. Qualitative Reasoning Group, 'What are Stars Made Of?', Northwestern University <http://www.qrg.northwestern.edu/projects/vss/docs/space-environment/2-what-are-stars-made-of.html> [accessed 9 July 2018].
79. Lispector, *A Breath of Life*, p. 5.

CHAPTER 17

Reflections in the *Porta-espelho*: Clarice Lispector's Literary Theory of the Object

Ami Schiess

> 'I must study the wardrobe before painting it. What do I see? I see that the wardrobe appears penetrable because it has a door. But when I open it, I see that penetration has been put off: since inside is also a wooden surface, like a closed door' — Clarice Lispector, *Água Viva*[1]

The narrator of *Água viva* (1973) presents her reader with a paradox: in a novel that explicitly begins by striving to do away with representational art in the traditional sense, the narration nevertheless returns repeatedly to a series of objects that she represents in painting.[2] Caves, a collection of flowers, a church portico, a mirror and eventually, a wardrobe, all serve as indices for a constellation of artistic and ontological questions concerning seeing and knowing the nature of the world that lies outside of the self. Working through Clarice Lispector's earlier exposition of the object-as-such in 'The Egg and the Chicken' (1964), this chapter presents the last of *Água viva*'s objects, the wardrobe with its mirrored door (the *porta-espelho*), as particularly emblematic of the Clarician 'theory' of looking at the object and of the nature of her object itself.

In these two texts, Lispector traces a theory of art that insists on the integrity of the object as essentially opaque. The central claim of my analysis is that the approach of the artistic object that I trace here helps us to understand an important thematic thread running through Lispector's late work: the ways of seeing, knowing and representing things in *Água viva* and 'The Egg and the Chicken' quite literally prefigure the ethics of representation that emerges in Lispector's last novel, *A hora da estrela* [*The Hour of the Star*] (1977). Beneath or beyond its visible surface, Lispector's object-as-such is inaccessible; it withdraws or flees under the scrutinizing gaze of the observer. By repeatedly figuring the failure to penetrate the enigma of the object, Lispector prepares her writing for an ethics of attempts and failures that will re-emerge in the problematic portrayal of Macabéa in her last novel.

The wardrobe in *Água viva* that will finally anchor my analysis has a telling antecedent. It appears in the very first paragraph of Lispector's debut novel, *Perto do coração selvagem* [*Near to the Wild Heart*] (1944):

> A máquina do papai batia tac-tac...tac-tac-tac...O relógio acordou em tin-dlin sem poeira. O silêncio arrastou-se zzzzzz. O guarda-roupa dizia o que? Roupa-roupa-roupa. Não não. Entre o relógio, a máquina e o silêncio havia uma orelha à escuta, grande, cor-de-rosa e morta. Os três sons estavam ligados pela luz do dia e pelo ranger das folhinhas da árvore que se esfregavam umas nas outras radiantes.
>
> [Her father's typewriter went clack-clack... clack-clack-clack ... The clock awoke in dustless tin-dlen. The silence dragged out zzzzzz. What did the wardrobe say? clothes-clothes-clothes. No, no. Amidst the clock, the typewriter and the silence there was an ear listening, large, pink and dead. The three sounds were connected by the daylight and the squeaking of the tree's little leaves rubbing against one another radiant.]³

The play of sounds that opens this novel is portentous: the 'three sounds' collected here (the clock, the typewriter, and the silence) announce themes that will provide perceptible structure to much of Lispector's work in the years to follow: the fleetingness of time, the act of writing, and the impossibility of capturing the ineffable in language.⁴ But amidst the onomatopoeia of typewriter clacking, clock ticking and silence droning, a fourth object briefly appears to have a voice: the wardrobe.

Does the wardrobe also speak, the narrator implicitly asks herself, and if it does, what does it say? The answer is mundane: 'clothes-clothes-clothes'. This conjecture is immediately followed by a 'No, no' that closes off any further questioning: whether negating the wardrobe's capacity to speak or simply sidelining its contribution as banal, Joana's response eliminates this object from the afternoon's chorus. This wardrobe dutifully fulfils its function ('clothes-clothes-clothes'); but because it *is* nothing but what it does, it fails to warrant 'listening'. Thus, while the questions of literary creation that accrue to the typewriter, the clock and the silence become perhaps the central themes of the author's body of work, the question of what a wardrobe might have to say resurfaces in her *oeuvre* only decades later, when the wardrobe appears as an uncanny figure for the obscurity of the non-self.

In an important sense, Lispector's theory of the artistic object can be seen as an extension of her career-long quest to pursue the aspects of existence that cannot be captured in language: as the child Joana concludes in the opening scene described above, 'Precisely the things that really mattered she couldn't say'.⁵ According to this view, the category of the object is akin to Lispector's many enigmatic phrases (the 'between-the-lines'; the 'inexpressive'; the 'interval'; the 'It'; and the 'X') through which the author attempts to represent the non-representable aspects of existence. Plínio Prado sees such phrases as a mark of Lispector's commitment to the sublime, and her return to them across various texts as a gravitation toward 'o impalpável, o incompreensível, o inomeável [na] tentativa atormentada de acolher o que simultaneamente repugna' [the impalpable, the incomprehensible, the un-nameable, [in a] tormented attempt to encircle that which simultaneously repulses]. He characterizes these repeated attempts to 'encircle the un-nameable' as an 'aesthetic of failure'.⁶

If 'precisely the things that can't be said' about direct experience preoccupied

Lispector for the bulk of her career, in her late phase the author came to grapple with aspects of the world outside the self that cannot be shown directly in representation. *Água viva*'s narrator formulates this problem clearly: 'Quando se vê o ato de ver não tem forma — o que se vê às vezes tem forma e às vezes não. O ato de ver é inefável. E às vezes o que é visto também é inefável' [When you see, the act of seeing has no form — what you see sometimes has form and sometimes doesn't. The act of seeing is ineffable. And sometimes what is seen is also ineffable].[7] In my analysis, what Lispector's rendition of objects in 'The Egg and the Chicken' and *Água viva* does for representation (and eventually for ethics) is what the rest of her 'failing' writing does for language: it performs the limits of knowing and expression as a practice of renewed attempts and always-partial failures.

The Hidden in Things and the Hidden in Men

On what grounds do Lispector's concerns for 'the hidden in things and the hidden in men' (as Gaston Bachelard once described the potential of the wardrobe-figure) intersect?[8] How can a study of objects address questions of ethics, and how can the extension of object-theory to the depiction of a human character be in any way ethical? In short, how will my analysis answer a valid concern, namely that pointing to resemblances between depictions of objects and of Macabéa, a character from an oppressed sector of Brazilian society, merely re-inscribes the objectification of the poor by Brazil's elites that Lúcia Sá critiques?[9]

Before turning directly to Lispector's texts, it is worthwhile to question the nature of the relationship that I ultimately propose between Lispector's literary sketches of objects and her forays into representing social alterity. First, over and above any similarities that might rightly be drawn between Macabéa's characteristics and an object's (her relative 'muteness', for instance, or what the narrator describes as her lack of awareness of herself), my reading focuses instead on the similarities between the procedures undertaken for seeing and representing these two orders of literary 'objects'. Second, the objection that such parallels serve to dehumanize Macabéa is only partially true, or only part of the story.

The question of how Lispector's approach to non-human alterity converges with her concern for the human other is a timely one. Since the 1990s there has been a growing concern, in both the humanities and the social sciences, with establishing a non-metaphorical ground of correspondence between people and things, often with the implicit or explicit aim of reformulating our concept of ethics. This has led to a systematic rethinking of hierarchical human/nonhuman relations from areas as varied as new materialisms, object-oriented ontology, ecological philosophy, animal studies, and Amerindian perspectivism. The preoccupation with the relation between the human and 'everything else' is such that Jacques Lezra argues it constitutes *the* general mood of our intellectual moment and 'the current disposition in Anglophone as well as European academic culture'.[10]

Why so much thinking about things? Timothy Morton has described this trend as a deep-seated 'churning' that is indicative of an ontological malaise, a repetitive return to a site of trauma. But to what trauma exactly? For Lezra, our interest in things represents an expression or even a fortification of our interest in ourselves, whereby categories 'such as "things", "objects", "matter", and companion terms rise up like positive, real conditions to designate the finitude of the human animal'.[11] For Morton, quite to the contrary, the return represents 'a kind of Stockholm syndrome' vis-à-vis the tyranny of human-style thought and consciousness; by returning to it time and again, we betray an underlying rejection of the line that separates humans from the nonhuman world.'[12] In quite a different vein from Morton's speculative realism, Bill Brown asserts that the allure of things for literature lies in a 'vertiginous capacity' of a thing to be both itself — a useful, uncomplicated material object whose appeal is a respite from theorizing — and to serve as a 'sign (symbol, metonym or metaphor) of something else'.[13]

These brief quotations illustrate some of the fundamental conundrums that arise when we theorize the thing. Does our current intellectual preoccupation with things represent a self-serving concern for the human, or are we truly engaged in a reconsideration of what separates us (or doesn't) from the material world around us? Do things serve as figures or as exempla that help us to concretize abstract phenomena, or do they allow us a respite from thinking? The debates surrounding our concerns for 'things, objects, matter, and companion terms' suggests that these questions are, in the last instance, unresolvable.

Lispector's objects in *Água viva*, and their uncanny similarities to the protagonist of *A hora da estrela*, embody many of these same dilemmas. Just as the literary in general is more amenable to contradiction than philosophical expositions that must make clean distinctions and adhere to principles of non-contradiction, so also the slippery genre of Lispector's prose works makes them even more capacious for housing the different orders of concerns and contradictory responses that characterize current thing theory debates. *Água viva*'s undeterminable genre, one that slides continually between the lyric, the epistolary and the mystical while only flirting with the narrative, makes room for many types of relationships between the writing subject and the object of her address. Similarly, Lispector's deployment of material things as images of the object-problem likewise leaves room for a variety of ontological relations between subjects and objects. In *Água viva* and elsewhere, Lispector opts not to draw hard distinctions between different philosophical categories of alterity and existence. In this way Lispector's literary style is a model for her literary theory: the object that is a subject and the subject that is an object continually spin a web around one another that, as Hélène Cixous has observed of the novel's narration generally, defies unravelling.[14]

Beyond its capacity for housing competing concerns, the literary genre of Lispector's object theory also allows the text to formally re-enact those concerns. Not unlike the philosophical 'churning' described by Morton, Lispector's literary approach of things is structured by returns and contradictions. As my analysis will make clear, the narrator continually revisits the question of the object, figuring and re-figuring it in a fugue of varying themes. As the text's specific object shifts and morphs, Clarice Lispector's literary sketches of objects enact a spiralling concern that is more significant than any single figure.

The identification of such a formal mimesis recalls Prado's 'aesthetic of the sublime', and it also echoes Carlos Mendes de Sousa's analysis of Lispector's posthumously published *Um sopro de vida* [*A Breath of Life*]. That text, assembled after the author's death from fragments of writing, maintains an 'unfinished' quality that Sousa reads as 'não um "puzzle," mas a própria figura do descentramento, do caos [...]. Uma não-figura ou a impossibilidade de figurar [que] é [aquilo] que se oferece na apresentação do inacabado' [Not a puzzle, but the very figure of destabilization, of chaos [...]. What is offered in [Lispector's] presentation of the unfinished is the non-figure, or the impossibility of figuring].[15] Analogously, in *Água viva* Lispector's narration mimics the approach of the unknowable: a study in obscurity that also underscores the limits of the capacities of the self.

Disentangling the Object

The word *objeto* appears in *Água viva* around twenty times, and designates different orders of objects that become entangled over the course of the novel. Given Lispector's multiple uses of the term, it would seem that 'object' names a problem, or a series of problems, rather than a single concept: it is the node where apparently heterogeneous concerns converge. In this *Água viva*'s object aligns with Brown's characterization of the thing's vertiginous capacity to be both itself and a sign of other things.

The word 'object' first appears in the novel's epigraph, which is taken from the writings of Belgian painter and art critic Michel Seuphor (1901–1999):

> Tinha que existir uma pintura totalmente livre da dependência da figura — o objeto — que, como a música, não ilustra coisa alguma, não conta uma história e não lança um mito. Tal pintura contenta-se em evocar os reinos incomunicáveis do espírito, onde o sonho se torna pensamento, onde o traço se torna existência.
>
> [There must be a kind of painting totally free of the dependence on the figure — or object — which, like music, illustrates nothing, tells no story, launches no myth. Such painting would simply evoke the incommunicable kingdoms of the spirit, where dream becomes thought, where line becomes existence.][16]

In Seuphor's words, the desire to do away with the object seems definitive.

Água viva comes very close to this ideal in that the narration does away almost entirely with traditional objects of literary representation such as people, places and events. In fact, the epigraph's last phrase ('where dream becomes thought, where line becomes existence') comes very close to a line from Lispector's *A cidade sitiada* [*The Besieged City*] (1949) that is often employed to sum up her own artistic aims: 'Nela e num cavalo a impressão era a expressão' [In her and in a horse, the impression was the expression].[17] If Clarice Lispector has an *ars poetica*, it is this: to produce a temporally and affectively immediate work of art, where expression cleaves as closely as possible to experience.[18] The author's intention of creating a nonrepresentative work of literary art in *Água viva* may well constitute the apex of a progressive move toward avant-garde abstraction, in the service of her aims for immediacy.

This progression is particularly germane to the late avant-garde movement of Brazilian *concretismo* in both the plastic and literary arts of which Lispector was a contemporary. Librandi notes the striking similarities between *Água viva*'s narration and this statement by Brazilian artist Hélio Oiticica in 1968, just a few years before the novel's publication:

> The Object is seen as an action in the environment within which objects exist as 'signs' and not merely as 'works'. It is the new phase of the pure vital exercise, where the role of the artist is to propose creative activities. The Object is the discovery of the world, and each instant. It does not have any a priori established existence but rather is the creation of what we would like it to be: a sound, a scream can be an object.[19]

Oiticica's declaration of the ephemerality of the artistic object conjures several parallels in Lispector's novel and also elicits a second understanding of the word 'object' in this text. The first of these parallels is the theme of disposability, a motif that Lispector applies at various moments in her prose to the act of looking, the use of language, and to her writing.[20] *Água viva*'s narrator poses her text not only as an object, but also as one that will be thrown away: 'Nunca lerás o que escrevo. E quando eu tiver anotado o meu segredo de ser — jogarei fora como se fosse ao mar' [You will never read what I'm writing. And when I've noted down my secret of being — I'll throw it away as if into the sea].[21] The gesture of disposal, of the concrete text as an ephemeral thing whose use is exhausted in its production, speaks to the notion of an artistic object-as-event, over one that is a closed and durable entity.

This raises a fundamental question for *Água viva*, namely, why a text so averse to referentiality and mimesis nonetheless contains such detailed representations of external objects. Brown argues that the emergent questioning of the role of literature in the modern era is precisely one of the dilemmas that is 'hypostasized' by the literary treatment of things: 'the question of things [in literature] becomes a question about whether the literary object should be understood as the object that literature represents, or the object that literature has as its aim, the object that literature is'.[22] In short, the confrontation in *Água viva* between the text as object and the text as object-free stages the modernist and avant-garde debates about the nature of art, an observation that resonates with Prado's assertion that in Lispector's work 'A escritura, como a musica (mas também como "a coisa"), deve ser *index sui*' [Writing, like music (and also like 'the thing') should be *index sui*].[23]

Finally, the narrator uses the term 'object' to refer to herself: 'Se tenho que ser um objeto, que seja um objeto que grita' [if I must be an object let it be an object that screams].[24] I analyse the 'screaming object' passage in further detail in this chapter's conclusion. In the context of *Água viva*'s many objects, however, it is worth noting the link between this phrase and the disposability motif just outlined. *Objeto gritante* (translated in some critical studies as 'Loud Object' but meaning literally 'screaming object') names an earlier and much more extensive manuscript of the novel. Marta Peixoto and others have noted that in addition to this title, what was extirpated from that manuscript in the editing process were its autobiographical details.[25] In excising a title that appears to refer to herself, it is as if the author wished, in some way, to get out of her own text — even if that proved possible in name only.

From Objects to Ethics?

A hora da estrela is both Lispector's most radical examination of the self-as-writer and the novel of hers that most clearly confronts the problems of Brazil's social inequalities. In it, Lispector creates a writerly alter ego, Rodrigo S.M., who in turn creates the fictional character Macabéa. The girl, a poor and uneducated migrant living precariously as a typist in Rio de Janeiro, remains as stubbornly opaque to her creator as her own existence, he presumes, remains to her. *A hora da estrela* thus revolves around the problematic representation of an 'object' that is neither fully a what nor a who.

Rodrigo S.M. battles a profound anxiety over putting into words a story 'that he has never lived' and a character that requires 'the creation of a whole person'.[26] This anxiety makes it nearly impossible for him to begin his narration, and results in a tug-of-war between the 'facts' of his story and his recurrent self-doubt. How does a writer 'create' a wholly other person? How does a member of the privileged classes represent the impoverished sectors of his or her own society? How to build a character that is realistic, give her a modicum of dignity, and yet be unflinchingly honest about the disdain of the dominant classes? How to presume to know experiences that are utterly alien and yet refrain from projecting one's own subjectivity onto the blank screen of the other's interiority?

The narrative poses these questions both explicitly and implicitly, while leaving undecided Rodrigo's capabilities for sincerely engaging with his class guilt. Lúcia Sá doubts the narrator's desire to transcend class divisions: 'Disposto a falar pelos oprimidos, ele não quer ouvi-los, nem conhecê-los de perto' [Pre-disposed to speak for the poor, he does not want to hear them, or get to know them up close].[27] Dalcastagnè agrees that Rodrigo's shortcomings 'prevent him from making [Macabéa] speak but say a lot about the difficult relationship between the intellectual and a great majority of Brazilians.' She nevertheless detects an ethics of sorts, one that manifests precisely in the narrative's 'deficiencies': in the formal clumsiness of Rodrigo's narration; in his inability to begin; in the frustrations to deciphering his character that constantly interrupt (or, arguably comprise) his narrative; in the prejudices toward her that he inadvertently lets slip, Dalcastagnè sees the formal replication of a 'deep discomfort in [the] face of his object of writing.'[28] Fuelled by the contradictory impulses of empathy and self-distancing, this discomfort is at least baldly, unflatteringly revealed.

In a similar vein, Daniela Mercedes Kahn argues that Rodrigo's stuttering narration 'mimetiza o embate entre cultura de elite e cultura periférica no interior dum país periférico' [mimeticizes the conflict between the culture of the elites and the culture of the peripheries inside of a country that is itself peripheral].[29] But Dalcastagnè's idea of a discomfort that arises from the *face-to-face* affirms that what she describes is not only the replication of a political problem, but indeed an ethics: a discomfiting encounter that imprints itself on the form of the novel by hijacking narration, and that discloses the subject's attitudes as flawed. It is, in other words, an ethics comprised of narrative failures. Working back from Lispector's social concerns in *A hora da estrela* to her earlier work, it becomes increasingly clear that the objects in her earlier texts, and more specifically how they are (or are not) seen, pave the way for Rodrigo's ambivalent presentation of his character. Macabéa should enjoy full subject status; however, insofar as she remains stubbornly inscrutable to the narrator, she is but a heightened form of the same gaze-defying objects one encounters in 'The Egg and the Chicken' and *Água viva*.

The *porta-espelho*

In a work that is so explicitly concerned with the writing of the self, the narrator of *Água viva* nevertheless presents us with three related external objects of representation: the church portico, the mirror, and the wardrobe. The narrator focuses on their physical properties: the solidity and opacity of the wooden surfaces of the portico and the wardrobe, the unfulfilled promise of interior space suggested by the presence of doors, and the equivocal capabilities of the reflective face of the mirror as emblematic of the problems of looking that characterize any approach of the object. The wardrobe with its half-ajar door, also hung with a mirror, functions as a fusion of these qualities:

> Mas eu também quero pintar um tema. E este tema será — um guarda-roupa, pois que há de mais concreto? Tenho que estudar o guarda-roupa antes de pintá-lo. Que vejo? Vejo que o guarda-roupa parece penetrável porque tem uma porta. Mas ao abri-la, vê-se que se adiou o penetrar: pois por dentro é também uma superfície de madeira, como uma porta fechada. Função do guarda-roupa: conservar no escuro os travestis. Natureza: da inviolabilidade das coisas. Relação com pessoas: a gente se olha ao espelho da parte de dentro de sua porta, a gente se olha sempre em luz inconveniente porque o guarda-roupa nunca está em lugar adequado: desajeitado, fica de pé onde couber, sempre descomunal, corcunda, tímido e desastrado, sem saber como ser mais discreto, pois tem presença demais. Guarda-roupa é enorme, intruso, triste, bondoso.
>
> Mais eis que se abre o porta-espelho — e eis que, ao movimento que a porta faz, e na nova composição do quarto em sombra, nessa composição entram frascos e frascos de vidro de claridade fugitiva.
>
> [But I also want to create a theme, I want to paint an object. And that object will be — a wardrobe, for what is more concrete? I must study the wardrobe before painting it. What do I see? I see that the wardrobe looks penetrable because it has a door. But when I open it, I see that penetration has been put off: since inside is also a wooden surface, like a closed door. Function of the wardrobe: to keep drag and disguises hidden. Nature: that of the inviolability of things. Relation to people: we look at ourselves in the mirror on the inside of the door, we always look at ourselves in an inconvenient light because the wardrobe is never in the right place: awkward, it stands wherever it fits, always huge, hunchbacked, shy and clumsy, unaware of how to be more discreet, for it has too much presence. A wardrobe is enormous, intrusive, sad and kind.

But suddenly the door-mirror opens — and suddenly, in the movement that the door makes, and in the new composition of the room in shadow, into that composition enter flask after flask of glass of fleeting brightness.]³⁰

'But I also want to paint a theme, I want to create an object,' Lispector begins, 'and that object will be — a wardrobe, for what is more concrete?' As I established in this chapter's second section, the narrator in *Água viva* openly intends for her text to relay, above all else, an unmediated expression of her own experience. The episode's introductory conjunction ('But I also') alerts the reader to an alternative, namely that the wardrobe's superlative concreteness serves as a late-arriving counterweight to the text's famously subjectivist perspective. The theme of the concrete, then, allows that which is external to the narrator to begin to contend for narrative space.

The second sentence of the *guarda-roupa* section reinforces the notion that the wardrobe is the nexus of themes of seeing, knowing and representing: 'Tenho que estudar o guarda-roupa antes de pintá-lo. Que vejo?' [I must study the wardrobe before painting it. What do I see?]. The verbs *pintar* and *criar* leave no doubt that the problematic addressed here plays out on the ground of the artistic act, while *ver* and *estudar* figure the difficulties to come in terms of a gaze seeking knowledge of the sort that ostensibly precedes representation. But the third sentence quickly runs up against the problem of appearances, of insides and outsides: 'Vejo que o guarda-roupa parece penetrável porque tem uma porta' [I see that the wardrobe looks penetrable because it has a door]. Finally, although the presence of a door suggests the possibility of accessing an interior essence, the wardrobe's apparent penetrability is (at least temporarily) thwarted: 'Mas ao abri-la, vê-se que que se adiou o penetrar: pois por dentro é também uma superfície de madeira, como uma porta fechada' [But when I open it, I see that penetration has been put off: since inside is also a wooden surface, like a closed door].

What will define Lispector's object in *Água viva*, then, is its intransigence. This wardrobe is no longer the mundane, utilitarian cabinet that Joana disdains in *Perto do coração selvagem*; it thwarts the seamless relation between user and used, seer and seen. Brown makes the point that such an intransigent object, one that will not make itself available for our practical or conceptual aims, initiates a shifted power dynamic between subject and object:

> We look through objects because there are codes by which our interpretative attention makes them meaningful as facts. A thing, by contrast, can hardly function as a window. We begin to confront the thingness of objects when they stop working for us: when the drill breaks, when the car stalls, when the windows get filthy [...]. The story of objects asserting themselves as things, then, is the story of a changed relation to the human subject.³¹

Whether it is the car engine that refuses to start or the philosophical thing that blocks the view of the concept, what defines the thing in Brown's analysis is precisely the moment at which it reveals that it was never 'for' us. The object that will not let itself be used, be known, be properly seen, is an object that both demands and defies our attention.

Lispector had already begun to explore this play of sight, surfaces and depths in an earlier exposition of the object, 'O ovo e a galinha' ('The Egg and the Chicken'; *A legião estrangeira* [*The Foreign Legion*], 1964). In this text, the formal dynamic between object and sight is so prevalent that Regina Pontieri reads the story as essentially structured by the polarity 'Egg vs. Eye'.[32] In it, problems of looking and knowing are framed in terms that specifically problematize the gaze, especially a penetrating one: 'O que não eu sei do ovo é o que realmente importa, o que eu não sei do ovo me dá o ovo propriamente dito, [...] Quem se aprofunda num ovo, quem vê mais do que o superfície do ovo, está querendo outra coisa: está com fome' [What I don't know about the egg is what matters. What I don't know about the egg gives me the egg properly speaking, [...] Whoever plunges deeper into an egg, whoever sees more than the surface of an egg, is after something else: that person is hungry].[33] But in the face of the penetrating gaze, the object stages a retreat: 'ovo visto, ovo perdido' [an egg seen is an egg lost].[34] One is reminded at this point of Brown's formulation of surfaces and depths, that the allure of the thing is precisely the challenge it presents to our interpretative habits: that the heuristic mind 'imagines, deep within the surface/depth dichotomy, overcoming it. However intriguing the inside might be, a sophisticated intelligence will make it disappear'.[35] In the end, we can't resist reading things, even if — or precisely because — they resist being read. We are attracted to the enigma, even if it refuses to offer itself up.

The egg that disappears upon capture, the reticent opacity of the wardrobe's receding wooden surfaces — all designate a robustly independent object that exceeds the sum of the human observer's knowledge. Morton describes the object's capacity to exceed apprehension as 'withdrawal', a term that he uses to designate the limits of knowledge: 'a single mode of access can never exhaust the thing; [...] the more we know about a strange stranger, the more he (she, it) withdraws'.[36] The idea of an object that withdraws from the totalizing gaze of the subject takes on an ethical cast when the object of observation is no longer a what, but a who. In *A hora da estrela*, Rodrigo complains: 'tenho um personagem buliçoso nas mãos e que me escapa a cada instante querendo que eu o recupere' [I have a fidgety character on my hands and who escapes me at every turn expecting me to retrieve her].[37] But at the same time as she withdraws from Rodrigo's attempts to describe her, Macabéa will not leave him alone. She has invaded even his physical space in her passive demand for attention: 'ela se me grudou na pele qual melado pegajoso ou lama negra [...] pois a datilógrafa não quer sair dos meus ombros' [she's stuck to my skin like some sticky treacle or black mud [...] the typist doesn't want to get off my shoulders].[38] The elusive object nevertheless gets under the skin.

What Lispector's object theory in *Água viva* offers to the discussion of withdrawal is two-fold. First, even before the introduction of a clearly human 'object' in *A hora da estrela*, the description of material objects in *Água viva* strongly implies that behind its surface of apparently inert material, the object might *feel*. In the pages preceding the wardrobe passage, Lispector describes the act of painting a church portal, whose wooden doors offer a precursor to the *porta-espelho*. This earlier description of wooden surfaces also begins with metaphors of impassibility: 'Sinto uma longa estrada e poeira até chegar ao pouso do quadro. Mesmo que os portais não se abram. [...] Crio o material antes de pintá-lo [...] Compacto, fechado como uma porta fechada' [I feel a long road and dust until I reach the resting-place of the painting. Even though the portals don't open [...] I create the material before I paint it [...] Compact, closed like a closed door].[39] And yet, despite the resistance offered to the gaze by the opaque impenetrability of this material, Lispector tells us that beyond the apparent finality of wooden surfaces, there is something much more vital than a void. The portal's matter itself bears the mark of what might be hidden beyond the closed doors: 'Mas no portal foram esfoladas aberturas, rasgadas por unhas. E através dessas brechas que se vê o que está dentro de uma síntese, dentro da simetria utópica. Cor coagulada, violência, martírio, são as vigas que sustentam o silêncio de uma simetria religiosa' [But onto the portal openings were flayed, scratched out by fingernails. And it's through those openings that you see what is inside a synthesis, inside the utopian symmetry. Coagulated color, violence, martyrdom, are the beams that sustain the silence of a religious symmetry].[40] There is surely something behind the church door, behind the inner wall of the armoire: beyond the visible surface of the object, beyond its representation, lies affect; fury, desperation, nails scratching; 'violence, martyrdom'. Cixous reads this passage as conferring a certain dignity upon the otherwise obscure object: 'The thing is standing upright, despite the torment inflicted upon it. [...] Matter is riddled with the hope of something.'[41] Nevertheless we can only glimpse this 'beyond' if we can see it at all: 'Função da guarda-roupa: conservar no escuro os travestis. Natureza: da inviolabilidade das coisas' [Function of the wardrobe: to keep drag and disguises hidden. Nature: that of the inviolability of things].[42]

Second, the wardrobe passage offers, at least provisionally, the possibility of a deferral for interpretation: 'vê-se que adiou o penetrar' [I see that penetration has been put off]. Rather than ending in aporia ('an egg seen is an egg lost'), the use of the verb *adiar* suspends the interpretative dance in mid-act. The question of seeing inside the wardrobe, of making the interior 'disappear' through exposition or through understanding, is left indefinitely unresolved. This deferral also guarantees that the interpretative cycle of attraction–repulsion will always renew itself. Just because the object-Other is uninterpretable, does not mean that we ignore it utterly; and yet we approach it knowing that the heuristic act will never be consummated or completed: 'Nature: that of the inviolability of things'.

If, as Brown's formulation suggests, the story of the object's resistance to penetration by the hungry gaze is 'the story of a changed relation to the human subject', what is the alternative relation that will arise between subject and object now that the wardrobe has asserted its capacity to withdraw? Lispector comes explicitly to the question of relation at this point in the *guarda-roupa* passage:

> Relação com pessoas: a gente se olha ao espelho da parte de dentro da sua porta, a gente se olha sempre em luz inconveniente porque o guarda-roupa nunca esta em lugar adequado: desajeitado, fica de pé onde couber, sempre descomunal, corcunda, tímido e distraído, sem saber como ser mais discreto, pois tem presença demais. Guarda-roupa é enorme, intruso, triste, bondoso.

> [Relation to people: we look at ourselves in the mirror on the inside of the door, we always look at ourselves in an inconvenient light because the wardrobe is never in the right place: awkward, it stands wherever it fits, always huge, hunchbacked, shy and clumsy, unaware how to be more discreet, for it has too much presence. A wardrobe is enormous, intrusive, sad, kind.][43]

Here, the narrator sensitizes the material object: 'a wardrobe is enormous, intrusive, sad, kind.' And precisely because the armoire has subject-like characteristics (awkward; standing wherever it fits; shy and clumsy; unaware of how to be more discreet), it makes itself inconvenient to its observer. The subjective object, inconveniently present to the observer who wishes to see herself, passively disrupts her self-contemplation. Perhaps we have seen the armoire, and it is Macabéa.

The alternative subject–object relationship that arises at this point in the *guarda-roupa* passage hinges upon an apparent change in the value of the mirror. Up until this point in *Água viva*, and also in other instances in Lispector's work, the mirror is presented as a foil to seeing the non-self. Tenuously capable of revealing infinite depths, the mirror also frequently represents the dangers of self-projection: 'Ao pintá-lo precisei de minha própria delicadeza para não atravessá-lo com minha imagem, pois espelho em que me vejo já sou eu' [When painting it I need my own delicateness in order not to cross it with my own image, since a mirror in which I see myself is already I].[44] This problem is re-enacted in *A hora da estrela*, when Rodrigo is famously unable to wrest his narration away from a description of his own personal and artistic struggles in order to conjure his character. Over the many pages of 'warm-up' that begin the novel, his attempts to portray Macabéa and her story in any detail slide back repeatedly into first-person narration ('Desculpai-me que vou continuar a falar de mim que sou meu desconhecido' [Forgive me but I'm going to keep talking about me who am unknown to myself]); but when Rodrigo finally manages to imagine Macabéa's physical appearance as she gazes at herself in a mirror, the image of her face is supplanted by his own: 'Vejo a nordestina se olhando ao espelho e — um rufar de tambor — no espelho aparece o meu rosto cansado e barbudo' [I see the northeastern girl looking in the mirror and — the ruffle of a drum — in the mirror appears my weary and unshaven face].[45]

An object that performs the role of self-affirmation resonates in Daniela Kahn's analysis of the role of alterity in Lispector's short fiction. Kahn pinpoints the persistence of 'um tipo peculiar de outro que, quer seja pessoa, animal ou coisa, tem uma função passiva no texto, servindo apenas de referência para o exercício de autoconhecimento do protagonista' [a particular kind of Other, whether person, animal or thing, that takes the passive role of serving merely as an index of the protagonist's self-recognition].[46] Kahn's description of alterity in Lispector's work thus recalls Lezra's critique of post-humanist disciplines that sees categories like 'things', 'objects', and 'matter' as proxies for 'the finitude of the human animal'.[47] In Kahn's analysis, Lispector's objects take the role of mirrors that merely display the contours of the self.

How has the mirror come to have a different value, and how has the relation that it incites with the viewer shifted from one of self-affirmation to one of awkward inconvenience? The key to this shifted relation is a question of angles. As an alternative to the direct or penetrating gaze, the narrator of *Água viva* repeatedly claims her point of enunciation from the sides and in the shadows: 'Por que não abordo um tema que facilmente poderia descobrir? Mas não: caminho encostada a parede, escamoteio a melodia descoberta, ando na sombra, nesse lugar onde tantas coisas acontecem. Às vezes escorro pelo muro, em lugar onde nunca bate o sol' [Why don't I tackle a theme that I could easily flush out? but no: I slink along the wall, I pilfer the flushed-out melody, I walk in the shadow, in that place where so many things go on].[48] The peripheral gaze, arriving at an angle from the margins, becomes a mark of respectful distance:

> A vida oblíqua? Bem sei que há um desencontro leve entre as coisas, elas quase se chocam, há desencontro entre os seres que se perdem uns aos outros entre palavras que quase não dizem nada. Mas quase nos entendemos nesse leve desencontro, nesse quase que é a única forma de suportar a vida em cheio, pois um encontro face a face com ela nos assustaria, espaventaria os seus delicados fios de teia de aranha. Nos somos de soslaio para não comprometer o que pressentimos de infinitamente outro nessa vida que te falo.
>
> [Oblique life? I am well aware that there is a slight detachment between things, they almost collide, there is a detachment among the beings that lose one another amongst words that almost don't say anything anymore. But we almost understand one another in this light discord, in this almost that is the only way to stand full life, since a sudden face-to-face encounter with it would frighten us, scare us off its delicate spider's web threads. We are askance in order not to jeopardize what we foresee is infinitely other in this life of which I speak to you.][49]

Standing askance to the Other, we are to understand, is another form of Lispector's ethics of failure. As we see in these two quotes, for Lispector it is the almost-but-not-quite quality of the encounter, the sideways glance from the margins, that allows for any encounter at all. Morton argues that this kind of partial encounter, the 'light discord' of Lispector's 'slight detachments between the beings that lose one another' is the only type of encounter that is possible. 'Objects', he argues, (including the objects that we, as humans, also are), 'encounter each other as operationally closed systems that can only (mis)translate one another'.[50]

At the same time, the narrator seems to suggest that by standing to the side we may finally manage a glimpse of an Other that is not a reflection of our Selves: 'Só uma pessoa muito delicada pode entrar no quarto vazio, e com tal leveza, com tal ausência de si mesma, que a imagem não marca. Como prémio, essa pessoa delicada terá então penetrado num dos segredos invioláveis das coisas: viu o espelho propriamente dito' [Only a very delicate person can enter the empty room where there is an empty mirror, and with such lightness, with such absence of self, that his image leaves no mark. As a prize, that delicate person will then have penetrated one of the inviolable secrets of things: he saw the mirror itself].[51] Is the object accessible, then, or isn't it?

The conclusion of the *guarda-roupa* episode comes as close as possible to achieving an answer to this question. In it, we see at last the half-open door hung with a mirror that gives its name to my discussion: 'Mas eis que se abre a porta-espelho

— e eis que, ao movimento que a porta faz, e na nova composição do quarto em sombra, nessa composição entram frascos e frascos de vidro de claridade fugitiva' [But suddenly the door-mirror opens — and suddenly, in the movement the door makes, and in the new composition of the room in shadow, into that composition enter flask after flask of glass of fleeting brightness].[52] As we have seen, up to this moment, the reflective capacities of the mirror have been presented mostly as a potential foil to seeing. But in the *porta-espelho* episode the angle of the door has permitted the object to interrupt; no longer with a lumbering presence of the wooden wardrobe, but with a luminous emission of its essence, of it-self. The verb in the last sentence in this passage is not 'reflect' or 'project', but 'enter'; the construction is active, not passive; and what enters are fragments of the material-made-ethereal: 'flasks of glass of fleeting brightness'. The object enters the creative space of the subject and transforms it. The angled mirror permits the subject and object to be co-present and to level, if only fleetingly, the exchange between them.

Matter, Riddled with the Hope of Something

After the conclusion of the *porta-espelho* episode, *Água viva* ends with an extensive rumination on subject–object elision. This shift in position, where the narrator will bind herself to her typewriter, echoes an earlier formulation of subject–object (or rather, object–object) solidarity when the narrator says of the mirror, 'Não descrevi o espelho. Fui ele' [No, I did not describe the mirror — I was the mirror].[53] In the exhaustion of the project of looking, the narrator moves from the position of observer (I didn't describe the mirror) to one of a companion-object (I was the mirror). The typewriter passage is even more unnerving, however, because it mixes a tone of solidarity with strains of complicity and responsibility: 'Sou uma maquina de escrever fazendo ecoar as teclas [...] Há muito não sou gente. Quiserem que eu fosse um objeto. Sou um objeto. Objeto sujo de sangue. Sou um objeto que cria outros objetos e a máquina cria a nós todos. Ela exige' [I am a typewriter making the dry keys echo in the dark and humid early hours. For a long time I haven't been people. They wanted me to be an object. I'm an object. An object dirty with blood. That creates other objects and the typewriter creates all of us. It demands].[54] The subject becomes an object among objects, and in the phrase's penultimate pronoun, involves us — her readers, all of 'us' — in a great web of relations beyond our control.

In the face of the mechanism that 'demands', Lispector leaves us with two resources. The first is the scream ('if I must be an object let it be an object that screams'). This scream is at once a protest against the objectification of self and of others by the 'mechanism', the anguished acknowledgement of the complicity of the writer in that objectification, and, as Oiticica proposed, an object-event in itself. The second recourse is the oblique encounter of subject to subject, object to object, mirror to mirror: 'Não são precisos muitos [espelhos] para se ter a mina faiscante e sonambúlica: bastam dois, e um reflete o reflexo que o outro refletiu, num tremor que transmite em mensagem telegráfica intensa e muda' [You don't need many [mirrors] to have the sparkling and sleepwalking mine: two are enough, and one reflects the reflection of what the other reflected, in a trembling that is transmitted in an intense and mute telegraphic message].[55] By placing herself to the side and looking into the mirror at an indirect angle, the narrator becomes the second mirror that reflects infinity. This is what she asks of us, as readers, as well.

In taking care not to overpower or obscure the object itself, the object is free to be itself, to maintain its 'it-ness'. This peripheral approach is described by Cixous in terms of non-intrusion: 'Clarice Lispector's endeavor consists in leaving the non-self alone'.[56] But while *Água viva* discreetly allows the object its space, it does not quite leave the non-self alone. In the repeated attempt to see past the object's opaque surface, and in their explicit failures; in the empathetic positioning of the self as object, and the acknowledgment of the object's disruptive potential; in the enduring, uncomfortable curiosity for what lies within, Lispector traces the complexities and ambivalences inherent in making an Other the object of representation. In the process, the author has drawn together the poles of the human and the non-human Other (the material and the sentient) to the point of co-contaminating their properties, without resolving whether the space that separates them is any different from the one that separates humans from each other: 'We are askance in order not to jeopardize what we foresee is infinitely other in this life of which I speak to you'. The result is a continuous field of alterity, of objects strange to one another (in which the narrator of *Água viva* includes herself, 'a typewriter making the dry keys echo'), where the repeated enactment of an always-partial encounter is the best hope for an ethics.

Works Cited

BACHELARD, GASTON, *The Poetics of Space*, trans. by Maria Jolas (Boston, MA: Beacon Press, 1964)

BROWN, BILL, *A Sense of Things: The Object Matter of American Literature* (Chicago, IL, and London: University of Chicago Press, 2003)

―― 'Thing Theory', in *Things*, ed. by Bill Brown (Chicago, IL, and London: University of Chicago Press, 2004), pp. 1–22

CIXOUS, HÉLÈNE, *Reading with Clarice Lispector*, ed. and trans. by Verena Andermatt Conley (Minneapolis: University of Minnesota Press, 1990)

―― *Coming to Writing and Other Essays*, ed. by Deborah Jensen (Cambridge, MA: Harvard University Press, 1991)

DALCASTAGNÈ, REGINA, 'Brazilian Contemporary Fiction and the Representation of Poverty', in *Literature and Ethics in Contemporary Brazil*, ed. by Vinícius Mariano de Carvalho and Nicola Gavioli (New York and London: Routledge, 2017), pp. 15–44

KAHN, DANIELA MERCEDES, *A via crucis do outro: identidade e alteridade em Clarice Lispector* (São Paulo: Associação Editorial Humanitas, 2005)

LEZRA, JACQUES, *On the Nature of Marx's Things: Translation as Necrophilology* (New York: Fordham University Press, 2018)

LIBRANDI, MARILIA, *Writing by Ear: Clarice Lispector and the Aural Novel* (Toronto: University of Toronto Press, 2018)

LISPECTOR, CLARICE, *Perto do coração selvagem* (Rio de Janeiro: Editora A Noite, 1944); *Near to the Wild Heart*, trans. by Alison Entrekin (New York: New Directions, 2012)

―― *A cidade sitiada* (Rio de Janeiro: Editora A Noite, 1949)

—— 'O Ovo e a Galinha', in *A legião estrangeira* (Rio de Janeiro: Editora do Autor, 1964), pp. 55–66; 'The Egg and the Chicken', in Clarice Lispector, *The Complete Stories*, trans. by Katrina Dodson (New York: New Directions, 2015), pp. 276–86

—— *Água viva* (Rio de Janeiro: Rocco, 1998 [1973]); *Água Viva*, trans. by Stefan Tobler (New York: New Directions, 2012)

—— *A hora da estrela* (Rio de Janeiro: Rocco, 1998 [1977]); *The Hour of the Star*, trans. by Benjamin Moser (New York: New Directions, 2011)

Morton, Timothy, *Humankind: Solidarity with Nonhuman People* (London and New York: Verso, 2017)

—— 'Here Comes Everything: The Promise of Object-Oriented Ontology', *Qui parle*, 19 (2011), 163–90

Moser, Benjamin, *Why This World: A Biography of Clarice Lispector* (New York: Oxford University Press, 2009)

Peixoto, Marta, *Passionate Fictions* (Minneapolis: University of Minnesota Press, 1994)

Pontieri, Regina Lúcia, *Clarice Lispector: uma poética do olhar* (São Paulo: Ateliê, 1999)

Prado, Plínio W., Jr., 'O Impronunciável: notas sobre um fracasso sublime', *Remate de males*, 9 (1989), 21–29

Sá, Lúcia, 'A hora da estrela e o mal-estar dos elites', *Estudos de Literatura Brasileira Contemporânea*, 23 (2004), 49–65

Sousa, Carlos Mendes de, *Clarice Lispector: figuras da escrita* (Braga: Universidade do Minho Centro de Estudos Humanísticos, 2000)

Notes to Chapter 17

1. Clarice Lispector, *Água Viva*, trans. by Stefan Tobler (New York: New Directions, 2012), p. 74.
2. I have taken English-language citations of Lispector's novel from Stefan Tobler's 2012 translation, which maintained the novel's title in the original Portuguese, while capitalizing the second word in accordance with English-language conventions for book titles. In this essay's notes, the titles of the Portuguese original and of Tobler's translation are distinguished by this variation in capitalization. Earl Fitz, the novel's first translator to English, rendered its title as *The Stream of Life*.
3. Clarice Lispector, *Perto do coração selvagem* (Rio de Janeiro: Editora A Noite, 1944), p. 9; *Near to the Wild Heart*, trans. by Alison Entrekin (New York: New Directions, 2012), p. 3.
4. Marília Librandi's study adds the act of listening, figured by the giant ear, to the list of structuring concerns that is announced by the opening paragraph of *Perto do coração selvagem*. See Librandi, *Writing by Ear: Clarice Lispector and the Aural Novel* (Toronto: University of Toronto Press, 2018), pp. 5–6.
5. Lispector, *Near to the Wild Heart*, p. 6.
6. Plínio W. Prado, Jr., 'O Impronunciável: notas sobre um fracasso sublime', *Remate de males*, 9 (1989), 21–29 (p. 28).
7. Lispector, *Água viva*, p. 89; *Água Viva*, p. 81.
8. Gaston Bachelard, *The Poetics of Space*, trans. by Maria Jolas (Boston, MA: Beacon Press, 1964), p. 89.
9. Lúcia Sá, 'A hora da estrela e o mal-estar dos elites', *Estudos de Literatura Brasileira Contemporânea*, 23 (2004), 49–65.
10. Jacques Lezra, *On the Nature of Marx's Things: Translation as Necrophilology* (New York: Fordham University Press, 2018), p. 14.
11. Lezra, *On the Nature of Marx's Things*, pp. 13–14.
12. Timothy Morton, *Humankind: Solidarity with Nonhuman People* (London and New York: Verso, 2017), p. 54.
13. Bill Brown, 'Thing Theory', in *Things*, ed. Bill Brown (Chicago, IL, and London: University of Chicago Press, 2004), pp. 1–22 (p. 11).

14. Hélène Cixous, *Reading with Clarice Lispector*, ed. and trans. by Verena Andermatt Conley (Minneapolis: University of Minnesota Press, 1990), p. 16.
15. Carlos Mendes de Sousa, *Clarice Lispector: figuras da escrita* (Braga: Universidade do Minho Centro de Estudos Humanísticos, 2000), p. 359.
16. Lispector, *Água viva*, n.pag.; *Água Viva*, n.pag.
17. Lispector, *A cidade sitiada* (Rio de Janeiro: Editora A Noite, 1949), p. 19; *The Besieged City*, trans. by Johnny Lorenz (London: Penguin, 2019), p. 15.
18. Librandi, *Writing by Ear*, p. 164; Prado, 'O Impronunciável', pp. 21–22; Benjamin Moser, *Why This World: A Biography of Clarice Lispector* (New York: Oxford University Press, 2009), p. 194.
19. Quoted in Librandi, *Writing by Ear*, p. 114.
20. In 'O ovo e a galinha', Lispector's narrator declares 'olhar é o instrumento necessário que, depois de usado, jogarei fora', *A legião estrangeira* (Rio de Janeiro: Editora do Autor, 1964) pp. 55–66 (p. 55); [Looking is the necessary instrument that, once used, I shall discard], Clarice Lispector, *The Complete Stories*, trans. by Katrina Dodson (New York: New Directions, 2015), pp. 276–86 (p. 276). In *Água viva*, the narrator uses 'a palavra como isca: a palavra pescando o que não é palavra [...] Uma vez que se pescou a entrelinha, pode-se com alívio jogar a palavra fora', *Água viva*, p. 22; [the word as bait: the word fishing for whatever is not word. [...] Once whatever is between the lines is caught, the word can be tossed away in relief], *Água Viva*, p. 15.
21. Lispector, *Água viva*, p. 73.
22. Bill Brown, *A Sense of Things: The Object Matter of American Literature* (Chicago, IL, and London: University of Chicago Press, 2003), p. 3.
23. Prado, 'O Impronunciável', p. 21.
24. Lispector, *Água viva*, p. 87; *Água Viva*, p. 79.
25. Marta Peixoto, *Passionate Fictions* (Minneapolis: University of Minnesota Press, 1994); pp. 66–68; Sousa, *Figuras da escrita*, pp. 348–49.
26. Clarice Lispector, *The Hour of the Star*, trans. by Benjamin Moser (New York: New Directions, 2011), pp. 40, 11.
27. Sá, 'A hora da estrela e o mal-estar dos elites', p. 61. Translation to English my own.
28. Regina Dalcastagnè, 'Brazilian Contemporary Fiction and the Representation of Poverty', in *Literature and Ethics in Contemporary Brazil*, ed. by Vinícius Mariano de Carvalho and Nicola Gavioli (New York and London: Routledge, 2017), pp. 15–44 (p. 31).
29. Daniela Mercedes Kahn, *A via crucis do outro: identidade e alteridade em Clarice Lispector* (São Paulo: Associação Editorial Humanitas, 2005), p. 120. Translation to English my own.
30. Lispector, *Água viva*, p. 82; *Água Viva*, p. 74.
31. Brown, 'Thing Theory', p. 4.
32. Regina Lúcia Pontieri, *Clarice Lispector: uma poética do olhar* (São Paulo: Ateliê, 1999), pp. 210–12.
33. Lispector, 'O ovo e a galinha', p. 56; 'The Egg and the Chicken', p. 277.
34. Ibid., p. 55; ibid., p. 276.
35. Brown, *A Sense of Things*, p. 11.
36. Timothy Morton, 'Here Comes Everything: The Promise of Object-Oriented Ontology,' *Qui parle*, 19 (2011), 163–90 (p. 166).
37. Lispector, *A hora da estrela*, p. 22; *The Hour of the Star*, p. 13.
38. Ibid., pp. 21–22; ibid., p. 13.
39. Lispector, *Água viva*, p. 77; *Água Viva*, p. 70.
40. Ibid.
41. Cixous, *Reading with Clarice Lispector*, p. 48.
42. Lispector, *Água viva*, p. 82; *Água Viva*, p. 74.
43. Ibid., p. 82; ibid., p. 74.
44. Ibid., p. 78; ibid., p. 71.
45. Lispector, *A hora da estrela*, 1977, pp. 15, 22; *The Hour of the Star*, pp. 7, 14.
46. Kahn, *A via crucis do outro*, p. 69. Translation to English my own.
47. Lezra, *On the Nature of Marx's Things*, pp. 13–14.
48. Lispector, *Água viva*, p. 81; *Água Viva*, p. 73.
49. Ibid., p. 70; ibid., p. 63.

50. Morton, 'Here Comes Everything', p. 165.
51. Lispector, *Água viva*, pp. 78–79; *Água Viva*, p. 71.
52. Ibid., p. 82; ibid., p. 75.
53. Ibid., p. 79; ibid., p. 72.
54. Ibid., pp. 76; 88; ibid., p. 78.
55. Ibid., p. 77; ibid., p. 70.
56. Hélène Cixous, *Coming to Writing and Other Essays*, ed. by Deborah Jensen (Cambridge, MA: Harvard University Press, 1991), p. 20.

CHAPTER 18

Lispector and the Illogic of Matter

Martin MacInnes

I first read about Clarice Lispector in 2009, in an article by Lorrie Moore included in the *Guardian* newspaper's complimentary sample of the *New York Review of Books*.[1] Moore was ostensibly reviewing Benjamin Moser's *Why This World: A Biography of Clarice Lispector*, but the piece served as a general introduction to Lispector's work. I remember one detail in particular: Moore was scrolling through readers' short reviews of Lispector's writing, quoting one that recommended buying the novels as an act of vengeance: you then send them to your worst enemy, who will be suitably wounded. Moore, I am sure, saw the wit in this. There is something unusually shocking and confrontational in Lispector's writing. I think the source of this is the way Lispector challenges, more than any other writer I am aware of, the idea of what a person is.

Around 2009, I contracted an undiagnosed infection, which alienated me from food. I wasn't the same person. An obvious truth became viscerally clear: I don't exist apart from world objects; my thinking voice functions within a biological network, an ecology. Looking out from this perspective, fiction frustrated me, presenting too often a stable and predictable world, a place I did not recognize. I did not recognize characters and narrators that existed beyond an environment, as if sealed off, whole, and prior to it. Characters who went unchallenged in their assumption that the world exists secondarily, a picturesque foundation for human affairs, a place that they lived 'on', rather than 'in'.

Lispector, accordingly, was a revelation. Lispector showed the possibility of writing with breadth, of incorporating spatial and temporal perspectives that are not familiar in day-to-day activity. She presented life as a crisis, an emergency that we struggle to apprehend. Importantly, for me, she wrote in a manner that did not assume the precedence of psychology over ecology, of man over world.

The Anthropocene, the period in which the biosphere is significantly affected by human industry, and where a new species, today, goes extinct every six minutes, carries in its name the promise of its brevity: this human dominance — even presence — will pass. The humility implied here — and in the origins of the word 'world' itself — 'the age of man' — is not shared by everyone. Technocrats such as Ray Kurzweil, at Google, plan to map every contour of an individual mind and reproduce it in digital form. These digital essences would extend humans indefinitely, theoretically populating the universe; this would be their post-human, or trans-human, identities. Lispector shows the mistake. 'The world', G.H. says, 'is not human, and [...] we are not human.'[2]

A person, in Lispector's novels, is not simply, or even primarily, a human. This remains a radical and dangerous step in fiction. One of the highest accolades a novel may still receive is the claim that it 'shows us what it is to be human'. Lispector reverses this trite platitude, assaulting fundamental assumptions about identity, and showing how, in the transformative natural world, 'human' is a cosmetic term, applied to something that is larger, stranger.

Throughout her novels, through their various narrators, there is a repeated determination to more fully wake up, aphorism upon aphorism attempting to confront the fact of being in the world. Firstly, necessarily, each character is alive unconsciously; thought is secondary. Lispector explores the body's mute, independent wisdom, a major part of our identity, and something that remains inaccessible to us. We do not understand, moment by moment, how we are able to continue being alive. What maintains this breathing structure? Where does the thinking voice fit into it? How can this voice continue to distract itself from its total absence of control? This pulsing bodily intelligence, the autonomic system, regulates vital processes including heart rate, blood circulation, breath, digestion, body temperature, and many others, with a wholly invisible effort. Lispector suggests — in all of her work, but most successfully so in *The Passion according to G.H.* — how remarkable it is that, outside of illness, we rarely think about these processes, aided as they are by the work of microorganisms. Generally, we turn the other way, like pedestrians avoiding the trauma of a road accident, trusting, without evidence, that things will be okay. Lispector refuses to do this, and as a result her narrators exhibit a creative, vital panic.

The prose carries a dissonant quality, simultaneously blank and radiant. G.H, especially towards the end of that novel, speaks in strange paradoxical pair groups: 'vibrant inexpressiveness'; 'violent, amorous unconsciousness of what exists'; 'neutrality, I'm speaking of the vital element linking things'; 'tranquil, neutral ferocity'; 'the great living neutrality striving'.[3] There is a jerking, almost atemporal cadence to this language: something is stated at the same time it contracts. I have sometimes thought that this style — this forward halt — mimics cellular turnover, the process of life, at a microscopic scale, continuing by repeatedly aborting itself. As if the profound example of this bio-structure is emerging in Lispector's voice. Lispector inspires this kind of earnest, overly ambitious interpretation — it is one of the great pleasures of reading her. There is the temptation to go on copying down passage after passage, to identify, once and for all, the point of revelation — this is unfashionable, embarrassing behaviour, but Lispector seems to give us permission.

I want to identify what I find vital in the writing. My reading of Lispector's unusual thinking — her alertness to the silent parts of her identity, including the autonomic system — might sound reductive. And reductive thinking, when applied to human identity, is often considered negative, limiting. Lispector shows, instead, that life is astonishing, miraculous, *because* it is matter. The human as auto-observant biology; the mind as infinite folds of a self-analysing surface. An extract from *Água Viva* expresses this particularly well: 'And there's a physical bliss to which nothing else compares. The body is transformed into a gift. And you feel that it's a gift because you experience, right at the source, the suddenly indubitable present of existing miraculously and materially'.[4] Time itself — every moment — as a staggering gift. This should all be impossible, but it is here. Life, independent of our will, prolonging strangely, through the present possibility of its unravelling.

Across her novels, Lispector shows affinity for non-human life. When *Água Viva*'s narrator says 'not having been born an animal is a secret nostalgia of mine', there is an irony. 'I don't humanise animals,' she says. 'I animalise myself. It's not hard'.[5] 'Biophilia' is the affiliation for life, the acceptance that people are part of a great, long interconnectedness, encompassing all orders of life, all of the vagaries of history and prehistory, and all possible futures. Really interrogating this idea — as Lispector does — reveals it as a position with promising aesthetic and moral possibilities: humility, empathy, fraternity following on from this original wonder.

The novels explore the perceptual opportunities that may come from an earned feeling of precariousness. Ermelinda, in *The Apple in the Dark*, in language that recalls tectonic upheaval — and I have often thought it apposite that Lispector lived, for a spell, near Vesuvius — speaks of '[taking] away the assurance of terrestrial life itself'.[6] Houses have been 'built too fragile', 'built without caution. [...] Houses and people were merely perching upon the earth, just as temporary as a circus tent'.[7]

The illusory quality of houses is clear; we do not live behind anything; the interior life is not fortified. There is no sheath. A passage in *Água Viva* describes the incorrigibility of the nerves through which we experience the world: they are 'dark strings that, when plucked, do not speak of "other things", they don't change the topic — they are in and of themselves'.[8] A nerve, despite the efforts of the associated mind, is impervious to metaphor; it cannot be made into something else. This, as I read it — the stuff that we are — is the 'tranquil, neutral ferocity' G.H. speaks of.

When I read Lispector, I am reminded that, from one perspective, the world is impossible. Matter is illogical. The earth, with its strange radiation of life, exceptional. Our present opportunity is almost overwhelming. Thinking like this is an amplifier; reading Lispector, one way of living keenly, and in fascination; experiencing, until the moment passes, the 'present of existing miraculously and materially'.

Works Cited

LISPECTOR, CLARICE, *The Apple in the Dark*, trans. by Gregory Rabassa (London: Haus, 2009 [1967])

—— *The Passion According to G.H.*, trans. by Ronald W. Souza (Minneapolis: University of Minnesota Press, 1988)

—— *Água Viva*, trans. by Stefan Tobler (London: Penguin Modern Classics, 2014)

MOORE, LORRIE, 'The Brazilian Sphinx', *New York Review of Books*, 56.14 (24 September 2009), 2–3

Notes to Chapter 18

1. Lorrie Moore, 'The Brazilian Sphinx', *New York Review of Books*, 56.14 (24 September 2009), 2–3.
2. Clarice Lispector, *The Passion According to G.H.* (1964), trans. by Ronald W. Souza (Minneapolis: University of Minnesota Press, 1988), p. 61.
3. Lispector, *The Passion According to G.H.*, pp. 135, 131, 92, 78, 84.
4. Clarice Lispector, *Água Viva*, trans. by Stefan Tobler (London: Penguin Modern Classics, 2014), p. 80.
5. Lispector, *Água Viva*, pp. 45, 42.
6. Clarice Lispector, *The Apple in the Dark*, trans. by Gregory Rabassa (London: Haus, 2009 [1967]), p. 316.
7. Lispector, *The Apple in the Dark*, p. 316.
8. Lispector, *Água Viva*, p. 74.

PART VI

Transmediality and Performance

CHAPTER 19

The Mute Wide-Open Eye of All Things

Kiran Leonard

In 2014 I was invited to contribute to a week-long artistic residency commemorating the re-opening of Manchester Central Library after a refurbishment. The resulting piece, *Derevaun Seraun*, is a work for voice, piano, and string trio, with each of its five movements dedicated to a separate author whose *oeuvre* I admire. This deliberately straightforward approach to the commission was intended as a defence of why I believe the library is such an integral social institution: chiefly, in that it treats all literature, even of the 'high-brow' variety, as fundamentally accessible beyond the class and intellectual paradigms that often serve to cloister 'difficult' writers within purely academic perspectives. We can be taught to understand a challenging book, but not to feel affection for it; what's more, all of us are capable of feeling such affection.

For me, the books written by Clarice Lispector perfectly embody the view that when a work resonates with a reader it is an instinctive experience before it is an intellectualized one. To describe her work as fundamentally accessible is not to say that the challenges and abstractions they present are meagre, and to deny that her style is intellectualized is *certainly* not to deny the depth of its intelligence. But you do not need to be well-read to understand Lispector; there are no arcane references of upmost importance, and little in the way of a canon or a context that must first have been studied. The provenance of most of the difficulty in her books is exactly the same as the source of their universality: her extraordinary capacity for perception, bafflingly precise and unexpected declarations that nobody else could articulate, observations that a reader may not understand word for word even as they feel that they have innately understood the whole, and that the whole has spoken to them. No amount of study can prepare you for a line such as (from *A paixão segundo G.H.*): 'It is forbidden to say the name of life. And I almost said it' (trans. Idra Novey). It is simply a lightning bolt from the aether.

Lispector is the focus of the piece's fourth movement, which is also its shortest and perhaps its most dissonant; I tried to straddle a line between 'nausea' and 'sweetness' which I hope is reflective of the lyrical subject matter. The title of the movement, 'The Mute Wide-Open Eye of All Things', is my translation of a description, from

Perto do coração selvagem, of a presence that the novel's protagonist Joana perceives as she emerges from a bathtub. It is another example of an image as peculiar as it is instantaneously relatable. After all, every one of us is shaped by the scrutiny and oppressive expectations of the outside world, created in part by our projected selves, often without our knowing it. In this sense, Lispector's work fulfils that which is implicit in the objectives of the public library: the remarkable and transformative poeticization of common experiences.

The Mute Wide-Open Eye of All Things

In her spacious apartment
in the demands of her children
she would feel the firm root of things
when silence of bathwater
and the blind and the buffalo
come disrupting womanhood
Composed with dramatic insistence
and in trembling mystery:
a happiness of the body
self-contained and not defined
I feel the nausea
and the resplendence of rotting tree trunks:
I sense the ties!

CHAPTER 20

Clarice Lispector: 'Unreal like Music'

Carlos Mendes de Sousa

Overture[1]

In a letter to her sister Elisa, written in Naples in early 1945, explaining how she plans to spend her days, Clarice Lispector mentions that she wishes to take singing classes: 'Quanto a estudar canto, vou tratar disso' [As for learning to sing, I'm going to sort that out].[2] Ten days later, she returns to the subject in another letter to her eldest sister and her doubts are presented in a humorous tone similar to one we will come across in much of her writing:

> Não tratei nada sobre o canto, sinceramente não me sinto muito animada a abrir a boca todos os dias e berrar. Mas certamente um dia desses resolvo e quando resolver você um dia acorda de madrugada e em vez de ouvir teus passarinhos ouve meus solfejos. Um dia desses fomos ouvir Lohengrin e não gostei. Ópera é chata como ela só. E apesar de ser Wagner era pau e cansava. Estou é com vontade de ter rádio, mas é dificílimo encontrar para comprar ou alugar.[3]

> [I didn't sort out the singing lessons. I honestly don't feel in the right mood to open my mouth every day and bellow. But one of these days I certainly will take care of it and when I do, one day you will wake up in the early hours and instead of hearing your little birds you'll hear me singing scales. A few days ago we went to hear Lohengrin and I didn't like it. Opera is annoying as only opera can be. And despite it being Wagner it was a drag and tiresome. What I'd really like is to have a radio, but it's incredibly difficult to find one to buy or hire].

Music was a constant presence in Clarice's daily life, adding a clearly identifiable lively dimension to many of her texts. One obvious assertion about what music meant to her appears in the *crônica* 'Brain storm': 'A eletrola está quebrada, o conserto é muito caro, e não viver com música é trair a condição humana que é cercada de música' [The gramophone is broken, it is costly to mend, and to live without music is to betray the human condition which is surrounded by music].[4] At the same time this need for the presence of music can be seen as a surrender that results from a quest, a permanent desire for knowledge. It comes about as the spontaneous externalization of sentiment, as the liberation of an ardently lived experience. In another letter, this time to her other sister, Tânia, from Berne, Switzerland (where she lived in the late 1940s), Clarice reveals how she was deeply moved by a phone call she had just received from Tânia. Overwhelmed with joy, she began to sing a famous aria from Camille Saint-Saëns's opera *Samson and Delilah*: 'Mon cœur s'ouvre à ta voix, comme s'ouvrent les fleurs aux baisers de l'aurore...' [Softly awakes my heart, as the flowers open at the kisses of dawn].⁵

In this chapter my intention is to highlight aspects of the relationships we can glimpse between music and writing in Clarice Lispector's universe, starting out by selecting illustrative examples drawn from the full range of her published works. I will include biographical information relating to the author's experiences of and with music that illuminate the reading of her texts. The most immediate consequence of these experiences, as we see from the quotation above, is to arouse feelings of exaltation in her.

The presence of music in her works will be discussed using a primarily thematic approach in order to identify patterns which, to a greater or lesser extent, express the works' wider potential meanings. I will also consider other fields which bring up relevant and related points such as narrative structure and elements that can be considered musical in the process of composition of the books, and style, more specifically the rhythmical effects of repetitions, of the reiteration of segments of text to create similarity or contrast. One thinks straight away of the profoundly musical effect of openings and endings, which function like preludes and codas, especially in the novels and short stories. From the perspective of composition there are very pronounced elements which back up this approach, such as, for example, in *A paixão segundo G.H.* [*The Passion According to G.H.*] (1964), with its repetitions at the beginning of each chapter of the segment which ended the previous chapter. We must bear in mind, in relation to this point, Clarice's assertion that *A maçã no escuro* [*The Apple in the Dark*] (1961) was the book which demanded the greatest investment from her in compositional terms, and stamina. In fact, we can see how the carefully orchestrated structure of that novel is the one which most closely resembles that of a symphony, with distinct movements and great breadth. And if the echoes of jazz are quite overt in *Água viva* (1973), there are other texts, especially the shorter and more difficult to classify, which we might say are very similar to chamber music, both figuratively, because of the restricted numbers of instruments and voices, but also materially: they are assemblages of fragments.

As I read through Clarice's *oeuvre*, I discover several ways in which, quite clearly, the presence of music hints at the author's concept of how literature works; particularly, the art of composing the novel and short story. Although occurring in her shorter, more fragmentary texts, it is above all in the novels that I am able to glimpse different literary techniques which echo musical conventions and perspectives which link music and words.

I

One means by which the impact of Clarice's work can be measured is the way single phrases extracted from longer texts have circulated and been recontextualized in a wide range of formats, and read as maxims.[6] I myself keep a note of certain phrases which have stuck with me over time and I began to realize that a significant number of them concern music or song, including two from the start of *A hora da estrela* [*The Hour of the Star*] (1977):

> Eu canto alto agudo uma melodia sincopada e estridente — é a minha própria dor, eu que carrego o mundo e há falta de felicidade.
>
> [So high-pitched I sing a strident and syncopated melody — it's my own pain, I who carry the world and there is a lack of happiness];[7]
>
> É que a esta história falta melodia cantabile. O seu ritmo é às vezes descompassado.
>
> [That's because this story lacks a *cantabile* melody. Its rhythm is sometimes discordant].[8]

Song is, in fact, a recurring motif in Clarice's work, associated primarily, especially in her earliest texts, with disharmonic music. At one point in *O lustre* [*The Chandelier*] (1946), Virgínia sings 'cantigas altas' [loud ballads], 'sem graça, puro som gritando, ultrapassando as coisas nos seus próprios termos' [awfully, pure sound screaming, going beyond things on their own terms].[9] The voice reaches a certain dimension that transports it from the realm of reality into the realm of invention.

This episode centres on the relationship between the siblings Virgínia and Daniel, and manifest tensions with the paternal figure. And the line of flight that leads Virgínia to inventiveness links to something which is not immediate: the realm of intensities. Singing overlaps with or blends with crying, as the sounds, notes and voices which transport her to another reality rise up. A sob is not just a sob, it is more than that, it is equal to the 'loud ballads', something from the domain of multiple voices, multiple rhythms.

The repercussions of this projection into inventiveness reveal a discordant way of living. Both the novels and short stories emphasize mismatches and unsuccessful encounters, such as the scene in *O lustre* where, in counterpoint, in an admirable set of intersections, Virgínia glimpses the school glee club.[10] In this sequence, a digression from the main storyline, the sounds resonate as they proliferate (the cockerel crowing, the chant of the rain as it falls) in a crescendo which creates an impressive kaleidoscopic-synaesthetic effect (involving visual sounds and audible visions), and captures very evocatively the subjective experience of a character who feels out of place in the world. Or much further on in the same novel, when, in a lovely passage about Virgínia wandering through the city, we come across an extraordinary metaphor used to describe her off-key singing:

> Saía à rua, andava lentamente pelo passeio mostrando-se, os olhos atentos, a sensação de que fulgurava ardente, séria. Era um duro inseto, um escaravelho, voava em linhas súbitas, batia de encontro às vidraças cantando com estridência.

> [She'd go out into the street, walk slowly down the sidewalk showing herself, her eyes watchful, the feeling that she was glowing ardent, serious. She was a hard insect, a scarab, flying in sudden lines, beating against windowpanes, singing with stridency].[11]

The metaphor of strident singing reflects Virgínia's intense, painful way of living, and the many obstacles she encounters in the city. This moment comes straight after a memorable episode (the dinner with Miguel) which has ended explosively. The song of the scarab translates magnificently the echoes of the dissonances of a hostile world.

In Clarice's works there are many more representations of tuneless singing, or songs sung in the wrong place or at the wrong time — the Portuguese woman in 'Devaneio e embriaguez de uma rapariga' [Daydream and Drunkenness of a Young Lady] in *Laços de família* [*Family Ties*] (1960), for example. In the same collection, in 'Amor' [Love], comes the 'canto importuno das empregadas' [the tiresome singing of the maids],[12] and in 'Feliz aniversário' [Happy Birthday], we witness a caricatured rendition of the song 'Happy Birthday', full of interruptions and wrong notes. Or even the chicken in 'A galinha' [The Chicken] who wasn't given to singing.[13] And there are so many occasions when we overhear the humming and warbling of Clarice's characters, in both major and minor keys. How can we forget Senhora Jorge B. Xavier, in 'A procura de uma dignidade' [In Search of a Dignity] in *Onde estivestes de noite* [Where were you at night], imagining an encounter with her beloved idol, the (now) veteran pop star Roberto Carlos, and recalling one of his greatest hits?

> Seus lábios levemente pintados ainda seriam beijáveis? Ou por acaso era nojento beijar boca de velha? Examinou bem de perto e inexpressivamente os próprios lábios. E ainda inexpressivamente cantou baixo o estribilho da canção mais famosa de Roberto Carlos: 'Quero que você me aqueça neste inverno e que tudo o mais vá para o inferno'.
> Foi então que a Sra. Jorge B. Xavier bruscamente dobrou-se sobre a pia como se fosse vomitar as vísceras e interrompeu sua vida com uma mudez estraçalhante: tem! que! haver! uma! porta! de saíííííííída!.
>
> [Were her lightly tinted lips still kissable? Or was it disgusting to kiss an old lady on the mouth? She studied her own lips up close and with no expression. And still with no expression she softly sang the chorus from Roberto Carlos's most famous song: 'I want you to keep me warm this winter and to hell with all the rest'.
> That was when Senhora Jorge B. Xavier abruptly doubled over the sink as if about to vomit up her guts and interrupted her life with an earth-shattering silence: there! must! be! an! exiiiiiiit!].[14]

One last example: the contrasting and overlapping musical sounds in 'A partida do trem' [The Departure of the Train] from the same story collection: Handel on one boy's transistor radio, girl scouts singing a hymn to Brazil in high voices in another carriage, Edith Piaf's 'J'attendrei' [I will wait] sounding out from another radio,[15] and the protagonist, Dona Maria Rita, with her 'tremor quebradiço de música de sanfona' [brittle tremor of accordion music].[16]

At the denouement of 'A procura de uma dignidade', music is one way of highlighting the mismatch between the old lady and the young pop idol. But it is important to say here, and relevant to the next example too, that this pop cultural reference corresponds to a change in style and form identifiable in Clarice's *oeuvre* after 1974 (when she brought out the short story collections *Onde estivestes de noite* and *A via crucis do corpo* [*The Via Crucis of the Body*] and the text 'Brasília: Esplendor' [Brasília: Splendour]). It was a moment when her work began to harbour texts that were tonally different from those published in previous decades.

One could look, for example, at the references to music playing on the transistor radio in 'A partida do trem'. Although the presence of a radio in her texts has been meaningful from early on (*A cidade sitiada* [*The Besieged City*] (1949) and *A maça no escuro* come to mind), from the 1970s onwards it becomes even more so, especially when it plays unexpected medleys, another way of translating the strangeness of worlds which engage with us. I am reminded of the Strauss waltz known as 'The Free Thinker', juxtaposed with the advertising jingle for 'Cremogema' [Cream of Wheat] in the story 'Onde Estivestes de Noite', or the moment in 'O Corpo' [The Body] in *A via crucis do corpo*, when Schubert's piano music, playing on the radio, is the unusual soundtrack to Xavier being murdered with kitchen knives by his two lovers. Or one last example: the explosion of references to different kinds of music in 'Brasília', playing on the radio as the narrator writes: Strauss, Chopin and Debussy alongside Carmen Miranda, Amália Rodrigues; and a *Te Deum* following a samba or a military march.[17]

2

Among the letters sent back and forth between Lispector and her sisters, when she was in Washington, there is one from 1955 which narrates an experience that might have come from one of her short stories, in a voice that could belong to one of her characters:

> Hoje de noite temos bilhetes para ver no teatro uma peça com Shelley Winters. Mas hoje de noite tem um único concerto de um pianista russo que dizem ser dos maiores, ele vai tocar uma sonata de Chopin que tem um tema, no quarto movimento, que me é muito querido e que eu ouvi no rádio quando tinha uns quinze anos e uma outra vez não sei quando — e sempre cantarolei o tema para quem entende música e ninguém conhecia, parecia até que eu tinha inventado. No sábado comprei uma sonata de Chopin e me deu esperança que nela encontrasse o tema. Estava ouvindo já sem esperança, quando no quarto movimento, a coisa estalou: ali estava ele. Então vim a saber que este 'quarto movimento' é considerado um dos pontos mais altos de Chopin, senão o mais alto. E, agora sabendo o nome da sonata (n. 3 em B menor), descobri no domingo que o pianista vai tocá-la. Então Maury vai com o filho de Mafalda ao teatro, e me deixa no concerto, se é que ele vai conseguir um lugar.
>
> [We have tickets for the theatre tonight, to see a play with Shelley Winters. But tonight there is one-off concert by a Russian pianist who they say is one of the best, he's going to play a Chopin sonata that has a theme, in the fourth

> movement, that's very dear to me and that I heard on the radio when I was around fifteen years old and another time, I don't remember when — and I've always sung it to people who understand music, but as nobody recognised it, it felt as if I'd invented it. On Saturday I bought a Chopin sonata and I was really hopeful that I'd find the theme there. I was listening to it and just when I'd given up hope, there in the fourth movement, the thing burst forth: there it was. Then I found out that this 'fourth movement' is thought to be one of Chopin's high points, if not the highest. And now I know what it's called (No. 3 in B minor) and I discovered on Sunday that the pianist will be playing it. So Maury will take Mafalda's son to the theatre and he'll drop me off at the concert, if he can get hold of a ticket, that is].[18]

What is Claricean in this episode, in literary terms? It refers to the manifestation of the yearning for discovery, the desire to recover an intense moment brought about by chance, and the way of experiencing it. I ought to highlight that what drives the narrative is the music that was lost and what the loss entailed, which in her account constitutes a nucleus close to what we will find in many of the author's texts: the element which corresponds, in the words of Benedito Nunes, to a 'determinado momento da experiência interior' [particular moment of internal experience].[19] In this case, the epistolary account might indicate some sort of 'aspiração ou devaneio' [aspiration or daydream],[20] like that experienced by the characters, flowing towards a lack of resolution that is unmistakeably Claricean.

The reference to Chopin and the impact caused upon hearing one of his sonatas recalls a biographical detail described by the author in one of her *crónicas* in the *Jornal do Brasil*, one that is crucial for any reading of the role of music in her work. The title, 'Lição de piano' [Piano Lessons], sets the tone, circumscribing the scope of the *crónica* which centres on her memory of learning to play the instrument chosen by her father for his daughters' musical education: 'Meu pai queria que as três filhas estudassem música. O instrumento escolhido foi o piano, comprado com grande dificuldade' [My father was keen that his three daughters should study music. The instrument of his choice was the piano, bought with enormous sacrifice].[21] The driving force here is the paternal figure, whose distinctive sensitivity and dignity are evoked. Chopin, the beloved composer, is associated with a negative sensation provoked by the presence of the piano teacher: 'Quando Dona Pupu tocava Chopin me enjoava, Chopin de quem eu gosto' [Whenever Dona Pupu decided to play Chopin I always felt quite sick; Chopin, who I really like].[22] The teacher's name is referred to repeatedly throughout the text to the point of distraction, like the trains of thought that lead the girl's mind away from the central purpose of the lesson (she was obese, what was her sex life like? how would she fit in her coffin?). Although the repetition of the teacher's nickname accentuates the comic nature of the tale, it also marks the psychological escape routes. The journey to the piano teacher's house and the appearance of an acacia tree at a particular bend in the road trigger a series of fantasies and streams of consciousness, beginning with the house hidden behind the yellow acacias ('quem morava ali?' [who lived in that house?]).[23]

There is one very short sentence which stands out and summarizes the lessons: 'Como eu errava' [How my thoughts would stray].[24] A layer of creativity imposes itself on top of rules and discipline. And it is here that the phantasmal figure of the mother emerges with all its strength:

> Tinha nove anos e minha mãe morrera. A musiquinha que inventei, então, ainda consigo reproduzir com dedos lentos. Por que no ano em que morreu minha mãe? A música é dividida em duas partes: a primeira é suave, a segunda meio militar, meio violenta, uma revolta suponho.
>
> [I was nine years old and my mother was dead. Even after all these years I can still play one of those tunes using two fingers. Why should this date from the year my mother died? The melody is divided into two parts: the first part is gentle, the second fierce and almost martial, perhaps expressing my rebellion].[25]

The account very clearly establishes a direct link between the paths to distraction and the ways to inventiveness. The child exercises a demarcation, a distancing of herself from the disciplining purposes of the piano lesson. In a certain way, this could be read as a projection of what the author's position will become, repeated frequently when she reflects upon her own art, asserting that she is not a professional. The girl gets distracted and it is during this process that creation occurs. Consequently, she is also distracted from pain and grief, even if the illness and death of her mother are simultaneously potential sources of inspiration. It is during the time when she was taking piano lessons that invented music imposed itself, in the year that her mother died. The structure of the piece of music reflects exactly that: the gentleness and fierceness, features that will come to mark the writing of the future author. It is also very interesting to note here the existence of a similarity between the musical terms of the composition invented by Clarice and the syntactic procedures of her writing where she highlights the rhythmic effect resulting from alternating between longer sentences and very short ones.

If the father equals presence, a motivating and supportive force, the mother is music, an open wound and a powerful trigger. Pain and guilt are pure sources of invention. At the end of the text, we find a reference to another pianist who taught the girl, a famous one this time: 'Acho que não tenho mais nada a dizer. Eu também passei para Ernani Braga[26] que disse que eu tinha dedos frágeis. Prefiro calar-me: este também morreu' [But I can think of nothing else of any interest. Like my sister, I also went on to have lessons with Ernâni Braga who commented on my delicate fingers. I shall say no more: he died some time ago].[27] The text's closing lines are impressively revealing. They offer us the metaphor and its key: the emphasis on the singularity of her determination to highlight what the master musicians could not see, the paradox of strength contained in apparent fragility. A circle concentrates the ambiguity which generates mystery and enigma. The father is the impulse behind the music lessons, but it is the absence, the shadow of the mother (a fertilizing immobility) that unleashes the creative process. At the denouement comes the key. Just as with the music, the force of the literature is in her 'dedos frágeis e delicados' [soft, weak fingers].[28]

The figurative description of the piano, as a metaphor or simile, occurs elsewhere, for instance in the *crônica* 'Lembrança da feitura de um romance' in which the author remembers 'The Making of a Novel'. This title invokes the image of the open instrument with its 'simultaneous keys' in order to reveal a process of composition in which everything was written at the same time.²⁹

The piano features many times in Clarice's books, especially the novels (particularly, the early ones), in scattered references which may be notes relating to characterization, elements propitiating specific situations that are part of the action, or similes and excuses for reflection. For example, in her debut novel, *Perto do coração selvagem* [*Near to the Wild Heart*], Joana, the protagonist, looks at the open piano and glimpses the possibility of a whole universe contained within:

> Por que não tocava sozinha todas as músicas que existiam? — Ela olhava o piano aberto — as músicas lá estavam contidas... Seus olhos se alargavam, escurecidos, misteriosos. 'Tudo, tudo.'
>
> [Why couldn't she play every piece of music in existence on her own? — She looked at the open piano — it contained all music... Her eyes widened, dark, mysterious, 'Everything, everything'].³⁰

The metaphor seems to announce the reflection that we find in the metadiscursive note in the *crônica* mentioned above about the making of a novel. The piano fits admirably well into the author's ongoing reflections on the naming of things, on the question of the word and the real. Here there is a clear disentangling of those thoughts which do not become reality and others which are profoundly transformational, able to create worlds, projecting themselves well beyond their limits. The music contained, potentially, in the piano is an amazingly apposite metaphor with which to express the links Clarice sees between the imagination and creative activity, as the next section will explore.

3

None of Clarice's main characters are musicians, nor are they associated directly or indirectly with any particular instrument, even though reflections about music are presented from their points of view. Nevertheless, although music is not the central focus of the action, we cannot say that it is absent from the diegesis of the novels or short stories. The instrument which plays the most important role in the settings described in the texts is, as I have already indicated, the piano.

A good example of this can be found in *O lustre*, when, still on the family farm in Granja Quieta, Virgínia and Daniel are planning to go and live in the city. Their departure is permitted by their father providing that they move there to study languages, business and piano. And a complementary piece of information about Daniel's skills is given: 'Daniel, que tinha tão bom ouvido e praticava algumas vezes num piano de Brejo Alto' [Daniel, who had such a good ear and practised sometimes on a piano in Upper Marsh].³¹ During their childhood (this is a novel which to a great extent portrays the role of childhood lived or relived) everything is marked by the relationship between the siblings. It is a link that is fortified by a strong desire to flee, and music becomes intimately associated with the idea of escape.

I would like to highlight two more occasions when the piano takes centre stage. It is played by secondary characters. The main focus, however, is on characters who are listening and effectively disrupt the performances: Otávio, in *Perto do coração selvagem* and Martim, in *A maçã no escuro*. The act of playing the piano and the identity of the pianist (Cousin Isabel in the former novel, and Ermelinda in the latter) become the pretext for the development of different tensions. In each case the sequence is fairly long, considering the narrative economy employed elsewhere in these two novels. In *Perto do coração selvagem*, Cousin Isabel plays waltzes by Chopin — music that Clarice knew well and loved. As for Otávio, he is full of pent-up tension: when he looks at his cousin, thoughts of conflicts in their relationship, going back to childhood, rise to the surface. With the passing of time, Cousin Isabel has aged and her piano playing has become full of hesitations and mistakes:

> Ela não conseguia dar mais aquela antiga suavidade entre uma nota e outra, como um desmaio. Um som prendia-se ao outro, áspero, sincopado, e as valsas explodiam fracas, saltitantes e falhadas. Às vezes as badaladas espaçadas e ocas do velho relógio vinham dividir a música em compassos assimétricos.
>
> [She was no longer able to move softly from one note to the next as she had in the past, like a faint. One sound would catch on the next, rough, syncopated, and the waltzes erupted weak, jumpy and full of gaps. Sometimes the slow, hollow chimes of the old clock would split the piece into asymmetrical bars].[32]

The way in which such scenes are captured suggests a process of alienation and transformation. In *A maçã no escuro*, we escape from mists and torpor through moments of tension, confrontations, explosions. The scene in the lounge, in that novel, which almost feels staged, is strangely familiar. It is the strangeness that marks it out as being very different from stereotypical representations of bourgeois life, where there is always a piano in the background. The complex, mismatched relationships between the members of the group rise to the surface. Like Cousin Isabel, who plays without sheet music and makes sure everybody knows it, Ermelinda plays 'sem olhar o teclado' [without looking at the keyboard],[33] and, likewise, emphasizes this to her listeners. Otávio's pent-up tension is released when he leaves the room. And while the performance of the music in the scene from *Perto do coração selvagem* quoted above is a complete failure, in *A maçã no escuro* it is the instrument which is out of tune and any exit from this knot of tensions simply intensifies the disharmony in the room. The scene becomes punctuated by another noise: the repetitive sound of the mallet Martim wields tightly as he, in an unexpected turn of events, begins to tan a hide outside: 'O cheiro de couro e as marteladas tiravam da cena a sua total imobilidade e deu-lhe um caminhar progressivo: pouco a pouco o cheiro mais intenso e as marteladas levaram a situação a um final' [The smell of the leather and the mallet-beats drew the total immobility away from the scene and gave it a progressive march. Little by little the stronger smell and the mallet-beats brought the situation to an end].[34]

This scene is the centrepiece of the second chapter of the third (and final) part of the novel. From the announcement that the Professor is coming and the preparations that, in the previous chapter, intrigued Martim ('seria o professor a mesma pessoa que o alemão?' [Could the professor be the same person as the German?]),[35] to the moment he is invited pointedly to join them in the lounge, he walks a tightrope of accumulated tensions. We might say that, against the backdrop of this apparently harmonious family get-together, music is, in fact, the pretext for the meeting, the real reason for which is to air suspicions. Ermelinda seems to be off stage, as if the piano is playing by itself. But in truth the sounds of the music and the mallet blows on the leather seem to punctuate the accusatory dissonance of the moment. Everything is latent and phantasmagorical and what is not spoken in words seems to emerge through these dissonant sounds.

4

If we embark on a reading of references to music in Lispector's novels in chronological order of publication, from *Perto do coração selvagem* to *Um sopro de vida* [*A Breath of Life*] (1978), we will find a clearly differentiated range of examples that reflect, homologically, the specific worldview of each of the narratives.

In the first chapter of the first part of *Perto do coração selvagem*, the child protagonist closes her eyes, pretending to hear the sound of the clock in the lounge and dancing to the 'som da música inexistente e ritmada' [the non-existent and rhythmic music].[36] Also in this first part (in the second chapter), there is a scene which foreshadows the short story 'O jantar' [The Dinner] from *Laços de família*. In the novel, in the sequence where Joana stares at the man eating, a soundless tune is described: 'As pernas sob a mesa marcavam compasso a uma música inaudível, a música do diabo, de pura e incontida violência' [His legs under the table kept time to an inaudible melody, the devil's music, of pure, uncontained violence].[37] The inexistent only exists when it is not thought about. The question of thought and naming as factors crucial to existence is central to Clarice's *oeuvre*. This becomes clear in relation to several things, music included. An abstract dimension prevails when music is glimpsed in the same realm of thought: 'A música era da categoria do pensamento, ambos vibravam no mesmo movimento e espécie' [Music was of the same category as thought, both vibrated in the same movement and kind].[38]

From the realm of abstraction we are led to another realm, and another recurrent motif imposes itself: music which manifests as vibration and translates excess. In Chapter 4 of Part II of *Perto do coração selvagem* we read: 'Sozinha no mundo, esmagada pelo excesso de vida, sentindo a música vibrar alta demais para um corpo' [Alone in the world, crushed by the excess of life, feeling the music vibrate too high for a body].[39] There are multiple descriptions of this state which builds up towards a certain limit, through which it breaks and explodes into excess. We can see it in images which translate accumulations, overlaps, intersections, like the tear in Joana's dress and the scream of the orchestra. Music conveys atmospheres, contradictions (oppositions, oxymorons), infinite things difficult to define such as the sound of silent footsteps like 'um cego ouvindo música distante' [a blind man listening to distant music].[40] Everything is excessive and replete with questions, from the deluge at the very beginning of the novel to the last pages: 'Fez-se muitas perguntas, mas nunca pôde se responder: parava para sentir' [She asked herself many questions but she could never answer herself: she'd stop in order to feel].⁴¹ Music also surfaces in Joana's endless list of questions: 'Onde se guarda a música enquanto não soa?' [Where does music go when it is not playing?].⁴²

In *A cidade sitiada*, matching perfectly with the artificial atmosphere of the book, the references to music reveal one of the fullest portraits of the city of São Geraldo: music that is associated with the outdoors, the music of marching bands, military music, *charanga* music,⁴³ the pealing of bells, the accordion, the flute-playing figurine, the open piano:

> A casa imersa no silêncio da eletricidade.
> E lá estava o seu quarto.
> Como um piano que se deixou aberto. Que susto ver as coisas. A composição das vigas no forro era estranha e nova, como de uma cadeira dependurada....
>
> [The house immersed in the silence of electricity.
> And right there was her room.
> Like a piano left open. How frightening to see things. The design of the beams in the ceiling was strange and new, like that of a hanging chair...].⁴⁴

The music from outside permeates into and echoes through buildings. Lucrécia, the protagonist, is glimpsed between light and shade. Although it is indoors, the image of the piano seems to translate the particular state of her home, as if it were outside. The keenness of the narrator's gaze makes her see things back to front and inside out, as if she were looking at a photograph and its negative. The light and the brilliance are revealed in a de-sentimentalized way, the interiors show structures as profoundly as if they were external surfaces. This is how Lispector achieves the strange effect of a kind of dismantling which runs throughout the whole book, influencing the presentation of sounds and music, of the evolving suburb, of the environments through which Lucrécia moves, herself an evolving being.

In Clarice's fourth novel, *A maçã no escuro* (the novel which is closest in structure to a musical symphony, as I mentioned before), what stands out is the way the text's greater length facilitates the theme of silence. A beautiful fit with the vast landscape is found in the silence, described as music of the night offered up by nature itself: 'aquela que é feita da possibilidade de alguma coisa piar e da fricção do silêncio contra o silêncio...' [fashioned from the possibility that things will chirp and from the soft rub of silence against silence].⁴⁵ From the outset we can tell that this is not music that will soothe the man, Martim. He is alert, he will not give in to gentleness, be ensnared by sweetness. In his speech to the stones, we come across a sentence which points in this direction: 'Mas também é verdade que os momentos de doçura eram muito intensos. E também é verdade que uma música ouvida antigamente podia fazer parar toda a máquina e estatelar por um instante o mundo' [But it is also true that the moments of sweetness were very intense. And it is also true that music heard in the past can make the whole machinery come to a halt and dumbfound the world for a moment].⁴⁶

In *A paixão segundo G.H.*, the opposite occurs. As I will explore in the next section, maximum concentration and the gradual overwhelming of the self mean that references to music are rendered abstractly, the vibrations of heat and light becoming 'paixões em forma de oratório' [passions in the form of an oratorio].[47] *Água viva* offers us a magnificent reflection along metaliterary lines whereby, alongside painting, the composition of music mirrors the process of writing. These brief examples lead us on to the explicit musical references in *A hora da estrela*, most specifically in the Author's Dedication, which celebrates music and musicians. And lastly, in *Um sopro de vida*, more than anywhere else, we find explicitness in the form of an explosion of references. Here too music (musicians, composers) appears, in sharp or soft focus, to represent writing and the processes of verbal creation. Both the characters, Ângela and the 'Autor' [Author], when they attempt to define themselves, bring music into play in very clear ways.

5

In the chapter 'O banho' [The Bath], from *Perto do coração selvagem*, there is an exquisitely beautiful passage, narrated in the first person, which describes Joana's visit to a church:

> Eu estava sentada na Catedral, numa espera distraída e vaga. Respirava opressa o perfume roxo e frio das imagens. E, subitamente, antes que pudesse compreender o que se passava, como um cataclisma, o órgão invisível desabrochou em sons cheios, trêmulos e puros. Sem melodia, quase sem música, quase apenas vibração. As paredes compridas e as altas abóbadas da igreja recebiam as notas e devolviam-nas sonoras, nuas e intensas. Elas transpassavam-me, entrecruzavam-se dentro de mim, enchiam meus nervos de estremecimentos, meu cérebro de sons. Eu não pensava pensamentos, porém música. Insensivelmente, sob o peso do cântico, escorreguei do banco, ajoelhei-me sem rezar, aniquilada. O órgão emudeceu com a mesma subitaneidade com que iniciara, como uma inspiração. Continuei respirando baixinho, o corpo vibrando ainda aos últimos sons que restavam no ar num zumbido quente e translúcido. E era tão perfeito o momento que eu nada temia nem agradecia e não caí na ideia de Deus. Quero morrer agora, gritava alguma coisa dentro de mim liberta, mais do que sofrendo. Qualquer instante que sucedesse àquele seria mais baixo e vazio. Queria subir e só a morte, como um fim, me daria o auge sem a queda. As pessoas se levantavam ao meu redor, movimentavam-se. Ergui-me, caminhei para a saída, frágil e pálida.

> [I was sitting in the Cathedral, in distracted, vague waiting. I was breathing oppressed the cold, purple perfume of the statues. And, suddenly, before I could understand what was going on, like a cataclysm, the invisible organ unfurled in full, tremulous, pure sounds. Without melody, almost without music, almost vibration alone. The church's long walls and high vaults received the notes and returned them sonorous, nude and intense. They pierced me, crisscrossed inside me, filled my nerves with tremors, my brain with sounds. I wasn't thinking thoughts, but music. Numbly, under the weight of the canticle, I slid from the pew and knelt without praying, annihilated. The organ fell silent with the same suddenness with which it had begun, like a flash of inspiration. I kept breathing quietly, my body still vibrating to the last sounds remaining in the air in a warm, translucent drone. And the moment was so perfect that I neither feared

nor gave thanks for anything and I was not drawn into the idea of God. I want to die now, cried something inside me freed, more than suffering. Any instant following that one would be lower and emptier. I wanted to rise and only death like an end, would give me the peak without the decline. People were getting up round me, moving about. I stood, walked to the exit, fragile and pale.]⁴⁸

The moment when the unexpected happens challenges everything that might be trapped by the narrow tools of comprehension: 'antes que pudesse compreender' [before I could understand]. The process of transformation is triggered by the weight of intensifications produced by the invisible instrument. And the description of sounds ('cheios, trémulos, puros' [full, tremulous, pure], '[s]em melodia, quase sem música' [without melody, almost without music]) is like one of the most extraordinary ways of translating the incessant quests which pursue themselves throughout Clarice's work, culminating here in a precise formulation: 'quase apenas vibração' [almost vibration alone]. The verbs expressively indicate the state provoked by the criss-crossing of the notes: 'transpassavam-me, entrecruzavam-se dentro de mim, enchiam meus nervos de estremecimentos, meu cérebro de sons' [they pierced me, crisscrossed inside me, filled my nerves with tremors, my brain with sounds]. The process of fusion leads to the annulling of limits — the space becomes a sort of sound box where inside and out, the walls of the church and the interior of the body connect, interlink, blend, become indistinguishable from one another and vibrate at the same wavelength, like a discharge that leads to a transfiguring horizon of expanded energy, beyond time and space, until it becomes a kind of dispossession. The chaotic accumulation of sounds, shattering losses of balance, and the thrilling sensations reflect a new state in which the minimum is equal to the infinite: 'Qualquer instante que sucedesse àquele seria mais baixo e vazio. Queria subir e só a morte, como um fim, me daria o auge sem a queda' [Any instant following that one would be lower and emptier. I wanted to rise and only death like an end, would give me the peak without the decline].

Later in this novel, through the character Otávio, we come across a force conceptualizing music and musical expression similar to that voiced by Ulísses in *Uma aprendizagem ou o livro dos prazeres* [*An Apprenticeship or the Book of Pleasures*] (1969) when he resorts to music to speak of his essay writing technique: 'Se um dia eu voltar a escrever ensaios, vou querer o que é o máximo. E o máximo deverá ser dito com a matemática perfeição da música, transposta para o profundo arrebatamento de um pensamento-sentimento' [If I ever write an essay again, I'll want it to be the greatest. And the greatest should be said with the mathematical precision of music, transposed to the deep rapture of a feeling-thought].⁴⁹ But for Joana, however, the process is very different, taking the form of the blind surrender of the corporeal, in which all the constraints of rationalization are suspended.

In Clarice's work there is another vivid moment which dialogues with the one above, or perhaps builds upon it: Chapter XII of *A paixão segundo G.H.*, when the protagonist comes face to face with the cockroach. The maid's room reveals itself intensely as reverberating silent music. This is the maximum point for the capture of vibrations experienced at the limit states at which opposites attract:

> Meu suor me aliviava. Olhei para cima, para o teto. Com o jogo de feixes de luz, o teto se arredondara e transformara-se no que me lembrava uma abóbada. A vibração do calor era como a vibração de um oratório cantado. [...]. Esperei que aquele som mudo e preso passasse. Mas a vastidão dentro do quarto pequeno aumentava, o mudo oratório alargava-o em vibrações até a rachadura do teto. O oratório não era prece: não pedia nada. As paixões em forma de oratório.
>
> [My sweat was relieving me. I looked up, at the ceiling. With the play of the beams of light, the ceiling had rounded and transformed itself into something that reminded me of a vault. The vibration of the heat was like the vibration of a sung oratorio. Only my hearing part was feeling. [...] I waited for that mute and imprisoned sound to pass. But the vastness inside the little room was growing, the mute oratorio was enlarging it in vibrations that reached the fissure in the ceiling. The oratorio was not a prayer: it was not asking for anything. Passions in the form of an oratorio.[50]

The progressive transformation of the space through the effects of light and heat, in the way they expand it, prefigure the path to an encounter characterized by fusion and revelation. The muteness which vibrates in singing makes visible the unlimited nature of the new lived experience: a depersonalizing profundity. Coming from a higher, but not superior, realm, the intense vibration of the vault is consubstantial to the deepest interior core of the self. It is the vibration and the musical elements existing within it that bring the nucleus of life closer: 'Minha carência vinha de que eu perdera o lado inumano — fui expulsa do paraíso quando me tornei humana. E a verdadeira prece é o mudo oratório inumano' [My neediness came from having lost the human side — I was banished from paradise when I became human. And the true prayer is the mute inhuman oratorio].[51]

But, yes, paradox is also a way forward. The mute reverberation triggers self-knowledge via the non-conscious. Here, the narrative itself almost becomes an oratorio which reflects G.H.'s experience. Words are not an accompaniment, like an ornamental choir. The various stages of the encounter (including fear, retreat, intensifying enlargement) are the same as those involved in the process of writing, of the sayability of the new state she has reached: 'Dentro dos sons secos de abóbada tudo podia ser chamado de qualquer coisa porque qualquer coisa se transmutaria na mesma mudez vibrante' [Within the dry sounds of the vault, everything could be called anything, because anything would be transmuted in the same vibrating muteness].[52]

What happens in *Água viva* is different: the character advances conscious of what she is searching for. The assertion of a complete corporeal surrender brings with it an adaptation to the creative process (writing, painting): 'escrevo-te toda inteira' [All of me is writing to you], 'é também com o corpo todo que pinto' [I also use my whole body when I paint]).[53] Here one finds an awareness of the process which takes music as its conductor: 'apóio de leve a mão na eletrola e a mão vibra espraiando ondas pelo corpo todo: assim ouço a eletricidade da vibração. Substrato último no domínio da realidade, e o mundo treme nas minhas mãos' [I gently rest my hand on the record player and my hand vibrates, sending waves through my whole body: and so I listen to the electricity of the vibrations, the last substratum of reality's realm, and the world trembles inside my hands].[54] The experimentation goes beyond the level of the sentence, approaching an admirably perceived new state, in terms of overcoming, plunging, surrendering. A central leitmotiv in *Água viva* is the introduction of the word into one realm which leads us to another: the fourth dimension. Through the body or the senses one reaches a phase in which the use of words encounters music: 'A palavra é a minha quarta dimensão. [...] O que pintei nessa tela é passível de ser fraseado em palavras? Tanto quanto possa ser implícita a palavra muda no som musical' [The word is my fourth dimension. [...] Can what I painted on this canvas be put into words? Just as the silent word can be suggested by a musical sound].[55] Music is not summoned up here as a romantic concept of the unattainable transcendentalized, but through a new kind of textual experimentation close to jazz. It is a mode of expression open to variations and modulations which translate the urgency of instants that are always new and the pulsing of multiple streams of energy:

> Para te dizer o meu substrato faço uma frase de palavras feitas apenas dos instantes-já. Lê então o meu invento de pura vibração sem significado senão o de cada esfuziante sílaba. [...] O que diz este jazz que é improviso? Diz braços enovelados em pernas e as chamas subindo e eu passiva como uma carne que é devorada pelo adunco agudo de uma águia que interrompe seu voo cego. Expresso a mim e a ti os meus desejos mais ocultos e consigo com as palavras uma orgíaca beleza confusa. Estremeço de prazer por entre a novidade de usar palavras que formam intenso matagal!
>
> [To tell you of my substratum I make a sentence of words made only from instants-now. Read, therefore, my invention as pure vibration with no meaning beyond each whistling syllable [...]. What does this jazz that is improvisation say? It says arms tangled with legs and the flames rising and I passive like meat that is devoured by the sharp hook of an eagle that interrupts its blind flight. I express to me and to you my most hidden desires and achieve an orgiastic beauty. I tremble with pleasure amidst the novelty of using words that form an intense thicket].[56]

Improvisation, explosion, networks, interweavings, that which whirls, intersects and prolongs as echo, visible in this text, are the rendering explicit of the restless and incessant experimentation in the search for the nucleus of the living word that has been underway since the first novel, in various different ways. In the passage from *Perto do coração selvagem* cited above, we read Joana's thought: 'Eu não pensava pensamentos, porém música' [I wasn't thinking thoughts, but music].[57] The different fictional experiences conform to the expression of a ceaseless search to reach the core — of the word, of the self, of being. Music is not just a vehicle in this process; the textual experiments incorporate the musical model as a major reference point.

One expressive formulation of this search can be found in the note 'to possible readers' at the beginning of *A paixão segundo G.H.*: 'a aproximação, do que quer que seja, se faz gradualmente e penosamente — atravessando inclusive o oposto daquilo que se vai aproximar' [the approach, of whatever it may be, happens gradually and painstakingly — even passing through the opposite of what it approaches].[58] Or, in other words, in a self-referential text which makes explicit that which she always sought and will continue to be her watchword until the end: 'chegar àquele ponto em que a dor se mistura à profunda alegria e a alegria chega a ser dolorosa — pois esse ponto é o aguilhão da vida' [to reach that point where sorrow mingles with deep happiness and happiness turns out to be painful — for at that point comes the sting of life].[59]

One of the most extraordinary examples of Clarice's reflections on music can be found in 'Hindemith', a text about a quartet by the eponymous German composer.[60] The content we read here is, in fact, very close to the way the author describes how she sees and speaks the world. In this sense, one could say that it is metapoetical: Clarice talks of the art of Paul Hindemith's music as a way of addressing her own literature, her means of capturing things. Not by chance was this text later incorporated into *Água viva* but modified so as to apply more explicitly to the realm of writing: 'Estou te falando em abstrato e pergunto-me: sou uma ária cantabile? Não, não se pode cantar o que te escrevo' [I am speaking to you in the abstract and wonder: am I a cantabile aria? No, you cannot sing what I am writing you].[61]

Nevertheless, it is in the original text about the composer (and not the version adapted for *Água viva*) that the Claricean universe is best revealed: 'Mas que *fato* tem uma noite que se passa inteira num atalho, onde não tem ninguém, e enquanto dormimos? História de escuridão tranquila, de raiz adormecida na sua força, de odor que não tem perfume' [But what *event* takes place at night in a deserted cul-de-sac while we are all asleep? A tale of tranquil darkness, rooted in spent forces, and without any perfume].[62] The discussion about the night in the cul-de-sac (what happens there, in that 'lugar onde tantas coisas acontecem' [place where so many things happen] while we sleep), centred on the music of the composer, is clearly and revealingly echoed in Clarice's characterization of her own literary project. Her reading of Hindemith's quartet is an amazing projection of her ideas into another form, and which touches on a point central to her prose: the question of representation. What shines out in Clarice's interpretation of the world is not the linear capture of the real. Writing about realism in Clarice's work, specifically *O lustre*, Ana Cristina de Rezende Chiara has described the predominance of the 'figura da circularidade' [figure of circularity].[63] The real is 'indeterminado, inorganizável' [indeterminate, un-organizable], she tells us, hence the 'ordem labiríntica' [labyrinthine nature] of her narratives. The *crônica* on the music of Hindemith leads us, precisely, to the ways of that which is not responded to. The labyrinthine nature of Clarice's literature shows that the ceaseless search along these circular paths is not that of the adamic or orphic encounter in which the word approaches the right word or the idealized music. The search is above all to do with intensity, an effect carried to paroxysm which exposes the dissonances, the discontinuities, the abysses, the latencies and, consistently, the research process itself:

> Pena que a palavra *nervos* esteja ligada a vibrações dolorosas, que 'nervos expostos' sejam expressão de sofrimento. Se não, seria quarteto de nervos. Cordas escuras que, tocadas, não falam sobre 'outras coisas', 'não mudam de assunto' — são em si e de si, entregam-se iguais como são.
>
> [What a pity the word *nervous* is associated with mournful vibrations, that exposed nerves are seen as an expression of suffering. Otherwise, the quartet could be described as one of nerves. Dark chords which are not played to evoke 'other things' or to touch on 'another theme'. These chords remain as they are and seek to explain nothing else.][64]

For Clarice, realism is inextricably associated with the interplay between figurative and abstract. She states it very directly in a very short, one-sentence-long text, entitled, precisely 'Abstrato é o Figurativo' ['The Abstract is Symbolic']: 'Tanto em pintura como em música e literatura, tantas vezes o que chamam de abstrato me parece apenas o figurativo de uma realidade mais delicada e mais difícil, menos visível a olho nu' [In painting, as in music and literature, what is often termed abstract strikes me as being simply representative of a more delicate and elusive reality which is barely visible to the naked eye].[65] Beyond the conventionally reducing spaces, beyond preconceived dualities, the figurative that Clarice refers to explains how art can reveal the most complex reality, which, like life itself, is not subject to any sort of categorical limits.

In a letter she sent from Naples to her sister Elisa on 20 April 1945, which she wrote while listening to a concert being broadcast on the radio, Clarice highlights an observation made by the announcer about the way the harp is used in the piece: '[o compositor] tirou o elemento decorativo da música' [the composer took the decorative element out of the music].[66] What the writer retains, in a point transmitted enthusiastically to her sister, is a kind of synthesis, illustrating what she does in her literature: 'Realmente a música que estou ouvindo não tem por assim dizer "história". Parece um bordado de sons, um manejar puro de notas. É belo, belo' [Actually the music I'm listening to doesn't have a 'story' as such. It's like embroidery done with sounds, a pure handling of notes. It's lovely, just lovely].[67]

Coda

On a final note, rather than a simple exercise of style, for Clarice bringing music and writing together is one of the ways in which the self comes into maximum confrontation with itself. Therefore, one of the references to music made by Ângela, in *Um sopro de vida*, admirably sums up Clarice's motto: 'Eu me defrontei com o impossível de mim mesma. Aí, eu desafinei sem querer. Irreal como música' [I came up against the impossible of myself. At that point, I went off key without meaning to. Unreal like music].[68]

Works Cited

CHIARA, ANA CRISTINA DE REZENDE, 'O cruel realismo de *O Lustre*', in Clarice Lispector, *O lustre* (Rio de Janeiro: Francisco Alves, 1992), pp. 1–6

LISPECTOR, CLARICE, *Perto do coração selvagem* (Rio de Janeiro: Francisco Alves, 1990 [1943]); *Near to the Wild Heart*, trans. by Alison Entrekin (New York: New Directions, 2012)

—— *Água viva* (Rio de Janeiro: Francisco Alves, 1990 [1973]); *Água Viva*, trans. by Stefan Tobler (London: Penguin, 2012)

—— *A paixão segundo G.H.* (Rio de Janeiro: Francisco Alves, 1991 [1964]); *The Passion According to G.H.*, trans. by Idra Novey (London: Penguin, 2012)

—— *Um sopro de vida* (Rio de Janeiro: Francisco Alves, 1991 [1978]); *A Breath of Life*, trans. by Johnny Lorenz (Penguin: London, 2012)

—— *O lustre* (Rio de Janeiro: Francisco Alves, 1992 [1946]); *The Chandelier*, trans. by Magdalena Edwards and Benjamin Moser (London: Penguin, 2019)

—— *A cidade sitiada* (Rio de Janeiro: Francisco Alves, 1992 [1948]); *The Besieged City*, trans. by Johnny Lorenz (London: Penguin, 2019)
—— *A maçã no escuro* (Rio de Janeiro: Francisco Alves, 1992 [1961]); *The Apple in the Dark*, trans. by Gregory Rabassa (New York: Knopf, 1967)
—— *Onde estivestes de noite* (Rio de Janeiro: Francisco Alves, 1992 [1974])
—— *A hora da estrela* (Rio de Janeiro: Francisco Alves, 1992 [1977]); *The Hour of the Star*, trans. by Benjamin Moser (New York: New Directions, 2011)
—— *Para não esquecer* (São Paulo: Siciliano, 1992 [1978])
—— *A descoberta do mundo* (Rio de Janeiro: Rocco, 1999); *Discovering the World*, trans. by Giovanni Pontiero (Manchester: Carcanet, 1992)
—— *Laços de família* (Lisbon: Cotovia, 2006 [1960])
—— *Minhas queridas* [My Dears], ed. by Teresa Montero (Rio de Janeiro: Rocco, 2007)
—— *The Complete Stories*, trans. by Katrina Dodson (New York: New Directions, 2015)
NUNES, BENEDITO, *O drama da linguagem: uma leitura de Clarice Lispector* (São Paulo: Editora Ática, 1989)
WILLIAMS, CLAIRE, 'A Brasília que Clarice construiu: o desmonte da nação nas crônicas lispectorianas', in *Fora do retrato: estudos de literatura brasileira contemporânea*, ed. by Regina Dalcastagnè and Anderson Luís Nunes da Mata (Vinhedo: Horizonte, 2012), pp. 145–65

Notes to Chapter 20

1. Translated by Claire Williams.
2. Letter dated 12 January 1945. Clarice Lispector, *Minhas queridas* [My Dears], ed. by Teresa Montero (Rio de Janeiro: Rocco, 2007), p. 70. All translations by Claire Williams unless otherwise indicated.
3. Letter dated 22 January 1945. Ibid., pp. 71–72.
4. Clarice Lispector, *A descoberta do mundo* (Rio de Janeiro: Rocco, 1999), p. 245; *Discovering the World*, trans. by Giovanni Pontiero (Manchester: Carcanet, 1992), p. 319. Clarice included a slightly altered version of this text, under the new title 'Tempestade de almas' in the collection *Onde estivestes de noite* [Where were you at night] (Rio de Janeiro: Francisco Alves, 1992 [1974]), pp.117–20; trans. by Katrina Dodson as 'Soul Storm' in *The Complete Stories* (New York: New Directions, 2015), pp. 501–03.
5. Letter dated 2 January 1947. Lispector, *Minhas queridas*, p. 149.
6. See chapter by Karyn Mota in this volume.
7. Clarice Lispector, *A hora da estrela* (Rio de Janeiro: Francisco Alves, 1992), p. 25; *The Hour of the Star*, trans. by Benjamin Moser (New York: New Directions, 2011), pp. 3–4.
8. Ibid., p. 30; ibid., p. 8.
9. Clarice Lispector, *O lustre* (Rio de Janeiro: Francisco Alves, 1992 [1946]), p. 29; *The Chandelier*, trans. by Magdalena Edwards and Benjamin Moser (London: Penguin, 2019), p. 25.
10. Ibid., pp. 60–62; ibid., pp. 55–57.
11. Ibid., p. 169; ibid., p. 161.
12. Clarice Lispector, *Laços de família* (Lisbon: Cotovia, 2006, p. 17); *The Complete Stories*, p. 115.
13. Ibid., p. 29; ibid., p. 130.
14. Lispector, *Onde estivestes de noite*, pp. 19–20; *The Complete Stories*, p. 430.
15. Ibid., pp. 23–24; ibid., p. 433.
16. Ibid., p. 30; ibid., p. 439.
17. On the 'soundtrack' to this text, see Claire Williams, 'A Brasília que Clarice construiu: o desmonte da nação nas crônicas lispectorianas', in *Fora do retrato: estudos de literatura brasileira contemporânea*, ed. by Regina Dalcastagnè and Anderson Luís Nunes da Mata (Vinhedo: Horizonte, 2012), pp. 145–65.
18. Letter dated 25 October 1955. Lispector, *Minhas queridas*, pp. 262–63. TN: Érico Veríssimo (1905–1975) was a Brazilian writer and diplomat who, along with his wife Mafalda, became

friends with Clarice and her family during their stay in Washington D.C. in the 1950s. Their son, Luiz Fernando Veríssimo (b. 1936), is a celebrated fiction writer and *cronista*.
19. Benedito Nunes, *O drama da linguagem: uma leitura de Clarice Lispector* (São Paulo: Ática, 1989), p. 83.
20. Ibid., p. 84.
21. Lispector, *A descoberta do mundo*, p. 51; *Discovering the World*, p. 71.
22. Ibid., p. 52; ibid., p. 71.
23. Ibid., p. 52; ibid., p. 72.
24. Ibid., p. 52; ibid., p. 72.
25. Ibid., p. 52; ibid., p. 71.
26. TN: Ernani Braga (1888–1948) was a Brazilian composer, conductor and pianist, who collaborated with Heitor Villa Lobos and participated in the famous 1922 São Paulo Modern Art Week. He lived in Recife in the 1930s and was one of the founders of the Pernambuco conservatoire.
27. Ibid., p. 52; Ibid., p. 71.
28. Ibid., p. 52; Ibid., p. 71.
29. Lispector, *A descoberta do mundo*, p. 284; *Discovering the World*, p. 371.
30. Clarice Lispector, *Perto do coração selvagem* (Rio de Janeiro: Francisco Alves, 1990 [1943]), p. 50; *Near to the Wild Heart*, trans. by Alison Entrekin (New York: New Directions, 2012), p. 32.
31. Lispector, *O lustre*, pp. 17–18; *The Chandelier*, p. 13.
32. Lispector, *Perto do coração selvagem*, p. 99; *Near to the Wild Heart*, p. 77.
33. Clarice Lispector, *A maçã no escuro* (Rio de Janeiro: Francisco Alves, 1992 [1961]), p. 201; *The Apple in the Dark*, trans. by Gregory Rabassa (New York: Knopf, 1967), p. 223.
34. Ibid., p. 204; ibid., p. 226.
35. Ibid., p. 193; ibid., p. 213.
36. Lispector, *Perto do coração selvagem*, p. 20; *Near to the Wild Heart*, p. 4.
37. Ibid., p. 26; ibid., p. 10.
38. Ibid., p. 54; ibid., pp. 36–37.
39. Ibid., p. 155; ibid., p. 129.
40. Ibid., p. 184; ibid., p. 157.
41. Ibid., p. 192; ibid., p. 164.
42. Ibid.
43. TN: In Brazil, *charanga* music is played by brass bands, most commonly to support sports teams.
44. Clarice Lispector, *A cidade sitiada* (Rio de Janeiro: Francisco Alves, 1992), p. 52; *The Besieged City*, trans. by Johnny Lorenz (London: Penguin, 2019), p. 56.
45. Lispector, *A maçã no escuro*, p. 18; Lispector, *The Apple in the Dark*, p. 13.
46. Ibid., p. 40; ibid., p. 44.
47. Clarice Lispector, *A paixão segundo G.H.* (Rio de Janeiro: Francisco Alves, 1991 [1964]), p. 86; *The Passion According to G.H.*, trans. by Idra Novey (London: Penguin, 2012), p. 79.
48. Lispector, *Perto do coração selvagem*, pp. 83–84; *Near to the Wild Heart*, pp. 62–63.
49. Clarice Lispector, *Uma aprendizagem ou o livro dos prazeres* (Rio de Janeiro: Sabiá, 1973), p. 99; *An Apprenticeship or The Book of Pleasures*, trans. by Stefan Tobler (London: Penguin, 2021), p. 80.
50. Lispector, *A paixão segundo G.H.*, p. 86; *The Passion According to G.H.*, pp. 78–79.
51. Ibid., p. 164; ibid., p. 169.
52. Ibid., p. 100; ibid., p. 96.
53. Clarice Lispector, *Água viva* (Rio de Janeiro: Francisco Alves, 1990), p. 14; *Água Viva*, trans. by Stefan Tobler (London: Penguin, 2012), p. 4.
54. Ibid, p. 15; ibid., p. 5.
55. Ibid., pp. 14–15; ibid., pp. 4, 5.
56. Ibid., p. 27; ibid., pp. 5, 16–17.
57. Lispector, *Perto do coração selvagem*, p. 84; *Near to the Wild Heart*, p. 63.
58. Lispector, *A paixão segundo G.H.*, p. 13; *The Passion According to G.H.*, p. xi.
59. Lispector, *A descoberta do mundo*, p. 201; *Discovering the World*, p. 264.
60. TN: Paul Hindemith (1895–1963) was a German musician, composer, conductor and music theorist.

61. Lispector, *Água viva*, p. 86; *Água Viva*, p. 73.
62. Lispector, *A descoberta do mundo*, p. 229; *Discovering the World*, p. 299.
63. Ana Cristina de Rezende Chiara, 'O cruel realismo de *O Lustre*', in Clarice Lispector, *O Lustre* (Rio de Janeiro: Francisco Alves Editora, 1992), pp. 1–6.
64. Lispector, *A descoberta do mundo*, p. 230; *Discovering the World*, p. 299.
65. Lispector, Clarice, *Para não esquecer* (São Paulo: Siciliano, 1992), p. 49; *Discovering the World*, p. 413.
66. Lispector, Clarice, *Minhas queridas*, p. 83.
67. Ibid., p. 84.
68. Clarice Lispector, 'irreal como música', *Um sopro de vida* (Rio de Janeiro: Francisco Alves, 1991 [1978]), p. 89; *A Breath of Life*, trans. by Johnny Lorenz (Penguin: London, 2012), p. 78.

CHAPTER 21

❖

The Body Speaks: Clarice Lispector on Screen

Magdalena Edwards

In November 2017, I presented a performance lecture titled 'The Body Speaks: Clarice Lispector's *The Chandelier*' at the AFTER CLARICE: LISPECTOR'S LEGACY conference in Oxford. This work required me to play several roles including the translator of *O lustre*, the main character Virgínia, and the author Clarice Lispector. I was terrified to attempt to transform into Lispector, even if for a moment. How could I dare? I watched her 1977 interview with Júlio Lerner numerous times as part of my preparation. What I didn't realize at the time was that I was practising a new way of engaging with Lispector's work. The essay that follows is an attempt to put my experience into words within a format that accomplishes the analytical and argumentative task of academic writing while maintaining the spirit of reading that Lispector recommends in her conversation with Lerner: reading that is motivated by feeling and entering into contact with Lispector. As she says to him on screen, 'Either it touches you or it doesn't'.[1]

★ ★ ★ ★ ★

Lispector on Screen: Speaking from the Tomb

On 1 February 1977, Clarice Lispector filmed her only television interview, a conversation with TV Cultura's Júlio Lerner in São Paulo.[2] The camera is on Lispector, who sits smoking in an armchair with an ashtray to her right. Lerner is off camera, such that when she speaks to him she is looking toward, but not directly into, the camera. The image is framed in a way that gives the interview an intimate and detached quality at the same time; the viewer watches Lispector watching Lerner as he asks each question, and sees Lispector get caught up in her own storytelling and train of thought. Her final words to Lerner on camera, which end the filmed conversation and respond to his question of whether she is reborn or renewed with each new work she publishes, are: 'Well, now I died... Let's see if I am reborn again. For now I am dead... I am speaking from my tomb'.[3] Her dramatic statement reiterates her earlier declaration during the interview: 'I think that when I do not write, I am dead'.[4] This declaration is hyperbolic, an exaggerated affirmation of how the act of writing is primordial for her; it is a testament to her sense that if she is between projects and not in the midst of the creative process, then she is not truly alive. Her repetition of this idea at the end of her interview — 'I am speaking from my tomb' — also functions, at first blush, as hyperbole because clearly she is in the television studio being filmed. On the day of filming, Lispector asked Lerner to promise the interview would not air until after her death, and he agreed.[5] Lispector would die of ovarian cancer — without knowing she had the disease because her doctors had not told her — on 9 December 1977.[6] The interview aired on the show *Panorama* less than three weeks after her death, on 28 December 1977, at 8.30pm, and the final footage is under 23 minutes. On the night of Lispector's television debut, and each time her interview has been viewed subsequently, her words — 'I am speaking from my tomb' — perform and enact what was only metaphorical on the day of filming.

Lispector's metaphorical-turned-uncannily-true statement — 'I am speaking from my tomb' — coupled with her request that the interview not be aired until after she dies, frames her conversation with Lerner, the only audiovisual footage of Lispector that we have, as the last word from a writer who controlled her image and maintained her artistic freedom fiercely. Lispector pre-emptively tackles the question of her legacy, including the posthumous publications and new editions that all writers of her stature face; no matter what critics, editors, publishers, biographers, and others might say about Lispector after her death, she has the last word in perpetuity. Her final statement also highlights the urgent nature of the footage, containing a message so serious it propels Lispector to speak from her tomb, as a posthumous performance given during a critical cultural and political period in Brazil, which in 1977 was in the middle of a twenty-one-year military dictatorship (1964–85) characterized by pervasive censorship.[7] In these ways, Lispector's one and only appearance on screen is provocatively aligned with the video art created in the 1970s by Brazilian artists, including Letícia Parente and Sonia Andrade, who were bent on 'projecting their own reality into televisual space, a form of feedback',[8] or talking back through words, sound, image, and silence. Lispector's performance, which includes several awkward moments when she prefers not to answer Lerner's questions, touches upon various topics: her childhood, her writing process, her insistence that she is not a professional writer, and her next novel, which she says she has finished writing, but does not name (though she does reveal it has thirteen titles). She is referring, of course, to *A hora da estrela*, first published in October 1977, two months before her death.

Lispector's interview with Lerner also functions as a map, drawn on an unquestionably 'anti-literary' grid, for reading her *oeuvre*. Adam Joseph Shellhorse argues that in Lispector's 'notes, fragments, chronicles, and interviews, one finds an entire archive of anti-literary statements' that put the process of writing, and not the literary outcome or product, front and centre: 'the text' is 'composed and decomposed, affirmed and critiqued, on an incessantly refractive plane of composition so as to charge the reader to see the present as entirely fabricated and a site of struggle, and in consequence, worthy of incessant critique and reconfiguration'.[9] In this way, Lispector's 'anti-literary' practice demands an active reader who is engaged in seeing and contending with her texts as dynamic entities. I argue in this essay that it is precisely the 1977 TV Cultura interview — where Lispector entrusts her readers with the active task of confronting her texts as dynamic and interconnected 'site[s] of struggle' and which I will discuss in more detail below — that illuminates the possibility of reading *A hora da estrela* as a rewriting of *O lustre* [*The Chandelier*], the novel Lispector first published in 1946 and which she said gave her the most pleasure to write.[10] The two women protagonists of these novels, Macabéa and Virgínia, can be provocatively seen and read alongside, and compared with, the blueprint offered by Clarice herself, through both her words and her body.

Lispector on Screen: An Anti-Interview

Lerner defines his encounter with Lispector as 'an anti-interview, pauses, silences', and highlights how difficult the experience was for him as an interviewer: 'Clarice is now fleeing to an uninhabited and unattainable galaxy, but she returns suddenly and, tolerant, supports all of my limitations'.[11] He also reads her body language, specifically the crossing and uncrossing of her legs, as indicative of the possibility she might get up and leave at any moment during the interview: 'her body expresses misgivings, she moves away from me, but again she brings me closer, her legs cross and uncross over and over and telegraph that suddenly she might get up and leave'. He describes his sense of being unsettled — 'I am completely disconcerted' — and explains that he has had no opportunity to prepare for the interview. Lispector arrived at the São Paulo television studios of TV Cultura, Channel 2, on 1 February 1977, to participate in a round table about film. Afterward, to everyone's surprise, she accepted an on-the-spot invitation to be interviewed one-on-one.

While Lerner is presumably the person in control — he describes himself as 'the man of the castle'[12] — Lispector maintains her ground firmly throughout the conversation, by refusing to answer certain questions and by taking her time in giving answers when she does. Lispector also challenges the interviewer's control over the proceedings in the way the footage is filmed — off the cuff without Lerner having the chance to prepare — and in her requirement that the interview only air after her death. Lerner's use of the word *'antientrevista'* or 'anti-interview' to describe the experience highlights this atypical distribution of power and, perhaps more to the point, highlights the fact that Lispector does not always behave in the way an interviewee is expected to behave. She does not follow the prescribed rules, and her 'anti-interview' fits squarely with the 'anti-literary' strategies highlighted by Shellhorse; just as Lispector's readers must engage actively with her 'anti-literary' texts as dynamic and unpredictable ecosystems, Lerner must struggle to keep up with Lispector's changes of topic and constant refusal to answer his questions.

Lispector, a seasoned interviewer herself with a series of interviews published in *Manchete* in the late 1960s and another set that appeared from 1976–77 in the magazine *Fatos & Fotos: Gente*, 'always controlled the interview and was not afraid to ask daring, insistent, or even impertinent questions'.[13] Until the televised

Lerner interview, the few times Lispector had accepted the role of interviewee had been in published written exchanges, and she 'was known to be difficult and not talk much, above all about her work'.[14] A new and as yet unseen dimension to Lispector-as-interviewee emerges in her Lerner interview because she is under the camera's constant and merciless eye. No matter how little she might say with words about herself and her work, her body speaks to the camera and the viewer. She is 56 going on 57, she has suffered the consequences of a devastating fire that ravaged her body and her home in 1966, and she is ten months shy of her death from cancer.[15]

The interview with Lerner is not easy to watch — and yet it is the very discomfort it produces in the viewer, and in the interviewer, that makes Clarice's performance powerful. The movements of her body and the deployment of her voice and her gaze, as well as her ability to sit in silence in front of the camera and her display of negative emotions, including exasperation, frustration, anger, fatigue, and resignation, create an unsettling experience. Lispector answers that she doesn't know — 'Eu não sei' — or some variation of the phrase numerous times during the interview. There are several instances when she declines to answer questions, about the name of the heroine of her latest novel or about the precise moment when adults become sad and solitary, by saying 'it's a secret' — and once she delivers the refusal, she smiles ever so slightly such that the balance of her response to Lerner is not entirely negative.[16] This resistance, whether unabashedly direct or more playful, is not the kind of performance television viewers would expect from the brilliant artist 'who pulled off the (unlikely) feat of being viable as both a woman and a writer'.[17] It is certainly not what Lerner was hoping for as he interviewed her. And yet Lispector's overall unyielding and devastatingly authentic audiovisual performance is precisely what entices viewers to watch her over and over again. Lispector's anti-interview with Lerner received the prize for the best interview of the year from the Associação Paulista dos Críticos de Arte (APCA) at the end of December 1977,[18] and the footage has been viewed millions of times through YouTube and Facebook since it first appeared online in 2012.

Lispector on Screen as 1970s Video Art

Lispector's unsettling performance — first, her unyielding presence and her sustained display of negative emotions; and second, the extreme constraints she places on the filming and distribution of her interview, specifically through a last-minute agreement that leaves Lerner without time to prepare, coupled with the requirement that the footage be shown only after her death — aligns her interview with the 1970s video art by Brazilian artists who 'perform uncomfortable and often tortuous confrontations with their bodies' as a way to make visible and condemn the military regime's use of violence and censorship.[19] For example, Letícia Parente in her work *Marca registrada* (1975) sews the phrase 'Made in Brasil' into the sole of her bare foot, 'which becomes a canvas for the slow and methodical process of stitching a series of letters, an uncomfortable tension the viewer must endure for the duration of the work', a total of nine excruciating minutes.[20] In

Fig. 21.1. Image from the TV Panorama interview. YouTube

Wire (1974–77), Sonia Andrade 'wraps a wire tightly around her head until she is no longer recognizable' and the 'ensuing face, unidentifiable and disfigured, deliberately summons the victims of torture'.[21] The viewer is placed in a bind, 'left feeling helpless, or even guilty, about their incapacity to deter' Andrade's actions. Meanwhile the artist is 'self-inflicting the pain and disfiguration' while playing a double role as 'active perpetrator' and 'passive recipient'.[22] There is a third aspect of Lispector's unsettling performance that makes the kinship between her presence on screen and that of 1970s video artists even more clear: the performance that occurs within Lispector's performance as interviewee. That is, the uncanny moment when she transforms herself, the way an actor becomes another person, into Mineirinho, the subject of one of her texts and a fatal victim of police brutality.

While Lispector does not inflict direct pain on herself in the way that Parente and Andrade did, she is clearly not at ease physically during her interview. Lerner writes that it was not only an extremely hot summer afternoon and the air conditioning was not working properly, but also the heat from the studio lights added to the uncomfortably high temperature.[23] A little more than a third into the conversation, Lispector says that she's not feeling well that day: 'I am only sad today because I am tired… usually I am happy'. Lispector then falls asleep on camera, a moment which lasts an astonishing 11 seconds punctuated by her audible deep breathing (8:11 to 8:22). She is out of sorts, but nonetheless accepts a last-minute invitation to give a television interview. Knowing that her conversation with Lerner will eventually be shown in homes throughout the country, Lispector chooses to deploy an audiovisual version of herself that is not optimal or even usual, and she says as much.

Lerner asks Lispector what the role of the Brazilian writer is today, and she responds that it is to 'speak as little as possible'.[24] Saying less and cultivating silence in late 1970s Brazil were political strategies for self-preservation.[25] To resist the potential consequences of speaking out of turn during Brazil's military dictatorship, the writer had to remain silent or deploy the next best thing — 'I don't know' and 'it's a secret'. One of the ways to make silence speak in an audiovisual narrative is to charge the body with the task of communicating. The body speaks when the writer cannot, or will not, utter the words: through a shrug, a smile, a laugh, a pause, a physical gesture with an arm or a toss of the head. Lispector's conversation with Lerner is filled with such performative moments. While Parente, Andrade, and others who produced video art in the 1970s were not able to disseminate their work widely — precisely because they were producing material meant to function as a 'critique of television and its relationship to the regime'[26] and thus circulate outside of the official, government-sponsored channels, such as TV Globo — Lispector seizes a unique opportunity to provide a critique that will appear on national television and — in the ultimate strategy to avoid the repercussions of not producing a performance that will satisfy the censors — her interview will air after her death.

When Lerner asks Lispector if writing can change anything, specifically in reference to her story 'Mineirinho' — about a Rio de Janeiro criminal gunned down by thirteen police bullets in 1962[27] — Clarice replies no: 'It doesn't change anything. It doesn't change anything. I write without the hope that what I write will change anything. It doesn't change anything [She takes a cigarette to smoke]'.[28] But prior to this statement of resignation — a trio of denials, with a biblical echo of Peter's denial of Christ — the most politically radical moment in Lispector's interview with Lerner occurs. This is when she performs, in a rather off-hand way, her transformation from Clarice-the-writer into Mineirinho-the-criminal, while she loosely cites her own text. As she speaks, her face turned away from Lerner and the camera, her palms turn upward and her extended arms stretch to mark the rhythm of her words: 'First shot I'm terrified. Second shot I don't know what. Third shot something. The twelfth hits me, the thirteenth it is me'. During the last phrase, 'the thirteenth it is me,' she begins to look up at Lerner and then she pauses. The transformation is complete. She takes in the moment where she *is* Mineirinho, and then she comments: 'I really became Mineirinho, massacred by the police. Whatever his crime might have been, one bullet was enough. The rest was the desire to kill. It was arrogance'. She uses the word 'massacrado' in reference to who she becomes in that moment when the thirteenth bullet hits, namely Mineirinho murdered, slaughtered, slain by Rio de Janeiro officers in 1962.

Yudith Rosenbaum argues that Lispector's 'Mineirinho' has a 'dual face — psychological/existential and ethical/political' and for this reason the text 'requires a comprehensive look, capable of understanding its multiple meanings.'[29] For Rosenbaum, the decision made by Lispector's narrator 'to *count the thirteen shots that killed Mineirinho*' instead of '*counting his crimes*' is an 'inversion in the literary subject matter' that 'shifts the focus to the act of killing a criminal'. While 'Mineirinho' was first published in the June 1962 issue of the Rio de Janeiro-based magazine *Senhor*, two years before the beginning of Brazil's military dictatorship (1964–85), Lispector's discussion of the text with Lerner in February of 1977 reactivates her *crônica* in the context of the dictatorship. Lispector is not known for her overt political writing, but she did produce explicitly political texts throughout her career. In mid-February 1968 Lispector published 'A Letter to the Minister of Education' arguing for funding for waitlisted students, so they might enrol in their university programmes. Lispector makes the following observation about the students' lack of agency: 'they could not even take to the streets for a protest march because they know the police could beat them up.'[30] Lispector's statement refers to tensions between the police and the student movement that had emerged in Brazil even prior to the dictatorship.[31] By late March 1968, one month after Lispector had published her letter, 'police killed a high school student [Edson Luís] participating in [a] protest. This proved a powerful catalyst — over a weeklong period that followed, there were 26 protests in 15 different cities.'[32] It seems no accident that Lispector makes her statement to Lerner about Mineirinho — '[O]ne bullet was enough. The rest was the desire to kill. It was arrogance' — in 1977, during the 'abertura' or 'opening up' years of the military dictatorship when President Geisel was slowly transitioning the country, not without a great deal of police force and brutality, toward what would eventually be democratization starting officially in 1985.

Lispector says that her writing changes nothing, and yet the transformative moment she performs on television, taken directly from her writing and loosely cited by her, is absolutely radical. She transforms herself from Lispector-the-writer to Mineirinho-the-criminal and, in essence, enacts the moment in her written text where the narrative voice says: 'The thirteenth shot assassinates me — because I am the other. Because I want to be the other'.[33] When Lispector clarifies that she becomes the other because she *wants* to be the other, she communicates — especially to those familiar with the published text of 'Mineirinho' — that she, or any Brazilian, could be the criminal, the other, subject to police violence at any time. By using the word 'assassinar' in her written text, she aligns the murder of Mineirinho with the assassinations of political figures of import; everyday people — including criminals — merit the same value and consideration, the same words, as politicians. Every murder is political.

Through her transformation into the 'other' — a process she says she wants — Lispector is able 'to communicate and denounce the violence of the regime and activate the viewer to reflect on their surroundings'.[34] Viewers numbering into the millions continue to experience an active kind of viewing charged with political implications by watching Lispector's interview online in the present day, which is a new critical moment both culturally and politically in Brazil given the divisive election in October 2018 of Jair Bolsonaro, who took office as the country's 38th president in January 2019. The critique of state-sponsored violence that Lispector, Andrade, and Parente provided in late 1970s Brazil — not only physical violence, but also the psychological violence brought on both the individual and the social fabric by censorship — becomes urgent in new ways during the Bolsonaro regime.

Lispector and Performance: On Screen, on Stage, on the Page

Lispector's 1977 TV Cultura interview is a performance, arguably posthumous, that is in sync with her lifelong artistic production. Her attention to performance and theatricality is consistently present in her writing through characters, scenes and dialogue attuned to the body and its performative work. In the opening pages of her first novel, *Perto do coração selvagem* [*Near to the Wild Heart*] (1943), it becomes clear that the main character, a child named Joana, approaches playing with her toys as a kind of psychological and physical performance: 'She always found a way to cast herself in the lead role precisely when events placed one character or another in the limelight. She was serious as she worked, in silence, arms by her side'.[35] In *O lustre*, Virgínia goes to the theatre to attend a concert with her boyfriend Vicente, a translator, and their friend Adriano. Once inside the performance space she 'felt grotesquely human' — and during the concert itself Virgínia has trouble settling into the experience: 'She couldn't manage to take pleasure in the music but she took refuge in the sound with a certain anguish, her white face angled toward the distant stage, her body contained and unmoving'.[36] Rodrigo, the narrator of *A hora da estrela*, talks about preparing his body to write Macabéa's story: 'I'm warming up my body to begin' and later he says: 'I'm not an intellectual, I write with my body'.[37] He even suggests he is an actor: 'Or I'm not a writer? Honestly I'm more of an actor'.[38] Macabéa tells her boyfriend Olímpico: 'You know what I wanted most in my life? In fact, to be a movie star.' When he responds negatively — 'You don't have the face or the body to be a movie star' — Macabéa is undeterred and responds with a question: 'You really think so?' He responds the same way again, so she changes the topic.[39] In an earlier conversation with Olímpico, which occurs on a bench in the public square more or less in the middle of the novel, their exchange is in pure dialogue format, as if the core of *A hora da estrela* were a script or a play.[40]

Lispector addresses performance and theatricality in her *crônicas*, as a ghostwriter (including a column for the actress Ilka Soares), as an interviewer, as the translator of numerous books of fiction, and as the co-translator of six plays with Tati de Moraes (Vinícius de Moraes's ex-wife), including works by Chekhov, Ibsen, Lorca, Hellman, Mishima, and McCullers.[41] In her 1964 book *A legião estrangeira* [*The Foreign Legion*], she published her one strictly dramatic piece, a one-act play titled *A pecadora queimada e os anjos harmoniosos* [*The Burned Sinner and the Harmonious Angels*] about a woman who commits adultery and is condemned to be burned at the stake. Lispector wrote this play between 1946 and 1948, right after publishing her second novel *O lustre* (1946), while pregnant with her first son Pedro, who was born in 1948, and while writing her third novel *A cidade sitiada* [*The Besieged City*] (1949), all during the time she lived in Bern, Switzerland with her diplomat husband.[42] The accused woman never speaks in the play: 'Hers, one might say, is a supremely eloquent and ironic discourse of silence'.[43] She remains silent 'even when to have spoken out would have quite possibly allowed her to save herself'. She does, however, speak with her body, specifically through her smile, a 'provocative act [...] in powerful contrast to the display of guilt and remorse her society would expect'.[44] The provocative smile performed by the protagonist of the only play Lispector

Fig. 21.2. Fauzi Arap, José Wilker, Glauce Rocha, Clarice Lispector and Dirce Migliaccio in conversation — 1965. Carlos Moskovics, Cedoc/Funarte

wrote resonates with her own playfully resistant smile as she deploys it in her 1977 interview with Lerner.

Between 1965 and 1966 the playwright, director, and actor Fauzi Arap staged the first theatre adaptation of Lispector's work, inspired by three of her books, *Perto do coração selvagem*, *A paixão segundo G.H.* [*The Passion According to G.H.*], and *A legião estrangeira*. The photographs, taken by Carlos Moskovics, of Lispector participating in rehearsal with Arap and the actors José Wilker, Glauce Rocha, and Dirce Migliaccio, depict a collaborative experience.[45] Arap also directed Maria Bethânia in her first show featuring Lispector's texts *Comigo me desavim* [*I'm at odds with myself*] (1967), where she recited 'Mineirinho' in its entirety for the first time.[46] According to Maria Bethânia, who has continued to perform shows featuring Lispector's work, Lispector was often present during Bethânia's rehearsals with Arap.

Fig. 21.3. Fauzi Arap, José Wilker, Glauce Rocha, Clarice Lispector and Dirce Migliaccio in conversation — 1965. Carlos Moskovics, Cedoc/Funarte

Lispector would take notes quietly in the dark, and she sometimes made suggestions for how to edit the texts for performance, which, for Bethânia, showed how Lispector 'had a thing for dramaturgy too'.[47]

In her May 1968 *crônica* about translation, 'Traduzir procurando não trair' [Translating by Trying Not to Betray], Lispector suggests the work of actors, translators, and writers share significant similarities. She describes how her co-translation with Tati de Moraes of Lillian Hellman's play *The Little Foxes*, in particular reading the dialogues out loud to get a sense of how they sounded, had an effect on her own voice and sound: 'From dealing so much with American characters, I "caught" an entirely American intonation in the inflection of my voice. I went on to sing the words, exactly the way an American who speaks Portuguese does'.[48] When Lispector complained about this to her friend, Moraes responded with great irony and demanded to know who had told Lispector 'to be an innate actress'.[49] Lispector goes on to reflect that she believes 'every writer is an innate actor' because a writer above all else plays herself in a very profound way, which is why writers get 'tired a lot' and end up making themselves 'nauseous' — because 'their intimate contact with themselves is by necessity overly prolonged'.[50]

The idea that all writers are innate actors because they have to play themselves sheds additional light on the fatigue Lispector displays in her interview with Lerner. The suggestion that Lispector is an 'innate actress' is interesting in the context of her upbringing, where Yiddish was spoken by the older generation at home though she spoke in Portuguese with family and at school. Coupled with her later travels where she functioned in Italian, French, and English, her multilingual upbringing and travel experiences reveal Lispector as 'an exemplary case of someone who writes language as a foreigner, making her especially responsive to hearing nuances, timbres, and intonations'.[51] One might say that for Lispector all writers and translators, like actors, are foreigners striving to perform, and to become, the other through language.

Lispector wrote letters throughout her life, and in many she makes references to going to the theatre or the movies.[52] She writes to her sisters from Paris in January 1947: 'We've gone to fantastic theatres. Today at lunch [...] (it was at the Ritz) [we saw] that movie star Victor Franceu [sic]. He is the same as on screen [...]. We saw Eugene O'Neill's *Electra*, magnificent'.[53] Overall her letters reveal 'details of a Clarice who struggles to be a regular woman, a wife and the mother to two sons, who writes letters feeling out the absence of her relatives and friends and also herself'.[54] The sensation that Lispector is trying to conjure herself through the letter-writing process particularly resonates throughout the letters she wrote to her confidant and fellow writer Lúcio Cardoso. The Cardoso letters also consistently raise questions of performance and theatricality. Silence hovers in an exchange about *O lustre*. She writes in September 1944: 'My book will be called O LUSTRE. It's finished, except it lacks what I cannot say'.[55] The need to include 'what I cannot say' in the novel Lispector wrote from 1943 to 1944 calls to mind the silences in her 1977 interview with Lerner, as well as the moments when she tells him 'I don't know' and 'it's a secret' in response to his questions.

Cardoso responds to Lispector's letter in December 1944: 'I haven't read your book, but I wanted very much to do so. I like the title *O lustre* but not too much. I think it's sort of Mansfield-like and a bit poor for someone as rich as you'.[56] She then responds in early 1945 and tells him why she disagrees with his critique: 'It made me a little sad that you did not like the title, *O lustre*. Exactly because of what you don't like, because of its poverty, is why I like it. I never quite managed to convince you that I am poor'.[57] Moreover, Lispector says: 'the poorer I am, the more adornments I use to adorn myself'.[58] The chandelier — *O lustre* — symbolizes wealth and luxury, but its poverty perhaps lies in its decorative nature as an object of illumination in a general sense, as well as in the specific narrative fact that in Virgínia's story it is the symbol of her family's former material wealth. Without question the title *O lustre* is a striking divergence from the title *Perto do coração selvagem*, Lispector's first novel: a decorative light versus a wild and presumably beating heart. What begins to emerge in this exchange between Lispector and Cardoso is a conversation about the poverty of silence versus the richness of language, or vice versa: the richness of silence (wild and beating heart) and the poverty of language (decorative light).

In *A hora da estrela* the narrator Rodrigo S.M. questions the poverty of the story he is telling, Macabéa's story. She is so poor, she does not even have the kind of poverty that can be dressed up or decorated. Her poverty is not only in her lack of material goods and exterior adornments, it is in her body and her spirit. Through this lack, to the bone, Rodrigo S.M. seeks to connect to the sacred. However, his experience of Macabéa's poverty, and his role in telling her story, does not always approximate a holy or transformative state: 'poverty is ugly and promiscuous. For this reason I don't know if my story is going to be — going to be what? I don't know anything, I still haven't worked myself up to write it. Will it have events? It will. But which ones? Again I don't know'.[59] Rodrigo repeats 'I don't know' three times, an echo of Lispector in her interview with Lerner. His repetition functions like an 'enfeite' — an adornment or decoration — for his silence, the lack of story. There is no story because he hasn't motivated himself to write it yet. He doesn't know why. Or he says he doesn't know, but really he resists the need to pin the narrative down; he declines the invitation to reveal the secret of what he is writing, the way Lispector repeats 'I don't know' in her interview with Lerner to protect her secret, to keep the power of the interviewer in check, and to perform the discomfort and difficulty of being a Brazilian writer during the dictatorship. The repetition of 'I don't know' also underscores the desire, on the part of both Lispector and Rodrigo, to focus on feeling, the way Virgínia, a girl from a once-wealthy family, dedicates herself to feeling instead of knowing: 'she didn't know what was happening to her and her only way of knowing it was living it'.[60]

The Body Speaks: Death

O lustre and *A hora da estrela* are novels adorned by poverty and silence, filled with feeling, and both contend with death from their opening moments: Virgínia and her brother believe they see a drowned man in the river, which they decide to keep a secret; and before Rodrigo can begin his version of Macabéa's story, an 'Author's Dedication' opens with 'old Schumann and his sweet Clara, who today are bones'.[61] Both novels also conclude tragically with female main characters who die by being run over: Virgínia is hit by an unidentified car and Macabéa by a yellow Mercedes. These deaths are presaged in the opening of Lispector's first novel *Perto do coração selvagem*, as Joana plays with her doll Arlete: 'She had already dressed her doll, undressed it, imagined it going to a party where it shone among all the other daughters. A blue car ran over Arlete, killing her'.[62] Lispector reveals a story from her own life in her conversation with Lerner that provides a throughline for Arlete's and Virgínia's and Macabéa's deaths. She says, when telling Lerner about what inspired her to write her latest novel: 'I went to a fortune-teller and I imagined [...] when I took the taxi back home, that it would be very funny if a taxi were to hit me, run me over, and if I were to die after having heard all those goods things'.[63]

This moment in the interview is awkward because while Lispector says that she imagined the scenario as funny, her face remains serious in the retelling. Lispector provides gallows humour with a completely deadpan delivery; there seems to be no pleasure or levity in the moment when she reveals her tragicomic daydream.

As Lispector begins to tell Lerner about the fortune-teller and the death by taxi that follows, her right arm and hand, both off screen, are preoccupied with putting out a cigarette she has been smoking slowly, as if the physical action of putting out the cigarette parallels the snuffing out of her own life or the life of her character. Lerner doesn't ask a follow-up question about her visit to the fortune-teller, but instead enquires about the name of the main character. Here Lispector replies, while smiling, that she does not want to say because 'it is a secret'. The protagonist in question, Macabéa, will echo this response when she tells her boyfriend Olímpico: 'I don't know what's inside of my name'.[64] The narrator of O lustre reveals that Virgínia's name is 'full of attentive peace' but that she could have a different name: 'she could be named Mary Magdalene or Hermione or even any other name except Virgínia […]. Yes, and she could also have been in small tranquillity Sybil, Sybil, Sybil'.[65] Sybil, the female oracle, would be an excellent name for Virgínia, whose story portends and prefigures the life of Macabéa.

When Lerner asks whether the title of the novel might be revealed, Lispector cuts him off and says, with a completely serious demeanour again: 'Thirteen names. Thirteen titles'. Here she sets up a connection that will become clearer later in the interview when she discusses the story of Mineirinho and the thirteen police bullets that hit him. Just as she transforms into Mineirinho, massacred by the police, Lispector can turn into Macabéa, a poor girl from the Northeast who is run over by a taxi after receiving good news from a fortune-teller. When Lispector reveals that her new novel has thirteen titles — and it is worth noting here that the thirteenth card in the tarot deck signifies death — Lerner understands immediately that she will not reveal any of them. The camera zooms out and Lispector's entire body is visible as she sits in the armchair with her arms stretched out on the armrests and her fingers stretched out too, her right leg crossed over her left, her body ready for the next question.

The Body Speaks: We Are All Stars

Earlier in the interview, Lerner asks Lispector a question about the moment she decided to pursue a career as a writer. She interrupts him and, shaking her head from side to side, tells him that she is not a professional. She clarifies that 'I only write when I want' and then looks at him straight on and takes a pause. She follows the pause with the statement that she is an amateur, and that she insists on being so and not being a professional. She ends her declaration by emphasizing that she does this 'in order to maintain my freedom'. An amateur is someone who engages in activity for pleasure, someone who is free from the responsibilities of paid labour; the Portuguese word for amateur is 'amador' or 'amadora' and incorporates the verb 'amar' or 'to love'. The 'amadora' is tied up in feeling, loving, taking pleasure freely, whereas the professional must be productive because there is a commitment, a contract, a deadline. Lispector does not want to be constrained by any of those professional requirements. Her insistence on being an amateur makes the title of the last novel she published during her lifetime, *A hora da estrela*, all the more interesting. What kind of star is she referring to? A star is somebody who is an expert and at the top of their professional field, or a celebrity, a luminary, as if predestined for fame because of an innate golden quality, in direct contrast to an amateur. The star is the best, the brightest, the most renowned and rewarded, whereas the amateur is off the official grid, unrecognized, invisible, uncompensated. Lispector's insistence on being an amateur is an additional invitation to consider her performance during the Lerner interview as aligned with the video art made by her female contemporaries as non-professional, or anti-professional, practitioners of film and television production.

Lispector's insistence on being an amateur to protect her freedom and her exploration of what it means to be a star in her final novel resonate with the zeitgeist of her time. Surely, she knew about *Jesus Christ Superstar*, the Broadway rock opera composed by Andrew Lloyd Webber with a libretto by Tim Rice, which was translated into Portuguese by Vinícius de Moraes. The Brazilian production opened in March 1972 in São Paulo's Teatro Aquarius where it played for over a year to full houses, and later opened in Rio de Janeiro's Teatro João Caetano for a season. There is also the Japanese writer, playwright, actor, and film director Yukio Mishima's 1960 novella *Star* that explores the burdens of celebrity and public life, which he wrote shortly after starring in the *yakuza* film *Afraid to Die* directed by Yasuzo Masumura. Lispector translated Mishima's play *Sotoba Komachi* (1956) with Tati de Moraes. These are two examples, directly in Lispector's orbit, of many works on the world cultural stage that engage with questions of celebrity, fame, notoriety, public life, and stardom. David Bowie's 1972 album *The Rise and Fall of Ziggy Stardust and the Spiders from Mars*, Barbara Streisand's 1968 Oscar-winning film debut *Funny Girl*, and George Lucas's *Star Wars: Episode IV — A New Hope*, a space-opera in medias res that premiered on 25 May 1977, also resonate.

Rodrigo S.M. says early on in *A hora da estrela*: 'Do not hope, then, for stars in what follows: nothing will sparkle'.[66] Macabéa dreams of becoming a film star, and at one point she tries to apply lipstick to look like Marilyn Monroe, but fails miserably and ends up staring at the grotesque 'figure in the mirror who in turn looked at her in fright'.[67] Macabéa tries to be the star and does not succeed, and yet Rodrigo predicts Macabéa's starry fate: 'certainly she would die one day as if earlier she had learned to play the role of the star by heart'.[68] To force stardom in life is to fail, but as life unfolds toward death every single person 'becomes a brilliant movie star, it is the instant of glory that belongs to each of us'.[69] The moments before her death are both physically gruelling and glorious: 'at this exact hour Macabéa feels a profound nausea in her stomach and almost vomited, she wanted to vomit what is not the body, vomit something luminous. A thousand-point star'.[70] In keeping with Rodrigo's prediction that nothing will sparkle in what follows, Macabéa is unable to vomit the luminous star from her body.

Unlike Macabéa, Virgínia does not seem to have aspirations, certainly not for stardom or celebrity of any kind. As a child she makes figures out of mud that can be star-like and human-like: 'Sometimes she made a small object with a shape that was almost starry but tired like a person'.[71] Virgínia's creative power — 'she could make what existed and what did not exist' — is in her hands from the beginning. The problem is that she does not know she has this power and nobody in her life — not Vicente, not her brother Daniel, not her father, not her friend Adriano, not any of her female friends or her sister or her mother — helps her to see it either. Virgínia, like Macabéa, has a star inside of her, but it remains forever unseen in the way she too remains largely invisible: 'nobody, nobody saw her — silence and solitude came to her from afar in a clear breath. [...] Only she herself would keep it like a violent point, a hot and white star at the centre of her body'.[72]

In many ways Macabéa has an improved fate compared to Virgínia's: she has a job as a typist and handles her own money, she has aspirations to be an actress, she envisions herself getting married, and she manages to stand up for herself in numerous situations, including when she calls her friend Glória ugly in response to Glória's initial insults. Sometimes Macabéa protects herself preventively, such as when she visits the doctor and says: 'I've heard it said that at the doctor's office you take off your clothes but I'm not removing a thing'.[73] Macabéa has a sense of agency, and she fights against abusive situations at least some of the time, whereas Virgínia seems to float along and receive everything that happens to her. But what Macabéa cannot avoid is the fate that eventually befalls everyone, death. If *A hora da estrela* is a somewhat more optimistic rewriting or translation of *O lustre*, the novel that gave Lispector the most pleasure to write, it is no less tragic. As Lispector says in her conversation with Lerner, her latest novel is about a girl from the Northeast of Brazil who lives in Rio de Janeiro and is so poor she only eats hotdogs; it's also the story of 'trampled innocence' and 'anonymous misery'.[74] The camera has Lispector in a close-up at this point in the interview, and when she says the words 'trampled' and 'anonymous' she looks directly at Lerner and toward the camera. Lerner begins to ask Lispector how she found a character like Macabéa in herself, and she cuts him off and clarifies that she too lived in Recife, that she lived and grew up in the Northeast. Virgínia is also a girl from the Northeast, Brejo Alto more specifically, and her name could have been Mary Magdalene or Sybil or Macabéa or Clarice.

★ ★ ★ ★ ★

Lispector once said the following about her early work as a journalist: 'I was a pioneer of female journalism in Brazil. At the time, I was the only woman working on the newspaper'.[75] Regarding her decision to pursue law school, she said: 'Everyone thought I would be a good lawyer because I was always concerned with attacking injustice'.[76] Lispector's pioneering spirit and her concern for injustice are clear in her Lerner interview, as are her attention to the performative power of the body and of silence. When she says, 'I don't know' or 'it's a secret', we can see that there is more to it than meets the ear or eye. By watching her interview over and over in preparation for my November 2017 performance lecture at Oxford, 'I began to feel my way through Lispector's fiction, *crônicas*, letters, and the traces of her life left behind [...] with a whole new sense [...] of ferociousness'[77] — and with a whole new sense of what I might be willing to say and how I too might attack injustice. As Lispector continues to speak from her tomb to this day, I believe she encourages us to do the same.

Works Cited

Aragão, Helena, 'A primeira vez de Clarice Lispector no teatro', *Brasil Memória das Artes* <http://portais.funarte.gov.br/brasilmemoriadasartes/acervo/foto-carlos/a-primeira-vez-de-clarice-lispector-no-teatro/> [accessed 14 December 2019]

Carvalho, Márcio Marconato, 'O ultimo encontro com Clarice', *Ângulo*, 121/122 (2010), 109–20

Edwards, Magdalena, 'Benjamin Moser and the Smallest Woman in the World', *Los Angeles Review of Books*, 16 August 2019, <https://lareviewofbooks.org/article/benjamin-moser-and-the-smallest-woman-in-the-world/> [accessed 15 December 2019]

Ferreira, Rony Márcio Cardoso, '"Traduzir pode correr o risco de não parar nunca": Clarice Lispector tradutora (um arquivo)', *Belas Infiéis*, 2.2 (2013), 175–204

Fitz, Earl, '"A pecadora queimada e os anjos harmoniosos": Clarice Lispector as Dramatist', *Luso-Brazilian Review*, 34.2 (1997), 25–39

Gomes, André Luís, *Clarice em cena: as relações entre Clarice Lispector e o teatro* (Brasília: Editora UNB, 2007)

Gotlib, Nádia Battella, *Clarice: uma vida que se conta* (São Paulo: Editora da Universidade e São Paulo, 2009)

Kushner, Rachel, 'Lipstick Traces: Clarice Lispector's Radiant Nothingness', *Music & Literature*, 4 (2013), 83–91

Lerner, Júlio, 'A última entrevista de Clarice Lispector', *Shalom*, 296.2 (1992), 62–69 <https://www.revistabula.com/503-a-ultima-entrevista-de-clarice-lispector/> [accessed 14 December 2019]

Librandi, Marília, *Writing by Ear: Clarice Lispector and the Aural Novel* (Toronto: University of Toronto Press, 2018)

'The Rise of Student Movements', in *Brazil: Five Centuries of Change*, Brown University, Center for Digital Scholarship <https://library.brown.edu/create/fivecenturiesofchange/chapters/chapter-7/student-movement/> [accessed 12 July 2020]

Lispector, Clarice, 'Mineirinho — um grama de radium', *Senhor*, 4.6 (June 1962), 16–19

—— *Perto do coração selvagem* (Rio de Janeiro: Rocco, 1998 [1944]); *Near to the Wild Heart*, trans. by Alison Entrekin (New York: New Directions, 2012)

—— *O lustre* (Rio de Janeiro: Rocco, 1999 [1946])

—— *A hora da estrela* (Rio de Janeiro: Rocco, 1999 [1977])

—— *A descoberta do mundo* (Rio de Janeiro: Rocco, 1999 [1984])

—— *Correspondências* (Rio de Janeiro: Rocco, 2002)

—— *Outros escritos*, ed. by Teresa Montero and Lícia Manzo (Rio de Janeiro: Rocco, 2005)

—— *Todos os contos* (Rio de Janeiro: Rocco, 2016)

—— *Todas as crônicas* (Rio de Janeiro: Rocco, 2018)

Lowe, Elizabeth, 'The Passion According to C.L.: Elizabeth Lowe Interviews Clarice Lispector,' *Review: Latin American Literature & Arts*, 24 (1979), 34–37

Montero, Teresa, *Eu sou uma pergunta: uma biografia de Clarice Lispector* (Rio de Janeiro: Rocco, 1999)

'Panorama com Clarice Lispector', *Panorama*, TV2 Cultura, 28 December 1977, <https://www.youtube.com/watch?v=ohHP1l2EVnU> [accessed 14 December 2019]

'Poesia & Prosa com Maria Bethania Episódio Clarice Lispector', online recording, YouTube, 3 August 2016, <https://www.youtube.com/watch?v=b5RuXB9kgi0> [accessed 12 July 2020]

ROSENBAUM, YUDITH, 'Ethics in Literature: Reading Clarice Lispector's 'Mineirinho', *Estudos avançados*, 24.69 (2010), 169–82

SHELLHORSE, ADAM JOSEPH, *Anti-Literature: The Politics and Limits of Representation in Modern Brazil and Argentina* (Pittsburgh, PA: University of Pittsburgh Press, 2017)

SHTROMBERG, ELENA, *Art Systems: Brazil & the 1970s* (Austin: University of Texas Press, 2016)

WILLIAMS, CLAIRE, 'Prefácio: Clarice 'entre-vistas', in Clarice Lispector, *Entrevistas* (Rio de Janeiro: Rocco, 2007), pp. 7–12

Notes to Chapter 21

1. All translations are mine unless otherwise noted.
2. 'Panorama com Clarice Lispector', *Panorama*, TV2 Cultura, 28 December 1977, <https://www.youtube.com/watch?v=ohHPIl2EVnU> [accessed 14 December 2019].
3. Nádia Battella Gotlib, *Clarice: uma vida que se conta* (São Paulo: Editora da Universidade de São Paulo, 2009), p. 573.
4. Ibid., p. 569.
5. Ibid., p. 564.
6. Teresa Montero, *Eu sou uma pergunta: uma biografia de Clarice Lispector* (Rio de Janeiro: Rocco, 1999), p. 291.
7. Elena Shtromberg, *Art Systems: Brazil & the 1970s* (Austin: University of Texas Press, 2016), pp. 97–102.
8. Ibid., p. 108.
9. Adam Joseph Shellhorse, *Anti-Literature: The Politics and Limits of Representation in Modern Brazil and Argentina* (Pittsburgh, PA: University of Pittsburgh Press, 2017), pp. 17, 42.
10. Gotlib, *Clarice: uma vida que se conta*, p. 254.
11. Julio Lerner, 'A última entrevista de Clarice Lispector', *Shalom*, 296.2 (1992), 62–69. Also published online in *Revista Bula* <https://www.revistabula.com/503-a-ultima-entrevista-de-clarice-lispector/> [accessed 14 December 2019]. I quote from the online version throughout this paragraph.
12. Ibid.
13. Claire Williams, 'Prefácio: Clarice 'entre-vistas', in Clarice Lispector, *Entrevistas* (Rio de Janeiro: Rocco, 2007), pp. 7–12 (pp. 7–8).
14. Williams, 'Prefácio: Clarice 'entre-vistas', p. 10.
15. Montero, *Eu sou uma pergunta*, p. 224.
16. Márcio Marconato Carvalho, 'O ultimo encontro com Clarice', *Ângulo*, 121/122 (2010), 109–20 (p. 120).
17. Rachel Kushner, 'Lipstick Traces: Clarice Lispector's Radiant Nothingness', *Music & Literature*, 4 (2013), 83–91 (p. 87).
18. Carvalho, 'O ultimo encontro com Clarice', p. 110.
19. Shtromberg, *Art Systems*, p. 122.
20. Ibid., pp. 108–09.
21. Ibid., p. 117.
22. Ibid.
23. Lerner, 'A última entrevista de Clarice Lispector'.
24. Gotlib, *Clarice: uma vida que se conta*, p. 571.
25. Carvalho, 'O ultimo encontro com Clarice', p. 120.
26. Shtromberg, *Art Systems*, p. 108.
27. Clarice Lispector, 'Mineirinho — um grama de radium', *Senhor*, 4.6 (June 1962), 16–19. <https://site.claricelispector.ims.com.br/en/2013/05/31/quem-foi-mineirinho-bastidores-de-uma-cronica/> [accessed 14 December 2019].

28. Gotlib, *Clarice: uma vida que se conta*, p. 570.
29. Yudith Rosenbaum, 'Ethics in Literature: Reading Clarice Lispector's "Mineirinho"', *Estudos avançados* 24.69 (2010), 169–82.
30. Clarice Lispector, 'Carta ao ministro da Educação', in *Todas as crônicas* (Rio de Janeiro: Rocco, 2018), pp. 77–78.
31. 'The Rise of Student Movements', in *Brazil : Five Centuries of Change*, Brown University, Center for Digital Scholarship <https://library.brown.edu/create/fivecenturiesofchange/chapters/chapter-7/student-movement/> [accessed 12 July 2020].
32. Ibid.
33. Clarice Lispector, *Todos os contos* (Rio de Janeiro: Rocco, 2016), p. 387.
34. Shtromberg, *Art Systems*, p. 122.
35. Clarice Lispector, *Near to the Wild Heart*, trans. by Alison Entrekin (New York: New Directions, 2012), p. 5.
36. Clarice Lispector, *O lustre* (Rio de Janeiro: Rocco, 1999), p. 218.
37. Clarice Lispector, *A hora da estrela* (Rio de Janeiro: Rocco, 1999), pp. 14, 16.
38. Ibid., p. 23.
39. Ibid., pp. 53–54.
40. Ibid., pp. 47–49; André Luís Gomes, *Clarice em cena: as relações entre Clarice Lispector e o teatro*, (Brasília: Editora UNB, 2007), pp. 158–59.
41. Rony Márcio Cardoso Ferreira, "Traduzir pode correr o risco de não parar nunca': Clarice Lispector tradutora (um arquivo)', *Belas Infiéis*, 2.2 (2013), 175–204.
42. Gomes, *Clarice em cena*, pp. 120–21.
43. Earl Fitz, 'A pecadora queimada e os anjos harmoniosos': Clarice Lispector as Dramatist', *Luso-Brazilian Review*, 34.2 (1997), 25–39 (p. 33).
44. Ibid., p. 33.
45. Helena Aragão, 'A primeira vez de Clarice Lispector no teatro', *Brasil Memória das Artes* <http://portais.funarte.gov.br/brasilmemoriadasartes/acervo/foto-carlos/a-primeira-vez-de-clarice-lispector-no-teatro/> [accessed 14 December 2019]
46. For details of the event, see 'Clarice na voz em drama De Bethânia', IMS, <https://ims.com.br/eventos/clarice-na-voz-em-drama-de-bethania/> [accessed 15 December 2019]
47. 'Poesia & Prosa com Maria Bethania Episódio Clarice Lispector', online recording, YouTube, 3 August 2016, <https://www.youtube.com/watch?v=b5RuXB9kgio> [accessed 12 July 2020].
48. Clarice Lispector, *Outros escritos* (Rio de Janeiro: Rocco, 2005), pp. 115–18, 115. This *crônica* was first published in Rio de Janeiro's *Revista Joia*.
49. Ibid., p. 116.
50. Ibid., p. 116.
51. Marília Librandi, *Writing by Ear: Clarice Lispector and the Aural Novel* (Toronto: University of Toronto Press, 2018), p. 19.
52. See Laís Botler's chapter in this volume.
53. Clarice Lispector, *Correspondências* (Rio de Janeiro: Editora Rocco, 2002), pp. 115–16.
54. Gomes, *Clarice em cena*, p. 23.
55. Lispector, *Correspondências*, p. 56.
56. Ibid., p. 60.
57. Ibid., p. 62.
58. Ibid.
59. Lispector, *A hora da estrela*, p. 22.
60. Lispector, *O lustre*, p. 144.
61. Lispector, *A hora da estrela*, p. 9.
62. Lispector, *Near to the Wild Heart*, p. 5.
63. 'Panorama com Clarice Lispector'
64. Lispector, *A hora da estrela*, p. 56.
65. Lispector, *O lustre*, p. 239.
66. Lispector, *A hora da estrela*, p. 16.
67. Ibid., p. 62.

68. Ibid., p. 29.
69. Ibid., p. 29.
70. Ibid., p. 85.
71. Lispector, *O lustre*, p. 45.
72. Ibid., p. 244.
73. Lispector, *A hora da estrela*, p. 68.
74. Lerner, 'A última entrevista de Clarice Lispector'.
75. Elizabeth Lowe, 'The Passion According to C.L.: Elizabeth Lowe Interviews Clarice Lispector', *Review: Latin American Literature & Arts*, 24 (1979), 34–37 (p. 37).
76. Ibid., p. 37.
77. Magdalena Edwards, 'Benjamin Moser and the Smallest Woman in the World', *Los Angeles Review of Books*, 16 August 2019, <https://lareviewofbooks.org/article/benjamin-moser-and-the-smallest-woman-in-the-world/> [accessed 15 December 2019].

CHAPTER 22

❖

Que(e)rying Femininities: Clarice Lispector's 'Correio Feminino' on TV Globo

Mariela Méndez

In 2013, to commemorate its fortieth year anniversary, the popular Brazilian Sunday newsmagazine programme 'Fantástico' aired 'Correio Feminino' [Ladies' Mail], a unique adaptation of the columns that Clarice Lispector crafted under the pseudonym Helen Palmer for the newspaper *Correio da Manhã* between 1959 and 1961. Blogger Mauricio Stycer praised the eight-episode series created by Luiz Fernando Carvalho as 'surpreendente e ousada' [surprising and daring]. It was indeed surprising, and daring, for a programme that usually favours 'hot' topics, and parades popular music icons like Shakira and Demi Lovato, to pick as one of its commemorative highlights the work of one of the most revered and hermetic Brazilian literary figures. Even though the tone of the series, in keeping with a newspaper column focused on so-called women's issues, was direct, colloquial and intimate (unlike Lispector's fiction), the choice made by 'Fantástico' was nonetheless unusual. Isaiana Carla Pereira dos Santos and Tobias Queiroz take this decision as a starting point for examining the reasons why the series received extremely low TV ratings and poor reviews. In their essay 'Correio Feminino e o Fantástico', they conclude that 'a série Correio Feminino não obteve o merecido prestígio porque o público não é condicionado a prestigiar esse tipo de programação' [the series Correio Feminino did not obtain the prestige that it deserved because the audience is not conditioned to value highly this type of programming].[1] The authors surmise that the typical audience of 'Fantástico' had neither the time for nor the interest in a cultural offering of this sort; conversely, those potentially interested would rather have had access to it through a medium other than television. The reasons outlined in the negative criticism that greeted the series pointed to the 'atemporalidade' [timelessness], '[o] ar ultrapassado' [the outdated appearance] of the series, an anachronism best exemplified by what critics viewed as a failure to address modern-day women, who in their view are, unlike the protagonists, 'mulheres independentes e resolvidas' [independent and resolute women].[2] This chapter sets out to dwell precisely upon the disjuncture between the apparent message(s) of

'Correio Feminino' and an underlying instability or uneasiness that may have gone unnoticed or possibly deterred prospective viewers.

At first sight, the series created by Carvalho offers us a glimpse into the lives of a female character at different stages of a life predicated by what Jack Halberstam calls the landmarks of a hetero-normative life: birth, marriage, reproduction, death. Upon closer examination, however, we catch glimpses of another subjacent, non-linear, non-straight temporal narrative that, following Halberstam, we can call *queer*. The theorist's examinations on *queer(ing)* time draw from Elizabeth Freeman's description of a chronobiological society, that is, one that rests, for its reproduction, on the pillars that sustain a chrono-normative life, namely, the landmark events above mentioned.[3] Even the objects displayed in the series invite interactions that help sustain chrono-normativity. And yet, interactions between characters and objects in the series veer off course, deviate, so to speak, from the straight line of heteronormativity. This act of going off-line is precisely what Sara Ahmed considers to be a *queering* of space and spatial configurations. I invoke these theories myself to *query* the series' apparent emphasis on hetero-reproductivity and, in so doing, I inscribe a *queer* reading that yields an interrogation of its sex and gender categories.

Lispector's column 'Correio Feminino: Feira de Utilidades' [Ladies' Mail: Home Goods Market], like other columns and sections of its type, was filled with recipes scripting the performance of an ideal of beauty, elegance, and moderation considered to be crucial for finding a good match or else making sure to keep it once found. By carefully and painstakingly drawing attention both to this performance and to the composition of the column itself as performance, Lispector's women's pages tested gender and sex categories, disturbing the hetero-normative ideology informing such a rigidly codified discursive space.[4] It came as no surprise that Luiz Fernando Carvalho decided to adapt the columns created for *Correio da Manhã*, since, particularly in the director's specials and series, as Eli Lee Carter points out, 'theatricality informs everything from the setting and space to the lighting and acting'.[5] Carvalho's staging of the columns succeeds in transposing the destabilizing uneasiness of the original columns and their que(e)ring of gender. This, alongside his well-known admiration and knowledge of Lispector's work, helps him succeed in transposing the destabilizing uneasiness of the original columns and their querying of gender and sex categories.[6] The starting point for my argument here is the tension underlying the hetero-reproductive ideology seemingly shaping the columns and, in particular, the Globo episodes.[7]

On a thematic level, half of the episodes evoke an ideal 'femininity' that was propagated in Brazil in the 1950s and 1960s through advertisements, shopping catalogues, beauty manuals, TV programmes, and even Hollywood films. Episode 1, 'Aulinhas de sedução' [Small Lessons in Seduction], Episode 2, 'Espelho mágico' [Magic Mirror], and Episode 5, 'Caprichos de mulher' [Women's Whims] summon the 'recipes' advanced by those discourses only to warn women against following them obediently. While the first episode insists that the secret to beauty lies in being oneself and developing self-confidence, and the second warns viewers against 'beleza de catálogo' [Catalogue Beauty], the fifth reminds them not to become slaves to fashion. The third episode, 'Ser mulher, ser moderna' [Being a Woman, Being Modern], administers advice on how women can best cope with the exhaustion and fatigue resulting from having entered the workforce in larger numbers. As a sort of counterpart to this episode, three other episodes focus on women's domestic selves. Episode 4, 'Receita de casamento' [A Recipe for Marriage], Episode 6, 'Ser mãe' [Being a Mother], and Episode 7, 'A fada do lar' [The Fairy in the House], as the titles make clear, unpack the secrets to building a happy home, as opposed to a house, and disallow at the same time the idealization of marriage and motherhood. The last episode, 'A mulher do futuro' [The Woman of the Future] presents viewers with flashbacks of key moments from the previous episodes as the voice-over asks them to embrace the future freely, with wide open arms, relying on their capacity for true happiness.

Written by Maria Camargo in collaboration with Carla Madeira, Carvalho's episodes each averaged seven to ten minutes in length with Helen Palmer embodied in the figure of model and actress Maria Fernanda Cândido. As viewers, we see Cândido only from behind, except at the very end of the series when she turns around to face us, always sitting on a revolving stool as she speaks her advice into a microphone, while we experience the voiceless staging of this advice through the performances of Alessandra Maestrini, a professional actress, and fashion models Cintia Dicker and Luíza Brunet. Dicker, Maestrini, and Brunet play a teenager, a young woman, and a mature woman, respectively, thus, together, compounding the implied viewer/reader addressed by Lispector's columns.

'Correio Feminino', like the columns where it originated, shares with genres like the soap opera and melodrama some sort of obsession with the idea of 'femininity' and with the figure of the housewife, an obsession that more often than not manifests itself in an attempt to create characters or delineate subject positions with whom an audience socially marked as feminine will likely identify. Carvalho's series is heavily reminiscent of soap operas, the genre that has gained him the most popularity, as it indulges in multiple close-ups of the characters' faces particularly during moments of intense emotional conflict oftentimes involving a love interest, namely, an actual or prospective husband. Close-ups can help build an intimate, personal connection between audience and characters, a phenomenon that feminist film theorist Jackie Stacey anatomized in her foundational work on cinematic identification with Hollywood stars of the 1940s and 1950s.[8] Throughout the interviews that Stacey carried out in her study, she discovered that the fragmentation of the female body in these Hollywood movies had an unexpected benefit largely overlooked within feminist film theory: spectators felt the stars they admired were friends and companions rather than distant unattainable models. Close-up shots did not just develop these 'heightened emotional connections between stars and spectators', but they also emphasized 'details of eyebrows, lashes, teeth' that spectators tried to emulate in their lives.[9] Significantly enough, the women's page set out to generate a similar identification as it fostered an intimate rapport between the author and the reader, 'a minha amiga e leitora' [my friend and reader] that Lispector would typically address as 'você' [you]. Close-ups of lashes, eyebrows, and hair were present in these spaces, including Clarice's, via drawings, photographs, or minutely detailed verbal descriptions. The emotional proximity between reader and columnist, supported by a prescriptive language, would, according to Tania Regina de Luca, harness the column's persuasive power.[10]

In using close-ups of the female characters' bodies, not only did Carvalho re-create the feature of the original columns just mentioned, he also hoped to facilitate a process of identification between characters and audience sustained in a strong emotional connection. As in the case of soap operas, emotions run high in the TV series, as the mute performance of the three actresses unavoidably overemphasizes sensations and affects transmitted and exacerbated through melodramatic body language. Carvalho's decisions in this respect are appropriate, since telenovelas had established themselves as one of the most popular TV genres in Brazil by the end of the 1960s with 'as donas de casa, como público-alvo' [housewives as the target audience], replacing in popularity their predecessors, 'fotonovelas', whose reading, 'como a de outras revistas femininas, ajudavam a integrar as mulheres na sociedade urbana, divulgando modos e modas a serem seguidos e copiados' [as in the case of other women's magazines, helped incorporate women into an urban society, disseminating manners and customs to be followed and copied].[11] Even though Carvalho's series borrows the telenovela's traditional over-dramatization of gestural and body language, the director resists the genre's extreme reliance on the spoken word, which helps explain both the mute performance of the actresses and the minimal appearance of language in the form of a handful of screens with intertitles interspersed throughout each episode.

The director's deep indebtedness to theatrical production is best described, in Carter's terms, as 'the construction of overtly antinatural and artificially hybrid fictional universes that emphasize theatrical staging and acting'.[12] Aware that Globo is one of the largest producers of telenovelas in the world, Carvalho takes it upon himself to make his mark in reinventing that genre. His artificial *mise en scène* oftentimes translates, in 'Correio Feminino', into an aesthetic akin to camp, bringing the visual construction of the narrative close to Spanish director Pedro Almodóvar's cult movies, which rely heavily on pop culture, melodrama, and glossy décor. Carvalho himself explains his predilection for glossy pop colours via an allusion to the visual aesthetic permeating the Brazilian press during the 1950s and 1960s, when both magazines and newspapers were undergoing profound transformations in production techniques, layout, typesetting, and graphic design under the marked influence of US models. He summarizes his own aesthetic in these terms:

> A linguagem do projeto, do ponto de vista estético, é uma homenagem às propagandas e aos ensaios de moda daquele período (anos 1950 e 1960). Nas revistas, encontrava-se página inteira em amarelo com a modelo vestida de vermelho, apoiada em carro azul e branco. Um minimalismo das cores e do não-cenário, muito característico do excelente design da publicidade da época. Na concepção, despojamos ao máximo os elementos cenográficos, centrando a dramaturgia nas cores e nos figurinos para que a voz se tornasse preponderante.

[The project's language, from an aesthetic point of view, pays homage to the advertisements and fashion photo shoots of that period (1950s and 1960s). You could find in magazines an entire yellow page with a fashion model dressed in red leaning against a blue and white car. A minimalism revealed in the colours and in the 'no setting', which was typical of the excellent design characterizing advertising at the time. In our conception of the series, we stripped all props, centring the dramaturgy on the colours and on the outfits so that voice would become dominant.][13]

Carvalho's 'camp aesthetic', his 'love of artifice and exaggeration',[14] is closely linked to dissatisfaction with naturalism 'which has become so ubiquitous that it has lost its communicative power'.[15] The Brazilian director's vision is in this sense once again reminiscent of Almodóvar, who understands his work not as mimetic reflection of reality but rather as stylized construction.[16] However, while Almodóvar's films treat viewers to profound dialogues, Carvalho's productions typically rely on other techniques for conveying characters' emotions, like exaggerated gestures and actions, anachronistic settings and costumes, and computer-generated images. Notwithstanding this difference, the end result remains the same, namely, a stylized portrayal that, in the case of Carvalho, points to a subversion of the telenovela genre.

Carvalho's highly aestheticized series for Rede Globo makes no attempt at a realistic representation; it does not hide its artificiality. While Dicker, Maestrini, and Brunet are the protagonists of soap-operaesque mini-stories that carry from one episode to another — lending the programme an air of verisimilitude — their actions, movements, and gestures unfold in brightly coloured open spaces where only a handful of relevant objects are scattered. Any semblance of a more or less realistic life narrative for each of the characters is disrupted in episode after episode of 'Correio Feminino', and this is reinforced particularly in 'Caprichos de mulher', where a photo shoot opens and later recurs throughout the episode. It starts with a close-up of studio lights and then immediately presents the viewer with the three women modelling stylish clothes from the 1950s and 1960s against a backdrop of the Rio de Janeiro's skyline [Fig. 22.1]. The series, like Lispector's columns, stages the construction of 'feminine' elegance and beauty, highlighting its artificiality and performative value. In doing so, 'Correio Feminino' also undermines the conventions of most women-centred narratives which, via a realistic representation, aim to foster a sense of proximity between the viewers' and characters' lives.

Both in this series and in the rest of his *oeuvre*, Carvalho defamiliarizes spaces 'so as to evoke an anachronistic time-space resembling 1960s pop art aesthetics'.[17] To this end, the director recycles objects from the decades that inspire him. This revival or revivification of antiquated objects is described by Eli Lee Carter as an 'aesthetically hybrid, anthropophagic model' that makes Carvalho an heir to Brazilian modernist aesthetics in the hands of artists like Oswald de Andrade, author of the famous *Manifesto Antropófago* (1928), where he argued for the development of a truly Brazilian artistic expression derived from the consumption and subsequent transformation of foreign cultural production.[18] The exaltation of technology as a salient feature of Brazil's *sociedade de consumo* [consumer society] is ubiquitous in the

Fig. 22.1. Scene from Episode 5 — 'Caprichos de mulher'.
Luis Fernando Carvalho.

programme created by Carvalho. At the very start of each episode, 'Helen Palmer' is wrapped up in a web of microphones, cables, and cameras, as various cameramen rush to get the episode started. Without this technology, no episode would be possible, but Carvalho's campy productions also include an overpowering presence of outdated objects in a 'no setting' which can be traced back to the inspiration he found in 1950s and 1960s advertising.

Each episode is populated with washing machines, stoves, refrigerators, and cars, among other things, technologies that, according to Carla Bassanezi, changed women's domestic lives during the period of economic developmentalism, urban growth, and industrialization that Juscelino Kubitschek's presidency (1956–61) launched.[19] This period witnessed the emergence of a strong, independent middle class financially capable of acquiring consumer goods like cars and domestic appliances meant to make women's lives easier. As Bassanezi explains:

> não foram só as máquinas que modificaram a repetitiva jornada do trabalho doméstico, aliviando seu fardo. A disponibilidade de produtos de limpeza industrializados poupava a dona de casa de ter que fabricá-los. Os utensílios de plástico substituíam os antigos, mais pesados e caros. Os tecidos sintéticos, mais 'leves e funcionais' que os de algodão, lã ou linho, facilitavam as tarefas de lavar e passar. [...] As roupas prontas vendidas em lojas e magazines concorriam com vantagens com as confeccionadas em casa, ainda que na máquina de costura.
>
> [it was not just machines that modified the repetitive work day, lightening its load. The availability of industrial cleaning products spared housewives the trouble of fabricating them. New plastic utensils replaced old ones, which were heavier and more expensive. Synthetic fabrics, 'lighter and more functional' than cotton, wool or linen ones, made easier the tasks of washing and ironing. [...] Ready-made clothes sold at stores and warehouses competed advantageously against those made at home, even with the aid of sewing machines.][20]

The powerful modernizing impulse traversing the country during the decades when Clarice created her columns was shaping 'a mulher como a grande consumidora, o público preferencial de toda a publicidade nos anos 60' [women as the greatest consumers, the target audience for all advertising in the '60s].[21] Interpellating readers/viewers socially marked as feminine as potential consumers has historically helped advance the reproduction of ideals of 'femininity' in the foundation of a hetero-reproductive ideology, and Brazil was no exception during the decades in question. The tone pervading these spaces frequently echoed that of advertising, solidifying the link between 'femininity' and consumption, or the 'feminization' of consumption. 'Não por acaso,' Tania Regina de Luca concludes in analysing the characteristics of the 'imprensa adjetivada de *feminina*', 'o tempo verbal mais frequente é o imperativo, configurando um discurso bastante próximo do publicitário' [It was not by chance that in the so-called feminine press the most frequent verbal tense was the imperative, configuring a type of discourse closely akin to that of advertising].[22] The association of beauty and consumerism was most prominent in the case of Lispector's column, which was sponsored by the cosmetics company Pond's. While the column itself did not include any ads, it was surrounded by them, as *Correio da Manhã* was one of the journals most sought after by a burgeoning advertising industry. A contract found among Lispector's papers informs us that 'Helen Palmer' agreed to persuade her reader subliminally, without mentioning specific names, to buy Pond's products.[23]

What is particularly relevant in the case of Carvalho's adaptation of Lispector's *Correio da Manhã* columns is how the perception of these older domestic technologies is renewed, intensified, and suspended through defamiliarization in an overtly artificial setting, and how this is closely associated with the staging of an unfamiliar relationship between objects and subjects. It is important to remember that the same Fordian mode of production characterizing consumer society during the years of Brazilian developmentalism informs the television industry's traditional output. As Carter rightly points out, nowhere is this more evident than in the case of telenovelas, where the process, 'refined and perfected by TV Globo', evokes 'an assembly line'.[24] Herein lies the appeal of these serialized narratives — themselves heirs to the *folhetim* — to television networks that 'explore[d] the most efficient ways to attract the largest possible audiences in exchange for revenues from the burgeoning advertising sector'.[25] Within consumer society, it is the usefulness, or profitability of an object, that matters. As if defying this logic that permeates all of mainstream television production, Carvalho's specials and series, including 'Correio Feminino', 'are fully set prior to airing', they involve a 'longer period of time for narrative preparation', but 'a shorter period of filming', and require 'larger budgets per episode'.[26] In a like manner, rather than appearing as instrumental or functional, to be consumed by the characters, the objects populating 'Correio Feminino' — cars, washing machines, radios, televisions, newspapers, among others — interrupt the visual narrative created by Carvalho, getting in the way of the performance of 'femininity'.

In the very first episode, 'Aulinha de sedução, it is, after all, the radio that gives out advice, not Helen Palmer, and we see the young woman glancing at it, smiling, responding to the advice offered by the machine with her body language. Right from the start, characters appear to be intra-acting with the objects around them, in the sense that Karen Barad gives to this dynamic.[27] 'All bodies,' claims Barad, 'not merely "human" bodies, come to matter through the world's iterative intra-activity — its performativity'.[28] Both the young woman and the radio in the scene in question actively engage with one another. Rather than being separate entities independent of their encounter, they both actualize their agency within the space-time of their encounter and entanglement. Objects in Carvalho's series constantly call attention to themselves as sources of action and, given that matter is, in Barad's words, 'always already an ongoing historicity',[29] they carry with them the marks of time; they bring along with them a life, a history, or histories, like the one(s) revealed by the accounts of Brazilian developmentalism already outlined.

In *Performing Objects and Theatrical Things*, a collection of essays aiming to rethink theatre and performance outside and against anthropocentric narratives, Marlis Schweitzer and Joanne Zerdy note: 'objects and things powerfully script, choreograph, direct, push, pull, and otherwise animate their human collaborators'.[30] During the fifth episode, 'Caprichos de mulher', which was devoted to fashion, the mature woman (played by Luíza Brunet) plays with big rolls of brightly coloured fabrics several times during the episode — touching them, smelling them, holding them close to her cheek, indulging in their materiality. As we see Brunet's character revelling in her entanglement with the fabrics — they literally enwrap her — we hear the voice of Cândido/Palmer announcing: 'decotes crescem ou minguam, saias sobem, saias descem, saias armam como abajures ou se estreitam como malha de ballerina [...] as fazendas brilham, tornam-se leves e alegres com flores e bordados ou ganham peso com cores obscuras' [necklines plunge or shorten, skirts go up, skirts go down, skirts get wider like lampshades or narrower like a dancer's leotard [...] fabrics shine, become lighter and cheerful with embroidered flowers or heavier with dark colours]. The 'tecidos sintéticos' that Bassanezi tells us flooded the market, and advertising, in the 1950s and 1960s, display in this episode their ability to become 'actants', to engage in intra-action, moving women to engage with them in return, prompting them to touch and smell them. The fabrics do not just dress Brunet's character; their sensuous qualities incite and excite her, demonstrating their capacity to make physical and emotional contact. Both the character and the fabrics perform their agency in/through/during intra-acting.

It is precisely through awakening the senses that several of the objects in the series display their status as 'actants' with the capacity to engage in intra-action. The evoked theatrical stage of 'Correio Feminino' is not unlike most productions by Carvalho, which, in Carter's words, 'invite[s] the audience to participate in an interpretive exercise for which the senses become the principal guide to understanding'.[31] As well as touching and feeling the fabrics, the viewer can also almost smell the 'cheiro de delícias no ar' [aroma of tasty treats in the air] when both the young and the mature woman present their families with pastries just out of the oven in Episode 7, 'A fada do lar', as if savouring these treats together with the characters on the screen, in an action evocative of that potentially provoked by the young woman devouring a whole box of chocolates in the second episode, 'Espelho mágico'. Similarly, one can hear the loud, intensified sound of typewriters whose image is also multiplied in the third episode, 'Ser mulher, ser moderna'. The typewriter in this episode lies on the lap of the young woman, a clear allusion to Lispector herself, who favoured that arrangement for typing her fiction. It is a well-known fact that Clarice had a life-long amorous relationship with her typewriters, 'as if they were something like a series of marriages', as Marília Librandi points out.[32] In several of Lispector's chronicles, typewriters even share with the writer the responsibility of having created the fiction that made her famous.

The entanglements of humans and non-humans throughout Carvalho's series defy the normative uses of objects either as just props in a 'theatrical' televised production or as things to be consumed and utilized. Stacy Alaimo's notion of 'trans-corporeality' can shape in this sense our understanding of the three main characters under the light of 'a new materialist and posthumanist sense of the human as perpetually interconnected with the flows of substances and the agencies of environments'.[33] 'Allowing a space-time for unexpected material intra-actions', Alaimo announces, offers opportunities for the more-than-human world to act,[34] and this intra-action unfolds outside an economy of causality and profit meant to yield measurable results. During the years of Brazilian developmentalism, even leisure was intimately tied to consumer society, and was seen as a benefit derived from time saved, which was in turn a direct product of 'a utilização de máquinas cada vez mais aperfeiçoadas e a racionalização do trabalho' [the utilization of ever improved machines and the rationalization of work].[35] Time saved meant larger gains and was therefore understood as an investment, as illustrated in the 1950s and 1960s by President Juscelino Kubitschek's famous campaign promise to facilitate fifty years' worth of progress in Brazil in just five years, or by 'produtos de beleza [que] garantiam "cinco horas de beleza [...] em 30 segundos"' [beauty products that guaranteed 'five hours of beauty [...] in just 30 seconds'].[36] Such a perception of time as an investment, as 'um bem valioso, uma mercadoria a ser vendida, adquirida, consumida' [a valuable product, a merchandise to be sold, acquired, consumed],[37] as something well utilized, resonates with the 'aesthetic of utility' permeating the press targeting consumers socially constructed as female. The logic of this idea of usefulness, practicality, efficiency definitely lies behind the original intent of the column that Lispector was invited to write, itself called 'Feira de utilidades' [Home Goods Market], a logic supported by the sponsorship of Pond's described earlier.

On the other hand, what we perceive in the TV series is a shift away from the 'usefulness' attached to objects. The characters in Globo's 'Correio Feminino' do not always use time 'efficiently'; we sometimes see them lost in thought, eating candy while listening to Palmer's advice, perusing their images in front of the mirror, despite the columnist's advice in Episode 4, 'Receita de casamento', that 'o ócio inspira os pensamentos mais desanimadores' [leisure inspires the most disheartening thoughts]. We do not always see them 'using' objects in a utilitarian sense, or even shopping, the preferred use for their time as the perfect consumers; they defy the logic of consumption. The consumer society conjured by Carvalho's homage to fashion ads of the 1950s and 1960s is also a 'chronobiological society', as Elizabeth Freeman describes it, where 'the state and other institutions, including

FIG. 22.2: Image featured on the DVD cover of *Correio Feminino*.
Luiz Fernando Carvalho.

representational apparatuses, link properly temporalized bodies to narratives of movement and change'.[38] These narratives, Freeman explains, are 'teleological schemes of events or strategies for living such as marriage, accumulation of health and wealth for the future, reproduction, childrearing, and death and its attendant rituals'.[39] In turn, these are all socioeconomically productive moments that are rendered necessary for the maintenance and reproduction (pun intended) of a hetero-normative ideology. They are also the moments that, within this ideology, determine 'what it means to have a life at all', to borrow Freeman's words.[40] The time that shapes a 'chronobiological society' is therefore one 'used to organize individual human bodies toward maximum productivity', a use of time Freeman refers to as '*chrononormativity*'.[41] Conversely, time in the series that occupies us here is not used productively, as we have just seen. Instead, time is *queered*; it is stalled and in turn stalls the characters' progression along key socioeconomically productive moments.

What is more, despite what might seem at first an overarching narrative oriented towards marriage and childbearing in each character's life, the episodes actually go so far as to stall linear, straight time, the time marked by the paradigmatic landmarks of birth, marriage, reproduction, and death.[42] In fact, this stalling of time recalls the image chosen, significantly, for the cover of the DVD release of the series [Fig. 22.2]. Multiple screens abound in the series, not only conjuring a pop art aesthetics, but also reinforcing simultaneity instead of highlighting linearity. The sequence ending in marriage is broken up, halted, and therefore defamiliarized, sometimes even thrown out of joint, as the wedding scenes appear halfway throughout the series, in Episode 4, 'Receita do casamento', and we then go backwards and forwards in relation to it in the following episodes. 'To make things queer', Ahmed states, 'is certainly to disturb the order of things',[43] and this entails disturbing times, spaces, and directions that are hetero-normative, that buttress 'chrononormativity'. In having domestic objects 'intra-act' rather than interact with humans, in placing them outside a logic of consumption and remuneration, the series disturbs chrononormativity and straight time and points 'toward different worlds — even if this "point" does not make such worlds within reach'.[44] These worlds, according to Ahmed, are in the background, behind us, and behind the straight line in front of us that orients us to certain objects within reach and dictates our engagement with them.

The series' staging of a queer, unfamiliar relationship between objects and subjects disrupts the reproduction and transmission of certain values through what Halberstam calls 'generational time within which values, wealth, goods, and morals are passed through family ties from one generation to the next.'[45] As the frame of human/non-human relations is queered by the trans-corporeal space-time informing the series, the narrative of evolution and progress shaping the whole developmentalist project falls apart, and, with it, the hetero-reproductive ideology underlying it. In the very first episode, the teenager fails to wear perfume the right way, the young woman spills a milkshake all over her dress on her first date, the mature woman loses her composure while washing clothes and therefore fails to appear at her best when welcoming home her husband. Still, their failure succeeds, as Halberstam would have it, in enacting a rupture in a narrative of growth, evolution, progress, and development geared towards a hetero-reproductive future. After all, as Ahmed concludes, 'a queer politics does involve a commitment to a certain way of inhabiting the world, even if it is not "grounded" in a commitment to deviation'.[46] For Ahmed, not following these conventions equates disorientation, and disorientation makes things oblique, out of line, bringing certain objects and worlds closer than they would be within straight ways of orientating the body. In the end, when we finally see Cândido's face, in the last episode, 'Mulher do futuro', we do not see finality or resolution, as in a soap opera, but openness, a glimpse into queer futurity.[47] The tensions underlying the hetero-reproductive ideology seemingly shaping both the Globo episodes and the original columns have unsettled the reproduction of dominant patriarchal culture by que(e)rying the sign 'woman'. This might be the reason why the series was reportedly a failure, or was it?

Works Cited

AHMED, SARA, *Queer Phenomenology: Orientations, Objects, Others* (Durham, NC: Duke University Press, 2006)

ALAIMO, STACY, *Exposed: Environmental Politics and Pleasures in Posthuman Times* (Minneapolis: University of Minnesota Press, 2016)

—— 'Trans-corporeal Feminisms and the Ethical Space of Nature', in *Material Feminisms*, ed. by Stacy Alaimo and Susan Hekman (Bloomington: Indiana University Press, 2008), pp. 237–64

BARAD, KAREN, 'Posthumanist Performativity: Toward an Understanding of How Matter Comes to Matter', in *Material Feminisms*, ed. by Stacy Alaimo and Susan Hekman (Bloomington: Indiana University Press, 2008), pp. 120–54

BASSANEZI, CARLA, 'Mulheres dos anos dourados', in *História das mulheres no Brasil*, ed. by Mary del Priore (São Paulo: Contexto, 1997), pp. 469–512

CARTER, ELI LEE, *Reimagining Brazilian Television: Luiz Fernando Carvalho's Contemporary Vision* (Pittsburgh, PA: University of Pittsburgh Press, 2018)

CARVALHO, LUIZ FERNANDO, *Helen Palmer em Correio Feminino da obra de Clarice Lispector*, dir. by Luiz Fernando Carvalho (Sonopress: 2013–2014) [on DVD]
—— 'Correio Feminino', <http://luizfernandocarvalho.com/projeto/correio-feminino/> [accessed 7 December 2018]
FIGUEIREDO, ANNA CRISTINA CAMARGO MORAES, *'Liberdade é uma calça velha, azul e desbotada:' Publicidade, cultura de consumo e comportamento político no Brasil (1954–1964)* (São Paulo: Hucitec, 1998)
FREEMAN, ELIZABETH, *Time Binds: Queer Temporalities, Queer Histories* (Durham, NC: Duke University Press, 2010)
HALBERSTAM, JACK, *In a Queer Time and Place* (New York: New York University Press, 2005)
LIBRANDI, MARÍLIA, *Writing by Ear: Clarice Lispector and the Aural Novel* (Toronto: University of Toronto Press, 2018)
LUCA, TANIA REGINA DE. 2013. 'Mulher em revista', in *Nova história das mulheres no Brasil*, ed. by Carla Bassanezi Pinsky and Joana Maria Pedro (São Paulo: Contexto, 2013), pp. 447–68
MIGUEL, RAQUEL DE BARROS, and CARMEN RIAL, 'Programa de mulher', in *Nova história das mulheres no Brasil*, ed. by Carla Bassanezi Pinsky and Joana Maria Pedro (São Paulo: Contexto, 2013), pp. 148–68
MUÑOZ, JOSÉ ESTEBAN, *Cruising Utopia: The Then and There of Queer Futurity* (New York: New York University Press, 2009)
PINSKY, CARLA BASSANEZI, 'A era dos modelos rígidos', in *Nova história das mulheres no Brasil*, ed. by Carla Bassanezi Pinsky and Joana Maria Pedro (São Paulo: Contexto, 2013), pp. 447–68
SANTOS, ISAIANA CARLA PEREIRA DOS, and TOBIAS QUEIROZ, 'Correio Femenino e o Fantástico: quando uma adaptação não se adapta a um programa generalista' <https://portalintercom.org.br/anais/nordeste2014/resumos/R42-0884-1.pdf> [accessed 10 August 2021]
STACEY, JACKIE, *Star Gazing: Hollywood Cinema and Female Spectatorship* (New York: Routledge, 1994)
SCHWEITZER, MARLIS, and JOANNE ZERDY, 'Introduction: Object Lessons', in *Performing Objects and Theatrical Things*, ed. by Marlis Schweitzer and Joanne Zerdy (New York: Palgrave, 2014), pp. 1–17
SONTAG, SUSAN, 'Notes on Camp' [1966], in *The Cult Film Reader*, ed. by Ernest Mathijs and Xavier Mendik (Maidenhead and New York: Open University Press, 2008), pp. 41–52
STYCER, MAURICIO, 'Novo quadro de "Fantástico" apresenta uma Clarice pouco conhecida', *UOL*, (27 October 2013) <https://mauriciostycer.blogosfera.uol.com.br/2013/10/27/novo-quadro-do-fantastico-apresenta-uma-clarice-lispector-pouco-conhecida/> [accessed 29 November 2018]

Notes to Chapter 22

1. Isaiana Carla Pereira dos Santos and Tobias Queiroz, 'Correio Femenino e o Fantástico: quando uma adaptação não se adapta a um programa generalista' <https://portalintercom.org.br/anais/nordeste2014/resumos/R42-0884-1.pdf> [accessed 10 August 2021].
2. Santos and Queiroz, 'Correio Femenino e o Fantástico', n.pag.
3. See Elizabeth Freeman, *Time Binds: Queer Temporalities, Queer Histories* (Durham, NC: Duke University Press, 2010).
4. This is a conclusion that I have elaborated upon elsewhere by substantively examining how Lispector's columns in both *Correio da Manhã* and *Diário da Noite* exacerbate the donning and acting out of all the accessories, attributes, accoutrements, and gestures associated with what is culturally constructed as 'feminine'.

5. Eli Lee Carter, *Reimagining Brazilian Television: Luiz Fernando Carvalho's Contemporary Vision* (Pittsburgh, PA: University of Pittsburgh Press, 2018), p. 75.
6. Carvalho's admiration and knowledge of Lispector's work is well known. His latest achievement has been the adaptation for the cinema of Lispector's signature novel *A paixão segundo G.H.* (1964), with Maria Fernanda Cândido in the leading role, launched in 2020. The director is already entertaining a second project called 'Objetos perdidos', where the main character will struggle with the same perturbation assailing Carvalho: adapting Clarice. See Guilherme Genestretti, 'Após "Lavoura Arcaica," Luiz Fernando Carvalho adapta obra de Clarice Lispector', *Folha de São Paulo*, 28 November 2018, <https://www1.folha.uol.com.br/ilustrada/2018/11/apos-lavoura-arcaica-luiz-fernando-carvalho-adapta-obra-de-clarice.shtml?fbclid=IwAR3z29XgpiKi5mqv-vN-OlvragkFpV7WBGEtIia01-klZNEMd4R2n5Rn6WI> [accessed 11 November 2019].
7. It is not within the purview of this essay to examine the columns, both because this analysis has been extensively carried out elsewhere and for lack of space. See Mariela Méndez, *Crónicas travestis: el periodismo transgresor de Alfonsina Storni, Clarice Lispector y María Moreno* (Rosario, Argentina: Beatriz Viterbo, 2017).
8. Jackie Stacey, *Star Gazing: Hollywood Cinema and Female Spectatorship* (New York: Routledge, 1994).
9. Stacey, *Star Gazing*, p. 210.
10. Tania Regina de Luca, 'Mulher em revista', in *Nova história das mulheres no Brasil*, ed. by Carla Bassanezi Pinsky and Joana M. Pedro (São Paulo: Contexto, 2013), pp. 447–68 (p. 448).
11. Raquel de Barros Miguel and Carmen Rial, 'Programa de mulher', in, *Nova história das mulheres no Brasil*, ed. by Pinsky and Pedro, pp. 148–68 (p. 152).
12. Carter, *Reimagining Brazilian Television*, pp. 92–93.
13. Luiz Carvalho, 'Correio Feminino', <http://luizfernandocarvalho.com/projeto/correio-feminino/> [accessed 13 August 2021].
14. Susan Sontag, 'Notes on Camp', in *The Cult Film Reader*, ed. by Ernest Mathijs and Xavier Mendik (London: Open University Press, 1964), pp. 41–52 (p. 42).
15. Carter, *Reimagining Brazilian Television*, p. 48.
16. See Alejandro Yarza, 'Iconografía religiosa y estética camp en ¡Átame! de Pedro Almodóvar', *Revista Canadiense de Estudios Hispánicos*, 22.1 (1997), 109–24.
17. Carter, *Reimagining Brazilian Television*, p. 29.
18. Ibid., p. 136.
19. Bassanezi, 'Mulheres dos anos dourados', in *História das mulheres no Brasil*, ed. by Mary del Priore (São Paulo: Contexto, 1997), pp. 469–512 (p. 500).
20. Carla Bassanezi, 'Mulheres dos anos dourados', p. 500.
21. Figueiredo, *'Liberdade é uma calça velha, azul e desbotada': publicidade, cultura de consumo e comportamento político no Brasil (1954–1964)* (São Paulo: Hucitec, 1998), p. 114.
22. De Luca, 'Mulher em revista', p. 448.
23. There are many instances where 'Helen Palmer' describes the benefits of a particular type of cream without saying its name, but it would be common knowledge to readers that it was one of Pond's many creams, such as, Creme Vitamina C, as Aparecida Nunes points out in her study of the women's pages. Aparecida Maria Nunes, *Clarice Lispector jornalista: páginas femininas e outras páginas* (São Paulo: Editora Senac, 2006), pp. 205–13.
24. Carter, *Reimagining Brazilian Television*, p. 47.
25. Ibid., p. 69.
26. Ibid., p. 71.
27. Karen Barad, 'Posthumanist Performativity: Toward an Understanding of How Matter Comes to Matter', in *Material Feminisms*, ed. by Stacy Alaimo and Susan Hekman (Bloomington: Indiana University Press, 2008), pp. 120–54 (p. 133).
28. Ibid., p. 146.
29. Ibid., p. 139.
30. Marlis Schweitzer and Joanne Zerdy, 'Introduction: Object Lessons', in *Performing Objects and Theatrical Things* (New York: Palgrave, 2014), p. 6.
31. Carter, *Reimagining Brazilian Television*, pp. 74–75.

32. Marília Librandi, *Writing by Ear: Clarice Lispector and the Aural Novel* (Toronto: University of Toronto Press, 2018), p. 117.
33. Stacy Alaimo, *Exposed: Environmental Politics and Pleasures in Posthuman Times* (Minneapolis: University of Minnesota Press, 2016), p. 112.
34. Stacy Alaimo, 'Trans-corporeal Feminisms and the Ethical Space of Nature', in *Material Feminisms*, ed. by Alaimo and Hekman, pp. 237–64 (p. 251).
35. Figueiredo, *'Liberdade é uma calça velha, azul e desbotada'*, p. 83.
36. Ibid.
37. Ibid., p. 84.
38. Freeman, *Time Binds*, p. 4.
39. Ibid.
40. Ibid., p. 5.
41. Ibid., p. 3. Italics in original.
42. See Jack Halberstam, *In a Queer Time and Place* (New York: New York University Press, 2005), p. 2.
43. Sara Ahmed, *Queer Phenomenology: Orientations, Objects, Others* (Durham, NC: Duke University Press, 2006), p. 161.
44. Ibid., p. 176.
45. Halberstam, *In a Queer Time and Place*, p. 4.
46. Ahmed, *Queer Phenomenology*, p. 177.
47. Defined by José Esteban Muñoz as 'a potential for a then and there that can be glimpsed in the here and now and disrupt straight time'; *Cruising Utopia: The Then and There of Queer Futurity* (New York: New York University Press, 2009), p. 32.

CHAPTER 23

Mutatis Mutandis: Communicating Absence

Sara André da Costa

Opening Credits

The relationship between literature and cinema has proved to be problematic, with terms such as *infidelity*, *betrayal* and *distortion* still featuring commonly in the criticism of screen versions of literary texts.[1] Nevertheless, critical developments over the last decades have actively contributed to demystifying literature's higher artistic status when compared to that of cinema. Robert Stam's work was precursor in new approaches that started questioning not only the multicultural and intertextual nature of the cinematographic image but also addressing the specificity of film itself as well as 'the migratory, crossover elements shared between film and other media'.[2] Even though the question of faithfulness might play a part in our subjective perspective of what a specific adaptation should capture as the fundamental narrative, thematic, and aesthetic features of its literary source, fidelity should not be considered as the most significant methodological criterion when approaching this discussion.[3] In this regard, the semiotic approach developed in the 1970s by Christian Metz, who is considered one of the first cinema theorists of filmic semiotics, acted as a reinforcement to the idea of film as a complex object, an idea that inspired a great variety of academic reflexions,[4] and led to a more comprehensive approach to the film adaptation processes, not in terms of 'fidelity' and 'faithfulness' but rather using, in Robert Stam's words,

> a rich constellation of terms and tropes — translation, actualization, reading, critique, dialogization, cannibalization, transmutation, transfiguration, incarnation, transmogrification, transcoding, performance, signifying, rewriting, detournement — all of which shed light on a different dimension of adaptation.[5]

Metz's work attracted the attention of film theorists like Stam, Linda Hutcheon,[6] and Thomas Leitch,[7] and contributed to the development of a multidisciplinary method which combined psychology, sociology, anthropology, linguistics, philosophy, and aesthetics so as to study film simultaneously as an artistic product, a social phenomenon, and a political object, drawing from the perspective that 'anything [...] could be constructed as a system of signs organized according to cultural codes or signifying processes'.[8] Stam's first reflexions on cinema took as a starting point the question of its linguistic nature — 'is cinema a language system (*langue*) or an artistic language (*langage*)?'[9] — and constituted a ground-breaking contribution to film theory, bringing concepts such as cinematographic writing, language of cinema, and cine-semiotics into film studies. By addressing film as an 'original creation' which expresses itself through a 'proper *writing*, which incarnates itself in each director in the form of a *style*',[10] Metz was one of the first to suggest the existence of a dynamic relationship between meaning and significance, whereby cinematographic language is condemned to disseminate the ambiguities caused by the clash between reality and its filmic image. It is through its imprecise nature that both cinematographic and poetic languages are brought closer together as film 'operates with the image of the objects, not with the objects themselves', revealing a 'fragment of quasi-reality to make it the element of a discourse'. In this sense, according to Metz, the surrounding worldly segments of either written or spoken language will be the ones which, organized and restructured, will produce an utterance.[11]

In the same vein, Pier Paolo Pasolini's texts from *Heretical Empiricism*, and the chapter 'The "Cinema of Poetry"' in particular, contributed in great measure towards a discursive approach of cinematographic image as units that incorporate an independent meaning, establishing a parallel between poetry and cinema in the sense that both separately constitute basic linguistic systems.[12] In this manifesto, presented in 1965 at the first *Mostra Internazionale del Nuovo Cinema de Pesaro*, Pasolini promoted the idea that although 'people communicate with words, not with images; [and] therefore, a specific language of images would seem to be a pure and artificial abstraction',[13] cinema does communicate as well. It communicates by a distinctive language — the language of cinema — a specific type of communication based on a system of visual signs that mediates the relations between the surrounding reality, on the one hand, and cinematic image, on the other. Pasolini's proposition is sustained by the idea that cinema is ruled by a linguistic system, in parallel to the basic linguistic system constituted by words (*lin-signs*). It is a system, however, which produces a different type of utterance. In his view, the linguistic system that rules cinema is a system of mimic signs (*im-signs*) and encompasses other forms of non-verbal language, such as 'the faces of people who pass by, their gestures, their signs, their actions, their silences, their expressions, their arguments, their collective reactions'. It communicates 'by means of significant images', even if

> the visual communication which is the basis of film language is [...] extremely crude, almost animal-like. As with gestures and brute reality, so dreams and processes of our memory are almost pre-human events, or on the border of what is human.[14]

In this scenario, images emerge as minimum units of a non-grammatical nature: 'they are pregrammatical and even premorphological',[15] for they are a result of the communication with ourselves and also between ourselves and a collective environment that produces, as poet Manuel Gusmão observes, 'um cinema metido na cabeça' [a cinema inside our heads],[16] or what Pasolini's described as 'a world of memory and of dreams'.[17] Therefore, a new *langue* (in the Saussurean sense) emerges, structured by a semiotic sequence of a *sign* that leads to a *cinematographic sign* which produces a specific *meaning*. Moreover, the filmic signs reflect a significant level of subjectivity, the director's editing process intensifies the metaphoric character of the cinematographic lexicon in the sense that

> [h]e chooses a series of objects, or things, or landscapes, or persons as syntagmas (signs of a symbolic language) which, while they have a grammatical history invented in that moment [...] do, however, have already lengthy and intense pregrammatical history.[18]

Cinema can therefore be regarded as a new instance of poetic language and approaching the screenplay can make this parallel more obvious. The screenplay demands the intervention of a reader who will lend to its text 'a "visual" completeness which it does not have, but at which it hints'.[19] Following this, and as Pasolini suggests when he writes about a '*structure that wants to be another structure*', the reader, in completing the meaning of the screenplay, contributes to a semantic expansion of the text in different terms to the reader of the literary text because it gives birth to images through the coordination of *kinemes* (*im-signs*), which in film language is the sign par excellence and through which, again, a new *langue* is presented. However, this procedure is not a typical selection of ideas because the filmmaker 'can never collect abstract terms' and '[t]he linguistic or grammatical world of the filmmaker is composed of images, and images are always concrete, never abstract'.[20]

Words, such as those present in a literary text, are already collected and available in dictionaries; they are, therefore, accepted by communities of languages as establishing linguistic relations between specific significants and significations. On the contrary, there is no dictionary of images which is previously available and ready to use, and the process of filmmaking would, consequently, generate an 'infinite dictionary' as 'the filmmaker [...] has infinite possibilities'.[21] This specific feature will, in this sense, highlight the difference between the literary writing and the cinematographic writing, even if (by their basic nature) they share, in Pasolini's words, ' "a will of the form to become another" above and beyond the form; that is, it captures "the form in movement" '.[22]

Pasolini's formulation 'the form in movement' proves useful for addressing the filmmaking strategies Suzana Amaral (1932–2020) adopted in her film *A hora da estrela* [*The Hour of the Star*] (1985), as it departs from a literary text — the novella of the same name by Clarice Lispector (1977) — towards a distinct artistic form. Her filmmaking process always follows the same route and, as Amaral has clarified in different interviews, in the first stage, the book is carefully read and analysed by her, in order to reach the subtext, followed by the selection of the most important facts narrated. Both levels will contribute to what the director considers to be her creative process, a more complex process than mere adaptation, which embraces the recreation of the story through a transmutable or trans-creative process that leads the literary work into a world of images, where, to some extent, as Linda Hutcheon puts it, '[t]he form changes [...] [but] the content persists'.[23] Hutcheon elaborates this definition of adaptation as follows:

> There are manifestly many different possible intentions behind the act of adaptation [...]. According to its dictionary meaning, 'to adapt' is to adjust, to alter, to make suitable. This can be done in any number of ways. [...] First, seen as a *formal entity or product*, an adaptation is an announced and extensive transposition of a particular work or works. [...] Second, as *a process of creation*, the act of adaptation always involves both (re-) interpretation and then (re-) creation.[24]

In the particular case of Amaral's *The Hour of the Star*, and taking into consideration that the novella is staged in three different narrative layers where the voice of Rodrigo S.M. is crucially important, what stands out in the process of inter-semiotic translation carried out by Amaral is the absence of the metalinguistic traces which are so abundantly present throughout Clarice's text. This absence can be regarded as, on the one hand, the most cautious transition from text to film, taking into consideration the difficulty in transposing Rodrigo S.M.'s complex and metalinguistic voice into the screen. On the other hand, the choice to exclude the narrator's presence in the film can be seen as an element that compromises the integrity of the Claricean universe from *The Hour of the Star*.

Even if one accepts at face value that the film adaptation process is that of a metamorphosis, whereby the director takes a complex literary text and recreates it, the question still remains: how, then, can the heterogeneity and the intricacy of this particular text survive the excision of something that appears to be essential, specifically, Rodrigo S.M.'s voice? By way of an answer, I argue in what follows that, in the film, the narrator conveys the impression of being assimilated by the only narrative that inspires the director: Macabéa's 'delicate and vague existence'.[25]

Negative Imprint: The Voice Underneath

In Clarice Lispector's novella the reader is introduced to three coexisting fictional realities: 1) the story of Macabéa (played in the film by Marcélia Cartaxo), a girl from the Brazilian Northeast, a typist and virgin who likes *Coca-Cola* and attracts the attention of a narrator on the streets of Rio de Janeiro; 2) the story of the narrator himself, Rodrigo S.M., who imposes his peculiar presence as a narrative voice while telling 'the lame adventures of a girl in a city that's entirely against her',[26] thereby transposing his own life onto the life of this character; and 3) the story of the writing process, telling 'the story of the story'[27] and regularly addressing the reader via an intense metalinguistic process which delays and sometimes interrupts the narration:

> Forgive me but I'm going to keep talking about me who am unknown to myself, and as I write I'm a bit surprised because I discovered I have a destiny. Who hasn't ever wondered: am I a monster or is this what it means to be a person?[28]

Simultaneously, Rodrigo S.M. searches for answers through his writing, and, in doing so, he projects himself into the text. Through an overtly declared 'false free will', he determines that the story 'will have around seven characters and [he is] obviously one of the more important',²⁹ and identifies also himself with his own creation, Macabéa. While each of the three coexisting fictional realities retain their distinctiveness, the uniqueness of an intradiegetic narrative voice which constantly interferes with its own process of storytelling entices the critic to focus on the strategies judiciously used in Amaral's film itself to reduce the distance between word and image in order to be *faithful* to Lispector's text, as will be shown later in this chapter.

In this sense, if the presence of the narrator throughout the book is clearly noticeable on three different levels, the last two levels (self-projection and self-identification) remain invisible in Amaral's film, which presents only his version of Macabéa's story. Nevertheless, when Rodrigo S.M.'s character is transcoded in the cinematographic narrative this process does not bring about his disappearance, and, in this chapter, we will try to tease out the traces of his projection and identification within both the narrative and the metalinguistic fields. While seemingly neglecting the metalinguistic nature of Lispector's text, Amaral's film evokes the unspoilt essence of Macabéa by pursuing, to some extent, Rodrigo S.M.'s narrative and allowing it to inhabit the cinematographic discourse in a purposefully subdued but no less determining fashion. In the cinematographic (re)telling of Macabéa's life story, the search for the poetical universe of Clarice Lispector's text relies largely on exploring the poetical devices of cinema (in Pasolinian terms). For that matter, the relationship between text and image established by Amaral are interspersed throughout the film, and one of the director's most aptly used techniques to bring together text and image is the use of close-ups. This technique will constitute the means through which the creative dialogue between word and image gains visibility at moments when the metalinguistic nature that characterizes the literary text would seem to seriously challenge the limitations of the cinematic medium. Further, Amaral's employment of this technique enables the screening of what, from her perspective, is essential and inherent to the literary work and becomes a privileged strategy when depicting crucial moments in Macabéa's story, revealing her personal traits and feelings, as we are about to discover.

At the start of the film, following the slow, punctuated sound of typewriter keys being pressed and led/guided by a travelling shot across a dark and busy warehouse, the viewer sees Macabéa struggling with her typewriter as she sniffs and wipes her nose on the collar of her blouse. During this sequence, the viewer is introduced to a sad and inept girl who neglects all acceptable social norms, a specific characteristic that Rodrigo S.M. also identifies in his first impressions of Macabéa. As soon as the narrator starts to focus on the construction of this character, he immediately sums up her attributes in a very concise and crude manner: 'she made too many typing mistakes, besides invariably dirtying the pages'.³⁰ Because 'all of her was a bit grimy since she rarely washed',³¹ a personal trait that in the film is underscored by a close up of her greasy hands, at the end of Sequence 2 (Fig. 23.1).³²

Macabéa's sensuality, upon which the text reflects, also finds itself inter-semiotically translated as the film gradually introduces Macabéa to the spectator. In

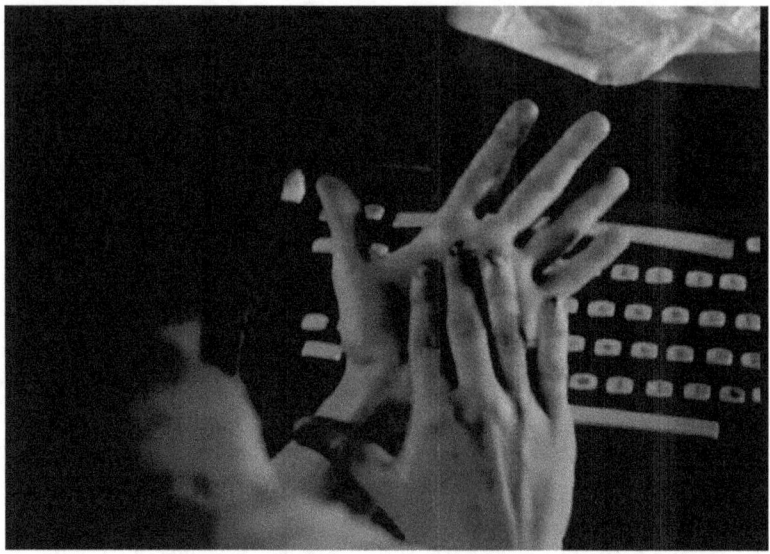

Fig. 23.1. Macabéa's hands (Sequence 2). Susana Amaral/Kino Video

the novella, Rodrigo describes his young character's simultaneously innocent and remorseful heightened sexuality:

> When she slept, she fitfully half-expected her aunt to knock her on the head. Or she strangely dreamed about sex, she who to all appearances was asexual. When she got up she felt guilty without knowing why, maybe because good things should be forbidden. Guilty and contented.[33]

Rodrigo's words are subtly transferred into images by Amaral's creative process in Sequence 15, through which the director engages with Macabéa's sexual awareness. In this scene, during the night, Macabéa rolls back and forth in the bed, squeezing her legs together, her hands pressing down between her legs. Suddenly, she coughs, wakes up and sits up in bed. Disturbed, she makes the sign of the cross and lies down, covering herself completely to the neck. This scene is the culmination of a slow revealing of Macabéa's sexual urges and immeasurable need for love. Macabéa is 'so dumb that she sometimes smiles at other people in the street' but '[n]obody smiles back because they don't even look at her'.[34] Her social relations always comprise a degree of deception as she often misreads the social cues, something we witness in her casual encounters with the men depicted in the film. In Sequences 11 and 13, the girl dreamily and seductively 'spies' on men who are clearly unaware of her: the first, a subway train security officer, stares at her just because she, without knowing it, is crossing the yellow safety line along the platform; the second, being blind, is facing in her direction just by chance. In a mixture of desire for love, disconcerting sexual desire and candid innocence, these encounters further evoke in both Macabéa and the viewer a feeling of loneliness and disappointment. In another sequence of a similar tone, Macabéa finds herself squashed between two young men cheerfully conversing inside the Metro. Inebriated by their bodies (and probably

Fig. 23.2. Macabéa holding a flower (Sequence 19). Susana Amaral/Kino Video

their masculine scents) she finds herself in a limbo of invisibility which allows her to enjoy an unexpected and fortuitous closeness.

Simultaneously, in Clarice's text, Rodrigo S.M. reflects on Macabéa as being a 'fresh flower' when he writes that 'there wasn't any human misery in her because she had within her a certain fresh flower', as if 'she was only fine organic matter'.[35] Here, the narrator appeals to the idea of the brevity of youth through the assumption of its ephemeral natural beauty (immediately creating a connection with Macabéa's tragic death) and thereby prefigures the specific symbol of femininity, sexuality and fertility which the film will come to explore. Interestingly enough, the scene in which Macabéa masturbates is followed by the first appearance within the film of a hibiscus which will come to play a symbolic role with regard to Macabéa's sexuality, as much in the film as it does in the novella. In the film, Amaral draws on the image of the flower as a symbol of sexuality and desire, connecting it with Macabéa and Glória, her confident and attractive office colleague. In Sequence 16, we see Glória steal Macabéa's hibiscus bloom from her desk when leaving the office to meet a new lover. The same hibiscus appears in a close-up that opens Sequence 19, where it is held by Macabéa while she sits on a park bench (Fig. 23.2). Superimposed over her lap, the flower plays a key element in the film in terms of Macabéa's destiny because it marks the moment when she encounters Olímpico, her future boyfriend (José Dumont).

Observing the progressive movement from when the flower first appears to the gradual construction of its symbolic meaning (Sequences 16 and 19), we can appreciate the way in which the actor-narrator living in the text is embodied at the cinematographic level: Rodrigo S.M.'s narrative voice inhabits the film on a technical level, with the camera taking on the role of the narrator, a constructor of the dramatic significance of images. This combination will result in a 'cinematic narrator', i.e., a dramatic camera that stands in for the literary narrator and allows the characters and their actions to emerge.[36]

Lispector's novella makes clear the discrepancy in social background between Macabéa and the narrator, but it appears that both in Clarice's novella and in Amaral's film Macabéa and Rodrigo S.M. rely on each other to confirm their individual existence. Macabéa depends on Rodrigo S.M. in the textual realm and Rodrigo S.M. depends on the physicality of Macabéa's image and action in the cinematographic realm. According to Pasolini, this technique draws on what he refers to as a cinematic 'free indirect discourse'.[37] Free indirect discourse triggers a transformation whereby the narrator becomes possessed by his own character's highly emotional thoughts, as though the one telling the story has become immersed in his character's soul and suddenly 'reveals not only the characters' but also where and with whom 'all the society and its contradictions emerge'.[38] This also takes place '[w]hen a writer recreates the speech of one of his characters [and] he immerses himself in his psychology, but also in his language'.[39] By strongly emphasizing a certain performative aspect of narration through the act of writing, and despite differing socially from the characters he creates, Rodrigo S.M. admits to the necessity of adopting unusual routines and language registers distinct from his own as he tries to experiment 'contrary to [his] normal habits to write a story with beginning, middle and "gran finale"':[40]

> It is not comfortable now: to speak of the girl I can't shave for days and must acquire dark circles under my eyes from lack of sleep [...]. Besides wearing old ragged clothes. All in order to put myself on the northeastern girl's level.[41]
>
> [...] I now see that I forgot to mention that for the time being I read nothing for fear of polluting the simplicity of my language with luxuries. [...] I juggle with intonation and force another's breathing to accompany my text.[42]

By trying to experience poverty in order to write about it, the narrator puts himself in the Northeastern girl's position and seemingly invites the reader to do so, as well. The ultimate aim, therefore, is to write a text that reveals the authenticity of its characters. While intertwining himself inside his own story and his own creation, the narrator continuously refers to Macabéa's solitude and invisibility, and the consequent unconscious need for love:

> Nobody looked at her on the street, she was cold coffee. [...] She didn't have that delicate thing called charm. I am the only one who finds her charming. Only I, her author, love her. I suffer for her.[43]

Furthermore, the story of *The Hour of the Star*, as stated by Clarice Lispector in an interview with Júlio Lerner for TV Cultura, in 1977, can be read as a story 'de uma inocência pisada, de uma miséria anónima' [of a trampled innocence, of an anonymous misery].[44] From this perspective, and engaging with the nature of this complex narrator, Macabéa appears to be the perfect pretext for Amaral, who read Clarice's novella as a 'lively metaphor' for contemporary Brazil,[45] to express her own political and social concerns through the camera. Adopting a creative attitude associated with a specific cinematographic movement in Brazil, 'Cinema Novo', whose aesthetics lie in the emphasis of the exposition of social and political issues in Brazil through an effort to promote economic reform, Amaral depicts a character, Macabéa, who is young and displaced. The director's dominant aspiration was, as she stated in the newspaper *Folha da Tarde* (18 February 1986), to make a 'universal film, with which all those who come to a large city without knowing the current cultural code, the way of speaking and the local customs, aspiring to a better life [...] could identify themselves'.[46] The universality of Macabéa's experience of loneliness, poverty and prejudice is also acknowledged by Clarice in the book when she states that

> this narrative will deal with something delicate: the creation of a whole person who is as alive as I am. Take care of her because all I can do is show her so you can recognize her on the street, walking lightly because of her quivering thinness.[47]

In this sense, the progressive process of the narrator's self-projection onto his character also contributes to an empathetic feeling towards this anonymous and ill-favoured girl. And while the writing is carefully constructed so as to conjure up images of affection and understanding of the Other's place in the world, both the narrator and the reader experience the same compassion.[48]

The key to Rodrigo S.M.'s position throughout the novel consists in the balance between the words 'writer' and 'actor'. From the beginning, Rodrigo S.M. determines with 'an illusion of free will that he is one of the most important characters of this story'.[49] He writes to unfold the trajectory of his unloved character, simultaneously undertaking an existentialist approach to his *métier* as a writer. In a spiral of doubt and uncertainty that leaves the reader in a type of limbo, he seeks a truth that 'is always an interior and inexplicable contact'[50] through the narration of a story about which he himself has 'no idea how things will turn out'.[51] Along the way, the world of perplexity so precariously inhabited by Macabéa, a world in which he is confronted with his own existence, is a world that appears to be veiled at the moment of the encounter with words, because the narrative aspires to communicate 'above all primary life that breathes, breathes, breathes',[52] at the same time as it reveals 'the lame adventures of a girl in a city that's entirely against her'.[53] In this writing scenario, imbued with an introspective point of view, Rodrigo S.M. is undermined by an epiphany in which he 'does not find himself, but the other',[54] and via which, in a process of subjective projection of ambivalent sense of identity and difference, he sees 'the northeastern girl looking in the mirror and — a ruffle of the drum — in the mirror appears [his] weary and unshaven face' since they 'are that interchangeable'.[55] Thereby, in Lispector's text, the architecture of both the narrative content and structure are the centre of the book itself, the product of the metalinguistic behaviour of a character-narrator who, according to Benedito Nunes, is anyone but Clarice Lispector, who, consequently, is Macabéa 'as much as Flaubert is Madame Bovary'.[56]

Picking up on this suggestion, Amaral composes and transforms her *The Hour of the Star*, as if she were subtly bringing Rodrigo's voice alive through Macabéa's presence on the screen. Traces of Rodrigo S.M.'s narration can be recognized

Fig. 23.3. Macabéa in the mirror (Sequence 17). Susana Amaral/Kino Video

throughout the film and they act as a testament to the poetic and imagistic vision of the director's attentive and transmuting reading. Amaral's film both elides and reveals the narrator's overwhelming presence. Indeed, throughout the film *The Hour of the Star*, the spectator frequently observes Macabéa's face being vaguely projected onto and reflected by mirrored surfaces, whereby her duplicated image emerges with quasi-phantasmagorical undertones (Fig. 23.3).

Macabéa's nondescript face seemingly disappears, as it does in Rodrigo S.M.'s narrative after receiving the warning that she might be fired:

> She went to the bathroom to be alone [and] mechanically looked at herself in the mirror atop the filthy and cracked sink, full of hairs, which matched her own life so well. It seemed to her that the dark and tarnished mirror didn't reflect any image. Could her physical existence have vanished?[57]

In fact, the transmutation process enacted by Amaral has a prior origin: echoes from the beginning of the text, which may very well account for the narrator's ghostly survival on-screen. Rodrigo's intention was (from the beginning) to write 'a book made without words [...] a mute photograph',[58] whereby '[t]he action of this story will end up with [his] transfiguration into somebody else and [his] materialization finally as an object'.[59] Possibly this was a story that would become a cinematographic object, the product of 'a story in Technicolor to add a little luxury which, by God, [he needs] too'.[60] Although Amaral chose not to make the narrator a character played by an actor to replace the narrator of *The Hour of the Star*, she did not neglect the main symbol that connects Macabéa to Rodrigo — the mirror — and it will be via the mirror's suggestion of doubling that the viewer will find him materialized in the film.

Fig. 23.4. Macabéa's death (Sequence 44). Susana Amaral/Kino Video

'Gran finale'

Given the complex relationship between Lispector's text and Amaral's film, it is hardly surprising that Macabéa's death, one of the most intricate episodes in *The Hour of the Star*, is a key contact point between the film and book, a privileged site where Amaral draws upon and elaborates Rodrigo S.M.'s direct communication.[61] Macabéa's tragic destiny is carefully set up by a series of seemingly banal events: Olímpico leaves her for Glória, and later, following the advice of a colleague, Macabéa visits a clairvoyant, Madame Carlota. This fortune teller spells out the sad succession of the events of Macabéa's past life and then announces, in an explosion of enthusiasm, that her life 'will change the minute [she] steps out of [the] house'.[62] The auspicious news has a profound effect on Macabéa's mood. Upon leaving the fortune teller's house, she was 'already a different person. A person pregnant with the future'.[63] Abruptly, however, while stepping off the pavement to cross the street, Macabéa is hit by a Mercedes-Benz. At this point, for Rodrigo S.M., the Northeastern girl 'was nothing more than a vague feeling on the dirty cobble stones'.[64] The narrator is ambivalent with regards to Macabéa's death, given his claims that he has been fatally wounded by the writing of this story. Suddenly he sees himself dispossessed from his own creation, for which he is no longer responsible since he is 'writing above and beyond' himself.[65] At the same time, he keeps her death suspended for as long as he can because 'the movie-star hour for Macabéa to die has not yet come'.[66]

Amaral similarly postpones Macabéa's death, and in Sequence 44 the camera begins by portraying the violent hit and run in a series of close shots and ends with a high-angle long shot of Macabéa's small, abandoned body lying on the pavement (Fig. 23.4).

Several close-ups of her hand, her legs, a shoe that has been knocked off, lead the viewer to the sight of her whole body, in the foetal position, suggesting a certain degree of suspense: what will happen, after all, to Macabéa? The viewer, though, witnesses the Mercedes' escape, whilst the girl lies in the middle of the street, like a 'sleeping beauty', embracing 'herself longing for the sweet nothing, and holding on to a 'thread of consciousness [...] [she] mentally repeated over and over: I am, I am, I am'.[67] The narrator's desire was to 'leave her lying on the street and simply not finish the story',[68] delaying (for several pages) her death as long as he can. But, suddenly aware of all the events he no longer controls and seeing himself now in the position of a spectator, he decides to 'go on where the air runs out [...]. And then — then the sudden rattling of a seagull, all at once the voracious eagle lifting to the high airs the tender lamb, the sleek cat mangling some dirty rat, life eats life'.[69]

Macabéa's death, however, appears to constitute also a critical point for the narrator himself, when Rodrigo, by the end of his writing journey, declares 'Macabéa killed me',[70] as if the girl's death meant his own death, therefore resolving the end of both stories. Nevertheless, death does not represent the end of their existence: it is rather 'an encounter with oneself'.[71] And it will be through his symbolic death, the moment the storytelling ends, that Rodrigo S.M. will experience the pleasure of resurrection. And by conceiving of a Macabéa who now dreams of and achieves a happy future, Amaral also announces a rebirth, that 'Yes' with which '[a]ll the world began', when she depicts in slow motion a jubilant Macabéa, running into the arms of a blond man, and ends the film with a close-up of the Northeastern girl smiling, with her hair loose and flowing, carefully made up: a new woman, a movie star (Fig. 23.5).[72]

After all, the secret behind the success of the transfiguration of the text into the film lies not in detachment as a method but rather in the construction of a presence that subtly communicates the narrative and the narrative features of the text through the cinematographic image.[73] Both the metaphorical image of the literary text and the cinematographic image in the film manifest the simultaneity of presence and absence, a characteristic which allows both media a certain amount of permeability to mechanisms of abstraction. In her film *The Hour of the Star*, Amaral not only depicts Macabéa, but also creates a space in which Rodrigo's negative fingerprints can be sensed. And masked behind Macabéa's character and storytelling techniques in the film, the presence of this unusual narrator is reinforced, while all the traces of his own reality are carefully placed throughout the entire film as a photograph waiting to be printed evermore by those who might be acquainted with the novel. By the end, while Rodrigo S.M.'s words shape our gaze and reaffirm his presence and importance for/throughout the storytelling process, in Amaral's film the viewer is offered a raw and austere, but nonetheless sensitive, narrative subtly but frequently suggesting Rodrigo S.M.'s seminal presence, acknowledging his importance beyond the text.

FIG. 23.5. Macabéa, movie star (Sequence 44). Susana Amaral/Kino Video

Works Cited

ARAÚJO, WASHINGTON ANDRADE DE, 'Macabéa vai ao cinema: *A Hora da Estrela* e a travessia da linguagem literária para a cinematográfica' (unpublished Master's thesis, Universidade de Brasília, 2008)

HUTCHEON, LINDA, *A Theory of Adaptation* (Routledge: London, 2006)

LAMAS, BERENICE SICA, *O duplo em Lygia Fagundes Telles: um estudo em literatura e psicologia* (Porto Alegre: EdiPUCRS, 2005)

LEITCH, THOMAS, *Film Adaptation and Its Discontents: From 'Gone with the Wind' to 'The Passion of the Christ'* (Baltimore, MD: Johns Hopkins University Press, 2007)

LISPECTOR, CLARICE, *The Hour of the Star*, trans. by Benjamin Moser (New York: New Directions, 2011)

MARTELO, ROSA MARIA, *O cinema da poesia* (Lisbon: Documenta, 2012)

MARTIN, MARCEL, *A linguagem cinematográfica* (Lisbon: Dinalivro, 2005)

MOUSINHO, LUIZ ANTONIO, and AFONSO BARBOSA, '*A hora da estrela*: adaptação e linguagem cinematográfica no filme de Suzana Amaral', *Revista Sessões do Imaginário*, 28 (2012), 42–50

NUNES, BENEDITO, *O drama da linguagem: uma leitura de Clarice Lispector* (São Paulo: Ática, 1989)

PASOLINI, PIER PAOLO, *Heretical Empiricism*, trans. by Ben Lawton and Louise K. Barnett (Washington, DC: New Academia Publishing, 2005)

PICK, ZUZANA M., 'Cinema as Sign and Language', *Canadian Journal of Political and Social Theory*, 5 (1981), 199–207

STAM, ROBERT, *Film Theory* (Oxford: Blackwell, 2000)

—— *Literature through Film: Realism, Magic, and the Art of Adaptation* (Oxford: Blackwell, 2005)

Notes to Chapter 24

1. For an earlier version of this chapter, see Sara Costa, 'A Hora da Estrela: texto-imagem', *Polifonia*, vol. 25, 40.1 (2018), 160–76.
2. Robert Stam, *Literature through Film: Realism, Magic, and the Art of Adaptation* (Oxford: Blackwell, 2005), p. 3.
3. Ibid.
4. Zuzana M. Pick, 'Cinema as Sign and Language', *Canadian Journal of Political and Social Theory*, 5 (1981), 199–207.
5. Stam, *Literature through Film*, p. 4.
6. Linda Hutcheon, *A Theory of Adaptation* (Routledge: London: 2006).
7. Thomas Leitch, *Film Adaptation and Its Discontents: From 'Gone with the Wind' to 'The Passion of the Christ'* (Baltimore, MD: Johns Hopkins University Press, 2007).
8. Robert Stam, *Film Theory* (Oxford: Blackwell, 2000), p. 107.
9. Ibid., p. 108.
10. Quoted in Marcel Martin, *A linguagem cinematográfica* (Lisbon: Dinalivro, 2005), p. 24. Emphasis in original. All translations from the Portuguese are mine unless otherwise noted.
11. Ibid., p. 24.[0]
12. Pier Paolo Pasolini, *Heretical Empiricism*, trans. by Ben Lawton and Louise K. Barnett (Washington, DC: New Academia Publishing, 2005).
13. Ibid., p. 167.
14. Ibid., pp. 168–69.
15. Ibid., p. 169.
16. Quoted in Rosa Maria Martelo, *O cinema da poesia* (Lisbon: Documenta, 2012), p. 170.
17. Pasolini, *Heretical Empiricism*, p. 168.
18. Ibid., p. 171.
19. Ibid., p. 189.
20. Ibid., p. 172.
21. Ibid., p. 169.
22. Ibid., p. 192.
23. Linda Hutcheon, *A Theory of Adaptation* (Routledge: London: 2006), p. 10.
24. Ibid., pp. 7–8.
25. Clarice Lispector, *The Hour of the Star*, trans. by Benjamin Moser (New York: New Directions, 2011), p. 7.
26. Ibid., p. 7.
27. Ibid., p. 34.
28. Ibid., p. 7.
29. Ibid., p. 5.
30. Ibid., p. 16.
31. Ibid., p. 19.
32. These sequences correspond to the screenplay written by Suzana Amaral and Alfredo Oroz as transcribed in Washington Andrade de Araújo, 'Macabéa vai ao cinema: *A hora da estrela* e a travessia da linguagem literária para a cinematográfica' (unpublished Master's thesis, Universidade de Brasília, 2008), pp. 106–15.
33. Lispector, *The Hour of the Star*, pp. 25–26.
34. Ibid., p. 7.
35. Ibid., p. 30.
36. Afonso Barbosa and Luiz Antonio Mousinho, '*A hora da estrela*: adaptação e linguagem cinematográfica no filme de Suzana Amaral', *Revista Sessões do Imaginário*, 28 (2012), 42–50 (p. 46).
37. Pasolini, *Heretical Empiricism*, pp. 79–101.
38. Araújo, 'Macabéa vai ao cinema', p. 14.
39. Pasolini, *Heretical Empiricisms*, p. 177.
40. Lispector, *The Hour of the Star*, p. 5.

41. Ibid., p. 11.
42. Ibid., p. 14.
43. Ibid., p. 19.
44. 'Clarice Lispector', *Panorama*, TV2 Cultura, 28 December 1977. The interview, which took place in February 1977, can be viewed online: <https://www.youtube.com/watch?v=ohHPrl2EVnU&t=3s> [accessed 29 January 2022].
45. Araújo, 'Macabéa vai ao cinema', p. 130.
46. Quoted in ibid., p. 131.
47. Lispector, *The Hour of the Star*, p. 11.
48. 'Even though I don't have anything to do with the girl, I'll have to write out all myself through her amidst frights of my own', ibid., p. 16.
49. Ibid., p. 15.
50. Ibid., p. 3.
51. Ibid., p. 8.
52. Ibid., p. 5.
53. Ibid., p. 7.
54. Berenice Sica Lamas, *O duplo em Lygia Fagundes Telles: um estudo em literatura e psicologia* (Porto Alegre: EdiPUCRS, 2005), p. 63.
55. Lispector, *The Hour of the Star*, p. 14.
56. Benedito Nunes, *O drama da linguagem: uma leitura de Clarice Lispector* (São Paulo: Ática, 1989), p. 169.
57. Lispector, *The Hour of the Star*, p. 28.
58. Ibid., p. 8.
59. Ibid., p. 12.
60. Ibid, p. xiv.
61. See also the chapter by Magdalena Edwards in this volume.
62. Lispector, *The Hour of the Star*, p. 67.
63. Ibid., p. 70.
64. Ibid., p. 74.
65. Ibid., p. 63.
66. Ibid., p. 73.
67. Ibid., p. 74.
68. Ibid.
69. Ibid., pp. 74, 75.
70. Ibid., p. 76.
71. Ibid.
72. Ibid., p. 3.
73. Martelo, *O cinema da poesia*, p. 169.

PART VII

Translating Clarice

CHAPTER 24

❖

Clarice Hebraica

Adriana X. Jacobs

for Edna Aizenberg, z"l

Fig. 24.1. Clarice Lispector's gravestone, Cemitério Comunal Israelita. Photo by Claire Varin. The stone on the bottom right corner was placed there by Varin.

The Hebrew Scriptworld

Clarice Lispector is buried in the Cemitério Comunal Israelita [Jewish Communal Cemetery] of Caju, in Rio de Janeiro. Pictured above is her gravestone, where a *magen David* [Star of David], a traditional symbol of Judaism, is visible at the top, flanked by the Hebrew letters <פ> and <נ>, an abbreviation for *po nitman/a*, here is buried, followed by a line of Hebrew text:[1]

חיה בת פנחס

Chaya daughter of Pinchas.

The gravestone records the date of her death according to the Jewish calendar — 29 Kislev 5738 — along with its corresponding date on the Gregorian calendar, 9 December 1977. At the foot of the gravestone, one finds a quotation in Portuguese from her 1964 novel *A paixão segundo G.H.*: 'Dar a mão a alguém sempre foi o que esperei da alegria' [Holding someone's hand was always my idea of joy].[2] The Hebrew and Portuguese texts encapsulate two of Lispector's major affiliations, but of these, her relationship to Judaism has remained the most opaque. Although Lispector grew up in a Jewish family and attended the Colégio Hebreo-Idisch-Brasileiro in Recife, throughout her life questions about her Jewish background and identity met with resolute reticence.[3] 'I am Brazilian, and that's final, once and for all', she declared in a frequently quoted 1976 interview with Edilberto Coutinho.[4] In a short biographical piece, titled 'Esclarecimentos: explicação de uma vez por todas' [One Final Clarification] and dated 14 November 1970, she notes 'I am a naturalized Brazilian, but for a matter of months, I could have been Brazilian by birth.'[5] The scant Jewish references in her fiction have presented a challenge to readers and critics invested in a Jewish reading of her work; at the same time, these traces have generated extensive readings and scholarship, as if, by gathering them together, like the broken shards of a vessel, a Jewish Clarice could be reconstituted.[6]

The Hebrew text on the gravestone draws us into her Jewish genealogy, a personal history that remained out of public view for much of her life. In his biography of Lispector, Benjamin Moser even goes so far as to refer to 'Chaya' as Lispector's 'hidden name'.[7] But Lispector's gravestone, and the way the Hebrew and Portuguese texts share this space, complicate this assessment. Lispector may have refrained from addressing her Jewish identity in public fora, but it was not uncommon for Jewish immigrants in Brazil, and elsewhere, to adopt a new name that better assimilated to the hegemonic language of their country of arrival (Pinchas became Pedro, for example), while continuing to use their Hebrew (or Yiddish or Ladino) name in Jewish religious and ceremonial contexts. Such practices would have been consistent with the internal diglossia characteristic of a number of Jewish communities.[8]

Lispector died on a Friday, and after her body was cleansed according to Jewish ritual it lay in state in an *oratório* (small chapel) at the cemetery until Sunday 11 December (Jewish law prohibits burial on the Sabbath). The following description of her funeral appeared in the Brazilian daily *Folha de São Paulo*:

Ainda no oratório, precisamente às 11 horas, o substituto do rabino [cantor-mór Joseph Aronsohn] deu início à liturgia lendo, em aramaico, o Salmo 91, do Antigo Testamento, seguido de cânticos em hebraico e de uma leitura, agora em português, de alguns Salmos. Ali, antes do caixão ser conduzido à sepultura, Joseph Aronsohn ainda fez a despedida do corpo, rezando o 'El Molê Rachamim'.[9] De lá o caixão seguiu até o túmulo 123, onde o filho de Clarice, Paulo Gurgel Valente (o filho Pedro não compareceu por se encontrar com o pai, o embaixador Mauri Gurgel Valente, em Montevidéu) chorou, sendo constantemente amparado pelas tias Elvira [sic] e Tânia, também escritoras.

A beira do túmulo, Joseph Aronsohn, tendo ao lado [Paulo] Gurgel Valente, rezou o 'Kadish' — oração fúnebre — , enquanto a última homenagem a Clarice Lispector era prestada com o lançamento de três pás de terra sobre o caixão, indicando que 'da terra viestes, à terra voltarás'. A cerimônia foi encerrada com o substituto do rabino pedindo aos presentes que se voltassem para a direita, em direção ao Oriente, indicando o sentido de Jerusalém.[10]

[In the oratory, at 11am sharp, the rabbi's proxy [chief cantor Joseph Aronsohn] began the liturgy by reciting, in Aramaic, Psalm 91 of the Old Testament, followed by songs in Hebrew and a reading, now in Portuguese, of some Psalms. There, before the coffin was taken to the grave, Joseph Aronsohn bid farewell to the body, praying 'El maleh rachamim'. From there the coffin was taken to Grave 123, where Clarice's son, Paulo Gurgel Valente wept (her son Pedro did not attend as he was in Montevideo with his father, the ambassador Mauri Gurgel Valente), comforted by his aunts Elisa and Tânia, who are also writers.

At the graveside, Joseph Aronsohn stood next to [Paulo] Gurgel Valente and recited the 'Kaddish', the funeral prayer — while final respects were paid to Clarice Lispector with the throwing of three spadefuls of dirt over her coffin, representing the fact that 'from dust you came, to dust you shall return'. The ceremony came to a close with the rabbi's proxy requesting that everyone present turn to the right, towards the East, in the direction of Jerusalem.]

Notably, *cantor-mór* [chief cantor] Joseph (Josef) Aronsohn presided over the funeral in place of Rabbi Henrique Lemle.[11] According to the paper, Aronsohn opened the liturgy with a recitation of Psalm 91, 'yoshev be-seter 'eliyon / be-tsel shadai itlonan' [He that dwelleth in the secret place of the most High shall abide under the shadow of the Almighty].[12] Traditionally known as a supplication for protection, it is repeated seven times during the procession to the grave. The newspaper reports that it is recited here in Aramaic, an ancient Jewish vernacular, though it's likely that the account has confused this text with the Mourner's Kaddish, an Aramaic prayer.[13] Given Lemle's commitment to the translation of Jewish liturgy into Portuguese, it is not surprising that Lispector's funeral featured liturgy in traditionally Jewish languages, as well as in the adopted language of Brazil's Jewish population.[14] In addition to members of Rio's Jewish community, the 200-strong procession that accompanied Lispector's coffin to its grave included the Brazilian writers Rubem Braga, Fernando Sabino, Nélida Piñon and José Rubem Fonseca, as well as the diplomat and family friend Vasco Leitão da Cunha. From these details, it is clear that the funeral was indisputably Jewish, and in a way that made it clear that the Lispector family was intimately integrated in Rio's Jewish community.

News reports about the funeral gave the public a glimpse into Lispector's Jewish background, to a degree that far surpassed the one she offered in real life, but it also underscored, as Carlos Mendes de Sousa has observed, how 'agora também a morte acabaria por ficar à mercê de apropriações e contraditórios trânsitos mitificadores' [now death would also end up at the mercy of appropriations and contradictory, mythmaking movements].[15] Separately, a group of Lispector's friends, as well as her publishers, organized a Catholic mass in her name, which took place on 15 December.[16] According to Piñon, Olga Borelli, who was Lispector's assistant and confidante (and herself a former nun), relayed in a private conversation that Lispector had wanted a Christian burial, 'as proof of her conversion'.[17] The friends decided against raising this issue with Lispector's family and plans for a traditional Jewish burial moved forward.

The inclusion of 'Chaya' on Lispector's gravestone acknowledges the role that the Hebrew name plays in the Jewish life cycle. Children receive their Hebrew name at their *brit mila* [circumcision ceremony] if one is a boy or *simchat bat* [name blessing] if one is a girl. It is a person's Hebrew name that appears in a Jewish *ketuba* [marriage certificate], as well as in a *get* [writ of divorce]. It is by their Hebrew names that Jewish congregants are called up to recite a blessing before the reading of the Torah (*aliya*). In the Yizkor (memorial) prayer, which is recited four times a year, the Hebrew name of the deceased is recited along with their father's name (according to Ashkenazi tradition), and in times of illness, prayers for the sick include one's Hebrew name as well as that of one's mother. I raise these details to call attention to the cultural work that the Hebrew text is doing on this gravestone next to, but also apart from, the Portuguese. If indeed it is the case that Lispector identified more with Christianity than Judaism, even going so far as to convert, the Jewish funeral and Jewish gravestone insist on asserting Lispector's Jewish identity in this world and in the *ha-'olam ha-ba* [the world to come, the afterlife].

As heard in a recording of Lispector's funeral, when Aronsohn performs the traditional Jewish funeral prayer, 'El male rachamim' [God full of mercy], there is a discernible shift from Ashkenazic Hebrew to Portuguese when he names the deceased, *Chaya bas Pinchos* Clarice Lispector *she-halkha le-'olama* [Chaya daughter of Pinchas... who has departed]. This shift is not just linguistic; like the interplay between Hebrew and Portuguese on the tombstone, Aronsohn's voice marks a movement between — and an interweaving of — the cultural and historical contexts that each language encompasses. The result is not a seamless translation or transition between these languages, but a clear collision of their distinct 'scriptworlds'. David Damrosch, who popularized this term in a series of articles published in the last decade, has called attention to the role of script in the circulation and translation of texts from ancient times to the present day. 'Learning a script', he observes, 'one absorbs key elements of a broad literary history: its terms of reference, habits of style, and poetics, often transcending those of any one language or country'.[18] The Latin script, for example, has been used by a number of languages and across long stretches of human history. In his own study on script, Damrosch cites the Epic of Gilgamesh and the Old Norse sagas as examples of texts that have come to influence a wide range of literary cultures in the Latin scriptworld via translation.[19] But the hegemonic status of 'the Latin scriptworld' can — and has — occluded the multiple linguistic worlds that comprise it, a reality that Sowon Park acknowledges when she describes the scriptworld as a 'a many-layered overlapping complex of multiple linguistic, political and cultural systems'.[20] Park's work, in particular, highlights shifts in power and cultural capital as texts translate *from* one scriptworld to another, as well as *within* a scriptworld, the Chinese scriptworld, for example, which has been used at different times and to varying degrees in China, Japan, Korea and Vietnam. Their work has prompted me to consider how the Hebrew translation of Lispector carries with it, in the square letters of the Hebrew alphabet, 'whole complexes of values, assumptions, and traditions' that have formed the history of this language, in this script.[21]

Attempts to romanize Hebrew in the early twentieth century met with swift opposition. Notably, the writer and editor Itamar Ben-Avi, who was born in Ottoman Jerusalem, spearheaded these efforts. The son of Eliezer Ben-Yehuda, a key player in the vernacularization of modern Hebrew, Ben-Avi was hailed as the region's first native Hebrew speaker. İlker Aytürk, who has studied the history of Hebrew romanization, notes that resistance to this effort came from religious and secular camps alike. The former saw in this script an inextricable bond to Jewish sacred text and tradition, and the latter, an opportunity to break from diasporic Jewish culture and languages, where the Latin script predominated.[22] While Ben-Avi was working to promote the Hebrew romanization effort, other proponents of Hebrew were devoted to expanding Hebrew script beyond the realm of religious texts, asserting its relevance in the administrative and bureaucratic matters that shaped Jewish daily life in Mandatory Palestine. In her comprehensive study of language politics in Mandatory Palestine, Liora R. Halperin relates the controversy that surrounded the British Mandate decision not to issue telegrams in Hebrew script, with a court upholding this ruling on the grounds that the script in which a language was written did not constitute a fundamental change to the language, 'any more than a message in English ceases to be in English when it is rendered in Morse Code'.[23] Language activists, including the Battalion for the Defenders of the Hebrew Language, pursued their case until the decision was overturned almost a decade later, in 1929.

In this period, the Hebrew poet Chaim Nachman Bialik had committed himself to the project of Hebrew translation, and specifically the translation of Jewish texts into Hebrew. He referred to this project as *kinus* [gathering], a word that carried theological as well as political implications, particularly at a time when the development of vernacular Hebrew was becoming increasingly synonymous with Jewish territorial nationalism. Underlying Bialik's project was also the understanding that the Hebrew language and Jewish identity were inseparable. For Jewish texts written in diasporic languages, the Hebrew language served as a homeland, a way out of exile through translation: 'For us only Hebrew can serve as a foundation and root. All that has been created in foreign languages does not exist unless it is later translated into Hebrew'.[24] In his 1930 essay 'On the Question of Languages in Israel', he notes that, as an exilic and diasporic language, Hebrew had attached itself to other 'living' languages as a means of survival, but as a national language, modern Hebrew's vitality no longer depended on this parasitic arrangement.²⁵ We may surmise from his silence on the matter of romanization that Bialik would not have been enthusiastic about the proposal.²⁶ Hebrew script distinguishes the language from a host of diasporic Jewish languages, but it is also an integral component of Jewish textual continuity, linking sacred scripture to modern literature. According to the treatise *Sefer yetsira* [Book of Creation], an early Jewish mystical text, God created the world out of the twenty-two Hebrew letters. This 'belief in the world-shaping power of the Hebrew letters', to quote Alan Mintz, had inspired works like Abraham Regelson's 1946 panegyric to the Hebrew language 'Chakukot otiyotayikh' [Engraved are Your Letters], but it also resonated in the language debates I have described above.²⁷

The examples offered here sketch in broad strokes the history of the modern Hebrew scriptworld into which Lispector's Portuguese texts were translated, highlighting the relation between language, script, ideology and (Jewish) identity in the twentieth-century history of modern Hebrew. Lispector may have resisted a Jewish reading of her work and biography, but Hebrew translation nonetheless activates religious and cultural relations that in her own life and writing remained in Nádia Gotlib's words, like 'um ar nebuloso' [a cloudy air].²⁸ And yet, as I show in the following section, translation into modern Hebrew draws Lispector's texts into the orbit of the Jewish textual tradition, revealing, but just as likely inventing, Jewish sites and echoes in her work.²⁹

קלריס ליספקטור

The first Hebrew translation of a work by Lispector was the collection *Kishrei mishpacha/ She'at ha-kokhav*, a 1999 volume that combined *Laços de família* [*Family Ties*] and *A hora da estrela* [*The Hour of the Star*], both translated by Miriam Tivon, a prolific Israeli translator of Portuguese and French fiction.³⁰ Tivon was born in Uzbekistan to Polish-born Jewish refugees of WWII and came to Israel with her family in 1950, after the establishment of the State of Israel.³¹ Her study of translation and Portuguese at the Université de Bordeaux in France provided the training that shaped her career as a literary translator, which now numbers over 60 titles. For most of her career, Tivon has worked as the in-house French and Portuguese translator of Ha-kibbuts ha-me'uchad, one of Israel's largest and most prominent publishers.³² In her translations of Portuguese and Brazilian Portuguese literature, which have garnered many reviews in the Hebrew press, she has focused primarily on the work of Jorge Amado, Lídia Jorge and José Saramago. Her major public recognition as a literary translator came in 1995 when she was awarded a Ministry of Education and Culture prize for her translations.³³ Despite her long résumé and accolades, Tivon largely refrains from participating in the public discourse on translation and remains reticent when it comes to discussing her translation choices and influences. In a rare 1996 interview, she described her process as follows: 'I translate like a medium… words come through the gut and only afterwards do I check and labour over them according to what I have learned.'³⁴

Tivon's Lispector translation appeared at the end of a decade that had seen a proliferation of scholarly works on Lispector, including an interest within Jewish Studies in tracing or excavating Jewish sources in her work,[35] and it was followed by *Osher samui*, her 2001 translation of the short story collection *Felicidade clandestina* [*Clandestine Happiness*]. Whether or not Tivon's Lispector translations were commissioned with an eye to capitalizing on this interest remains a matter of speculation, but the absence of further translations of her work in the first decade of the new millennium was notable, given that each Hebrew translation had sold around 5000 copies. This represented 'a respectable figure for a non-novel', according to Menachem Perry, the editor of the series in which these translations appeared.[36] But despite Perry's contention that the books were 'well-received and highly regarded', their reception was muted at best, with very few reviews appearing in the Israeli press.[37] Perry himself conceded that the bestseller status of a book in its home literary market was hardly a predictor of how a book would fare when translated into Hebrew, but that he was 'proud' nonetheless ('if not more so') to support translations that injected into 'the bloodstream of contemporary Hebrew literature' the kind of literary values and writing styles that he felt it needed and desired.[38]

The last decade has seen a marked shift in the Hebrew reception of Lispector's work, in part because of the renewed attention that Moser's 2009 biography *Why This World: A Biography of Clarice Lispector* brought to Lispector's Jewish background, as well as the flurry of translations and retranslations of Lispector's novels that have circulated in the global anglophone market.[39] The publication of Moser's biography was covered in the Israeli press, notably in Maya Sela's 2009 *Haaretz* interview with the author.[40] It was in this interview that Perry was quoted promising new translations of Lispector.[41] Several years later, he fulfilled this promise by bringing out Yael Segalovitz's highly praised translation of *A via crucis do corpo* [*The Via Crucis of the Body*] published in Hebrew as *Derekh ha-yesurim shel ha-guf*. Segalovitz's translation appears now to have been the harbinger of greater interest in Lispector's work in the Hebrew literary market, though the impending centennial of her birth was certainly not incidental. The years since have seen the publication of *Karov la-lev ha-piri* [*Near to the Wild Heart*, 2018] and *Ha-teshuka 'al pi G. H.* [*The Passion According to G.H.*, 2019], both translated by Tivon, as well as reissued editions of *Kishrei mishpacha* and *She'at ha-kokhav* published in 2020 as separate volumes.

The reissued *She'at ha-kokhav*, the focus of the reading that follows, includes a critical afterword by Segalovitz that offers an overdue reframing of the novella for the Hebrew reader, and specifically for readers more attuned to the book's explicit and implicit Jewish references and allusions. Jewish readings of *A hora da estrela*, first published in October 1977, tend to focus on the name of its protagonist, Macabéa, which, in Segalovitz's words, 'hints at Lispector's own Jewish identity'.[42] But although Segalovitz signals the relation between the name Macabéa and the biblical Maccabees, she otherwise focuses her discussion on points of connection between Macabéa and Lispector (both grew up in the Northeast of Brazil, both end up living, and dying, in Rio).[43] Jewish readings of Lispector's *oeuvre* have amply covered the relation between Macabéa and the Maccabees, and I am going to surmise that a Hebrew readership in Israel, where these translations primarily circulate, would likely be familiar with this story: how a group of Jewish rebels, active in second century BCE Ancient Judea, protested against the imposition of Hellenism, and following a revolt led by Judah Maccabee and his brothers, seized control of the region and established the Hasmonean dynasty, which ruled from 167 BCE to 63 BCE, when it was conquered by the Romans. According to rabbinic sources, when the Maccabees regained control of the Temple in Jerusalem the rebels were only able to procure enough oil to light the sacred Temple lamp for one day. By some miracle, the oil lasted for eight days, giving them time to replenish this supply, an event commemorated in the Jewish celebration of Hanukkah, the eight-day 'festival of lights' which usually falls in December. But other relations become visible when *A hora da estrela* enters the semantic field of Hebrew.

The word itself, Maccabee, or in Hebrew מכבי (*ma-ká-bi*), has been traced to the Hebrew word מקבה (*makaba*), designating a hammer, from the root נ-ק-ב to pierce, bore a hole, excavate. Throughout her translation, Tivon renders Macabéa's name as מַכַּבֵּיָה, including diacritical marks as a phonetic aid for the Hebrew reader. This rendering reveals מכה (*maka*), a blow or wound (the latter meaning appears in rabbinic Hebrew texts), from the root נ-כ-ה, to strike or blow, as well as כבה (*kabe*) meaning to extinguish or put out, as in a light or lamp. The word *bea*, from the Latin *beatus*, may no longer be as visible here, but the linguistic relations Hebrew forges nonetheless prove meaningful in the context of the novella. Macabéa's moments of hurt and disillusion, as well as sudden joy and revelation, are repeatedly marked with the parenthetical '(explosão)', explosion.[44] There are also physical blows — her face bursting when Olímpico drops her to the ground or the yellow Mercedes hitting her when she crosses the street. Rejecting the premise that opens the novella ('Do not [...] expect stars in what follows for nothing will scintillate'), Macabéa, who loves movie stars, becomes, at the moment of her death, a 'star with a thousand pointed rays' and, an instant later — as her own name signifies — her light flickers out.[45]

The name Macabéa is arguably the most explicitly Jewish reference in this book, if not in Lispector's *oeuvre* as a whole. Segalovitz teases out others (which I will return to), but reading *A hora da estrela* in Hebrew translation I am drawn to the ways that the Hebrew language itself opens up the possibility of a different kind of Jewish reading. For the remainder of this section of my chapter, I will offer an exegesis on Tivon's translation of the Portuguese 'piedade' [mercy, pity], a word that appears — for the first of many times — in the novella's opening pages, when Rodrigo S.M. explains his relation to Macabéa:

> Se em vez de ponto fosse seguido por reticências o título ficaria aberto a possíveis imaginações vossas, porventura até malsãs e sem *piedade*. Bem, é verdade que também eu não tenho *piedade* do meu personagem principal, a nordestina: é um relato que desejo frio.
>
> If, instead of a full stop, the title were followed by dotted lines, it would remain open to every kind of speculation on your part, however morbid or *pitiless*. It is true that I, too, feel no *pity* for my main character, the girl from the North-east: I want my story to be cold and impartial.

אם במקום נקודה היו באות אחרי הכותרת שלוש נקודות היא היתה נשארת
פתוחה לדמיונות אפשריים שלכם, אולי אפילו חולניים וחסרי רחמים.
טוב, נכון שגם בלבי אין רחמים על הדמות הראשית שלי, הבחורה הנורדֶסטית:
זהו סיפור שאני רוצה אותו קר.⁴⁶

Derived from the Latin *pietas* [pity, piety], the Portuguese 'piedade' carries resonances of the Italian *pietà*, the popular title for artistic representations of Mary cradling the dead body of Jesus. Tivon translates Lispector's 'piedade' as the Hebrew רחמים (*rachamim*), which is typically translated into English as pity, compassion, or mercy (the same is true for English translations of 'piedade'). In the novella, Lispector critiques the limits and failures of 'piedade' in the context of Brazil's religious landscape, where Catholicism predominates. But when 'piedade' is translated into רחמים, a Jewish ethical reading also emerges.

In the Talmud, the set of teachings and commentaries that form the basis of Jewish law, God is frequently referred to as *Rachamana*, Aramaic for compassionate. Psalm 103 describes God's relationship to human beings as a compassionate parent to a child: *ke-rachem av 'al banim*, as a father has compassion for his children.⁴⁷ There is also a maternal association inherent in *rachamim*, which shares a root with the word רחם (*rechem*), 'womb'. This theological intimacy is particularly poignant in relation to *A hora da estrela* given the attention paid to Macabéa's body, the repeated affirmations that she is a virgin (and will die a virgin), and the narrator's wrangling over the book's closure, where he considers writing her out like 'murdering an infant child'.⁴⁸ According to the Talmud, to be compassionate is one of the three distinguishing marks (*simanim*) of the Jewish people.⁴⁹ *Bereshit Rabba* 12:15 teaches that God created the earth with *midat ha-din* [a measure or principle of judgement] and *midat ha-rachamim* [a measure or principle of compassion]. God is merciful and bestowed this attribute on the Jewish people; therefore, to be without compassion or pity was to be 'unfit to be part of the Jewish people'.⁵⁰ In Ashkenazi Jewish tradition, the prayer 'El male rachamim' [God full of mercy], is dedicated to the souls of the dead and is usually recited during a funeral service (as it was at Lispector's funeral) or on the anniversary of a relative's death. Though the exact dating of this prayer is not known, in its current form and variations, it appears to date back to the early seventeenth century, when it was recited among European Jewish communities as a prayer for victims of anti-Jewish violence.⁵¹ The prayer asks that the soul of the deceased be granted a proper rest — in Hebrew, a *menucha nekhona* — and underlying this request is the belief that souls are not guaranteed this rest even in *ha-'olam ha-ba*. One's own achievements in life determine the quality of one's rest in the world to come but attaining this state also relies on those who remain in the world of the living. The prayer makes this explicit in its request that the one praying 'contribute to charity in remembrance of [the departed's] soul',⁵² constituting a kind of cosmic ledger where every prayer and deed is taken into account.

In her translation, Tivon's interweaving of *rachamim* and its cognates creates the possibility of a rich intertextual reading that brings Jewish liturgical texts to the fore, as I have noted above, but for the remainder of this chapter I will focus in particular on echoes that I discern between this translation and modern Hebrew literary texts, and specifically the work of the Israeli poet Yehuda Amichai (1924–2000). Amichai was born Ludwig Pfeuffer in Würzberg, Germany, in 1924 and emigrated to Mandatory Palestine when he was a young boy, later changing his name to Yehuda Amichai (עמי חי, ami-chai, my people lives). Like Lispector, Amichai's work has inspired readings that seek out traces of his early biography, particularly with respect to his German childhood and Germanic traces in his Hebrew poems.[53] But where I discern a relation between these writers is with respect to how each one interrogates the principle of *rachamim* or *piedade* in their work. Across many poems in his long career, Amichai frequently addressed and problematized *rachamim* as both a divine and human virtue. This preoccupation is evident in early poems like 'El male rachimim' [God Full of Mercy] which takes its title from the aforementioned prayer and 'Elohim merachem 'al yaldei ha-gan' [God Has Pity on Kindergarten Children], one of his most popular poems. The latter was published in Amichai's 1955 debut collection *Akshav u-ve-yamim acherim* [*Now and in Other Days*]; written in the aftermath of the 1948 war, it is frequently read as Amichai's meditation on the struggle to reconcile faith and tradition with lived, often brutal and violent, realities. It opens with the following startling stanza:

אֱלֹהִים מְרַחֵם עַל יַלְדֵי הַגַּן,
פָּחוֹת מִזֶּה עַל יַלְדֵי בֵּית-הַסֵּפֶר.
וְעַל הַגְּדוֹלִים לֹא יְרַחֵם עוֹד,
יַשְׁאִירֵם לְבַדָּם,
וְלִפְעָמִים יִצְטָרְכוּ לִזְחֹל עַל אַרְבַּע
בַּחוֹל הַלּוֹהֵט,
כְּדֵי לְהַגִּיעַ לְתַחֲנַת הָאִסּוּף
וְהֵם שׁוֹתְתֵי דָם.[54]

> God has pity on kindergarten children.
> He has less pity on school children
> And on grownups he has no pity at all,
> he leaves them alone,
> and sometimes they must crawl on all fours
> in the burning sand
> to reach the first-aid station
> covered with blood.
> (trans. by Stephen Mitchell).[55]

This poem seeks to reconcile the belief in a compassionate god, *Rachamana*, with a world that appears to be full of unrelenting suffering and poverty. Children have God's compassion not because they are more deserving, but because they have not yet stepped out of the 'garden' into the real world. Once they leave the safe space of the garden — and here an association with the biblical Garden of Eden is strongly insinuated — they are subject to a pitiless world. The speaker then pivots into a reflection on accountability and responsibility — in a world bereft of God's mercy, it falls upon 'us' to tender, in the poet's words, 'the last rare coins of compassion'.[56] Such acts are mutually beneficial, a poetic 'pay it forward'. Counting on God's mercy, human beings may find themselves reluctant to invest in acts of pity and charity, but from the very opening lines of the poem, Amichai's speaker explicitly exposes the very idea of a merciful God as a false cosmic safety net.

In his next collection, *Be-merchak shtei tikvot* [*Two Hopes Away*], published in 1958, Amichai included the poem 'El male rachamim', which further elaborates this idea of an unmerciful God in the poem's opening lines:[57]

אֵל מָלֵא רַחֲמִים,
אִלְמָלֵא הָאֵל מָלֵא רַחֲמִים
הָיוּ הָרַחֲמִים בָּעוֹלָם וְלֹא רַק בּוֹ.

> God full of mercy,
> If God were not full of mercy
> There would be mercy in the world and not just in Him.

Human beings exercise compassion in the hopes that they will be repaid in kind in the hour of their greatest need. Amichai, on the contrary, points to the futility of these prayers through the counterfactual conditional 'if God were not'. In Hebrew, the conditional conjunction 'if not' — *ilmale* — contains the letters that form *el* [god] and *male* [full], a pun that suggests that this condition is not hypothetical. Through this grammatical sleight of hand, Amichai advances the idea of a god who is, in Chana Kronfeld's words, 'a selfish child' who gorges himself on mercy and leaves nothing for human beings.[58]

In *A hora da estrela*, we repeatedly encounter the refusal of other characters to extend pity or compassion towards Macabéa. Of the doctor who treats her, we are told that 'O médico simplesmente se negou a ter piedade' [[he] resisted any temptation to be compassionate].[59] In Tivon's translation, this becomes, 'ha-rofe pashut sirev le-rachem', the doctor simply refused to pity.[60] When Madame Carlota exclaims, 'Mas, Macabeazinha, que vida horrível a sua! Que meu amigo Jesus tenha dó de você, filhinha! Mas que horror!' [Poor little Macabéa, what a terrible life you have! May my friend Jesus have pity on you, my child, how awful!], her words implore a divine compensation for Macabéa's sufferings, thereby releasing her from any personal responsibility to dispense this compensation directly.[61] Here, Tivon also translates Lispector's *dó* [pity] from the Latin *dolor*, as *lerachem*, to take pity ('she-yeshu yedidi ketsat yirachem alaykh' [may my friend Jesus pity you a bit]).[62] This scene with Madame Carlota is also where Segalovitz locates a reference to Zwi Migdal, a Jewish crime organization involved in the sexual trafficking of Eastern European Jewish women in the early twentieth century. Active in Brazil, the group left its mark on Brazilian Portuguese slang, for example, when Madame Carlota describes her former work as a 'caftina' [madam]. Segalovitz notes that this word recalls the Portuguese slang term for pimp, 'cafetão', which in turn derives from caftan (in Hebrew, *kapota*), denoting Hasidic traditional dress. She concludes that 'Lispector thus ends her tale of this female version of Judah the Maccabee with a reminder of Jewish violence against Jews in Brazilian society', a history that resonates in this meeting between the two women.[63] Like the false promises made to the Jewish women who fell victim of Zwi Migdal, the future that Madame Carlota presents to Macabéa proves fatal.

As he narrates Macabéa's prolonged death scene, Rodrigo S.M. sees a violinist busking on the street, possibly the same musician he referred to at the opening of the story, whose 'plangent tones' would serve as a soundtrack for his narration.[64] Here, the levitating fiddlers of Marc Chagall's paintings come to mind; in fact, it may not be incidental that Lispector's Portuguese translation of *Brenendike likht* [*Burning Lights*], a memoir by Bella Rosenfeld Chagall, the painter's first wife, was published posthumously in 1975, just two years before *A hora da estrela*.[65] Like the violinist who appears at the beginning and end of the novella, Chagall's fiddlers are translational figures on the threshold of past and present, life and death, but they also connect powerfully to Jewish history and tradition as figures associated, for Chagall, with the vanished world of East European Jewry. The scene may be full of Christian references, but Tivon's Hebrew translation invokes the language of Jewish lament and consolation. The Portuguese 'violino' [violin, fiddle], for example, becomes 'kinor' in Hebrew, a word that in biblical Hebrew denotes an ancient instrument akin to the harp or lyre, the instrument that David plays to soothe a tormented Saul (1 Samuel 16. 23). It is the instrument that the exiled Israelites 'hang on the poplars', as they grieve the loss of Zion from the shores of Babylon (Psalm 137). I also want to note that when Rodrigo S.M. asks the reader to 'pray for [Macabéa] and interrupt whatever you're doing in order to breathe a little life into her', Tivon translates Lispector's 'sopra-lhe vida' as 'ru'ach chayim', a phrase that appears a few times in the biblical story of Noah, notably when God informs Noah that the coming flood will destroy 'all flesh that has within it the breath of life' (Genesis 6:17).[66] The story of the flood is exceedingly cruel — elevating the life of the few over the many — but here Lispector, via Tivon's translation, refuses to forsake Macabéa. Prayer may not save Macabéa but the act of prayer, even when it is self-serving, acknowledges her humanity. Standing by Macabéa's broken body, the violinist's tin can collects 'the rattling coins' of bystanders who, in Rodrigo S.M.'s words, were grateful that he played 'the dirge of their lives'.[67] These coins allude to Charon, the figure in Greek mythology who ferries the dead across the river Styx in exchange for a coin, but they are also the coins of charity and compassion that Amichai describes in 'God Has Pity on Kindergarten Children'. As the strangers dispense these coins, Rodrigo S.M. reflects on the possibility — and even wish — that this music will play at the time of his own death, which may suggest that paying the busker now invests in that future possibility.

Amichai further explores the economy of *rachamim* in a later poem, 'Be-khol chumrat ha-rachamim' [The Full Severity of Compassion], which opens with the following lines:

מְנֵה אוֹתָם.
אַתָּה יָכוֹל לִמְנוֹת אוֹתָם. הֵם
אֵינָם כַּחוֹל, אֲשֶׁר עַל שְׂפַת הַיָּם. הֵם
אֵינָם כַּכּוֹכָבִים לָרֹב. הֵם כַּאֲנָשִׁים בּוֹדְדִים.
בַּפִּנָּה וּבָרְחוֹב.[68]

> Count them.
> You can count them. They are
> Not like the sand on the seashore. They are

> Not like the countless stars. They are like lonely people.
> On the corner and on the road.

In the Hebrew bible, stars and sand represent limitless quantities; they feature notably in God's promise to the biblical Abraham (which Amichai alludes to here): 'Look up to the heavens and count the stars, if you can count them [...]. So shall be your seed' (Genesis 15:5). Although the 'they' in the poem is never identified, the reference to 'ruined houses' in the stanza that follows likely refers to the Arab villages razed in the 1948 war and in the years that followed.[69] I have translated the Hebrew expression *ka-anashim bodedim* as 'lonely', but 'single' or 'solitary' are possibilities. For Amichai, to count 'them' means to acknowledge an individual's existence and humanity, their 'hopes, unbandaged'.[70] This ethic of compassion is present from the beginning of *A hora da estrela*, when Rodrigo S.M. notes that '[t]here are thousands of girls like this girl from the Northeast to be found in the slums of Rio de Janeiro', but the novella will focus on just one, 'the creation of an entire human being who is as much alive as I am'.[71] As the story of Macabéa unfolds, Rodrigo S.M. openly struggles between feelings of repulsion towards his protagonist and his commitment to acknowledge her existence.

In her translation of the scene of Macabéa's death, Tivon's Hebrew renders Lispector's 'rezem por' [pray for] as 'titpalelu 'aleya'. The translation of the Portuguese is straightforward, but the preposition *'al* may imply that one is praying *over* someone or something.[72] It is a small detail, and one that involves a hyper-literal reading of the Hebrew; regardless, when I read the Hebrew translation, this *'al* stages the scene in a way that recalls (among other things) a funeral, like the one that opened this chapter, as if the bystanders were graveside, praying for Macabéa. I want to offer here one final detail about Lispector's gravestone: along the bottom a series of Hebrew letters are engraved on the stone, the acronym for תהיה נפשו/נפשה צרורה בצרור החיים, 'may his/her soul be bound in the bundle of life' (I Samuel 25:29). These words also appear in the prayer 'El male rachamim', in the line 'the Merciful One will bind her/his soul in the bundle of life'. The prayer 'El male rachamim' may insist that our acts of charity on earth shape the state of our soul in the world to come, but in Amichai's poetry, as in Lispector's story, it is in the present moment that our acts of compassion, pity and mercy matter. As Naomi Sokoloff has observed, 'A God full of mercy remains at a remove from the world of fulfilment, of efforts, disappointments, realizations and change'; rather, she argues, '[Amichai] deals directly with [the world], and, indeed, with a very concrete, physical world'.[73] If compassion is the distinguishing mark of being human, of being part of humanity, then we can understand Rodrigo S.M.'s final realization of his own mortality as a sign that he has attained this virtue. As Macabéa's light goes out, she fulfils the other possibility of her Hebrew name, becoming, like the Maccabean miracle of light, the spark of this affirmation.

Works Cited

ALTER, ROBERT, trans., *The Book of Psalms: A Translation with Commentary* (New York: W. W. Norton, 2007)

—— trans., *The Hebrew Bible: A Translation with Commentary*, vol. 1 (New York: W. W. Norton, 2018)

AMICHAI, YEHUDA, *Shirim 1948–1962*, vol. 1 (Jerusalem: Schocken, 2002 [1962])

—— *The Selected Poetry of Yehuda Amichai*, trans. and ed. by Chana Bloch and Stephen Mitchell (Berkeley and Los Angeles: University of California Press, 2006 [1986])

AYTÜRK, İLKER, 'Attempts at Romanizing the Hebrew Script and Their Failure: Nationalism, Religion and Alphabet Reform in the Yishuv', *Middle Eastern Studies*, 43.4 (2007), 625–45

BENOR, SARAH BUNIN, 'On Jewish Languages, Names, and Distinctiveness', *The Jewish Quarterly Review*, 16.4 (Fall 2016), 440–49

BIALIK, CHAIM NACHMAN, "Od 'al kinus ha-ru'ach' (February/March 1926), *Ben Yehuda Project*, <https://benyehuda.org/read/3998> [accessed 23 May 2021]

—— 'She'elat ha-leshonot be-yisra'el', *Ben Yehuda Project*, <https://benyehuda.org/read/3553> [accessed 25 May 2021]

DAMROSCH, DAVID, 'Scriptworlds: Writing Systems and the Formation of World Literature', *Modern Language Quarterly*, 68.2 (June 2007), 195–219

DIANTONIO, ROBERT, and NORA GLICKMAN, eds, *Tradition and Innovation: Reflections on Latin American Jewish Writing* (Albany, NY: SUNY Press, 1993)

EISENBERG, RONALD L., *Jewish Traditions: A JPS Guide* (Philadelphia: Jewish Publication Society, 2004)

FETTHAUER, SOPHIE, 'Josef Aronsohn', in *Lexikon verfolgter Musiker und Musikerinnen der NS-Zeit*, ed. by Claudia Maurer Zenck, Peter Petersen and Sophie Fetthauer (Hamburg: Universität Hamburg, 2017)

GOTLIB, NÁDIA BATTELLA, *Clarice: uma vida que se conta* (São Paulo: Ática, 1995)

HALPERIN, LIORA R., *Babel in Zion: Jews, Nationalism, and Language Diversity in Palestine, 1920–1948* (New Haven, CT: Yale University Press, 2015)

INSPIRAÇÃO LITERÁRIA (channel), *Enterro de Clarice Lispector, 11 de Dezembro de 1977*, online video recording, YouTube <https://www.youtube.com/watch?v=koho64RggMg> [accessed 2 February 2021]

KOREN, YEHUDA, 'Bedidut ha-metergemet', *Yediot Achronot*, 22 March 1996, p. 28

KRONFELD, CHANA, *The Full Severity of Compassion: The Poetry of Yehuda Amichai* (Stanford, CA: Stanford University Press, 2016)

LISPECTOR, CLARICE, *A paixão segundo G.H.* (Rio de Janeiro: Francisco Alves, 1991 [1964]); *The Passion According to G.H.*, trans. by Idra Novey (New York: New Directions, 2012)

—— *A hora da estrela*, 23rd edn (Rio de Janeiro: Francisco Alves, 1995 [1977]); *The Hour of the Star*, trans. by Giovanni Pontiero (New York: New Directions, 1992 [1986])

—— *A descoberta do mundo* (Rio de Janeiro: Francisco Alves, 1994 [1984]); *Discovering the World*, trans. by Giovanni Pontiero (Manchester: Carcanet, 1992)

—— *Kishrei mispacha/ She'at ha-kokhav [Family Ties/ The Hour of the Star]*, trans. by Miriam Tivon (Bnei Barak: Ha-kibbuts ha-me'uchad/Siman kri'a, 1999)

MINTZ, ALAN, *Sanctuary in the Wilderness: A Critical Introduction to American Hebrew Poetry* (Stanford, CA: Stanford University Press, 2011)

Miriam Tivon, Leksikon ha-sifrut ha-'ivrit ha-chadasha, <https://library.osu.edu/projects/hebrew-lexicon/00718> [accessed 23 August 2020]

MOSER, BENJAMIN, *Why This World: A Biography of Clarice Lispector* (New York: Oxford University Press, 2009)

NATKOVITCH, SVETLANA, 'Miriam Tivon', *Heksherim Lexicon of Israeli Literature*, <https://heksherimlexicon.bgu.ac.il/lexicon-entry/טבעון-מרים/> [accessed 23 August 2020]

'No enterro de Clarice Lispector, 200 pessoas', *Folha de São Paulo*, 12 December 1977: http://almanaque.folha.uol.com.br/ilustrada_12dez1977.htm [accessed 2 February 2021]

PARK, SOWON S., 'Introduction: Translational Scriptworlds', *Journal of World Literature*, 1 (2016), 129–41

PERI, MENACHEM, 'Ma hem 'osim sham mul ha-tekst' [What do they do in front of a text?], *Ha-sifriya ha-chadasha*, <https://www.newlibrary.co.il/article?co=13162> [accessed 8 February 2021]

PIÑON, NÉLIDA, *Livro das horas* (Lisbon: Círculo de Leitores, 2013 [2012])

SEGALOVITZ, YAEL, '"Ha-sefer ha-ze hu demama": Novelat ha-anti kokhav shel Lispektor' ['This Book is a Silence': Lispector's Anti-Star Novella], in Clarice Lispector, *She'at ha-kokhav*, trans. by Miriam Tivon (Bnei Barak: Ha-kibbuts ha-me'uchad/Siman kri'a, 2020 [1999]), pp. 83–94

SELA, MAYA, 'Clarice Lispector: Ha-sfinks mi-Rio de Janeiro', *Haaretz* (13 August 2009), <https://www.haaretz.co.il/gallery/1.3339126> [last accessed 6 September 2020].

SOKOLOFF, NAOMI B., 'On Amichai's El male raḥamim', *Prooftexts*, 4.2 (May 1984), 127–40.

SOUSA, CARLOS MENDES DE, 'Dizer a morte de Clarice Lispector', *Revista Caliban* (20 July 2016), <https://revistacaliban.net/dizer-a-morte-de-clarice-lispector-aaea284fa52a> [accessed 1 July 2021]

VARIN, CLAIRE, *Clarice Lispector: rencontres brésiliennes* (Laval, Québec: Trois, 1987)

VIEIRA, NELSON H., *Jewish Voices in Brazilian Literature: A Prophetic Discourse of Alterity* (Gainesville: University of Florida Press, 1995)

Notes to Chapter 24

1. I am grateful to Claire Varin for the permission to use her photograph, which first appeared in Claire Varin, *Clarice Lispector: rencontres brésiliennes* (Laval, Québec: Trois, 1987), p. 220.
2. Clarice Lispector, *A paixão segundo G.H.* (Rio de Janeiro: Francisco Alves, 1991 [1964]), p. 21; *The Passion According to G.H.*, trans. by Idra Novey (New York: New Directions, 2021), p. 9.
3. Her sister Elisa Lispector's autobiographical novel *No exílio* [*In Exile*] provides the most extensive portrait of the Lispector family's Jewish ties. Elisa Lispector, *No exílio: Romance* [In Exile: A Novel] (Rio de Janeiro: Irmãos Pongetti, 1948).
4. Quoted in Nelson H. Vieira, *Jewish Voices in Brazilian Literature: A Prophetic Discourse of Alterity* (Gainesville: University of Florida Press, 1995), p. 117.
5. Clarice Lispector, *A descoberta do mundo* (Rio de Janeiro: Francisco Alves, 1994 [1984]), p. 345. All translations from the Portuguese and Hebrew are mine unless otherwise noted. Giovanni Pontiero renders this line as 'I am a naturalized Brazilian and, had my parents set out a few months earlier, I should have been born in Brazil.' Clarice Lispector, *Discovering the World*, trans. by Giovanni Pontiero (Manchester: Carcanet, 1992), pp. 418–19.
6. In Lurianic Kabbalah, a school of Jewish mysticism, the creation of the universe was preceded by *shevirat ha-kelim*, the breaking of vessels which contained the divine light. This event brought chaos and disorder into the world. The broken shards of these vessels contain sparks of the divine light that humans must now gather if the world is to become whole again, a process called *tikkun 'olam*, repair of the world.
7. Benjamin Moser, *Why This World: A Biography of Clarice Lispector* (New York: Oxford University Press, 2009), p. 385.
8. As Sarah Bunin Benor has shown in her work on Jewish English, the pressure to assimilate, at least outwardly, contributed in part to the concealment of Hebrew names and Jewish languages in the early to mid-twentieth century. Benor, 'On Jewish Languages, Names, and Distinctiveness', *The Jewish Quarterly Review*, 16.4 (Fall 2016), 440–49.
9. The orthography here corresponds to the Ashkenazic pronunciation of the prayer, whereas my transliterations, out of personal habit, reflect the Sephardic pronunciation that is more common in Israeli Hebrew.
10. 'No enterro de Clarice Lispector, 200 pessoas', *Folha de São Paulo*, 12 December 1977, <http://

almanaque.folha.uol.com.br/ilustrada_12dez1977.htm> [accessed 2 February 2021]. In my English translation of the passage, I have corrected the name of Lispector's sister, which is Elisa and not Elvira as reported in the newspaper and also corrected the misidentification of Lispector's son Paulo.

11. Joseph Aronsohn (1918–1993) fled Germany during World War II and lived for several years in Shanghai before emigrating to Brazil in 1949, where he joined the Associação Religiosa Israelita (ARI), an organization for Jewish immigrants founded by Henrique (Heinrich) Lemle (1909–1978), in 1942. Lemle, a rabbi, was affiliated with Reform Judaism and led Rio de Janeiro's largest Jewish congregation for many years. Aronsohn and Lemle had met at Buchenwald concentration camp in 1938. Sophie Fetthauer, 'Josef Aronsohn', in *Lexikon verfolgter Musiker und Musikerinnen der NS-Zeit*, ed. by Claudia Maurer Zenck, Peter Petersen and Sophie Fetthauer (Hamburg: Universität Hamburg, 2017) <https://www.lexm.uni-hamburg.de/object/lexm_lexmperson_00005268 [accessed 2 February 2021]; 'Henrique Lemle Dead at 68', *Jewish Telegraphic Agency*, 27 September 1978, <https://www.jta.org/1978/09/27/archive/henrique-lemle-dead-at-68> [accessed 2 February 2021].
12. English translation from the King James Version. Until recently, a short recording of the beginning of Lispector's burial ceremony was available online. Inspiração Literária (channel), *Enterro de Clarice Lispector, 11 de Dezembro de 1977*, online video recording, YouTube <https://www.youtube.com/watch?v=koho64RggMg> [last accessed 2 February 2021].
13. Jewish funerals do not follow a prescribed liturgical order; the order in which some prayers appear during the burial ceremony can vary between communities and even, as was likely the case for Lispector's family, may be determined by the family and congregation.
14. On his own and in collaboration with Rabbi Fritz Pinkuss, Lemle translated a number of Jewish liturgical texts into Portuguese, among them the *siddur*, the Jewish daily prayer book.
15. Carlos Mendes de Sousa, 'Dizer a morte de Clarice Lispector', *Revista Caliban*, 20 July 2016, <https://revistacaliban.net/dizer-a-morte-de-clarice-lispector-aaea284fa52a> [accessed 1 July 2021].
16. The announcements for this 'missa de ressurreição' appeared in *O Globo*, 14 December 1977, p. 18. I am grateful to Claire Williams for sharing these materials with me.
17. 'assim dando prova de sua conversão', Nélida Piñon, *Livro das horas* (Lisbon: Círculo de Leitores, 2012]), p. 67.
18. David Damrosch, 'Scriptworlds: Writing Systems and the Formation of World Literature', *Modern Language Quarterly*, 68.2 (June 2007), 195–219 (p. 200).
19. Ibid., p. 209.
20. Sowon S. Park, 'Introduction: Translational Scriptworlds', *Journal of World Literature*, 1 (2016), 129–41 (p. 130).
21. Damrosch, 'Scriptworlds', p. 208.
22. İlker Aytürk, 'Attempts at Romanizing the Hebrew Script and Their Failure: Nationalism, Religion and Alphabet Reform in the Yishuv', *Middle Eastern Studies*, 43.4 (2007), 625–45.
23. Liora R. Halperin, *Babel in Zion: Jews, Nationalism, and Language Diversity in Palestine, 1920–1948* (New Haven, CT: Yale University Press, 2015), pp. 107–08.
24. Chaim Nachman Bialik, "Od 'al kinus ha-ru'ach' (February/March 1926), *Ben Yehuda Project*: <https://benyehuda.org/read/3998> [accessed 23 May 2021]. I discuss Bialik's *kinus* project in my article 'The Forgers of World Literature: Translation, *Nachdichtung*, and Hebrew World Poetry', in *The Cambridge Handbook of World Literature*, ed. by Debjani Ganguly (Cambridge: Cambridge University Press, 2021), pp. 544–65.
25. Chaim Nachman Bialik, 'She'elat ha-leshonot be-yisra'el', *Ben Yehuda Project*, <https://benyehuda.org/read/3553> [accessed 25 May 2021].
26. Aytürk, 'Attempts at Romanizing the Hebrew Script and Their Failure', p. 636.
27. Alan Mintz, *Sanctuary in the Wilderness: A Critical Introduction to American Hebrew Poetry* (Stanford, CA: Stanford University Press, 2011), p. 70.
28. Nádia Battella Gotlib, *Clarice: uma vida que se conta* (São Paulo: Ática, 1995), p. 115.
29. For a trenchant critique of the tendency to force a Jewish reading onto Lispector's texts, see Naomi Lindstrom, 'Judaic Traces in the Narrative of Clarice Lispector: Identity Politics and

Evidence', in *Latin American Jewish Cultural Production*, ed. by David William Foster (Nashville, TN: Vanderbilt University Press, 2009), pp. 83–96.
30. Clarice Lispector, *Kishrei mispacha/ She'at ha-kokhav* [*Family Ties/The Hour of the Star*], trans. by Miriam Tivon (Bnei Barak: Ha-kibbuts ha-me'uchad/Siman kri'a, 1999).
31. I have drawn this biographical information from Svetlana Natkovitch, 'Miriam Tivon', *Heksherim Lexicon of Israeli Literature*, <https://heksherimlexicon.bgu.ac.il/lexicon-entry/טבעון-מרים/> [accessed 23 August 2020].
32. For a comprehensive list of her published translations (last updated in 2012), see 'Miriam Tivon', *Leksikon ha-sifrut ha-'ivrit ha-chadasha*, <https://library.osu.edu/projects/hebrew-lexicon/00718> [accessed 23 August 2020].
33. Natkovitch, 'Miriam Tivon'.
34. Yehuda Koren, 'Bedidut ha-metergemet', *Yediot Achronot*, 22 March 1996, p. 28. I am grateful to Tafat Hacohen-Bick for making this interview available to me.
35. Cf. Robert DiAntonio and Nora Glickman, eds., *Tradition and Innovation: Reflections on Latin American Jewish Writing* (Albany, NY: SUNY Press, 1993); Naomi Lindstrom, 'The Pattern of Allusions in Clarice Lispector', *Luso-Brazilian Review*, 36.1 (Summer, 1999), 111–21; Vieira, *Jewish Voices in Brazilian Literature*.
36. Quoted in Maya Sela, 'Clarice Lispector: Ha-sfinks mi-Rio de Janeiro', *Haaretz*, 13 August 2009, <https://www.haaretz.co.il/gallery/1.3339126> [accessed 6 September 2020].
37. Menachem Peri, 'Ma hem 'osim sham mul ha-tekst' [What do they do there in front of the text?], *Ha-sifriya ha-chadasha*, <https://www.newlibrary.co.il/article?co=13162> [accessed 8 February 2021].
38. Ibid.
39. See Cynthia Beatrice Costa's and Luana Ferreira de Freitas's chapter in this volume.
40. Sela, 'Clarice Lispector: Ha-sfinks mi-Rio de Janeiro'. None of the major biographies of Lispector, including Moser's, has been translated into Hebrew.
41. Ibid.
42. Yael Segalovitz, '"Ha-sefer ha-ze hu demama": Novelat ha-anti kokhav shel Lispektor' ['This Book is a Silence': Lispector's Anti-Star Novella], in Clarice Lispector, *She'at ha-kokhav* [*The Hour of the Star*], trans. by Miriam Tivon (Bnei Barak: Ha-kibbuts ha-me'uchad/Siman kri'a, 2020 [1999]), pp. 83–94 (p. 87). See Yael Segalovitz's chapter in this volume.
43. Ibid.
44. Clarice Lispector, *A hora da estrela*, 23rd edn (Rio de Janeiro: Francisco Alves, 1995 [1977]). The word occurs in too many pages to cite here and has been translated as '(bang)' by Giovanni Pontiero and '(explosion)' by Benjamin Moser.
45. Clarice Lispector, *The Hour of the Star*, trans. by Giovanni Pontiero (New York: New Directions, 1992 [1986]), pp. 16, 84.
46. Lispector, *A hora da estrela*, p. 27; *The Hour of the Star*, p. 13; *She'at ha-kokhav*, p. 135. My emphases.
47. Robert Alter, trans., *The Book of Psalms: A Translation with Commentary* (New York: W. W. Norton, 2007), p. 359.
48. Lispector, *The Hour of the Star*, p. 82. I have Roni Masel to thank for the expression 'theological intimacy' and for her comments on this chapter.
49. Yevamot 79a, *Sefaria*, <https://www.sefaria.org/79a> [accessed 29 May 2021].
50. Ibid. The English translation comes from the William Davidson Talmud, a free digital edition of the Babylonian Talmud.
51. This is distinct from the prayer 'Av ha-rachamim' [Father of Mercy], which was composed in the wake of the First Crusades and explicitly calls for vengeance on behalf of Jewish martyrs.
52. Ronald L. Eisenberg, *Jewish Traditions: A JPS Guide* (Philadelphia: Jewish Publication Society, 2004), p. 87. I have used the translation provided in this description.
53. Cf. Nili Scharf Gold, *Yehuda Amichai: The Making of Israel's National Poet* (Lebanon, NH: University Press of New England, 2008) and Na'ama Rokem, 'German–Hebrew Encounters in the Poetry and Correspondence of Yehuda Amichai and Paul Celan', *Prooftexts*, 30.1 (1 January 2010), 97–127.
54. Yehuda Amichai, 'Elohim merachem 'al yaldei ha-gan', *Shirim 1962–1948*, vol. 1 (Jerusalem: Schocken, 2002 [1962]), p. 15.

55. Yehuda Amichai, 'God Has Pity on Kindergarten Children', *The Selected Poetry of Yehuda Amichai*, trans. and ed. by Chana Bloch and Stephen Mitchell (Berkeley and Los Angeles: University of California Press, 2006 [1986]), p. 1.
56. Ibid. Stephen Mitchell translates the Hebrew *chesed* as 'compassion' but another possible translation is 'lovingkindness'.
57. Yehuda Amichai, *Shirim 1948–1962*, pp. 86.
58. For a different translation of these lines, and of the full poem, see Yehuda Amichai, 'God Full of Mercy', trans. by Chana Bloch and Chana Kronfeld, in Chana Kronfeld, *The Full Severity of Compassion: The Poetry of Yehuda Amichai* (Stanford, CA: Stanford University Press, 2016), p. 89. These lines repeat at the end of the poem in a slightly altered form.
59. Lispector, *A hora da estrela*, p. 86; *The Hour of the Star*, p. 68.
60. Lispector, *She'at ha-kokhav*, p. 183.
61. Lispector, *A hora da estrela*, p. 94; *The Hour of the Star*, p. 75.
62. Lispector, *She'at ha-kokhav*, p. 190.
63. Segalovitz, 'Ha-sefer ha-ze hu demama', p. 92.
64. Lispector, *The Hour of the Star*, p. 23.
65. Bella Chagall (née Rosenfeld) was Marc Chagall's first wife. Her memoir was published posthumously in 1946, two years after her death. Although the book was originally written in Yiddish, Lispector's translation was based on the French translation. Bella Chagall, *Luzes acesas*, trans. by Clarice Lispector (Rio de Janeiro: Nova Fronteira, 1975); Nádia Battella Gotlib, *Clarice fotobiografia* (São Paulo: EDUSP and Imprensa Oficial, 2007), p. 538. Many thanks to Claire Williams for pointing out this connection.
66. Lispector, *The Hour of the Star*, p. 82; *A hora da estrela*, p. 102; *She'at ha-kokhav*, p. 197; Robert Alter, trans. *The Hebrew Bible: A Translation with Commentary*, vol. 1 (New York: W. W. Norton, 2018), p. 27.
67. Lispector, *The Hour of the Star*, p. 82.
68. Amichai, *Shirim 1948–1962*, p. 297.
69. For a fuller consideration of the figure of the ruined Arab village in modern Hebrew poetry, see Haggai Rogani, *Mul ha-kfar she-charav: ha-shira ha-'ivrit ve-ha-sikhsukh ha-yehudi-'aravi 1929–1967* [Facing the Ruined Village: Hebrew Poetry and the Jewish-Arab Conflict 1929–1967] (Haifa: Pardes Press, 2006).
70. I have translated this stanza into English. For Chana Bloch and Chana Kronfeld's translation of the poem (from which I have quoted the words 'hopes, unbandaged'), see Kronfeld, *The Full Severity of Compassion*, p. 136.
71. Lispector, *The Hour of the Star*, pp. 14, 19.
72. Lispector, *A hora da estrela*, p. 102; *She'at ha-kokhav*, p. 197.
73. Naomi B. Sokoloff, 'On Amichai's El male raḥamim', *Prooftexts*, 4.2 (May 1984), 127–40 (p. 132).

CHAPTER 25

Marketing Lispector: Life Writing as Literary Criticism

Júlia Braga Neves

Clarice Lispector's life has always been of great interest to her readers, including her critics. Indeed, many of Lispector's works, such as the chronicles and short stories, can be seen to put forward fictionalized accounts of autobiographical events. Lícia Manzo argues that none of Lispector's books can be considered autobiographical, but they nevertheless provide 'um percurso irreversível em direção à primeira pessoa, ao texto confessional, ao "eu", [...] acabando por converter-se no personagem principal de seus escritos' [an irreversible movement towards the first person, the confessional text, the 'I', [...] converting herself into the central character of her writings].[1] Although Lispector frequently denied that her literature was autobiographical, Manzo contends that her writing became an 'unplanned autobiography' to the extent that her novels, short stories, chronicles and press contributions negotiated between her life and her fiction.

The entanglement between Lispector's life and work has become a compelling critical approach, especially with the publication of several biographies over the last forty years. This chapter will examine how Lispector's biographies have consolidated a widely established critical reading of her fiction through the lens of her biography. In particular, I will focus on Nádia Battella Gotlib's 1995 biography *Clarice: uma vida que se conta* [Clarice: A Life that Tells Itself], Teresa Montero's 1999 *Eu sou uma pergunta: uma biografia de Clarice Lispector* [I Am a Question: A Biography of Clarice Lispector] and Benjamin Moser's 2009 *Why This World: A Biography of Clarice Lispector*, all three of which are biographies that resulted from academic research that explored how Lispector's life and writing are deeply related.[2] Although the biographical approach to Lispector's works goes back to translations published before Gotlib's, Montero's and Moser's biographies, I will argue that their books have strengthened readings of Lispectorian literature as autobiographical. Furthermore, I contend that the emphasis on Lispector's life has become a marketing strategy for her literature. This has intensified since the publication of Moser's *Why This World*, a book frequently referenced as pivotal in the international promotion of Lispector's literary legacy and for the expansion of her readership worldwide.[3]

It is important to stress, however, that the first book to introduce this parallel between life and work was Olga Borelli's memoir *Clarice Lispector: esboço para um possível retrato* [Clarice Lispector: Sketch for a Possible Portrait], which was published in 1981. The book includes some of Lispector's unpublished fragments and correspondence with her sisters, along with Borelli's own memories of Lispector. In a note to the reader, Borelli, who was one of Lispector's closest friends, anticipates that hers is a *depoimento* [testimony], rather than a biography, 'onde procurei tornar explícita certas características pessoais' [where [she seeks] to make explicit [Lispector's] personal characteristics] and describe the 'particularidades que constituem o que se poderia chamar de "trajetória espiritual" de Clarice Lispector' [particularities that constitute what one may call Clarice Lispector's 'spiritual trajectory'].[4] Earlier translations of Lispector's literature also included information about her life, but usually as an introduction to the author and not as an overall approach to her fiction. One exception is Giovanni Pontiero, one of the most prominent translators of Lispector into English, who does mention overlapping aspects between her life and work in prefaces, introductions and afterwords to his translations that came out after her death in 1977.

In the translation of *Laços de família* [*Family Ties*], which was released in 1972, Pontiero introduces the collection of short stories by briefly noting life events and, instead of correlating biography and fiction, presents her literature as part of a tradition of existential writing comparable to that of Albert Camus and Jean-Paul Sartre.[5] In his 1986 translation of *A legião estrangeira* [*The Foreign Legion*] and 1992 translation of *Selected Crônicas*, however, the connection between life and work already features as a selling point. While Pontiero asserts, in the afterword to *The Foreign Legion*, that in these short stories 'we encounter Clarice Lispector in a number of guises: woman, mother, artist and mystic', who 'confides her own vulnerability, her personal phobias and obsessions', in the introduction to *Selected Crônicas* he states that some of the chronicles provide 'autobiographical details' that 'offer a reliable account of her origins and background'.[6] This approach was introduced to anglophone readers in the decades since up to the present day, and has been particularly buttressed by Moser's editorship of the New Directions translations of Lispector's works.

Of course, Gotlib's and Montero's biographies also paved the way for the interpretation of Lispector's texts alongside her life by introducing unpublished documents, photographs and testimonies, and discussing them side by side with her literature. However, Gotlib's biography has only been translated into Spanish and Montero's only exists in Portuguese, whereas Moser's book came out in English with a translation into Portuguese and several other languages, such as French, German, Dutch and Spanish. This information is relevant and important due to the disparities in the circulation of these biographies, considering that Gotlib's and Montero's books circulated mostly among Portuguese speakers who already had an interest in Lispector whereas Moser's arguably has had a greater impact because it was published in English and thereby achieved substantial visibility and circulation, not least by being widely reviewed by the North American, European and Brazilian press. Moser's professional and personal network and his role as a transnational figure also give him more power in the international publishing world certainly than Montero, who is a central figure in the promotion and edition of Lispector's works in Brazil, but even Gotlib, who is a highly renowned academic worldwide in the field of Brazilian literature, especially due to her research on Clarice Lispector. Moser's book came out with Oxford University Press in the US and Haus in the UK, and in 2014 the UK paperback was issued by Penguin. Montero and Gotlib had nowhere near that sort of advantage.

The influence of Moser's biography can also be perceived in the newly published editions of Lispector's work by New Directions, a major independent US publisher, which were edited by Moser himself. Colm Tóibín's introduction to *The Hour of the Star* [*A hora da estrela*], for instance, explicitly references Moser's biography, and asserts that although Lispector's novella cannot be regarded as an autobiography, it 'is an exploration of a self that is sometimes glimpsed, but barely known'.[7] Tóibín's reputation as an internationally acclaimed Irish author can be regarded as a further gesture of authority to Moser's biography in comparison with Gotlib's and Montero's.[8] Alongside Tóibín's introduction, Moser's forewords to the new translations of *Água viva* [*Agua Viva*], *Perto do coração selvagem* [*Near to the Wild Heart*], *A cidade sitiada* [*The Besieged City*], *Um sopro de vida: pulsações* [*A Breath of Life (Pulsations)*] and to *The Complete Stories* follow that reading, making reference to his own research about Lispector and the family's migration from Ukraine to Brazil.

Since Lispector was often reticent about personal aspects of her life, there seems to be an attempt in her biographies to unravel the enigmatic image she displayed publicly. What Gotlib, Montero and Moser share in their portrayal of Lispector is the ways that they often turn to her fiction to narrate her life or try to find aspects of her life within her fiction, narrowing the gap between the author's life and work. Occasionally, this relationship may create tension in the process of writing in a genre (biography) that relies on the premise of its non-fictionality and, at the same time, employs strategies — such as the construction of plot, description of characters, and the recreation of real-life situations through language — that pertain to the realm of fiction, which is based on the assumption of imagination and inventiveness and, in the case of Lispector's biographies, is used as a source to narrate her life.

Recent studies about life writing have frequently addressed the genre in the context of postmodernism with respect to the way that 'historical truth confronts narrative truth', but recognizing that 'the alliance is often uneasy'.[9] In these readings, there is a deliberate recognition that biographies borrow narrative techniques from fiction, since the construction of reality, in Ira B. Nadel's words, aims 'to present truthful characters in a convincing, realistic world' that is constructed by language and by 'the authenticity of events'.[10] Along similar lines, Hermione Lee upholds that 'biography is a form of narrative, not just a presentation of facts', since all biographies involve the collection and selection of stories from family, friends, co-workers and acquaintances, and of information compiled through archival and bibliographical research that is to be turned into a narrative.[11]

Lee also postulates that 'the biographer has a responsibility to the truth, and should tell us what actually happened in [the person's] life.'[12] While this might be an obvious statement, Lee warns us that it is a rule that is easy to break. She explains that authors of biographies may construct 'narratives with descriptions of emotions, highly coloured scene-setting, or strategies of suspense' to the point of composing works that 'read more like fiction than history'.[13] Janet Malcolm, however, suggests that what is established as truth and how the truth is represented is actually more complex than its narration, as she defines the biography as 'the medium through which the remaining secrets of the famous dead are taken from them' and exposed to the world.[14]

For Malcolm, a person cannot own their life, particularly if they are a public figure. In this sense, she compares the work of a biographer to that of a burglar who breaks into someone's private property in search of valuable items that will make their enterprise successful. Malcolm's comparison points to the role played by both the editorial market and the reader in this venture, as she stresses the ways that, on the one hand, the biographer 'is portrayed almost as a kind of benefactor' for their hard work and dedication, and the reader is plunged into 'a kind of collusion between him[self] and the biographer in an excitingly forbidden undertaking', which consists in 'tiptoeing down the corridor together, to stand in front of the bedroom door and try to peep through the keyhole'.[15] This, according to Malcolm, is what constitutes the very transgressive aspect of biographies.

Nevertheless, the transgression inherent to the biographical narrative must also be discussed in tandem with the ethics of life writing. Paul John Eakin disputes Malcolm's argument by explaining that ethics in life writing cannot be contained in 'a traditional model centered on privacy and property',[16] as Malcolm's burglar analogy postulates. Eakin identifies the following contradiction: if a person cannot own what others say about their own lives, especially if they are public figures, then the biographer cannot necessarily 'steal' information about the person they are writing about. For Eakin, the ethics of life writing lies in the biographer's commitment to the genre's non-fictional character, and in morality, for he understands that one's identity is produced through moral standards that should be considered by the biographer when writing about their subject.[17]

In the case of Lispector's biographies, the issues of fictionality, truth and ethics are particularly relevant. Firstly, because her fiction is used by Gotlib, Montero and Moser to compose narratives about her life. As we will see, Gotlib and Montero are more careful in establishing underlying truths about how Lispector's life is fictionalized in her literature. While Gotlib traces clear lines between life facts and how they were represented in Lispector's fiction, Montero counts on intertextual references from Lispector's literature that are not always marked as such, but rather function as parts of Montero's own narrative, creating a kind of patchwork text. Both Gotlib's and Montero's biographies are very much invested in newly found documents and testimonies about Lispector, although Montero's book deliberately shows how the lines between fictional and non-fictional are often blurred. However, it is relevant to note that her biography, like Gotlib's, still relies on historical documentation and ethical responsibility in the narration of Lispector's private life, especially in relation to the Lispectors' journey to Brazil, the writer's love affairs, and her elder son's mental illness.

In this sense, the venture of 'peeping through the keyhole' that binds reader and biographer in Gotlib's and Montero's biographies is curbed by ethical and moral guidelines that take into account Lispector's own image as a public figure, primarily as an author, since they are cautious about recounting episodes that cannot be entirely confirmed, and in consolidating them as overarching truths. Some examples of these episodes include the illness of her mother, Mania Lispector, the family's journey to Brazil, and events that compromise friends' or relatives' public portrayal, as is the case with her elder son. This is not to say that the public should not know about Lispector's private life, but rather to understand that not all aspects of it are relevant to the discussion of her literature or her role as a writer.

Moser's biography did certainly explore these 'blind spots', as it were, in Gotlib's and Montero's biographies, as I will show, most strongly in his account of the family's escape from Ukraine. Although he was the first to make public new information about their journey to Brazil, which was found in an unfinished manuscript written by Lispector's eldest sister, Elisa Lispector, Moser also, at times, offers speculative versions for the events that took place when the family was struggling to leave their home country. This latter aspect has become a significant point of contention in his biography, especially his allegation that Lispector's mother, Mania, was raped by Russian soldiers. This information has not been confirmed either by Lispector's family and friends, or by historical documentation, yet Moser has established it as an underlying truth that, according to his biography, permeates much of Lispector's literature. Moser's narration of Lispector's life can be deemed as transgressive in terms of how Malcolm understands the biography, as a way of 'stealing' and exposing the secrets of a public figure. However, his account of Lispector's life leads to discussions about ethics in life writing, and about legal debates regarding the publishing of his biography in Brazil.

While in the United States, Eakin argues, the right to privacy is 'legally ineffective', in Brazil this has been a feature strongly protected by law.[18] Until 2015, when the law was repealed by the Brazilian Supreme Court, all biographies had to be legally authorized by the person about whom it was written, if they were still alive, or by their heirs. In Lispector's case, this is of particular significance, since the three biographies discussed in the following sections had to be authorized by Lispector's family before they were published in Brazil. As we will see, this becomes an interesting point of discussion with respect to Moser's biography, since it is possible to compare the original version in English, which did not need the family's consent, with its translation into Brazilian Portuguese, which did, and in which some information was left out and, at times, modified from the English version.

Biography as Literary Criticism

In 1995, Gotlib published *Clarice: uma vida que se conta*, the first complete biography of Lispector, interweaving the author's life, work and a critical reading of her literature.[19] Gotlib's book was the first piece of life writing about the author that displayed unpublished photographs, original testimonies, and thorough research about the Lispector family in Brazil. This was also the first publication to systematically describe Lispector's life events in parallel to her work. In her introduction, Gotlib puts forward her objective in a 'universo em que o documental e o fictício se misturam' [a universe in which the documentary and the fictional merge] and in which biographical information and critical examination of Lispector's texts 'alternam-se e complementam-se, sem que, equivocadamente, se estabeleçam mútuas relações de dependência' [alternate and complement each other without, mistakenly, establishing mutual relations of dependency].[20] For Gotlib, Lispector's literature is not necessarily autobiographical in the sense that one could read her biography to understand her fiction or vice versa. Rather, her literary texts function, at most, as a fictionalization of the author herself: 'A prática do inventar outras ou de dramatizar-se em inúmeras máscaras será a condição da própria produção ficcional de Clarice' [The very production of Clarice's fiction would come to rely upon the practice of inventing other [selves] or of dramatizing herself behind countless masks].[21]

In each of Gotlib's readings, this perspective is corroborated by the juxtaposition of biographical narrative and literary criticism, where the author draws clear limitations between both. While the excerpts that recount Lispector's life are narrated according to testimonies, interviews and documents, Lispector's works are mostly presented chronologically in tandem with her life events. When discussing her literature, Gotlib's analyses often go back to what she has already narrated about Lispector's life as a means of creating a parallel between life and work and to provide a critical reading of this parallelism. Lispector's chronicles and short stories play an important role in the narrative, since the first-person narrator in these texts frequently refers to the author's life. For example, as Lispector openly states in a letter to the prominent chronicle writer, Rubem Braga: 'É fatal, numa crônica que aparece todos os sábados, terminar sem querer comentando as repercussões em nós de nossa vida diária e de nossa vida estranha' [It is inevitable, in a chronicle that appears every Saturday, to end up unwittingly commenting on the repercussions on oneself of daily life or about one's own strange life].[22] Even when Gotlib approaches these texts that are written in the first person, she is cautious about affirming that the 'I' that narrates the story corresponds to the reality of a specific life event: the narration is, in this sense, a representation of a memory and does not necessarily correspond to the reality of the event itself.

One example is Gotlib's interpretation of the chronicle entitled 'Medo da eternidade' [Fear of Eternity], which describes one of Lispector's childhood memories in Recife.[23] Her sister has given her a piece of gum and tells her that she can chew it forever, an episode that reminds Lispector of how scared she was of the 'peso da eternidade' [weight of eternity].[24] As she introduces the story, Gotlib emphasizes that the central motif of the chronicle is not really the gum, 'mas o que [ele] significa' [but its wider meaning], which is precisely the notion of eternity.[25] Gotlib makes sure to separate the episode that took place in childhood from the one that is narrated in the chronicle, for, as she explains, the piece of gum 'chega até a Clarice adulta que se lembra do que lhe aconteceu, mantendo, quem sabe, a seqüência dos fatos, mas já interpretando-lhes o significado' [reaches the adult

Clarice who remembers what happened to her, retaining, who knows, the sequence of facts, but now interpreting their meaning].[26] In Gotlib's reading, with which I concur, it is the piece of pink gum that turns grey and bland when it is chewed that triggers this fear of eternity, a theme that is reworked again, as Gotlib notes, in 'Amor' [Love], from *Laços de família* [*Family Ties*].

While testimonies, letters and Lispector's short stories and chronicles are important sources for Gotlib's research, the diverging official information about the writer's birthdate, the scarce availability of documents about the Lispector family's journey from Ukraine to Brazil and the circumstances of their emigration are described as obstacles.[27] In the first section of her biography, Gotlib explains that there are conflicting dates for Lispector's birth, since there are no traces of the original certificate issued in Ukraine. The available documents are translations from Russian, in which the first attests to Lispector being born on 10 December, and the other on 10 October 1920. In 2007, Lispector's original Ukrainian birth certificate was made public by the family, confirming her date of birth as 10 December, a new piece of information that Gotlib included in the revised biography.[28]

Gotlib also points out that it is difficult to trace reliable sources about the Lispectors' migration to Brazil and exposes the uncertainties and hypotheses that emerge:

> [Clarice nasceu] em Tchechelnik. Mas os pais não eram dali. Vinham de outro lugar da Ucrânia. De onde exatamente? *Não se sabe*. [...] Quando passaram por uma aldeia chamada Tchechelnik... nasceu Clarice, nessa aldeia pequena [...]. Depois, seguiram viagem. Em direção a Odessa, [...] *onde talvez tenham embarcado num navio*.

> [(Lispector) was born in Chechelnyk. But her parents were not from there. They came from somewhere else in Ukraine. Where, exactly? *No one knows*. [...] When they passed through a village called Chechelnyk... Clarice was born, in that little village [...]. Later, they continued their journey. Towards Odessa [...] where *they may have boarded a ship*.][29]

We notice in this passage that Gotlib is careful to reveal how much information is still unknown about the family's migration, as she is quite clear and open about not knowing the birthplaces of Lispector's parents, Pinkhas and Mania, and emphasizes that Odessa *could be* the place where they started their journey to Brazil. Further on, she writes that it is likely that they left Russian territory 'atravessando a fronteira pelo rio Dniester' [by crossing the border at the Dniester river] and asks, rhetorically, 'teriam, então, atravessado a fronteira para Bucareste (Romênia), de lá para Budapeste (Hungria), para, então, chegar a um porto?' [had they, therefore, crossed the border to Bucharest (Romania), gone from there to Budapest (Hungary), in order to, at last, reach a harbour?].[30] The same ambivalence is employed when referring to Mania's illness, which was 'possivelmente por causa de uma infecção que lhe atingiu o sistema nervoso e a parte motora' [possibly caused by an infection that affected her nervous system and motor skills], and left her paralysed for the rest of her life.[31]

Gotlib's hesitation before asserting uncertain events as facts alongside her theoretical and critical reading of Lispector's work might come across as an overly academic tactic to the average reader, who seeks the writer's biography as a gateway into the most private and intimate aspects of Lispector's life. However, this caution is significant, especially because it prevents the consolidation of hearsay or gossip as well-known established facts, since the documentary traces of the Lispectors in Brazil are mostly based on the testimonies of friends and relatives.

As well as the biography, which is now in its seventh edition, in 2008, Gotlib also published an acclaimed photobiography, *Clarice: fotobiografia*, in which she brings together many unpublished photographs and documents. Gotlib's research has become a milestone in Lispector scholarship, and her books have made her one of the greatest authorities about Lispector worldwide. As we will see in the following sections, Gotlib's pioneering archival research also inspired Montero's and Moser's biographies, having encouraged them to search for new documents, photographs and interviews, about, of and with Lispector.

Intertextuality between Fiction and Life Writing

Released in 1999, Montero's *Eu sou uma pergunta: uma biografia de Clarice Lispector* pursues a strategy that employs intertextuality as a way of including Lispector's works directly in Montero's own narrative about Lispector's life. Whereas Gotlib offers critical readings of the literary texts along with her biography, and demarcates clearly between her narrative voice and Lispector's, Montero uses entire sentences picked out from testimonies, correspondence, chronicles, and short stories and incorporates them as part of her narrative. Unlike Gotlib, Montero often does not offer citations for this material, but rather marks them in italics in order to stress how Lispector's fiction and life often merge. For example, when Montero reports the incident of the fire in Lispector's apartment, which seriously damaged the author's right hand, she cites a passage from the chronicle 'A morte de uma baleia' [The Death of a Whale]:[32]

> Todos os que a visitaram foram recebidos por ela *gemendo de dor, como numa festa: eu tinha me tornado falante e minha voz era clara: minha alma florescia como um áspero cáctus.* Clarice desconhecia que estava no limiar da morte. Parecia-lhe que *enquanto sofresse fisicamente de um modo tão insuportável, isso seria a prova de estar vivendo ao máximo.*

> [Everyone who visited was greeted by her *moaning with pain: as if at a party I had become talkative and my voice was clear: my soul was flowering like a spiky cactus.* Clarice did not know that she was at the brink of death. It seemed to her that *although she was suffering physically in such an unbearable way, that suffering would be the proof she was living life to the maximum.*][33]

Montero uses Lispector's literary fragments as part of her own text, and through this intertextuality creates a new one that displaces the original and its connotations. Recycling material was, in fact, a well-known method for Lispector, who often wrote passages haphazardly on scraps of paper and used them for different textual purposes. In Lispector's chronicle, the anecdote focuses on a whale that was washed up at a beach in Rio de Janeiro and which suffered eight hours of pain before it was shot. Lispector associates the whale's pain with her own while she was in hospital after a fire in her home, caught between life and death. The chronicle is thus about suffering, life, death and humanity; Lispector reflects on the ways she has died several times, sometimes of suffering, other times of happiness.

In reproducing this passage to narrate Lispector's recovery, Montero reuses the fragment of an autobiographical chronicle and turns it into a source for her own biography. Although her book was the result of academic research, the edition published by Rocco does not display quotation marks or bibliographical references. The interweaving of the biographer's writing with Lispector's highlights the latter's own writing process. It is a tactic which can be read as a way of openly addressing the intertextual nature of Lispector's literature, as well as making explicit the ways that Lispector's life often inspired and was used in her fiction.

The intertextual references not only appear in the form of direct citation, as noted above, but also in paraphrases of Lispector's own stories. For instance, Montero retells the writer's anecdote, published as 'Viajando por mar (1a parte)' [Traveling by sea (1st part)], in which Lispector remembers her journeys on different ships. In the chronicle, the author recalls that she was crying because she did not want to leave Brazil and, therefore, was not in the mood to enjoy a party held to celebrate crossing the equator.[34] Montero reproduces Lispector's story, in her own words (in the third person), without referencing the chronicle:

> Chorando de saudades do Brasil, Clarice não conseguiu se animar durante a viagem, nem mesmo quando houve uma grande festa no navio, devido a sua passagem pela linha do Equador no dia 7 de setembro de 1952. Assistindo aos passageiros serem jogados vestidos na piscina, limitou-se a beber champanha gelado, ultra-seco.
>
> [Crying because she missed Brazil, Clarice could not bring herself to cheer up during the journey, not even when there was a huge party on the ship, when it crossed the equator on 7 September 1952. Watching the fully clothed passengers being thrown in the swimming pool, she limited herself to drinking cold, ultra-dry champagne.][35]

In Lispector's chronicle, she mentions that she cried during the journey, that she drank chilled champagne and that she did not join in the party. She does not allude to watching the other passengers, although she does explain the reason for the party. Montero understands Lispector's chronicle as the narration of a true-life episode and, in her own text, she changes the perspective of the narrator. Whereas in Lispector's chronicle the narrator describes a high-spirited episode involving 'jogar as pessoas mesmo vestidas na piscina' [throwing fully dressed people in the swimming pool],[36] in which she did not participate at all, Montero's account suggests that Lispector was present at the party, watching the passengers jump into the swimming pool. Lispector's first-person narrative voice in the chronicle implies that she did not join in and therefore did not necessarily see the passengers in the pool, although she did drink champagne. On the other hand, Montero's third-person narration of the voyage focuses on Lispector as if she had been present during the party and therefore fictionalizes the author's own version of the chronicle.

As well as producing a fictional and intertextual narrative, Montero's biography also featured newly accessible documents, testimonies and photographs.[37] The most important of these are Pinkhas's passport and a letter written by Lispector to the President of Brazil, Getúlio Vargas, asking for his support in the legal process by which she would become a naturalized Brazilian. The former's relevance lies in the fact that inside the passport is the only photograph of the whole family before they migrated to Brazil and the latter's in representing an official document that registers Lispector's request to obtain Brazilian citizenship (which was granted in 1943).

Montero's biography is also extremely relevant because it was the first one to contextualize Lispector's life and work within the framework of Brazilian and European history. She added more background information than Gotlib and constructed a detailed narrative that interwove the dangers of the Ukrainian pogroms with the family's escape in the context of Brazilian and European history in the 1920s. Though less hesitant than Gotlib in her narration, Montero is also cautious with affirmations about the family's escape from Ukraine: 'é *provável* que Pinkas tenha pagado uma determinada quantia a um dos homens que ajudavam os imigrantes a atravessarem a fronteira [para Romênia]' [it is *likely* that Pinkhas paid a certain amount to one of the men who helped immigrants to cross the border [to Romania]].[38] Regarding Mania's disease, Montero provides another version, stating that she suffered from 'uma afecção neurológica paralisante, *provavelmente* oriunda de um parkinsonismo' [a paralysing neurological condition *probably* deriving from Parkinson's disease].[39]

Like Gotlib, Montero is prudent in describing events that cannot be verified by documents or testimonies. Yet, her narrative strategy in recounting Lispector's life is more literary than academic and relies on intertextuality, especially with Lispector's chronicles, short stories and correspondence, to shed light on the ways that they are interrelated and, to a certain extent, autobiographical. While Gotlib tries to show that, in spite of their intricate relationship, Lispector's life and fiction should be separated, Montero's argument revolves around the fact that it is very challenging to dissociate both. On the one hand, Gotlib stresses that, in her fiction, Lispector is always inventing herself by putting on different masks. On the other, Montero's biography suggests that all of these reinventions are, in fact, fragments of Clarice Lispector's life.

The Ethics of Life Writing

Moser's *Why This World* is currently the most internationally well-known biography of Lispector. His book draws on many testimonies, documents and narrative strategies from both Gotlib's and Montero's biographies and includes new findings and testimonies. He builds on Gotlib's intention to produce literary criticism of Lispector's literature by reflecting on the ways that her life is represented in her fiction. Like Montero, he adopts a detailed historical and cultural contextualization of the places that constitute Lispector's itineraries at different moments of her life.[40]

In spite of the largely positive reviews the biography has received, in Brazil its academic reception was controversial. The polemical aspects of Moser's text relate to what can be seen as a sensationalist tone with respect to Lispector's romantic relationships and private life and to his tendency to turn speculative information, particularly the allegation that Mania Lispector had been gang-raped by Russian soldiers during a pogrom and hence contracted syphilis, into a widely consolidated truth. This rather shocking event that he claims Mania had suffered was widely disseminated by the Brazilian and international press,[41] and is also mentioned in Moser's introductions to *The Complete Stories* and *A Breath of Life (Pulsations)*.[42] The rape episode was mentioned by the reviewers in the Brazilian daily newspapers *Folha de S. Paulo*[43] and *Estado de São Paulo*,[44] which used this upsetting story to generate interest in the biography.

In *Why This World*, the source Moser cites to corroborate the story is dubious: 'Clarice confided to her closest friend that her mother was raped by a gang of Russian soldiers',[45] yet the name of the 'closest friend' is never disclosed. In an endnote, Moser claims that he obtained this information from the Canadian scholar Claire Varin. Gotlib has publicly disputed Moser's claim that Mania's illness was the result of rape, asserting that there is no proof, since the death certificate gives 'progressive paralysis' as the cause of death.[46] In a 2011 interview with Rachel Cozer, just as Gotlib was about to launch her edition of Elisa Lispector's *Retratos antigos*, the author once again contested Moser's conclusion that Mania had been raped and contracted syphilis: 'A única pessoa que falou em estupro foi ele. Nunca ninguém falou isso' [The only person who has mentioned rape is him. Nobody else has ever said that].[47]

Cozer's article points to the fact that the alleged rape is disputable and cites a footnote from the 2009 edition of Gotlib's biography, where she claims that the possibility of Mania having syphilis was put forward by Henrique Rabin, a cousin in Recife, as a hypothesis for the origin of her paralysis.[48] This, however, was deemed only a possibility and was never confirmed. Varin is also quoted in Cozer's article explaining that the account of Mania's rape and illness was passed on to her by Olga Borelli: 'Clarice contou a Olga. Nunca usei a informação porque não cabia nas minhas pesquisas. Acho a doença da mãe mais relevante que sua causa para entender Clarice' [Clarice told Olga. I never used this information because it didn't fit into my research. I think the mother's illness is more relevant to understanding Clarice than its cause].[49]

As Benjamin Abdala explains, Moser's speculation about Mania's rape relies on Elisa Lispector's testimony in *Retratos antigos*[50] (some excerpts of which were first published in his biography) and on her novel *No exílio* [In Exile],[51] which describes a Ukrainian family's escape from the pogroms and their journey to Brazil.[52] The novel is clearly based on the Lispectors' own journey, since Elisa Lispector was old enough to remember it, although it is fictionalized and the names changed. Nevertheless, even in the novel, there are no passages which describe the mother being raped. Moser attempts to strengthen his hypothesis with historical facts about the pogroms, asserting that '[e]very account of the pogroms records the prevalence of rape', since 'rape is an essential element of ethnic cleansing, designed as much to humiliate a people as to kill and expel them' and 'Ukraine of the civil war era was no different'.[53] This historical argument could be perceived as the most compelling one, for it is here that we can find some kind of evidence that Mania's rape was a possibility. Yet, the fact that this episode is a possibility still does not prove that it is true, nor does it confirm that she had, or died of syphilis.

Reflecting on Eakin's premise that the biographer should be concerned with the biography's 'potential for harm' and with the violation of telling the truth within 'a literary convention [that governs] nonfiction as a genre',[54] one can question the ethics of using such a violent and traumatic story as the basis for many of the readings of Lispector's literary texts. This story is frequently brought up implicitly and explicitly in Moser's narrative, as he constructs Mania's illness and death as an underlying influence on her daughter's writings. And since Mania's illness and death cannot, in Moser's work, be dissociated from her having been raped, this story becomes an established truth about the Lispector family and about Clarice Lispector's life and work.

At times, even Lispector's letters and archival material are reworked to fit Moser's hypothesis. In narrating Lispector's years in Berne, Switzerland, Moser quotes a letter sent to her sisters, which was originally published in Borelli's memoir, providing a disputable translation into English to uphold his argument. The letter describes Lispector's daily life in Berne and her difficulties in dealing with the elitist diplomatic community. She criticizes their behaviour, opinions and ideas, disclosing that she often had to lie in order to be able to fit in. In the original, the excerpt states that, because she was always pretending, Lispector felt harmed, hurt or injured ['*fiquei lesa*'[55]], which Moser translates in a way that links Lispector's feelings of helplessness with her mother's death: '"From lying so much to try to have the same opinion as everyone else, because there's no point in arguing, I've been *paralyzed*." The connotation cannot be accidental'.[56] Although it is left to the reader to reflect on the connotations of Lispector's apparent 'paralysis', the association of the word with Mania's illness is implied in the following paragraph (and several other places in the biography),[57] when Moser writes that 'the sense of uselessness [in Berne] oppressed [Lispector], and the possible reference to the mother she failed to rescue echoes the helplessness she felt toward the victims of a more recent tragedy [the Holocaust]'.[58]

Another example is Moser's reading of the killing of the cockroach in *A paixão segundo G.H.* [*The Passion According to G.H.*]. Although his interpretation of the novel starts with the existential, philosophical and religious meanings of the cockroach and its killing, after which the protagonist feels disgusted and even guilty, Moser links the evocations of 'mãe' [mother] in the novel directly with Mania Lispector: 'Hidden within G.H.'s confrontation with the dying cockroach is a memory of Clarice Lispector's own dying mother. The identity [sic] of her mother with the roach is one of the most shocking aspects of this whole unsettling book.'[59] He goes further by analysing an excerpt in which G.H. reflects on her pregnancy, on having had an abortion and on love: 'Se era, então amor é muito mais que amor: amor é antes do amor ainda: é planctum lutando, e a grande neutralidade viva lutando. Assim como a vida na *barata presa pela cintura*' [If so, then love is much more than love: love is something before love: it's plankton struggling, and the great living neutrality struggling. Just like the life in the roach *stuck at the waist*.][60] For Moser, the waist is 'an allusion to the location of Clarice's mother's wound' and he concludes that '[l]ike Mania Lispector, the cockroach is paralyzed, awaiting death'.[61] While Lispector's references to maternity, death, life and the materiality of the body in *The Passion According to G.H.* can be read in terms of a wide range of themes that touch upon universal questions of being in the world, Moser puts forward a reading that endorses his own version of Lispector's relationship with her mother and her illness, and reminds the reader once again of Mania's paralysis and its alleged origins.

The differences between the English and Brazilian Portuguese editions of Moser's biography should also be taken into account. Most of the episodes that have been redacted or modified from the Brazilian edition refer to Lispector's elder son Pedro (who was diagnosed with schizophrenia as a teenager), the author's relationship with her ex-husband, and her affair with the author Paulo Mendes Campos.[62] In the English version, Moser often describes Pedro in terms that emphasize his mental illness: 'First [Lispector] had failed to save her mother. Now she had to look on helplessly as her son went mad',[63] or '[e]ven a person in much better shape than Clarice would have had a hard time in dealing with a son so far gone'.[64] In Portuguese, these descriptions have been toned down: '[Lispector] deixara de salvar a mãe. Agora assistia impotente à doença do filho' [Lispector had not been able to save her mother. Now she looked on powerlessly at her son's illness];[65] 'Clarice teria passado apuros para lidar com um filho tão problemático' [Clarice must have had a hard time dealing with such a problematic son].[66] As is widely known among Lispector scholars, Clarice and her family have always been very careful to protect Pedro's image in the public sphere by avoiding exposing his illness, the details of which are irrelevant to discussions of Lispector's literature. Moser, however, includes testimony from Isabel Gurgel Valente (Maury's second wife and the boy's stepmother), that offers an unnecessarily graphic description of Pedro's crises.[67] This paragraph was entirely suppressed from the Brazilian edition.

Also, in the Brazilian Portuguese edition, the endnote that attributes a source to the allegation that Mania had been raped differs from the one in English. Note 7 in the Chapter entitled 'O *pogrom* básico' [The Average Pogrom] in the Brazilian edition, acknowledges Moser's interview with Claire Varin in January 2006, yet it also explains that Lispector's sisters did not confirm the episode:

> Outras fontes atribuem a paralisia de Mania a um choque traumático (possivelmente um espancamento) ocasionado pela violência do *pogrom* ou por outra doença. Não se conhecem depoimentos das filhas de Mania, Tânia Kaufmann e Elisa Lispector, que confirmem a hipótese do estupro.
>
> [Other sources attribute Mania's paralysis to a traumatic shock (possibly a beating) caused by violence during the pogroms or another illness. There are no known testimonies by Mania's daughters, Tânia Kaufmann and Elisa Lispector, that confirm the hypothesis of rape.][68]

This comment does not appear in the US and UK editions, which only include the reference to the interview with Varin.[69] When the Brazilian Portuguese translation was published, Brazilian law still prohibited the publication of a biography without the family's authorization, so it is possible that Lispector's family asked for certain passages to be left out or modified. UK and US legislation on biographical writing, on the other hand, does not require the family's consent. There is no doubt, however, that Moser's biography increased Lispector's readership around the globe, and this is perhaps the greatest achievement of his book.

Conclusion

All three biographies are remarkable contributions to the preservation of Lispector's memory and legacy as a writer. Nonetheless, by narrowing the gap between her life and work all three encourage her fiction to be read as an autobiography, even an 'unplanned' one, as Manzo contends. Analysing Lispector's literary legacy through the events in her life could diminish the relevance and power of her literature, since the language that she uses to represent universal features that pertain to human suffering, questioning and solitude are then reduced to narcissistic projections of the author onto her writing.

While translations and criticism that were published before Lispector's death described her fiction as introspective, psychological and existential, much contemporary criticism of Lispector's work succumbs to the temptation to analyse her literature alongside her biography. Gotlib's argument that literature allowed Lispector to fictionalize herself behind different masks and Montero's merging of fiction and biography have become popular approaches to Lispector's work.[70] Both Gotlib's and Montero's biographies have strongly influenced contemporary criticism on Lispector's work, whether critics explore the relationship between life and work or not. Edgar Cézar Nolasco, for instance, builds upon their studies, defining Lispector's literature as 'biográfico-literária' [biographical-literary], as he attempts to 'retraçar o traço biográfico-literário que sustenta e mantém o projeto escritural e, por conseguinte, a escritura clariceana' [retrace the biographical-literary tracks that uphold and maintain the scriptural project and, as a consequence, Claricean writing].[71] In her book about Lispector's use of language as a means of nomadism and displacement, Simone Curi reads the 'foreignness' in Lispector's literature in the context of her Jewishness and biography (relying on Gotlib's, in particular).[72]

Although Gotlib's and Montero's biographies were positively received and their books are central to critical studies about Clarice Lispector, Moser's book is still the most popular biography worldwide. However, the reception of *Why This World* also reawakened interest in Lispector's Portuguese-written biographies in Brazil. A revised and extended version of Gotlib's *Clarice: uma vida que se conta* was reprinted in 2009. A revised second edition of Montero's biography was published by Rocco in November 2021 with a new title, *À procura da própria coisa: Uma biografia de Clarice Lispector* [In Search of the Thing in Itself: A Biography of Clarice Lispector]. In 2018, Montero published a different kind of biography, *O Rio de Clarice: passeio afetivo pela cidade* [Clarice's Rio: A Personal Trip Through the City], which is based on the walking tours she organizes in Rio de Janeiro that bring to life Lispector's relationship with the city.[73]

It is true that Moser's biography has promoted Lispector's works, particularly among anglophone readers. Nevertheless, his book has often overshadowed the importance not only of Gotlib's and Montero's biographies, but also of scholars and translators who have dedicated their efforts to Lispector's literature. While Gotlib's and Montero's books have influenced biographical readings of Lispector's works, as I have shown, their critical perspectives combining the author's life and work have not featured in the most recent translated editions of Lispector's books. The New Directions and Penguin editions that came out under Moser's supervision have turned Lispector's life into a marketing strategy, or a selling point to appeal to the anglophone readership, and his perspective on her literature has established itself as an overwhelming voice in contemporary criticism.[74] Placing Lispector's biography before her fiction has encouraged a view of the author as an unapproachable 'mythical figure'. But if her literary legacy is to endure, her work — which speaks to universal existential concerns — cannot be restricted to her life story alone.

Works Cited

ABDALA, BENJAMIN, 'Biografia de Clarice, por Benjamin Moser: coincidências e equívocos', *Estudos Avançados*, 24.70 (2010), 282–92

ALMODÓVAR, PEDRO and BENJAMIN MOSER. 'Exchange on A Breath of Life, in *A Breath of Life (Pulsations)*, trans. by Johnny Lorenz (New York: New Directions, 2012), pp. vii–xii

BORELLI, OLGA, *Clarice Lispector: esboço para um possível retrato* (Rio de Janeiro: Nova Fronteira, 1981)

CURI, SIMONE, *A escritura nômade em Clarice Lispector* (Chapecó, SC: Argos, 2001).

EAKIN, PAUL JOHN (ed.), *The Ethics of Life Writing* (Ithaca, NY, and London: Cornell University Press, 2004)

GOTLIB, NÁDIA BATTELLA, *Clarice: uma vida que se conta* (São Paulo: Ática, 1995)

—— *Clarice: uma vida que se conta*, rev. edn (São Paulo: EDUSP, 2009)

—— *Clarice: fotobiografia* (São Paulo: EDUSP, 2008)

LEE, HERMIONE, *Biography: A Very Short Introduction* (Oxford: Oxford University Press, 2009)

LISPECTOR, CLARICE, *A paixão segundo G.H.* (Rio de Janeiro: Rocco, 1998 [1964]); *The Passion According to G.H.*, trans. by Idra Novey (New York: New Directions, 2012)

—— *A descoberta do mundo* (Rio de Janeiro: Rocco, 1999)

—— *Family Ties*, trans. by Giovanni Pontiero (Austin: University of Texas Press, 1972)

—— *The Foreign Legion*, trans. by Giovanni Pontiero (New York: New Directions, 1986)

—— *Selected Crônicas*, trans. by Giovanni Pontiero (New York: New Directions, 1992)

LISPECTOR, ELISA. *No exílio* (Rio de Janeiro: José Olympio, 1948)

—— *Retratos antigos*. ed. by Nádia Battella Gotlib (Belo Horizonte: Editora UFMG, 2012)

MANZO, LÍCIA, *Era uma vez: Eu. A não-ficção na obra de Clarice Lispector* (Juiz de Fora: Templo, 2001)

MALCOLM, JANET, *The Silent Woman: Sylvia Plath and Ted Hughes* (London: Granta Books, 1994)

MONTERO, TERESA CRISTINA FERREIRA, *Eu sou uma pergunta: uma biografia de Clarice Lispector* (Rio de Janeiro: Rocco, 1999)

—— *O Rio de Clarice: passeio afetivo pela cidade* (Belo Horizonte: Autêntica, 2018)

MOSER, BENJAMIN, *Clarice, uma biografia*, trans. by José Geraldo Couto (São Paulo: Cosac Naify, 2009)
—— 'Glamour and Grammar', in *The Complete Stories*, trans. by Katrina Dodson (New York: New Directions, 2015), pp. ix–xxiii.
——, *Why This World: A Biography of Clarice Lispector* (London and New York: Penguin, 2014).
NADEL, IRA B., 'Narrative and the Popularity of Biography', *Mosaic*, 20.4 (1987), 131–41
TÓIBÍN, COLM, 'A Passion for the Void', in Clarice Lispector, *The Hour of the Star*, trans. by Benjamin Moser (New York: New Directions, 2011), pp. vii–xii.

Notes to Chapter 25

1. Lícia Manzo, *Era uma vez: Eu. A não ficção na obra de Clarice Lispector* (Juiz de Fora: Templo, 2001), p. 4. All translations from the Portuguese are mine unless otherwise noted.
2. Gotlib's biography was the result of research done for her *livre docência* at the University of São Paulo, which concerns promotion to the second highest position as a professor at the institution. Her book was first published by the educational publishing house Ática in 1995 and republished in 2009 by EDUSP (University of São Paulo Press). Montero's biography was the outcome of her Master's dissertation at the Catholic University of Rio de Janeiro and was first printed by Rocco, a Brazilian publishing house that is also, currently, largely responsible for the editions of Lispector's works. Moser's 2009 publication *Why This World: A Biography of Clarice Lispector* (New York: Oxford University Press, 2009) was the result of his doctoral research.
3. See Fernanda Eberstadt, 'Untamed Creature', *New York Times*, 19 August 2009, Sunday Book Review, p. BR8; Marguerite Itamar Harrison, 'The Other of Others', *The Women's Review of Books*, 27.4 (2010), 25–27.
4. Olga Borelli, *Clarice Lispector: esboço para um possível retrato*, 2nd edn (Rio de Janeiro: Nova Fronteira, 1981), p. 5.
5. Giovanni Pontiero, 'Introduction', in Clarice Lispector, *Family Ties*, trans. by Giovanni Pontiero (Austin: University of Texas Press, 1972), pp. 13–23.
6. Giovanni Pontiero, 'Afterword', in Clarice Lispector, *The Foreign Legion*, trans. by Giovanni Pontiero (New York: New Directions, 1986), p. 217; Giovanni Pontiero, 'Introduction', in Clarice Lispector, *Selected Crônicas* trans. by Giovanni Pontiero (New York: New Directions, 1992), p. vii. The second of these volumes of translations is made up of texts selected from the first.
7. Colm Tóibín, 'A Passion for the Void', in Clarice Lispector, *The Hour of the Star*, trans. by Benjamin Moser (New York: New Directions, 2011), pp. vii–xii (p. ix).
8. As well as Tóibín, singer Caetano Veloso and film director Pedro Almodóvar have also written introductions to the New Directions/Penguin editions of, respectively, *A paixão segundo G.H.* [*The Passion According to G.H.*] and *Um sopro de vida: pulsaçõe s* [*A Breath of Life (Pulsations)*].
9. Ira B. Nadel, 'Narrative and the Popularity of Biography', *Mosaic*, 20.4 (1987), 131–41 (p.135).
10. Ibid., p. 140.
11. Hermione Lee, *Biography: A Very Short Introduction* (Oxford: Oxford University Press, 2009), p. 49.
12. Ibid., p. 46.
13. Ibid., p. 47.
14. Janet Malcolm, *The Silent Woman: Sylvia Plath and Ted Hughes* (London: Granta Books, 2011), p. 19, ebook.
15. Ibid., p. 20.
16. Paul John Eakin, *The Ethics of Life Writing* (Ithaca, NY, and London: Cornell University Press, 2004), p. 9.
17. Ibid., pp. 2–4.
18. Ibid., p. 6.
19. For this essay, I have used the first edition of Gotlib's biography, from 1995. The revised and

extended edition, published in 2009, by the University of São Paulo, was also consulted and it is cited where relevant, particularly when referring to the discussions that arose over the publication of Moser's biography just one month prior to the release of Gotlib's.
20. Nádia Battella Gotlib, *Clarice: uma vida que se conta* (São Paulo: Ática, 1995), p. 15.
21. Ibid., p. 81.
22. Lispector quoted in ibid., p. 375.
23. Lispector, 'Medo da eternidade', in *A descoberta do mundo* (Rio de Janeiro: Rocco, 1999), pp. 289–91; 'Fear of Eternity', in *Selected Crônicas*, pp. 144–45.
24. Lispector, *A descoberta do mundo*, p. 310; *Selected Crônicas*, p. 145.
25. Gotlib, *Clarice* (1995), p. 75.
26. Ibid., p. 76.
27. In the 2009 edition of Gotlib's biography, the author incorporated newly found information about the family's migration to Brazil. However, even in this edition Gotlib is at pains to point out that, despite new documents, testimonies and memoirs about the family's journey having surfaced in the last decades, there are still aspects of the Lispectors' history that remain unresolved or even unclear. For her 2009 biography, Gotlib was able to access Elisa Lispector's *Retratos antigos* [Old Portraits], the unfinished manuscript telling the Lispector family's history and which she edited for publication (Belo Horizonte: Editora UFMG, 2012). Gotlib had also interviewed surviving family members living in the northeast of Brazil to collect testimonies about the family's arrival in the country and gained access to other documents which had featured in her 2008 photobiography and in Montero's research.
28. Nádia Battella Gotlib, *Clarice: uma vida que se conta* (São Paulo: EDUSP, 2009), p. 32.
29. Gotlib, *Clarice* (1995), p. 62. My emphasis added.
30. Ibid., p. 63.
31. Ibid., p. 67.
32. Lispector, 'A morte de uma baleia', in *A descoberta do mundo*, pp. 125–27; *Discovering the World*, pp. 168–70.
33. Teresa Montero, *Eu sou uma pergunta: uma biografia de Clarice Lispector* (Rio de Janeiro: Rocco, 1999), p. 225. Montero's emphasis.
34. Lispector, 'Viajando por mar (1ª parte)', in *A descoberta do mundo*, pp. 349–50; 'Sea Voyage', in *Discovering the World*, pp. 459–60.
35. Montero, *Eu sou uma pergunta*, p. 179.
36. Lispector, *A descoberta do mundo*, p. 350.
37. Montero's research was particularly relevant due to the original interviews she held with Lispector's family members in the northeast of Brazil and the archival research she carried out in institutions in Recife and Rio de Janeiro, and in private archives which Gotlib had not visited.
38. Montero, *Eu sou uma pergunta*, p. 26. My emphasis.
39. Ibid., p. 47. My emphasis.
40. Moser acknowledges both Montero's and Gotlib's biographies in the Acknowledgements section of his book (Moser, *Why This World*, p. 390), in which he cites them frequently.
41. See Eberstadt, 'Untamed Creature', p. BR8; Harrison, 'The Other of Others', p. 25; Natasha Randall, ' "Why This World: A Biography of Clarice Lispector" by Benjamin Moser', *LA Times*, 2 August 2009, <https://www.latimes.com/entertainment/la-ca-clarice-lispector2-2009aug02-story.html> [accessed January 2020]; Guilherme Freitas and Leonardo Cazes, 'Benjamin Moser fala sobre Clarice Lispector', *O Globo*, 14 November 2009, < https://blogs.oglobo.globo.com/prosa/post/benjamin-moser-fala-sobre-clarice-lispector-240928.html> [accessed January 2020]; Ian Thomson, ' "She's the most important Jewish writer since Kafka!" ', *The Spectator*, 11 January 2014, < https://www.spectator.co.uk/2014/01/why-this-world-by-benjamin-moser-review/> [accessed January 2020].
42. Pedro Almodóvar and Benjamin Moser, 'Exchange on A Breath of Life, in *A Breath of Life*, trans. by Johnny Lorenz (New York: New Directions, 2012), pp. vii–xii (p. viii); Benjamin Moser, 'Glamour and Grammar', in Clarice Lispector, *The Complete Stories*, trans. by Katrina Dodson (New York: New Directions, 2015), pp. ix–xxiii (p. xvii).
43. 'Biografia sobre Clarice Lispector chega às livrarias nesta semana', *Folha de S. Paulo*, 16 November

2009, <https://www1.folha.uol.com.br/folha/livrariadafolha/ult10082u652882.shtml> [accessed December 2018].
44. Antonio Gonçalves Filho, 'Clarice, uma esfinge que virou gente', *Estado de S. Paulo*, 21 November 2009, <https://www.estadao.com.br/noticias/geral,clarice-uma-esfinge-que-virou-gente,469769> [accessed December 2018].
45. Moser, *Why This World*, p. 27.
46. See the round table discussion held at the VI Fliporto literary festival in 2010, 'Clarice Lispector: como se constrói uma biografia', <https://www.youtube.com/watch?v=yFFiAl5CC-8>, (28'30"-30') [accessed August 2019].
47. In Rachel Cozer, 'O resgate de Elisa: o que a irmã de Clarice Lispector deixou para a história', *Folha de São Paulo*, 4 December 2011, <https://www1.folha.uol.com.br/fsp/ilustrissima/12756-o-resgate-de-elisa.shtml> [accessed April 2020].
48. Gotlib's footnote reads as follows: 'Henrique Rabin [...] vale-se de sua experiência de médico para lançar a hipótese de que o processo infeccioso [de Mania Lispector] pode ter sido proveniente de uma sífilis contraída, possivelmente, durante os *pogroms*, quando mulheres eram violentadas e aldeias inteiras eram destruídas' [Henrique Rabin makes use of his experience as a physician to raise the hypothesis that [Mania Lispector's] infection might have stemmed from the contraction of syphilis, possibly during the *pogroms*, when women were raped and entire villages were destroyed], Gotlib, *Clarice* (2009), p. 53.
49. Cozer, 'O resgate de Elisa', n.pag.
50. Elisa Lispector's posthumous and unfinished memoir about the family actually contradicts Moser's claim, since according to her, Mania suffered from hemiplegia (the paralysis of one side of the body). Elisa Lispector, *Retratos antigos*, p. 111.
51. Elisa Lispector, *No exílio* (Rio de Janeiro: José Olympio, 1948).
52. Benjamin Abdala, 'Biografia de Clarice, por Benjamin Moser: coincidências e equívocos', *Estudos Avançados*, 24.70 (2010), 282–92 (pp. 288–89).
53. Moser, *Why This World*, pp. 27–28.
54. Eakin, *The Ethics of Life Writing*, pp. 2–3, 4.
55. Borelli, *Um esboço para um possível retrato*, p. 122, emphasis in the original.
56. Moser, *Why This World*, p. 171, my emphasis.
57. The words 'paralyze' or 'paralyzing' appear ten times throughout Moser's biography and in five of them a link is established with Mania.
58. Moser, *Why This World*, p. 171, my emphasis.
59. Ibid., p. 266.
60. Clarice Lispector, *A paixão segundo G.H.* (Rio de Janeiro: Rocco, 1998 [1964]), p. 92; *The Passion According G.H.*, trans. by Idra Novey (New York: New Directions, 2012), p. 91. My emphasis.
61. Moser, *Why This World*, p. 267.
62. Gotlib and Montero put forward discreet accounts about Lispector's relationship with Paulo Mendes Campos that only suggest a love affair (Gotlib, *Clarice*, p. 239; Montero, *Eu sou uma pergunta*, p. 217). Montero compares it with the impossible love Lispector felt for Lúcio Cardoso (Ibid., p. 277).
63. Moser, *Why This World*, p. 254.
64. Ibid., p. 307.
65. Benjamin Moser, *Clarice, uma biografia*, trans. by José Geraldo Couto (São Paulo: Cosac Naify, 2009), p. 368.
66. Ibid., p. 446.
67. Moser, *Why This World*, p. 253.
68. Moser, *Clarice, uma biografia*, p. 566.
69. Ibid., p. 399.
70. For example, Manzo, *Era uma vez: eu*; Katiuscia Corrêa Ricardo, 'Clarice Lispector e o pacto autobiográfico: paradoxo entre realidade e ficção', in *Clarice em cena: 30 anos depois*, ed. by André Luis Gomes (Brasília: Petry, 2008), pp. 171–75; and Edson Ribeiro da Silva, 'Jogos ficcionais como máscaras em obras de Clarice Lispector', *Patrimônio e Memória*, 10.1 (2014), 222–43.
71. Edgar Cézar Nolasco, *Restos de ficção: a criação biográfico-literária de Clarice Lispector* (São Paulo: Editora Annablume, 2004), pp. 22–23.

72. Simone Curi, *A escritura nômade em Clarice Lispector* (Chapecó, SC: Argos, 2001).
73. See Teresa Montero's chapter in this volume. See also Claire Williams, ' "Putting the Fish in the Stream": The Intersection of Literature and Biography in Guidebooks to (Clarice Lispector's) Rio and (Maria Ondina Braga's) Braga', in *Women in Transition: Crossing Boundaries, Crossing Borders*, ed. by Maria-José Blanco and Claire Williams (London: Routledge, 2021), pp. 166–84.
74. Cf. Magdalena Edwards, 'Benjamin Moser and the Smallest Woman in the World', *LA Review of Books*, 16 August 2019, <https://lareviewofbooks.org/article/benjamin-moser-and-the-smallest-woman-in-the-world> [accessed January 2020].

CHAPTER 26

Clarice Lispector in English: Translation and Reception

Cynthia Beatrice Costa and Luana Ferreira de Freitas

In the 2001 volume *Closer to the Wild Heart: Essays on Clarice Lispector*, editors Cláudia Pazos Alonso and Claire Williams described Clarice Lispector as 'arguably Latin America's most celebrated female writer'.[1] A decade later, *The Guardian* listed Lispector as one of the world's best short story authors, introducing her as 'a darkly addictive Brazilian writer'.[2] In recent years, such statements have resonated in the anglophone literary system more than ever. Lispector has been frequently translated, retranslated, reviewed and studied in English, a phenomenon that was felt most acutely when *The Complete Stories* came out in 2015. Translated by Katrina Dodson and edited by Benjamin Moser, the anthology received rave reviews and entered *The New York Times*'s list of best books of that year. 'Since her death in 1977, Lispector's literary reputation has grown enormously, thanks to her nine unsettling novels', critic Larry Rohter wrote in his review. 'Whatever the form, Lispector is enigmatic, mystical, confounding and philosophical'.[3]

More recently, in 2018, the Brazilian author reappeared in the pages of US newspapers when *The Chandelier*, Moser and Magdalena Edwards's translation of *O lustre* (1946), was finally released, the last of her novels to be translated into English. It is regarded as difficult to read even by those accustomed to Lispector's often bewildering style; regardless, its overall anglophone reception was once more positive. 'Did I mention that this novel is charming? Punishing, yes, and maniacally overwritten, but a vulnerable and moving performance — with a heart-stopping payoff', wrote Parul Sehgal in *The New York Times*.[4] Interestingly, Christina Soto van der Plas declared never having been able to admire what she considered to be Lispector's 'self-centered, hermetic and dull' literary body of work until she read *The Chandelier*, which she described in the *Los Angeles Review of Books* as 'daring, dense, intricate, and difficult, and [...] without a doubt Lispector's most challenging work', praising Edwards and Moser's effort to create 'their own version of the novel, following the tone and rhythm more than the actual meaning of words — an un-reading'.[5]

As the table in the Appendix shows, more than fifty years after its English-language debut, Lispector's fictional work is now largely accessible to anglophone readers. With all her novels and short stories (not counting those for children) and most of her *crônicas* issued in English,⁶ it is possible for the English-language reader to travel into her world thanks to the efforts of various anglophone translators and publishing houses. That being said, many of her non-fictional texts — journalistic articles, interviews, and letters — are still in need of translation. As for her five books for children, at least one is slated for publication in 2022: Moser's translation of *A mulher que matou os peixes* [*The Woman Who Killed the Fish*] (1968), once more by New Directions.

An interesting phenomenon regarding the publishing of the short story collections is that, despite the relative popularity of *Family Ties*, with at least three different editions of Giovanni Pontiero's translation issued (1972, 1984, 1995) by two different publishers (Carcanet and University of Texas Press), only *A legião estrangeira* [*The Foreign Legion*] and *A via crucis do corpo* [*The Via Crucis of the Body*] have been published in English as independent short story collections. The collections *Felicidade clandestina* [*Clandestine Happiness*], *A imitação da rosa* [*The Imitation of the Rose*], *Onde estivestes de noite?* [*Where Were You at Night?*], and *A bela e a fera* [*Beauty and the Beast*] have not (yet) been published as stand-alone volumes in English. Nevertheless, *The Complete Stories* reunites all of Lispector's short stories including those that were published inside and outside of anthologies and literary journals. A valid discussion around Moser's editorial organization of these texts for the volume was raised by some scholars, among them Nádia Battella Gotlib,⁷ who has argued that even though the title points to 'stories', other types of texts were included as well, such as the chronicle 'Brasília' from *Visão do esplendor* [*Vision of Splendour*]. Additionally, the criteria for organizing the stories were not entirely clear. For example, some stories that were first published in the volume *Alguns contos* [*Stories*] (1952) — like 'Amor' [Love] — appear in *The Complete Stories* in the section 'Family Ties', the title of Lispector's second collection of short stories, *Laços de família*, published in 1960. Given that her short story collections often introduced new stories while reissuing old ones, this discrepancy foregrounds that there is no straightforward way to distinguish between Lispector's genres or to organize her body of work.

Over the years, a number of Lispector's short stories have been incorporated into various compilations. In 2018, Penguin included *Daydream and Drunkenness of a Young Lady*, a micro-collection of three short stories from *Laços de família*, translated by Katrina Dodson, as the fifteenth book in its Penguin Modern series, 'celebrating the pioneering spirit of the iconic Penguin Modern Classics, with each one offering a concentrated hit of its contemporary, international flavour'.⁸ Various short stories have been featured in numerous literary and art magazines as well. Examples include 'One Hundred Years of Forgiveness' and 'A Story of Great Love' (respectively, 'Cem anos de perdão' and 'Uma história de tanto amor', from *Felicidade clandestina*), both translated by Rachel Klein and published in *The Paris Review* (2011). Also, Dodson's translations 'The Fifth Story' ('A quinta história', from *Felicidade clandestina*) and 'Day After Day' ('Dia após dia', from *A via crucis do corpo*) were featured in *The Scofield*, in an issue 'dedicated to the life and writing of Clarice Lispector'. Dodson's translation of 'The Smallest Woman in the World' ('A menor mulher do mundo' from *Laços de família*) also appeared online in *Tablet*, a daily online magazine of Jewish news, ideas, and culture.[9]

These Anglo-American publications and platforms underscore Lispector's status as both a Latin American and Jewish woman writer, a relation that a number of scholars have explored, as we will address further on. The availability of Lispector's works to anglophone readers is a remarkable accomplishment for a literature originally written in Brazilian Portuguese. Also notable is the number of translators involved in the task of presenting Lispector in English: at least twenty translators have had their translations published in the form of books or single short stories featured in collections and journals. Retranslations of Lispector's works, especially in the case of most of her novels, are further proof of her marketability in the anglophone global literary market (see Appendix).

Following this brief history of the circulation of Lispector's works in the anglophone literary system, we will now introduce some of the central figures who have been involved in the process.

Lispector in the Anglophone World: Key Players

Clarice Lispector's introduction into and dissemination within the anglophone literary system is the result of the initiative of a few key players who have endeavoured to make her work available to English-speaking readers. The first among these was US poet Elizabeth Bishop who published, in June 1964, three of Lispector's short stories in issue 26 of *The Kenyon Review*, under the title 'Three Stories by Clarice Lispector — Translated from Portuguese by Elizabeth Bishop'. These were: 'The Hen' ('Uma Galinha'), 'The Smallest Woman in the World' ('A Menor Mulher do Mundo'), and 'Marmosets' ('Macacos').

Lispector herself was supposedly happy with the translations, but never explicitly so.[10] It seems that Bishop told friends — among them the US poet Robert Lowell — that she had translated some of Lispector's stories, which came to the attention of publisher Alfred A. Knopf. It was Knopf, in fact, who introduced Lispector's novelistic work into English, bringing, for the first time, significant attention to the Brazilian author in the United States through the publication of *The Apple in the Dark* (1967), Gregory Rabassa's translation of the novel *A maçã no escuro* (1961). According to Rabassa, Knopf, who had been married in Rio de Janeiro and had already published books by Gilberto Freyre, was interested in publishing more Brazilian literature and offered him Lispector's book. Rabassa considered the conditions to be 'ideal'. He was preparing to leave for Brazil on a Fulbright scholarship and 'Clarice would be available' in case he needed help. Of his positive experience translating Lispector, Rabassa wrote: 'Clarice writes a clear, flowing, and evocative prose. A translator following her words should be led right along by them and have no trouble'.[11] The book's reception, on the other hand, was not uniformly positive. Writing for *The New York Times*, critic C. D. B. Bryan declared her 'an inspired and beautiful writer, but she lacks control; her overwriting flaws the novel'.[12]

Translator Giovanni Pontiero also played a fundamental role in Lispector's circulation in the English language. A Lecturer in Latin American Literature at the University of Manchester, and the first translator of José Saramago's work into English, Pontiero began by rendering the short story collection *Laços de família* (1960) into English as *Family Ties* (1972). In 1986, Pontiero's translations of *A legião estrangeira* (1964), another short story collection, and the novella *A hora da estrela* (1977) came out, respectively, as *The Foreign Legion: Stories and Chronicles* and *The Hour of the Star* with the UK publishing house Carcanet Press, which had already published his *Family Ties* in the UK in 1984. Pontiero's translation of Lispector's first novel *Perto do coração selvagem* (1943) [*Near to the Wild Heart*] came out in 1990, this time with the US publishers New Directions. Two years later, Carcanet launched *Discovering the World*, 'a miscellaneous collection of aphorisms, diary entries, reminiscences, travel notes, interviews, serialized stories, essays, loosely defined as *chronicles*; a genre peculiar to Brazil which allows poets and writers to address a wider readership on a vast range of topics and themes'.[13] Always one to provide insightful information in the prefaces and notes that accompanied his translations, Pontiero expressed, in the preface to *Discovering the World* (1992), great admiration for the Brazilian writer and her radical style, affirming that 'such is the intensity and vehemence of her prose that it unleashes everything which is gentle and violent in this world of ours'.[14] Pontiero's last translation of Lispector was *The Besieged City* (*A cidade sitiada*), which he completed before his death in 1996 but which still remains unpublished.[15]

In the last decade, New Directions has played a further key role in expanding Lispector's legacy through its partnership with Moser, whose *Why this World: A Biography of Clarice Lispector* (2009) was described by Fernanda Eberstadt as 'lively, ardent and intellectually rigorous' in the *New York Times*[16] and as a good 'biographical essay' by *Folha de São Paulo*, in a review written by Ruy Castro.[17] In 2015, news of her positive reception in the US awakened a fresh interest in the writer. *Clarice Lispector: todos os contos*, the Brazilian version of *The Complete Stories*, was launched soon after its US counterpart. Though the Brazilian volume follows the US edition, it excludes Katrina Dodson's 'Translator's Note' and the acknowledgments section. Published by Rocco, it became a relative commercial success, entering best-seller lists the following year.[18] In 2018, Rocco continued its mission to republish Lispector's entire body of work, bringing out *Clarice Lispector: todas as crônicas*, a compilation of her chronicles edited by Pedro Karp Vasques.[19]

In Brazil, Lispector's fame and positive reception date back as early as 1944, just after the release of her first novel, which attracted the attention of important literary critics like Sérgio Milliet and Antonio Candido, the latter observing, 'If we discount possible foreign sources of inspiration, the fact remains that, within our literature, it is a top-quality performance'.[20] In the 1960s, other luminaries of Brazilian literary criticism, such as Roberto Schwarz, Assis Brasil, and Luís Costa Lima, also wrote about Lispector. Year after year, the rising appreciation and insights of scholars contributed to the development of a body of critical work on Lispector, thereby consolidating her place in the Brazilian literary canon. These included studies by Benedito Nunes, who authored the first academic work, *O mundo de Clarice Lispector* (Manaus: Edições Governo do Estado do Amazonas, 1966);[21] Affonso Romano de Sant'Anna, who published multiple texts on Lispector in the 1970s, and later on;[22] and Judith Grossmann and Lúcia Helena, who both wrote articles on Lispector's fiction in the 1970s.[23] This critical reception from the 1970s onwards was also actively echoed in — and aided by — her reception among foreign readers and critics, as detailed below.

US scholar Earl E. Fitz began publishing on Lispector's fiction in 1977 (Rabassa supervised his dissertation 'Clarice Lispector: The Nature and Form of the Lyrical Novel').[24] In 1979, scholar and translator Elizabeth Lowe published an important interview with Clarice Lispector under the title 'The Passion According to C.L.'.[25] That same year, Lowe had translated *Chronology: Clarice Lispector*, by Brazilian critic Bella Jozef, into English (published in New York by the Center of Inter-American Relations), and would later translate the novel *The Stream of Life* [Água viva] in collaboration with Fitz. That same year, in Brazil, Olga de Sá published *A escritura de Clarice Lispector*, which is, to date, considered to be one of the major scholarly investigations on narrative form in Lispector's writings.

At the same time, a turning point in Lispector's literary path abroad was instigated by Jewish-Algerian-French literary critic Hélène Cixous. Her extensive work on Lispector, much of it translated into English, played a fundamental role in providing a theoretical framework for reading Lispector on a global scale as an example of *écriture féminine*.[26] Establishing relations between Lispector and Rilke, Heidegger, and Derrida, among others, Cixous outlined a philosophical, sometimes psychoanalytical, yet very personal, way of approaching her texts; personal because Cixous constantly sees 'Clarice' behind her fictional creation, imagining her internal struggles and ideologies. In her analysis of *Água viva*, she writes: 'Who in me puts me outside myself, Clarice wonders', and then 'Clarice tells herself that she must speak, because to speak saves. But she has no words and nothing to say. There is an abyss'.[27] Describing Cixous's relationship towards Lispector's fiction as a 'textual *coup de foudre*', Anna Klobucka argues that, from the 'fateful year of 1978' on — or since Cixous 'fell in love' with Lispector, a year after the author's death — the Brazilian writer 'has come to achieve considerable prominence on the Franco-American literary and academic circuit due precisely to Hélène Cixous's passionately personal involvement in the propagation of Lispector's writings'.[28] Cixous found in Lispector 'a companion and a contemporary woman',[29] as the French writer put it, thus establishing a rapport beyond scholarly work. Although Cixous's influence on critical readings of Lispector has waned over the years, particularly as more translations have become available in English, it remains arguable that a personal, passionate engagement towards the Brazilian author can still be perceived among Anglo-American critics, as well as a tendency to relate Lispector's fiction to her life and identity as a woman writer — an inclination shown by Cixous and seemingly influential on how Lispector is still approached by some of her contemporary readers.

Cixous's impact on the Anglo-American reception of Lispector extended to Brazilian scholars as well, as noted by Haroldo de Campos in the introduction to Olga de Sá's *A travessia do oposto* [The Crossing Between Opposites] (1993), which was clearly influenced by Cixous's philosophical approach. Yudith Rosenbaum names Cixous as the one responsible for launching Lispector internationally, together with Canadian writer Claire Varin, who has published on the Brazilian author both in French and Brazilian Portuguese.[30] It was Varin who first presented a more detailed account of Lispector's life in her 1987 study *Rencontres brésiliennes*, indicating 1920 — and not 1925, as Lispector used to say — as the true year of her birth.[31]

Varin seems to have inaugurated a 'new wave' of biographical studies that would increase in amplitude and intensity in the next decades. Under Cixous's ongoing influence, studies about Lispector rarely failed to establish some sort of relation between her fictional creation and her identity as a woman writer, and her biographical persona was considered increasingly pertinent to the understanding of her work. Olga Borelli's reflections in *Clarice Lispector: esboço para um possível retrato* [Clarice Lispector: Sketch for a Possible Portrait] (1981) actually showed how difficult it was to understand Lispector as a person, but this did not appear to have intimidated future biographers.[32] Nádia Battella Gotlib devoted various essays to Lispector as a woman writer before publishing, in 1995, the first full biography of the author, *Clarice Lispector: uma vida que se conta* [Clarice Lispector: A Life that Tells Itself].[33] Four years later, Teresa Montero published her biography of Lispector, *Eu sou uma pergunta: uma biografia de Clarice Lispector* [I am a Question: A Biography of Clarice Lispector].[34] In *Clarice Lispector: uma poética do olhar* [Clarice Lispector: A Poetics of the Gaze] (1999), Regina Lúcia Pontieri also sought to decipher literary devices adopted by the author, such as epiphany, while commenting on what was already known by then about her life.[35] Outside of Brazil, books like Marta Peixoto's *Passionate Fictions: Gender, Narrative, and Violence in Clarice Lispector* (1994) and the aforementioned *Closer to the Wild Heart: Essays on Clarice Lispector* (2001), in addition to Diane Marting's *Clarice Lispector: A Bio-Bibliography* (1993), are just a few of many scholarly works that have contributed to the writer's distinction in the English-speaking literary system and beyond.[36]

So vast is the contemporary interest in Lispector's legacy that we are able to assess major approaches towards her work and biography. One central field is Sexuality and Gender studies, as well as Feminist Studies, which have been shaped by Cixous's direct or indirect influence, as well as Fitz's and Peixoto's examinations. Another is Jewish Studies, which seeks to understand Lispector's relation to Judaism and how this is expressed in her body of work. This approach has been carried out by scholars such as Naomi Lindstrom,[37] Nelson Vieira,[38] and Nathan Goldman,[39] and was also explored in Moser's biography.[40] Race- and class-related issues are part of an emerging area of inquiry in the twenty-first century as well in the work of Lesley Feracho and Lucia Villares.[41]

Then there is the more personal approach, echoing Cixous's *coup de foudre*. For instance, poet and translator Idra Novey stands out for her creative engagement with Lispector's work. After completing her translation of *The Passion According to G.H.* (2012), Novey published *Clarice: The Visitor*,[42] a *cahier* of poems that address in part the translation process, as well as the novel *Ways to Disappear* (2016), which tells the story of an American translator who travels to Brazil in search of her vanished author (a character that, at least partially, appears to be based on Lispector).[43] In general, contemporary anglophone translators have been more vocal about the ways in which Lispector has influenced their writing and thinking about literature.[44] In the aforementioned issue of *The Scofield*, a sense of being mystified and deeply touched by Lispector's way of writing seems to appear, in one way or another, in all the interviews given by her translators, including Moser, Dodson, Alison Entrekin, Johnny Lorenz, and Novey.

The translators, reviewers, critics, scholars, publishers and editors mentioned above have helped to forge, over the years, Lispector's reputation in the English-speaking world. There is no question that this process has been indebted to translation. In the next section, we will turn our attention to the practice of translation through close readings of two texts translated by Dodson: the short story 'Amor' and the *crônica* 'Mineirinho'. Our focus on Dodson acknowledges the critical success of *The Complete Stories*, and in what follows, we will consider the extent to which Dodson's translations take into consideration Lispector's phenomenological approach to writing.

Translating Clarice Lispector

One of the greatest challenges for a reader and, above all, for a translator of Lispector's texts is their linguistic originality. Lispector seems to be in constant conflict with language, searching for the right word or expression to grasp the experience of her character. She subverts syntax, collocations, punctuation, but at the same time her texts seem, paradoxically, to be both sophisticated and hesitant, as though participating in a continuous game of trial and error. As Cixous and Fitz have observed, phenomenology can serve as a key to Lispector's work.[45] According to phenomenology, objects do not exist objectively, but rather intuitively as the subject apprehends them. This apprehension of a phenomenon, because it is intuitive, must suspend judgments and all sorts of theorizations about the observed object. Thus, the object is analysed as something unexplored, unknown, without preconceptions. In this way, the struggle between language and experience in Lispector's writing consists of a conscious method of creation. Her use of a seemingly reluctant and subversive language seeks to account precisely for the phenomenon as it is apprehended by the character when the encounter takes place; hence her unusual lexical choices, surprising collocations, strange syntax, and peculiar punctuation. There is also, in her tentative use of language, the feeling of incompleteness, of sensing a phenomenon. As Fitz has noted:

> Whenever this one to one connection between words and reality breaks down, as it does for Lispector's protagonists, chaos, fear, despair, confusion, anxiety and loss of identity result. It is at this point, at the breakdown of language in its attempt to name and therefore control reality, that Clarice Lispector's style and basic theme merge into an insoluble whole.[46]

In Lispector's writing the action does not take place outside of the character: a programmed life is interrupted by unexpected encounters that lead to self-knowledge. The character's routine is encroached upon by an external element that provokes reflection and an attempt to apprehend the object, resulting in a series of experiences that will give her a glimpse of herself. In 'Amor' and 'Mineirinho', the elements generating conflict are a blind man chewing gum and a murder, each one triggering the fragmentation of a reality, a routine or a worldview that the protagonists had created for themselves.

The phenomenological approach in Lispector is achieved through defamiliarization, as theorized by Russian formalist Viktor Shklovsky. According to Shklovsky, this is when language is no longer a mere vehicle for a message, when reading is deautomatized by a linguistic resource that imposes itself in the decoding process, a use of language that draws attention to itself.[47] Here we are interested mainly in Lispector's use of language as opposed to an everyday and prosaic linguistic experience, that is, an automatic process in which language is expected to be transparent so as to convey a clear, unequivocal message. Language in Lispector is not a simple vehicle for ideas nor does it have an instrumental function that leads the reader to an automatized perception. Lispector's use of language is singular in her struggle to name things and experiences as if the narrator had never seen them before, leading us to perceive the object under a different light, to experience her vision of the object rather than the simple recognition of the object itself.

We will focus our attention now on three recurrent devices in Lispector's writing — repetitions, unexpected collocation, and antithesis — and the strategies Dodson uses to deal with these devices in her translations. In our approach, we have relied on Antoine Berman's theory of translation. According to Berman, when considering prose translation, 'from a formal point of view, the language-based cosmos that is prose, especially the novel, is characterized by a certain shapelessness [...]. In effect, the masterworks of prose are characterized by a kind of "bad writing", a certain "lack of control" in their texture'.[48] This 'bad writing' is also part of the richness of prose or what makes it unique. Contrary to the domesticating tendency in literary translation, the French intellectual challenges the primacy of meaning and argues instead for a more literal translation, 'Here literal means: attached to the letter [*la lettre*] (of works)'.[49] For example, the nonstandard way Lispector arranges her texts into paragraphs, and how translators like Dodson have rendered it, illustrates Berman's 'bad writing' and his preference for 'literal translation'.

Before the publication of *The Complete Stories*, the stories 'Amor' and 'Mineirinho' were already available to anglophone readers in Pontiero's translations: 'Amor' [Love] in *Family Ties* (1972) and 'Mineirinho' in *The Foreign Legion* (1986). As one of us has already published an article analysing Pontiero's *Near to the Wild Heart* translation[50] and a second contrasting Pontiero's and Dodson's translations of 'The Smallest Woman in the World', as well as Pontiero's and Entrekin's translations of *Near to the Wild Heart*,[51] we will focus here on Dodson's translations of these two stories and the strategies she employs in their translation. Dodson's project appeared when interest in Lispector was growing significantly in the anglophone literary market and that also plays a part in our interest in a close reading of her translations, and these stories in particular.

'Amor'

Ana, the protagonist of 'Amor', has organized her entire routine around her house and her obligations as a mother and wife. With a past of 'unbearable happiness', Ana is part of a lineage of Lispector characters that repress their imagination for an expectation of normalcy, a process of self-detachment during which emotions must be controlled. She consciously represses her youth of restlessness and trepidation and fills her days without leaving room for reflection until she meets a blind man chewing gum. Somehow, this sight intrigues her and she cannot get it out of her head. Nevertheless, Ana is reluctant to start the reflective process triggered by the blind man: 'Ana still had a second to think about how her brothers were coming for dinner'.[52] But her resistance is useless: 'He was chewing gum in the dark. Without suffering, eyes open. [...] A facial expression, long unused, had reemerged with difficulty, still tentative, incomprehensible'.[53] The protagonist returns to the state of restlessness of her youth and is violently thrown into a chaotic process of apprehending this scene and how it affected her.

The phenomenological construction of the narrative is carefully thought out, starting with the disruption which jolts Ana away from her surrounding reality:

> A rede de tricô era áspera entre os dedos, não íntima como quando a tricotara. A rede perdera o sentido e estar num bonde era um fio partido; não sabia o que fazer com as compras no colo. E como uma estranha música, o mundo recomeçava ao redor. O mal estava feito. Por quê? teria esquecido que havia cegos? [...] Mesmo as coisas que existiam antes do acontecimento estavam agora de sobreaviso, tinham um ar mais hostil, perecível... O mundo se tornara de novo um mal-estar.

> [The knit mesh was rough between her fingers, not intimate as when she had knit it. The mesh had lost its meaning and being on a tram was a snapped thread; she didn't know what to do with the groceries on her lap. And like a strange song, the world started up again all around. The damage was done. Why? could she have forgotten there were blind people? [...] Even the things that existed before this event were now wary, had a more hostile, perishable aspect... The world had become once again a distress.][54]

One of the most interesting aspects of Lispector's phenomenological writing is the defamiliarization she establishes by using hesitant language, which seeks to convey meaning upon the world and upon the character's internal revolution. This is notable in two aspects. The first is repetition, sometimes as if the protagonist were trying to convince herself, as in 'That was what she had wanted and chosen',[55] or sometimes to try to account linguistically for the phenomenon. For example:

> Ela plantara as sementes que tinha na mão, não outras, mas essas apenas. E **cresciam** árvores. **Crescia** sua rápida conversa com o cobrador de luz, **crescia** a água enchendo o tanque, **cresciam** seus filhos, **crescia** a mesa com comidas.

> [She had sown the seeds she had in her hand, no others, but these alone. And trees **were growing**. Her brief conversation with the electric bill collector **was growing**, the water in the laundry sink **was growing**, her children **were growing**, the table with food **was growing**.][56]

The second is by means of unexpected collocations, alien to Brazilian Portuguese. Listed below are some fragments representative of Lispector's creative language, followed by the translations proposed by Dodson.

> Enquanto a vida que descobrira continuava a pulsar e **um vento mais morno e mais misterioso rodeava-lhe o rosto**.
>
> [While the life she had discovered kept pulsating and **a warmer, more mysterious wind whirled round her face**.][57]
>
> Sua alma batia-lhe no peito — o que sucedia? **A piedade pelo cego era tão violenta** como uma ânsia, mas o mundo lhe parecia seu, sujo, perecível, seu.
>
> [**Her soul pounding in her chest** — what was happening? **Her compassion for the blind man was as violent** as an agony, but the world seemed to be hers, dirty, perishable, hers.][58]
>
> Acabara-se **a vertigem da bondade**.
>
> [The **dizziness of benevolence** was over.][59]

In Dodson's translations, great care is taken with the rhythm of the text: the translator replicates the length of paragraphs and sentences, the position of ellipses, indentations, repetitions and all kinds of marks of hesitation in the narrative. The rhythm of the narrative is one of disorder and vertigo, which subverts orthodox punctuation. Contrary to Pontiero's translation, in which there is some reorganization of the textual structure, Dodson maintains, in her text, the vertiginous rhythm of Lispector's prose. We observe that the repetitions of 'piedade' and 'bondade' were diligently followed by Dodson in her choice of 'compassion' and 'benevolence'. As for the unusual collocations quoted above, Dodson maintains them, and with the added benefit of beautiful alliteration: 'wind whirled'. Pontiero was more reserved, as we can observe, in his translation 'her heart beating in her breast'[60] for 'sua alma batia-lhe no peito', which Dodson translated more literally as 'her soul pounding in her chest', thus maintaining the strangeness and deautomatization of perception present in Lispector's description of the protagonist's anguish.

In Lispector's *oeuvre*, examples of defamiliarization such as *a soul pounding in a chest* instead of the idiomatic *heart pounding in a chest* are recurrent. Readers are constantly reminded of the instrument with which fiction is created and, in that moment, language ceases to have an instrumental role in literary production, leading to an asymmetry that has as its objective an aesthetic effect. In this respect, deautomatization is associated with an idiosyncratic use of language.

In addition to unusual collocations, like those mentioned above, there are also several cases of antithesis throughout the story:

> A decomposição era profunda, perfumada...
>
> [The **decomposition was deep, perfumed**][61]
>
> De que tinha vergonha? É que já não era mais piedade, não era só piedade: **seu coração se enchera com a pior vontade de viver**.
>
> [What was she ashamed of? That it was no longer compassion, it wasn't just compassion: **her heart had filled with the worst desire to live**.][62]

These examples not only present antithetical ideas but they are also true to Lispector's style, i.e., they create tension and surprise. Phrases like *perfumed decomposition* or *the worst desire to live* are not difficult to translate: the conflict they present is recognizable across many cultures, and they do not represent a challenge in lexical terms. The difficulty or the mentioned conflict lies in their unpredictability and how this would be received by an English-language reader. In Lispector's writings contrasting ideas are usually related to a character's thought process. The device gives the reader a glimpse of a character's mindset, how they (usually she) combine ideas and try to make sense of their experiences. Dodson is attentive to Lispector's use of antithesis and follows it closely in her translation, thus maintaining the strangeness proposed by the author, even if, by doing so, there may be, as in Portuguese, an ungrammatical construction, or 'bad writing' as Berman would say.

'Mineirinho'

Published originally in 1962, this *crônica* recounts the real-life murder of a thief and murderer known as Mineirinho, an event that occurred a month prior to its publication. The predominant tone of the text is one of perplexity, revolt and compassion. The narrator tries to understand why it took the police thirteen shots to stop the murderer. Hence her use of climax: 'But there is something that, if it makes me hear the first and second gunshots with the relief of safety, at the third puts me on the alert, [...]. The thirteenth shot murders me — because I am the other.'[63] Despite its brevity, 'Mineirinho' nonetheless contains some of the characteristics of Lispector's technique, such as the use of repetition as a rhetorical device (especially the words 'tiro' [shot], 'erro' [error], 'doido' [crazy] and 'justiça' [justice]), her unusual collocations, as in 'assustada violência' [frightened violence] and 'violência inocente' [innocent violence] and antithesis, as the following excerpt illustrates:

> Até que treze tiros nos acordam, e com horror digo tarde demais — vinte e oito anos depois que Mineirinho nasceu — **que ao homem acuado, que a esse não nos matem**. Porque sei que ele é **meu erro**. E de uma vida inteira, por Deus, o que se salva às vezes é apenas o **erro**, e eu sei que não nos salvaremos enquanto **nosso erro** não nos for precioso. **Meu erro** é meu espelho, onde vejo o que em silêncio eu fiz de um homem. **Meu erro** é o modo como vi **a vida se abrir na sua carne e me espantei**, e vi a matéria de vida, placenta e **sangue**, a lama viva.

> [Until thirteen gunshots wake us up, and in horror I plead too late — twenty-eight years after Mineirinho was born — **that in killing this cornered man, they do not kill him in us**. Because I know that he is **my error**. And out of a whole lifetime, by God, sometimes the only thing that saves a person is **error**, and I know that we shall not be saved so long as **our error** is not precious to us. **My error** is my mirror, where I see what in silence I made of a man. **My error** is the way I saw **life opening up in his flesh and I was aghast**, and I saw the substance of life, placenta and **blood**, the living mud.][64]

As in 'Amor', Dodson follows the rhythm of the text, reproducing punctuation, indents and the length of paragraphs and sentences. Along with improvisation, inversions, and emphases, which we will address in the next paragraph, punctuation helps set up the conversational tone proposed by Lispector, mainly through the use of long sentences.

Lispector's use of emphasis can be observed in a more explicit way in the clause '**digo** tarde demais — vinte e oito anos depois que Mineirinho nasceu — **que ao homem acuado, que a esse não nos matem**'. The sentence is constructed in an intricate manner, and initially its meaning is not clear. The main difficulty here lies in the inversion of subject-verb-object order: Lispector opts for an object-verb order, omitting the subject, quite common in written Portuguese. The emphasis in the clause 'que ao homem acuado, que a esse não nos matem' is crucial to understanding its meaning. Lispector chooses to highlight that the man was cornered by positioning this information before the verb, isolating it with a comma, and then she uses the demonstrative pronoun 'esse' as an object referring to 'cornered man', so, effectively she mentions him twice, emphasizing Mineirinho as a victim. Moreover, the proposition 'a' in 'que **ao** homem acuado, que **a** esse' with a direct object is used because of its position before the verb, thereby emphasizing the latter. Dodson's translation is correct, but by using 'kill' twice, the emphasis is weakened.

In her translation, Lispector's repetitions are maintained, which also points to the confessional nature of the text and the relevance of emphasizing the pain and guilt that permeate the text. The last sentence, 'My error is the way I saw life opening up in his flesh and I was aghast, and I saw the substance of life, placenta and blood, the living mud', presents us with a striking antithesis, as death is described in terms of 'the substance of life': flesh, placenta and blood. The narrator invokes these symbols to call attention to the brutality of Mineirinho's death, and then, after seeing what he is made of, she realizes too late that they are both made of the same substance.

Our brief analysis of two short stories translated by Dodson examines how Lispector subverts the use of language and what kind of strategies a translator like Dodson adopts when faced with such language in the source text. The anglophone literary system has benefited from gaining access to Lispector's stories in translation and, above all, from Dodson's diligence in translating Lispector's unique use of language.[65] Dodson has managed to introduce readers to a version that approximates closely our original and linguistically subversive Brazilian Lispector. Lispector's literary universe cannot be recreated if it is subordinated to the lexical and syntactic expectations of another language. The author's originality lies precisely in the enigma of naming what has no name, of qualifying the amazement of the discovery of consciousness through a phenomenological approach. An acceptance of Lispector's creative technique, in which language seems to be in a state of constant reinvention, is the key to a good translation.

In this chapter, we have presented Lispector's readers with a panoramic view of her reception in the anglophone literary system, from the first translations into English to the 2018 publication of *The Chandelier*. Lispector's literary works are, by now, almost completely available to anglophone readers, which not only allows for a deep immersion into her writing but also encourages Lispector scholars who read her work in the original Portuguese to reflect on aspects that become visible through the processes of translation and close reading. Over the years, anglophone editors, translators, and literary critics have contributed fresh perspectives on Lispector's work, highlighting peculiarities of her style and the challenges her language has imposed on her readers, many of whom — ourselves included — are impelled to unravel the mysteries of her craft.

Works Cited

ALONSO, CLÁUDIA PAZOS, and CLAIRE WILLIAMS, *Closer to the Wild Heart: Essays on Clarice Lispector* (Oxford: Legenda, 2001)

BERMAN, ANTOINE, 'Translation and the Trials of the Foreign', trans. by Lawrence Venuti, in *The Translation Studies Reader*, ed. by Lawrence Venuti (London: Routledge, 2000), pp. 240–53

BRYAN, C. D. B., 'Afraid to Be Afraid', *New York Times*, 3 September 1967, pp. 22–23

CARRERA, ELENA, 'The Reception of Clarice Lispector via Hélène Cixous: Reading from the Whale's Belly', in *Brazilian Feminisms*, ed. by Solange Ribeiro de Oliveira and Judith Still (Nottingham: University of Nottingham Press, 1999), pp. 85–100

CASTRO, RUY, 'Obra sobre Lispector não é biografia, mas ensaio biográfico', *Folha de São Paulo*, 5 December 2009, <https://www1.folha.uol.com.br/fsp/ilustrad/fq0512200913.htm> [accessed 20 January 2020]

CIXOUS, HÉLÈNE, *Reading with Clarice Lispector*, ed., trans. and intro. by Verena Andermatt Conley (Minneapolis: University of Minnesota Press, 1990)

DODSON, KATRINA, 'Understanding is the Proof of Error', *The Believer*, 119 (2018) <https://believermag.com/understanding-is-the-proof-of-error/> [accessed 28 January 2020]

EBERSTADT, FERNANDA 'Untamed Creature', *New York Times*, 19 August 2009, <https://www.nytimes.com/2009/08/23/books/review/Eberstadt-t.html> [accessed 20 January 2020]

EDWARDS, MAGDALENA, 'Benjamin Moser and the Smallest Woman in the World', *Los Angeles Review of Books*, 16 August 2019, <https://lareviewofbooks.org/article/benjamin-moser-and-the-smallest-woman-in-the-world/> [accessed 13 January 2020]

FITZ, EARL E., *Clarice Lispector: The Nature and Form of the Lyrical Novel* (unpublished doctoral dissertation, City University of New York, 1977)

GOTLIB, NÁDIA BATTELLA, 'De Cuentos reunidos a Todos os contos', *Cult*, 19 June 2017, <https://revistacult.uol.com.br/home/de-cuentos-reunidos-todos-os-contos/> [accessed 10 January 2020]

GROSSMANN, JUDITH, 'A soberania do eu em O lustre, de Clarice Lispector', *Estudos lingüísticos e literários*, 12 (1971), 117–40

KLOBUCKA, ANNA, 'Hélène Cixous and the Hour of Clarice Lispector', *SubStance*, 23 (1994), 41–62

LISPECTOR, CLARICE, *Family Ties*, trans. by Giovanni Pontiero (Austin: University of Texas Press, 1972)
—— *Discovering the World*, trans. by Giovanni Pontiero (Manchester: Carcanet, 1992)
—— *The Complete Stories*, trans. by Katrina Dodson (New York: New Directions, 2015)
—— *Todos os contos* (Rio de Janeiro: Rocco, 2016)

O'GRADY, KATHLEEN, 'Guardian of Language: An Interview with Hélène Cixous (March 1996)', *Women's education des femmes*, 12.4 (Winter 1996–67), 6–10, <http://bailiwick.lib.uiowa.edu/wstudies/cixous/index.html> [accessed 13 January 2020]

PECHMAN, ALEXANDRA, 'It's Complicated — Clarice Lispector and Elizabeth Bishop's Fraught Relationship', *Poetry Foundation*, 29 September 2015, <https://www.poetryfoundation.org/articles/70270/its-complicated> [accessed 20 January 2020]

POWER, CHRIS, 'A Brief Survey of the Short Story, Part 56: Clarice Lispector', *Guardian*, 5 March 2014, <https://www.theguardian.com/books/booksblog/2014/mar/05/clarice-lispector-short-story-survey> [accessed 29 January 2020]

RABASSA, GREGORY, *If This Be Treason: Translation and its Discontents — A Memoir* (New York: New Directions, 2005)

ROSENBAUM, YUDITH, *Clarice Lispector* (São Paulo: Publifolha, 2002).

ROHTER, LARRY, 'Review: Clarice Lispector's "The Complete Stories" Sees Life with Existential Dread', *New York Times*, 11 August 2015, <https://www.nytimes.com/2015/08/12/books/review-clarice-lispectors-the-complete-stories-sees-life-with-existential-dread.html> [accessed 28 January 2020]

SEHGAL, PARUL, '*The Chandelier* Offers an Early Glimpse of Clarice Lispector's Power', *New York Times*, 27 March 2018, <https://www.nytimes.com/2018/03/27/books/review-chandelier-clarice-lispector.html> [accessed 20 January 2020]

VAN DER PLAS, CHRISTINA SOTO, 'Un-Reading Clarice Lispector's The Chandelier', *Los Angeles Review of Books*, 27 March 2018, <https://lareviewofbooks.org/article/un-reading-clarice-lispectors-the-chandelier> [accessed 13 January 2020]

Appendix

1. Novels[66]

Perto do coração selvagem (1943)
- *Near to the Wild Heart*, by Giovanni Pontiero (New Directions, 1990)
- *Near to the Wild Heart*, by Alison Entrekin (New Directions, 2012)

O lustre (1946)
- *The Chandelier*, by Magdalena Edwards and Benjamin Moser (New Directions, 2018)

A cidade sitiada (1949)
- *The Besieged City*, by Giovanni Pontiero (Carcanet Press, 1997 [unpublished])
- *The Besieged City*, by Johnny Lorenz (New Directions, 2019)

A maçã no escuro (1961)
- *The Apple in the Dark*, by Gregory Rabassa (Alfred Knopf, 1967)

A paixão segundo G.H. (1964)
- *The Passion According to G.H.*, by Ronald W. Sousa (University of Minnesota Press, 1988)
- *The Passion According to G.H.*, by Idra Novey (New Directions, 2012)

Uma aprendizagem ou O livro dos prazeres (1969)
- *An Apprenticeship or The Book of Delights*, by Richard A. Mazzara and Lorri A. Parris (University of Texas Press, 1986)
- *An Apprenticeship or The Book of Pleasures*, by Stefan Tobler (New Directions, 2021)

Água viva (1973)
- *The Stream of Life*, by Elizabeth Lowe and Earl Fitz (University of Minnesota Press, 1989)
- *Água Viva*, by Stefan Tobler (New Directions, 2012)

A hora da estrela (1977)
- *The Hour of the Star*, by Giovanni Pontiero (Carcanet Press, 1986)
- *The Hour of the Star*, by Benjamin Moser (New Directions, 2011)

Um sopro de vida (1978)
- *A Breath of Life*, by Johnny Lorenz (New Directions, 2012)

2. Short story collections

Alguns contos [Stories] (1952)

—

Laços de família (1960)
- *Family Ties*, by Giovanni Pontiero (University of Texas Press, 1972)

A legião estrangeira (1964)

The first editions of *Legião estrangeira* included a section called 'Fundo de gaveta' [Bottom of the Drawer] which was composed of chronicles, fragments and the play 'A pecadora e o anjo queimado' [The Sinner and the Burned Angel]. Pontiero included them in his translation, and some are included in *The Complete Stories*.
- *The Foreign Legion: Stories and Chronicles*, by Giovanni Pontiero (Carcanet Press, 1986)

Felicidade clandestina [Covert Happiness] (1971)
- Included in *The Complete Stories*.

A imitação da rosa [The Imitation of the Rose] (1973)

This contains stories from *Laços de família* and *Legião estrangeira*

O ovo e a galinha. — Amor. — A imitação da rosa. — Miopia progressiva. — Come, meu filho. — Mistério em São Cristovão. — Uma galinha. — Os desastres de Sofia. — A menor mulher do mundo. — O crime de professor de matemática. — Devaneio e embriaguez duma rapariga. — A legião estrangeira. — Macacos. — Perdoando Deus. — Feliz aniversário. —

A via crucis do corpo [The Via Crucis of the Body] (1974)
- *Soulstorm: Stories by Clarice Lispector*, by Alexis Levitin (New Directions, 1990)

Onde estivestes de noite? [Where were you at night?] (1974)
- *Soulstorm: Stories by Clarice Lispector*, by Alexis Levitin (New Directions, 1989)

A bela e a fera [Beauty and the Beast] (1977)
- Included in *The Complete Stories*

3. Chronicle collections

Visão do esplendor: impressões leves [Vision of Splendour: Fleeting Impressions] (1975)

—

Para não esquecer [So I Don't Forget] (1978)

These correspond to the chronicles from the 'Fundo de gaveta' section of *Legião estrangeira*.

—

A descoberta do mundo (1984)
- *Discovering the World*, by Giovanni Pontiero (Carcanet Press, 1992)
- *Selected Crônicas*, by Giovanni Pontiero (New Directions, 1996)

4. Stories in Collections

A menor mulher do mundo
    'The Smallest Woman in the World', by Elizabeth Bishop
- *The Eye of the Heart: Short Stories from Latin America* (Bobbs-Merrill, 1973), edited by Barbara Howes

A imitação da rosa
    'The Imitation of the Rose', by Giovanni Pontiero
- *Other Fires: Short Fiction by Latin American Women* (Three Rivers Press, 1985), edited by Alberto Manguel

Amor Laços de família
- 'Love' and 'Family Ties', by Giovanni Pontiero
- *Women's Fiction from Latin America: Selections from Twelve Contemporary Authors* (Wayne State University Press, MI, 1988), edited by Evelyn Picon Garfield

Amor
    'Love', by Giovanni Pontiero
- *A Hammock Beneath the Mangoes: Stories from Latin America* (Plume, 1990), edited by Thomas Colchie

A procura de uma dignidade
    'Looking for Some Dignity', by Leland Guyer
- *Short Stories by Latin American Women: The Magic and the Real* (Arte Público Press, 1990), edited by Celia Correas de Zapata

Laços de família
    'Family Ties', by Giovanni Pontiero
- *The Oxford Book of Jewish Stories* (Oxford University Oress, 1998), edited by Ilan Stavans

Para acabar de 'fundir a cuca'
    'No More Worries', by Giovanni Pontiero
- *The House of Memory: Stories by Jewish Women Writers of Latin America* (The Feminist Press at The City University of New York, 1999) edited by Marjorie Agosín

Amor
    'Love', by Giovanni Pontiero
- *The Vintage Book of Latin American Stories* (Vintage/Penguin, 2000), edited by Carlos Fuentes and Julio Ortega

O búfalo, A galinha, A menor mulher do mundo, A repartição dos pães; A quinta história; Miss Algrave; O corpo; Praça Mauá; Bela e a Fera, ou a ferida grande demais

'The Buffalo', by Giovanni Pontiero; 'The Chicken', by Elizabeth Bishop; 'The Smallest Woman in the World', by Elizabeth Bishop; 'The Breaking of the Bread', by Eloah F. Giacomelli; 'The Fifth Story', by Eloah F. Giacomelli; 'Miss Algrave', by Alexis Levitin; 'The Body', by Alexis Levitin; 'Plaza Mauá', by Alexis Levitin; 'Beauty and the Beast, or, The Wound Too Great', by Earl Fitz

- *Oxford Anthology of the Brazilian Short Story* (Oxford University Press, 2006), edited by K. David Jackson

Amor
    'Love', by Giovanni Pontiero
- *Oy, Caramba! An Anthology of Jewish Stories from Latin America* (University of New Mexico Press, 2016), edited by Ilan Stavans

5. Children Stories

O mistério do coelho pensante (1967)
- *The Mystery of the Thinking Rabbit*, translated by Suzanne Jill Levine, *Fiction* 62 (2016 [1973]) pp. 61–66

A mulher que matou os peixes (1968)
- *The Woman Who Killed the Fish*, by Earl Fitz (*Latin American Literary Review*, 11.21 (1982), 89–101

A vida íntima de Laura [The Intimate Life of Laura] (1974)
—

Como nasceram as estrelas — Doze lendas brasileiras [How the Stars were Born: Twelve Brazilian Legends] (1977)
—

Quase de verdade [Almost True] (1978)
—

Notes to Chapter 26

1. Cláudia Pazos Alonso and Claire Williams, *Closer to the Wild Heart: Essays on Clarice Lispector* (Oxford: Legenda, 2001), p. 1.
2. Chris Power, 'A Brief Survey of the Short Story, Part 56: Clarice Lispector', *Guardian*, 5 March 2014 <https://www.theguardian.com/books/booksblog/2014/mar/05/clarice-lispector-short-story-survey> [accessed 29 January 2020].
3. Larry Rohter, 'Review: Clarice Lispector's 'The Complete Stories' Sees Life with Existential Dread', *New York Times*, 11 August 2015, < https://www.nytimes.com/2015/08/12/books/review-clarice-lispectors-the-complete-stories-sees-life-with-existential-dread.html> [accessed 28 January 2020].
4. Parul Sehgal, '*The Chandelier* Offers an Early Glimpse of Clarice Lispector's Power', *New York Times*, 27 March 2018 <https://www.nytimes.com/2018/03/27/books/review-chandelier-clarice-lispector.html> [accessed 20 January 2020].
5. Christina Soto van der Plas, 'Un-Reading Clarice Lispector's *The Chandelier*', *Los Angeles Review of Books*, 27 March 2018, <https://lareviewofbooks.org/article/un-reading-clarice-lispectors-the-chandelier> [accessed 13 January 2020]. Magdalena Edwards recounts her experience of translating *The Chandelier* in 'Benjamin Moser and the Smallest Woman in the World', *Los Angeles Review of Books*, 16 August 2019 <https://lareviewofbooks.org/article/benjamin-moser-and-the-smallest-woman-in-the-world/> [accessed 13 January 2020].
6. For example, *The Foreign Legion: Stories and Chronicles* (1992) and *Selected Crônicas: Essays* (1996).
7. Nádia Battella Gotlib, 'De Cuentos reunidos a Todos os contos', *Cult*, 19 June 2017, <https://revistacult.uol.com.br/home/de-cuentos-reunidos-todos-os-contos/> [accessed 10 January 2020].
8. 'Daydream and Drunkenness of a Young Lady', book description, Penguin website, <https://www.penguin.co.uk/books/308490/daydream-and-drunkenness-of-a-young-lady/9780241337608.html> [accessed 27 March 2020].
9. Lispector, 'The Smallest Woman in the World', trans. by Katrina Dodson, *Tablet*, 27 July 2015, <https://www.tabletmag.com/jewish-arts-and-culture/192365/the-smallest-woman-in-the-world> [accessed 27 March 2020].
10. This fact is discussed in Alexandra Pechman's enlightening essay about Lispector and Bishop's relationship, 'It's Complicated — Clarice Lispector and Elizabeth Bishop's Fraught Relationship', *Poetry Foundation* , 29 September 2015, <https://www.poetryfoundation.org/articles/70270/its-complicated> [accessed 20 January 2020].
11. Gregory Rabassa, *If This Be Treason: Translation and its Discontents — A Memoir* (New York: New Directions, 2005), p. 73.
12. C. D. B. Bryan, 'Afraid to Be Afraid', *New York Times*, 3 September 1967, pp. 22–23.
13. Giovanni Pontiero, 'Preface', in Clarice Lispector, *Discovering the World*, trans. by Giovanni Pontiero (Manchester: Carcanet, 1992), pp. 21–32 (p. 21).
14. Pontiero, 'Preface', in *Discovering the World* (Manchester: Carcanet, 1992), pp. 21–30 (p. 23).
15. See the excerpt by Giovanni Pontiero in this volume.
16. Fernanda Eberstadt, 'Untamed Creature', *New York Times*, 19 August 2009, <https://www.nytimes.com/2009/08/23/books/review/Eberstadt-t.html> [accessed 20 January 2020].
17. Ruy Castro, 'Obra sobre Lispector não é biografia, mas ensaio biográfico', 5 December 2009, <https://www1.folha.uol.com.br/fsp/ilustrad/fq0512200913.htm> [accessed 20 January 2020]. See also Júlia Braga Neves's chapter in this volume.
18. *Todos os contos* was Rocco's best-seller in the fiction category in 2016, even though it sold a little less than 28,000 books — the other four best-selling books of their catalogue were foreign fiction. See <https://www.publishnews.com.br/ranking/anual/9/2016/6/0>
19. For Lispector's translation into French, Hebrew and Chinese, respectively, see the chapters by Julie Côté, Adriana X. Jacobs, and Min Xuefei in this volume.
20. All translations into English are ours, unless otherwise indicated. Original text: 'se deixarmos de lado as possíveis fontes estrangeiras de inspiração, permanece o fato de que, dentro da nossa literatura, é performance da melhor qualidade', Antonio Candido, 'Perto do Coração Selvagem',

first published in *Folha da Manhã*, 16 July 1944). In *Folha de S.Paulo*, 1 December 2001, <https://www1.folha.uol.com.br/fsp/ilustrad/fq0112200109.htm>.

21. Later, Nunes reaffirmed his literary and philosophical approach to Lispector's fiction in *O drama da linguagem: uma leitura de Clarice Lispector* (São Paulo: Ática, 1989).
22. Among them, analyses of *Laços de família* e *A legião estrangeira* in *Análise estrutural de romances brasileiros* (São Paulo: Ática, 1973) and 'A leitura de Clarice Lispector' (*Littera*, 1973).
23. Judith Grossmann, 'A soberania do cu em *O lustre*, de Clarice Lispector', *Estudos lingüísticos e literários*, 12 (1971), 117–40; Lúcia Helena, 'Aprendizado de Clarice Lispector', *Littera*, 5.13 (1975), 99–104.
24. Later, Fitz would publish the monographs *Clarice Lispector* (Boston, MA: Twayne, 1985) and *Sexuality and Being in the Poststructuralist Universe of Clarice Lispector: The Différance of Desire* (Minneapolis: University of Minnesota Press, 2001), in addition to various other essays.
25. Elizabeth Lowe, 'The Passion According to C.L.', *Review: Literature and Arts of the Americas*, 13.24 (1979), 34–37.
26. Her first publication about Lispector was the bilingual *Vivre l'orange / To live the Orange* (Paris: des Femmes, 1979). Later, a collection of essays was translated by Verena Andermatt Conley in *Reading with Clarice* (Minneapolis: University of Minnesota Press, 1989). .
27. Hélène Cixous, *Reading with Clarice*, pp. 29, 37. For more on Cixous as a reader of Lispector, see Julie Côté's chapter in this volume.
28. Anna Klobucka, 'Hélène Cixous and the Hour of Clarice Lispector', *SubStance*, 23.1 (1994), 41–62 (pp. 41, 42–43).
29. Kathleen O'Grady, 'Guardian of Language: An Interview with Hélène Cixous (March 1996)', *Women's education des femmes*, 12.4 (Winter 1996–97), 6–10 <http://bailiwick.lib.uiowa.edu/wstudies/cixous/index.html> [accessed 13 January 2020].
30. Yudith Rosenbaum, *Clarice Lispector* (São Paulo: Publifolha, 2002), p. 89.
31. Claire Varin, *Clarice Lispector: rencontres brésiliennes* (Laval, Québec: Trois, 1987).
32. Olga Borelli, *Clarice Lispector: esboço para um possível retrato* (Rio de Janeiro: Nova Fronteira, 1981).
33. Nádia Battella Gotlib, *Clarice Lispector: uma vida que se conta* (São Paulo: Edusp, 2013).
34. Teresa Montero, *Eu sou uma pergunta: uma biografia de Clarice Lispector* (Rio de Janeiro: Rocco, 1999).
35. Regina Lúcia Pontieri, *Clarice Lispector: uma poética do olhar* (Cotia: Ateliê Editorial, 1999).
36. Marta Peixoto, *Passionate Fictions: Gender, Narrative, and Violence in Clarice Lispector* (Minneapolis and London: University of Minnesota Press, 1994). Diane Marting, *Clarice Lispector: A Bio-Bibliography* (Westport, CT: Greenwood Press, 1993).
37. Naomi Lindstrom, 'The Pattern of Allusions in Clarice Lispector', *Luso-Brazilian Review*, 36.1 (1999), 111–21.
38. See Nelson H. Vieira, 'A expressão judaica na obra de Clarice Lispector', *Remate de Males*, 9 (1989), 207–09; Nelson H. Vieira, 'Clarice Lispector — A Jewish Impulse and a Prophecy of Difference', in *Jewish Voices in Brazilian Literature: A Prophetic Discourse of Alterity* (Gainesville: University Press of Florida, 1996).
39. Nathan Goldman, 'On the Heterodox Jewishness of Clarice Lispector: A Writer of The Diaspora, In Search of God', *Literary Hub*, 27 September 2016, <https://lithub.com/on-the-heterodox-jewishness-of-clarice-lispector/> [accessed 13 August 2021].
40. See also the chapters by Yael Segalovitz and Adriana X. Jacobs in this volume.
41. Lesley Feracho, 'Authorial Intervention in *A hora da estrela*: Metatextual and Structural Multiplicity', in *Linking the Americas: Race, Hybrid Discourses and the Reformulation of Feminine Identity* (Albany: State University of New York Press, 2005); Lucia Villares, *Examining Whiteness: Reading Clarice Lispector through Bessie Head and Toni Morrison* (Oxford: Legenda, 2017).
42. Idra Novey, *Clarice: The Visitor* (London: Sylph Editions, 2014).
43. See also the chapters by Idra Novey and Claire Williams in this volume.
44. See the chapter by Katrina Dodson in this volume.
45. Cixous, *Vivre l'orange*; Earl E. Fitz, *Clarice Lispector: The Nature and Form of the Lyric Novel* (unpublished doctoral dissertation, City University of New York, 1977).
46. Fitz, *Clarice Lispector: The Nature and Form of the Lyric Novel*, pp. 234–35.

47. Viktor Shklovsky, *The Theory of Prose* (Champaign, IL: Dalkey Archive Press, 1991).
48. Antoine Berman, 'Translation and the Trials of the Foreign', trans. by Lawrence Venuti, in *The Translation Studies Reader* (London: Routledge, 2000), pp. 240–53.
49. Ibid. p. 253.
50. Luana Ferreira de Freitas, '*Perto do coração selvagem* em inglês', *Cerrados*, 16.24 (2007), 279–85.
51. Luana Ferreira de Freitas, 'Clarice Lispector's Radicality Translated into the English-Speaking Literary System', *Cadernos de Tradução*, 38.3 (2018), 244–58.
52. Ibid., p. 117.
53. Ibid., p. 118.
54. Lispector, *Todos os contos*, p. 148; *The Complete Stories*, pp. 118–19.
55. Lispector, *The Complete Stories*, pp. 116–17.
56. Lispector, *Todos os contos*, p. 145; *The Complete Stories*, p. 115. Our emphasis.
57. Lispector, *Todos os contos*, p. 152; *The Complete Stories*, p. 122. Our emphasis.
58. Lispector, *Todos os contos*, p. 155; *The Complete Stories*, p. 122. Our emphasis.
59. Lispector, *Todos os contos*, p. 155; *The Complete Stories*, p. 126. Our emphasis.
60. Lispector, *Family Ties*, p. 44. Our emphasis.
61. Lispector, *Todos os contos*, p. 151; *The Complete Stories*, p. 121. Our emphasis.
62. Lispector, *Todos os contos*, p. 153; *The Complete Stories*, p. 123. Our emphasis.
63. Lispector, *The Complete Stories*, p. 363.
64. Lispector, *Todos os contos*, p. 387; *The Complete Stories*, p. 363. Our emphasis.
65. See also the chapter by Min Xuefei in this volume.
66. In all of the sections, with the exception section 4, all titles are listed in chronological order according to their original publication date. In section 4, the titles are listed in chronological order according to the translation publication date.

CHAPTER 27

Counterfeit Clarices: Performing Lispector

Katrina Dodson

I. Clarice, the Mystic

At a reading I gave in Seattle in 2016, on the occasion of translating Clarice Lispector's *The Complete Stories*, a man with white hair raised his hand to tell me he had once lived in Brazil and had named his daughter after the writer.[1] Later, he handed me a piece of paper on which he'd scrawled 'Katrina: I've often thought of Clarice as something of a mystic. Thanks'. The note was written on a photocopy of the opening page from Evelyn Underhill's 1911 book *Mysticism: A Study in the Nature and Development of Man's Spiritual Consciousness*.

Forty years after her death, Clarice, as she is known in Brazil, has become one of those writers whose persona is inextricably intertwined with her books. No longer a mere author, she has taken on the aura of a myth, a goddess, a sphinx, a sorceress, even a kind of internet self-help oracle, with nearly a thousand inspirational aphorisms attributed to her daily on Twitter, fake quotes blending seamlessly with the real. It seems to me that 'something of a mystic' is among the best ways to characterize Clarice Lispector.

Beneath the man's handwritten note, I read the heading, CHAPTER 1: THE POINT OF DEPARTURE, and a summary of topics that could have passed as a thematic index for Clarice's work, beginning with, 'The mystic type — its persistence — Man's quest of Truth', and ending on, 'It claims direct communion with the Absolute.' Underhill's descriptors made me consider how Clarice's constantly inquiring approach to her subjects also brings us to the 'foundations of experience' and the 'logical end of Intellectualism' in a burst of dark laughter or with a simple, unanswerable question. 'Religion — Suffering — Beauty — Their mystical aspect' could serve as shorthand for any number of Clarice's texts, particularly *A paixão segundo G.H.* [*The Passion According to G.H.*] (1964).[2] This fictional account of a profoundly transformative encounter that leads to spiritual awakening recalls personal narratives by sixteenth-century saint Teresa of Ávila and modern-day mystic Simone Weil — except the woman known as G.H. is a 1960s chain-smoking bourgeois dilettante sculptor trapped in the tropical heat of her Copacabana apartment, and the Eucharist that leads her to God is a cockroach.

Like mysticism, Lispector's work is hard to define. Both are shrouded in a distrust of language's ability to capture truth. The Greek root of *mysticism*, μυω, means 'to conceal', while the word mystic derives from *mystikos*, one initiated into secret religious rites. 'It's a secret', Clarice would say when she didn't want to answer an interview question. Reading her for the first time can feel like being led down a passage toward esoteric mysteries that will never be completely illuminated. I imagine Clarice's most devoted readers practising a form of bibliomancy, opening her books at random to let one of her arresting lines set them at a new angle to life, like a tarot card pulled from the deck:

> É que eu olhara a barata viva e nela descobria a identidade de minha vida mais profunda.
>
> [Because I'd looked at the living roach and was discovering inside it the identity of my deepest life.]
>
> Continuo com capacidade de raciocínio — já estudei matemática que é a loucura do raciocínio — mas agora quero o plasma — quero me alimentar diretamente da placenta.
>
> [I can still reason — I studied mathematics, which is the madness of reason — but now I want the plasma — I want to eat straight from the placenta.]
>
> A lei geral para continuarmos vivos: pode-se dizer 'um rosto bonito', mas quem disser 'o rosto' morre; por ter esgotado o assunto.
>
> [The general law for us to stay alive: one can say 'a pretty face,' but whoever says 'the face,' dies; for having exhausted the topic.][3]

Her sentences shake you out of complacent rationality and faith in totalizing knowledge with their unblinking intensity and uncanny mix of the familiar and the strange, often with a dose of absurdist humor. In the Claricean version of the mystic's quest to dissolve the boundaries between the self and a divine other, that other can be a cockroach, a placenta, a face, a clock named Sveglia. In the story 'Perdoando Deus' [Forgiving God], a somewhat parodic B-side to *The Passion According to G.H.*, a woman's mystical union with all of creation gets rudely interrupted when she nearly steps on a huge dead rat on Avenida Copacabana, her transcendent rapture punctured by God's practical joke.[4]

The two years I spent translating Lispector's *The Complete Stories* sometimes felt like a mystical journey, or at the very least a vision quest in which her sentences rose up like feral hallucinations as I groped at their meaning. I didn't exactly pray my way through the translation, but I often spoke to an image of her I'd tacked above my desk, her hands covering her famously gorgeous face. I liked that it could be a gesture of anguish or a sign of retreat into an interior world, corresponding to my own oscillations between frustration and focus. Magic crystals and *palo santo* came into play in moments of desperation. I might have gone to a psychic and summoned Clarice. There's only so much the dictionary can help you with.

II. The Gospel of Clarice

Lispector's frequent invocations of God raise questions about her relationship to religion. Her family came from Podolia, a region in Ukraine known for a remarkable concentration of Jewish mystics.[5] Clarice was born Chaya Pinkhasovna Lispector on 10 December 1920, as the family was fleeing the pogroms, and they landed in northeastern Brazil less than two years later. Her grandfather and father studied the Holy Scriptures, and she grew up going to synagogue in Recife. Yet her own approach to faith turned away from religious orthodoxy, reflecting a more Brazilian syncretism. Clarice embraced the divine alongside the occult, the sacred with the profane, without fear of contradiction, as if inventing her own form of spiritual practice. She read Kabbalistic texts and was deeply interested in Catholicism. Her writing references both the Old and New Testaments, as well as Afro-Brazilian religious rituals that mix Christian saints with Yoruba *orixás*. She followed astrology and saw a fortune-teller on a regular basis. Delighted to be an invited speaker at the First World Congress of Sorcery in Bogotá in 1975, she mystified the international witches and warlocks with a reading of 'The Egg and the Chicken' [O ovo e a galinha], one of her most puzzling stories — but not one that deals overtly with magic.

Clarice has been a significant literary figure in Brazil since the publication of her startling debut novel, *Perto do coração selvagem* [*Near to the Wild Heart*], in 1943, when she was twenty-three. Reviewers were intrigued by this writer with the strange name whose Portuguese sounded foreign. It has taken several decades for her reputation abroad to approach her stature at home, but various champions have sought to elevate her to the firmament of literary genius. Clarice is one of the great innovators of Brazilian literature and the Portuguese language, according to literary critic Antonio Candido;[6] a possible Rilke, Rimbaud, Heidegger, or Kafka who happened to be a Brazilian Jewish mother, as French feminist Hélène Cixous suggests;[7] 'the greatest Jewish writer since Kafka' and 'a female Chekhov on the beaches of Guanabara', to quote Benjamin Moser, her biographer and the series editor for her most recent English translations.[8] She has been called 'the Brazilian Virginia Woolf', a label to which Chanel designer Karl Lagerfeld took a fancy,[9] and 'the premier Latin American woman prose writer of this century' in a blurb from *The New York Times*.[10] Yet beyond this literary cachet, it is her mystical quality — more evocative of a charismatic cult leader than of just a talented writer with a cult following — that has kept a hold on readers. 'Be careful with Clarice', the writer Otto Lara Resende used to warn. 'It's not literature. It's witchcraft'.[11]

The stakes are high when you translate a book with the aura of a sacred text. *The Complete Stories* 'might even become your bible', one reviewer wrote, while another predicted it was 'bound to become a kind of bedside Bible or I Ching for readers of Lispector'.[12] 'It's not the Bible', my editor reminded me at one point when I was worried about maintaining the traceability of certain key words across the collection, in solidarity with readers prone to exegesis but cut off from direct access to the original. Only the most celebrated works receive multiple translations into English, and this was a rare opportunity to recuperate the singular force of

Lispector's originality (about two-thirds of the stories had already been translated). I was the sixth translator in a new series intended to grant the Gospel of Clarice its proper glory by lovingly restoring every comma, semicolon, abrupt paragraph break, insistent repetition, and nonsensical turn of phrase that had been excised or steamrolled in previous, apocryphal versions.

This linguistically remastered version of Clarice invades your body with subtly jarring choices that establish her own rules of reality and grammar. In this realm, the verb *morrer*, 'to die', takes on transitive properties: 'Ai que te amo e amo tanto que te morro' [Oh how I love you and I love so much that I die you]. I still don't know what it means *to die* someone, but I didn't have to in order to transmit it. If she says that 'tudo ficou de carne, o pé da cama de carne, a janela de carne, na cadeira o fato de carne que o marido jogara' [everything became flesh, the foot of the bed made of flesh, the window made of flesh, the suit made of flesh her husband had tossed on the chair], so be it. A previous translator had decided this violated the rules of reality and fixed it to read 'everything took on the appearance of flesh'. Elsewhere, when a woman's spontaneous smile is an *abismo* it's not a 'charm', as he had deemed more acceptably feminine, but a goddam *abyss*.[13]

I did my best to divine where Clarice's significant distortions of language lay and how I might convey them faithfully, to use a fraught term for translators. Yet we know there is no such thing as a perfect translation — the pieces that make up different languages never correspond exactly. In the end, it's someone's grubby fingerprints all over the Word of another, no matter how much the translator wants to let the spirit take over and speak through her. Translation is interpretation. I had to decide when a *mulher* was just a 'woman' and when she was a 'wife' (it's the same word in Portuguese). Was a *mulher vulgar* a 'common' or 'vulgar' wife-woman? At one point, I wrote a memo to my editor outlining a three-point argument for why *galinha* had to be 'chicken' instead of 'hen'.[14]

There were also reminders of the limits of blind adherence to the authority of the original — that first editions are not in fact Holy Scripture. I quietly got rid of the extra 'l' in the misspelled last name of the beloved singer-songwriter Caetano Veloso and amended the slightly-off *They Do Kill Horses, Don't They?* to the correct title *They Shoot Horses, Don't They?* to maintain a reference to the 1969 film. These kinds of slips could have come from Clarice herself, an editor, or the typesetter, and I relied on my own growing recognition of the rhythms of her deliberate distortions to distinguish between distinctly Claricean linguistic deviations worthy of preservation versus trivial typos of uncertain provenance that would be unnecessarily distracting. Still, it wasn't exactly a fail-safe algorithm. And any translator's eyes and brain can falter in a fateful instant, causing *verão* to become 'winter' instead of 'summer'. Or perhaps you think, *Sure, 'Russian mountain ride' sounds weird, but what doesn't in these stories?* until a friend points out that *montanha-russa* just means 'roller coaster'.

III. 'Your Birth Is My Death.'

A few months after the Seattle reading, I went to a writers' conference in Los Angeles, where I met the only living translator of Lispector's short stories into English from the previous generation. I had worried about his response to my new translations, about whether he would feel my work rendered his obsolete. After watching a panel on translating Brazilian women writers, we made eye contact across the room, and he shuffled up in his tweed blazer, stretched his upturned palms toward me, and intoned, 'Your birth is my death'. My eyes went wide as he chuckled wistfully. Later, I wondered what it meant to live and die through Clarice.

There should be a word for the ambiguous kinship between translators who share an author. It's a bond marked by tender antagonism or light rivalry, mixed with a uniquely intimate solidarity. This polygonal relationship lies somewhere between familial and erotic, all of us vying to be closest to the object of desire: the author's body and soul, textually speaking. We're like lovers who have lived with the same romantic partner — or, to take a more sinister view, vampires who feed off the same life essence.

Lispector's most famous and perhaps least possessive translator was Elizabeth Bishop, her onetime neighbour in Rio de Janeiro. An established poet in her own right, Bishop translated just three of Clarice's stories. Had she published more, as she'd once planned, I might not have dared to compete with my favourite poet and the subject of my dissertation, completed in three frantic months after the translation came out. Though Bishop lived in Brazil for over fifteen years, her Portuguese wasn't strong enough to follow Clarice's sophisticated linguistic manoeuvres. Still, her Lispector vibrates with a singular harmony between two brilliant voices. It felt like killing one mother to claim another when I retranslated one of my favourite stories, 'The Smallest Woman in the World', and changed Bishop's titles for 'Macacos' and 'Uma Galinha' from 'Marmosets' and 'A Hen' to what I believed were the more fitting 'Monkeys' and 'A Chicken' (cf. that memo).

Yet the main spectre hanging over Clarice's prior reception in English is the late Scots-Italian translator Giovanni Pontiero, a University of Manchester professor responsible for three of the novels, her two most famous story collections, *Laços de família* [*Family Ties*] (1960) and *A legião estrangeira* [*The Foreign Legion*] (1964), as well as the *crônicas*, or short literary sketches, collected posthumously in *A descoberta do mundo* [*Discovering the World*] (1984). Pontiero is the translator most associated with smoothing Clarice's language in English into something more conventionally elegant and akin to realism than the original. Before I began translating the stories, I regularly joined other Lispector scholars in nit-picking his choices.

When I crossed over from critic to fellow translator, however, I began to respect my predecessor more. I still believed Clarice needed to be retranslated with a keener eye for her subtle use of Portuguese and an ear more attuned to the cadences of her voice. Yet the more I experienced the difficulty of keeping her syntax straight — or properly crooked — without going cross-eyed, the more Giovanni, as I now called him, became my ally. The turning point came when I translated *The Foreign Legion* using an edition that had belonged to him (his partner had passed it on to my editor). Its bright pink cover was coming loose, and the browning pages were in such a fragile state that I kept it in a ziplock bag so it wouldn't crumble before I was done.

At first I resented having Giovanni in the room with me. I'd squint while working so I wouldn't be distracted by his spidery notes and suggestions in the margins. I was angry at him for messing up the repetitions, for not allowing one-sentence paragraphs, for tweezing out the commas and reducing colons to periods, for not letting the foot of a bed or a window be made of aching flesh, because that would break the rules of reality. I scoffed at him for not knowing Brazilian vegetables like *maxixe*, a spiky gherkin, or *chuchu*, chayote. But the translation process was so solitary, so fraught with the threat of not understanding Clarice's meaning, that after a while I came to appreciate his company. 'Poor, dear Giovanni', I'd say, sighing, or 'Giovanni, why?' Whenever I'd come across a question mark in blue ink, sometimes doubled or tripled, or a prickly row of asterisks or a forest of exclamation points, I'd shake my head and think, I know, right? WTF. Every so often I'd army-crawl through a sentence that kept turning corners, getting tangled in confusing prepositions and ambiguous modifiers, all of it complicated by words with multiple meanings, each equally plausible. Then I'd breathe deeply and take comfort in Giovanni's scrawls: *?? !!! ★★★ +++*

My thoughts exactly.

IV. Women on the Verge

Clarice Lispector's stories as a whole are more deeply embedded in the language and rhythms of women's everyday lives than any of her other works. Of the eighty-five stories I have translated, at least seventy have a presumably female narrator or protagonist. I was particularly drawn to characters whom I referred to privately as 'women on the verge,' a nod to Pedro Almodóvar's film *Mujeres al borde de un ataque de nervios* [*Women on the Verge of a Nervous Breakdown*] (1988). Like Almodóvar's memorable heroines, Clarice's women are over-the-top in ways that feel tragicomic, slapstick, disturbing, and very real; their manias conjure precisely those moments when your grip on the world starts to waver, but you know that everything going haywire in your head is still really happening. They are on the verge of exaltation, greatness, dissolution, spiritual ecstasy, blossoming into womanhood, becoming nuns, leaving their husbands, forgetting their families, getting assaulted, being abandoned, murdering someone, losing their minds. I was a woman on the verge over and over for two years.

Looking back on that time now, I see something like a film montage of women in front of mirrors — an image that recurs throughout Clarice's body of work. Her women literally recompose themselves in mirrors, smoothing the contours of identities that have been ruptured or threatened. They steady their existential distress by smiling politely at themselves or combing their hair, reaching for their lipstick to put things right again. My favourite mirror scene occurs after a woman believes her male makeup artist and rival has diabolically erased her face. Checking her reflection in a rising panic, she slaps herself hard. Then: 'No espelho viu enfim um rosto humano, triste, delicado. Ela era Aurélia Nascimento. Acabara de nascer. Nas-ci-men-to' [In the mirror she finally saw a human face, sad, delicate. She was Aurélia Nascimento. She had just been born. Nas-ci-men-to].[15] *Nascimento* means 'birth' in Portuguese, and I liked the idea of slapping oneself into rebirth. While I never hit myself, I did resort to 'putting on my face' in the bathroom at 2 or 3 a.m., then returning to my desk with renewed focus.

As I acted out these scenarios in English, I knew instinctively how these women would think, talk, and act. I've been a distracted teenager and a lover who has betrayed and been betrayed, but I have never been a housewife, mother, elderly widow, or exotic dancer. Yet I felt the pulse of their presence in the world. 'Como é que sei? Sabendo' [How do I know? Knowing], Clarice wrote of inventing characters.[16] My own assurance came from recognizing my obsessive mind and emotional intensity in these women at different stages of their lives, and from drawing on that detailed archive of womanhood that most girls unconsciously accumulate, first-hand or through representation, as they try to piece together how to be a 'woman'.

The narrator of 'Encarnação involuntária' [Involuntary Incarnation] describes a propensity for this kind of body snatching:

> Às vezes, quando vejo uma pessoa que nunca vi, e tenho algum tempo para observá-la, eu me encarno nela e assim dou um grande passo para conhecê-la. E essa intrusão numa pessoa, qualquer que seja ela, nunca termina pela sua própria autoacusação: ao nela me encarnar, compreendo-lhe os motivos e perdoo.
>
> [Sometimes, when I see someone I've never seen before, and have some time to observe that person, I incarnate myself in the other person and thus take a great step toward knowing who it is. And this intrusion into a person, whoever it may be, never ends in self-accusation: once I incarnate myself in someone else, I understand her motives and forgive.][17]

To think and write beyond our own experience is a necessary transgression if we are to expand our understanding of the world. To translate the stories, I had to perform a double incarnation, to inhabit Clarice inhabiting her various characters. It was fascinating and brutal to live through so many women's crises, to experience the neediness and love of husbands and children when I had none of my own, to feel the loneliness and unfulfilled desire of elderly, forgotten widows when I was thirty-five — roughly the midpoint of Clarice's age range when she wrote these stories. She herself started publishing them as a nineteen-year-old law student and journalist, then as a Brazilian diplomat's wife for sixteen years, and, after they separated in 1959, as a single mother of two sons. I was a graduate student who hadn't written any books, and this was my first full-length translation, yet working through the collection in chronological order, I experienced the trajectory of Clarice's writing life as though in compressed real time.

Approaching the end of the volume, I felt the excruciating weight of four decades of writing coming to a close, the words suffused with her fatigue and mine. In a TV interview recorded in 1977, the year of her death from ovarian cancer, Clarice declares that she's tired of herself. Sitting in an easy chair, fiddling with a pack of cigarettes, her face solemn, with its characteristic heavy-lidded gaze under a dark slash of eyeliner, she says, 'Por enquanto eu estou morta. Estou falando de meu túmulo' [For now I'm dead. I'm speaking from my grave].[18]

V. What the Psychic Said

In the last days of December 2014, I saw a psychic astrologer in San Francisco.[19] I was starting to feel delirious — the manuscript was due in January, and I was racing to get through edits, experiencing the terror of making all those minute decisions irrevocable. My personal life also felt out of control. At the end of Clarice's final novel, *A hora da estrela* [*The Hour of the Star*] (1977), the pathetic heroine, Macabéa, goes to see a fortune-teller. It ends badly. I was more hopeful.

The psychic was a friend of a friend, welcoming but no-nonsense, with bold glasses, dark Louis XIV curls, and an overall queer-witch vibe that seemed equal parts intuitive and highly cultivated. Adding to her mystical aspect were a gold tooth and one eye that appeared to do its own thing while the other homed in on me. We spent most of the hour on my family, specifically the patterns that women on my mother's side have repeated for generations, leading to an explanation of why I was stuck in a four-year relationship with someone that was making both of us lonely and miserable. With just five minutes left in a very expensive reading, I interrupted her: 'Um, when I say "Clarice Lispector", or just "Clarice", do you get anything?' She consulted whatever she was seeing with her third eye, snapped her attention back to me, and said, 'I see. You're fangirling with a dead woman'. I laughed nervously; it came out more like a shriek.

She said she saw a figure who was *zaftig*, a word from Yiddish that she said meant 'thick and curvy in a sexy way'. The medium further described the presence she was channelling: 'She was a passionate woman… She's crass in a poetic way. Like, there's something very voluptuous about her processing style'. Raising her voice, the psychic explained, 'She's kind of a projector, so I kind of want to yell at you when I'm talking. She's intense!' And then, 'This is a woman with balls, OK? She has HUGE BALLS'. She was refracting Clarice's personality through her own, and the result struck me as surprisingly accurate, even if the wording was nowhere near what I'd have chosen.

There was one message from Clarice that helped free me from the mania of perfectionism that had been closing in. The medium assured me:

> She doesn't want you to get it perfect. If you got it perfect then you'd be her and she doesn't want you to be her. She doesn't want you to perfectly capture her. Because that would be insulting. If you could, she feels like she wouldn't be that complex, and she felt like a complex woman. So she wants you to feel really good about what you've done. She wants you [*long pause*] to be suspicious of men. She doesn't want men owning anything of her.

This incarnation of Clarice had now become my personal self-help oracle, telling me that I should write my own kind of poetry, that she didn't really care about my boyfriend, that I should never let myself go for another person. 'And you have sat there communicating with her,' the psychic continued, 'telling her what you wanted, apologizing, asking, asking, asking, and she says sometimes she wants to shake you and say, *It's fine*. She feels respected and honored by you. But she doesn't need you to get her completely. That's not your job.'

The final directive from this Clarice was for me to put a glass vessel in a cloth and break it. 'Destroy it', the psychic said. 'Maybe you'll do that as a celebration for the new year or for when you get the book done. So whenever you do it, she'll be with you'. I did it on New Year's Eve and on New Year's Day explosively and unexpectedly ended that flailing four-year romance. At the close of the month, I turned in the manuscript.

VI. Imitation of Clarice

The Complete Stories came out in July 2015 to much fanfare in the corner of the publishing world that cares about strange and difficult writers. It was no Ferrante Fever, but Lispectormania hit the cover of *The New York Times Book Review*, and the first print run sold out within two weeks. As Clarice's star has risen on the international stage, increasing attention has been paid to her looks: a certain whiff of glamour, helped along by the prominent use of her image on book covers and by sound bites like translator Gregory Rabassa's endlessly reverberating remark that she 'looked like Marlene Dietrich and wrote like Virginia Woolf'.[20]

'What if Clarice Lispector had not been a disconcerting beauty?' Miranda France wondered in *The Times Literary Supplement*. 'The question needs to be asked because the Brazilian writer's appearance has become inseparable from an appreciation of her writing.'[21] Though I agreed with France's concern that the emphasis on Clarice's looks came at the expense of her writing, I also cringed at an unfortunate irony: the photo accompanying the piece was not of Clarice but of a Brazilian doppelgänger named Rita Elmôr. It's a still from *Que mistérios tem Clarice?* [What Mysteries Does Clarice Hold?], a one-woman play from 1998 in which Elmôr starred at the age of twenty-four. The resemblance is striking, but Elmôr is more gamine, lacking those full cheeks, and posing much more theatrically, her head resting dreamily on a hand delicately balancing a cigarette. There is a self-possession in the real Clarice's eyes, an unsettling directness in her gaze that I find more compelling than her beauty.

In the months following the release of the story collection, I spotted fake Clarices in other reputable literary publications. One magazine paired Lispector's bio with a photo of the writer Alice Denham from her July 1956 *Playboy* centrefold spread. In an exaggerated fantasy of the seductive woman writer, Denham also holds a cigarette while leaning suggestively over a typewriter. As my evangelical fervour for guarding the Word of Clarice extended to her image, I made it my vigilante business to right this wrong. Yet after several rounds of emailing editorial staffs, I realized I was playing a futile game of Whac-A-Mole against the mighty forces of misinformation. Like the fake #claricelispector quotes proliferating across social media, these ersatz Clarices are impossible to weed out.

On the poster for a Lispector conference to which I was invited in 2017, there was Rita Elmôr again. The organizers were duly mortified when I pointed out the error and quickly commissioned a new poster, but a cosponsoring department insisted on using the original one, on the basis that it foregrounded the theme of performance. (My presentation happened to be called 'Performing Clarice's "Women on the Verge"'.) Shortly after, a Brazilian online magazine published an interview with me, accompanied by a collage of Elmôr against a backdrop of Lispector phrases in English that I hadn't translated. When I objected to the image, the editors claimed it had been intentional, that the artist was creating an analogy between my own representation of Clarice in translation and a photograph of an actress who, like me, wasn't Clarice but was *representing* her.

Point taken. I had to accept that, to a certain extent, *Rita Elmôr, c'est moi*. Through my crusade against these false icons, I came to suspect that my distress was provoked in part by a recognition that I, too, was a counterfeit Clarice. Did these impersonators hold up a mirror in which I, too, was staring into the distance, cigarette in hand? Another Lispector translator confessed to having pondered, half in jest, whether, given the timing of her birth some months after Clarice's death on 9 December 1977, she might have absorbed some of the recently departed writer's cosmic matter in transit. I understand the desire, though ultimately none of us — translators, performers, mediums — can be her, even as we try to channel her. We do all we can to convey her to others through our voluntary incarnations, but we also have a responsibility to maintain a respectful distance from the original.

Throughout Clarice's work, there's something I think of as an ethos of error. 'Understanding is the proof of error', she writes in 'The Egg and the Chicken'.[22] In another of her stories, 'A imitação da rosa' [The Imitation of the Rose], a perfectionist housewife named Laura recalls how, as a Catholic schoolgirl, she'd read the spiritual handbook *The Imitation of Christ* 'com um ardor de burra' [with a fool's ardor], but also with the fear that 'quem imitasse Cristo estaria perdido — perdido na luz, mas perigosamente perdido' [whoever imitated Christ would be lost — lost in the light, but dangerously lost].[23] In the end, she grows ominously attached to a bouquet of roses and relapses into former obsessions that leave her stranded from the logic of the ordinary world, somewhere between hysteric and mystic. Clarice's characters keep striving for the kind of flawless performance society expects of women — to be the ideal wife, ideal mother, ideal daughter, ideal student. But salvation can come in the form of failure, often the failure to follow a fixed set of commandments.

One spring night in New Orleans, I crashed a cocktail gathering at the home of a successful photographer who was close to my mother's age. My status shifted from anonymous interloper to person of interest when she learned that I had translated *The Complete Stories*. Plucking the hardcover from her shelf, she asked me to sign it. Then she asked me to sign again, as Clarice. Horrified, I told her I could never do that! I was just the translator — how could I write in Clarice's name? I didn't want to be a cheap impersonator; it went against my code of honour. Yet the photographer insisted. In the passion of the moment, my self-righteousness dissolved, and I relented. I asked if she had any red lipstick. She did. So I painted my lips carefully in the entryway mirror. Then I picked up the book, closed my eyes, and kissed it for Clarice.

Works Cited

ANASTAS, BENJAMIN, 'A Passion for the Void', *The New Republic*, 27 July 2015, <https://newrepublic.com/article/122379/passion-void> [accessed 26 December 2018]

CANDIDO, ANTONIO, 'No começo era de fato o verbo', preface to *A paixão segundo G.H.*, ed. by Benedito Nunes, Coleção Arquivos, 2nd edn (Paris: Edições Unesco, 1996 [1964]), pp. xvii–xix

CASTELLO, JOSÉ, 'A senhora do vazio', *Inventário das sombras* (Rio de Janeiro: Record, 2006), pp. 28–29

CIXOUS, HÉLÈNE, 'Reaching the Point of Wheat, or A Portrait of the Artist as a Maturing Woman', *New Literary History*, 19.1 (Autumn 1987), 1–21

—— 'By the Light of an Apple', in *'Coming to Writing' and Other Essays*, ed. and trans. by Deborah Jenson (Cambridge, MA: Harvard University Press, 1992), pp. 132–35

DODSON, KATRINA, 'Understanding is the Proof of Error', *The Believer*, 119 (June/July 2018), 3–10, <https://believermag.com/understanding-is-the-proof-of-error/> [accessed 12 August 2021]

FRANCE, MIRANDA, 'Caustic Soda', *Times Literary Supplement*, 4 September 2015, p. 20

LAGERFELD, KARL, Q&A WITH EDDIE ROCHE, 'Ring! Ring! Ring! Catching Up with Karl Lagerfeld', *The Daily Front Row*, 11 September 2015, <https://fashionweekdaily.com/ring-ring-ring-catching-up-with-karl-lagerfeld/> [accessed 20 September 2019]

LISPECTOR, CLARICE, *Family Ties*, trans. by Giovanni Pontiero (Austin: University of Texas Press, 1972)

—— *Água viva* (Rio de Janeiro: Artenova, 1973); *Água Viva*, trans. by Stefan Tobler (New York: New Directions, 2012)

—— *A via crucis do corpo* (Rio de Janeiro: Artenova, 1974)

—— *A paixão segundo G.H.*, ed. by Benedito Nunes, Coleção Arquivos, 2nd edn (Paris: Edições Unesco, 1996 [1964]); *The Passion According to G.H.*, trans. by Idra Novey (New York: New Directions, 2012)

—— *The Complete Stories*, trans. by Katrina Dodson (New York: New Directions, 2018)

—— *Todos os contos* (Rio de Janeiro: Rocco, 2016)

LUISELLI, VALERIA, 'The Complete Stories', *Publishers Weekly*, 22 June 2015, <https://www.publishersweekly.com/978-0-8112-1963-1> [accessed 26 December 2018]

MACADAM, ALFRED, 'Falling Down in Rio', *The New York Times*, 18 May 1986, Section 7, p. 27

MOSER, BENJAMIN, *Why This World: A Biography of Clarice Lispector* (Oxford: Oxford University Press, 2009)

RABASSA, GREGORY, *If This Be Treason* (New York: New Directions, 2005)

Notes to Chapter 27

1. A version of this essay originally appeared in *The Believer*. Katrina Dodson, 'Understanding is the Proof of Error', *The Believer*, 119 (June/July 2018), 3–10 <https://believermag.com/understanding-is-the-proof-of-error/>.
2. Evelyn Underhill, *Mysticism: A Study in the Nature and Development of Man's Spiritual Consciousness*, 3rd edn (London: Methuen, 1912), p. 3.
3. Clarice Lispector, *A paixão segundo G.H.*, ed. by Benedito Nunes, Coleção Arquivos, 2nd edn (Paris: Edições Unesco, 1996), p. 38; *The Passion According to G.H.*, trans. by Idra Novey (New

York: New Directions, 2012), pp. 51–52. Clarice Lispector, *Água viva* (Rio de Janeiro: Artenova, 1973), p. 9; *Água Viva*, trans. by Stefan Tobler (New York: New Directions, 2012), p. 3. 'O ovo e a galinha', in *Todos os contos* (Rio de Janeiro: Rocco, 2016), p. 305; 'The Egg and the Chicken', in *The Complete Stories*, trans. by Katrina Dodson (New York: New Directions, 2018), p. 282. All references to *The Complete Stories* refer to the 2018 corrected paperback edition, unless otherwise noted.

4. Lispector, *The Complete Stories*, pp. 383–87.
5. See Benjamin Moser, *Why This World: A Biography of Clarice Lispector* (New York: Oxford University Press, 2009), pp. 14–15.
6. Antonio Candido, 'No começo era de fato o verbo', preface to *A paixão segundo G.H.*, Coleção Arquivos, xvii–xix.
7. Cixous makes these comparisons throughout her writing, most succinctly here: 'If Kafka had been a woman. If Rilke had been a Jewish Brazilian born in the Ukraine. If Rimbaud had been a mother, if he had reached the age of fifty. If Heidegger had been able to stop being German, if he had written the Romance of the Earth'. In 'By the Light of an Apple', in *'Coming to Writing' and Other Essays*, ed. and trans. by Deborah Jenson (Cambridge, MA: Harvard University Press, 1992), pp. 132–35 (p. 132).
8. Cixous declares Clarice Lispector 'is the greatest writer in the twentieth century. I rank her with Kafka', in 'Reaching the Point of Wheat, or A Portrait of the Artist as a Maturing Woman', *New Literary History*, 19.1 (Autumn 1987), 1–21 (p. 7). Moser echoes this line in his most-repeated Lispector talking point, 'the greatest Jewish writer since Kafka', in various interviews and essays. The jacket copy for his Lispector biography, *Why This World*, proclaims her 'the true heir to Kafka'. The epithet 'a female Chekhov' is the closing line to Moser's introduction to *The Complete Stories*, p. xxii.
9. Lagerfeld mentions he's currently reading 'All the books by Clarice Lispector, who is the Brazilian Virginia Woolf' in a Q&A with Eddie Roche, 'Ring! Ring! Ring! Catching Up with Karl Lagerfeld', *The Daily Front Row*, 11 September 2015 <https://fashionweekdaily.com/ring-ring-ring-catching-up-with-karl-lagerfeld/> [accessed 20 September 2019].
10. The *New York Times* blurb appears on the cover copy of several Lispector books, published by Book-of-the-Month Club, Carcanet, and New Directions. It comes from Alfred MacAdam's review of Lispector's *The Hour of the Star*, translated by Giovanni Pontiero, and published by Carcanet: 'Falling Down in Rio', *New York Times*, 18 May 1986, Section 7, p. 27.
11. Journalist José Castello recounts receiving this warning from Resende in a bar, only to discover later that he'd given the same warning to French Canadian writer Claire Varin while she was researching a book on Clarice. In 'A senhora do vazio', *Inventário das sombras* (Rio de Janeiro: Record, 2006), pp. 28–29; 'Clarice Lispector: Madame of the Void', trans. by Katrina Dodson, The Paris Review Daily, 10 December 2020, <https://www.theparisreview.org/blog/2020/12/10/clarice-lispector-madame-of-the-void/> [accessed 30 January 2022].
12. Benjamin Anastas, 'A Passion for the Void', *The New Republic*, 27 July 2015, <https://newrepublic.com/article/122379/passion-void> [accessed 26 December 2018]. Valeria Luiselli, 'The Complete Stories', *Publishers Weekly*, 22 June 2015, <https://www.publishersweekly.com/978-0-8112-1963-1> [accessed 26 December 2018].
13. Lispector, 'Brasília', *Todos os contos*, p. 607; 'Brasília', *The Complete Stories*, p. 591; 'Devaneio e embriaguez duma rapariga', *Todos os contos*, p. 141; 'Daydream and Drunkenness of a Young Woman,' *The Complete Stories*, p. 118. Previous translation by Giovanni Pontiero, 'The Daydreams of a Drunk Woman', in *Family Ties* (Austin: University of Texas Press, 1972), p. 34. While adding this footnote, I discovered, to my dismay, my inexplicable addition of 'once more' after the phrase 'everything became made of flesh'. I have corrected it here and it will be corrected in subsequent editions of *The Complete Stories*. The potential to err remains infinite, as careful as we may be. 'The explorer tried to smile back at her, without knowing exactly to what abyss his smile responded...'. Lispector, 'The Smallest Woman in the World', *The Complete Stories*, p. 177. Pontiero's translation diverges at: 'to which charm his smile was replying', same title, in *Family Ties*, p. 95; 'O explorador tentou sorrir-lhe de volta, sem saber exatamente a que abismo seu sorriso respondia...', *Todos os contos*, p. 200.

14. First, the colloquial tone and several punchlines in the stories work better in English with *chicken*: the figure of the *galinha* in Clarice is often ridiculous, fearful, and unfortunate, even if she temporarily gains respect, which produces a lot of dark humour, especially in contrast to the impassive and perfect egg. Both *galinha* and *chicken* can also mean 'coward'; chickens are often the butt of jokes and the word has a colloquial feel, whereas *hen* has a more elevated, literary register, at least in American English. Second, Clarice's *galinhas* are characters who tend to end up on the dinner table. *Chicken* more aptly captures that connection between live animal and everyday meat — people don't often say they ate hen unless it's perhaps a special Christmas hen or Cornish game hen. Third, the story 'The Egg and the Chicken' plays on that conundrum, *Quem veio primeiro, o ovo ou a galinha?* — which gets inverted in English to: Which came first, the chicken or the egg? 'The Egg and the Hen' loses this echo.
15. Lispector, 'Ele me bebeu', *A via crucis do corpo* (Rio de Janeiro: Artenova, 1974), p. 58; 'He Drank Me Up', *The Complete Stories*, p. 542. I quote from the original story collection here instead of the usual citation of *Todos os contos* (Rocco, 2016) because the latter mistakenly leaves out the hyphens in the last word.
16. In the 'Explanation' to the collection *A via crucis do corpo* [*The Via Crucis of the Body*] and echoed as, 'How do I know? Look, I just know...', by the narrator of 'Before the Rio-Niterói Bridge' in the same collection. Lispector, *The Complete Stories*, pp. 509, 555. Also 'Como é que sei? Ora, simplesmente sabendo', in '*Explicação*' and '*Antes da Ponte Rio-Niterói*', *Todos os contos*, p. 527, 571.
17. Lispector, *Todos os contos*, p. 428; *The Complete Stories*, p. 408.
18. My translation. Interview with Júlio Lerner for *Panorama*, TV Cultura, São Paulo, 1 February 1977. <https://www.youtube.com/watch?v=w1zwGLBpULs> [accessed 26 December 2018].
19. All quotes in this section are transcribed with permission from a recorded session with psychic medium Jessica Lanyadoo on 19 December 2014 in San Francisco, CA.
20. 'I was flabbergasted to meet that rare person who looked like Marlene Dietrich and wrote like Virginia Woolf'. Gregory Rabassa, *If This Be Treason* (New York: New Directions, 2005), p. 70.
21. Miranda France, 'Caustic Soda', *The Times Literary Supplement*, 4 September 2015, p. 20.
22. My original translation of 'é a prova do erro' was 'is the proof of making an error' but I revised it for the paperback to 'is the proof of error' to maintain the concision of the original. Lispector, *The Complete Stories* (2015), p. 277; *The Complete Stories* (2018), p. 281; *Todos os contos*, p. 304.
23. Lispector, *Todos os contos*, pp. 160–61; *The Complete Stories*, p. 138. *The Imitation of Christ* is the influential Christian devotional book written by German-Dutch monk and theologian Thomas à Kempis between 1418 and 1427, originally in Latin as *De Imitatione Christi*.

CHAPTER 28

We Are All Children of Babel: On Clarice Lispector's Chinese Translation

Min Xuefei

I

I initially translated Clarice Lispector into Chinese for a very pragmatic reason: I needed to complete my doctoral thesis on Clarice's writing.[1] Doing so, I soon realized the immense difficulty of reading Clarice, and the great difference between this and my previous experience with other Portuguese-speaking writers. Her sentences and meanings are so often capricious and untrammelled. I had to give up fast reading and slow down. I made a copy of *Felicidade clandestina* [*Clandestine Happiness*] and took notes in my own language in the margins. When the Chinese publisher Peng Lun invited me to translate the same book, I was very happy to accept because I already had completed most of the translation. In the act of reading, I was literally translating at the same time.

It is no exaggeration to say that Clarice changed my life and my mind. Before reading her, I had assembled some vague and unsystematic thoughts on important topics such as happiness, existence, goodness and evil, but it was in Clarice's writing that I encountered the most profound and beautiful approach to these topics in the form of great literary expression.

From my point of view, Clarice's work would allow me to combine translation and research, and in the process, deepen my understanding of certain topics that are of vital importance to me as a human being. There is no better intensive reading than translation, and no more wonderful experience than translating my favourite writer into Chinese in order to give people who do not speak Portuguese an opportunity to know her and understand her particular philosophy.

For a long time, the greatness of Brazilian literature was ignored in China, often overshadowed by Latin American literature in Spanish. Except for Jorge Amado, few Brazilian writers have been translated into Chinese. Thus, the recognition of Brazilian literature in China contrasts sharply with that of Spanish-speaking Latin American literature, chiefly represented by Gabriel García Márquez, Julio Cortázar and Jorge Luis Borges. My Chinese writer friends often ask me: Why are there no great writers in Brazil? Why isn't Brazil's literature as brilliant as that of its Spanish-speaking neighbours? When Cristovão Tezza came to China in 2014 most of the writers he met and journalists who interviewed him insisted on asking him the following two questions: Why doesn't your book resemble Magical Realism? What do you think about Paulo Coelho?[2] This does not mean that the Chinese readership knows more about Hispanic Latin American literature, but rather that their view of this literature tends to be narrow and full of stereotypes. Under such circumstances, translating Clarice can convey simultaneously to Chinese readers that she is a great writer, that Brazil has excellent literature, and that Brazilian literature does not equal Magical Realism.

The most attractive aspect of Clarice's writing is her elimination of dichotomies, a feature that is very important for Chinese women, especially at this critical moment. Given that eighty percent of all Chinese women work and are financially independent, one may think that they enjoy a high social status and that gender equality has been achieved in China. However, it is paramount to realize that our social positions are not due to a collective awakening, but rather have been given to us by a government that, after the republic's foundation in 1949, mainly consisted of men. Men give, men can take away. Today, the biggest crisis in China is that under its new economic model, the traditional family structure — working father, stay-at-home mother — is rapidly disintegrating at the same time that the birth rate is rapidly declining. The authorities are aware of this change, but their solutions have been rather unsettling. So-called traditional values embodied in the figures of the 'good wife and good mother' are highly promoted. As the authorities try to dictate the discourse of female happiness, it is vital for women to express their own needs and perceptions.

Women like me can benefit from Clarice's understanding of happiness as conveyed in her portrayals of women. Clarice's women are eager to find someone with whom they can communicate and share their experience of seeking strength through what others may deem as evil actions. Reading Clarice's work, Chinese women may find the courage to 'do evil' and thereby encounter their true selves. Clarice was never afraid to write about evil, but her discussion on the theme of good and evil actually transcends morality; rather, evil is a mode of revelation, of making existence and reality visible. For Clarice, human beings must be free in order to have subjective consciousness. The consciousness of 'evil', or the courage to practise 'transgression', plays an important role in facilitating this freedom. We see this in many of her works, such as Joana's invasion of her husband's intellectual territory in *Perto do coração selvagem* [*Near to the Wild Heart*]; the formation of consciousness through the act of writing a story that does not conform to mainstream moral values, as in 'Os desastres de Sofia' [Sofia's Disasters]; Ana's brief departure from her normal life in 'Amor' [Love]; and so on. I don't know if Chinese women can find happiness by reading Clarice Lispector, but I hope they learn that misfortune or disobedience is not a big deal, because, in the end, we all belong to the ancient race of 'a galinha tonta, desocupada e míope' [the silly, idle and short-sighted hen].[3]

2

My editor and I decided to debut the Chinese translation of Clarice with my translation of *A hora da estrela* [*The Hour of the Star*]. Accustomed to Chinese novels, Chinese readers tend to pay more attention to story and plot than to unique narrative techniques. Since *A hora da estrela* is the only one of Clarice's works that has a plot with 'começo, meio e "gran finale"'[4] [a beginning, middle and grand finale], we thought this book would ease Chinese readers into the process of reading and accepting Clarice. My translations of *A hora da estrela* [《星辰时刻》] and *Felicidade clandestina* [《隐秘的幸福》] were published in 2014 and 2016, respectively, by Shanghai Literature and Art Publishing House. While it is still too early to draw any conclusions about their Chinese reception, as of 2020 more than 20,000 copies of my translation of *A hora da estrela* have been sold, and the first printing of *Felicidade clandestina* is already out of stock. Several Chinese writers have read and expressed their appreciation for Lispector's books and have recommended these works on various occasions. The famous Chinese writer Zhang Yueran even stated that *A hora da estrela* has had the most influence on her work in recent years.[5] Wu Tiao Ren, a popular Chinese rock band, recommended Lispector and posted the cover of *A hora da estrela* on Weibo, a popular microblogging website.[6] To date, on douban.com, a major literary website in China, the first edition of *A hora da estrela* has received 1,492 short reviews, as well as 582 for the second edition. *Felicidade clandestina* has garnered 578 reviews for the first edition and 172 reviews for the second. Here are a few highlights:[7]

> 1. Best novel I've read in the last six months. She's almost writing fiction in the same way (Elizabeth) Bishop used to write poetry. Such writing is pure ashes produced by the burning of the author's flesh.
> 2. The whole text wanders and agitates in a kind of drifting, barren realm... There is no difference between the beginning and the end; all we have is the present, and the present is eternity. Between this explosion of life and death is the moment of the stars.
> 3. There are always words that make you feel sweaty and shaky inside, that wake you up from the inertia of everyday life and make you re-examine your own definition of joy and happiness.

Some readers have commented specifically on my translation:

> 4. Internally exhausting, frenetic writing. Min's translation is excellent, and the final epilogue is solidly written. 'Yes', the beginning and the end. 'Yes', not the beginning and not the end. I thought it was a closed loop structure, but the first paragraph self-consciously dissolves everything. I have never read a narrative like it.
> 5. A real painstaking effort was put into the translation of this little book.
> 6. A protagonist with a completely different life experience from the author — race, homeland, profession, family — the only similarity is that they are all women, and yet I am also alienated from her in many female experiences, and yet I feel the emptiness of existence in an incredibly tangential way. The author is too sensitive and communicative. I knew Min would translate well, but upon reading I found it better than I expected, smooth, strong, and full,

but I wonder if there was some slight obscuring of some of Clarice's mystery? 'I don't have a ball but I play with a ball' [a quotation from the novel], has given me a wonderful new insight into writing and translation.

Despite achieving my preliminary goal of introducing Clarice to the Chinese reading public, two good friends, both well-known poets and literary critics, who will remain anonymous, insisted that I do more translations of Fernando Pessoa and not waste time on minor writers like Clarice. Though I did not appreciate their advice, their words made me think that perhaps there had been in a flaw in my plan: *A hora da estrela* is the last work Clarice published in her lifetime, but without any knowledge of her previous works, readers are not able to appreciate Clarice in full. Maybe if they had read *Perto do coração selvagem* and specifically the scene where little Joana runs over Arlete the doll with a toy car, they would better understand Macabéa's crushing death in *A hora da estrela*. They would gain a deeper understanding of how carefully Clarice crafted her characters and how cunningly she developed their subjectivity and hers as an author.

For Chinese readers, even writers with discerning literary judgment, *A hora da estrela* and *Felicidade clandestina* did not suffice for fully understanding and accepting Clarice. More translations of her works were required, and to this end, I continued to translate Clarice into Chinese. Recently, I have completed the translation of *Laços de família* [*Family Ties*] and next I will translate *A paixão segundo G.H.* [*The Passion According to G.H.*]. But it is my hope that other Chinese translators will join me in bringing Clarice to Chinese readers.

3

My translation of Clarice into Chinese is a matter of great curiosity for Lispector scholars. But I wonder if perhaps what people really want to know is how much and how far I twisted Clarice's words in Chinese.

I am not comfortable explaining my translation strategies or techniques; for me translation is a mystical process.[8] I have read some translation theories that accord with my translation practice, but traditional theories of translation tend to accentuate the conversion process between languages and treat translatability as the most essential feature of a translation.[9] I am a translator, not a scholar of Translation Studies. In fact, I doubt very much whether Western translation theories, which mainly focus on Indo-European languages, can be applied to the conversion that takes place between Portuguese and Chinese. For me, the only translation theory that applies to both East and West is Walter Benjamin's 'The Task of the Translator'.[10] I am in complete agreement with the main point of his essay, namely that so-called 'translatability' exists but depends on the translator.

To illustrate how a translator may achieve translatability, I offer three examples from the history of literary translation:

1. Edward FitzGerald's translation of Rubáiyát of Omar Khayyám[11]

The global circulation of the Rubáiyát is not due to Khayyám, its original author, but to its translator, the famed British poet Edward FitzGerald (1809–1883). FitzGerald was not a faithful translator; instead, he used his translation to showcase his own outstanding literary talent and unique poetic style. In the words of Borges — 'Perhaps, around 1857, Omar's soul took up residence in FitzGerald's. In the Rubaiyat we read that the history of the universe is a spectacle that God conceives, stages, and watches; that notion (whose technical name is pantheism) would allow us to believe that the Englishman could have recreated the Persian because both were, in essence, God or the momentary faces of God'.[12]

2. Ezra Pound's translations of Chinese classical poetry[13]

Pound (1885–1972) did not understand Chinese very well, if at all. From a linguistic point of view, there were many mistakes in his translation. But this does not mean that what Pound did was not a great translation. Anyone writing Chinese classical poetry in English must do it Pound's way, as Eliot argued: 'As for *Cathay*, it must be pointed out that Pound is the inventor of Chinese poetry for our time. I suspect that every age has had, and will have, the same illusion concerning translations, an illusion which is not altogether an illusion either. When a foreign poet is successfully done into the idiom of our own language and our own time, we believe that he has been "translated"; we believe that through this translation we really at last get the original.'[14]

3. Fu Lei's translations of Honoré de Balzac[15]

Fu Lei (1908–1966) was a famous Chinese translator of French literature and one of the translators of the complete works of Balzac (1799–1850) into Chinese. Some translation scholars consider Fu Lei's language to be very elegant, but this is not a reflection of Balzac's language. The truth is that Balzac wrote quickly in order to pay off his debts, which resulted in unrefined language. Chen Weifeng, Professor of French at Fudan University, wrote in an article entitled 'On Fu Lei's Translation' that 'Balzac was used to writing quickly, and without much revision, the style is long and laggy. But Fu's translation of Balzac's novel is clearly articulated and layered. So, one can say without exaggeration that on a linguistic level Fu's translation is much better than the original.'[16] However, for the general Chinese reading public, Balzac in Chinese is Fu Lei's Balzac, to the extent that this readership has come to believe that if Balzac had written in Chinese, he would have written in Fu Lei's style.

In his famous 1978 essay 'The Position of Translated Literature within the Literary Polysystem', Itamar Even-Zohar observed that translated literature is an indispensable part of a literary polysystem. In this spirit, I offer these three examples as literary translations that joined a national literature together with its original literature.[17] These three examples illuminate how a translation can gain autonomy and independence from the original text. They show how a translated work can cross national boundaries, becoming part of anglophone or Chinese literary canons. They also show that a successful translation need not be a faithful translation, as Benjamin argues in 'The Task of the Translator', a position that George Steiner also shares in *After Babel*.[18]

In my translations, I try to integrate Clarice into Chinese literature, making her literary texts an intrinsic part of the literature of my own tongue. That being said, my translation of Clarice Lispector is very faithful to her style, which Olga de Sá described in her pioneering study *A escritura de Clarice Lispector* (1979) as:

> a quebra de linearidade discursiva, metáforas estranhas como oposição ao lugar comum, comparações, paradoxos, metalinguagem, pontuação particular, repetições, frase fragmentada, predominância da terceira pessoa narrativa
>
> [a break with linear discourse, strange metaphors rather than commonplaces, comparisons, paradoxes, meta-language, unusual punctuation, repetitions, fragmented sentences, a narrative predominantly in the third person].[19]

For example, in 'Amor', Clarice writes:

> Agora que o cego a guiara até ele, estremecia nos primeiros passos de um mundo faiscante, sombrio, onde vitórias-régias boiavam monstruosas. As pequenas flores espalhadas na relva não lhe pareciam amarelas ou rosadas, mas cor de mau ouro e escarlates. A decomposição era profunda, perfumada... Mas todas as pesadas coisas, ela via com a cabeça rodeada por um enxame de insetos, enviados pela vida mais fina do mundo. A brisa se insinuava entre as flores. Ana mais adivinhava que sentia o seu cheiro adocicado... O Jardim era tão bonito que ela teve medo do Inferno.[20]

I rewrite her words into Chinese as follows:

> 现在:盲人引她来到此处:她颤颤巍巍地 出了最初的脚步:步入一个晶光烁烁、昏昏沉沉、王莲如怪兽一般漂浮的世界。草丛里的小花星星点点。看上去既不黄也不粉:而是暗沉的金色与红色。世界的解体深沉而芳香......但是:在她观看这林林种种的沉重之物时:总有一群虫子:由世界上最精微的生命派遣而来:绕着她的头颅飞舞。微风潜藏于花间。与其说安娜闻到了它的甜味:不如说是猜到了......花园如此美丽:竟让她害怕地狱。[21]

If you understand Chinese, you can feel the same breath between these two passages. To translate Clarice, the most important thing is to grasp the rhythm. *Adjetivação* [adjectivation], one of her most amazing stylistic techniques,, is usually troublesome for readers and translators but isn't a problem for Chinese readers because lexicality is changeable in Chinese, where many words can be both nouns and adjectives. Therefore, Clarice's most surprising modifiers can be directly translated into Chinese. Since even more exotic descriptions abound in traditional Chinese poetry, the Chinese reader has no trouble accepting Clarice's language. Additionally, words that cannot be directly translated can be expressed through metaphor. For example, the paragraph above presented two challenges, the first being 'vitórias-régias boiavam monstruosas' [giant water lilies floated monstrous]. 'Monstrous' is difficult to express in Chinese, so here I translate the line as 'the water lilies were like a monster floating in the world'. Some of Clarice's puns can be solved through intertextual references to ancient Chinese poems, an example being 'A brisa se insinuava entre as flores', where 'insinuar' is a core verb that if translated directly as '进入 [to enter] may lose its other associations. I translate it as '微风潜入花间 [the breeze dives into the flowers], using the verb 'to dive'. Chinese readers will not find this awkward; they will understand the meaning of the word because there is a famous Chinese poem by Du Fu that figuratively refers to 'rain' as '随风潜入夜:润物细无声 [With the wind diving into the night, moistening the air]. Though destined to lose some of its meaning, Clarice's language nonetheless gains new life in another culture.

Except for a few cases, translating Clarice was not a very difficult task. I just stopped when Clarice stopped. When she repeated something, I said it again. When she was vague, I became confusing as well. I followed her style by not doing anything, by just letting her speak and write freely in Chinese, as if she were a Chinese writer. What is translatable is not the language, but rather the style, and my task was to create in translation a language appropriate to Clarice's style.

As Benjamin stated, a translation is not simply the transmission of information. The disparity between a translator's linguistic adequacy and the translatability of a difficult text must urge her to endeavour to mend the gap, one that might function like the 'historical distance' between a classical text and an interpreter's horizon, as observed by Hans Gadamer.[22] In the preface to his translation of Balzac's *Le Père Goriot*, Fu Lei stresses that 'an ideal piece of translation should be like a Chinese version written by the author of the source text'.[23] By using a structurally different language, I have actually rewritten Clarice in Chinese by imitating her narrative structure, her rhythmic patterns, the relationship she draws between various senses and concepts, and her unique sensuality. Through such rewriting, the ambition of such translated literature is no less than competing with the most prominent works of contemporary Chinese literature.

Clarice's writing style has been a strong influence on my own translating-writing process: for her, to write was always to 'dizer o indizível', that is, to express what cannot be expressed.[24] Writing must be an endeavour to exhaust all possible expressions for the purpose of coming across the ideal one, even though it might finally prove to be a failed attempt. The Sisyphean task undertaken by the translator may paradoxically exaggerate the linguistic variance of correspondence between the target and the source texts, while narrowing the gap of understanding between the target reader and the original. Perhaps, in such a paradox lies the dynamic creativity of translation in overcoming this interpretative tension. Clarice kindly dedicated the egg to the Chinese people in 'O Ovo e a Galinha' [The Egg and the Chicken], which she called her most mysterious short story. Rewriting her under the spell of her own language is the only way I can repay her.

Works Cited

BARBOSA, VÂNIA MARIA CASTELO and VERA LUCIA ALBUQUERQUE DE MORAES, 'A linguagem de Clarice Lispector como desautomatização da vida', *Revista de Letras*, 1/2.29 (2007/2008), 81–84

BENJAMIN, WALTER, 'The Task of the Translator' [1923], trans. by Harry Zohn, in *The Translation Studies Reader*, ed. by Lawrence Venuti (New York: Routledge, 2001), pp. 15–23

BORGES, JORGE LUIS, *Selected Non-Fictions*, trans. by Eliot Weinberger (New York: Viking, 1999)

CHEN, WEIFENG, 'On Fu Lei's Translation', in *Chinese Translators Journal* (Original title: *Correspondence of Translation*), 5 (1983) (Beijing: The Translators Association of China), 9–10

ELIOT, T. S., 'Introduction' to Ezra Pound, in *Selected Poems* (London: Faber & Gwyer, 1928), pp. 14–15

EVEN-ZOHAR, ITAMAR, 'The Position of Translated Literature within the Literary System' [1978], in *Translation Studies Reader*, ed. by Laurence Venuti (London and New York: Routledge, 2000), pp. 192–97

FU, LEI, 'Preface to the Retranslation of *Le Père Goriot*', in *Twentieth-Century Chinese Translation Theory: Modes, Issues and Debates*, ed. by Leo Tak-hung Chan (Amsterdam and Philadelphia: John Benjamins, 2004)

GADAMER, HANS, *Truth and Method*, rev. edn, trans. by Joel Weinsheimer and Donald G. Marshall (London and New York: Continuum, 2004)

KHAYYAM, OMAR, *The Rubáiyát of Omar Khayyám*, trans. by Edward FitzGerald (Boston, MA: Houghton, Osgood and Company, 1859)

LISPECTOR, CLARICE, *Laços de família* (Rio de Janeiro: Editora Rocco, 1998); 克拉丽丝·李斯佩克朵《家庭纽带》:闵雪飞译: trans. by Min Xuefei (北京: 人民文学出版社:2021)

—— *A legião estrangeira* (Rio de Janeiro: Rocco, 1999)

—— *A hora da estrela* (Rio de Janeiro: Francisco Alves, 1992 [1977]); 《星辰时刻》trans. by Min Xuefei (Shanghai: Shanghai Literature and Art Publishing House, 2014)

—— *Complete Stories*, trans. by Katrina Dodson (London: Penguin, 2015)

—— 《隐秘的幸福》[Felicidade clandestina], trans. by Min Xuefei (Shanghai: Shanghai Literature and Art Publishing House, 2016)

MIN, XUEFEI, 'Diluindo fronteiras: mal, amor, morte, corpo e mente em Clarice Lispector', (unpublished doctoral thesis, University of Coimbra, 2018)

POUND, EZRA, *Cathay* (London: Elkin Mathews, 1915)

SABINO, FERNANDO, and CLARICE LISPECTOR, *Cartas perto do coração* (Rio de Janeiro: Record, 2002)

'Short Reviews of *Xingchen Shike* [*A hora da estrela*]', *Douban*: <https://book.douban.com/subject/25699387/comments> [accessed 6 July 2021]

STEINER, GEORGE, *After Babel: Aspects of Language and Translation* (Oxford: Oxford University Press, 1975)

ZHANG, YUERAN, '2009–2019: Zhongguo Zuojia Xiaoxiang [Portraits of Chinese Writers]' *GQ Report* (25 August 2019), <https://mp.weixin.qq.com/s/3YlQ8bOv_ZiQJfOSDz4q-Q> [accessed 6 July 2021]

Notes to Chapter 28

1. Min Xuefei, 'Diluindo fronteiras: mal, amor, morte, corpo e mente em Clarice Lispector' (unpublished doctoral thesis, University of Coimbra, 2018).
2. Cristovão Tezza (b. 1952) is a prize-winning Brazilian novelist, best known internationally for his novel *O filho eterno* [The Eternal Son] (2007), which has been translated into nine languages, including Chinese: 永 的菲利普, trans. by Ma Lin (马琳) (Beijing: People's Literature Publishing House, 2014). In 2014, when Tezza was visiting China, he gave interviews to several Chinese newspapers and magazines, the most famous being *Sanlian Life Week Magazine* on March 20. Excerpts from this interview were republished by several media outlets under the title 'Brazilian Writer Cristovão: Magical Realism Has Little Influence in Brazil'.
3. Clarice Lispector, 'O ovo e a galinha', in *A legião estrangeira* (Rio de Janeiro: Rocco, 1999 [1964]), pp. 51–60 (p. 55). All translations into English are mine unless otherwise noted.
4. Clarice Lispector, *A hora da estrela* (Rio de Janeiro: Francisco Alves, 1992 [1977]), p. 27
5. Zhang, Yueran. '2009–2019: Zhongguo Zuojia Xiaoxiang [Portraits of Chinese Writers]', *GQ Report*, 25 August 2019, <https://mp.weixin.qq.com/s/3YlQ8bOv_ZiQJfOSDz4q-Q> [accessed 6 July 2021].
6. Wu Tiao Ren, 'Yiban Yishujia, Yiban Liulangzhe [Half Artist, Half Nomad]', *Shishang Xiansheng* [Mr. Fashion], 26 September 2020, <https://mp.weixin.qq.com/s/R5792RG74Yqjhe7WV5YOCA> [accessed 6 July 2021].
7. 'Short Reviews of *Xingchen Shike* [*A hora da estrela*]', *Douban* <https://book.douban.com/subject/25699387/comments> [accessed 6 July 2021].
8. On translation and mysticism see also Katrina Dodson's chapter in this volume.
9. On conversion and translation see also Adriana X. Jacobs's chapter in this volume.
10. Walter Benjamin, 'The Task of the Translator' (1923), trans. by Harry Zohn, in *The Translation Studies Reader*, ed. by Lawrence Venuti (New York: Routledge, 2000), pp. 15–23.
11. Omar Khayyam, *The Rubáiyát of Omar Khayyám*, trans. by Edward FitzGerald (Boston, MA: Houghton, Osgood and Company, 1859).
12. Jorge Luis Borges, *Selected Non-Fictions*, trans. by Eliot Weinberger (New York: Viking, 1999), p. 368.
13. Ezra Pound, *Cathay* (London: Elkin Mathews, 1915).
14. T. S. Eliot, 'Introduction' to Ezra Pound, *Selected Poems* (London: Faber & Gwyer, 1928), pp. 14–15.
15. As the most famous translator of French literature, Fu Lei translated fifteen works by Balzac over the course of twenty-two years (1944–66). In 2017, Henan People's Publishing House brought out a nine-volume collection of Fu Lei's translations of Balzac's works.
16. Chen Weifeng, 'On Fu Lei's Translation', in *Chinese Translators Journal* (Original title: *Correspondence of Translation*), 5 (1983) (Beijing: The Translators Association of China), 9–10.
17. Itamar Even-Zohar, 'The Position of Translated Literature within the Literary System' (1978), in *The Translation Studies Reader*, ed. by Laurence Venuti (London & New York: Routledge, 2000), pp. 192–97.
18. Benjamin, 'The Task of the Translator', pp. 20–21; George Steiner, *After Babel: Aspects of Language and Translation* (Oxford: Oxford University Press, 1975).
19. As paraphrased by Vânia Maria Castelo Barbosa and Vera Lucia Albuquerque de Moraes, 'A linguagem de Clarice Lispector como desautomatização da vida', in *Revista de Letras* (Fortaleza: Universidade Federal de Ceará), 1/2.29 (2007/08), 81–84 (p. 82).
20. Clarice Lispector, *Laços de família* (Rio de Janeiro: Editora Rocco, 1998), pp. 33–34. 'Now that the blind man had led her to it, she trembled upon the first steps of a sparkling, shadowy world, where giant water lilies floated monstrous. The little flowers scattered through the grass didn't look yellow or rosy to her, but the color of bad gold and scarlet. The decomposition was deep, perfumed... But all the heavy things, she saw with her head encircled by a swarm of insects, sent by the most exquisite life in the world. The breeze insinuated itself among the flowers. Ana sensed rather than smelled its sweetish scent... The Garden was so pretty that she was afraid of Hell', *The Complete Stories*, trans. by Katrina Dodson (London: Penguin, 2015), p. 121.

21. 克拉丽丝•李斯佩克朵《家庭纽带》:闵雪飞译:(北京: 人民文学出版社:2021), pp. 7–8.
22. Benjamin, 'The Task of the Translator', p. 21; Hans Gadamer, *Truth and Method*, rev. edn, trans. by Joel Weinsheimer and Donald G. Marshall (London and New York: Continuum, 2004), p. 290.
23. Fu Lei, 'Preface to the retranslation of *Le Père Goriot*', in *Twentieth-Century Chinese Translation Theory: Modes, Issues and Debates*, ed. by Leo Tak-hung Chan (Amsterdam and Philadelphia: John Benjamins, 2004), p. 103.
24. Fernando Sabino and Clarice Lispector, *Cartas perto do coração* (Rio de Janeiro: Record, 2002), p. 118.

INDEX

Abdala, Benjamin 381
Abercrombie, Joan 77
absurdist motifs, humour 243, 412
adaptations (film/theatre/dance) 8, 11 n. 8, 20, 102 n. 27, 102 n. 47, 200, 309, 321, 327, 334, 337–38
adjetivação 430
aesthetic, aesthetics 81, 109, 111, 140, 256, 259, 275, 324, 325, 329, 330, 335, 343, 400
affect 127, 128, 133, 135
Africa 46, 64
After Clarice, conference 1, 301
Agência Nacional 105
Agualusa, José Eduardo, 199, 206, 207
Ahmed, Sara 63, 64, 65, 66, 322, 330, 331
Almeida, Elizama 76
Almeida, Mauro de, 24
Almodóvar, Pedro:
   Mujeres al borde de un ataque de nervios 324, 325, 386 n. 8, 416
Alonso, Cláudia Pazos 227
Alphen, Ernst van 48
Alter, Robert 148
Alves, Francisco, 20, 21, 231
Amado, Jorge 358, 425
Amaral, Suzana, 8, 95, 337, 338, 339, 340, 342–46, 348 n. 32
   A hora da estrela 337–46
amateur, 313–14
analysis, as distancing reader from work (Lispector) 110
Andrade, Mário de, 73, 106, 110, 117 n. 27, 217
   Macunaíma 12, 106
   'Ode ao burguês' 110
Andrade, Oswald de 106, 325
   Manifesto Antropófago 325
   Memórias sentimentais de João Miramar 106
Andrade, Sonia, *Wire* 302, 305–07
Angelides, Sophia 42
Anglophone (translation, influence, world) 2, 3, 203, 257, 359, 372, 385, 391–92, 393, 397, 398, 402–03, 430
angústia 130, 131
animistic strategies 243
anthologies of short stories inspired by Lispector 200
   Extratextos 1: Clarice Lispector — Personagens reescritas 200
   Feliz aniversário, Clarice 200
Anthony, Saint 24

Anzaldúa, Gloria (theory of the shapeshifter/*la naguala*) 6, 240, 241–43, 245, 246, 249
   shapeshifting subjectivity, 242
appropriations (of Lispector's writing) 142, 165, 217, 218, 219, 220, 221, 225, 227, 229, 231–32, 356
'aproximação' (*A paixão segundo G.H.*) 106, 202, 295
Arap, Fauzi, 20, 309–10
archive 1, 2, 4, 35 n. 20, 57, 73–84, 89, 90, 91, 92, 97, 98, 120, 200, 209, 232, 302, 373, 378, 382, 387 n. 37, 417
   as accomplice 91
   see also library, manuscripts
Arêas, Vilma 95, 143, 145
Arrojo, Rosemary 161, 162, 167 n. 9 & 11
art 64, 82, 100, 108, 115, 173, 175, 177, 209, 255, 259, 282, 296, 297, 302, 304, 306, 314, 325, 330, 392, 427
   of composition 7
   traditional, representational 255
Artenova, publisher 21
artifice 87, 175, 291, 324, 325, 327, 336
artist (artistic expression) 9, 20, 21, 26, 29, 31, 42, 60, 84, 110, 111, 117 n. 27, 255, 256, 259, 260, 263, 266, 279, 302, 304, 305, 308, 325, 335, 337, 361, 372, 416, 420
   'Clarice's gallery' 29
   in Leme 15, 17, 29
Asia Minor 66
Augé, Marc, 39, 40, 45, 46, 51
   non-place 3, 39–41, 44–47, 49–52
   'supermodernity' 39
   see also travel
Austen, Jane 200
autobiography 9, 153 n. 15, 205, 206, 209, 260, 367 n. 3, 371, 372, 373, 376, 379, 380, 384
   and fiction, overlap 206, 372
avant-garde 4, 40, 259, 260
   concretismo 260
   see also vanguard
Aytürk, İlker 357
Azevedo, Heloisa, 28
Azevedo (Padre) 209
Azulay, Jacob David 79

Bachelard, Gaston, *The Poetics of Reverie* 49, 84, 257
Bakhtin, Mikhail 174
Balzac, Honoré de 429, 433 n. 15

Bandeira, Manuel 35 n. 8, 81, 86 n. 19, 110, 117 n. 27
'O anjo da guarda' 110
Barthes, Roland 87
  'death of the author' 162
  Mourning Diary 87, 88
  'The Preparation of the Novel' 99
Bauman, Zygmunt, *Liquid Modernity* 40, 47
belonging, sense of 3, 39, 41, 47, 48, 50–52, 64, 67, 169, 195, 225
  connection to Brazil though lens of life abroad 48
  rootlessness 50
Ben-Avi, Itamar 357
Benjamin, Walter, 'The Task of the Translator' 428
Bennett, Jane, *Vibrant Matter* 245, 251 n. 18
Bergson, Henri 127
Berman, Antoine, 'bad writing' 398, 401
Berne 40, 43, 45, 48, 51, 83, 121, 204, 281, 382
Bethânia, Maria 20, 309, 310
  Comigo me desavim 20, 309, 310
  'minha Clarice' 183
Bezerra, Elvia xi, 4, 72–84
Bialik, Chaim Nachman 357, 258
Bible (Hebrew) 5, 140, 142, 143, 144, 145, 146, 148, 154 n. 38, 155 n. 42, 160, 193, 365, 413
  manipulations of biblical text 140
  Noah 364
biography 154 n. 28, 199, 200, 205, 206, 215 n. 45, 273, 354, 358, 359, 362, 371–85
  marketing strategy 371
  see also autobiography
biographer 1, 40, 80, 183, 302, 373, 374, 375, 379, 382, 396, 413
biographical writing 200, 384
  see also life writing
Bishop, Elizabeth 16–17, 117 n. 26, 393, 406, 407 n. 10, 415, 427
  An Anthology of Twentieth Century Brazilian Poetry 16
  'The Burglar of Babylon' 17
body 5, 7, 21, 22, 63, 64, 65, 93, 99, 112, 128, 130, 139, 145, 147, 154 n. 24, 160, 177, 185, 191–92, 194, 199, 201, 202, 205, 239, 241, 242, 244, 245, 247, 248, 252 n. 39, 274, 275, 280, 285, 290, 292–95, 301–16, 323, 324, 327, 331, 345–46, 354, 355, 359, 361, 364, 383, 388 n. 50, 392, 414, 415, 417
body language 303, 324, 327
Bolsonaro, Jair 307
Bonomi, Maria 29, 31
Bopp, Leon, *L'Art de vouloir, d'aimer et comprendre: nouveaux exercices spirituels* 82
Bopp, Raul, *Cobra Norato* 15
Borelli, Olga 8, 22, 23, 24, 27, 30, 78, 89, 91, 97, 100, 243, 247, 356, 371–72, 381, 382, 396
  Clarice Lispector: esboço para um possível retrato 371–72
Borges, Jorge Luis 172, 174, 183, 425, 429
  'The Aleph' 172
  the Aleph as metaphor for global coexistence (of cultures) 172

bossa nova 17, 31
Botler, Lais Maria Rosal xi, 3, 39–52
Boyarin, Daniel 140
Braga, Rubem 79, 110, 355, 376
Braidotti, Rosi, *The Posthuman* 67, 239–41, 242, 246, 247–48
Brasil, Assis 394
Brazil:
  canonical Brazilian writers in social media 217
  climate, weather 62
  diegetic world 139–41
  historic and economic circumstances 120
  internal migration 170
  Lispector's new view of 48
  northeastern plight of subalternity and marginality 176
  North/South divide (northeast) 29, 33, 112, 117 n. 27, 170, 175, 176, 242, 243, 266, 313, 315, 338, 342, 343, 345, 346, 359, 360, 365, 387 n. 27 & 37, 413
  patriarchal society 139, 140, 141, 177, 331
  spiritism and Catholicism 170
Broadbent, Laura, *In on the Great Joke* 207, 208
Brown, Bill 285
Bryan, C. D. B. 393
Butler, Judith 59, 142, 143, 149, 151
  The Psychic Life of Power 59
Buzzati, Dino *Il deserto dei Tartari* 83

Cabral, Melo Neto João de 110, 117 n. 27, 134
  'Psicologia da composição' 110
Callado, Antônio 105
Camargo, Maria (with Carla Madeira) 323
Campos, Haroldo de 15, 395
Campos, Paulo Mendes 78, 79, 83, 84, 383
  A palavra escrita 79
  Homenzinho na ventania 79
  'O amor acaba' 79
  'Relógio de Sol' 79
Candido, Antonio 105–07, 109, 394, 413
  'No raiar de Clarice Lispector' 105
Cândido, Maria Fernanda 323, 328, 331, 333 n. 6
capitalism 170, 244
Carcanet publishing house 119, 120, 392, 394, 422 n. 10
caricature 1, 200, 284
  and graffiti, memes 200
Cardinale, Claudia 17
Cardoso, Lúcio 29, 42, 52, 86 n. 25, 105, 311–12
Carrera, Elena 161, 162, 167 n. 9
Carrero, Natalia, *Soy una caja* 6, 205, 207, 215 n. 55
Carvalho, Luiz Fernando 8, 321–30, 333 n. 6
Casanova, Pascale, *The World Republic of Letters* 171, 172
Cass, Rosa 22, 31
Castro, Ruy 394
Catholicism (Roman) 170, 361, 413
Caullery, Maurice *Les Problèmes de la sexualité* 82
celebrity 20, 105, 177, 219, 314, 315, 394
Chagall, Bella Rosenfeld 364, 370 n. 65

Chagall, Marc 364
Charon, figure of Greek mythology 364
Chekhov, Anton 308, 413
Chen Weifeng 429
Chiara, Ana Cristina de Rezende 296
chiaroscuro effects 123
childhood 40, 76, 94, 100, 122, 288, 289, 302, 362, 376
children 16, 17, 18, 19, 20, 24, 26, 27, 32, 34, 66, 79, 87, 117 n. 27, 118 n. 49, 193, 208, 280, 356, 361, 362, 364, 370 n. 55, 392, 399, 406, 417, 425
    children's literature 406
Chinese 3, 9, 357, 407 n. 19, 425–31
    lexicality being changeable 430
    Shanghai Literature and Art Publishing House 427
    see also translation
Christianity 24, 139, 242, 356
    Lispector's identification with Christianity 356
    Roman Catholicism of Brazil 170, 361
    see also Jesus, Catholicism (Roman)
Christie, Agatha 82
cinema 11 n. 8, 18, 46, 78, 98, 121, 225, 323, 333 n. 6, 335–37, 339, 341–42, 344, 346
    'Cinema Novo' 342–43
    filmmaking strategies 337
    poetical devices of 339
city 16, 40, 46, 48, 107, 307, 338, 343, 384–85
Cixous, Hélène 4, 5, 10, 157–66, 201, 203, 208, 240, 258, 265, 269, 395, 396, 397, 413
    criticism that she 'colonized' Lispector 158, 165
    écriture féminine 5, 10, 157, 158, 159, 161, 165, 395
    effect of Lispector on her work 157–66
    Eve (Biblical) 160, 163
    L'Heure de Clarice Lispector [*The Hour of Clarice Lispector*] 159
    'Le Rire de la Méduse' 157
    Vivre l'orange 159, 161, 167 n. 5
Clarice na Cabeceira 183
Clarice Lispector: todas as crônicas (Rocco, ed. Pedro Karp Vasques) 83, 394
class 2, 60, 62, 107, 113, 170, 172, 175, 176, 231, 244, 261, 279, 326, 396
    see also society
classic status (of Lispector) 200
Clifford, James, *Routes: Travel and Translation in the Late Twentieth Century* 170
Coelho, Paulo 426
Closer to the Wild Heart: Essays on Clarice Lispector 391, 396
Colasanti, Marina 110
comic (tragicomic) 31, 96, 243, 286, 313, 416
Complete Stories, The [*Clarice Lispector: todos os contos*] 9, 373, 381, 391, 392, 397, 398, 411, 412, 413, 419, 420
consciousness 113, 127, 128, 129, 133, 135
    non-conscious processes 294
consumerism (*sociedade de consumo*) 8, 170, 173, 176, 225, 325, 326, 327, 329, 327
Copacabana beach 15, 17, 23, 25, 30, 33, 93, 411, 412

Copland, Aaron, *What to Listen for in Music* 82
copyright infringement 227
Correia, Hélia xi-xii, 5–6, 189
    'Captura' 5, 189–96
Correio feminino 8, 20, 85 n. 16, 321–31
Correio da Manhã, pen name Helen Palmer 20, 32, 83, 321, 322, 327, 332 n. 4
Corrêa dos Santos, Roberto 227, 235 n. 28
    As palavras 227
    O tempo 227
Cortázar, Julio, *Cronopios and Famas* 183, 425
Costa, Cynthia Beatrice xii, 9, 391
Costa, Sara André da xii, 8, 335
Costa Lima, Luís 394
Côté, Julie xii, 5, 157
Coutinho, Edilberto, *Brazilian Literature as World Literature* 354
Coutinho, Sonia 212
Couto, Rui Ribeiro 74–77
Cozer, Rachel 381
creation, creativity 2, 3, 8, 27, 41, 42, 44, 45, 59, 64, 80, 90, 114, 118 n. 44, 144, 149, 150, 172, 199, 204, 217–32, 241, 242, 245, 256, 260, 261, 268, 274, 286, 287, 288, 292, 294, 315, 336, 337–39, 342–45, 358, 365, 367 n. 6, 373, 395–97, 400, 402, 412, 431
    creative process 41, 42, 44, 45, 90, 204, 229, 230, 231, 232, 287, 294, 302, 337, 340
cultural:
    capital 357
    code 335–36
    commodity 232
    critics 201
    cross-pollination 178
    gestures 142
    icon 169
    impact 1
    inequalities 218
    masculinity 177
    relations 358
    sensitivity 176
    strata 113
    tool (Portuguese language) 115
    tradition, deliberate distortions of 151, 242
Cunha, Vasco Leitão da 355

Dabul, Ligia 42
Dalcastagnè, Regina 261
Damrosch, David 171, 356
Dawkins, Richard, *The Selfish Gene* 218
death 8, 24, 26, 73, 87, 91, 94, 96, 98, 100, 107, 119, 122, 160, 162, 177, 190, 194, 196, 199, 200, 209, 240–44, 246–49, 259, 287, 293, 304, 312, 330, 341, 345–46, 354, 356, 360–65, 372, 378–79, 381–83, 384, 391, 394, 395, 402, 417, 420, 427, 428
    Eros and Thanatos 248

defamiliarization 327, 398, 399, 400
Deleuze, Gilles 127, 239, 240, 241
Delorme, Renée 16
Denham, Alice 419
Depierre, Marie-Ange, *Paroles fantomatiques et cryptes textuelles* 201
Derecho, Abigail 200
Derrida, Jacques 200, 214 n. 34, 239, 395
detective novels 78, 82
dictatorship 21, 93, 302, 306, 307, 312
digital culture 6, 217–33
   Digital Humanities 232, 233
diplomatic life, travels (consulate) 42, 48–49, 57, 74, 78, 204, 382
disguise 122, 262, 265
displacement 38, 40, 169, 173, 170 n. 4, 384
   geographic displacement 40
dissemination of Lispector's works 227, 393
distortions 140, 141, 146, 148, 150, 151, 154 n. 38, 335, 414
Dodson, Katrina xii, 3, 9, 154 n. 38, 391, 392, 392, 394, 397–98, 400–02, 410–21
Donga 24
Dow, Gillian 200
Doyle, Plínio 73
Drummond de Andrade, Carlos 80, 81, 110–11, 116, 117 n. 27, 134, 217
   'Poema das sete faces' 110
Du Fu 431
Duvivier, Edgar, bronze statue 23, 33

Eakin, Paul John 374, 375
Eberstadt, Fernanda 394
écriture féminine, *see* Cixous, Hélène
Edwards, Magdalena xii, 12, 301–16, 391, 407 n. 5
Eliot, George 252
Eliot, T. S. 429
emotion 42, 54 n. 33, 87, 88, 106, 111, 122, 124, 127–29, 132, 133, 134, 175, 178, 201, 203, 207, 222, 242, 249, 304, 323–24, 325, 328, 342, 374, 399, 417
emotional disturbance 111
English language (Lispector's works in) 391–410
   see also Anglophone
enigma (enigmatic) 123, 132, 133, 255, 256, 264, 287, 373, 391, 402
Entrekin, Alison 397, 398
epigraph 67, 138, 140, 144, 145, 147, 148, 151, 154 n. 38, 169, 241, 244, 259
epiphany 4, 66, 127, 133, 203, 222, 223, 343, 396
Escorel, Lauro 105, 116 n. 4
ethics 174, 175, 241, 255, 257, 261, 262, 269, 374, 375, 382
   of failure 267
   of life writing 374–75, 380
Europe (European) 31, 44, 63, 64, 66, 240, 257, 361, 363, 364, 372, 380, 428
Even-Zohar, Itamar, 'The Position of Translated Literature within the Literary Polysystem' 429

exile 47, 48, 50, 51, 58, 148, 357, 364, 381
   longing, nostalgia 48, 54 n. 33
existentialism 173, 220–21, 306, 372, 385, 416
experiment 2, 7, 21, 79, 107, 109, 123, 143, 200, 202, 203, 205, 294, 295, 342
evil 122, 180 n. 37, 425, 426

fake, counterfeit, ersatz versions of Lispector 411–21
Fanon, Frantz 63
Farge, Arlette, *The Allure of the Archives* 89
Fatos & Fotos: Gente 303
favela 15–17, 25–26, 36 n. 36, 66
feminine 64, 113, 122, 130, 137 n. 37, 157, 158, 160, 161, 165, 192, 241, 323, 325, 327, 332 n. 4, 414
   beauty, futility of 95
feminism 4, 5, 6, 140, 142, 145, 146, 148, 158, 241, 242, 323, 396, 413
Feracho, Lesley 396
fiction:
   fictional/non-fictional, blurred line 174
   'fictional traps' 202, 203
   fictiveness/realness (subjectivity) 59
Filho, Adonias 110
fire accident (1966) 20–21, 26, 29, 79, 304, 378, 379
First World War 40
Fitz, Earl 149, 153 n. 7, 270 n. 2, 395, 397
   'Clarice Lispector: The Nature and Form of the Lyrical Novel' 395
FitzGerald, Edward, poet 429
   Rubáiyát of Omar Khayyám 429
Folha da Manhã (*Folha de São Paulo*) 105, 408
Fonseca, José Rubem 110, 117 n. 27
Fontes, Mora 110
foreignness 171, 202, 384
Foucault, Michel 42, 62, 241
   heterotopias 62
fragment, fragmentation 1, 59, 74, 77, 78, 80, 90, 91, 92, 93, 95, 97–98, 117 n. 27, 121, 201, 215 n. 45, 218, 219, 227, 230, 232, 246, 259, 268, 282, 302, 323, 336, 372, 378, 379, 380, 398, 400, 405, 430
   fragmentary writing technique 232
   of female body 323
   of a reality 398
France, Miranda 419
Franceschi, Antonio Fernando de 80
Franceschi, Humerto 28
freedom 110, 114, 122, 142, 143, 145, 177, 219, 220, 302, 313, 314, 426
   see also liberation
Freitas, Luana Ferreira de xiii, 390–406
Freud, Sigmund 96, 153 n. 16, 154 n. 24
   on humour 96
Friis, Elisabeth 240
Frohwein, Fábio 232
Fu Lei 429, 431
Fundação Casa Rui Barbosa 29, 57

Index

Gadamer, Hans 431
García Márquez, Gabriel 245
Geisel, Ernesto 307
gender 2, 8, 58, 63, 64, 107, 130, 131, 132, 142, 149, 150, 153 n. 20, 154 n. 24, 168 n. 19, 170, 172, 175, 176, 177–78, 200, 242, 251 n. 10, 322, 396, 426
Genette, Gerard 139
Gide, André 78, 82
globalisation 115, 170, 176
God 76, 78, 98, 141, 146, 147, 160, 163, 173, 187, 247, 293, 344, 356, 358, 361–65, 401, 411–13, 429
gods (goddesses) 170, 191, 207, 411
Goldman, Nathan 396
Gomes, Carlos Magno 149
Gotlib, Nádia Battella xi, 2, 4, 8, 40, 41, 42, 79, 80, 81, 82, 105–16, 236 n. 43
  Clarice: fotobiografia 378
  Clarice: uma vida que se conta xi, 8, 82, 137 n. 37, 371, 375, 384, 396
Grossmann, Judith 395
Guardian, The xiii, 273, 391
Guimarães, Adalberto Rafael 42, 43
Guimarães Rosa, João *Grande sertão: veredas* 114, 117 n. 44, 173, 217
Gullar, Ferreira 209
Gurgel Valente, Maury 22, 73, 355
Gurgel Valente, Paulo 11 n. 8, 15, 25, 32, 34, 73, 89, 227, 231, 235 n. 32, 355
Gurgel Valente, Pedro 15, 22, 25, 30, 49, 308, 355, 383
Gusmão, Manuel 336

Halberstam, Jack 239, 322, 331
Halperin, Liora R. 357
Hanson, Clare 200
Hawton, Hector, *Philosophy for Pleasure* 82
health and physical appearance 82
Hebrew 2, 3, 5, 8, 140, 142, 144–48, 154 n. 40 & 41, 68 n. 21, 353–65
  Israeli Hebrew 2, 397 n. 9
  language politics in Mandatory Palestine 357
  poetry 142, 357
  romanization of 357–58
Heidegger, Martin 395, 413, 422 n. 7
Helena, Lúcia 395
Hellman, Lillian, *The Little Foxes* 308, 310
Himmelseher, Cecília 83
Hindemith, Paul 296
history 3, 65, 79, 93, 110, 160, 176, 200, 218, 245, 275, 328, 337, 354, 356, 357, 358, 363, 364, 374, 380, 387 n. 27, 393, 428, 429
  and prehistory 90, 97, 275
Holocaust, the 382
Holy Land imagery 4, 57
hooks, bell 39, 47, 50, 52
  'culture of place' 50
  sense of place of origin 47

home 15, 17, 23, 26, 31, 40, 47–48, 49–50, 61, 63–64, 66, 74, 77, 79, 80, 93, 101, 121, 122, 132, 195, 207, 208, 219, 291, 304, 305, 311, 312, 322, 323, 326, 329, 331, 357, 359, 375, 379, 413, 420, 426, 427
  a human being's first microcosm 49
  in construction of identity 49
Hornike, Dafna xiii, 3–4, 57–68
Hoyos, Hector 170, 172–73, 178
  Beyond Bolaño: The Global Latin American Novel 170
human (the), humanity 6, 7, 24, 44, 67, 84, 115, 147, 191, 194, 239, 241, 243, 248, 257–58, 263, 264, 265, 266, 269, 274, 281, 294
  decolonizing 6
  dominance, Anthropocene period 273
  humanitarian issues 44
  human rights 85, 113
  interconnectedness 275
humour 95–96, 143, 149, 281, 313, 412, 423 n. 14
Hutcheon, Linda 335, 337

I Ching or *Book of Changes* 82, 209, 413
identity 2, 40, 49, 50, 51, 52, 65, 122, 130, 131, 142, 146, 151, 169, 225, 227, 230, 231, 246, 274, 289, 343, 354, 356, 358, 359, 374, 382, 395, 396, 397, 412
  deconstruction of 50
  rootlessness 50
imagination 22, 174, 193, 213 n. 4, 242, 244, 246, 288, 373, 399
immigration 22, 174, 193, 242, 244, 246, 288, 373, 399
indigenous 28, 242
  arts and crafts 28
individual (the) 5, 48, 63, 109, 124, 153 n. 16, 171, 175, 189, 194, 218, 229, 241, 246, 247, 273, 307, 330, 342, 365
  inner life 65
  rhythm 124
influence (on other writers) 1–8, 165, 168 n. 33, 201, 203, 205, 215 n. 55, 373, 395, 397, 431
innocence 112, 175, 315, 340, 342
innovation 105
  innovative style 105, 107
  innovator (Lispector as) 413
Instituto Moreira Salles (IMS) ix, 9, 4, 25, 35 n. 20, 73–75, 81, 84, 90–92, 97, 232, 236 n. 43
Instituto Pró-Livro 217
intellectualism 115, 411
intensity (quality, effect in Lispector) 79, 100, 128, 135, 207, 208, 296, 394, 412, 417
internationalization 1, 170, 225, 227
interpretation (resistance of) 132
interviews, interviewer 115, 209, 246, 303, 304, 308, 312
intimacy 1, 2, 5, 41, 143, 145, 183, 206, 207, 208, 239, 361
intuition 150, 209
irony 81, 122, 130, 177, 247, 275, 311, 419

Ivo, Lêdo 105, 171

Jacobs, Adriana X. xiii, 1, 10, 120, 168 n. 21, 353–66
Jesus (Christianity) 149–50, 149, 163, 314, 361, 363
Jesus Christ Superstar 314
Jewish Studies 359, 396
  see also Judaism
Jornal do Brasil 2, 18, 19, 20, 21–22, 32, 83, 121, 143, 144
journalism 2, 19, 22, 23, 115, 153 n. 15, 155 n. 45, 315
Jozef, Bella 395
Judaism 354, 356, 368 n. 11, 396
  Jewish exegetical tradition 139, 140, 142, 151
  Kabbalah 367 n. 6, 413
  liturgy 140, 147, 355, 361, 368 n. 13–14
  Macabéa as a Jewish name 359, 360
  Midrash 139, 140, 147
  Talmud 139, 361
  Zion (and loss of) 148, 364

Kafka, Franz 387 n. 41, 413
Kahn, Daniela Mercedes 261, 266
Kama Sutra 82
Kärrholm, Mattias 239, 243
Kauffmann, Gisel 80, 383
Kirsch, Adam 171, 172
  The Global Novel: Writing the World in the 21st Century 171
Klein, Rachel 392
Klobucka, Anna 158, 161, 167 n. 12, 395
Knopf, Alfred A. 393
knowledge, self-knowledge 9, 109, 111, 116, 173, 175, 208, 232, 245, 251 n. 10, 263, 264, 281, 294, 397, 398, 412
Kronfeld, Chana 139, 363, 370 n. 70
Kurzweil, Ray 273

Lage, Claudia, 'Near to the Heart of Language' 200, 204, 207
Lagerfeld, Karl 413
Landy, Joshua 175
Laor, Yitzhak 142
language:
  antithesis 398, 400, 401, 402
  as politicizing act 113
  collocations 397, 398, 400, 401
  communicating through words 123
  devices in Lispector's writing 396, 398
  distortions of 414
  drawing attention to itself 398
  improvisation 295, 402
  Portuguese language 113, 115, 413
  pre-verbal psychic states 135
  punctuation 61, 91, 92, 397, 402, 430
  repetition as rhetorical device 401
  subversive 397, 402
  the unsayable 83, 135, 175, 177, 189, 207

  the word as bait 99, 135, 271 n. 20
  word order 402
  see also style
Latin 141, 150, 186, 356–57, 361, 363, 423 n. 23
Latin America (and literature) 1, 3, 4, 170, 172, 174, 177, 178, 183, 242, 251 n. 10, 391, 393, 394, 405–06, 413, 425–26
  Magical Realism 426, 433 n. 2
law 5, 140, 146, 148, 150, 152, 153 n. 12, 160, 163, 164, 165, 166, 247, 354, 361, 375, 384, 412, 417
  study of (Lispector) 113, 315
Leal, Aurelino 24
Lee, Hermione 373
legacy (Lispector) 1, 2, 3, 5, 6, 84, 166, 183, 200, 209, 247, 301, 302, 371, 384, 385, 394, 396
Leitch, Thomas 335
Lerner, Júlio 7, 230, 235 n. 42, 301, 317 n. 11, 342, 423
  '*antientrevista*' 303
  TV Cultura interview with Lispector (1977) 230, 312, 313
  see also interview
letters:
  epistolary genre 41
  'Letters to C.' 208
  see also Novey, Idra
  Lispector's letters 3, 7, 18, 39–46, 49–52, 54 n. 19, 73, 77–78, 285, 311, 382
  public and private spheres 41
  and self-understanding 43
  sense of belonging 52
  spontaneity 41
Leme 3, 15–35
Leonard, Kiran xiii, 7, 279–80
  Derevaun Seraun 279
Lessa, Elsie 17, 18, 19
Levy, Tatiana Salem 87, 202–03, 212
  'As Vítimas de Clarice' 203
Leys, Ruth 128
Lezra, Jacques 257, 266
liberation 4, 109, 112, 281
  see also freedom
Librandi, Marília 260, 270 n. 4, 329
library, libraries 26, 84, 87, 119, 120, 279, 280
  Clarice's library 80–84
life:
  as a crisis 273
  force, *zoe* 241
life writing 8, 200, 240, 371, 373, 374, 375, 378, 380
Lindstrom, Naomi 242, 368 n. 29, 396
Lisboa, Adriana 202, 203
Lisbon 46, 74, 76, 77, 78
Lispector studies — three waves (Gotlib) 2
Lispector, Clarice:
  cancer 22, 302, 304, 417
  Chaya Pinkhasovna (birth name) 354, 356, 413
  children, *see* Gurgel Valente, Paulo and Gurgel Valente, Pedro

death (on 9 December 1977) 1, 6-8, 22, 36 n. 27, 73, 84, 154. n. 28, 167. n. 5, 199, 243, 245, 259, 302–04, 354, 372, 378–79, 384, 391, 395, 411, 417, 420
funeral of 23, 354, 355–56, 361, 365
hospital 22, 29, 89, 100, 379
marriage 122, 193
see also Gurgel Valente, Maury
national literary and cultural icon 169
pogroms 380, 381, 383, 413
pop star status 218, 225
   Brazilian muse 221, 222
sisters 39, 40, 41, 42, 43, 51, 52, 78, 206, 213 n. 4, 285, 311, 382, 383
see also Lispector, Elisa and Kaufmann, Tânia
works:
   Água viva 6, 21, 91, 111, 127, 130, 143, 157, 164, 165, 207, 235 n. 32, 239, 240, 255, 257–60, 262–64, 266, 267, 268, 269, 275, 282, 292, 294, 296, 373, 395, 404
   Alguns contos 20, 405
   'Amor' (*Laços de família*) 129, 132, 284, 377, 392, 397, 398–401, 402, 405–06, 426, 430
   A bela e a fera 392, 405
   'Berna' (*A descoberta do mundo*) 43, 83
   'Brasília' (*Visão do esplendor*) 137 n. 30, 285, 392, 422 n. 13
   Caderno de Bordo (Log Book/Travel Journal) 75, 76, 89, 236 n. 43
   'Cem anos de perdão' (*Felicidade clandestina*) 214 n. 18, 392
   A cidade sitiada 4, 44, 107, 119, 285, 291, 308, 373, 404
   The Complete Stories 9, 373, 381, 391, 392, 397, 398, 405, 411, 412, 413, 419, 420
   De corpo inteiro 21
   'Correio Feminino' page in the *Correio da Manhã* 8, 20, 320–31
   Correspondências 39–52
   'Os desastres de Sofia' (*A legião estrangeira*) 129, 132, 405
   A descoberta do mundo 83, 405
   'Desenhando um menino' (*A legião estrangeira*), later 'Menino a bico de pena' (*A descoberta do mundo*) 129
   'Devaneio e embriaguez de uma rapariga' (*Laços de família*) 128–29, 284, 405, 422 n. 13
   'Dia após dia' (*A via crucis do corpo*) 392
   'Encarnação involuntária' (*Todos os contos*) 417–18
   'Esclarecimentos: explicação de uma vez por todas' (*A descoberta do mundo*) 354
   'Explicação' (*A via crucis do corpo*) 143,
   'Explicação' (*A descoberta do mundo*) 423 n. 16
   Felicidade clandestina 214 n. 18, 359, 392, 405, 425, 427, 428
   'Uma Galinha' (*Laços de família*) 393, 405, 415
   'Uma história de tanto amor' (*Felicidade Clandestina*) 392
   A hora da estrela 4, 8, 10, 22, 74, 90, 92, 97, 100, 143, 170, 206, 232, 240, 255, 258, 261, 262, 266, 283, 292, 302, 303, 308, 312, 314, 315, 337, 358, 359, 360, 361, 363–65, 373, 394, 404, 418, 427–28
   'Idle Chatter' in *Discovering the World* 173
   'A imitação da rosa' (*Laços de família*) 5, 21, 129, 134, 392, 405, 420
   Laços de família 20, 129, 132, 201, 284, 290, 358, 372, 377, 392, 393, 394, 405, 406, 428
   'A legião estrangeira' (*A legião estrangeira*) 4, 18, 32, 83, 129, 132, 308, 309, 372, 394, 405, 408 n. 22, 415
   A legião estrangeira 4, 18, 32, 83, 129, 132, 308, 309, 372, 394, 405, 415
   'A Letter to the Minister of Education' 307
   'Literatura de Vanguarda no Brasil' 105–18
   O lustre 76, 77, 79, 288, 296, 301, 303, 308, 311, 312, 313, 315, 404
   A maçã no escuro 16, 79, 173, 239, 275, 282
   'Macacos' (*A legião estrangeira*) 393, 405, 415
   'Medo da eternidade' (*A descoberta do mundo*) 387 n. 23
   'A menor mulher do mundo' (*Laços de família*) 76, 392–93, 398, 405, 406, 415, 422
   'A Mensagem' (*A legião estrangeira*) 129, 130, 132, 134
   'O milagre das folhas' (*A descoberta do mundo*) 82
   'Mineirinho' 141–42, 149, 305–07, 309, 313, 397, 398, 401–03
   Minhas queridas 38–52, 78
   'Mistério em São Cristóvão' (*Laços de família*) 132, 405
   'A morte de uma baleia' (*A descoberta do mundo*) 378–79
   'Observações sobre o direito de punir' 113
   'Onde estivestes de noite' (*Onde estivestes de noite*) 82, 285, 298, 392, 405
   Onde estivestes de noite? 82, 285, 392, 405
   Outros escritos 107, 116 n. 13, 117 n. 39
   'O ovo e a galinha' (*A legião estrangeira*) 264, 271 n. 20, 405, 413, 431
   A paixão segundo G.H. 11 n. 8, 28, 58, 82, 117 n. 27, 127, 158, 162, 165, 166, 168 n. 33, 202, 208, 239, 282, 291, 293, 295, 309, 333 n. 6, 354, 382, 404, 411, 428
   Perto do coração selvagem 7, 74, 77, 83–84, 105, 107, 219, 220, 221, 255, 280, 289, 290, 292, 295, 308, 309, 311, 373, 394, 404, 407 n. 20, 413, 426, 428
   'A pesca milagrosa' 135
   'A quinta história' (*A legião estrangeira*) 392, 406
   'Só para Mulheres' page for *Diário da Noite* 20
   Um sopro de vida 4, 74, 78, 80, 111, 127, 134, 165, 206, 239, 259, 290, 292, 297, 373, 404

'Traduzir procurando não trair' (*A descoberta do mundo*) 310
A via crucis do corpo 5, 139–49 *passim*, 151, 285, 359, 392, 405
'Viajando por mar (1a parte)' (*A descoberta do mundo*) 379
Visão do esplendor: impressões leves 21, 393, 405
works of, translated into English 404–06
Lispector, Elisa 375, 383, 388 n. 50–51
  No exílio 367 n. 3, 381
  Retratos antigos 381, 387 n. 27
Lispector, Mania 40, 375, 377, 382, 383
Lispector, Pinkhas 40, 377, 380
literary afterlives (of Clarice) 6, 199–210, 211
literary craft 114, 188, 403
Lorenz, Johnny 119, 397, 404
Lowe, Elizabeth 395, 404
  Chronology: Clarice Lispector (Bella Jozef) 395
  'The Passion According to C.L.', interview 316, 395
Lunardi, Adriana 203, 211

MacInnes, Martin xiii, 7, 273–76
machista culture 112
madness 99, 195, 248, 412
Madureira, Pedro Paulo Sousa 21
Malcolm, Janet 374, 375
Malini, Fábio 217
Mallarmé, Stéphane 134
Manchete 20, 21, 24, 32, 36 n. 45, 85 n. 10, 303
Mandarin 2, 3, 9
Mann, Thomas 82
Mansfield, Katherine 83, 84, 86 n. 25, 133, 137 n. 32–37, 311
  Bliss 133
  The Doll's House and Other Stories 84
  Lettere 83, 84
Manovich, Lev 229–30, 231
  non-narrative nature of 'new media objects' 229–30
manuscripts 4, 21, 28, 42, 71, 73, 74, 77, 78, 80, 86–101, 108, 120, 121, 232, 235 n. 32, 260, 275, 387, 418, 419
Manzo, Lícia 371, 384
Marchi, Siléa (nurse) 22
Marsack, Robyn 119
Marting, Diane, *Clarice Lispector: A Bio-Bibliography* 396
Martins, Justino and Lucinda 24, 25
Mary, mother of Jesus 201, 206, 361
  Lispector painted as compassionate Mary 201, 206
Mary Magdalene 313, 315
mass culture 170
Massumi, Brian 128
Masumura, Yasuzo *Afraid to Die* 314
material world 258
materiality 61, 240, 243, 244, 328, 383
materialisms 241, 257
Matisse, Henri 84

matter 112, 163, 245, 248, 258, 265, 266, 268–69, 272–75, 328, 341, 420
  animating power of 245
McDermott, Annie xiii–xiv, 6, 197 n. 2
  translation of Hélia Correia's 'Captura' 190–96
Mediterranean 66, 68
memes 2, 200, 206, 217–33
Méndez, Mariela xiv, 321–31
Merquior, José Guilherme 115
metaphor 58, 59–60, 131, 133, 142, 143, 148, 150, 170, 172, 175, 205, 207, 208, 248, 257, 258, 264, 275, 283, 284, 287, 288, 302, 337, 342, 346, 430
  the star metaphor 248
Metz, Christian 335, 336
Miguel-Pereira, Lúcia 106, 107
Milliet, Sérgio 105, 394
military dictatorship (Brazil 1964–85) 302, 306, 307
Milne, Esther 43
Min Xuefei xiv, 9, 424–31
Mishima, Yukio 308, 314
  novella *Star* 314
  Sotoba Komachi (co-translated by Lispector with Tati de Moraes) 314
'mistakes' 5, 139–52, 206, 289, 339, 429
Mizumura, Minae, *The Fall of Language in the Age of English* 171, 172, 174
modern world 244
modernism (postmodernism) 241, 373
modernity (postmodernity) 39, 40, 46, 50, 251 n. 10
  progress 44–45, 121, 122, 329, 331
  sameness 46
Montero, Teresa xiv, 3, 8, 15–34, 42, 78, 133, 137 n. 32, 225, 371, 374, 379, 380, 384, 388 n. 62, 396
  À procura da própria coisa: Uma biografia de Clarice Lispector xiv, 384
  Eu sou uma pergunta: uma biografia de Clarice Lispector 8, 371, 378, 396
  O Rio de Clarice: passeio afetivo pela cidade xiv, 3, 14–34, 384
  Todas as cartas xiv
Moore, Lorrie 273
Moraes, Emanuel de 144
Moraes, Tati de 308, 310–11
Moraes, Vinícius de 17, 79, 308, 314
Morton, Timothy 257–58, 264, 267
Moser, Benjamin 8, 57, 100, 144, 175, 199, 273, 354, 359, 371, 372–73, 374, 375, 378, 380–85, 391, 392, 394, 396, 397, 404, 413
  The Chandelier, with Magdalena Edwards (trans. of *O lustre*) 391, 404
  A mulher que matou os peixes 392, 406
  Why This World: A Biography of Clarice Lispector 8, 199, 273, 359, 371, 380, 394
Mota, Karyn xiv, 6, 206, 216–33
motherhood 154 n. 27, 323
Motta, Zezé 30

Moure, Erín 201–02, 211
Moutonnier, Denise 83
music 7, 17, 18, 24, 36 n. 35, 73, 82, 170, 218, 248, 259, 260, 281–97, 308, 320, 364, 399
   Chopin, beloved composer 285–86, 289
   disruption of performances 289
   jazz 282, 295
   João Gilberto, Tom Jobim, Vinícius de Moraes and Chico Buarque 17
   Kiran Leonard, composition 279–80
   'Lição de piano' 286
   organ in *Perto do coração selvagem* 292–93
   samba, bossa nova 17, 22, 24, 31, 285
   and thought 290
   voice, singing 7, 281, 283–84, 294
   yearning for discovery 286
mystery 4, 20, 106, 132, 190, 191, 220, 248, 280, 287, 406, 428
mystic (L. as) 411, 412
mysticism 242, 367 n. 6, 411, 412
myth, mythology 57, 65, 112, 123, 149, 241, 259, 364, 411

narrative 6, 21, 96, 111, 114, 130, 145, 158–59, 168, 170, 172, 175, 209, 217, 230, 221, 231, 232, 241, 246, 248, 261–63, 282, 290, 311, 312, 322, 324, 327, 330, 335, 338–39, 343, 346, 373–74, 376, 378–80, 382, 395, 400, 411, 430
   addressivity 174
   anthropocentric 328
   audio-visual 306, 327
   biographical 376
   border between reflection and narrative 98
   economy 289
   experimental 21, 176
   female 416
   of growth 331
   irony 122, 130, 177, 247, 275
   labyrinthine nature of 296
   layers 338
   male narrator 174–76, 244
   metafiction 170, 173, 174, 176, 209
   as oratorio 294
   phenomenological construction of 399
   playfulness 143, 205
   project 114
   radical intertextuality 140
   in the realm of internet 217, 229
   the right to narrate 104, 113
   rejecting commonplaces of victimization 96
   sequencing of life's disorder 170
   strategy 380
   structure, form 175, 431
   technique 373, 427, 373, 427
   traditional narrative structure challenged 173, 176, 177, 248, 325
   voice 178, 307, 341

Negrete, Fernanda 240
Neves, Júlia Braga xi, 371–86, 407 n. 17
New Directions 372, 373, 392, 394
New York Times 391, 393, 394, 413, 419
Nina, Cláudia 47, 58
A Noite 105
Nolasco, Edgar Cézar 212, 384
nomadic 57–59, 60–61, 64–65, 67, 68
notetaking (Lispector) 83, 232, 310
Novey, Idra xiv–xv, 5, 183–87, 202, 208, 212, 279, 396, 404
   Clarice: The Visitor 183–87
   Ways to Disappear 212, 215 n. 65, 396
Nunes, Aparecida Maria 80, 85, 333
Nunes, Benedito 2, 115, 118 n. 49, 286, 394
   O mundo de Clarice Lispector 394–95

O Povo, online portal 225
object:
   artistic object 255, 256, 260
   ephemeral nature of 260
   gaze 262, 264
   mirror, *porta-espelho* 7, 254, 262, 264, 267, 268
   Objeto gritante 260
   theory of 254–69
   wardrobe, *guarda-roupa* 6, 254–57, 262–66, 268
   see also theory
occult 9, 413
   fortune-teller 78, 98, 312, 313, 313, 418
Oiticica, Hélio 260, 268
Oliveira, Ilca Vieira de 42, 43
D'Oliveira, Manoela Purcell 81
Oliveira, Marly de 110, 27
Olympian gods 170
Orient, the 63, 64, 66
Orientalism 58, 63, 64, 68
originality 115, 202, 204, 207, 397, 402, 414
orixá, female deity 64, 413
otherness 61–67
outsider 47

Pagu (Patrícia Galvão), *Parque industrial* (1933) 107
painting 29, 45, 255, 259, 262, 263, 264, 265, 266, 292, 294, 297, 364
Parente, Letícia, *Marca registrada* 302, 304–06
Paris 22, 23, 87, 100, 101, 311
Park, Sowon 357
Parks, Tim, *Where I'm Reading From: The Changing World of Books* 173
Pasolini, Pier Paolo 336–37, 339, 342
   Heretical Empiricism 336
Paulino, Simone, *Como Clarice Lispector pode mudar a sua vida* 214, 235
Pearce, Lynn 50
Peixoto, Marta xv, 4–5, 127–35, 260, 396
Pellegrino, Hélio 79

Penguin UK 119, 183, 227, 373, 385, 392, 407 n. 8
Pensador, popular Brazilian website 219
performance 7, 63, 106, 172, 176, 218, 278, 289, 301, 302, 304, 305, 306, 308, 310, 311, 314, 315, 322, 323, 324, 327, 328, 335, 391, 394, 407 n. 20, 420
   performativeness 90, 149, 150, 306, 308, 315, 325, 342
Perry, Menachem 359
Pessoa, Fernando 428
phenomenology 397
   see also object, language
photograph 25, 28, 31, 36 n. 43, 47, 61, 92, 93, 201, 205, 291, 309, 324, 344, 346, 372, 375, 378, 380, 420
philosophy 82, 118 n. 49, 127, 251 n. 27, 257, 335, 425
Pino, Claudia Amigo 90
Piñon, Nélida 22, 24, 31, 110, 117 n. 27
Pinto, Sobral 80
Piskorski, Rodolfo 239
pleasure 16, 82, 96, 140, 152, 224, 274, 293, 295, 303, 308, 313–14, 315, 346, 404
plot, story 113, 144, 203, 205, 232, 243, 245, 373, 427
police 7, 24, 305, 306, 307, 313, 401
Pontieri, Regina Lúcia, *Clarice Lispector: uma poética do olhar* 45, 264, 396
Pontiero, Giovanni xv, 2, 3, 4, 9, 10, 118–24, 372, 392, 394, 398, 400, 404, 405, 406, 415
   afterword to *The Besieged City* 118, 121
   Lya Luft's *The Red House* 120
popularity 6, 20, 217, 218, 323, 324, 392
postcolonial (reading, thinking) 161, 241
   decolonial, Lispector's work as 240
posthumanism 6, 239, 240, 241
postmodernism 223, 373
postmodernity 46
   postmodern world 39
poststructuralist theory 239, 408
Pound, Ezra 9, 429
   translations of Chinese classical poetry 429
power (and discourse) (Foucault, Braidotti) 241
Prado, Plínio 73, 256
   'aesthetic of the sublime' 259
present, the:
   place can only be felt through the lens of 48
   absolute present 129
private sphere of Lispector's life 41, 47, 52, 58, 356, 374, 375, 375, 381
   sense of belonging held on to 47
   value of privacy for Lispector 209
   privacy in context of life writing 374, 375
Probyn, Elspeth 47
prosopopeia 201
Proust, Marcel 82
psychic (pre-verbal state, individual) 59, 135, 142, 191, 248, 412, 418, 419

'quarteto de Minas' 78–79
Que mistérios tem Clarice?, play 419
Queiroz, Rachel de 106

Rabassa, Gregory 393
Rabin, Henrique 381
race 2, 58, 63, 64, 242, 251 n. 10, 396, 426, 427
Ravikovitch, Dalia 142
reader:
   the haunted/reader 6, 162
   readers' admiration for/devotion to Lispector 7, 202, 333 n. 6, 394
   reading, the act of, as process 135, 158, 209, 425
'radical receptivity' 207
realism 7, 258, 296, 297, 415, 426, 433 n. 2
reality 59, 93, 96, 121, 123, 129, 134, 143, 154 n. 28, 171, 174, 226, 283, 288, 294, 297, 302, 325, 336, 346, 357, 373, 376, 397, 398, 399, 414, 416, 426
   in state of constant transformation 123
   'trans-corporeality' 329
relationship(s) 6, 41, 44, 114, 121, 122, 123, 158, 161, 165, 166, 175, 199, 219, 243, 246, 258, 282, 289, 381
   interdependent, interchangeable nature of 123, 241
religion (religious) 24, 64, 68, 94, 122, 142, 201, 205, 242, 265, 354, 357, 358, 361, 382, 411, 412, 413
   relation between fandom and religious devotion ('cult', 'icon', etc.) 201
repetition, *see* language
Resende, Otto Lara 78, 80, 84, 413
resistance, political strategy of 149
Rilke, Rainer Maria 395, 413
Rimbaud, Arthur 413
Rio de Janeiro 3, 15, 16, 20, 22, 40, 61–68, 78, 81, 88, 93, 94, 100, 101, 113, 243, 261, 306, 314, 315, 325, 338, 354, 365, 378, 385, 393, 415
   see also Brazil
Robinson, Marie N. *The Power of Sexual Surrender* 82
Rocco, publishing house 4, 107, 227, 231, 379, 384, 394
Rosenbaum, Yudith 306, 396
roses 6, 18, 20, 134, 189, 190, 191, 195, 196, 420
Rubião, Murilo 110, 117 n. 27
Russian Revolution 40

Sá, Olga de 64, 395, 430
   A escritura de Clarice Lispector 430
   A travessia do oposto 395
Sabiá, publisher 21
Sabino, Fernando 42, 43, 52, 79, 184, 185, 186, 204, 355
Sager, Juan 120
Said, Edward 63
Salermo, Ronaldo 81
Salles, Walther Moreira 74, 81
Sampaio, Gustavo 23
San Tiago Dantas, Francisco de 100

Sant'Anna, Affonso Romano de 115, 118 n. 49, 136 n. 3, 212, 395
Sant'Anna, Sérgio, 'A bruxa' 110, 117 n. 27, 209, 212
Saramago, José xv, 358, 394
saudade 44, 47, 48
Schiess, Ami xv, 6–7, 254–69
Schwarz, Roberto 394
Scofield, The 392, 397
scriptworld 354, 356–58
sea, the 15–16, 19, 31, 260, 364
Second World War 39, 46
Segalovitz, Yael xv-xvi, 3, 5, 139–52, 359, 360, 363
  Derekh ha-yesurim shel ha-guf 359
Sela, Maya, *Haaretz* 359
self 3, 42, 50, 63, 65–68, 96, 114, 136 n. 3, 177, 203, 240, 242, 249
  as joining tree of life 249
self-help (messages) 1, 206, 214 n. 20, 225, 411, 418
  use of fragments as 227
Sell, Roger D., *Communicational Criticism: Studies in Literature as Dialogue* 171
  addressivity 174–75
  communicational ethics 174–75
Senhor 18, 36 n. 39, 85 n. 5
  'Children's Corner' 19
Seuphor, Michel 259
sex 2, 8, 82, 112, 122, 130, 132, 139, 143, 144, 145, 148, 154 n. 27, 157, 241, 251 n. 10, 286, 322, 340, 341, 363, 396, 418
Shakespeare, William 82, 219
Shaviro, Steven, 'Two Lessons from Burroughs' 239
Shellhorse, Adam Joseph 302, 303
Shklovsky, Viktor, Russian formalist 398
Shouse, Eric 128
silence 27, 43, 91, 93, 121, 131, 141, 143, 164, 256, 265, 280, 384, 291, 302–06, 308, 311, 312, 315, 336, 358, 401
Simenon, Georges 82
Smith, Jess, archivist 120
Soares, Ilke 20, 24, 83, 308
society (social):
  classes 107, 113, 261
  margins 66, 143
  paradoxes 176
  points of view 170
  position 145, 426
  prejudice 121, 176, 343
  see also class
social media, *see* digital culture
Sociedade Pestalozzi do Brasil 27
Sokoloff, Naomi 365
soul 23, 67, 144, 146, 196, 207, 245, 342, 361, 365, 378, 400, 405, 415, 429
  matter as more mysterious than 244–45
Sousa, Carlos Mendes de xvi, 7, 10, 78, 259, 280–97, 356

Spinoza, Baruch de 82, 127, 241, 251 n. 27
spirit 66, 106, 109, 121, 169, 178, 182, 201, 209, 259, 301, 312, 315, 392, 414, 439
  spectral encounters (with Clarice Lispector) 199–202, 208
  spirituality 46, 50, 123, 175, 411, 413, 416, 420
  spiritism 82, 170, 198
Spivak, Gayatri 175
Stam, Robert 335–36
Steiner, George, *After Babel* 430
style (esp. of Lispector) 9, 11 n. 3, 107, 127, 143, 144, 177, 199, 203, 205, 227, 242, 243, 258, 274, 282, 285, 297, 336, 359, 391, 394, 397, 401, 403, 418, 429–31
subalternity (narrative, identification) 176
  see also Brazil *and* society
subjectivity 4, 6, 41, 58, 59, 60, 67, 168 n. 12, 239, 241, 242, 244–46, 261, 337, 428
  and death 240
  posthuman and posthuman death theory 240
suburb, the 44–45, 121, 122, 291
supernatural 209
  see also occult
Suzuki, D. T., *An Introduction to Zen Buddhism* 82
Switzerland 40, 57, 121, 204, 219, 282–83, 308, 382

Tablet online magazine 393
taxis 18–19, 22, 23, 100, 312, 313
Teresa of Avila, Saint 411
Tezza, Cristovão 426
theatre 1, 7, 20, 145, 169, 175, 200, 218, 225, 285, 286, 308, 309, 311, 328
  adaptations, collaborative, Lispector 309
theory 4–7, 201–02, 232, 239, 254, 255
  affect theory 127–29, 135
  of art, of object ('thing theory') (Lispector) 7, 255–58, 264
  (feminist) film theory 323, 336
  of performativity 142
  posthuman theory (and of death) 240
  post-structuralist 239
  of shapeshifter 240–43
  of translation 398, 248
    see also translation
  twentieth-century turn from liberal humanism to critical posthumanism 239
Tivon, Miriam 8, 358–59, 360–61, 363–65
  Ha-teshuka 'al pi G. H. 359
  Karov la-lev ha-piri 359
  Kishrei mishpacha/ She'at ha-kokhav 359
  Osher samui 359
Tóibín, Colm 2, 175, 373
translation:
  as collaborative process 208
  domestication 398
  as interpretation 414, 431
  issues 429, 430

Lispector's translations (for Artenova and Imago) 21
Lispector unhappy with translator's job 83
Portuguese translation of the Bible 146
rhythm of the text 400
theory of 428
translator 1–5, 7, 9, 83, 119, 120, 149, 183, 201, 208, 215 n. 65, 231, 301, 308, 310, 311, 358, 372, 385, 392–98, 400, 402–03, 414–15, 419, 420, 428–31
   kinship between translators 415
   Sisyphean task of 431
transience (as perspective) 47
travel 59, 170, 194, 311, 392, 394
   travel journal/log 74–76, 78, 236 n. 43
Trevisan, Dalton 110
truth 47, 50, 96, 99, 114, 159, 162–63, 164, 165, 166, 167 n. 12, 174, 190, 199, 273, 290, 343, 373–74, 375, 381, 382, 411, 412, 429

Ukraine 9, 29, 40, 242, 373, 375, 377, 380, 382, 413, 422 n. 7
Última Hora, newspaper 22
Una Rosa Per Tutti, film 17
Underhill, Evelyn, *Mysticism: A Study in the Nature and Development of Man's Spiritual Consciousness* 411
universal themes (in Clarice's works) 173, 180 n. 37
unsayable, the 83, 135, 175, 177, 189, 207, 256–57
urban (culture, crisis) 44, 61, 66, 117 n. 27, 170, 173, 324, 326

Van der Plas, Christina Soto 391
vanguard 4, 105–16
   eschewing conceptual norms 111
   'false vanguards' 115
   lecture 'Literatura de Vanguarda no Brasil' 107
   new point of view 111
   see also avant-garde
Valente, Mariana ix, 9
Valéry, Paul 134
Vargas, Getúlio 380
Varin, Claire, *Rencontres brésiliennes* 45, 211, 353, 381, 383, 384, 396

Veríssimo, Mafalda and Érico 24, 298 n. 18
Veríssimo, Luis Fernando 24
Vidal, Paloma xvi, 3, 4, 87–103
   'And now' (*crônica*) 4, 87–103
video art 7, 302, 304, 305, 306, 314
Vieira, Nelson xvi, 5, 169–78, 242, 251 n. 27, 396
Vilela, Luiz 110, 117 n. 27
Villares, Lucia 396
violence 25, 94, 140–41, 144, 146, 203, 243, 265, 290, 304, 307, 361, 363, 383, 396, 401
violin-player 100, 363, 364
   see also Chagall

Wainer, Bluma 100
Weil, Simone 411
Weltliteratur 169
Wiggins, Bradley E. 218–19, 222
Williams, Claire xvi–xvii, 1, 2, 4, 6, 35 n. 1, 58, 118–20, 130, 198–213, 298 n. 17, 368 n. 16, 389 n. 73, 390
women 10, 21, 22, 47, 62, 83, 91, 106, 122, 140, 141, 144, 154 n. 27, 157, 159, 183, 200, 205, 303, 231, 322–28, 388 n. 48, 405–06, 420, 426, 427
   allegorical fallen 148
   characters 122, 140–41
   Chinese women 426
   domestic lives 326
   emotional fragility (Lucretia) 122
   Jewish women 363
   sexuality 143
   societal expectations of 420
   writers 202, 203, 204, 415, 416–17, 418, 420
Woolf, Virginia 84, 200, 214 n. 35, 413, 419
writing, act of 28, 52, 61, 99, 162, 209, 256, 302, 342, 426
   writers as innate actors 311

Zaytoun, Kelli D. xvii, 6, 329–49
Zhang, Yueran 427
Zular, Roberto 90
Zweig, Arnold, *Les Pages immortelles de Spinoza, choisies et expliquées par Arnold Zweig* 82

www.ingramcontent.com/pod-product-compliance
Lightning Source LLC
Chambersburg PA
CBHW081156230426
43666CB00016B/2836